Managing the Electronic Library

Managing the Electronic Library

A Practical Guide for Information Professionals

Edited by
Terry Hanson and Joan Day

London • Melbourne • Munich • New Providence, NJ

British Library Cataloguing in Publication Data
A catalogue record for this book is available from the British Library.

Library of Congress Cataloging-in-Publication Data
A catalog record for this book is available from the Library of Congress.

Published by Bowker-Saur
Windsor Court, East Grinstead House
East Grinstead, West Sussex RH19 IXA, UK
Tel +44 (0) 1342 326972   Fax: +44 (0) 1342 336198/190
E-mail: lis@bowker-saur.com
Intemet Website: http://www.bowker-saur.com service/

Bowker-Saur is part of REED BUSINESS INFORMATION LIMITED

ISBN 1-85739-184-5

Cover design by
Printed on acid-free paper
Typeset by The Florence Group, Stoodleigh, Devon
Printed and bound in Great Britain by Antony Rowe, Chippenham, Wilts, UK.

About the Authors

John Akeroyd is Director of Learning and Information Services at South Bank University where his responsibilities include libraries, IT centres, the LRC and Learning Technology. He has published well over 100 papers mainly concerning IT and libraries and information handling and has been Project Director of both European and UK research projects.

Jane Arthur has worked at Cranfield University, the University of Abertay, Dundee and is currently at the University of Hertfordshire. She was Project Officer for the Hatfield Learning Resources Centre new building development and is now an Assistant Director in the Department of Learning and Information Services.

John Blagden is Chief Librarian at Cranfield University Library. He is Chair of Bedfordshire and Buckinghamshire Information and more recently Chair of the Library and Information Co-operation Council (LINC), and has written extensively on performance assessment and information retrieval. Previous appointments include McKinsey, Greater

London Council, British Institute of Management, and Zinc and Lead Development Association. He is a former member of the Library Advisory Council, the Council of Aslib and the British Library's Advisory Committee on Interlending.

Lynne Brindley is Pro-Vice-Chancellor (Communications and Information Technology) at the University of Leeds. She also retains her position as University Librarian. As a member of JISC she led the Electronic Libraries Programme and has been involved in the development of the JISC Information Strategies Initiative.

Jackie Brocklebank is an Information Specialist for business and law at Aston University Library and Information Services. She is a member of The British and Irish Association of Law Librarians and the Association of Law Librarians in Central England. Prior to working at Aston she worked as librarian for a firm of consulting engineers and before that as Head of Information Services at the British Leather Confederation.

Peter Brophy is Professor of Information Management and Director of the Centre for Research in Library and Information Management (CERLIM) at the Manchester Metropolitan University. Until March 1998 he was University Librarian and Head of the Library and Learning Resource Services at the University of Central Lancashire. He has directed a large number of library and information management research projects and has published widely in the field. Currently he is President-Elect of the Institute of Information Scientists.

Graham Bulpitt was appointed University Librarian at Sheffield Hallam University in 1990, and since September 1996 he has been Director of the Learning Centre. He is currently Chair of the Library Association University College and Research Group and a member of the SCONUL Executive Board. He is also a member of the Advisory Council on Libraries, which advises the Secretary of State, Department of Culture, Media and Sport, on public library provision.

Jane Core is currently Assistant Head of Information Services at the University of Abertay Dundee and Associate Director of EduLib. Jane has worked in higher education libraries for many years and has both delivered and managed the delivery of extensive programmes of user education/information skills to undergraduate and post-graduate students. Jane was involved closely in TAFIS (Tayside and Fife Information Skills Gateway) – a regional collaborative project lead by the University of Abertay Dundee Information Services.

John Cox is Head of Library IT Services in the Boole Library at University College Cork. Previously he managed the Information Service at the Wellcome Centre for Medical Science in London. He has published widely on electronic information services.

Robin Davis is Associate Librarian, University of Stirling (Acting Director of Information Services 1996/97). He is a founder member (1996) of Stirling University and has also worked at University College London, University of Liverpool, and McMaster University (Ontario). He has published widely mainly on bibliographical topics and on the writer Samuel Beckett.

Joan Day is Professor and Head of Department of Information and Library Management at the University of Northumbria at Newcastle. She has been co-director, with Graham Walton, of the IMPEL research team, investigating the Impact on People of Electronic Libraries since 1992. She has lectured and published widely on user aspects of using Information Technology in Library and Information Services and was co-editor, with Terry Hanson, of *CD-ROM in Libraries: Management Issues* (Bowker Saur, 1994).

Marilyn Deegan is an expert in humanities computing and electronic research. Currently Project Manager of the Refugee Studies Programme Digital Library Project at the University of Oxford, she was formerly Professor of Electronic Library

Managing the Electronic Library

Research at De Montfort University. She has published widely on these subjects, and is currently Editor of the major journal *Literary and Linguistic Computing* published by the Oxford University Press. Dr Deegan is also a medievalist specialising in medieval medical and herbal manuscripts, and she has an interest in crime and adventure literature of the early twentieth century. She recently edited the John Buchan novel *The Dancing Floor* for Oxford World's Classics.

Catherine Edwards is a Research Associate in the Department of Information and Library Management at the University of Northumbria at Newcastle. She has been involved with the IMPEL research team since 1993, investigating the organizational and cultural aspects of the increasingly electronic environment in Higher Education Library and Information Services.

Helen Edwards is Head of Library and Databases at London Business School, having held various other positions there for ten years previously. Prior to this she was Assistant Librarian at the University of Sussex. She is a committee member of UK MISG and has published the *Biography of Finance and Investment 2nd edition* with R. Brealey.

Colin Galloway is currently Acquisitions Librarian at Glasgow University Library, a post he has held for the past seven years. Previous posts he has held include Serials Librarian, Social Sciences Subject Librarian, Reference Librarian, and Official Publications Librarian in Glasgow and Oxford.

Thomas Graham is Librarian of the University of Newcastle upon Tyne. He previously held the same position at the University of York and worked earlier in his career at the universities of Glasgow, Aberdeeen and Hull. He is a member of SCONUL's Advisory Committee on Scholarly Communication and of the Funding Councils' Steering Group on the National Electronic Site Licence Initiative.

Andrew Green took up the post of Librarian of the National Library of Wales in October 1998. Previously he was Director of Library and Information Services at the University of Wales Swansea, where he was responsible for library, academic IT, networking and media services. He has also worked in university libraries in Aberystwyth, Cardiff and Sheffield, is Chair of the SLS User Group and the joint JISC/CURL COPAC Policy Group, Covener of the Swansea Bay Information Society Group, and is a member of the Executive Board of SCONUL. His professional interests include access to libraries and information, strategic planning and inter-library cooperation.

Terry Hanson is currently Sub-Librarian: Information Services at the University of Portsmouth where he has worked since 1980. During 1994/95 he was Head of Reference and Information Services at the University of Connecticut. He has published widely on electronic information services and library management issues.

Elizabeth Heaps is Acting Librarian at the University of York Library. Prior to this she has held a variety of posts at York, including subject librarian for social sciences, systems librarian, head of reader services and systems and head of subject services and information systems. She started her professional career at the University of East Anglia Library.

Ruth Jenkinson has worked in higher education libraries for many years, and for the last fourteen years as Head of Library Services and then more recently as Head of Library and Information Services at Edge Hill University College. She is actively involved in management development and staff training initiatives in both academic libraries and computing services.

Paula Kingston has worked extensively in higher education libraries, including at Aston, Swansea and Loughborough universities. She has also worked for the National Council for

Educational Technology where she managed the information service and a wide range of projects. Whilst working at Loughborough she managed Project ACORN, an Electronic Libraries project to develop an electronic short loan collection.

Derek Law is Librarian and Director of Information Strategy at the University of Strathclyde, having worked previously in the Universities of London, Edinburgh, St Andrews and Glasgow, mainly in technical services. The author of over 100 articles, conference papers and monographs, he lectures widely, mainly on topics to do with electronic libraries and management in higher education. Throughout the nineteen-nineties he has been much associated with the development of electronic library services delivered nationally and with the Follett Report and its various outcomes. This has led to service on a large number of committees concerned with national policy. He is at present a member of the Library and Information Commission, chairing its international sub-committee and is Treasurer of the International Federation of Library Associations.

Patrick McGlamery works in the Map and Geographic Information Center (MAGIC) at the University of Connecticut. Coming to the university in 1980 from the Library of Congress, he developed MAGIC as a spatial data library. He is active in ALA's LITA and Map and Geography Roundtable and in IFLA. He is a frequent speaker nationally, regionally and internationally.

David McNamara is currently Director of EduLib. He is based at the University of Hull where he is professor of education. He has particular interest in the relevance of the social sciences to education theory and the practice and training of teachers. He is also concerned with providing training and support in teaching methods for university staff and he contributes to the higher education teaching methods programme at Hull. He has researched and published extensively in the fields of policy and practice in primary and higher education.

John Morrow works in the Robinson Library of Newcastle University Library where he is responsible for Reader Services. He is also the University Library's Staff Development Officer and is a committee member of the Personnel Training and Education Group of the Library Association.'

Martin Myhill is Deputy Librarian, University of Exeter. His interests include electronic library resourcing in former Soviet States, WWW development (Chair of the university's Joint Liaison Group of information providers and member of the University of Exeter's Electronic Information Working Group) and Chair of the national group: Librarians of Institutes and Schools of Education (LISE).

Bernard Naylor has been Librarian of the University of Southampton since 1977, where he was also Co-ordinator of Information Services 1988–93. He has been a member of the British Library Board since 1995. His experience in applying computer technology to library and information matters extends over thirty years, and includes most of the specialist areas.

Kath O'Donovan is Head of Information Systems and Technical Services at the Library of the University of Sheffield. From 1977 to 1993 she worked in the Library of the University of Newcastle upon Tyne, as Engineering Librarian, Medical Librarian and finally as Sub-Librarian: IT and Liaison. She has also worked in special libraries.

Keith Renwick has recently retired from the post of Head of Technical Services and Administration at UMIST Library and Information Service in Manchester, where he was employed in various posts for 25 years. He has retired from UMIST to take up the post of UK Sales Manager for W.H.Everett & Son Ltd., the London-based International Library Supplier established in 1793. He has many years experience in the field of library acquisitions and served on the Executive Committee of the National Acquisitions Group from 1989 to 1997.

Norman Russell has been University Librarian at the Queen's University of Belfast since 1990 having previously worked in McMaster University, Canada and the University of Ulster. He currently chairs the Library and Information Services Council (Northern Ireland) and is a member of the Library and Information Commission's Research Sub-Committee and the British Library Advisory Council. In less busy days he had a considerable number of publications, mainly in the area of staff management.

Michele Shoebridge is Assistant Director for Public Services within Information Services at the University of Birmingham which involves responsibility for front-line services across 12 sites. She has worked in a variety of posts in the University Library prior to convergence in 1995 including Head of Administration and Planning, Systems Librarian and running the Sports Documentation Centre.

Jean Steward has worked at the University of East Anglia Library since 1974 when she joined the Library as a cataloguer. She successively became Head of the Cataloguing Department, Head of Technical Services and Head of Services and in 1998 was appointed Director of Library and Learning Resources. Jean has been an active member of the Library Association, and has served as Chair of the East Anglian Librarians' Consultative Committee, President of the Association of Assistant Librarians, and Editor of the *UC&R Newsletter*. She has been a member of the L.A. Council and the Board of the *L.A. Record*. Jean has also undertaken consultancy work in Nigeria, Ethiopia and Bulgaria as well as co-directing British Council workshops in England and abroad.

Phil Sykes originally trained as a lawyer before becoming a librarian. He has worked at Leeds Polytechnic, Hatfield Polytechnic and until recently managed 'the ARC' at Liverpool John Moores University, an innovative resource centre which provides a 'converged' computing and library service. His main professional interests are in staff management and motivation, liability for information provision, the convergence of academic support services, and electronic information provision. He was the originator of the 'On Demand Publishing in the Humanities' project, funded by the JISC under the 'eLib' programme, which explores the issues surrounding electronic supply of course readings. He has recently taken up an appointment as Director of Library Services at the University of Huddersfield.

Jill Taylor-Roe is Sub-Librarian, Liaison and Academic Services at Newcastle University, where she leads the team of Faculty Liaison Librarians, and manages the Library's acquisitions budget. She also chairs the NEYAL Purchasing Consortium which comprises 22 academic libraries in the North, North East, Yorkshire and Midlands

Ian Tilsed is the Computing Development Officer for the University of Exeter Library and Information Service. An experienced Web author, he is Editor of the Library Web site and teaches HTML authoring within the University.

Will Wakeling has recently taken charge of collection management at Northeastern University, Boston, Massachusetts. Between 1991 to 1998 he was Assistant Director for Collection Management in the University of Birmingham's Information Services where he had University responsibility for licensing and copyright matters. He has previously worked in technical services at BLDSC and the Universities of Bristol and York, has a special interest in journal management and publishing and has been an active member of the UK Serials Group.

Margaret Watson is Principal Lecturer/Head of Subject Division in the Department of Information and Library Management at the University of Northumbria at Newcastle. Teaching areas include user education, communication of information, interpersonal skills and communication theory. Margaret's research interests are lifelong learning, information skills, and staff training and development. She has run several courses on delivering information skills programmes, staff training, customer care and presentation skills. She is currently Chair of the Library Association: Northern Branch and a member of the Northern Training Group.

Keith Webster is Sub-Librarian, Document Delivery Services at the University of Newcastle upon Tyne where he manages the core areas of library activity including Reader and Technical Services, Information Systems and Special Collections. Previous posts include Reference Librarian at Glasgow Caledonian University and Manager of the Scottish Library and Information Council. He is currently Honorary Secretary of the Institute of Information Scientists.

Roy Williams has worked at the University of North London for ten years and is currently Director of Information Systems and Services.

Robin Yeates is the Senior Researcher/Manager of the Library Information Technology Centre (LITC) at South Bank University in London. LITC's mission is to undertake and communicate applied research to inspire and assist 'libraries' of the future. Robin is joint Editor of *Library Technology*, and a member of the Board of Program: electronic library and information systems. He is the co-ordinator of the NewsAgent current awareness alerting project and is also actively involved in large-scale European and UK development projects concerning digital library management, interoperability and access control.

Foreword

The idea of the electronic library has been with us for a long time and whether we date the thinking from the seminal 1944 paper by Vannevar Bush (Bush, 1945) or earlier it is clear that the ideas are rapidly turning into reality. It may not be the reality of (all of) our dreams and predictions but the rapid progress of the last few years has taken us to the point where the terrain is becoming clearer and real products and services are becoming available in significant numbers. In particular the development and rapid adoption of the open World Wide Web protocol, with its simple hypertext navigation system and ability to handle multimedia, has been the platform on which much of this progress has been built.

In our previous book (Hanson and Day, 1994) we looked at how libraries were dealing with the management implications of an earlier stage of this evolution, the impact of CD-ROM. For the present work we continue with the management theme in the context of a more mature and far more complex electronic library situation. We are looking at how libraries cope with the enormous effects of new service possibilities, with the constant re-definition of their role, and with the necessity to forge strategic partnerships on campus.

The general approach of the book is to take a comprehensive look at how libraries in a broadly similar situation grapple, theoretically and practically, with the transition to the electronic library. Though the issues identified in the book are universally applicable, across library sectors and countries, we decided, nonetheless, to concentrate attention on one sector in one country, UK academic libraries. This focused approach, with its clear basis for comparison between different libraries, will, we believe, be of greater value not just to the UK academic library community but also to academic librarians in other countries and to public and special librarians anywhere. International coverage is not entirely absent though with chapters describing experience in Cork and Connecticut.

The structure of the book is similar to the earlier work. The chapters have been commissioned on the basis of a designed structure. There is a mix of 'overview' papers which identify themes and issues, and practical case studies from individual libraries. Most sections have an overview and two case studies though the section on Management Issues at Campus Level has two overviews and four case studies while the Management Information section, as a new area of concern, has only the overview. In addition there is a section devoted to management of specific services, such as electronic reserve and geospatial data collections, and a final section devoted to general case studies covering all the issues from the perspective of individual libraries. In general the chapters have been commissioned with a view to providing a representative collection of universities by size, age and geographic location within the UK.

The main theme of the book is change. It is about how university libraries are responding to the rapidly changing higher education system in the UK with its increasing student numbers and their greater diversity and requirement for flexibility of access. At one level the response is, of necessity, political and strategic. It is about how libraries re-think their traditional roles and see the value and necessity of re-positioning themselves on campus. At another level it is concerned with:

- the constant pressure to do more with less;
- the recognition of the potential for new service possibilities;
- the implementation of these services;
- the adoption of more flexible working practices and management structures;
- making a reality of end user empowerment;
- the effective management of the change process (for both staff and users).

There is inevitably much repetition, or reinforcement, as different authors emphasise some of the same fundamentals and acknowledge the same influences from their different perspectives.

In Britain the electronic library debate is informed by a burgeoning literature that includes major reports such as Dearing (NCIHE, 1997) at the general higher education level and Follett (HEFCE, 1993) which looks at the changing role of university libraries. Combined with these high-level contributions there have also been a number of key developments that have had an enormous influence on UK academic libraries.

At the strategy and policy level there has been a particularly active convergence debate in the UK and more recently, since Follett, this has been set in the context of the development of unversity information strategies. The latter has been promoted by Follett and Dearing and, as a practical requirement, by the Funding Councils' Joint Information Systems Committee (JISC), as a framework for the effective development of information resources, in all areas, in universities. After an introduction on the nature of the electronic library we begin the book with a section devoted to these strategic issues with overview chapters from Lynne Brindley on information strategies and from Derek Law on convergence. These are followed by four case studies looking at how individual universities have dealt with these issues.

At a more practical level it is important to mention major initiatives such as:

- the development, and continued improvement, of the universities' computer network JANET (Joint Academic NETwork);
- the evolution of what is now called the Distributed National Electronic Resource (DNER). This is an ongoing programme to collect together, by commercial procurement or by generation within the sector, scholarly information resources ranging from bibliographic databases (such as the ISI Citation Indexes via BIDS), statistical datasets (such as census statistics via MIDAS), geospatial datasets (such as Ordnance Survey Strategi via EDINA), other research collections such as the Arts and Humanities Data Service, and Internet Subject Gateways such as OMNI and SOSIG. The DNER is the responsibility of JISC's Committee for Electronic Information (CEI);
- the Electronic Libraries (eLib) Programme. This has been a very important development in British academic librarianship. It has provided, at just the right time, an opportunity for innovative projects to be supported and a focus for the entire community on the issues involved in the development of the electronic library. This has provided for a collective learning experience, with extensive participation across the sector. It has in fact illustrated the potential, and necessity, for national and international cooperation in the development of library and information services.

It is of course very difficult to say how this development process would have proceeded without the support and guidance of JANET, the DNER and the eLib Programme, but it is clear that these initiatives have been very influential and beneficial. This is made clear throughout the book, in both the overviews and case studies.

In the current, third, phase of the eLib Programme one of the two main themes is the development of 'hybrid libraries';

the notion of a mixed library environment incorporating large print holdings with increasing quantities of electronic information accessible via local and Internet sources. The book might perhaps be more accurately, if a little less snappily, entitled *Managing the Hybrid Library* as it is clear that all university libraries are in the midst of a long transition that will shift the balance between print and electronic sources, but which will never result in a purely electronic library.

Finally, we would like to thank all of our contributors for their readiness to share their thoughts and experiences. The general picture painted by the book is, we think, of an energetic sector keen to experiment and innovate and to meet the challenges of an uncertain but unquestionably exciting future. There has never been a more interesting time to be an academic library manager!

References

Bush, V. (1945) As we may think. *Atlantic Monthly*, **176**(1), 641–649

Hanson, T. and Day, J. (1994) *CD-ROM in libraries: management issues.* London: Bowker Saur

Higher Education Funding Council for England, et al. (1993) *Joint Funding Councils' Libraries Review Group: Report.* (Follett Report). Bristol: HEFCE

National Committee of Inquiry into Higher Education (1997) *Higher education in the learning society.* (Dearing Report). London: HMSO

Terry Hanson
Joan Day
August 1998

Contents

Section 1: Introduction

Section 2: Management issues at campus level

Figures

Tables

SECTION 1
Introduction

CHAPTER ONE

The Electronic Library in Teaching and Research

Marilyn Deegan

The library world is currently undergoing a period of great change, and university and research libraries are finding themselves at the forefront of some exciting new developments. With the growth in the use of new technologies, the increasing availability of digital information in the form of electronic publications and networked resources, and the pervasiveness of the Internet, a new concept is emerging: the 'electronic (or digital) library'. This is a much discussed notion at the moment in both the USA and Europe; it has many enthusiastic proponents, and with the ubiquity of electronic networks and global connections, it seems likely to revolutionize the way academic libraries throughout the world deliver their information. Research monies are being spent on a plethora of electronic library projects, and some scholars and librarians are becoming alarmed at the rapid progress being claimed in the race to full digitization of scholarly materials. There are a number of different definitions of the electronic library which it might be useful to discuss and contrast, but first perhaps we need to think a little about the concept of the research library and its main functions. It is something which librarians, scholars and students take for granted every day, but perhaps in a time of such great change it is useful to look at some of the assumptions we make and see how they are going to change in these new environments.

Most people in the academic world think of a library first of all as a defined place where they go to do some or all of their scholarly work. Indeed, many academics spend their lives, or certainly their summers, travelling around the libraries of the world consulting unique documents which make up the their holdings. In a recent article, Lynne Brindley (Brindley, 1993, p. 176) gives a list of libraries used regularly by one scholar working in a history-related discipline. This list includes thirteen libraries in the UK, as well as libraries in Moscow, St Petersburg, and Helsinki. We can regard this as a typical practice, certainly in the humanities. The library, therefore, is a central site to which information is brought, and if you want access to that information, you have to go to the site.

For many scholars and students, in the humanities in particular, the library is the prime location of research and scholarship: it is their laboratory. While one would not deny that the library is also an important source of information for scientists, they are less likely to use the range of legacy material which is still of vital use in the humanities. They are much more likely to need rapid access to the latest research results, the provision of which is one of the many areas where the electronic library might have significant advantages over the traditional library. In the humanities, it is not just a question of preserving information for a small and specialist band of researchers: the information which is preserved in libraries, and in other repositories such as museums and art galleries, is our culture, which must be secured from harm and obsolescence if we are to remain civilized. This culture is produced, enhanced and augmented through a complex, interdependent and rather mysterious set of processes, in which researchers in the humanities play an important role. The major activity of the humanities scholar is the sifting of information about cultural artefacts, which include texts, images, objects, sounds, languages and performances. Some of the artefacts are the product of our material culture, and some are products of the imagination. In the study of these artefacts, each generation of scholars and students finds new meanings and new interpretations. These accretive layers of interpretation become themselves part of the meaning encoded upon the artefacts, and therefore part of the objects of study. This is a rather different process from that which takes place in the sciences, where new information generally replaces the old, rather than supplementing it.

Librarians and libraries, of course, play an equally, if not more important role in cultural preservation and enhancement. Traditionally, they are concerned with the acquisition, preservation and organization of information. That is, they acquire documents, preserve them, and catalogue them so that they may be found and used by those who need them. This may seem very obvious, but it is important to descibe the function of a traditional library in order to understand the extent of the changes which are taking place. In the definitions given, organization is the key to distinguishing a library from other collections of documents: if you don't organize, you can't find things, and if you can't find them, you can't use them. The move from handlist to card catalogue to computerized OPAC is a revolutionary; one instead of finding holdings according to when you acquired them, or who wrote them, it is now possible to find holdings according to any of the structured parameters by which a document is described. With the card catalogue, if a reader wished to search by author, by title or by subject, then there had to be three catalogues, and searching by any other parameter was impossible. With the OPAC, redundancy of information is avoided: there is one catalogue containing information structured in such a fashion that it can be ordered from many different points of view. But, however sophisticated the management of digital information about the physical objects in a library may be, this is not yet an electronic library. The objects are just as they were, although they are perhaps easier to find. An electronic library, rather, contains digital versions of the actual materials which the library holds and which the user needs. When a critical mass of material is held by a library in digital form, then that library is on the way to becoming an electronic library. One definition of the electronic library might be that it is a conventional library which has converted some proportion of its holdings to digital form, but there are significant properties of digitized media which could make the library more than that.

Digital documents are just a series of electronic impulses. Whether they are represented as searchable ASCII text or as bitmap page images, they are still in the same form at the lowest possible level. Of course, this does not only apply to documents, it also applies to anything which has been digitized or produced as digital from the start. So sound, video, images and text are all represented by patterns of bits. The implications of reducing all media to this set of digital patterns are that, firstly they can all be stored the same way (although there are differences of orders of magnitude in the amount of storage required by different media). Secondly, the boundaries are effectively removed between media, between institutions which hold the media, between countries, and between types of repositories. Whereas in the physical world there is a huge difference between a painting, a museum object (vase, sculpture, coin etc.), a document (book, manuscript, journal etc.), a satellite image or a medical image, there is almost no difference in the digital world: they are all represented by a pattern of bits and bytes, they need the same kind of machine to allow their display and manipulation and they can all be transmitted through networks. The main difference between digital representations of different media is size: searchable text is very compact; detailed images, sound and video are all very large. But that is a difference of degree, not kind. This means that the electronic library can therefore, in theory, integrate all the kinds of materials a researcher might need, and can transcend institutional and national boundaries. A student or academic could bring to his or her desktop a whole variety of media, from different kinds of institutions and many countries, and integrate them on the screen of his or her personal workstation. What we have when this is possible is not just an electronic library, which might be a physically identifiable library with staff and facilities, but which delivers the information it holds through digital means, but a 'virtual library' which means that when one is virtually anywhere, one can be virtually everywhere. The 'virtual' library has an element of illusion about it: the searcher may think that he or she is retrieving information from a local source, when in fact it is being collected without his or her knowledge from all corners of the world and being integrated seamlessly at the desktop. The virtual library is therefore potentially enormous, as it could comprise all the electronic libraries in the world linked together. It is also potentially very small and personal, being the set of information which a scholar identifies and accesses as a personal virtual workspace. The purpose of libraries, even huge research libraries like the British Library, is shifting from acquisition to access: libraries are gateways to resources as much as they are custodians of some of those resources. Given these definitions, one might ask if Internet or the World Wide Web are electronic libraries. They are certainly going to be the means through which electronic libraries disseminate their information, but they are not themselves electronic libraries as they lack the organizational principles necessary for the delivery of scholarly information in a structured and economical fashion. In libraries, information is delivered to us by skilled professionals, and this is how it should be delivered in electronic or virtual libraries.

One question we might consider is the status of the book in the digital world, and, related to this, the role of the publishing industry. The book, some say, is dead. Others, notably Sven Birketts (1994) in his lament for the book '*The Gutenberg Elegies*', plead for the familiarity of the physical object which offers an immediacy of experience unmediated by the interposition of technology. The book, a medium which encourages depth and reflectiveness, is posed against the computer and the Internet, which offer speed and shallowness. But between those tolling the death knell for the book and those who regard technology as the spawn of the devil is a middle way, in which we can consider the appropriateness of a particular medium for a specific task. Encyclopaedias and large dictionaries such as the Oxford English Dictionary, for instance, are probably best delivered electronically. Large corpora of art-historical images, too, which are prohibitively expensive to print, can be digitally delivered to the desktop for a fraction of the cost. A number of electronic library projects are currently engaged in building large image archives: the HELIX project, for instance [funded by the Electronic Libraries Programme (eLib)] which, during 1998, will be delivering more than 50,000 images of art objects, furniture, ceramics and early photographs, among other things; and the Joint Information Services Commitiee (JISC) Image Digitization Initiative which is working with 16 archives in UK higher education to provide a large number of diverse images. Studies of film technique too, which offer the opportunity to view film clips as part of the argument rather than read a description, offer a valuable enhancement to the subject. Perhaps, though, the latest novel, or a volume of verse, are best in the traditional book format.

Academic journals are an interesting case perhaps for dual delivery: the electronic version for the speed with which issues can appear, crucial in some subjects – physics or medicine, for instance; and the paper version for archiving – at least for the present while there is still uncertainty about the long-term preservability and stability of the digital media. There is an interesting debate in progress in some academic circles on the role of the publisher in the production and dissemination of scholarly findings now that it is possible to carry out most of the attendant processes electronically. The argument advanced is: the university pays the academic to do the research and write up the findings. The academic publishes a journal article or monograph, which the university then purchases. Is the university then paying twice for the same thing, and would there be a way to cut out the intermediate stage? Several proposals have been advanced to remove publishers from the loop. It has been suggested that universities should act as publishers of materials produced by their own employees, keep the materials on their own servers, and charge for access to them from outside. Another idea which is being tested is electronic journals which are entirely managed and controlled within the academic world. In physics, for instance, the Los Alamos National Laboratory Electronic Preprint Archive for physics literature, started by Paul Ginsparg in 1991, is now used globally by researchers in most areas of physics, and is estimated to have captured over 70 per cent of the current physics journal literature. This archive has succeeded in dispersing the stereotype which dismisses electronic publishing as an inferior publishing medium: most authors in physics now routinely substitute their Los Alamos preprints with electronic versions of the final, refereed, published versions of their articles. There are two examples later of electronic journals in the UK which are produced without any paper cognates. On the other hand, while academic books and journals are expensive to purchase from publishers, perhaps there would be losses, some unforeseen, if we were to dispense with publishers entirely. The processes of editing, refereeing, book design, marketing, etc. are more complex, time-consuming and therefore expensive than many assume, and there is several centuries' worth of experience in the publishing industry. There need to be many changes in the era of electronic publication, but we should be wary of any attempts to get rid of babies along with the bathwater.

The move from the print world to the electronic world, though beneficial for some of our materials, is a difficult, time-consuming and expensive process. We should also not be carried away by the possibilities of digitization: just because we can digitize resources, doesn't mean that we must. It has been calculated, for example, that it would cost billions of pounds to digitize all the holdings of the British Library, and so we perhaps need to be selective in what we choose to digitize, at least in these early stages. A note of caution should be sounded here however: there is a danger that only very popular texts and other artefacts will be made available, and this will reinforce a narrowly canonical approach to scholarship. Another point which also needs to be made is that there is a difference between retrospective conversion, and the provision of originals in electronic form or in simultaneous printed and electronic form. In the matter of text, because books, journals, etc. are now being produced by computer, an electronic product could easily be one of the outputs alongside the printed version, and we are seeing many more electronic journals and magazines either alongside the printed versions, or, increasingly, produced as only electronic. In the artefactual disciplines, computers are being used in the practice of the discipline, and again an electronic output is a possible product. A good example of this is illustrated by the electronic journal, *Internet Archaeology*, funded by eLib, which is making exciting and innovative use of the structures and modelling techniques available through digital technologies for the representation of non-linear, three-dimensional archaeological information. The journal publishes the results of archaeological research, including excavation reports (text, photographs, data, drawings, reconstructions, diagrams and interpretations), analyses of large data sets along with the data itself, visualizations, programs used to analyse data and applications of information technology in archaeology: for example, geographical information systems and computer modelling. Conventional publication via the printed page cannot do justice to the rich diversity of archaeological information. Electronic publication, by contrast, offers opportunities to overcome these difficulties. In chemistry, the eLib Programme has funded the establishment of an electronic version of the journal *Chemical Communications*, a forum for the dissemination of preliminary accounts of important developments in chemistry. This is using Internet technologies such as Java to allow the display of three-dimensional molecular information attached to numerical and symbolical data in order to enhance the value of the information.

Some of the world's major research libraries which hold valuable and rare or unique materials are embarking on large-scale programmes of digitization as means to preservation and wider dissemination. For some of these projects, digitization is a means to the production of a paper surrogate, as in the Cornell Brittle Books Program, where printed books which are deteriorating badly are scanned to produce a digital paper facsimile, which is then bound to replace the crumbling volume in the stacks. This process has as a by-product a digital intermediate surrogate which is also being made available online. In other projects, the digital facsimile itself is the end product, particularly in libraries which are dealing with fragile and unique manuscript materials where access to the originals is restricted, providing a surrogate for the use of scholars and students from their desktops. Damage to the manuscripts caused through handling can (hopefully) be halted, while the needs of scholarship are served by the digital surrogates. If one has the appropriate technology, in particular a large screen, one can view side-by-side manuscripts from, say, Prague, New York, Paris and London. Palaeographers no longer need to rely on capacious memories, or the vagaries of the post which can deliver photographs months late; now at the click of a mouse many resources are available. There are several projects to which one could draw attention: the Beowulf manuscript studies being carried out at the British Library; the Celtic Manuscripts project at Oxford University; and the Aberdeen Bestiary at Aberdeen University are good examples.

There are still a considerable number of problems which need to be solved, however, in the provision of high-quality images of complex and rare originals, including the management of such images over a long period of time. Microfilm, the main surrogate storage medium at the moment, is accessible using relatively simple technology, though it does deteriorate over time, in particular if colour film is used. Digital images require highly sophisticated hardware for their display, and this hardware rapidly becomes obsolete.

This is a problem which has also been found in the uses and storage of electronic text. Some key texts were captured in the 1960s, the early days of textual computing, and the media of capture (punch cards, punch tape, etc.) are no longer available. If the texts are not moved up consciously through generations of hardware and software, then the life of an electronic text is potentially very short, shorter even than that of a text printed on the most fragile acid-based paper. If we are to spend vast amounts of money capturing digital images, then we need to ensure that the images survive as long as possible. We also need to preserve these secondary images as a means of conserving the originals, and controlling access to them. If the surrogates are sufficiently good, then use of the fragile originals can be restricted; but if we have to keep rescanning the originals, the use of surrogates as a conservation method becomes pointless. One great advantage which digital technology has over photography of medieval manuscripts is that the colours, if calibrated properly, are 'true', unlike colour photography, which varies with the brand of film and the chemicals used to develop it. Also, digital images do not degrade over time in the way photographs can. Much work is being done at the moment to calibrate colour targets, scanners, monitors and printers so that accurate colour reproduction at all stages is possible.

The delivery of digital information in a structured, reliable, organized and timely fashion has been seen as so crucial by various national bodies in the UK and elsewhere that funding has been mobilized for various electronic library initiatives. In the UK, a major report on academic libraries was produced in 1993 as the findings of a committee chaired by Sir Brian Follett (HEFCE, 1993). The Follett Report suggested that information technology could be mobilized to help meet the needs of library users and library managers over the next decade, and that substantial funding should be made available for a range of projects to investigate electronic library issues and to develop some of the content, resources and management structures needed for digital libraries. As a direct response to the Follett Report, the JISC established eLib. The programme was initially given a budget of £15 million over 3 years to fund projects in a variety of areas. The main aim of the eLib Programme, through its projects, has been to engage the higher education community in developing and shaping the implementation of the electronic library.

The first two phases of the eLib Programme have so far yielded almost 60 projects funded in different programme areas. These areas are:

- Document Delivery;
- Access To Network Resources;
- Training and Awareness;
- Electronic Journals;
- Digitization;
- Images;
- Electronic Short Loan Collections;
- On Demand Publishing;
- Pre-Prints and Grey Literature.

The Programme has also funded the Higher Education Digitization Service at the University of Hertfordshire. The thrust of these initial stages has been to create some of the components of the electronic library: a building blocks approach. Particularly important is the ACORN (Access to Course Reading via Networks) Project, which is exploring the potential of information technology to deliver high-demand material electronically to students across the campus, via networked computers, and has developed and implemented a model for effectively managing the whole process, from requesting reading lists from academic staff to the consultation of the text by students; and EDDIS (Electronic Document Delivery – the Integrated Solution) which aims to produce an integrated, end-user-driven identification, holdings discovery, ordering and electronic supply service for non-returnable items (typically journal articles), which could be used by all UK higher education institutions.

Also important in these first two phases are the various subject gateway projects such as:

- OMNI: Organizing Medical Networked Information;
- ADAM: Art, Design, Architecture and Media Information Gateway;
- EEVL: Edinburgh Engineering Virtual Library;
- SOSIG: Social Science Information Gateway.

Content building, too, is a priority for the Programme: important here are the HELIX project mentioned above; the Internet Library of Early Journals, whose aim is to offer expanded access over the Internet to digitized page images of substantial runs of 18th- and 19th-century journals, and to evaluate these in terms of use and acceptability; and MIDRIB: Medical Images: Digitized Reference Information Bank, which is creating, maintaining and delivering a comprehensive collection of medical images in digital form for use in teaching and research in medical and healthcare faculties of universities and teaching hospitals. A third phase of eLib has recently begun, with a small number of larger projects than in the earlier phases. These fall into two main areas: hybrid libraries and large-scale resource discovery. Worldwide there have been a large number of electronic, digital or virtual library projects which are producing a wide range of alternative technologies. The challenge now is to bring together technologies from these new developments, plus the electronic products and services already in libraries, and the historical functions of our local physical libraries, into well-organized, accessible hybrid libraries. These hybrid libraries must deal with materials in every kind of format, both digital and non-digital, and should integrate them through some system which is presented to the user through a single interface (this is discussed further below). The UK's higher education libraries contain an incomparable set of bibliographic resources, which are not fully exploited outside the individual institutions holding them. The Anderson report has highlighted the problems inherent in institutions building adequate research collections on their own, and the increasing imperative to share resources, particularly at a regional level. Some of the eLib phase three projects will build integrated bibliographic resources ('clumps') which could serve regions or specific user groups. There is another strand of eLib phase three which is investigating the issues around preservation of digital data in library environments.

Another key national development in the UK in the route to the collection and dissemination of digitized materials for scholars is the establishment of the Arts and Humanities Data Service. In 1994 a feasibility study was funded by the JISC of the Higher Education Funding Councils in the UK to report on the potential for scholarship of such a service, and the study recommended that the service should indeed be set up; its finding were quickly endorsed by the funding councils, and a substantial annual budget was allowed for the purpose. The original study recommended that the role of the Service should be to promote effective, low-cost access to the widest range of relevant digital resources by UK academics in the humanities; and that a distributed structure should be established with some services provided centrally and others by specialist data and service providers in different subject areas or dealing with different media. The executive for the Service has been set up at King's College in London, with Dr Daniel Greenstein as Director, and five service providers have been selected: the History Data Unit at the University of Essex to provide historical data, the Oxford Text Archive to serve the literature and linguistics communities, a centre for archaeology at York, a centre for music and time-based data at Glasgow (PADS), and a centre for the visual arts at Surrey Institute of Art and Design (VADS). All the projects described above which are being funded by the UK Higher Education Funding Councils are contributing to the Distributed National Electronic Resource (DNER); a major initiative to make available teaching and research resources.

Outside of the UK higher education sector there are, of course, many electronic library projects. The Telematics for Libraries Programme of the European Union DG XIII funds a number of pan-European projects, many of which have UK partners, and this programme has had great impact on developments throughout Europe. In the US, there are six federally-funded digital library projects led by universities which comprize the National Science Federation (NSF)/Advanced Research Projects Agency (ARPA)/National Aeronautics and Space Administration (NASA) Digital Library Initiative (DLI). The individual projects are:

- University of California, Berkeley: An Electronic Environmental Library Project;
- University of California, Santa Barbara: The Alexandria Project: Towards a Distributed Digital Library with Comprehensive Services for Images and Spatially Referenced Information;
- Carnegie Mellon University: Informedia: Integrated Speech, Image and Language Understanding for Creation and Exploration of Digital Video Libraries;
- University of Illinois at Urbana-Champaign: Building the Interspace: Digital Library Infrastructure for a University Engineering Community;
- University of Michigan: The University of Michigan Digital Library Project;
- Stanford University: Stanford University Digital Libraries Project.

There are also many other initiatives and centres throughout the USA; they are too numerous to mention individually, but details about them can be found at the dLib Magazine Ready Reference Web site. The commercial world, too, has become heavily involved in digital library developments: IBM, for instance, have been building digital library systems in partnership with a range of institutions: the Vatican Library, with nearly 1.5 million books; Indiana University's Variations project for distributing multimedia information across a campus network; and the Institute for Scientific Information, for example. In the UK, they are partnering De Montfort University in the IBM/DMU Digital Library Project which is building a digital library for the ten distributed campuses of the university, as well as for access from outside.

So far, this chapter has looked at some of the underlying concepts which are important for understanding the digital library, and also some of the initiatives which are brokering the realization of the digital library. But in practical terms what is currently available is a diverse number of projects in several countries, dealing with different kinds of electronic media, and funded by different agencies and funding models with their own agenda, a veritable Tower of Babel of information with a vast diversity of management structures. How is this to be welded together into something which can be accessed and understood by all? A number of issues need to be mentioned here: first of all, the problems of cataloguing electronic resources (Hanson, 1998). Should they be integrated into the main library OPAC, or should this deal only with the physical resources of the library? In the new eLib hybrid library models there might be any number of possible solutions to this. I offer two suggestions: firstly that we should remove the ontological distinction between a physical and a digital object, and consider only 'objects' or perhaps 'library objects' or even 'information objects'. A library object might be a book, a manuscript, a letter, a CD-ROM, a microfilm, a video, an electronic document or other kind of electronic entity. The reader/user interrogates the OPAC as a one-stop shop for the data he or she seeks: the data could reside in one or more object types; this is irrelevant to the reader/user up to the point when the located object needs to be retrieved, when the ontological status will need to be known for pragmatic reasons: is one to click on an icon or walk to a shelf? The second suggestion is that we preserve the distinction between objects at a catalogue level, and thus have book catalogues, manuscript catalogues and other structured information about physical objects on the one hand, with different kinds of catalogue information about the electronic objects on the other hand. For the reader/user there would be a 'catalogue of catalogues' which would offer the same one-stop shopping experience described above, with the distinctions between object types hidden until the point of retrieval. These two strategies would offer the same experience to the reader/user, but would have different underlying organizational principles.

Another issue closely related to cataloguing is metadata. If we are to build durable collections of quality electronic resources, the data we store with those resources needs to be rich, accurate, extensible, reliable and structured in some standard format. This metadata (or data about data) is arguably as important as the data itself. Three type of metadata have been identified by the National Digital Library Project of the US Library of Congress as being relevant to digital collections. These are intellectual metadata (cataloguing records, finding aids, etc.), structural metadata (information which links digital objects to make up a logical unit such as a journal article or archival folder) and administrative metadata (which allows the repository to manage the digital collection, including scan date and resolution, storage format and filename). Metadata is a burning question in the electronic library world, and indeed for any groups or individuals concerned with providing, distributing or maintaining electronic information in a networked environment. Many groups have been established to address the question in different communities and are working hard on offering some guidelines. A good start for understanding metadata in the context of electronic libraries is Paul Miller's article in *Ariadne* (1996).

Standards and protocols are different but related issues: standards allow us to produce materials which we know will be exchangeable on different media if we only adhere to the international standards. The most well-worked out approach to standards is probably in the area of digital text. The Text Encoding Initiative has produced a set of complex, definitive standards for the encoding and interchange of digital text based on the Standard Generalized Markup Language, SGML. HTML (Hypertext Mark-up Language), the encoding standard of the World Wide Web, is a subset of SGML, as is the newly-emergent XML (eXtensible Mark-up Language) standard. These standards are now widely accepted by the scholarly community and also by the publishing industry. There is another set of standards also being promulgated by the publishing industry, in particular for the presentation of electronic journals: Portable Document Formats or PDFs, a good example of which is Adobe Acrobat. The main differences between these are as follows: SGML enables the creation of user-defined markup languages which identify what textual elements are, rather than how they should appear, which is what PDFs specify; it is the difference between marking up a piece of text as 'Title' rather than as '24 point Times Roman, bold, centred'. The main advantage of PDFs is that they describe documents in such a way as to enable them to be presented in an attractive visual form on screen. There are some search facilities available in PDF-presented documents, but unlike SGML marked-up documents, they cannot be easily exchanged between systems. This is a disadvantage for the scholar, but a benefit for the commercial publisher of an electronic journal, who may be seeking to prevent any such easy exchange. The standards situation for images is less well-established and there are a number of image standards on the market: TIFF, BMP, etc. Digital sound and video standards are also much less well understood and finalized than standards for text, as are standards for the compression of images, video and sound.

Protocols allow the interchange of information between systems of hardware and software which are different and which hold materials which are of different standards. For instance, the Internet Protocol allows the interchange of information world-wide between sites which locally adhere to many different standards. An exciting and relatively new protocol, which is being used by a number of electronic library projects is the Z39.50 network protocol which is establishing an international standard for network information searching and retrieval. This allows the user to access remote database records by specifying criteria to identify appropriate records, and then requesting the transmission of some or all of the identified records. The crucial point about Z39.50 is that it allows remote databases to be interrogated and integrated without their having to be compatible, and without the interrogator necessarily knowing anything about the structure: the search is as familiar as searching local, known databases. This is a vital development for the integration of various electronic libraries into a global virtual library. A good example of the use of Z39.50 for digital library exchange is the ELISE (Electronic Library Image Server for Europe) Project based at De Montfort University. This is funded by the EU to develop connected image servers running on different hardware platforms with different software systems in four countries. Cross-domain search and retrieval will be possible across the sites using the Z39.50 protocol.

Copyright/intellectual property rights are probably the thorniest problems faced by those developing electronic libraries, but without relatively straightforward and, hopefully, electronic means of managing these issues, there will be a paucity of resources which can be accessed via an electronic library. What makes this a particularly difficult area to deal with is the fluidity of the situation, and the intransigence of some of the copyright owners who fear the opening of the floodgates of illegal usage if they give an inch. In many ways, the copyright situation is no different if you want to digitize material and make it available than if you want to make materials available in some form other than digital. Permission is required from the owner of the rights (generally with printed materials this means both the author and the publisher) before making any use of it other than for personal research. Great complications arise with multimedia materials, since different kinds of materials are restricted by different rights, and may have various licensing agencies dealing with those rights. Music is different from printed materials, which is different from film or drama, for instance. There are also new rights established when the material is copied into a different form. For example, if a photograph is taken of a painting, the photographer owns the rights to that photograph, unless he or she is working on behalf of another person or organization. If someone else digitizes that photograph, they then hold the rights to the digital copy, and permissions have to be obtained for every stage of the copying of protected materials. Publishers of complex multimedia systems have sometimes found themselves with a very difficult and expensive rights management situation on their hands, and it may necessitate thousands of individual negotiations. In the electronic library environment, in-copyright materials have to be managed in such a way that infringements are minimized and fees are paid to rights-holders as appropriate. There are some eLib and EU projects, as well as commercial organizations, which are working on electronic rights management systems: the EU-funded Decomate Project has information about a plethora of these.

Finally, and probably most important for librarians, how, in the electronic networked environment, are we to ensure the preservation of the materials we digitize? I mentioned above the problems of the survival of electronic information which is a different one from the survival of artefacts: artefacts are subject to physical deterioration over time because of external or internal environmental factors. We are all aware of the problems caused by the deterioration of books which were printed on acid-based paper. With the digital versions of artefacts the survival problems are different, and possibly even more costly to prevent. As I mentioned above, the potential survival of electronic materials can be very short, not because they are inherently fragile, but because they rely on other entities, namely hardware and software, to allow access to them, and the life of these is limited because of advances in technology which mean that obsolescence is rapid. We are therefore at the mercy of commercial forces which dictate that hardware has to be changed at least every four years, and software perhaps even more frequently. The necessary migration of materials up through the rapidly evolving generations is a cost which is often missed in electronic libraries programmes. In order to address this problem, the US Commission on Preservation and Access and the Research Libraries Group (RLG) created a Task Force on Archiving of Digital Information, charged with investigating and recommending means to ensure 'continued access indefinitely into the future of records stored in digital electronic form'. The final report of the task force was produced in 1996 and is available on the RLG Web site. In response to the RLG work, JISC and the British Library Research and Innovation Centre (BLRIC) held a workshop in Warwick in 1995 to look into the issues raised. Subsequent to this, a number of studies were funded to raise awareness, promote best practice and help the community understand more fully the nature of electronic materials and the particular preservation problems they pose. BLRIC is overseeing these studies, and the various reports are being placed on the BLRIC web site.

New opportunities and new challenges are being offered to libraries with the advances in digital media. The great research libraries can reach out to readers scattered over a wide geographical distance, the less well endowed institutions have the opportunity to provide access to a greater range of research materials and tools than ever before. There are, of course, problems and blockages, but there is a spirit of goodwill and co-operation between libraries and librarians throughout the international community to overcome these.

References

Aberdeen Bestiary: http://www.clues.abdn.ac.uk:8080/besttest/alt/comment/best_toc.html

Anderson Report: http://ukoln.ac.uk/services/elib/papers/other/anderson/

Arts and Humanities Data Service (AHDS): http://www.ahds.ac.uk

Beowulf manuscript studies at the British Library: http://www.bl.uk

Birketts, Sven. (1994) *The Gutenberg Elegies: the fate of reading in an electronic age.* New York: Fawcett Columbine

Bloch, R. H. and Hesse C. (1995) (eds) *Future Libraries*. Berkeley, Los Angeles and London: University of California Press

Brindley, L. (1993) 'Research Library Directions in the 1990s'. In *Electronic Information Resources and Historians: European Perspectives*, ed. S. Ross and E. Higgs, pp. 176–183. St. Katharinen: Scripta Mercaturae Verlag

British Library Research and Innovation Centre (BLRIC): http://bl.uk/index.html

Celtic Manuscripts Project, Oxford University: http://image.ox.ac.uk

CLIC: Consortium Electronic Journal Project (*Chemical Communications*): http://www.ch.ic.ac.uk/clic/

Communications of the ACM, April 1995. An issue devoted to digital libraries.

Cornell Brittle Books Project: http://www.library.cornell.edu/preservation/brittle.htm

Decomate Project: http://www.lse.ac.uk/decomate/related.htm

De Montfort University Digital Library Project: http://www.dlib.dmu.ac.uk/

dLib Magazine Ready Reference: http://mirrored.ukoln.ac.uk/lis-journals/dlib/dlib/reference.html

Electronic Libraries (eLib) Programme: http://www.ukoln.ac.uk/services/elib/

EU Telematics for Libraries Programme: http://www.echo.lu/libraries/en/libraries.html

Hanson, T. (1998) The access catalogue: gateway to resources. *Ariadne*, 15, 6–7.

HELIX Project: http://severn.dmu.ac.uk/elib/helix/

Higher Education Funding Council for England, et al. (1993) *Joint Funding Councils' Libraries Review Group: Report*. (Follett Report). Bristol: HEFCE

IBM Digital Library Projects: http://www.adfa.oz.au/Mail/Ausepub/0261.html

Internet Archaeology: http://intarch.ac.uk/

Joint Information Services Committee (JISC): http://www.jisc.ac.uk

Miller, P. (1996) Metadata for the masses. *Ariadne*, (5): http://www.ariadne.ac.uk/issue5/

Physics Preprint Archive: http://xxx.lanl.gov/ or http://xxx.soton.ac.uk/ See also MacColl, J. (1996) E-print archives key To paperless journals. *Ariadne*, (2): http://www.ariadne.ac.uk/issue2/

Research Libraries Group: http://www.rlg.org/

Text Encoding Initiative: http://www.tei.uic.edu/orgs/tei/

Zephyr: http://www.rlg.org/zephyr.html

Management Issues at Campus Level

CHAPTER TWO

Information Strategies

Lynne Brindley

Introduction

This chapter aims to give an overview of the concept of information strategies, particularly through their development in UK higher education institutions. It is within the context of an information strategy that the more specific challenges of managing the electronic library will need to be set. To date the only thing that unites writers about information strategies is an agreement that there is terminological and conceptual confusion about exactly what an information strategy is or ought to be. Many senior decision-makers in universities now recognize that their institution should develop such a strategy but are still grappling with how to do it and what to include.

For that reason it is not the intention to commence with lengthy and competing definitions: rather the emergence of information strategies in higher education will be approached from an historical perspective, identifying some of the main influences that have helped to shape the UK national initiative in this area, led by the Joint Information Systems

Committee (JISC) and its immediate predecessor the Information Systems Committee (ISC). The chapter will build up a rich and complex picture of these influences and the different emphasis that each brings, thus working towards some clarity of scope, if not certainty of definition. The progress of the JISC initiative will be charted and the major issues that are emerging in practice will be highlighted. The added impetus that has recently been given to information strategies by the Dearing report on higher education in the learning society (NCIHE, 1997) will be assessed, and finally some comment will be made on the implications for libraries and their role in the management of electronic information resources and service development.

From Information Technology (IT) to Information Systems (IS) Strategies

Information strategies in higher education in the UK have had a long gestation in concept and in implementation. As early as 1990 this author was in discussion with the Computer Board for Universities and Research Councils on the need to develop a methodology for information systems strategies in UK universities. The Computer Board had outline guidelines on producing an IT and Computing Strategy, to provide support to the formal review and visit of the Computer Board in connection with the academic computing procurement cycle, at that time centrally controlled and funded. By late 1990 it was known that this national procurement process was going to cease – the concept of large, mainframe procurements on a seven year cycle had become obsolete – and in preparation for a different role, when in 1991 the Computer Board became the ISC of the University Funding Councils, arguments were made to the Funding Councils for a programme of work to be initiated to help institutions develop their independent information systems strategies.

The case for this work was accepted by the UFC, interestingly with Sir Ron Dearing as Chairman. The new, broader remit of the ISC included oversight of management, administrative and library computing, as well as academic computing. At this stage a deliberate shift of emphasis away from IT towards IS was signalled, in the scope and terms of reference of the new committee, with IS embracing 'the use of computer and communications hardware, software and networking facilities and services in support of research, teaching, library or administrative functions in universities'. Thus began the decoupling of a central funding regime for university computing in the UK from the provision of advice on institutional information systems strategy formulation on a more integrated basis.

The ISC was short-lived, but this broadening of remit, together with, for the first time, the inclusion in its membership of two librarians and a senior administrator, reinforced this change. The shift was reinforced by speakers at an Inter-University Committee on Computing Conference in 1992, who referred to information systems as the new focus of attention and to the importance of information management. A more detailed discussion of this early period can be found in a special issue of the British Journal of Academic Librarianship (1991), which is devoted to the topic of IS strategies, and in particular the article by Breaks (1991).

From Information Systems Strategies to Information Strategies

The JISC was set up in April 1993 to take over from the ISC and to reflect in membership and scope of activities the newly merged polytechnic and university sectors after the abolition of the binary divide. JISC endorsed the information systems strategy initiative and set up a sub-committee to develop an IS strategy framework. As part of its wider remit JISC was developing a major programme of national electronic information services, negotiating national dataset deals and mounting these resources for access by the whole higher education community at national datacentres, hosted by three universities. Information strategy and electronic content, as well as networking and other technology infrastructure issues, were firmly on the JISC agenda.

Another endorsement of IS strategies during 1993 came from the Chief Executive of the Higher Education Funding Council for England (HEFCE) who indicated that institutions would be required to have IS strategies and submit them to the Funding Councils. This resulted in guidance being issued by the Funding Council (HEFCE, 1994) which since then has required that institutions include an 'information and library systems strategy' as part of their overall annual return of a strategic plan and financial forecast, alongside estate and staffing strategies. In more recent guidance from all funding councils specific reference is made to the JISC guidelines.

The scope of the IS strategy envisaged in this context is 'the exploitation of information systems for teaching and learning, research and administration, showing the extent to which an institution has developed an integrated information strategy (*sic*), addressing areas such as networking, library provision, management information systems, access to information sources, electronic information dissemination, telephony and computational facilities for research'. It is interesting to note that the term information strategy is emerging as the umbrella term for what is required.

The sub-committee of JISC met for the first time in November 1993 and very deliberately decided on two changes: it dropped information systems in favour of information strategies in its title, and became a group instead of a sub-committee, signalling its intention to treat the development in information strategy guidelines as a finite project. Information strategies in higher education had reached a starting point, at least as far as national involvement was concerned.

At the same time there were other developments within and outside the sector which were important influences on the way in which JISC thinking developed on what an information strategy should be. These are selectively described below and indicate clearly the evolving nature of work in this field.

Review of Libraries in Higher Education – the Follett Report

The Follett Review of libraries in higher education was set up in 1992 and issued its report in December 1993 (HEFCE, 1993). The background and driving force behind the Review was high level concern across the newly unified higher education sector that university libraries were not able to cope with the pressures of a massively increased student population and that resource pressures on libraries continued to be particularly acute. Given this background to the review it was inevitable that its references to information strategies would be perceived to have a library orientation. In fact the recommendations of the report in this area are framed very broadly, and only in part can be seen as a context for reviewing the role of the library.

In the introduction (p.5) the report states that institutions 'need a sea change in the way they plan and provide for the information needs of those working within them'. The report recommends that each institution should develop an information strategy setting out how it proposes to meet the needs of those working within it (para. 83–4), and the place of the library in meeting these needs. The report was concerned that frequently there was not a close link between institutional strategy and the planning for library and information service developments. The report specifically made a connection with the information systems strategy (*sic*) initiative proposed by JISC (para. 268) and recommended that an institutional information strategy 'should be sufficiently widely drawn' to encompass the JISC guidelines. Overlapping membership between the two committees facilitated this relationship. The report endorsed the funding councils' thinking that institutional strategies should be required to have a component dealing with library and related services, based on the institutional information strategy, and a more integrated review of information resources.

The Follett Report also touches on information strategies and their relationship with convergence, although the report deliberately steered clear of being prescriptive in its organizational and managerial recommendations. It did, however, highlight the need for some convergence, at least in the sense of better integration of provision. The advantages of organizational convergence were suggested, namely that they might enable an integrated information strategy to develop. The importance of designating a senior person to be responsible for this area and to be involved in the high level management of the institution was stressed. Ultimately though, the report leaves it to institutions to decide which approach they wish to take (paras. 91–4).

The Follett Report has been an important influence in many ways in the development of information services and libraries over the past several years. It provided a timely focus on information as a strategic resource to be managed at a high level, it stressed the need for integration with the strategic plans of institutions, and it questioned organizational and management arrangements. All of this gave the information strategies initiative of JISC an additional high profile and helped to bring it to the attention of vice-chancellors and other senior decision makers in universities.

Strategic Information Systems Planning

The broad field of strategic information systems planning now has an enormous literature, but there was not a significant amount available on IS or information strategies in the public sector on which the JISC initiative could draw. There existed guidelines on IS and information management for government departments; most consultancies were using their own adopted formal methods for IS strategies in the corporate sector, and companies such as ICL were developing frameworks for IS strategy formulation. However, there was a gap which needed to be filled to assist higher education institutions to develop their information strategies in their own particular settings. Universities were looking for advice on good practice, case studies and checklists of key questions that they needed to address. Feedback to the JISC suggested that institutions wanted non-prescriptive guidelines for practitioners and help in raising the awareness of vice-chancellors and pro-vice-chancellors of the importance of information strategies.

An early contributor to the JISC initiative was Michael Earl, one of two UK academics making major contributions to this field, the other being Galliers (1987, 1991). Earl's work (1989, 1990) and thinking was influential at this stage and his experience fed directly into a workshop for the community early in 1994, the third joint information services conference held at Stirling, at which it was apparent that most participants were grappling to conceptualize what an information strategy should be.

A useful starting point was his IT strategy triangle (Figure 2.1) which includes three dimensions of strategy: the IS strategy, owned by senior management, business and applications focused and linked closely to institutional priorities (the what of the strategy); the IT strategy, supply oriented, technically focussed architecture and infrastructure to support the performance and delivery of the IS functions (the how of the strategy); and the IM, information management strategy, the organizational and management aspects of the strategy (the wherefore of the strategy).

Taking this framework together with the Follett emphasis on information services (comprising the information content, information resource allocation, balancing the holding of information locally or accessing it remotely, the integration of information provision within course design and planning, the life cycle of information sources, and so on) begins to give a sense of the broad scope of what might generically emerge as an information strategy.

Earl warned against too strong a dependence on any 'off the shelf' formal methods for IS strategy planning. His own

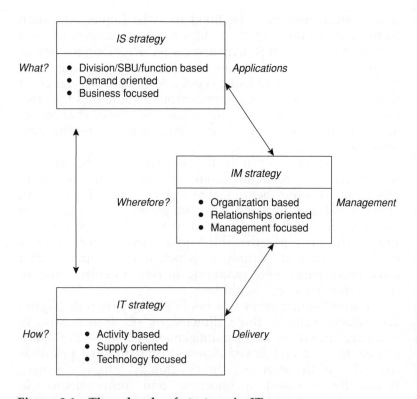

Figure 2.1 Three levels of strategy in IT
Diagram originally published in *Management Strategies for information technology*, Prentice Hall, 1989

research (Earl 1992) argued for a multiple methodology framework, showing that in practice no one method works in isolation. He proposed three types of approach: 'top down', in relation to any significant change in business strategy; 'bottom up', through audit and evaluation of current systems; and perhaps most significantly for universities, 'inside out' whereby innovation for IS comes from all parts of the organization involved in different processes and activities, and that many of the best applications of IT for competitive

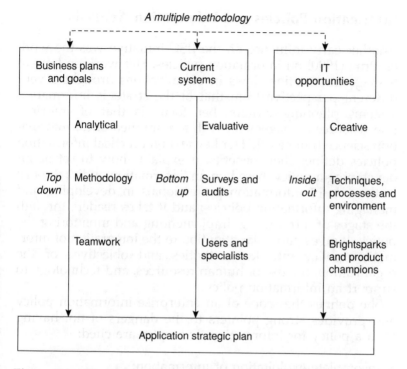

Figure 2.2   IS strategy formulation: a multiple methodology
Diagram originally published in *Management Strategies for information technology*, Prentice Hall, 1989

advantage are derived from the ideas and exploits of users within the organization.

His work also emphasizes the need to combine different approaches (Figure 2.2), which he terms business led, method driven, administrative, technological and organizational, recognizing the pros and cons of different approaches and the possibility of 'mixing and matching' them. This flexible and non-prescriptive approach seemed to have much to commend it in the context of higher education, and institutions early in to information strategies development commonly drew from Earl's work.

Information Policies and Information Analysis

Another early influence on the JISC initiative was the work of Orna (1990) on information policies. Her work on how to manage information flows in organizations brought a very different perspective from that of the strategic information systems planning writers: her focus is that of information resource management, with a more theoretical information science framework. Her key text on practical information policies defines their benefits: it explains how to set about developing a policy, based on an 'information audit'; it looks at the role of information professionals in developing and managing information policies; and it takes readers through the stages of introducing, implementing and monitoring the policy. It gives particular attention to the integration of information policy into key activities and objectives of the organization, the use of human resources, and technology to support an information policy.

She defines the scope of an enterprise information policy and provides strong pointers to the dangers of not having such a policy for information. Examples are cited:

- incomplete exploitation of information;
- implementation of office automation systems without due consideration of information handling concepts such as indexing and edition control;
- information products continuing well beyond their useful life or presented in entirely unhelpful formats;
- technical investments made without linkage to overall objectives.

Librarians will probably feel most comfortable with this approach and it takes little to extrapolate what might be appropriate roles for library and information professionals in this wider information policy development.

Orna introduces consideration of the tools of information audits and information mapping techniques. The conduct of a total or partial information audit can be a vital part of information strategy development. She also usefully makes a link with others' work on information management (Burk and Horton, 1988) and work on the relationship between information technology and organizational change (Eason, 1986). A useful review article by Ellis *et al.* (1993) provides an assessment of a range of information audit, communication audit and information mapping techniques to support information strategy development.

Information Assets in the Corporate Sector

During 1995 an important report emerged from the private sector which reinforced the importance of the JISC information strategy initiative, by reflecting many shared concerns, albeit couched in the language of business. The Hawley Committee report (KPMG, 1995) was undertaken under the auspices of the KPMG IMPACT programme, a club of major organizations seeking to share experience in information management in its broadest sense. The committee sought to put together a set of guidelines for boards of directors on information as an asset, recognizing that all significant information in an organization, regardless of its purpose, should be properly identified even if not in an accounting sense, for consideration as an asset of the business.

It proposed that the board of directors should address its responsibilities for information assets in the same way as for other assets – e.g. property, plant. This implied a new approach to how information should be treated and requires a board to make clear to management what actions it wishes to be taken and who is responsible for action and compliance. The report sets out a checklist of actions that should be taken by the board in considering the proper direction and supervision of their information assets. Interestingly the report notes that whilst most boards feel comfortable with most subjects on their agenda – financial, marketing, personnel, business strategy – the area of information management is considered difficult. This problem is mirrored in Dearing (NCIHE, 1997), which urges institutions to 'introduce managers who have both a deep understanding of C & IT [Communications and Information Technology] and its application to higher education, and senior management experience. There is a shortage of such individuals within higher education'. It does not take much imagination to see the relevance of this corporate approach to higher education.

JISC's Information Strategy Initiative

Throughout 1994 the JISC working group was building up a complex picture of the many possible approaches to an information strategy, primarily, but not solely, through the influences described above. Feedback on the Follett Report and informal contact in the sector suggested that guidance was seriously and urgently needed by the sector. The group tendered for this work and commissioned Coopers & Lybrand to assist with the development of guidelines for sites wishing to prepare information strategies. The first phase of the work, conducted in the early part of 1995, identified the generic functional activities in universities and outlined a possible framework for information strategy development.

Late in 1995 saw the production of more detailed guidelines for developing an information strategy (JISC, 1995). In the preface Professor Arbuthnott, Chair of JISC staked a claim for information as the lifeblood of higher education institutions, a key resource which needs managing as such and on a par with finance and human resources. The emphasis in the executive briefing is on flexibility of approach and the non-prescriptive nature of the guidelines. In the view of Coopers, 'the best way to think of an information strategy is as a set of attitudes rather than as a report' (p.9). This is indeed a far cry from formal methods-driven strategic information systems planning (SISP). The document spells out that an information strategy should embrace:

- 'teaching and learning materials (in all media);
- research information and data;
- the management information needed to plan and monitor the delivery of teaching, learning and research. Such information may or may not be held on computers and may or may not be found in libraries' (p.9).

The guidelines (Figure 2.3) contain pointers to the relationship between information strategies and IS and IT strategies. 'For the sake of clarity we define an information

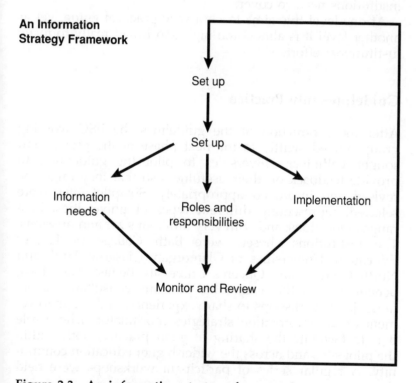

Figure 2.3 An information strategy framework
Diagram originally published in *Guidelines for developing an information strategy*, JISC, 1995

system strategy as the computer systems needed to support the information strategy; in turn, the information technology strategy defines the technical infrastructure covering standards, hardware and software, operating systems, networks and technical policies. This document and guide is not directly concerned either with information systems or with information technology' (p.14).

The practitioners' guide provides information on how to develop an information strategy through six main steps and is complemented by examples of tools and techniques to support its development and checklists of key points that institutions need to cover.

At one level this aims to be a very practical guide, yet at another level it is almost too high and broad really to focus institutional effort.

Guidelines into Practice

After the production of the guidelines the JISC working group moved swiftly to the next phase of the project and sought volunteer universities to pilot the guidelines, to provide feedback on their usefulness so that they might be revised and improved appropriately. Six pilot sites were selected, representing different types of universities, in a range of locations, and with very different sizes and missions. The institutions chosen were Bath College of Higher Education, Universities of Glamorgan, Glasgow, Hull, and North London, and Queen's University Belfast. They have benefited from the availability of some consultancy assistance, joint workshops to share experience, and the involvement of the information strategies coordinator, whose role it is to facilitate the sharing of good practice, both within the pilot sites and across the wider higher education community. A regular series of participant workshops were held through 1996.

Many lessons have been learned and there are significant issues emerging:

- pilots were slow in getting started as it often proved difficult to put resources in place;
- maintaining momentum has been difficult because of the extended timescale of the exercise and the often nebulous nature of the work;
- it is easy to get overwhelmed with the size of the task, and especially in very large universities with significant devolved responsibilities it has proved difficult to be focused and agree on priority activity;
- skills such as information auditing and mapping and project management are often lacking;
- an approach which uses exemplar projects has been found to be useful, but carries the danger of lack of integration;
- associated management of change, e.g. in processes, procedures and activities is critical, but often poses major challenges and is seen as threatening;
- it is encouraging if a few 'quick wins' can be identified and carried through;
- more centrally managed universities are finding it easier to establish a direct linkage between academic plans and information strategy.

Perhaps none of these points is surprising, nor that the process is both time consuming and resource intensive. After a major open conference held in November 1997 the pilot sites' experience was reviewed, and this led to a revision of the strategy guidelines and the framework. Revised guidelines with accompanying case studies were issued in Spring 1998 (JISC, 1998).

Other Activities

Meanwhile a significant and complementary set of activities has been under way at Sheffield University Department of Information Studies, particularly through the work of Professor T. Wilson and David Allen. In 1995 with the support of JISC, SCONUL and UCISA, Allen carried out a survey through questionnaire of four major stakeholders in information strategy development – librarians, academics, chairs of IS/IT committees and directors of IT (Allen, 1995). The aim of the survey was to explore process, content and use of the two intertwined concepts of information strategies and IT strategies. For the purpose of the survey the information strategy was differentiated from the IT strategy and defined as 'a strategy evaluating information gathering, processing, storing or dissemination within your institution'.

He found that the majority of higher education institutions (HEIs) had or were currently developing information strategies, and were not on the whole just waiting for the JISC guidelines. The primary reason for this rapid uptake seems to be that the JISC initiative came at precisely the right time for many HEIs. The concept has been used by some as an internal political tool with which they can push information issues up the organizational agenda. There was common concern about the difficulties of resourcing the IT infrastructure needed to support exponentially growing demands. There was dissatisfaction with the IT centre in terms of service and IT resources, as well as dissatisfaction with management information provision.

In the light of a realistic assessment of likely resources and spiralling costs of information and IT there seemed to be a strong awareness of the need to reassess the information provided to user communities and the way in which it should be provided. At least half of the institutions surveyed perceived the information strategy as potentially changing radically or transforming the way in which their institutions operate. It was found that the process of information strategy formulation was being approached in a fairly consensual manner (more so than with previous IT strategies), with librarians and IT directors generally working well together during the process.

Sheffield University also hosted two conferences during 1996 on information strategies, the latter of which was reported in *Ariadne* (MacColl, 1996). From this report it is clear that there are mixed views on the value of information strategies and different motivations for their development, including compliance with Funding Council instructions; as a convenient trigger for convergence of library and computing services, and so on. Some have questioned the value of information strategies as a tool for competitive advantage (Allen and Wilson, 1995). Most encouragingly Professor Gareth Roberts, Vice Chancellor of the University of Sheffield, and at that time Chair of the committee of vice-chancellors and principals (CVCP), stated that 'information is the foundation on which any strategic plan is based'.

Recent International Initiative

So far this chapter has concentrated on leading work in the UK higher education sector. However, early in 1997 the Coalition for Networked Information (CNI) in the USA issued a white paper entitled 'Institution-Wide Information Strategies' as a background to a proposed initiative in this area (CNI, 1997). The initiative aims to promote institution-wide strategies in several key areas of networked information resource and service development. The focus of this initiative is on information – its use, its users, and the strategic allocation of resources in support of networked information across an entire institution. Its definition of information strategies embraces IT resources and infrastructure, financial resources – budget, cost models and price structures, organization and human resources information policies and practices and strategic alignment of the information strategy to the mission and business strategy of the institution.

The view is taken that most organizations cannot address all the issues involved in a comprehensive, institution-wide strategy on their own, and what is proposed is a collaborative approach where participants work on a 'manageable piece of the challenge', to produce best practice case studies. Some examples of strategic information initiatives are suggested as follows:

- a user-centred design programme to integrate diverse information resources and tailor them to the needs of specific groups;
- an information policy programme to establish standard rules for information use, access, sharing, disclosure, protection, etc.;
- an electronic licence programme to negotiate and fund institution-wide agreements for acquiring digital content or widely-used commercial software;
- a collaborative user service programme which builds teams or other structures that cross a variety of organizational boundaries – library and technology, central and departmental – to support the use of information resources institution-wide.

The UK is participating in this initiative through the JISC information strategies coordinator and it is anticipated that the programme will enrich any further stages of the work on UK guidelines.

Implications of Dearing

In the immediate aftermath of the appearance of the Dearing Report (NCIHE, 1997), it would appear that information strategies have been given another significant boost in importance. Dearing uses the phrase 'Communications and Information Technology' (C & IT) widely through the report, especially in connection with teaching and learning, and reinforces many of the messages about information strategies that have been developed in the JISC initiative. Dearing recommends specifically that all higher education institutions in the UK should have in place overarching communications and information strategies by 1999/2000 (Recommendation 41). The Committee recognizes that its vision of the future in which a world market in learning materials based on educational technology will develop depends on the successful management of institutional change. The Committee believes that 'the development and implementation of an integrated C & IT strategy will be one of the main challenges facing managers of higher education institutions' and is in itself a process for change.

Effective management through the development of information strategies and through programmes of training and support is seen to be at the heart of the effective use of C & IT in higher education. This is expressed diagrammatically in Figure 2.4:

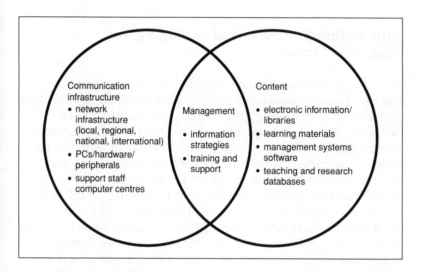

Figure 2.4 Effective use of communications and information technology in higher education
Diagram originally published in *Higher education in the learning society*, NCIHE, 1997

The scope of such a strategy is suggested as covering:

- information resources;
- the facilitation of staff/student communication;
- the development (purchase or production) of learning and teaching materials and other content;

- the development of effective management information systems in an integrated manner.

The current requirement of the funding bodies for institutions to have information strategies is suggested as a good basis for extension to all aspects of C & IT. This positive, almost ringing, endorsement of the importance of C & IT and information strategies is likely to be used to bring information issues to the fore in most universities.

Information Strategies and Managing the Electronic Library

This chapter has deliberately avoided attempting a precise definition of information strategies: by now it will be obvious that the concept is emerging and evolving constantly. However, in whatever form or interpretation it emerges within a particular university, it will be the context for electronic library developments (and indeed traditional library developments), and one within which they will need to be managed. The process of information strategy development within an HEI is thus extremely important for libraries. There are in addition opportunities for librarians to be key players in information strategy development, but in some institutions they are excluded or marginalized. There is no set pattern and much will depend on the political relationships within each individual institution.

What is clear is that the management of electronic library developments will require continuing engagement well beyond the boundaries of the traditional library. It requires the forging of new working relationships across campus, collaboration at many levels of the university, the imaginative application of library skills to non-library situations and an appreciation of the opportunities that are opened up for the library to play a leadership role – for example, in electronic publishing, in copyright management, and in content negotiation – well beyond traditional bibliographic and library confines.

References

Allen, D.K. (1995) *Report on survey results on information and information technology strategies in UK higher education institutions,* unpublished.

Allen, D.K. and Wilson, T.D. (1995) The context of information strategies: competition or collaboration? *The New Review of Academic Librarianship,* **1,** 3–14

Breaks, M. (1991) Information systems strategies. *British Journal of Academic Librarianship,* **6,** (2) 65–70

British Journal of Academic Librarianship (1991), **6** (2), whole issue

Burk, C.F. and Horton, F.W. (1988) *Infomap: a complete guide to discovering corporate information resources.* London: Prentice Hall

Coalition for Networked Information (1997) *White paper: institution-wide information strategies (IWIS), a CNI initiative.* http://www.cni.org/projects/iwis/www/IWIS-wp.html

Earl, M.J. (1989) *Management strategies for information technology.* London: Prentice Hall

Earl, M.J. (1990) (ed.) *Information management: the strategic dimension.* Oxford: Clarendon Press

Earl, M.J. (1992) *Strategic information systems planning: the contribution of formal methods.* Centre for Research in Information Management working paper 92/7

Eason, K. (1986) *Information technology and organizational change.* London: Taylor & Francis

Ellis, D *et al.* (1993) Information audits, communication audits and information mapping: a review and survey. *International Journal of Information Management,* **13,** 134–51

Galliers, R.D. (1987) (ed.) *Information analysis: selected readings.* Maidenhead: Addison-Wesley

Galliers, R.D. (1991) Strategic information systems planning: myths, reality and guidelines for successful implementation. *European Journal of Information Systems*, 1, 55–64

Higher Education Funding Council for England (1994) *Strategic plans and financial forecasts*, Circular 5/94. Bristol: HEFCE

Higher Education Funding Council for England, et al. (1993) *Joint Funding Councils' Libraries Review Group: Report*. (Follett Report). Bristol: HEFCE

Joint Information Systems Committee (1995) *Guidelines for developing an information strategy*. Bristol: JISC

Joint Information Systems Committee (1998) *Guidelines for developing an information strategy: the sequel*. Bristol: HEFCE

KPMG (1995) *Information as an asset: the board agenda; a consultative report* (Chairman Dr Robert Hawley). KPMG Impact Programme

MacColl, J. (1996) Information strategies get down to business. *Ariadne*, (6), 1 and http://www.ukoln.ac.uk/ariadne/

National Committee of Inquiry into Higher Education (1997) *Higher education in the learning society*. (Dearing Report). London: HMSO

Orna, E. (1990) *Practical information policies: how to manage information flows in organizations*. Aldershot: Gower

CHAPTER THREE

Convergence of Academic Support Services

Derek Law

Introduction

The first converged services in the UK, bringing together library and computing centre under a single manager are already over a decade old. Indeed, as early as 1988, the *British Journal of Academic Librarianship* devoted a whole issue to the topic, seeing a trend which 'is gathering momentum' (BJAL, 1988, p. 121). Since then the progress of convergence has appeared inexorable, although occasional distinguished voices have spoken out against it, arguing that 'at the very least the priorities and management needs in two such diverse bodies are incompatible' (Ratcliffe and Hartley, 1993). Yet even in 1993 this comment from the then Librarian and Computing Centre Director at the University of Cambridge appeared to say more about the distinctiveness of Cambridge than the merit of the argument. Since then, very few higher education (HE) institutions have consciously rejected the opportunity for convergence when it occurred and none has yet chosen to revert to the previous structure when offered the opportunity, although one or two may be considering it. Sidgreaves (1995) has perceptively pointed out that convergence is a logical consequence of libraries and computer centres moving towards the same point and that senior institutional managers can see this quite as clearly as those directly involved. Like many others he also stresses that there is no single optimal model. The fullest description of the background to convergence has come from the Impact on People of Electronic Libraries (IMPEL) project conducted by Day. The project has undertaken case studies in six institutions, but has also looked critically at the growing literature on the topic. A follow up project, IMPEL2 has carried out further studies in 1996 and 1997 (Edwards 1997) in twenty-eight institutions and has again conducted an extensive literature review on monitoring organisational and cultural change.

Impact of the Follett Report

It is popularly, if erroneously, supposed that it was the Follett Report (HCFCE, 1993) which produced the pressure for convergence and yet the Report is curiously ambivalent on the topic. Its sole recommendation comes in Paragraph 91 and reads:

> 'The Review Group considers that there are many advantages in organisational convergence, particularly in enabling an integrated information strategy to develop. While it must be for each individual institution to decide which approach it wishes to take it is important that these organisational issues are addressed, and that the place of the library and of other information providers is assessed within the context of an overall information management strategy'.

Elsewhere the report says, 'There is no single model of a future library or information service which can or should be imposed on individual institutions or libraries within them'. It seems reasonable to suppose that this less than ringing endorsement was, however, sufficient to cause university management to focus on the issue of academic support services. A whole series of other reports and initiatives ranging

from Al Gore's very public support for the Information Super-
highway in the U.S.A, the G7 digital library initiative and the
several Bangemann Reports in Europe have given great
prominence to the concept of the Information Society. In
turn, lay members of university governing bodies would be
increasingly familiar with the notion of a Chief Information
Officer at board level in commercial companies. Follett too
stressed the idea of information policies and most librarians,
aware of the way that things were moving, will have been
pressing for such strategies, expecting them to be led by institutional mission rather than driven by technology.

The Fielden Report

The Fielden Report (John Fielden Consultancy, 1993) was
commissioned by the Libraries Review Group and has a
rather fuller review of the issues surrounding convergence.
The report is concerned in general with human resource
issues and in it Fielden helpfully distinguishes between two
types of convergence:

- organizational, in which library and computing come
  together for management purposes. The most limited
  example of this is where a single manager is appointed
  but no other change takes place;
- operational, in which detailed functions or operations are
  brought together. This can be brought together through
  strategic co-operation and does not require a single manager.

Yet despite all this it appears that at the time of writing
approximately half the HE sector has adopted a converged
structure. Over fifty institutions * appear to have a professional

---

* These figures are derived from a survey undertaken by Bruce Royan while he
was librarian at the University of Stirling. It was published as 'Are you being
merged?' in the *SCONUL Newsletter* no. 1, 1994, and subsequently maintained
and circulated privately to directors of converged services. Allowance has been
made for additions since the survey was undertaken in 1994.

head of information services bringing together the library and computing services, while a further dozen have an academic pro-vice-chancellor in charge. Further institutions continue to make the change on a regular basis and although opportunities have occurred, no institution in the UK has yet reverted to its previous structure. To the core of library and computing centre is often added a range of other, often smaller, academic services, not least as a convenient device for organizing line management. In addition to obvious areas such as learning resources, one may find included telephony, administrative computing and media production as well as such exotica as the university chapel, the careers service or hazardous waste disposal.

Fielden (John Fielden Consultancy, 1993) notes that the head of the converged service may now manage a large enough part of the organization to justify a place on the central management team of the university. This brings valuable political clout as well as an information flow. Further, where the budgets are combined and virement is allowed, this flexibility gives managers much greater scope for effecting change. Several areas have proved most susceptible to such change:

- joint strategic planning. The funding councils' requirement for an information strategy is most often driven within the organization by a converged service, while the development of teaching and learning strategies again benefits from convergence;
- joint use and development of networks. As services such as campus-wide information servers, networked CD-ROMs or mirrored resources become more common, joint planning becomes ever more important;
- increased physical co-location. The most visible manifestation is in the provision of open access terminal areas within learning centres and libraries, but convergence also allows more effective space utilization of everything from offices to common rooms. As new buildings and extensions begin to emerge in the post-Follett era, one can also

see a growing number of commonly managed service delivery points;

- shared training in information management skills. This is more often talked about than happening, although the various training projects funded under the eLib programme are likely to have a marked impact on this. Another useful extension of this is in the provision of common documentation describing either resources or services;
- physical sharing of resources in various media. Books Computer assisted learning (CAL), audio, video and online may be 'owned' or purchased by different budgets but are presented together to users.

As Buckland (1988) has noted:

'With convenient telecommunication, the physical location of an electronic text is substantially irrelevant. Databases (which are copied not borrowed) at a distance are likely to be more reliably accessible than paper documents owned by one's local library. What is needed, then, is a bibliography of what is conveniently accessible rather than the much narrower concept of a catalog of what happens to be locally owned'.

Fielden (John Fielden Consultancy, 1993) expected organizational convergence to continue (as has happened), and operational convergence to expand in some areas. It was thought unlikely that any single model would become dominant (again true), but the report perhaps expected more multi-skilling of individuals to take place than has happened. At least in discussion the multi-skilling appears to be most likely to develop amongst teams of specialists with complementary skills than through individuals with multiple skills. This seems more plausible than developing a superbreed of renaissance men and women.

Winners and Losers?

At first convergence was seen as a turf war issue and in terms of winners and losers. But it soon became clear that more often than not, the institutional librarian was being chosen to head the converged service. And yet there was no discernible logic to this. Most institutions have claimed that there were particular local circumstances which dictated the outcome, and Fielden (John Fielden Consultancy, 1993) appears to accept that the trend largely follows a fairly random pattern dictated by retirement and job vacancies. Yet nationally the ratio of appointments appears to run at perhaps 5:1 in favour of librarians. This appears to stretch the bounds of coincidence rather far. However only the most superficial of examinations suggests that one group is more competent than the other. One perhaps unexpected benefit of convergence is that once the turf wars are over, there emerges a growing respect for each other's professional skills. Computing centres have faced impossible pressures over recent years and have tended quite unfairly to become institutional whipping boys. In 1985 the Computing Centre of King's College London supported perhaps 500 users from an essentially centralized mainframe based service. In 1995 it supported some 15,000 users in a largely decentralized PC-based service, with very few additional staff. A 3000 per cent increase in users has been combined with only a 10 per cent increase in staff. Worse, the level of desktop support required even by experienced users has increased by further orders of magnitude, while the constant upgrading of networks and workstations has given computing centres a quite unfair reputation for financial insatiability coupled with eroding levels of service. The inability and/or unwillingness of most universities to adopt a standard PC configuration and a standard suite of office software means that almost every installation is unique and every upgrade fraught with difficulty.

A recent report suggests that there are also clear problems of image: 'they have a poor attitude to their non-IT colleagues, are politically naïve at work and even promote a bad image through their dress and posture.' (Kavanagh, 1997) The same report notes that IT people have traditionally been loyal to IT, not their employer, whereas Norman

Higham, former librarian of the University of Bristol famously remarked that he was a university man first and a librarian second. It is also indicative that many computing centres see themselves as precisely that and have failed even to make the cosmetic but symbolic change of title to computing services. Libraries have, of course, suffered over the same period, but not to anything like the same degree. During this period of time there has been a significant professional focus on customer care and quality assurance which has mitigated the effects of cuts, while librarians have effectively and skilfully passed all of the blame for poorer provision on to journal publishers. In summary, skilful manipulation of stereotypes has benefited one group rather than the other.

Management Structures

At its most extreme the services are merged. The University of Birmingham is a case in point where existing departmental barriers have been completely removed and a quite new structure developed. Perhaps more common is a structure in which the traditional departmental structures continue to exist, but joint working groups are set up to address specific problems or issues. At the other end of the spectrum lies the situation where a joint manager is appointed, perhaps on a rotating basis as at Southampton, but where the existing management structures remain largely untouched and the two major services produce development by committee and co-operation. Day *et al* (1996) notes that the IMPEL Project found a distinction between the success of convergence at institutional level and on the ground. Generally the organizational convergence was felt to be successful. University managements felt that their objectives had been achieved. The same may be true of converged service directors. In the summer of 1997 it was proposed to close the listserv for this group due to lack of use. After a flurry of e-debate the list was retained although it appeared that the decision was based as much on nostalgia as realism. This 'success' was not true at an operational level. Many staff saw (and see) convergence as a fad to save money and while accepting the need for departments to work together saw convergence as a threat to their professional skills. This cultural lag was seen at one institution where '... professional identity [was] fiercely defended by both sides, and attempts to instigate a joint Help Desk for students [were] thwarted. Communication lines remained vertical, with little horizontal contact even between systems staff and computing advisers.' (Day, 1996). This lack of horizontal contact seems to be a widespread problem and the one which needs to be addressed most if converged services are to succeed.

The Emerging Model

The findings of those libraries with most experience in the electronic future are quite consistent. Students use the library as a physical place more and more, while faculty members use it less and less, expecting to find resource available at the desktop. This has been most clearly articulated by Geleijnse (1995) describing the experience at Tilburg University. If this pattern does persist, it has implications for user support activities, which is one of the areas where convergence has most to offer. The post-Follett building programme has concentrated on learning and resource centres and on information centres, where the two groups of user support staff from library and computing centre are brought together. It does seem plausible to suppose that a joint model can develop in which support and basic training for undergraduates is delivered within the library/information centre and support for research is delivered in the office/laboratory by multi-skilled teams of library and computing staff. Another view is that we should expect the development of hybrid staff where the individuals are multi-skilled. In either case it is important that such teams have an early impact on academic departments. Many academic staff have no perceived information shortage and there is a danger that a growing band of the satisfied inept will emerge, who under-value information management skills and confuse ease of use with quality of response. The team approach has the advan-tage that it acknowledges a spectrum of skills from book cataloguing to network installation, assuming some common-ality of skills only in the user support area, rather than assuming a common skills set applicable to all staff in infor-mation services.

Advantages of Convergence

In management terms the biggest single advantage is the creation of a single very large budget-holder. Where a library has typically managed perhaps 3–5 per cent of the institu-tional budget, a converged service may well be managing close to 10 per cent of the institutional budget when equip-ment costs are included. For the manager this means that anything is possible, anything is achievable. Of course the resources are not sufficient to make everything possible, which leads to a quite proper concentration on information strategies and the prioritization of ambitions. With a larger budget, there should be opportunities for improved value for money. This can be in areas as varied as library system procurements, space utilization or furniture purchases.

But perhaps the biggest potential lies in the area of shared services. These can range from new services such as elec-tronic journals, campus wide information server (CWIS) or CD-ROM networks to the sharing of service points where issuing documentation and printout or selling diskettes sit happily and commonly with both services. The recent Pilot Site Licence Initiative gives a good example of this. Libraries were expected to make an average saving of £10 000. No thought was given at national level to the knock-on effect on computing provision. Quite apart from the availability of suitable hardware, there was a need, at least in principle, to load a standard Netscape browser and Adobe Acrobat –

and commit to appropriate upgrades as new software was released. If the task were to be performed properly, the computing centre would have to recruit perhaps two extra desktop support staff in order to save the library its journal subscriptions. In a converged service it should at least in theory be practical to have a seamless introduction of such a service.

Similarly, as JISC begins to propose charges for JANET usage* based on international traffic, institutions will begin to look at what traffic is being sent and received by the site. We may confidently expect that mirroring and cacheing strategies will be developed and that converged services will be well placed to act to provide economic information management.

Training and instruction is the second area where change may be expected. The IMPEL2 study has found that there is a general consensus among library and information services (LIS) staff that the clearest impact of the changing LIS environment is a shift in their role towards more instruction and teaching of users. The experience in learning resource centres and previous knowledge of the practices of academic staff lead one to suppose that converged services could perform the critical role in operationalizing computer assisted learning.

The broad area of user support is the third area where convergence has the potential to show real benefit. There are many reasons why systems will not perform as users might expect, and there is no good reason to expect them to perform the diagnosis of why failure or imperfect performance has occurred. User-centred support where and when the customer requires it should be a fundamental objective of converged services.

It is also worth remarking that the main thrust of funding council policy has been led by content-focused national initia-

---

*   This is discussed in the letter of 22 September 1997 from Dr M. Read, secretary of JISC to Vice-Chancellors. It is available on the JISC and NISS home pages and provoked much debate on LIS-UCISA

tives ranging from the Teaching and Learning Technology Programme (TLTP) to dataset provision. Institutions may reasonably expect new structures to maximize the benefit from these programmes.

Disadvantages

The disadvantages – or perhaps better the challenges – facing converged services are equally clear. Firstly is the fact that apart from the possibility of an all too brief honeymoon period, institutions have not faced up to the reality that they are under-resourcing academic services. A new management structure offers some room for economy and for innovation, but this is essentially at the margin. The institution will often place impossible demands on the new service. The director of a converged service does well carefully to articulate strategy and the optimum resource requirements while making clear the limited outcomes that can be achieved with the resources actually provided.

Secondly, there will be unrealistic expectations of the speed and impact of such a change. But at least initially, the same staff, are usually in the same roles as formerly, with the same skills set and the same attitudes. It takes both time and patience to weld the different approaches together.

It is a commonplace belief that libraries and computing centres have different cultures. What is perhaps more important is that each of these cultures has positive and productive areas rather than one being superior to the other. It may be partly for this reason that very few institutions have attempted wholesale merger of the two departments, preferring to recognize the value of cultural diversity and to build on the strengths of each tradition. There is however the danger of cultural lag: the need for all parts of the culture to catch up with and understand that which is changing most rapidly.

Finally, and as noted previously, in most cases convergence is usually managerial rather than operational at least in the first instance. If much of the institutional thrust for convergence is concerned with strategic planning and development this is not necessarily a bad thing, as it gives time for a climate of trust to develop between the services. We may then expect a further IMPEL study to show these barriers of cultural lag eroding. If however they remain, convergence will come to be seen as a marriage of convenience rather than a love match.

Conclusion

One last question remains. This is a particularly British phenomenon (although there are examples in other countries), but why in the UK? And why now? When reviews of academic services are undertaken in universities, the local administrators always say that they are considering convergence as a local response to local issues – and yet a clear national pattern has emerged. If we cannot attribute this to the Follett Report we can perhaps attribute it to a whole series of reports on various aspects of higher education, culminating in the Dearing Report (NCIHE, 1997). Although British higher education may now be the most over-analysed anywhere, several key strands have emerged, which appear to lead towards convergence. One is the importance of strategic planning; one is the pervasiveness of Information Technology; a third is a belief in the inevitability of computer-assisted learning; fourthly, as Dearing puts it, 'Communications and Information Technology is too big, too expensive and too fundamental to the operation of the institution as a whole to be decided at faculty level' (p. 207); and finally the report acknowledges that this whole enterprise is a senior management issue and must be handled at that level. '. . . We believe it will be necessary for institutions to introduce managers who have both a deep understanding of C and IT, and its application to higher education, and senior management experience. There is a shortage of such individuals within higher education' (p. 207).

It is that central area of management that seems likely to keep some form of convergence firmly within institutional structures and on institutional agenda. Dearing's Recommendation 42 seems destined to become engraved on as many hearts as Parry's famous recommendation that 6 per cent of the institutional budget should be spent on the library. Recommendation 42 says that 'All higher education institutions should develop managers who combine a deep understanding of C and IT with senior management experience'. It seems difficult to disagree.

References

British Journal of Academic Librarianship (1988) Issue devoted to convergence **3**, (3).

Buckland, M. (1998) Bibliography, library records and the redefinition of the library catalog. *Library Resources and Technical Services*, **32**, 299–311

Day, J. (1996) *The culture of convergence in electronic library and visual information research: papers from the Third ELVIRA Conference, 1996.* London: ASLIB

Day, J. et al. (1996) *Higher education, teaching, learning and the electronic library*: a review of the literature for the IMPEL2 project: monitoring organisational and cultural change. *New Review of Academic Librarianship*, **2**, 131–204. And at: http://www.unn.ac.uk/~liy8/impel2/abstr.htm

Edwards, C. (1997) Change and uncertainty. *Ariadne*, **11**, 6–8. And also at http://www.unn.ac.uk/~liy8/impel2/cni4.htm

John Fielden Consultancy (1993) *Supporting expansion: a study of human resource management in academic libraries.* Bristol: HCFCE.

Geleijnse, H. (1995) A strategy for information access. In *Networking and the future of libraries 2: managing the intellectual record.* London: Library Association.

Higher Education Funding Council for England, et al. (1993) *Joint Funding Councils' Libraries Review Group: Report.* (Follett Report). Bristol: HEFCE

Kavanagh. J. (1997) Why IT staff are losers with an attitude problem. *The Times Interactive Section,* 27 August 1997, p. 10.

National Committee of Inquiry into Higher Education (1997) *Higher Education in the Learning Society.* (Dearing Report). London: HMSO

Ratcliffe, F. and Hartley, D. (1993) Library services: letter. *Times Higher Education Supplement,* 5 March 1993, p. 17.

Sidgreaves, I. (1995) Convergence – an update. *Relay: Journal of UC & R Group,* **42**, 3–6

CHAPTER FOUR

Case Study: Converged Working at Liverpool John Moores University

Phil Sykes

Introduction

In February 1993 Liverpool Polytechnic created a new division of 'Learning Services' which brought together staff from the polytechnic library with their 'user services' colleagues in the Division of Computer Services. The Division of Computer Services merged with the Management Information Unit of the polytechnic, and continued to maintain the infrastructure of the computer network and to look after hardware. Learning Services, however, assumed responsibility for direct support to users in the use of networked software, including answering enquiries, writing documentation, and providing advice and tuition in computer use.

Senior managers within computer services, library services and the open learning unit already reported to the same senior manager prior to the 'big bang' merger decision described above, and discussions had been taking place about operational convergence since the summer of 1992. The actual decision taken by senior management at the Polytechnic was not informed by these discussions, and resulted in a form of convergence which was not ideal: the computing staff who joined Learning Services felt that they had been sundered from their erstwhile colleagues in the central computing unit, and computing and library staff now reported to the Rector through completely different hierarchies.

The creation of Learning Services was the first stage in a gradual process of 'convergence' of library and computer user services which is still continuing. Convergence is rather like European Union: a dynamic process which begins with a treaty but does not end with it. The following sections describe the steps we have taken down the road of convergence, outline the form of converged working adopted and analyse the impact of convergence upon users and staff.

Stages in the Development of Converged Working

The immediate impact of the formal creation of Learning Services upon staff duties and the service to users was limited. Computing and library staff generally worked in different buildings, so opportunities for practical collaboration were limited. Trades unions strongly committed to resisting change meant that any idea of 'organic' transition to converged working was a non-starter. At that time, substantial changes to working practices took place through formal negotiation or not at all.

The months after between February and October 1993 were largely devoted to working through the consequences of the decision to merge library and computer user services in terms of organizational structure and job descriptions. This was a very fraught period. A strongly adversarial climate between managers and trades unions made any change difficult to implement. Changes of the magnitude required for convergence were bound to excite strong feelings. These factors, combined with mistakes made in the presentation of the aims and purposes of convergence to staff, meant that almost all library and computing staff were opposed to convergence in early 1993.

A dramatic improvement in the climate of relations was achieved when working parties, involving members of staff from every level, were formed to create appropriate job descriptions for a converged environment. Though there was still a distrust of the idea of convergence, staff began to feel more of a sense of ownership of the new structure when they themselves were involved in creating it. These working parties, chaired by the Librarian and the Deputy Librarian, also presented managers with an opportunity to explain the reasoning behind convergence in a way that the set-piece, unavoidably confrontational, meetings with the trades unions had not.

As a result of the progress made after the formation of these working parties, an agreement was finally concluded with the unions in October 1993. The form of convergence agreed upon in these negotiations still forms the basis of converged working at JMU, and is described in the section below. It was some time before the structure agreed in October 1993 could become a working reality: computing and library staff were still, by and large, working in separate buildings and could only co-operate at the margins in service provision.

The most significant stage in the practical implementation of convergence came in July 1994 with the opening of the Aldham Robarts Centre (ARC). This was a purpose-designed learning resource centre, and the physical integration of library and computing facilities had been central to the design process. The ARC was divided into a series of 'subject floors', each of which attempted to provide a comprehensive selection of both computing and library facilities for users in a particular subject area. For the first time, then, we had a building and a layout which allowed, and even required, the implementation of the converged working practices described below.

Between 1994 and 1997 the ARC represented the most thoroughgoing example of converged working at Liverpool JMU. Converged working was slower to take root at other campuses, partly because of the geography of service provision, partly because of the preferences of individual managers and partly because the degree of residual resistance to the notion of convergence differed from area to area. In August 1997 the main 'geographical' obstacles to the spread of convergence were finally overcome with the opening of a second major learning resource centre: the Avril Robarts Centre, 'ARC 2'. Whether ARC 2 embraces convergence with the enthusiasm of ARC 1, or whether there will continue to be a degree of pluralism as regards working practices between the different sites, is uncertain at the time of writing of this case study.

Because of the different speeds at which JMU sites have moved towards convergence, most of the examples of the implications and effects of convergence are drawn from the experience of staff at ARC 1 which has the longest experience of thoroughgoing convergence.

The Form of Convergence at Liverpool JMU

Staff roles and duties: the 'core duties' approach

As described above, Learning Services at Liverpool JMU brought together two groups of staff: library staff and 'User Support' staff from the previously separate Computer Services Division. Members of Computer User Support were already, as the name implies, skilled at providing direct frontline support to users. In the JMU model of convergence, the job descriptions of all staff contain a common core of basic duties drawn from what, previously, were exclusively 'library' or 'computing' job descriptions. At the non-professional level, for example, these 'core duties' include such tasks as issuing material (previously a library duty) and selling laser-printer output and computer consumables (previously a computer services duty). An example of JMU's 'Information Assistant' job description (the category into which library assistants were subsumed) is given in Appendix 1.

Almost all jobs, however, still retain a specialist computing or information content. It is important to note that JMU did not aim at total merger of job descriptions, and actively encourages most staff to see themselves as either computing or information specialists working together to provide a converged service. The aim was to achieve a sufficient degree of flexibility for the converged service to function in an integrated manner, without losing the benefits of specialization and without undermining staffs' sense of professional identity and pride.

Staffing structure: the 'subject team' approach

The key feature of the staffing structure is that most staff are members of teams which contain both library and computing specialists and report to managers who are responsible for both library *and* computing services. This applies at senior management level, but more significantly it also applies to middle managers. At the ARC, for example, the service divides into an operations team and a series of subject teams, all of which contain both computing and information specialists. The subject teams correspond to subject floors in the building which provide both the computing facilities and library services appropriate to users in a particular subject area. Each subject floor has a single subject team leader responsible for all aspects of the floor's operation. The staff structure is, therefore, focused on the subject affiliation of the user, not the professional affiliation of the service provider.

Reasons for Convergence

The foregoing sections describe the context in which convergence took place, and the form of convergence adopted. This section outlines some of the reasons why, as early as 1992, managers of learning support services at JMU formed the view that converged working was a worthwhile goal to pursue.

There were two principal reasons for the adoption of a converged structure at JMU: firstly, the need to adopt the most efficient structure in the face of declining unit funding and an increasing workload; and secondly, the need to create a structure which would improve quality and facilitate the development of new services, particularly the provision of networked electronic information and multimedia learning materials. Among the particular benefits convergence was intended to bring about were the following:

Economies of scale

Convergence can bring about the same kind of economies of scale as integrating two or more libraries – provided, firstly, that there is an overlap between the roles of 'library' and 'computing' staff and, secondly, that the physical configuration of the service permits co-operative working in practice. Front line computing specialists and information specialists at JMU can help one another in the areas covered by their core duties. This makes it easier to deal, for example, with peaks of activity at service desks, because the greater total volume of staff on which managers can draw enables queues to be dealt with more quickly. It also allows the service to function with slightly fewer staff at quieter times – evenings, weekends, vacations – because fewer staff are needed simply to open up and supervise separate physical areas, or to respond to intermittent flurries of activity.

Better access to advice and support

Under the JMU model of convergence, information specialists have a basic knowledge of computing facilities available, and computing specialists have a basic knowledge of library facilities available. This increases the likelihood of a user with a relatively low-level query receiving prompt assistance. Taking a typical computing enquiry – 'How do I log on to the network?' or 'How do I send my output to the single-sided printer?' – there are approximately 30 people within

JMU's ARC who could deal with this, rather than the eight there would have been if the building operated with an unconverged structure.

Better 'Customer Focus'

The subject floor approach described above makes the layout both more intelligible to users and more convenient. Initial orientation to the ARC is made easier, because the layout corresponds more closely to an individual user's instinctive sense of his own requirements. Bringing computer and library facilities together saves users' time because they find printed information side by side with electronic information and together with the applications software needed to manipulate and process that information.

The subject floor approach was also intended to humanize a large and potentially impersonal service for the benefit of both staff and users. It was felt that users would feel more comfortable with this approach, and grow used to a group of familiar faces on 'their' subject floor. It was hoped that, for staff, job satisfaction would be enhanced by closer identification with a particular group of users, and that staff would take more readily to the hitherto unfamiliar aspects of their jobs if they saw them as meeting the needs of a known and familiar group of students.

Supporting electronic services

There are a number of developing areas, which are clearly going to be of massive significance in the future and require computing and library experts to work side by side if they are to be supported properly. One area is electronic information. Providing access to networked information within a university requires the skills of computing specialists, who can look after technical, hardware and networking matters. Clearly, however, it also requires the librarian's skill of organizing large amounts of information and making it easily retrievable. This fact is, perhaps, insufficiently appreciated.

When computer networks had only very limited numbers of (chiefly) applications software packages on them it was easy to succumb to the illusion that there were no problems in organizing networks, or that crude solutions were all that were required. It is now becoming more apparent that librarians are needed to enable users to find the cyber-needle in the electronic haystack. One of the first fruits of convergence at JMU was the way in which computing and library and information service (LIS) specialists worked together to improve the interface to the JMU network. The interface that resulted is both simpler and more powerful than that which was developed by computer specialists working in isolation.

If electronic information sources require the complementary skills of librarians and computer specialists the same is true, to an even greater degree, of multimedia learning materials. A multimedia approach to learning is very important to Liverpool JMU's sense of itself and its future path, and has been an important influence on the development of Learning Services. Multimedia brings with it learner support problems that simply do not arise with traditional library material or with the kind of applications software computer centres have developed to support. Users need computing specialists to load the software in the first place, to make sure that it interfaces successfully with other software packages and to help with any technical problems which arise in use. They need librarians to make informed selection decisions about what multimedia materials should be put on the network, to organize those materials for easy retrieval, and to help find multimedia material either on local area networks or at remote Internet locations.

Service development

Though convergence was intended to bring about specific types of service development it was also hoped that 'in a more general sense' bringing computing and information specialists together would generate new ideas for service improvement, and engender a climate of greater creativity.

Staff in different organizational units can work together to bring about improvement, but the structures needed for this – working parties, task groups, liaison meetings etc. – can inhibit spontaneity and stifle the attitude to change and innovation often summed up as 'Ready, Fire, Aim'.

Training required for convergence

This topic merits a separate article in itself. Convergence generates a huge need for additional training. This is not merely a matter of 'skills' training, which is, in a sense, merely the tip of the training iceberg. Equally important is the need to reassure staff, to explain the reasons for convergence (which an acrimonious period of negotiation had tended to obscure rather than clarify at Liverpool JMU), and to enable people to understand the new context in which they will be working. A brief overview of the topic of training for convergence is provided in the published papers of the ARCLIB 1996 conference (Architecture Librarians' Group, 1996, pp.24–30).

The impact of convergence at Liverpool JMU

A converged service has now been operating at JMU's ARC for three years. This is a relatively short time in the history of an organization, and convergence still *feels* new, but it is possible to make some assessment of its impact upon staff and students.

Impact upon users

The ARC (ARC) currently embodies the most thoroughgoing model of converged service delivery within JMU. The opening of this new centre, on July 18 1994, did not 'cause' convergence, but it allowed convergence to be implemented in full, in a way that the geography of other JMU sites prevents. It is interesting to compare the 1993/94 usage figures for the two libraries and two computer centres that were merged into the ARC with the figures for 1994/95, the year in which the ARC opened. The difference is spectacular. Against a background of relative stability in student numbers an estimated 75 per cent increase in the exit gate count took place, enquiries rose by over 400 per cent, and there was an increase in excess of 70 per cent in a variety of computing transactions including sales of computer consumables and output of laser print. Though a certain amount of this increase can be attributed to the excellence of the building in which the services are now housed – and its novelty value – it is hard to believe that none of the increase is attributable to the way that the services are organized, including the 'subject floor' approach. Certainly, a new custom-built library opened by JMU at a suburban site some three years previously enjoyed nothing like this increase in activity, though the 'new building' factor can be presumed to have been equally potent.

Measures of student satisfaction tell a similar story (Table 4.1). It is fortunate that in February 1994, before the ARC opened, Liverpool JMU instituted a practice of systematically measuring the level of student satisfaction with various facilities on an annual basis. Students rate their satisfaction with services on a scale of one to five with responses ranging from 'very dissatisfied' to 'very satisfied'. The tables below shows the change in the percentage of ARC-based students who considered themselves 'satisfied' or 'very satisfied' with library and computing services between February 1994 (before the building opened) and February 1995, six months after it opened, and February 1996 (when the 'honeymoon period' with the new building/new service can reasonably be presumed to have finished).

The students in each of the six schools directly served by the ARC were asked 'How satisfied are you with library services?' 'How satisfied are you with computing services?'

The ARC has certainly realized a number of the benefits mentioned earlier. Convergence has proved to be a more

Table 4.1 Computing and library services satisfaction survey results

School	Computing			Libraries		
	1994	1995	1996	1994	1995	1996
Built Environment	50.9	57.9	61.8	55	78.8	73.9
Business	33.9	62.4	57.8	45.1	72.9	71.2
Art & Design	47.3	63.8	67.8	63	72.6	81.8
Languages	44.4	74.5	67.8	35.5	90.6	76
Law	36.8	51.2	58.1	50.5	78.3	71.5
Media/Humanities	29	54.3	60.9	41.9	59.1	58.4
Average (unweighted)	40.3	60.6	62.4	48.5	75.3	72.1

efficient mode of operation than separate library and computer services. The tangible benefits of this have been the ability to cope with the huge increase in demand for our services without additional staff, the extension of opening hours and the extension of availability of particular services. Significantly, service points have continued to operate at times when, under an unconverged service, they would have had to close. The predicted advantages in terms of a wider base of staff knowledge for students to draw upon have also materialized. While we presume that there is a relationship between these improvements and the improvement in student satisfaction noted above, this cannot be proven.

Impact of convergence upon staff

Given the amount of resistance to convergence originally manifested at JMU most staff have adapted to their changed roles remarkably well. Ex-library staff answer basic level computing queries competently, and are capable of running computer service desks in the absence of computer specialist colleagues. Although many staff regard their achievements with respect to networked computers as modest, most have achieved a degree of expertise far in advance of what is required by their job descriptions. The information officers in particular have moved from being unusually unfamiliar with computer technology five years ago to a very high level of expertise in certain packages. Despite the resistance which the move to convergence originally engendered, morale within the service seems reasonably high – even despite the huge increase in workload noted above – though this is inevitably a subjective impression.

Convergence has taken root more readily in some areas than others. Those aspects of convergence that are concerned with efficiency and immediate support to users are well established and, indeed, it would now be difficult to imagine how the service could be maintained without them. Perhaps less successful has been our aim of engendering creative co-operation between information and computing officers within subject teams. Although the juxtaposition of computing and information expertise has resulted in the odd improvement 'for example the change to the network interface described earlier' examples are still quite sparse. In many ways, the huge increase in activity that the launch of a new building and a converged service brought in its wake inevitably means that much of the time of professional information and computing officers is taken up with meeting the insistent needs of present users. There is, perhaps, little time left for devising imaginative solutions to the problems of future users.

It also seems true to say that convergence, as yet, has had more impact upon the roles of ex-library staff than upon ex-computer services staff. There are two reasons for this. The first is that the increase in demand has taken place chiefly on the computing side of JMU's activities so that, though both groups of staff are required to be equally flexible with regard to core duties, in practice ex-library staff are more likely to have needed to help with computing duties than ex-computer centre staff are to have needed to help with library duties. The second is that, in absolute terms, the number of computing specialists is small. Inevitably, that means that ex-library staff are called upon to solve computing problems in the absence of specialist colleagues more often than computing specialists are obliged to cope with 'library' problems in the absence of LIS specialists.

Overall, the degree of adaptation to converged working that has taken place at Liverpool JMU has been encouraging. However, it has to be admitted that there is still a feeling that convergence goes against the grain of many staffs' inclinations – not perhaps of recently recruited staff, but certainly of many long-standing members of staff, both on the computing and library sides. There is still a powerful nostalgia for the old structures and although relations between most ex-library and most ex-computer centre staff are amicable, a certain social separation is still apparent between them. Although most staff would probably acknowledge that convergence has been a success from the users' point of view a substantial minority would still, if their own preferences alone were consulted, prefer to revert to their former mode of working. Reactions to the subject team approach do perhaps form an exception to this slightly gloomy generalization. The subject team idea is popular with staff, and seems to have changed working patterns in a way that went *with* the grain of staffs' inclinations.

References

Sykes, P. (1996) Convergence of library and computer services at Liverpool John Moores University: a tale of two cultures? In *Finding and Meeting users' needs. Proceedings of the 7th annual conference of the Architecture Librarians' Group*. Architecture Libraries' Group.

Appendix 1

LIVERPOOL JOHN MOORES UNIVERSITY
LEARNING SERVICES
JOB DESCRIPTION

1. Job Title   : Information Assistant
2. Grade   : Scale 1–3[1]

3. Salary   :

4. Full/Part-Time hours :

5. Location   : Aldham Robarts Learning
                               Resource Centre[2]

6. Job Summary   :

   The general purpose of all user services assistant posts
   within Learning Services is to provide efficient and
   effective information and computing services to users.
   Information Assistants have a particular responsibility
   for processing, maintaining, storing, accessing and circu-
   lating information and learning materials.

7. Responsible to   : Operations Manager via Senior
                               Information Assistant for service
                               desk work
                             : Subject Team Leader for Subject
                               Work

8. Responsible for   :

9. Duties   :

   Information Assistants perform two set of duties:

   – **Core duties**. These are performed in common with all
     user services assistants, and relate to both information
     and computing provision

   – **Information duties**. These are performed by Informa-
     tion Assistants only and relate specifically to the provi-
     sion of information and learning materials

   9.1 Core Duties

      9.1.1 Service Desk Duties
            – Issuing and returning Learning Services items
              and other transactions immediately arising from
              these operations
            – Sales and cash handling
            – Sorting and distributing printer output

9.1.2 User Assistance
- Answering basic location and information enquiries
- Helping users to gain access to basic network facilities and gain assistance via E-Mail

9.1.3 Equipment
- Basic operation of Learning Services equipment[3]
- Switching equipment on and off
- Recognising and reporting equipment faults
- Replacing consumable materials in equipment – eg. paper and printer ribbons
- Photocopying duties, including replacing paper, clearing simple jams and reporting breakdowns

9.1.4 Learning Services Area Duties
- Assisting with opening and securing Learning Services areas
- General supervision and basic security of Learning Services areas

9.1.5 Other Core Duties
- Collecting simple statistical data
- Collecting and distributing post within Learning Services areas
- Light stock and equipment moves
- [Duties necessary to comply with Health and Safety legislation – guidance awaited from Personnel]
- Any other duties commensurate with the grade as deemed necessary by the Director of Learning Services

9.2 Information Duties
Core duties as above plus

9.2.1 Overdues and reservations work

9.2.2 Staffing the security system (passing items round the system and challenging users who trigger the alarm)

9.2.3 Processing of stock: receipt, trigger, label, repair, transfer, reservation and withdrawal of stock as directed. Collection of newspapers from newsagent.

9.2.4 Checking item orders

9.2.5 Shelving, moving, and tidying Learning Services Stock. Location (or otherwise) of stock from shelves

9.2.6 Photocopying as directed by Operations Manager

Notes to the text

1. Staff will normally be recruited to Sc. 1. After satisfactory completion of the probationary period they will be transferred to the bottom point of scale 2. There is a bar at the top of scale 2. Transfer to scale 3 is contingent upon satisfactory performance of a specialised duty or responsibility.
2. Staff will be recruited, initially, to a particular site, but may subsequently be required to move between sites
3. An Information Assistant is required to be sufficiently familiar with Learning Services equipment to enable a user to begin using the equipment. Advanced knowledge of equipment or applications software is not required.

Signature   :

Name (Print) :

Date   :

CHAPTER FIVE

Case Study: The Queen's University of Belfast

Norman Russell

Introduction

The Queen's University of Belfast, incorporated in 1908, is the successor to one of the three university colleges, called the Queen's Colleges, founded at Belfast, Cork and Galway in 1845. The College recognized from the outset the need to provide a library for its staff and students but while funds were set aside for the purchase of books as early as 1850 it was more than a decade later before the first library building opened its doors. For almost a century this was the only library, serving all disciplines, but as the university expanded away from the main site so new branches of the library were developed: first the Medical Library, then the Science Library, the Agriculture and Food Science Library and finally, in 1997, a 'Follett' legacy, the Seamus Heaney Library.

Over the years the Library has developed a collection which is certainly of considerable significance within Northern Ireland and has elements within it which are of national and even international importance. While much within the latter categories relates to Irish history and culture the library has been able to acquire, through purchase and donation, important material of a more general nature. Collection-building went into rapid decline in recent years with a startling contrast between the late 1960s, when a previous Librarian could bid at Sotheby's for desired collections, and the late 1980s, when Queen's was spending less per student on books than any other institution then designated as a university.

It is fair to say that Queen's Library, like many other libraries of 'larger civic universities', focused largely on collection-building as its primary activity and this was reflected in the deployment of its professional staff. Unfortunately it has to be said that Queen's was later than most in moving away from this focus. In recent years, however, it has been going through a period of considerable change due both to a re-orientation towards the development of a user-centred service, of which the collection is but one part, and to the integration of information technology into almost every aspect of the library's activities.

Finally, in this scene-setting introduction, it may be helpful to give some indication of the scale of the operation of Queen's library. The library has a core staff of around 130 of whom just over 20 are part-time. The number of staff in academic-related posts, which had risen to 36, is due to fall to around 30, mainly through a reduction in the number of such posts in technical service areas. Total library expenditure in the current year is close to £4 million but over 25 per cent of this is from income generated outside the university and used to serve non-university users. In 1996–97 student numbers stood at approximately 10,000 full-time and 5,000 part-time.

Convergence at Queen's

It is possible to date fairly precisely the beginning of consideration of convergence issues at Queen's using two markers: the report of the working group established to recommend changes to committee structures subsequent to the Jarratt Report on efficiency in universities (CVCP, 1985) and the resignation of the previous Librarian. The recommendations in the final report of the university's Jarratt group, approved in December 1988, included the replacement of separate committees for the library and computing by a Library and Information Services Committee. Among the terms of reference of this new committee was the production of an 'overall rolling plan'. While this was a move towards convergence the resignation of the Librarian in 1989 saw organizational convergence considered and rejected.

The Library and Information Services Committee did not lead to any convergence between the library and the computer centre. An overall plan was not prepared and the Committee would typically have two sub-agenda: library business and computing business. Meeting by meeting these would alternate in the order in which they were considered, in the interests of fair play; elected members were seen as being library-interest or computing-interest and an attempt was made to balance the numbers; and at its worst the members associated with one area or the other would leave when consideration of their part of the agenda was complete.

Such co-operation as did exist arose from informal contact between the Librarian and the Director of the Computer Centre and meetings between staff of the two departments. This did produce some useful cross-fertilization such as when the library initiated discussion on what in 1992 was described as a campus-wide information service before allowing the computer centre to run with the initiative. When an open access computing area was provided in the main library the computer centre was happy to assist in making its opening the occasion for the launch of what was referred to as '*The Electronic Library: Phase one*'.

Formal consideration of organizational convergence did not recur until the resignation of the Director of the Computer Centre at the end of 1994. Before moving to appoint a replacement the vice-chancellor established what was called the Information Services Review Group. Although its terms of reference related mainly to the development of an information strategy the Group was asked to consider 'the organization of computer and information provision within the University . . . as well as the necessity of a replacement for the Director of the Computer Centre'. In performing this task the Group consulted widely throughout the university and it was clear that there was little support for the sort of convergence which would have led to the appointment of a director to manage both library and computing operations. Having said that, the arguments in favour of such a move were not presented and most will have operated on the basis of a belief that each job was a significant enough challenge in itself and had differing requirements in the type of person called upon to fill them.

A new Director of Computing Services was appointed and he and the Librarian are expected to work together, just as the Director would need to do with any head of department in the university. The Librarian and Director both report to the same senior administrator who would have to arbitrate if there should be a dispute which they cannot resolve between them. Although the Information Services Review Group aimed to reform the committee structure in this area no decisions have been made and the existing merged committee continues much as before.

The Review Group, when considering convergence, had concluded that although there are areas of activity which bring the two departments close to one another the majority of their activities are quite separate. The extreme examples quoted were the library's care for its special collections and Computing Services' support for high-power computing. It is also true to say that the aspect of computing support which has been receiving most attention is what might loosely be called administrative computing. From a library perspective, the present situation in relation to convergence can be characterized as one in which the need for the library and computing services to work together has never been greater, but where the structures to allow this to happen have not been developed. Convergence at Queen's is incidental rather than planned and arises from two information service departments having roles which at times bring them into contact, and occasionally conflict, with one another.

It is one of life's little ironies that the Review of Information Services, and the subsequent appointment of a new Director of Computing Services, have coincided with events such as the opening of a new library with major IT provision, the migration to a new library computer system, the development of Web-based services and a new process for setting the budget of the library and computing services. As these took place there were instances of the Librarian and the Director taking different stances, usually supported by their respective committees.

An example may be helpful. The new student library, the Seamus Heaney Library, had been planned by the Librarian as one which would have half of its 500 places equipped with PCs, emphasizing that it would be a workplace for students where they could study in the traditional fashion and also access electronic resources and software. Provision for student computing had been through a number of computing services-managed open access centres, two of which were based in libraries, and the Director saw the facilities in the Seamus Heaney Library as an extension of these. The Librarian wanted use of the computer areas to be on the usual library model of individual use while the Director saw them as bookable for classes.

The situation will doubtless be familiar throughout the land but the point in relating it here is to emphasize that the only mechanism for resolving the disagreement at Queen's was by referring it to a line manager with a wide range of responsibilities of which information services is but one. The hope that an information strategy might help clarify roles and responsibilities was one reason why the Librarian welcomed the opportunity for the university to pilot the Joint Information Services Committee's approach, as described in its 'Guidelines for developing an information strategy' (JISC, 1995).

Information Strategy

Strategic planning is a relatively new activity at Queen's, as in most similar institutions. Before its arrival planning related almost exclusively to student numbers and was driven by the information demanded by the funding council in its planning circulars. Even in its 1992 plan the word 'strategy' appears only in a reference to the university's information systems strategy. However, by 1996 the university had decided to carry out a comprehensive strategic review which would build on the work already carried out in response to requests for documents such as an estates strategy, and reflect the context in which it must operate after the 1995 Budget Statement. This report of the Strategic Review Group was not presented until after the Dearing Committee had reported and the university's new vice-chancellor had arrived.

The former computer centre had for several years produced an annual rolling plan, which in 1990 metamorphosed into what was referred to as the Information Technology Strategy 1990–93. (Much of this activity was stimulated by the Computer Board.) Although this did aim to set the scene for development during the specified period it was essentially procurement-driven: achieve agreement on the plan and use this in bids for funding to procure equipment. The IT strategy was drafted by computer centre staff only but library staff had some input when in 1993 an Information *Systems* Strategy was produced. This was very similar in form and purpose to the previous strategy and the process was heavily criticized for not allowing wider input.

The library did not have such a long history of planning and one of the recommendations of the Library Review Group, which reported in 1989, was that 'a rolling strategic plan' should be produced. This duly appeared as a duty in the job description when a new Librarian was recruited later in that same year. As was said earlier, the creation of a joint committee for the library and computing was supposed to bring a combined plan but this did not occur. The Information Systems Strategy, insofar as it dealt with the library, referred only to those activities which involved the use of IT. The library prepared and won agreement for its own statement of aims and objectives, and its strategic direction, without ever gracing it with the title of a strategy.

When the funding council began to ask for details of the university's Information and Library Systems Strategy (1994), and then its Information Services Strategy (1995-), some difficulty was encountered in delivering the coherent response which was sought. There were also indications that all was not well in that area of the university's activities. The Information Services Review Group referred to earlier was called upon to determine the framework necessary for the development of an information strategy and it was during its deliberations that the 'Guidelines for developing an information strategy' were produced and that JISC invited bids to pilot their approach.

In his letter accompanying the Queen's bid to be a pilot site the vice-chancellor described the university as being committed wholeheartedly to the formulation of an information strategy. He welcomed the support that JISC would offer to the pilot sites and expressed a ready willingness to share our experiences with other institutions. The Librarian was wholly in support of the bid because he favoured the emphasis in the Guidelines on information as distinct from information technology. He also believed that being a pilot site would impose a discipline which would ensure that the strategy would be completed within a reasonable timescale and not overtaken by what might have been seen as more pressing matters. Undoubtedly others would not have been so keen to volunteer, whether because of scepticism about the very concept of an information strategy or a reluctance to have someone watching over our shoulder as we went through the process of developing one.

In its bid the university stated that it seeks to be an information-led institution and that it believes that this can best be achieved through the development and implementation of an appropriate information strategy. The bid spoke of 'islands' of information which had been created without recognition of the need for a coherent approach to information management. It was acknowledged that there is both an enthusiasm for the possibilities of the new technology and a scepticism based on past disappointments.

The university expressed the hope that, against a background of declining funds, a coherent information strategy would assist decisions in relation to resource allocations. Without a strategy it would become more and more difficult to reconcile the competing demands for resources in support of its teaching, research, administration and library activities. In addition, the strategy would provide a framework for the development of operational policies and, through its implementation, lead to the change in culture necessary if the institution was truly to become information-led. High hopes and expectations indeed.

The Library and Information Services Committee was charged with delivering the strategy, operating through a Working Group which was chaired by a pro-vice-chancellor. Although the Guidelines state at the outset that an information strategy is not just about libraries or computing the Librarian and Director of Computing Services were the next members of the group, followed by a faculty administrative officer. Queen's was unique among the pilot sites in involving academic staff, from the School of Management, as Project Director and Assistant Project Director. They immediately gave the project considerable impetus and helped to dissociate the strategy from the previous information technology and systems strategies which, as was said earlier, were basically computer centre initiatives. They also brought with them the opportunity to involve postgraduate students in the survey work.

The Working Group adopted a number of guiding principles including the use of the university's Mission Statement as its starting point. In other words, the task would be to consider information in the context of corporate aims, which can be summarized as excellence in research and teaching. A second principle, recognizing our role as a pilot site, would be that we would use the Guidelines as much as possible even though there was some headscratching at the statement that 'the best way to think of an information strategy is as a set of attitudes rather than a report'! A third guiding principle was that every effort would be made to involve as many as possible in the development of the project, and to disseminate information about it as work in progress, in an attempt to ensure that there was ownership of the strategy throughout the institution.

The methodology comprised an investigation of information use and information provision in the hope that an analysis of the findings would help to identify any gaps or duplication. A contrasting range of sample sites was chosen (two academic departments, a faculty office and the Research Office) and the plan was that some interventions would be undertaken at these sites, and their usefulness monitored. The work is still in progress but a number of the most likely conclusions can be presented.

It seems clear that the analysis of findings will show clearly that there is a need for an information strategy, suggesting that there is evidence that the management of information use and provision at an institutional level needs the cohesion and sense of direction which such a strategy can deliver. However, those who are expecting a document similar to the university's estates strategy will be disappointed to discover that the report of the working group may well argue that the university is not ready to produce one. The view which has emerged is that the university will have to undergo such a profound culture change that the structures currently in place could not cope. What will be produced will be offered as a first step, a 'metastrategy'; it will seek to enable rather than proscribe. Any other type of document would be destined to become 'shelfware', as so many strategic documents have been before.

While the investigators tried to encourage those they were interviewing to think of information management in the broadest sense they encountered a mind set which tended to overemphasize issues relating to information technology. This seemed to arise more from the previous association of strategic development in this area with computer centre initiatives and less from dissatisfaction with present hardware. On the contrary, dissatisfaction focused on what have been characterized as 'soft' issues such as training, coordination, access and incompatibility.

Just as in the deliberations of the Information Services Review Group (referred to in the section above on convergence) the library received comparatively little attention except when referred to specifically in questions. In the minds of many academic staff, probably a majority, the library remains the most important information resource in support of their teaching and research but it is seen as distinct from what they understand to be the university information system. This, of course, is not the view from within the library.

The interviews with staff and students added comparatively little to the library's understanding of the views of its users. (Books and journals, inter-library loans and online databases are all considered to be of great importance; library staff are highly regarded; and the provision of books and journals is considered to be inadequate.) However, the investigators were not attempting a small scale library survey but rather were laying the groundwork for the information strategy which the university wishes to develop and the library wishes to see developed. In the concluding paragraphs of this section the position of the Queen's University Library within the development of an information strategy, and the implications for convergence issues, will be explored.

What Next at Queen's?

Queen's College Belfast began with a full-time Librarian, albeit one who was expected to run the library single-handedly and had to resort to paying an assistant £40 *per annum* out of his own £150 salary. Although this Librarian was regarded as a success he was succeeded in 1880 by a professor and Queen's then had a series of part-time librarians for the next fifty years. While this may have appeared a retrograde step Moody and Beckett (1959, p.503) were able to write that in the mid-1920s the library was 'the most important unifying force in the intellectual life of the university' and that the Librarian, who was also Professor of English Literature, played a considerable part in the administration of the university. In 1930 the university reverted to appointing a full-time Librarian, by now a professional, and the position of Librarian became, and remains, one which is important in its own right but does not involve the holder in wider responsibilities.

The purpose of this reflection on the place of the Librarian at Queen's is to demonstrate the need to be open-minded in anticipating what lies ahead. Clearly the precise role of the Librarian in the development of the information strategy is of considerable significance for the future of Queen's Library. While in other institutions the interest in information strategies is seen as having arisen from the Follett Report this is not the case at Queen's where the work of the University's Information Services Review Group, and Information Strategy Working Group, revealed a concentration on management information systems and on technology. It is difficult to argue that the Librarian *ex officio* should lead the process but there must be sufficient involvement to ensure that the role of the library as the main information provider in support of teaching and research is fully integrated into the strategy.

The aim of library involvement will be to avoid too much concentration on technology and systems issues and to direct thinking towards what we need to do in relation to information management if the university is to achieve its overall strategic aims. We will want to see the university include library planning in its academic planning so that, for example, the contribution that the library might make to coping with major increases in student numbers is considered. We will want to see a clearer link between strategic development and funding so that decisions on the budget are better informed, more responsive and less based on history.

It seems inevitable that when the university considers the organizational change which will be necessary if the strategy is to be successful it will have to revisit the question of convergence and in particular the respective roles of the library and computing services. It is impossible to predict what the outcome of this may be, especially at a stage when a new vice-chancellor has just taken up his post. The fact that the university has rejected organizational convergence on two occasions when the post of one or other of the heads of service was vacant would suggest that it will not rush down that particular path.

Allen (1995, p.17) claims that an information management strategy must be a key component of an information strategy and will be concerned with how the information services are organized. The trend at this point in time is still towards convergence in one of a myriad number of forms and there seems little doubt that library and computer professionals at Queen's, as elsewhere, will have to make fundamental changes in the way they work and the way they relate to one another. The library is no longer simply a customer of computing services but is a provider of information resources, many of which are now computer-based. If greater convergence is not to occur then the re-examination of roles must lead to a strict definition of remits and this will neither be easy to achieve nor necessarily helpful from a user point-of-view.

It is generally thought that change is more difficult to achieve in older institutions, where traditional ways of operating are deeply entrenched but, while conscious that it is almost a truism, it has to be said that there has been as much change at Queen's in the past ten years as in the previous fifty. Change has come about through global developments, such as in network and communication technologies; through national initiatives such as SuperJANET, eLib and BIDS; through a transformation of the University itself by, among other things, huge increases in student numbers and the introduction of modularity and semesterization; and last, but by no means least, through initiatives arising within the library itself. There is no reason to suggest that the pace of change will slow, and the need for the university and its library to exert greater control over its destiny has never been greater. In Queen's University the implementation of an information strategy, and the organizational and culture change which must precede it, are seen as vital in this process.

Postscript

In March 1988 JISC published a set of revised guidelines for developing an information strategy (JISC, 1998a) and a set of case studies from the six pilot sites (JISC, 1998b).

References

Allen, D. (1995) *Information strategies in context: a report commissioned by the SCONUL Advisory Committee on Information Systems.* London: SCONUL

Committee of Vice-Chancellors and Principals (1985) *Report of the Steering Committee on Efficiency Studies in Universities.* London: CVCP

Moody, T. W. and Beckett, J. C. (1959) *Queen's, Belfast, 1845–1949: the history of a university.* London: Faber and Faber

Joint Information Systems Committee (1995) *Guidelines for developing an information strategy.* Bristol: HEFCE

Joint Information Systems Committee (1998a) *Guidelines for developing an information strategy:* Bristol: HEFCE

Joint Information Systems Committee (1998b) *Case Study – Developing an information strategy: The Queen's University, Belfast.* Bristol: HEFCE

Case Study: Information Strategy and Convergence of Academic Support Services at the University of North London

Roy Williams

Introduction

This case study deals with aspects of convergence at the University of North London and charts the more recent development of a University Information Strategy. Links are made between these two developments although they are mostly described separately. Efforts have been made to provide an objective account of events and to set them in a wider context where this might be of interest.

The University of North London

The former Polytechnic of North London is now a medium sized, mainly teaching university based in an inner city location on Holloway Road (the A1). Student numbers grew from around 7000 in 1990 to 14 800 in 1997. The university has a clear access mission 'to provide the best possible educational experience leading to a range of employment, social and economic opportunities for the widest possible clientele'. This is reflected in the distinctive student profile which shows that some 76 per cent of UNL students are classed as mature. Many students come from ethnic minority backgrounds and most of them are from Greater London. Fifty-six per cent of UNL students are women.

This case study is mainly concerned with the period 1990–1997. During this time the number of University sites was reduced from four to two. Amongst the new buildings acquired was a large mirror factory which was successfully converted into a new Learning Centre which opened in 1994. The old campus library was itself converted during 1995 to form the Information Technology Teaching Centre encompassing eight IT studios.

Part One: Convergence of Academic Support Services

It could be said that the history of convergence is much more about the interaction of people than it is about technology. This is certainly the case at UNL, where the convergence was effected on the initiative of two service Heads.

A history of UNL convergence

Less than ten years ago the polytechnic's 'electronic library', not untypically for the time, was centred around computerized housekeeping systems (as part of the BLCMP co-operative) and limited access to online searching of remote databases. Each of the five site libraries had one of the still novel 'personal computers' and there was emerging use of e-mail, particularly for internal communication. The Head of Library and Media Services, appointed in late 1987, was evidently not required to have a clear vision of the electronic future, nor to be particularly IT literate. Vision and momentum in this context were the province of the Library Systems Office, the staff of which had developed a mission to cajole their colleagues into the new library world.

The enthusiasts of the Library Systems Office were frustrated by the inability of the polytechnic's Computing Service (PNLCS) to provide resources for developmental projects like the campus-wide information service. Worse still, there was an uncertainty in PNLCS about sharing any sort of vision. Computing staff were still focused on and structured around a mainframe-based service, as would be the case in many universities of the time. The library had allied itself to the institution's drive to establish effective academic quality systems, whilst the computing service was perceived to be remote in its organization and out of step with the rapidly developing modular scheme of things.

In 1991 the opportunity arose to appoint a new Head of PNLCS. There was no serious discussion about converging academic support services and a new Head, from a commercial rather than educational background, duly arrived and began flattening structures and changing priorities. A good informal working relationship was established with the Head of Library and Media Services and eventually the new Head suggested that the Media Service might be transferred to PNLCS, so that a critical mass of technical support staff could be established at site level. During a fateful lunchtime meeting in a local pub, a more radical counterproposal was put forward : rather than hive off the Media Service, why not merge the two departments together and bring all three services under joint management?

Rationale for convergence

The arguments used to support this proposal went along the lines that were becoming well documented in the professional press at the time, for instance in the *British Journal of Academic Librarianship* (1988). Technologies were seen to be converging and information itself was becoming the focus of students', researchers' and administrators' needs. Traditional boundaries were becoming both blurred (for example in terms of presentational technologies and 'multi-media') and unhelpful (as with the campus-wide information service).

The potential of electronic, network based services was becoming increasingly clear (even to a 'Chief Librarian') and staff in the different professional areas of the department had what were seen to be complementary information-related skills.

Converged services were being established in a range of different universities at the time, although a recently published report on computer-based information services had (rather cautiously) stopped short of openly advocating convergence (IUCC/SCONUL, 1990, p.30). My own feeling was that somewhere down the line a convergence would be proposed at PNL and that to avoid possible resource-driven expediency it would be better to be proactive and bring forward more rational arguments. There was similar pragmatic reasoning concerning the place of a converged service in the political landscape of the institution. This was dominated by the four faculties, with academic support services and other departments in competition with one another for resources. A combined service would find it easier to move IT and information on to the polytechnic's big agenda and key issues could be presented and dealt with in a positive and strategic context.

A proposal to combine the two departments was made to the then Deputy Director (Academic) who was the senior line manager to the two Heads. She welcomed the idea immediately and saw its potential to benefit the Polytechnic. The Polytechnic Director was then persuaded, making it clear that he had not previously considered the matter much. It was agreed that a presentation could be made to the Senior Executive Team and, later, to the Board of Governors. That only left the staff of the two departments and the rest of the polytechnic and these were won round through a series of presentations and workshops.

Features of convergence at North London

In 1991 the creation of a new department, prosaically called Computing Library and Media Services (CLMS), was a proactive and pre-emptive move by two managers soon supported by two enthusiastic groups of staff. As any department can only have one Head, the two protagonists demonstrated their commitment through a 'gentlemen's agreement' rather than cloud the merger issue with a formal recruitment process. The Head of Computing would assume the title of Head and the former Head of Library and Media Services would become the Associate Head of the new department. Each would continue to report to the Deputy Director/Vice-Chancellor (Academic). More significantly, the two erstwhile Heads agreed that they would support each other through an open and frank personal partnership. This commitment provided the lasting foundation for the development of the department over the next six years and continues in the considerably different climate of today.

The restructuring and reorganization of the services and staff were largely left in the hands of the two main players and their colleagues. The lack of an institutional blueprint gave the opportunity to consult widely about user needs and priorities and to act accordingly in the light of this. The department could set its own agenda and timescales whilst promoting its services and presenting its case to the institution at large.

From CLMS to ISS

One early and largely unforeseen outcome of the way that the new department came into being was that additional areas of responsibility were added to its portfolio. This started with the assimilation of technical support staff from four academic Schools. A few years later, reorganization of certain corporate services saw the University Print Centre and telephone service join the department, which, as part of a process review of its own, was then re-designated Information Systems and Services (ISS). Two Director posts were created, one for Information Systems and IT and the other for Information Services.

To chart the detailed history of the converged department would be merely tedious. However it is worth listing a number of milestones along the way. These include the development of a university IT Strategy in 1993; the series of interlocking planning and implementation projects which led to the opening of the Learning Centre (see Williams, 1996); the design, development and delivery of the new IT studios and the Media Centre; monthly reports to customers; development of institutional World Wide Web strategy and policy; and a growing recognition of the importance of information, information management and IT, not just within the department but as institutional issues in their own right (hence, in time, the information strategy).

Of course all of the achievements listed could and probably would have occurred without convergence. For the two managers concerned however the value of mutual support and joint problem solving cannot be overestimated and change management was greatly assisted. The political and tactical elements of the merger were achieved and there was greatly enhanced flexibility in dealing with new projects and unforeseen developments. Not least, any barriers to the strategic development of user-based services and facilities were removed and the student experience in these areas was positively transformed, largely over a three year period 1993–1996.

The impact of convergence

An e-mail survey by Bruce Royan (the results of which were sent to lis-sconul in December 1993) described 'five broad patterns of convergent service management'. North London has elements of at least three of these : 'goodwill and commonsense', a 'peer coordinator' and a 'PVC/Deputy Principal' (in UNL terms a deputy vice-chancellor, albeit one with a brief wider than information services). The initial rationale for convergence at UNL was part strategic and part tactical. One of the outcomes has been the effective saving of a senior post when compared to Royan's classic 'Executive Director' model of convergence, apparently adopted by 36 of his 75 respondents.

The criteria for measuring the success or otherwise of converged services have yet to be agreed. Collier (1996, p.75) suggests that a fully converged department would have nine characteristics, including avoidance of internal overlap or competition, rationalized administration, flexibility of human resource management, flexible resource allocation and integrated management. UNL scores heavily on these features but less well on others, such as breakdown of professional demarcations and multi-disciplinary teams (other than when convened for projects). In addition, our move towards developing a one-stop-shop approach to customer services is precluded by the realities of local accommodation and we have instead concentrated on complementary provision.

Overall, Information Systems and Services at the University of North London score perhaps seven out of ten on the Collier scale as a converged department. It is possible to argue that the focus of the department, which was information, has been diluted by some of the responsibilities acquired along the way and the notion of a centre to the department has at times been difficult to sustain. As the department has grown, it, in turn, has become a natural target for the faculties and others. However, the tensions inherent in these shifts of fortune have done little to undermine the co-operative relationship between the two directors who, six years on, still view the merger as a win/win development.

Part Two: Information Strategy and the UNL Strategic Plan

There is a conundrum concerning the relationship between information strategy and converged academic support services. Is convergence an inevitable outcome of information strategy development or is information strategy a product of convergence? Whatever the ins and outs of this, at UNL it can be said that the development of an institutional Information Strategy seems logical within the context of the converged service. Thus this part of the case study gives some background as to how the development of an Information Strategy came to be an integral part of the UNL Strategic Plan and how the university came to be one of the JISC Pilot Sites for implementing the published guidelines on developing an information strategy (JISC, 1995b). A description is given of the structure set up to develop and manage the Information Strategy and of progress made during 1996/7 in developing a framework for the strategy and its implementation.

It has already been demonstrated that a concern with information in a broad sense was a factor in the original convergence proposals. Consideration of information issues soon moved outside the parochial boundaries of library, media and computing service areas into the institutional arena and beyond. As elsewhere, such considerations have also moved beyond the provision of services and facilities into the realms of teaching and learning. The publication of the Follett Report (which openly encouraged convergence) brought this into sharper focus. The report stated that: 'the way in which information can be stored, accessed and disseminated is changing fundamentally. In the light of these changes, each institution should develop an information strategy setting out how it proposes to meet the needs of those working within it . . .' (HEFCE, 1993, p. 71).

Opportunities to discuss this arose as part of the institutional consideration of Follett and, as has been shown, such discussion coincided with a period of intense activity at North London on such areas as the development of an IT Strategy, the Learning Centre and, from 1994, a reappraisal of the existing Corporate Plan. This combination of strategic debate and practical implementation highlighted the scope for an information strategy to link developments. When the university was required to respond to a funding council circular in June 1994, interest was sharpened, since recipients were asked to demonstrate: 'the extent to which the institution has developed an integrated information strategy, addressing such areas as networking, library provision, management information systems, access to information sources, electronic information dissemination, telephony and computational facilities for research'. (HEFCE, 1994, p.4).

Becoming a JISC Pilot Site

At UNL an informal group was set up to investigate the idea of an information strategy further and to advise the Deputy Vice Chancellor (Academic). The group met three times over about a six month period and produced some general statements highlighting both the nature and the potential of an information strategy. This meshed neatly with the parallel reconsideration and redrafting of the new Strategic Plan. Task Groups were set up to work on various aspects of the plan and a draft was circulated, revised and adopted by December 1995. It contained explicit mention of an Information Strategy which was set out in Strategic Aim 30. Targets for the delivery of the various Strategic Aims were then discussed and agreed by May 1996. It was during this same period, December 1995 to May 1996, that the JISC Guidelines belatedly appeared and invitations to bid to become a pilot site were issued.

Strategic Aim 30 of the university's Strategic Plan seeks: 'to formulate a University Information Strategy in accordance with the strategic aims. The development of this strategy will provide a framework for communication and information flows within which academic, management and administrative systems will operate. The strategy will inform and integrate with a review and development of academic and administrative processes'. It would be fair to say that this was, and has been proved to be, an ambitious statement, but with such a strategic aim in place it was natural that we were keen to become a JISC pilot site and pleased to be invited to be so. It is not unlikely that the link with the Strategic Plan was a prime factor in our selection.

The objectives of the UNL Information Strategy

The UNL Strategic Plan sets out the key objectives of the Information Strategy. These are to 'support the delivery of the strategic aims of the university; support the operational and functional aspects of the university's work and the management processes; and to facilitate the involvement and participation of all members of the university in delivering the strategic aims and engaging in ongoing development'. The Information Strategy was therefore seen as contributing to and facilitating the management of change. It was to be about the way people work and the way things do or do not get done. It was to involve staff throughout the university.

The Information Strategy is also intended to support the interaction between staff and students, recognizing the centrality of students to the university's Mission and to the type of university which UNL is. The Information Strategy will also deliver external requirements and support accountability as well as supporting external relations and partnerships.

Setting the context

The work done in preparation for the Strategic Plan and the publication of JISC's own Issues paper (JISC, 1995a), enabled the university to move smoothly through the initial stages of implementing the JISC Guidelines. These suggest that there are four contextual factors to be considered, three of which were summarized in the first part of the published UNL plan. The one exception was the managerial and organizational context of the institution, the subject of some debate amongst members of the Information Strategy Task Group. The setting the context exercise was concluded by using a proforma checklist of the key points to be considered, recording on the proforma relevant documents and logging milestone dates.

Structural framework

In accordance with the Strategic Plan a structural framework for the Information Strategy was established by March 1996.

This employs an Information Strategy Steering Group (ISSG), with an overarching executive role, and the Information Strategy Task Group (ISTG). The ISSG, which is chaired by the Deputy Vice Chancellor (Academic), is in effect an augmented meeting of the UNL Senior Management Team. In addition to the four Deans and the Registrar, the Group contains the Director of Information Systems and IT and the Head of Educational Development.

The ISTG, which is charged with developing the strategy and taking practical steps towards implementation, is convened by the Director of Information Services. Membership brings together the Deputy Dean of the Business School, the Deputy Registrar, the Head of Management Information, the Head of the School of Historical, Philosophical and Contemporary Studies, a senior lecturer from the School of Information and Communication Studies and the university's Development Officer for Learning Innovation. Several of these members were part of the original informal information strategy group.

In addition to its own resources, UNL, as a JISC Pilot Site, was also afforded a defined amount of assistance from a Coopers & Lybrand consultant, access to and support from the JISC Information Strategy Coordinator and the advantage of regular exchange of experience meetings with colleagues from the other pilots.

Following the JISC Guidelines

Eighteen months on from our start date it is clear that we need to go back to the Strategic Plan and the various contextual documents, and perhaps spell out more clearly the information strategy implications of the statements they contain. We have also had a lot of debate about determining priorities for implementing the emerging strategy. The Coopers & Lybrand consultant worked with each individual member of the ISSG to facilitate their thinking on this and to link the Information Strategy with their individual operating plans and Strategic Plan accountabilities.

Even though (perhaps because?) we are a Pilot Site, it is worth pointing out that a good deal of the ISTG's thinking and the approach it has taken to the Information Strategy project have been influenced by published research and alternative views of information management not always in line with the methodology articulated in the JISC Guidelines. The Hawley Committee (1995) and Orna (1990) are but examples and, at times, we have felt that we had a broader perception than our consultant, although we were grateful for her advice on some of the more fundamental project management issues.

A broader view, of course, does not always facilitate decision making and action and at various stages of the project the ISTG found difficulty in knowing whether or not it was progressing the project at the right level. On the one hand there were discussions relating to the information management aspects of the Strategic Plan, at the other was a detailed pilot information audit of the assessment function in the university. The Coopers & Lybrand consultant and, particularly, the JISC Information Strategy Coordinator were helpful in assisting the Group to refocus its work and to marry up the various levels of the project. Were the university working solely from the published Guidelines however, it is doubtful if such a resolution would have been achieved so readily.

Resources

Developing the Information Strategy has been more onerous and time consuming than predicted and inevitably other projects and priorities have had to be accommodated by ISTG members. This has necessitated changes in working practice and meant that progress has not always been as swift as would have been wished. The university was unable to allocate staff resources to the Information Strategy project at a time when additional support became a pressing need. After a period of slow progress the position was retrieved with the assistance of JISC funding (£5000) which ensured that virtually all project targets for 1996/7 were met. A more ambitious request for resources was submitted in accordance with the university's internal budget allocation timetable for 1997/8 and was successful, renewing optimism for the year ahead. Project plans were agreed by the ISTG and the ISSG but much of the work is being carried out by external or project specific staff.

General approach

The implementation of the UNL Information Strategy is to be based on developing good information management practice across the university via a series of key projects during 1997/8. As part of the preparatory work for this, a practically-oriented Information Policy, highlighting good practice, was drafted and included in a Framework Document agreed with the ISSG. This also contains an updated exposition of aims, objectives and definitions along with draft statements on human resources. Linked to the development of concrete policy will be a suite of 'tools' which, ultimately, will provide a coherent framework for managers and others to carry out information management projects in their own areas of work. Currently these tools include an information audit questionnaire, a methodology for translating responses into a functional analysis of an individual's tasks, and the use of a software package for mapping information flows. Performance indicators of good information management practice are also being developed.

Defining information needs

As a way into the third section of the Guidelines, a detailed audit case study was carried out within the assessment function of the university. This involved academic and administrative staff and students. Flow diagrams for individuals, for specific roles and for different faculties were produced and discussed with those engaged in assessment work. The expectation was that defining a streamlined system would be made easier through an information management approach and that duplicated effort and waste could be reduced. At the time of writing there are concrete indicators that this has been the case. The audit has also highlighted aspects of roles and responsibilities (academic/ administrative staff) and differing practice in various parts of the university.

Further projects have been identified as part of the implementation phase during 1997/8. This was done through the ISSG and the Senior Management Team. The key areas for attention were those related to the delivery of sections 2 and 3 of the UNL Strategic Plan (Academic Identity and Academic Profile). The information management topics which emerged as important across the university included: information for students (a life cycle analysis); the information implications of implementing technology-based course units; the use of information audit practices in departmental process reviews; linking the Information Strategy with a reworking of the UNL IT Strategy; knowledge management; and strategic management information needs.

As has been stated earlier there are elements of the Information Strategy project which are almost dauntingly ambitious. The level of senior management commitment is likely to be tested as further work during the implementation phase takes place and current practice is challenged and remodelled. A significant effort will be necessary to ensure that the aims and purposes of the Information Strategy are widely understood and that the benefits are quantified through the monitoring and evaluation of projects. Now that resources are available, much progress is being made through the academic year 1997/98. Actual outcomes and deliverables will perhaps form the substance of a future case study.

Conclusion and Postscript

It can be reiterated that, although much of the UNL experience in the fields of convergence and information strategy is unremarkable, some perspective is given to significant sectoral and professional developments *by* charting local activity. The impact and influence of individuals and institutional circumstances have been demonstrated and these have been further highlighted by more recent events. In March 1997 the early retirement of the Deputy Vice Chancellor (Resources) led to the secondment to the university's Senior Executive Team of the Director of Information Systems and IT. To cover for his absence the Director of Information Services became Acting Head of ISS reporting to his former colleague. These arrangements have subsequently been made permanent although the internal management structure of ISS is now the subject of a process review. The emerging Information Strategy is a significant factor which will ensure that a converged service model, albeit in modified form, continues at UNL.

Postscript

In March 1988 JISC published a set of revised guidelines for developing an information strategy (JISC, 1998a) and a set of case studies from the six pilot sites (JISC, 1998b).

Acknowledgements

I am grateful to Kevin Harrigan, Mike O'Reilly, Eileen Milner, Mike Heery and a host of UNL colleagues for their contribution to this chapter. However, the views expressed in this case study are those of the author and not necessarily those of the university or its officers.

References

British Journal of Academic Librarianship (1988) **3** (3) [This issue is largely devoted to convergence case studies]

Collier, M. (1996) The context of convergence. In *Staff Development in Academic Libraries,* ed. M. Oldroyd, pp.68–80. London: Library Association.

Hawley Committee (1995) *Information as an asset – the board agenda*. London: KPMG IMPACT

Higher Education Funding Council for England, et al. (1993) *Joint Funding Councils' Libraries Review Group: Report*. (Follett Report). Bristol: HEFCE

Higher Education Funding Council for England (1994) *Strategic plans and financial forecasts, Circular 15/94*. Bristol: HEFCE

IUCC/SCONUL (1990) *Report on information technology penetration and co-ordination on university campuses*. Joint Information Services Working Party

Joint Information Systems Committee (1995a) *Exploiting information systems in higher education : an issues paper*. Bristol: HEFCE

Joint Information Systems Committee (1995b) *Guidelines for Developing an Information Strategy*. Bristol: HEFCE

Joint Information Systems Committee (1998a) *Guidelines for Developing an Information Strategy: the sequel*. Bristol: HEFCE

Joint Information Systems Committee (1998b) *Case Study – Developing an information strategy: the University of North London*. Bristol: HEFCE

Orna, E. (1990) *Practical information policies*. Aldershot: Gower

Williams, R. (1996) The Learning Centre at the University of North London. *SCONUL Newsletter*, **7**, 7–11

CHAPTER SEVEN

Case Study: University of Stirling

Robin Davis

Background

The University of Stirling was founded in the wake of the 1963 Robbins report into UK higher education. It received its first students in 1967, and rejoiced in being the first completely new university established in Scotland for four hundred years. There was competition within Scotland for this privilege but Stirling won because it had a 'green field' site and was easy to reach – Glasgow and Edinburgh are less than an hour away. Indeed its situation is extremely beautiful, a factor which has always been an attraction to students and staff at the same time as a constraint on physical development. Thirty years later the university has about 6000 students and has no plans to exceed 7000 in the foreseeable future, which will mean its remaining relatively small by UK standards. The original academic plan was to establish teaching and research in the arts, social sciences and natural sciences. Subjects such as engineering, law and medicine were specifically excluded as being already adequately catered for in existing universities. We now have four faculties – Arts, Human Sciences (including Education), Management and Natural Sciences (the latter concentrating on the life sciences). New is the development of Nursing and Midwifery (Human Sciences faculty), which involves the delivery of education in these subjects to students in the Highlands and Islands through campuses at Inverness and Stornoway as well as in the Stirling and Falkirk areas of central Scotland. It presents particular challenges at a time when the future is full of uncertainties – political, financial, pedagogical and technical, but we feel Stirling is as well prepared as any to face these.

Academic support services have always been a priority at Stirling. The Librarian was among the first principal officers to be appointed, well before the first students appeared, to 'play an active educational role within the University, with the emphasis on the exploitation of resources rather than conservation. It is desirable that provision should made for some teaching to be done within the Library building' (from the brief for the original library building). Although physical development was seen very much in terms of growth of the collections, this emphasis on liaison and education has remained, as has the intention that the building should be able to cope with change in the way services are delivered. Computing services operated initially as a service to all departments based on a central mainframe (ICL 4130) computer, while audio-visual services came under the umbrella of the education department which had a brief that included initial teaching training and which was the main user of such facilities. Administrative computing began with the appointment in 1969 of a systems analyst/programmer within the administration to operate a small number of batch processing systems. Management of these services continued separately for many years, with the one change that the audio-visual services became independent of the education department as the university grew in size and diversity.

Convergence

In 1988, both the Librarian and the Director of Computing gave notice, within a short time of each other, of their intention to retire early, and the Principal of the university, Professor John Forty, began discussions involving users of the central services and the staff of these services which led in October 1989 to the appointment of a Director of Information Services. The remit of the new post was to manage library, computing, audio-visual and lecture-room support, printing and management computing services. The office of University Librarian remained, as it was enshrined in the University Statutes, but was subsumed into the Director's post. Professor Forty had been chairman of the University Grant Committee's Computer Board (a UK body) and on the Board of the British Library. He foresaw a growing reliance by librarians on technology, an increase generally in the demands made on computing by the needs of teaching and research, and possible synergies developing from harnessing the energies of staff in computing and library services who were involved in tendering advice to their academic colleagues. He was aware of the increasingly competitive environment in which universities were having to operate, and the absolute necessity for a small university such as Stirling to be ahead of the field if it was to survive. Staff in these services, though not happy at the loss of separate identity, were keen to show commitment to this desire for change, pointing out, for example, the library's early development – in the 1970s – of online information retrieval and their harnessing of automation; the Dynix system was installed in Stirling in 1986. Users were less sure of the advantages of the proposal, fearing that books would take second place to technology, and assuming that the university's real aim was to save money.

The period that followed was, and remains, one of constant change and development. Bruce Royan, the Director, had two major tasks to perform at the outset: to integrate the academic and administrative support services for which he was now responsible and to implement a new computing strategy which depended less on a central mainframe and moved towards a future involving client-servers working on distributed open systems computers across a wired campus. Integration was assisted by bringing into action classic management ploys such as away-days and weekends for the staff to try and foster the spirit of working together towards a common goal. Stirling is small, so this was made easier by most people knowing already at least a little of their colleagues from other sections, but cultural differences showed – the librarians fond of their image of being helpful to all and particularly supportive of undergraduates, the computer staff accustomed to providing almost individual support to staff and research students and very much aware of their users' often complete dependence on their services. Proposals for restructuring the organization were accepted by the university within two months of Bruce Royan's appointment: it was necessary to demonstrate quickly how Information Services could be meaningfully knit together. The opportunity was taken to rectify several staff grading anomalies, to recruit some additional staff, to link liaison in the library and computing services directly to the Schools (as the faculties were then known), and to put in place a clear operating structure – see the attached organization structure (Appendix 1). This structure, which was built on the concept of divisions whose heads reported to the Director, demonstrated that management of policy was to be coherent but failed to show the myriad cross-links between divisions on which the actual service delivery so vitally depends. Staff were aware of their inter-dependence as a team but had, and continue to have, some difficulty in persuading users to appreciate it.

Implementing a new computer strategy meant convincing a sceptical audience that the staff who had operated an old-style centralized system could adapt to the new concept of distributed services, and supporting computer staff, some of whom felt undervalued by their academic colleagues or were resistant to change. The procurement exercise involved tough negotiation with the suppliers but the creation of a local area network went ahead steadily. Some users continued to prefer their own packages to those now supported by computer services, and the Information Services Committee (ISC) had to act as arbiter on occasion. (ISC was the new single committee that replaced the former separate committees for the library and the computer unit.) In general however, it was the improvements in communication that were the most applauded. Users hitherto baffled by the technicalities of remote logging on to the library's OPAC now found this an easy task. A campus information system was inaugurated, and e-mail began to flourish. Thus Stirling's academic support services were converged, and early benefits realized.

Subsequent revisions in 1992 of the staff organization chart saw Media Services transferred from the Resource Management to computing services to form a Computing and Media Services Division (CMSD) ostensibly on the grounds of a convergence of technology, though in practice this had more to do with some critical personnel management issues which stem from the period pre-1989 when audio-visual services had been, managerially-speaking, in a sort of limbo, operating as a remote arm of Administration. Creating clear line management has helped, as has the demonstration of dependence on other branches of Information Services. Convergence in this sense has assisted the resolution of difficult problems. Also in 1992, responsibility for the university art collection was handed to the director. At Stirling, this is not a large collection – three to four hundred items only, but a significant proportion, garnered in the early years of the University, are of national importance. There is no gallery, but the main items are on display in one building. The art collection had been latterly administered as an appendage to the Estates and Buildings department. Once in Information Services, the collection was registered with the Museums and Galleries Commission, and proper governance was put in place – yes, we set up a committee that reports to the University Court. Again the significance of this was that the university recognized the competence of the new directorate to take on and manage effectively an additional sphere of responsibility.

In 1996, the Director resigned to take up an appointment outside the university sector, and the university, after a period of due reflection, agreed to replace him. Though some users remain unconvinced about the achievements of Information Services, university senior management showed no hesitation in its support of the principle of converged services: the debate was over the kind of person we wanted to attract rather than the post itself – a leader with experience of senior management, and one whom staff in a multidisciplinary department could trust, and was not associated solely with (say) librarianship or computing. This paragon also had to have vision. A new director was however found – Peter Kemp – and he took up his duties in August 1997.

This extent of responsibility is a challenge. The training of professionals in the different disciplines has traditionally been very different, and while bringing such people together can be very productive it can produce tensions. The service also employs people on the whole gamut of categories employed in the university – manual, clerical, technical, administrative and academic. It can be difficult to relate easily to all these people and easy to be remote from them. Virtually every member of the university is a customer of one or more of the services offered, so that on a bad day you seem to be the scapegoat for everyone else's misdemeanours. And the budget is necessarily large.

The environment is a testing one. Information Services must give support to academics undergoing Teaching Quality Assessment and Research Assessment, and itself has to undergo periodical internal reviews by the university (moderated by external assessors) and have its operations audited. Efficiency and economy are thoroughly scrutinized and management information, statistics, performance indicators, benchmarks, are all further and continual tests of the organization. The planning environment is particularly demanding. Information Services now has a five year rolling plan, annually reviewed with a strong input from the user community, and which itself makes reference to, and is guided by, the institutional Information Strategy.

Information Strategy

It was of course the Follett report that recommended that 'each institution should develop an information strategy setting out how it proposes to meet the needs of those working within it' (para. 323), and that the funding councils should themselves seek evidence of this as part of the overall strategic planning they regularly demand from institutions. When the Joint Information Systems Committee (JISC), on behalf of the funding councils, wrote to the universities in March 1994, Stirling's Principal was able to report acceptance of the concept, and some progress that had already been made:

'I can report that the Planning and Resources Committee (PRC) of the University of Stirling has asked its Information Services Committee to coordinate the development of an Information Strategy for the whole institution, which would be the basis of a component of the University's overall strategic planning.

As a result of its earlier strategic thinking, the University in 1989 achieved organisational and managerial integration in the provision of library, computing, networking and media services for students, teachers, researchers and administrators, by setting up a Directorate of Information Services.

Information Services, after extensive consultation, has established and published a Policy Statement, setting out its Purpose, Values, Priorities and Divisional Aims. Within this framework, an annual Statement of Objectives is produced for the Library, the Management Computing Group and the Computer and Media Services Division. In addition a rolling 5-year plan for Computer Services Provision is maintained on a an annual basis. Elements of these planning papers are already utilised where appropriate, in the writing of the University's external planning statements.

The recent PRC decision reflects a desire to move beyond strategic planning for Information Services, towards the development of an Information Strategy for the whole institution.

In this regard the most valuable contribution that JISC could make would be to produce a model framework or methodology for the development of an Information Strategy in the Higher Education environment.

I note that it is Information Strategy Steering Group's intention to publish such a framework in 1995. In the meantime, I can confirm that my Director of Information Services would be happy to provide feedback on draft sections of this documentation, as and when they are produced.'

It is interesting to note that the reply begins by pointing out the managerial and organizational convergence that took place in 1989. Follett (HEFCE, 1993) saw there were many advantages in organizational convergence 'particularly in enabling an integrated information strategy to develop' (para. 91) but left it to individual institutions to decide the best way forward. What was important was that the issue should be addressed. We shall discuss below whether convergence actually helped at Stirling.

The discussions held by Bruce Royan with information services staff after his arrival eventually led to the suggestion that the new department should have a mission statement. What was eventually accepted after much debate (and some scepticism over the value of the exercise) was a statement of the 'purpose' of Information Services, and the 'values' and 'priorities' that went with this (see Appendix 2). It is true to say that the majority of Information Services staff accepted the spirit behind this though found the business jargon inappropriate and not always meaningful. The essential point here is that we all accepted the need to work to a common goal and to plan properly for that. Planning was of course not a new idea. What was new for many sections was the idea of bringing the user into the picture. Computer and Media Services had for several years prepared annual policy statements linked to purchasing plans for the year ahead. These statements were agreed with the users through formally constituted meetings, and included Heads of School (faculties); the latter group of people were often the most constructively critical of all the user groups. A review of the library in 1995 highlighted the need for more open and forward planning, and this led, as indicated in the Principal's letter to JISC, to the production of Service Provision Plans, the first of which was approved in 1996 for the years 1996–2001. There is a timetable, agreed by all parties, for the annual consultations that lead to the final draft which is accepted by the Information Services Committee and forwarded to the Planning and Resources Committee.

The Principal was therefore able, as we have seen, to point out that the academic support services had already been brought together, that they had an agreed information services strategy, and that this was in turn subordinate to the institution's strategic plan.

The Principal also wrote to the Scottish Higher Education Funding Council: 'I should like to underline our acceptance of the need for an institution-wide strategy for information. We see this as a vital framework for further use of scarce resources'.'

It was originally intended that the ISC should take on this work. The PRC, 1 February 1994, agreed that 'ISC should continue to advise this Committee on information strategy as a component of the University's planning process'. However, PRC later changed its mind. It noted, 25 October that year, that 'the University is committed to produce an Information Strategy. Agreed to ask the Principal's Management Group, after consulting Heads of Schools, to form a group for this purpose, on the basis of a paper to be prepared by the Director of Information Services'.'

Professor Forty had by this time retired, and been succeeded as Principal in August 1994 by Professor Andrew Miller. Professor Miller readily accepted the message that what was being sought was a strategy that could be applied throughout the university, and that the development of such a strategy should not be left solely to the ISC. In recruiting to the working group, he made known his desire for Schools to nominate members who would be 'young and enthusiastic people with ideas' and prepared to work; he would chair the group. It was his first year in office and wheels moved slowly so that it was another six months before the group came into being. There were twelve members representing all areas of the university, and including the Director of Information Services and two of his staff.

The JISC's *Guidelines for developing an information strategy* were published in December 1995 (JISC, 1995) by which time the Stirling group had produced three drafts and had received comments from the ISC. It was decided that while much of the advice in the JISC document was sound, to adopt the framework at this point would cause considerable delay in the production of the strategy, and that the immediate priority was to consult widely within the University on what the group had achieved to date. A 21-page document – the fourth draft – was distributed around the university in February 1996 to:

- Heads of Departments, Sections and Schools;
- those who had attended a staff development session on the topic;
- Information Services user groups – library, computing, media services;
- policy committees – Information Services, the Committee on Teaching Learning and Academic Standards, Research, Management Information Systems;
- Planning and Resources Committee, Academic Council, University Court.

The aim was for the plan to be in place to influence service provision plans for 1996/97 and the university's strategic plan for 1998–2003.

The draft that was eventually passed in the autumn of 1996 to Academic Council at the University Court had increased in size to 24 pages. (See Appendix 3 for a copy of the contents, and the executive summary.) The information strategy joined the other strategies – teaching, research, estate, finance – in forming the university's Strategic Plan.

What are its strengths? The principal strength must be the recognition that information is a key institutional resource.

To state this explicitly in this kind of document is a major step forward. In that sense, it can act as a catalyst for change. At the very least it provides a statement of goals agreed following a university-wide process of consultation, and can be used from now on as a point of reference for other plans and activities. Because it is a university strategy it is not tied solely to Information Services, and indeed it is not constrained by the existing way the university is organized.

It is comprehensive, covering teaching and research, administration, finance, estates and buildings, communications and public relations, and looking at every activity where information is required – the environment in which we operate, how our competitors are faring, the potential for co-operation, management decision-making, ensuring the right information reaches the right people, and so on. Its scope is information, not information systems.

The university has embraced information technology in its operations. It has endorsed the concept of information being communicated, for preference, electronically around the campus, and is anxious to see that good use is made of the Scottish Metropolitan Area Network, to which Stirling is linked.

A less sympathetic view is that information strategy is yet another example of an externally driven unproductive and time-wasting exercise foisted on universities, which should have better things to do, such as research and teaching. The 'strategy' according to such critics is a mere wish list and not a plan for action. The working group may have been full of enthusiasm but the committees that received the product of the group's work, though dealing with it conscientiously, did so with a marked absence of enthusiasm. It is not linked to budgets, as is say the estate strategy, but more to the way we do things. Already in an era of rapid change, the strategy demands yet another series of changes, and indeed a new culture, particularly in the sharing of information rather than the withholding of it. Stirling's document perhaps does not emphasize this enough.

It also requires links to the other university strategies (finance, estates, etc.) to bring home its pervasive relevance, and should be part of regular audit and assessment. Management will have constantly to be reminded, and to remind others, that we have this information strategy, and much will depend on the Director of Information Services succeeding in retaining the full backing of the Principal and senior university management, for the gradual fulfilling of the goals set out in the strategy. (There will always be a danger that anything to do with 'information' is seen only as the preserve of Information Services). The production of the first edition was certainly dependent on the Director's full involvement – and leadership. He came to it with the authority of the manager of a converged service, not just of one of the academic support services, and was able to harness, for example, not only technical expertise (from computer services) but also project expertise (in the Management Information Systems Division).

It is clear that such leadership will continue to be required. The Dearing report recommends (NCIHE, 1997, recommendation 41) 'That all higher education institutions in the UK should have in place overarching communications and information strategies by 1999/2000'. There is however some ambiguity here: the context of this recommendation is a discussion of Communication and Information *Technologies*. We are going to have to bang the drum of *Information* for some time yet.

Appendix 1

Service Structure Chart

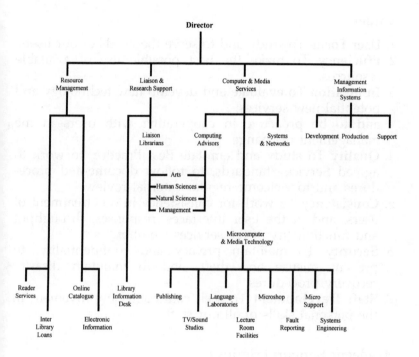

Appendix 2

University of Stirling: Information Services

Purpose, Values and Priorities

Purpose

Information Services exists to support the library, media, computing, networking and other information needs of all the teachers, researchers, students and administrators of the University of Stirling and to contribute to the local community and the wider academic world.

Values

1. **User Focus** To study and to serve the needs of our users.
2. **Efficiency** To make the best possible use of available resources.
3. **Innovation** To evaluate and develop new technology and potential new services,
   and to be proactive in cooperating with users in the management of change.
4. **Quality** To study and emulate Best Practice, to work to agreed Service Standards, to follow documented procedures and to welcome regular external review.
5. **Consistency** To work for consistency in our treatment of users, and in the user interfaces, responses, throughput and functionality of the services we offer.
6. **Security** To maintain privacy and confidentiality, to prevent misuse and theft, and to maintain disaster recovery procedures.
7. **Staff Development** To seek continuous improvement in the personal skills of all our staff.

Academic Support Priorities

1. Support of Teaching
2. Support of Current Research in top-ranked departments
3. Support of Current Research in all departments
4. Support of possible Future Research
5. Support of the Wider Scholarly Community in areas of existing strengths
6. Support of the Wider Scholarly Community in all areas.

Appendix 3

University of Stirling Information Strategy

Contents

Executive Summary

Strategic direction

Information is a strategic resource in the activity and development of the University. Appropriate mechanisms must exist to facilitate its collection, selection, analysis and communication.

Teaching and learning

Because success in teaching and learning requires both an appropriate Teaching and Learning Strategy and effective delivery capability, strategies for Information and for Teaching and Learning are necessarily intertwined. The creation and maintenance of an excellent teaching and learning environment also requires current awareness of developments and good practice in curriculum design, teaching methods and assessment. The University will create an information environment appropriate to the continued pursuit of excellence in teaching and learning.

Research and consultancy

The University recognizes the need to promote excellent research and commercial activity. Information systems to facilitate the identification of funding, preparation of proposals, conduct of research and its dissemination/ exploitation will be put in place and will also support submission to the Research Assessment Exercise.

Resource management

Information systems and services play an important role in the efficient management of resources and in the continued development of the University. Initiatives will be pursued to encourage the development of an integrated, flexible and high quality information system for everyone involved in the University.

References

Higher Education Funding Council for England, et al. (1993) *Joint Funding Councils' Libraries Review Group: Report.* (Follett Report). Bristol: HEFCE

Joint Information Systems Committee (1995) *Guidelines for Developing an Information Strategy.* Bristol: JISC

National Committee of Inquiry into Higher Education (1997) *Higher Education in the Learning Society.* (Dearing Report). London: HMSO

SECTION 3
Managing Change

CHAPTER EIGHT

Overview: Managing Change

Joan Day and Catherine Edwards

Introduction

'The libraries of colleges and universities are changing faster than
their respective parent institutions. Essentially everything in and
around the library is changing: services, technologies, organizational
constructs, ownership and access policies, values and most of the
rest.' (Riggs, 1997)

Most people involved in Library and Information Services
(LIS) are acutely aware that their service is the focal point
where political, educational and social changes combine
with technological change. This chapter gives an overview
of change surrounding and within LIS, particularly in the
United Kingdom, leading to consideration of the management of change. So much of a manager's work now involves
looking outwards to the external environment as well as
inwards to staff and resources, in an attempt to position the
service most appropriately within the institution.

The IMPEL Projects

Since late 1993, the Department of Information and Library Management and the Information Services Department at the University of Northumbria at Newcastle, UK, have been collaborating on a range of projects which include IMPEL1 (IMpact on People of Electronic Libraries) and IMPEL2 (Monitoring Organizational and Cultural Change). IMPEL1 took as its focus the qualified librarian working in the increasingly electronic environment of Higher Education (HE) LIS. Its successor, IMPEL2, broadened the scope by studying not only LIS staff and their training and development needs, but also academic staff as users of electronic information systems and sources, and the impact on LIS of institutional resource based learning policies. By taking a qualitative case study approach involving approximately 350 in-depth semi-structured interviews, with a wide range of library and related support staff and teaching staff across a spectrum of disciplines, it has been possible to obtain deep insight into the impacts of change upon LIS in the 1990s. The data collected for the IMPEL Projects provides not only a source of knowledge of the extent of change occurring in LIS in higher education institutions, but also of current practice in the management of change. As a project funded under the Electronic Libraries Programme, eLib, dissemination of its findings to the widest community is a priority, and are the basis for this chapter.

Forces for Change

The chief forces for change in higher education in the United Kingdom stem from political influence on the sector as a whole. They can be identified principally as:

- expansion of the student population with a target of one in three young people entering HE in the UK by the year 2000;

- increased numbers of 'non-traditional' students such as mature, female, overseas, part-time, returning and distant learners who may not have qualified for entrance through the previously typical route of success in Advanced-level public examinations;
- increased financial pressure on students to contribute to the cost of their higher education, making them more demanding as paying 'customers' and less flexible in attendance through part-time employment;
- the breakdown of the distinction between further and higher education;
- increased financial accountability and quality assessment of research and teaching activity;
- the adoption of new structures for teaching programmes, such as modularization, and semesterization;
- new, increasingly student-centred methods, with a move from teaching to more independent learning;
- continual reduction in the unit of resource;
- increase in partnerships with franchised or affiliated institutions and in multi-site institutions;
- influence of entrepreneurial management styles previously more typical of the business sector than of universities and colleges, with emphasis on value for money and customer satisfaction.

Change is not new to the HE sector, but would appear to have accelerated since the early 1980s. Ashworth (1993) traces the beginnings of this acceleration to the 1981 funding cuts which unsettled the whole system. When polytechnics were removed from local authority control in 1988, a parallel university/polytechnic system dependent upon central government developed. Within four years this binary line disappeared and through various methods a radically new HE culture has been created. The positive aspects of the new culture might include:

- a system of HE offering university education to a broader spectrum of the population;

- a HE system which ensures that financial resources are maximized;
- a HE system which dismantles its 'ivory towers' and becomes more responsive to society in general.

On the other hand, negative aspects of the new culture might include:

- loss of autonomy and academic freedom;
- unhealthy effects of competition between institutions;
- short-termism resulting from new methods of account-ability such as the separate research and teaching quality assessment exercises;
- doubt over appropriateness of business approaches in academia.

The climate of change has impacted most acutely upon the 'new' universities, the former polytechnics. Doubling of student numbers since achieving university status in 1992 has been reported in such an institution (Heery, 1995) but the experience of this institution is not unique. It is typical of many universities and colleges across the UK. The 'unstop-pable forces of political dogma and economic stringency that were the hallmarks of the Conservative government' have been implicated. No imminent period of consolidation and reflection can be anticipated with a new Labour government in power, and the implications of the National Committee of Inquiry into Higher Education (NCIHE, 1997) yet to be realised. What Dearing does emphasize is the need to harness communications and information technologies in the delivery of HE within a framework of lifelong learning, reinforcing the need for LIS to move towards electronic delivery of services and user support.

Developments in Australia, the USA and Canada mirror the UK experience overseas, where the twin constraints of increased student numbers and declining unit of resource exert similar pressures. The pressure will continue to be of a conflicting kind, namely the desire for expansion of student numbers and more industry-oriented research coupled with a continued unwillingness to pay for either (Miller,1995). Sources of conflict and turbulence in the HE sector are similarly described by Day *et. al.* (1996) and Edwards (1993). The issue is vividly illustrated by figures for the increase in the total number of students in HE in the UK, rising from around 40 000 in 1965/66 to over 1 600 000 in 1995/96. Compare these with official government figures from the Department for Education and Employment, which put unit costs per FTE student (costed in 1995/96 real terms) as almost £7000 in 1989/90, dropping to around £4500 in 1997/98 and predicted to fall thereafter (THES 1996, DfEE 1997).

The effects of such figures inevitably impinge directly on the student experience. A student in the late 1990s is far less likely to be an academically-minded, middle-class school leaver. Some argue that the UK has not yet achieved the mass HE system advocated by Robbins (1963), and anticipate further expansion. Students have less money and time to spend on their education and more have personal, social and study skill problems (Goodwin, 1995). Large undergraduate numbers plus increased demands on teaching staff for administration and research output put pressure on traditional lecture and tutorial-based teaching, so that student-centred learning approaches may provide an attractive alternative to conventionally taught courses (Clark, 1995).

It is possible to differentiate between alternative types of learning approaches, namely distance learning, open and flexible learning, student-centred learning and resource based learning. Resource based learning may be defined in various ways which all assume that 'the student will learn from his or her own direct confrontations, individually or in a group, with a learning resource or a set of resources or activities, rather than from conventional exposition by the teacher' (Beswick, 1977). The implications for LIS of shifting to student-centred approaches are becoming recognized. The traditional library may change physically to become a 'learning resource centre' housing a wide range of print, electronic, multimedia and audiovisual sources; the instructional role of

LIS staff increases; LIS staff must collaborate to a greater extent with staff in teaching and other central departments; they must keep abreast of new developments in technology and give technical assistance to enable staff and students to make use of them. There are also implications for in-service training of LIS staff and redeployment of staff at different grades to exploit and develop skills at different levels.

The impact that National Vocational Qualifications (NVQs) will make in this sector has yet to be felt, but undoubtedly The Information and Library Services Standards will have an effect on in-service training and in education. Since the widespread adoption of the Management Charter Initiative approach to training and staff development there has been more understanding of the role of NVQs, which provide a highly structured and detailed map of training and educational needs (Herzog 1996).

There is an increased awareness of the importance of the competency approach to training in employment. The demands for full utilization of staff throughout libraries and information services together with the need for flexible staff with a range of abilities and a lack of funding to provide full time or part time education has meant that NVQs may become an attractive option for many managers. The qualities of the programmes and their portability have yet to be proved.

Change in the Workplace

We should look to the wider environment for social trends which are reflected in LIS administration. These trends include:

- the concept of life-long learning where training and education, whether in traditional or non-traditional formats, becomes the means of sustaining a flexible workforce which recognizes that jobs are no longer for life;
- changing work and family patterns with greater numbers of women entering the workforce;

- recognition of current, rapid and accurate information as an important 'commodity' in keeping pace with change;
- the importance of technology such as digitization, networking, electronic mail, discussion lists and video conferencing in giving access to information and enabling new forms of communication;
- increasing pervasiveness of hardware and software in the home;
- raised expectations and demands for accountability and value for money in consumer-driven economies.

This list could go on. Other trends such as the 'information explosion', greater technological complexity, scarcity of appropriately qualified personnel, continuing emphasis on quality, teamworking, 'customer-ism', restructuring and demands for innovation and flexibility may be added (Moore, 1995). Moore's view is that many of these new factors are in conflict with the environment of the past, resulting in conflicts of culture at the organizational level, in the nature of LIS work itself and in the role of library administrators. She concludes:

> 'Library administrators must become facilitators. They must under-
> stand how the world is changing and how the library must change.
> And they must also learn to be masters at persuasion, since wher-
> ever there is change there will be resistance'.

Neal (1996) also looks beyond the confines of academia for the trends which he considers will have significant impact on LIS. His '12 revolutions' which will shape delivery of service are not dissimilar to Moore's: Quality, Re-engineering, Demographics, Personal Computing, Electronics, Network, The MTV Generation, Values, Accountability, Higher Education, Partnership and the Knowledge Worker. Competence as evidenced by NVQs should also be added to this list. These external factors point to the key role that libraries and librarians have as technology develops and the significance of sharing and collaboration as a vital part of that role. The challenges that LIS face in positioning themselves prominently both locally in campus activities and in the wider HE and social scene are immense.

Access versus Holdings

The advent of electronic technology to LIS brings its own management imperatives adding to the social and organizational aspects of LIS management. While electronic sources have become a fact of life, they are not yet proving to be cheaper than print sources; they provide extensive, rapid delivery of text, video and graphics but are technologically dependent; the potential of the Internet is enormous but it is chaotic; there are problems of copyright, licensing agreements, maintenance and replacement of equipment, inequality of access and long-standing practices and policies to which publishers continue to adhere (Lynden, 1996). This complex and delicate balancing act of 'access versus holdings' will continue for many years. Each institution is seeking the most appropriate sustainable mix to suit its needs. Kane's (1997) solution of seeking a balance between access *and* ownership is only partly helpful:

> 'By combining the best features of both the traditional warehouse idea and the electronic library idea, libraries in the future will not only survive but flourish to to become the hub of the information community.'

This approach only partly satisfies because it states the obvious – achieving the appropriate balance is at the very heart of managing LIS at this time when the 'hybrid library' with 'multiple media' rather than 'multimedia' is the desired objective.

Approaches to Change

In the light of irresistible trends and pressures which have been described, it is clear that the LIS manager's role in managing change is paramount. Techniques borrowed from commerce and industry are increasingly forming part of the armoury with which to grapple with complex issues such as organizational structures, staff roles, technological innovation, collaboration, position within the institution and HE community and service delivery, all within the context of falling units of resource and increasing demand. There is fundamentally little difference in managing a library from managing any other service. Management problems for LIS are common for all types of service – time management, leadership, quality of service, good communications, enabling staff to achieve maximum potential, staff training and development. However, as well as managing people; librarians are also managing information (James, 1994). The broad management skills must be brought to managing the core activities; however, amidst such a profound climate of change, definitions of the core activities in LIS become more elusive.

As users' expectations have risen and LIS have striven to adopt more user-oriented approaches, it becomes ever more difficult to live up to the demands. While on the one hand LIS staff are seeking greater equality with academic colleagues, becoming partners in the business of teaching and learning, institutional policies see central services such as LIS and computing centres as targets for budget cuts, so that developing and delivering the kind of information-handling skills with fewer and fewer staff becomes problematical. At least one 'new' university has so severely cut its central services budgets that the LIS has been forced to withdraw any 'teaching' of its users apart from basic library induction tours. Other LIS are adopting the opposite policy that supporting students through information technology and information-handling skills is indeed a core activity within the institution and confirming the policy by building teaching suites, acquiring hardware and training staff accordingly in teaching skills. This is just one example of the kinds of choice which are to be made. (See chapters 21 to 23 on approaches to training).

The concept of 'the learning organization' is a useful approach for LIS to borrow from the business sector:

> 'The learning organization offers a splendid forum for the entire library to engage in self-examination. What can it stop doing? What must it maintain? How can it innovate by substitution? These are examples of questions that the learning organization should pose and answer.' (Riggs, 1997)

A learning organization is characterized by the acquisition and transfer of knowledge and insights which are then taken on board in order to modify behaviour. This process involves a change of culture for LIS which traditionally have been characterized by clearly defined areas of responsibilities and division of labour. In theory, rigid organizations which fail to adopt concepts of learning and reflection are less capable of exploiting creativity in new ways of thinking, behaving and communicating. They may be less able to seize opportunities offered to them by new technology. Clearly, any notion of LIS as independent 'havens of peace' within HE institutions is entirely inappropriate. Many LIS directors now are adopting an increasingly – in some cases, entirely strategic role, devolving operational management aspects to junior colleagues, in order to ensure that their service plays a full part in the learning and development of the whole institution. Carr (1977) makes an important point:

> 'There is much in the notion of the learning organization that assumes managers will be in a 'partnership' of learning with other managers and indeed with employees. In the learning relationship with other employees a climate of trust and open dialogue is a minimum requirement.'

Such a climate of trust and open dialogue is clouded by the level of uncertainty pervading HE and the role of LIS within it. The speed of change and the complexity of issues involved, as described earlier in this chapter, create uncertainty for institutional direction and vision. LIS directors and managers seek commitment and strategic direction from the top, which all too often appears lacking; they may feel vulnerable and inhibited by the perception that the value and significance of information and information technology is under-appreciated. There may be tension between central initiatives and devolvement of decision-making and spending power to faculty or department level. At the same time, LIS need to forge closer relations with these groups and with other central service providers, particularly computing centres, as well as administration, staff and educational development units. Unbending hierarchical structures do not fit well with more flexible concepts such as the learning organization.

The potential for developing 'partnerships' with teaching departments may be undermined by perceptions that the contribution of the LIS is somehow secondary, more akin to a kind of clerical support role. Subject specialism in LIS may be diluted by the pressure to provide 'lower level' support for users, technical fixes, basic induction tours, giving access rather than deep knowledge of sources. LIS staff feel uncertain about how to support research activity despite the higher profile currently being afforded to research in HE. They are experiencing uncertainty amidst organizational change which directly affects their jobs and working relationships. They experience difficulty keeping up with technological developments in networking, telecommunications, new electronic systems and information sources. They are uncertain of their responsibilities vis-à-vis the Internet, how to present it to users, how to control its use and how to integrate it with existing provision. They fear for the quality of end-user searches, particularly by remote users, and for the ultimate impact of poor searching techniques on teaching and research.

The management of change involves exploiting the positive aspects of uncertainty. Here again, the world of business management gives a lead. It has recognized that the future is less and less predictable and that uncertainty is a permanent feature of life which it is better to try to accept, understand and incorporate than to fear (Wack, 1991).

Mindful of the need for flexibility and responsiveness in accommodating change and uncertainty, LIS managers recognize that organizational structures may need to change, although it can be observed that often some catalyst, such as a severe funding cut, is present before dramatic restructuring occurs. LIS managers and their staff often prefer to retain the status quo, the traditional hierarchy, sections and reporting lines, rather than go in for radical change. Experience in the UK is supported by that in the US; Fatzer (1996) believes that:

> 'Budget reductions, normally viewed as barriers to change or causes of negative changes, can be forces for creativity, innovation and positive change.'

Staff, however, can be forgiven for suspecting hidden agendas behind restructuring and suspect that behind the text-book theory that the integrated nature of information, computing and telecommunications require more integrated and less hierarchical working patterns, lies the wish to 'downsize' and destabilize the workforce, or, as Kelleher puts it, ' . . . technology [as] the pretext for organisational change.' (interview by MacColl, 1997). Referring again to a business technique which has been much in vogue in HE institutions, business process re-engineering (BPR), Martinsons and Revenaugh (1997) describe how massive reorganizations associated with BPR have been viewed with suspicion:

> 'BPR is now commonly associated with two things: 1) inflated consultancy bills and 2) slash and burn corporate 'downsizing' . . . This has in turn created or strengthened suspicions about the organizational impacts of IT, since IT is the enabling agent, and often the driver for BPR.'

They attribute the high failure rate for BPR in the corporate sector to poor change management, resulting in 'demoralized workers and a proliferation of process modelling documentation [which] stifled rather than encouraged creativity and dynamism.' LIS managers appreciate the difference between the potential for IT to reduce the need for human input in housekeeping, secretarial and cataloguing processes on the one hand and IT for information storage and retrieval purposes. The latter imposes an additional workload and level of complexity on LIS which at the present time are also maintaining and delivering traditional print-based services.

Institutional managers, however, may confuse 'IT for processes' and 'IT for information provision', and take the line that, 'if you have fewer books and journals, then you need fewer staff.' Managing an increasingly hybrid library service is the current challenge, and is reflected in the latest eLib programme projects (eLib 1997).

Corrall (1995a) identifies the challenge for LIS managers as 'judging the pace of change, striking the right balance and managing the inherent tension between tradition and transformation.' She and Bluck (1994) agree that in theory, 'teams provide the flexibility to cope with change, together with improved communication and participation through delegated decision-making'. Smith (1996) considers that a radical new structure at Aston University LIS, where staff were reorganized into self-managed teams linked directly to Schools:

> . . . 'is ideally suited to transport us into the fluid, but turbulent, electronic future – it will enable our information specialists to develop into para-academics and our information assistants into para-professionals; it could readily absorb computer officers and networking specialists if we ever 'converge', and, ultimately, it would enable us to converge with academic departments, if the library as a physical entity eventually disappears.'

In practice, however, the manager must support staff through restructuring. They will undoubtedly be suspicious, uncertain of their roles and position within the structure and fearful of redundancy. Openness, good communications, clear vision, leadership and training are essential.

The field of cognitive psychology offers the technique of 'reframing' for managing change. The technique encourages the manager to see a situation and then 'resee' it through another frame. Reframing offers a contemplative methodology to support managers in their response to change through a range of different frames:

- the structural frame – analysing change through the lens of the structural frame to understand how formal parts of an organization function while being ready, at the same time, to act when it is necessary to restructure;

- the human resources frame – focusing upon workers and how well the organization meets their needs;
- the political frame – viewing organizations as a series of complex power relationships;
- the symbolic frame – focuses upon the realities of the organizational culture, norms and values.

This technique represents a formal way of understanding the external and internal environments which have been alluded to throughout this chapter. It implicates an increased level of flexibility, experimentation and creativity. The writers stress the importance of communication and involvement to avoid staff apathy, dissatisfaction and low productivity (Head and Brown, 1995).

Training and Staff Development

The role of training and development is well recognized in enabling staff to achieve objectives, manage change and in maintaining good morale (Wetherby 1994). Increased workloads and reduced staffing levels, coupled with more powerful computer systems cause greater fluidity in the way work is carried out. As many housekeeping tasks can be handled by computers, staff can be deployed elsewhere. A good example is in cataloguing, which in past times was the province of professionally qualified librarians but which now, with online cataloguing, has in many LIS been handed down to support staff. Technology integrates library processes so that it is no longer appropriate for staff to have expertise in a single process, but must understand how the various functions interact. Information work is increasingly complex, so that no one individual is capable of acquiring and sustaining skills in every aspect of the work from knowledge of traditional reference sources, to familiarity with a range of CD-ROM interfaces, to technical expertise, to faculty and user support and to management. Team working can pool and share expertise so that pressure on individuals may be eased. A multiskilled workforce is required in order to maximise resources both financial and human. Multiskilling depends upon effective and continuing training programmes. Experience shows that achieving a multiskilled workforce is not a rapid process; staff may be reluctant to break from their accustomed secure niche and may feel uncomfortable with the changes in reporting structures which may ensue. Effective use of the NVQ programmes will help.

Hard-pressed managers are handing over decision-making to more junior levels, so that overlapping of the roles of professionally qualified and support staff begins to occur, as does the emergence of the so-called 'paraprofessional' role. The skilled and able library assistant or senior library assistant is becoming more crucial to the running of LIS. Experience in the UK suggests that in many HE institutions, the jealously-guarded professional status of librarians inhibits greater blurring of the divisions between professional and support staff. Problems of appropriate grading and remuneration are difficult to resolve. Decision-making and supervisory duties are welcomed by some but resented by others; these duties had not been there when they applied for the job. Middle-grade professionally qualified staff begin to wonder what their role is when much of it is handed over to non-qualified colleagues. The chief barrier to overcoming the question of overlapping roles may be at root a cultural one:

> 'Changing roles for professionals and paraprofessionals come up against a very powerful force within libraries – their culture. Culture is the system of norms, values and beliefs and assumptions that determine how people in the organization act.' (Johnson, 1996)

Training for all levels of staff should be systematic and ongoing. Casserly (1995) proposes a cyclic model which involves identifying needs, allocating resources, designing training plans, designing and developing training programmes, delivering programmes, evaluating training, and round again to the beginning of the cycle. She suggests that organisational change may mean the adoption of new techniques for doing work, changes in job design and/or responsibilities, technological change and new emphases. Change may involve how people make decisions, the tasks they carry out, the initiatives they take and the level of creativity they bring to the job. Training and development are without doubt fundamental both to bringing about and managing change.

Cultural Change

The reality for LIS is much more complex than early advocates of the electronic solution might suggest, involving a greater degree of collaboration than in the past. As has been suggested earlier, LIS in the electronic age need to broaden and strengthen their links inside and outside the institution: with other institutions, publishers, funding bodies, hardware and software houses, with senior managers, teaching departments, academic and administrative computing centres, with their own staff operating in different spheres of activity and with their various user groups – students, research staff, tutors, both on and off-site, full and part-time. Allen (1995) relates the need for collaboration directly to technological innovation although the culture of the mass HE system is also implicated here. He suggests that barriers to collaboration relate to clashes of organizational cultures, personal incompatibilities and different approaches to change, and that managers should develop appropriate organizational structures, select staff who work well in a collaborative environment and show leadership in organisational flexibility.

The issue of clashes of organizational culture, particularly between LIS and computing centres, persists. Indeed, in a number of institutions visited for IMPEL1 and IMPEL2, relations between the services had at best remained static and at worst, perceptibly deteriorated. Good working relations between the services do not necessarily require formal organizational convergence, but are strengthened by good communications both horizontally and vertically, joint staff training programmes, encouragement to share values and respect skills, recognition that key post-holders (e.g. library computing officer) can be influential in forging links, leadership, clear strategic direction and genuine organizational commitment to change (Day et al, 1997).

'Information professionals would do well to become more than responsive technicians cultivating a level of comfort with ambiguity and change, and becoming more flexible and creative in their information-seeking habits.' (Rice-Lively and Racine, 1997)

They take up the theme of collaboration, 'boundary spanning' across departmental and organizational boundaries to enable cross-disciplinary and cross-departmental projects. This approach places responsibility not only on managers but on individual information professionals.

Strategy

Many LIS managers are engaged in collaboration with other individuals and groups in the creation of information strategies, which in themselves represent significant efforts to manage change, although they have sometimes been criticized for lack of pragmatism. Information strategies have been seen to contain expositions of external and internal factors in the context of the institution and to be rather weaker in the 'nuts and bolts' department. These documents, however, may be significant in that they do symbolize the kind of collaborative effort which the information era demands. LIS managers may 'feed up' to the process the outcomes of collaboration with staff, such as Strengths, Weaknesses, Opportunities and Threats (SWOT) analyses, reports from planning groups, library reviews, user surveys and environmental scanning exercises. The planning process presents an opportunity to managers to increase staff awareness and involvement and to develop effective methods of communication.

Walster (1995) differentiates between 'strategic planning' and 'tactical planning', suggesting that these should combine into an overall system for making decisions. Strategic planning involves:

- Creating a mission statement;
- Developing policies and long range goals;
- Predicting possible outcomes;
- Writing long range plans;
- Evaluating, reviewing and revising.

She stresses that the process is more important than the plan itself and that the process is associated with problems, notably the fact that libraries are smaller components of large organizations and may be caught in the conflict between user needs and organizational necessity.

Parallel tactical plans for integrating technology in libraries are the mechanisms for managing problems created by the new technologies. They involve:

- Developing action plans to match strategic plans with specific timelines;
- Creating appropriate activities;
- Identifying resources: financial, personnel, space, facilities etc.;
- Establishing outcomes and assessment criteria.

Walster continues by explaining the value of planning – saving time, saving money and increasing effectiveness, but stresses that these may not be the most important goals for libraries as non-profit agencies: 'The intangibles of values, feelings and attitudes may be more important to libraries than money, time and work effectiveness.'

Her view is another indication of the complexity of managing change in libraries, whose value to the institution or to the individual user may not be revealed by accounting methods.

Conclusion

Higher Education Library and Information Services are experiencing unprecedented levels of change associated with a radically altered educational landscape. This chapter has identified the forces for change, shared experiences from within the UK sector and identified some of the theories of change being adopted in several countries.

A sense of being overwhelmed by the enormity of the task was evident at all levels in the institutions investigated by the IMPEL team (Edwards, 1997). Change can, however be a creative force. To quote one university librarian interviewed:

> 'This is a great opportunity to sit back for a minute and say, this is a rather big institution now ... we have got a tremendous lot of people needing different types of information at different times. What sort of systems, both IT based and personality based have to be in place to make those information flows work for the benefit of the whole institution? So you are finding establishing the philosophy is much more important initially than looking at the IT issues or looking at the individual information needs of certain sections'.

Rather than see change as loss of management control, take Sheila Corrall's advice and adopt a radical/dynamic view of change. Informed by chaos theory, this interpretation

> 'rejects the notion of managing change as an incremental, evolutionary, linear and orderly process, and instead sees it as inherently transformational, revolutionary, circular/spiral, and essentially chaotic – but ultimately productive and beneficial'. (Corrall, 1995b)

Some of the 'best practice' in managing various aspects of change found in the UK institutions visited is contained in a series of IMPEL Guides (IMPEL URL, 1997). A key theme throughout is the need for LIS managers and directors to think creatively in pursuing a new vision. Clinging to a mechanistic management model only leads to sidelining of library services. Insecurity and uncertainty are now the norm, and LIS communities need to assimilate continual innovation into their culture if they are to meet the challenge of the electronic library.

References

Allen, B. (1995) Academic information services: a library management perspective. *Library Trends*, **43**, 645–662

Ashworth, J.M. (1993) Higher Education foundation lecture: universities in the 21st centuries – old wine in new bottles or new wine in old bottles? *Reflections on Higher Education*, 5 July, 46–61

Beswick, N.W. (1997) *Resource based learning.* London: Heinemann

Bluck, R. (1994) Team management and academic libraries: a case study at the University of Northumbria. *British Journal of Academic Librarianship*, **9**(13), 224–240

Carr, A. (1997) The learning organization: new lessons/thinking for the management of change and management development. *Journal of Management Development* **16**(4), 224–231

Casserly, T. (1995) The implications of change for staff training and development: some thoughts on the contribution which training can make. In *Managing Organisational Change, Proceedings of Joint Annual Seminar of the Institute of Information Scientists (Irish Branch) and the Library Association of Ireland, 21st May, 1993 Dublin,* eds. V. Mckernan and J. Donnelly, pp. 27–34.

Clark, E. (1995) Open learning: educational opportunity or convenient solution to practical problems in higher education. In *Flexible learning strategies in higher and further education,* ed. D. Thomas London: Cassell

Corrall, S. (1995a) Academic libraries in the information society. *New Library World*, **96** (1120), 35–42

Corrall, S. (1995b) An evolving service: managing change. In *Networking and the future of libraries: managing the intellectual record,* eds. L. Dempsey, D. Law and I. Mowat. London: LAPL

Day, J.M., Walton, G. and Edwards, C. (1996) The culture of convergence. In *Proceedings of the 3rd International ELVIRA Conference* (April 30-May 2)

Day, J.M., Walton, G., Bent, M., Curry, S., Edwards, C. and Jackson, M. (1996) Higher education, teaching, learning and the electronic library: a review of the literature for the IMPEL2 project: monitoring organisational and cultural change. *The New Review of Academic Librarianship*, **2**, 131–204

Department for Education and Employment (DfEE) education facts and figures (1997) http: www.open.gov.uk/dfee/edufact/edufacts.htm#POST

Edwards, C., Day, J.M. and Walton, G. (1993) Key areas in the management of change in higher education libraries in the 1990s: relevance of the IMPEL Project. *British Journal of Academic Librarianship*, **8**(3), 139–177

Edwards, C. (1997) (ed.) Organizational and cultural change in Higher Education LIS. *Information UK Outlooks*, **29**, November 1997

eLib: http://www.ukoln.ac.uk/services/elib/

Fatzer, J.B. (1996) Budget stringency as a stimulus to innovation: the cases of Louisiana and Ohio. *Journal of Library Administration*, **22**(2/3), 57–77

Goodwin, P. (1995). What is your problem?: the present day realities of higher education in libraries. *SCONUL Newsletter*, **4**, 33–35

Head, A.J. and Brown, K. (1995) Reframing techniques in managing change within the library setting. *Journal of Library Administration*, **22**(1), 1–12

Heery, M. (1995) A change is as good as a rest? *Library Manager*, **10**, 20

Herzog, J. (1996) *Implementing S/NVQs in the Information and Library Sector: a guide for employers*. London: LAPL

IMPEL: http://ilm.unn.ac.uk/impel

James, S. (1994) The manager and the library: a review of some general and industrial management books and their relevance to library management. *Library Review,* **43**(1), 39–45

Johnson, P. (1996) Managing changing roles: professional and paraprofessional staff in libraries. *Journal of Library Administration,* **22**(2/3), 79–99

Kane, L.T. (1997) Access vs. ownership: do we have to make a choice? *College and Research Libraries,* **58**, 59–67

Lynden, F.C. (1996) Tradeoffs of not: the pros and cons of the electronic library. *Collection Management,* **21**(1), 65–92

MacColl, J. (1997) A View from the hill. *Ariadne,* **7**, 5

Miller, H.D.R. (1995) *The management of change in universities: universities, state and economy in Australia, Canada and the United Kingdom.* London: The Society for Research into Higher Education & Open University Press

Martinsons, M.G. and Revenaugh, D.L. (1997) Re-engineering is dead; long live re-engineering. *International Journal of Management,* **17**(2), 79–82

Moore, M. (1995) Impact of the changing environment on academic library administration: conflicts, incongruities, contradictions and dichotomies. *Journal of Library Administration* **22**(1), 13–36

National Committee of Inquiry into Higher Education (1997) *Higher Education in the Learning Society.* (Dearing Report). London: HMSO

Neal, J.G. (1996) Academic libraries: 2000 and beyond. *Library Journal,* **121**(12) 74–76

Rice-Lively, M.L. and Racine, D. (1997) The role of academic librarians in the era of information technology. *Journal of Academic Librarianship,* **23**(1), 31–38

Riggs, D. E. (1997) What's in store for academic libraries? Leadership and management issues. *Journal of Academic Librarianship,* **23**(1), 3–8

Robbins report. *Higher Education*. Report of the Committee under the Chairmanship of Lord Robbins (1963). Cmnd 2154. London: HMSO

Smith, N.R. (1996) *Turning the library inside out: radical restructuring to meet the challenge of sudden change*. Proceedings of the 20th Annual Computers in Libraries International, February 20–22 pp. 71–82. Oxford: Learned Information, Europe Ltd.

THES (1996) Snapshots of universities in flux. *The Times Higher Education Supplement*, iv-v, 1996 September 27

Wack, P. (1991) Scenarios: uncharted waters ahead. In *Managing Innovation 2121*, eds. J. Henry and D. Walker, pp. 200–210. London: Sage Publications

Walster, D. (1995) Planning for technology. *Journal of Library Administration*, **22**(1), 39–50

Wetherby, J. (1994) *Management of training and staff development*. London: Library Association Publishing

CHAPTER NINE

Case Study: Managing Change at the University of Wales, Cardiff Libraries

Catherine Edwards

Introduction

The University of Wales, Cardiff (UWC) is a major civic university dating back to 1883. The five faculties and 25 departments cater for around 14,000 students, of whom a quarter pursue postgraduate courses. The city centre campus, which is fully networked, is served by 11 distributed libraries situated close to teaching departments. The University's mission is to establish itself 'as an innovative research-based institution recognised locally, nationally and internationally.' It aims to achieve a research performance ranked among the top twelve in the UK.

A major survey of library users was conducted in 1993 (Davies, 1994) and repeated in 1996; the message from both surveys was that users indicated their wish for greater cohesiveness across the libraries. The surveys indicated a catalyst for change, the libraries' response being to adopt Quality Standards, addressing issues which users perceived as less than satisfactory and taking steps to improve the public face of the libraries. As a result, user documentation was improved across the board and a more integrated approach to the issue of teaching skills for Library and Information Service (LIS) staff adopted. User instruction had long been given a high priority within the service.

This chapter is based on a case study of the Cardiff libraries conducted in 1994 and followed up in 1996 for the IMPEL2 Project, funded by the Joint Information Systems Committee under the eLib programme.

Background Factors

All universities have undergone a period of rapid and profound change, particularly so for Cardiff which emerged with a new identity from the merger of the former UCC and UWIST in 1988. The social and cultural impacts of the merger are slow to fade from the memory of many of those library staff who were affected. Technological developments have been added to the list of changing circumstances to which the library was responding most positively.

It was perhaps fortunate for the present library service that the Librarian, former longstanding Librarian of one pre-merger institution, had wide knowledge and lengthy experience of technological developments in the library, lending a degree of stability amidst a high level of turbulence. Around the time of the merger, developments world-wide in telecommunications and networking were accelerating, providing the opportunity for the library and Computing Service to capitalise on them, and the merger could be seen to offer the both necessity and the opportunity.

Impressive efforts had been made to understand the impacts on staff of cultural and organisational change through the work of Davies, Kirkpatrick and Oliver (Davies, 1992). As part of its approach to management, the library had typically conducted a great deal of internal research and generates regular reports of activity. In terms of the access versus holdings issue, the aim is to achieve a healthy balance between the two. In the past there had been a tendency for technology to drive initiatives but it had been realized that this approach did not support top quality research. A study had been undertaken in the university related to the provision of information for research (Bell, 1997). These studies and reports indicated an encouraging responsiveness to the views and reactions of both library staff and users and a commitment to use the knowledge gained through research for future planning.

The Librarian had been involved in library automation and cataloguing since the 1970s and with networking since the early 1980s. The concept of networking was fundamental to the acquisition of a new Libertas library system in the mid 1980s. Post-merger the campus was linked by a joint network running from one end to the other, linking in the library and all departments along its length in a high speed procurement exercise. The speed and capacity of the network had been increased dramatically in the last two years.

Funding

Despite a lower level of funding than competitor institutions, the library at Cardiff had achieved a high level of activity. In the past, the library benefitted from 5 per cent of the University's disposable income, a stable figure which allowed forward planning. This figure had recently been raised to 5.75 per cent. The library was also financed by income from departments who therefore had the power (if they so wished) to influence the development of collections and services for their own benefit. Heads of Departments were key people in these decisions. While the dual system of financing has clear benefits for individual departments, it brings with it a level of difficulty in terms of decision-making and the potential for imbalance of service provision. Such an empowered, devolved structure presents considerable challenges for service departments.

The separate Computing and Library Committees had recently been merged under an Academic Services Committee with the aim of integrating the two services more fully; the

Committee was moving towards a joint funding budget for library and Computing Centre. The library had received a recent 1 per cent increase destined for stock development, easing the immediate funding situation and lessening the disparity between funding of Cardiff's research collections and those of peer institutions. In practical terms, the increase in funding for stock had been achieved partially at the expense of the operating budgets for both Libraries and Computing Service. The Welsh Funding Council allocated an increase of 1.26 per cent for Cardiff in 1996/97 which, although it compared favourably with other Welsh Higher Education institutions, was less than the rate of inflation and amounted to a funding cut.

Institutional structure

Cardiff is a highly devolved institution with a large degree of autonomy accorded to the 25 schools, although there are currently some indications of increased centralisation of policy making. Alongside the Academic Services Committee, a Quality Board and a Teaching and Learning Policy Committee have been formed with a remit to improve teaching and learning within the university, to investigate the potential of resource based learning techniques and to disseminate good practice; its first task is to discover what practices currently exist. The Teaching and Learning and Research Committees had succeeded in developing a policy reflecting increased emphasis on research activity.

These central initiatives were beginning to make an impact institutionally. Initiatives stemming from the Planning and Resources Committee and the Standing Committee as well as from the Academic Services Committee created a complex picture. Achieving a balance between schools-based initiatives and central initiatives continued to present opportunities and problems. This current phase could be described as 'an uncomfortable middle stage' as a triangle of senior institutional managers, academics and service departments held to their own agenda and all standing their ground rather than setting a common agenda. This dilemma is not untypical of most Higher Education institutions.

Perhaps the most pertinent background factor of all at Cardiff was the distributed nature of the 'Library' with 11 libraries within walking distance of each other. Popular with departments, and maintained as a policy decision, the distributed system was a selling point to students. The associated problems of managing several physically and culturally different libraries present a continuing challenge.

Information Strategy

An Information Strategy was under development. The strategy had not so far fully addressed the question of administrative information, concentrating on library and academic computing information. Senior Library managers were somewhat critical of the proposed strategy in that it appeared to reflect earlier library planning documents and failed to address wider institutional aspects. The tradition in the libraries of continuous evaluation and improvement may explain this perceived library bias in the strategy in that a great deal of content was ready to hand. This imbalance also reflected some lack of central institutional vision and direction for a campus-wide approach to information management and provision. The strategy was to be reviewed in 1998, in line with an ongoing, iterative approach.

Library Staffing Structures

A changing environment ideally depends on a flexible and responsive workforce capable of exploiting the benefits afforded by change. Staffing structures by their very nature tend to be inflexible and managers are bound to ask how well existing structures can reflect the changing demands of a more electronic environment.

The present, traditionally hierarchical line management structure within the majority of the 11 libraries had remained fairly static since the merger. Retention of the status quo had provided stability over that at times traumatic period. Senior managers were exploring ways in which the strict hierarchy may be relaxed. Cross-library task and working groups had become increasingly active. Those who favoured a move towards a team approach felt that the structure which had been in place (since merger in 1988) needed to be continually appraised in view of the imperatives of service provision, of teaching and involvement in academic departments. However, the internal organisation of individual libraries in the system was the responsibility of individual operational managers.

A team structure operated extremely successfully in the Law area, a small, discrete unit which lent itself readily to this pattern of working; the law librarians felt that this type of collaborative approach was more appropriate to an increasingly electronic department, exploiting more fully the complementary skills and attributes of team members and spreading knowledge more widely, thereby improving the service level.

There had been a small increase in LIS staff numbers over the two year period, particularly, contrary to earlier expectations, of qualified staff, because of the range of skills needed, the level of complexity of work, the IT expertise and management skills required. Graduates were being appointed to 'library assistant' posts again reflecting the diversity and complexity of tasks, even on issue desks. At times, support staff were tempted by electronic systems into activities which their level of understanding did not prepare them for and where they were quickly out of their depth.

The phenomenon of 'stratification' among middle grade staff can be found, some of these individuals becoming increasingly involved in higher level tasks while some retained lower level tasks. Stratification may also be observed at all levels in LIS – directors and senior managers being more and more drawn into strategic matters, and site librarians into management roles, leaving operational matters to colleagues or more junior staff.

Despite the cautious approach to the modification of structures in the Cardiff Libraries, the possibility remained of greater fluidity in the future, as electronic developments grow and change the nature of information work. Historical and structural factors, including the legacy of the 1988 merger, the large staff working in varying units with different cultures and physical environments, acted as impediments to change.

Relations with Computing Services

The Library and Computing Services had remained separate with no formal convergence although there had been a long-standing history of cooperation. The position of the Computing Service vis a vis the library had come under increasing scrutiny as, inevitably, points of contact and overlap became more visible. The institutional Committee structures had been realigned but merging the Library and Computing Committees alone may not have provided strong enough direction for the services. As far back as 1994, the Principal's Advisory Group believed that:

a) there was a need for a study to be made of the IT needs of the library and its interface with the Computing Service, and
b) the Director of Computing should be asked to produce proposals for refocusing the role of the Computing Service in the light of the many existing and predicted technological and other changes that were occurring in its environment.

The Academic Services Committee may be seen as a formal attempt to coordinate the efforts of the LIS and Computing Service, but this had proved more difficult in practice than in theory. Some convergence of views, if not of service, was occurring, with more library staff embracing the inevitable approach of IT and some Computing Service staff grasping the concept of a user-driven service. The services were to be subject to joint internal quality review rather than separate reviews, which may have significant effects.

There were strong feelings of territoriality between the two services, possibly even increasing because of the high level of library activity which could be seen to overlap with Computing Service activity. The lines of demarcation between the services was at times unclear and made more complex by historical factors: Computing had traditionally delivered training to research students and staff, while the library had traditionally offered training to everyone, including undergraduate students. While the work of the library had been based on subject divisions, that of Computing had been based on functional divisions.

Recent attention has focused on four main areas of activity where a common approach would produce clear benefits for the University:

- Training of staff and students;
- Web development;
- Access to PC workstations;
- Publications.

Concerning training, there had been differing opinions between the library and computing over what constituted IT learning skills and what constituted core IT skills. The University approach to this was somewhat uncoordinated, with IT skills being delivered by computing, by the library and by individual departments, with some students inevitably falling through the net. This problem had been recognised at senior institutional levels and was therefore likely to be addressed in the near future. Teaching suites had been built in libraries where space allowed. This significant trend for the library had not been entirely welcomed by Computing Services who saw their territory being invaded. The library had been proactive in the area of IT training (including core skills) to the extent that they were being invited by departments to deliver skills courses to their students, thus bypassing Computing Services.

A joint LIS/Computing/Marketing Web Development Group had been more successful. It was responsible for drawing up a coordinated framework for University Web pages. The Group worked well together and had made considerable progress.

The question of access to and support of PC workstations was complex and a potential source of conflict. Three levels of PC access existed across campus – open access, open access and bookable, private access. While open access PCs may be sited in libraries but provided by Computing, both services clearly had a stake in their use and support which, understandably, neither wished to relinquish. Computing were unwilling to allow open access workstations to be booked, so the library had acted unilaterally to provide bookable teaching suites.

The library has a long-standing Publications Group and Computing were invited to send a representative(s) to try to coordinate leaflets and other publications across campus. While significant progress had been made to coordinate library publications, the question of a unified image for library and computing documentation had yet to be addressed.

As the research mission of the university and the general needs of the library users continues to drive the need for close cooperation between library and Computing Services, it is evident that a clear structure and formal exposition of the roles of both services in relation to each other would be beneficial.

Information Skills for Users

Increasingly in recent years the library has been developing the area of IT and information skills teaching by library staff. Four libraries had acquired funding to create teaching suites.

While Library staff had long been engaged in teaching activities, it now had a higher profile. The library had seized the initiative offered by quality assessment requirements for academic departments which scrutinise IT and information skills provision. The library was defining its role within the university as the department skilled in electronic information.

In conjunction with new hardware to assist in teaching, the form and content of teaching had also been addressed by an Information Skills Teaching Task Group. This library initiative grew from the objectives and targets of the Quality Procedure on User Education and resulted in an impressive Information Skills Teaching Manual. It did not, of course, deal solely with electronically-based systems and sources. The manual covered curriculum development, promotion, lesson materials, teaching aids, lesson structure and content, assessment, lesson delivery, evaluation and instructor training. The aim was to gain uniformity of user experience across libraries, and to provide guidelines for trainers. It also served as formal evidence for departments of what the library could offer and as an inducement to include information skills in teaching modules. It had both promotional and pedagogical potential.

The quality manual had been adopted across all libraries and a full evaluation was due to be carried out. Those members of staff who had used it to plan and structure their teaching praised it highly. Library staff who undertook teaching were required to attend the in-house teaching skills sessions which were specially tailored for their needs. Combined with the use of the manual, this requirement went a long way to ensuring highly professional information skills teaching across the campus.

Links with teaching departments were stronger in some areas (such as Law, Architecture, the Business School, Maritime Studies, Psychology and the School of English Studies, Communication and Philosophy), than in others, but growing. The formation of partnerships with departments was also a growing feature, the most recent partnership being with Preclinical Sciences. In this department a new Teaching and Learning Resource Centre was in use, a joint arrangement with the School of Molecular and Medical Biosciences.

Library Staff Training

It was acknowledged that there was an enormous training need from the very basic level upwards. This included an awareness of what staff did not know as well as what they should know. The problem of delivering training and development at the right time was recognised. Staff responded well to the 'learn a bit, do a bit, learn a bit, do a bit' sequence of training, in order to put into practice and not forget what had been learned. Of course, the logistics of that approach were problematical.

Most staff were satisfied with the level of training they received, which they considered generous. Senior staff, though percieved that more training could be done, stressing that the need for training both in IT and behavioural aspects was ongoing. A list of competencies for library assistant level had been drawn up, so that identified needs may be addressed. A programme of management training for professional staff had been developed, covering topics such as the art of delegation and problems with teams. The problem of keeping up to speed with new products was well recognised; a proposal to share out in-depth knowledge of particular sources between professionals had met some resistance, as time to become familiar with sources was so short. Organising training for non-professionally qualified middle grade staff had proved more problematical because of the range of tasks undertaken by that group.

'Technofear' among staff was reducing as electronic systems and sources became more and more a way of life. The problem persisted of timing of IT training, which tended to be clustered during quiet times of the year, whereas a more continuous process or programme would be ideal.

Conclusion

Many of the problems facing library managers at Cardiff had a historical basis. These included:

1. Hangover from 1988 merger of two culturally-different institutions.
2. Long-term planning hampered by devolvement of power to Heads of Department.
3. Lack of central institutional direction.
4. Distributed library system providing additional management problems.
5. Differing physical and cultural environments of distributed libraries.
6. History of limited cross-library communication.
7. Lack of clarity surrounding relationship between Library and Computing Services.
8. Persistence of traditional hierarchical structures.

These factors will not disappear overnight. Indeed some are unlikely ever to disappear, particularly points 1, 2, 4 and 5. However, the major management issues which need to be addressed relate to points 3, 6, 7 and 8.

Cardiff libraries were building on their strengths, notably:

1. Concentrated effort in the area of IT and information-handling skills teaching.
2. Responsiveness to views of staff and users.
3. Systematic compilation of documentation (reviews, reports, surveys etc).
4. Improved technical support.
5. Commitment to good provision of staff training and development.
6. Closer links with academic departments.
7. Campus-wide network with increased capacity.

The management approach in the Cardiff libraries had been deliberately proactive. The 'go it alone' attitude on teaching was achieving results; how much greater they would be if Library and Computing Services joined forces here?

Institutionally there were signs that increased central direction may come, although the devolved structure would ensure that tensions between the centre and departments would persist. In the minds of academic teaching staff and of institutional managers, the perpetuation of a devolved, schools-based structure acted as a safeguard to academic freedom and autonomy. Academics and senior managers may be fearful of the concept of strengthened central service departments.

Cardiff was not immune to the major external factors affecting HE. The LIS funding had received an injection of funds for stock but subsequent funding allocation failed to keep up with inflation. In developing a professional approach to teaching IT and information skills, the library had positioned itself well to contribute to the twin corporate mission of high quality teaching and research.

Postscript

Following internal review, Computing, Library and Administrative Computing are converging to form Information Services from August 1st 1998.

References

Bell, A. (1997) The impact of electronic information on the academic research community. *New Review of Academic Librarianship*, **3**, 1–24.

Davies, A., Kirkpatrick, I. and OLIVER, N. (1992) *Merger and Cultural Adjustment: a report on the UWC library system.* Cardiff: Cardiff Business School.

DAVIES, A. and Kirkpatrick, I. (1994) *Service Quality in the UWC Library: Report on Questionnaire Findings.* Cardiff: Cardiff Business School.

CHAPTER TEN

Case Study: Managing change at Edge Hill University College

Catherine Edwards and Ruth Jenkinson

Introduction

This chapter is based on a case study of Edge Hill University College Learning Resource Centre (LRC) conducted in 1996 (and since updated) for the IMPEL2 Project, funded by the Joint Information Systems Committee (JISC) under the Electronic Libraries Programme (eLib).

The development of Edge Hill University College from its beginnings as a teacher education college in 1885 to its present five school structure indicates the extent to which the college has been, and still is, responsive to change. Around half of the student body is mature and many are part-time. Student numbers rose from 2,488 in November 1990 to 6,600 in 1997, but are not expected to rise significantly in the near future.

While teacher education remains an important element of the programmes on offer to students, the college is continuing to develop its range of BA and BSc degrees in the areas of Health Studies, Humanities and Arts, Management and Social Sciences and Sciences and Technology. Degrees are

awarded by the University of Lancaster in accordance with
the college's accredited status with the university. Modular
schemes are being developed and reviewed in order to
respond to changing patterns of demand. The college's
research activity has traditionally centred on taught postgraduate work, and is now developing further with participation in the Research Assessment Exercise. A new appointment, that of Head of Research, has recently been made.
Most of the college's activity takes place at the main campus,
with two smaller remote sites.

The college has been subject to the same pressures affecting
the university sector: a larger student body, financial
constraints, increased accountability and quality assessments
of teaching and research. It would appear, however, that the
college has been able to maintain its clear focus, that is, the
teaching and learning experience of the students. The good
match between the college's mission, structure, strategy and
culture is a significant feature; the development of the electronic environment both strengthens and is strengthened by
this cohesion.

Mission and Vision

The college's mission is as follows:

> 'Edge Hill is a major centre of excellence providing a high quality
> university experience in a responsive learning environment. Working
> with a range of partners, and committed to equality of opportunity,
> Edge Hill provides its students with the knowledge and skills
> to make key contributions to communities and organizations
> throughout their lives.'

The mission makes clear that it is the students' needs which
are paramount. This policy is applied in practice through, for
instance, the first priority always being given to the provision of high specification IT equipment for students in
open-access areas.

The college's flat management structure is designed to
avoid hierarchical barriers between senior management and

their clientele. Only the Director of Academic Affairs and Quality Management sits between the Chief Executive and the Heads of School, the Head of Library Services, the Head of Teaching, Learning and Programme Development and the Head of Research. Student support has been streamlined, moved towards a one-stop-shop model where the Student Information Centre (SIC) and main computing facility are housed within one building, adjacent to the Learning Resource Centre.

The teaching and learning policy has been developed to support 'autonomous learners, capable of both independent and interdependent learning' through a range of opportunities and resources. The teaching and learning 'culture' emerges as one of the college's strengths. IT is seen as a tool in the teaching and learning process. A number of subjects are introducing information retrieval skills into their courses. The culture embraces the concept that library staff are essentially in the same business as academic teaching staff, that of facilitators and supporters of learning, opening the way for greater academic convergence for library staff.

Crucial to the development of IT at Edge Hill was the strong vision of the previous and current chief executives who saw its potential for society as a whole and not least for Higher Education. This vision is shared by the current Head of Library Services. The role of visionary leadership in pushing forward IT development is a significant factor at Edge Hill The vision of a fully networked campus has been achieved, apart from halls of residence (one new one has cabling built in). The capacity of the network is adequate for present needs. The ratio of students to PCs is an impressive 7:1. Institutional commitment to IT provision on campus is clearly present despite some tensions at senior levels between whether IT provision is really an 'added-on bonus' to teaching and learning or a replacement for traditional methods. The balance between 'added on' and 'instead of' may change in the light of financial stringency, an enlarged and diffuse student body and other pressures affecting higher education in general.

Along with the vision for an IT-intensive campus came that for a new Learning Resource Centre which opened in 1994, a central facility with books, journals and multimedia materials and extensive IT provision. The staffing is comparatively small for the diversity of services offered, 21.9 FTE (36 people), two thirds of whom are part-time. Additional IT support is provided by students of the college and placement students from Liverpool John Moores University (LJMU). The capacity of the building is expected to be adequate for future needs. The building itself is significant, housing 150 PCs and multimedia workstations as well as traditional print-based collections. It is possible for the learning resources centre (LRC) to take advantage of developments and knowledge gained elsewhere, more painfully, at an earlier stage. The building symbolizes the convergence between information and computing technologies; both computing and library staff work within it.

ASSIST (Access for Students and Staff to Information Services and Technology)

ASSIST is a co-operative grouping of four services: Library Services, Computer Services, Learning Development Unit and MediaTech services. Thinking again of the fit between mission, strategy, structure and culture, ASSIST would appear to be central to the philosophy of the student learner at the centre of college activities.

The model developed around the time that the new LRC was being planned and built, in response to the clear need for the services to work more closely together. ASSIST does not appear formally in the college management structure but has a high profile on campus. The model was not imposed by senior management but grew in a more bottom-up way. It avoids any form of organizational convergence, each service retaining its own head. Operationally, however, there is a significant degree of convergence. ASSIST is a pragmatic, functional solution to the convergence issue. It brings the services together in a fairly seamless way without the turbulence of a formal convergence. Among the benefits of the ASSIST grouping are listed below:

- Services have the flexibility necessary to respond to changing needs;
- A higher profile institutionally is better than four completely separate services;
- It helps people learn in more than one way;
- It is able to respond to new types of learning such as modularization. It integrates well into the academic environment;
- It minimizes suspicion and jockeying for position;
- The services have common aims;
- There is peer pressure between the services to perform well;
- Technical support for the LRC is good.

Possible disadvantages of the grouping are that:

- it lacks permanence and could be broken up by a change in institutional management;
- it is possibly personality-dependent.

Help leaflets available in the LRC are all ASSIST leaflets; these are available also on the World Wide Web and it is planned that eventually they will only be accessible via the Web. The college is developing its own Intranet, which will include information and guidance for students and staff, policy documents and procedures and, in due course, specialized learning materials. There is joint registration held in the LRC – students register at the same time with the college and all four ASSIST services, receiving computer passwords at the same time. Joint training, joint projects and end-user support are facilitated. LRC staff are conscious of some disparity in service standards between themselves and computing staff and that computing staff could learn from them in this area. The reliance on student placements from LJMU and on students from Edge Hill for the delivery of front-line IT support has highlighted the need to ensure that service standards and levels are consistent and fully understood by all staff, and these issues have to be regularly revisited in view of the short-term nature of student contracts.

The ASSIST model relies upon good communication between its heads and staff, with a recognition that 'the people are more important than the model'. The LRC management group includes computing staff. There are regular heads of ASSIST meetings and working relations between the services are good. The model does not encourage a 'blame culture' as any inevitable disagreements would be very obvious. The ASSIST model works well for Edge Hill, a relatively small and stable college. How well it would work in a large, very complex institution is more doubtful.

LRC staff work with computing staff in many ways, including First Week (introduction to services for new students), drop-in sessions for users, college open days, joint training on customer care and help desk work and creating a list of frequently asked questions.

An extremely good working relationship and strong affinity has grown up between the LRC and MediaTech whose role in supporting staff and students in new ways of working (e.g. use of video and camcorder technology) is growing. The two services have worked together on video production. It is tempting to conclude that ASSIST has in fact developed its own culture.

Information Strategy

The college is working on a campus-wide information strategy, an outline of which appears in the Strategic Plan. Early attempts to create this using a bottom-up approach resulted in plenty of ideas which failed to come to fruition through lack of coordination. The initiative has since been taken at the senior management level although all Schools have recently been invited to make proposals for consideration. The top-down approach is felt to be a better way of getting the job done, another instance of pragmatism at work. Interestingly the JISC guidelines for information strategies (JISC, 1995) are being used more as a checklist or a benchmark in the process, than as strict guidance.

The Chief Executive holds the view that the strategy is not simply about technology although that is part of it. More important are issues of communication. The main value of the information strategy lies in clarifying objectives and in reinforcing the 'teaching and learning culture' of the college.

LRC Staffing Structure

More evidence of pragmatism can be found in the way staff are deployed in the LRC. Up until the move into the new LRC, the library had not offered a school liaison service. Since then the liaison role has grown in importance and popularity. All liaison staff also have an operational function; for instance, the science and technology liaison librarian also has responsibility for document delivery, requests and journals management, and is also involved generally in support services and collection development. This type of multi-skilling operation does not lend itself to easy diagrammatic illustration but offers a solution to low levels of staffing and to the changing demands on library services.

Staff effectively work in non-static teams and because they are multi-skilled they are responsive to change. This type of working arrangement tends to blur hierarchies, reflecting again the flat institutional hierarchy. It also mirrors the integrated nature of information work where services and systems become inseparable. At Edge Hill, this flexible structure engenders an enabling culture whereby senior staff are encouraged and enabled to take greater responsibility and library assistants have individual responsibilities. In theory, job satisfaction should be enhanced; however, some staff have reacted more positively than others to this type of structure as reporting lines are not straightforward.

The rapid expansion of services which the LRC delivers, and in particular that of the School liaison service, has prompted some concerns about the very varied roles of LRC staff and, in particular, those of the senior staff. Some academic staff and students would welcome greater specialism among the staff with more clearly defined and limited roles so that, for example, LRC input into the information requirements of research-active staff and students could be increased.

Pressure to specialize has been resisted by the Head of Library Services because staff numbers are too small to make this viable and essential flexibility would be reduced. LRC staff also seem to appreciate the variety and scope of their roles, despite some inevitable practical problems in managing so many varied tasks and responsibilities at the same time. There is a general philosophy that information-handling skills are more valuable in the Edge Hill context than deep subject specialist knowledge, again, probably, for practical reasons, but with reducing staffing resources in the sector as a whole, this is an issue not by any means unique to Edge Hill.

The 'paraprofessional' role is a key one in the successful operation of the LRC . The role has developed as a result of necessity rather than any changes in working practice relating to IT. Paraprofessional staff are recognized as capable individuals who work mainly in a supervisory or organizational capacity, for instance enquiry desk management. The role has caused some minor tension at both senior and junior levels; however it does provide able assistants with some career progression and most importantly, is an effective way of deploying staff within tight budgets.

Signifying again the enabling culture within the LRC, library assistants and paraprofessionals are encouraged to handle as many queries as they feel able to, and do receive training in the use, for instance, of CD-ROMs and in Internet searching. Library assistants' meetings are held and outcomes reported. Staff report that issues relevant to the LRC are well communicated, a policy which helps to discourage fragmentation within the staff. Some staff at junior levels do perceive that a hierarchy exists within LRC and are somewhat resentful of this. The increased responsibility accorded to non-professionally qualified staff is a sign of change. They have, for example, been involved in designing the ground floor counter. A presentation by library assistants on customer care has been greatly valued by all staff and is a good example of their involvement in the team.

Users

The LRC has only recently been in the position of needing to cancel some hard copy journal runs, so here the concept of the electronic library as an 'add-on' rather than an 'instead-of' has largely held. Edge Hill is a site for the UK Pilot Licence Scheme which promises to have a significant impact on access to documents and on journal provision.

There is patchy uptake of use of electronic systems and sources by academic teaching staff. They are seen by LRC staff in this to be to some extent driven by their students. An important impact of electronic library developments on LRC staff is promotion of these services, and how and when to promote them. They are constantly seeking new approaches; personal approaches, for instance by e-mail, have been successful, but time-consuming. Some teaching staff lack confidence in dealing with IT developments and some need convincing. LRC staff have been disappointed that two School staff training days (one for Management and Social Sciences, one for Education) were poorly attended. The liaison librarians realize that they have a major promotional task on hand.

The opening of the LRC caused a surge of activity amongst student users whose IT competence and awareness was variable, being particularly shaky among mature students who had been out of education for some time. A great deal of staff time and effort goes into supporting autonomous use of electronic systems. The ASSIST services have developed an impressive, systematic induction process where maximum effort goes into 'First Week'. The aim of First Week is to engage all new students in a rolling programme of induction including hands-on experience. The thinking here is that time spent during First Week will be time saved later. This is an excellent demonstration of successful collaboration by ASSIST. Staff recognize that more effort should go towards meeting the needs of part-time and mature students. As time is short for much one-to-one user training, a wider range of help sheets is available (with many also on the Web site), providing a practical solution to that problem.

Joint LRC and computing effort has also gone into 'drop-ins', which students with particular queries may attend. Drop-ins have proved to be extremely popular early in the year but to tail off significantly as the year progresses. Consequently, a decision has recently been taken to concentrate staff time on drop-ins at the start of the year and then on specific workshop sessions on identified aspects of information handling, supplemented by an appointments system with the school liaison librarians for specific subject-based requirements. LRC staff enjoy working alongside computing staff in this context and feel there is a genuine sharing of knowledge.

There is an enquiry desk on each of the three floors of the LRC staff, the ground and first floor desks staffed by LRC, the second floor desk by computing staff close to the large PC suite. Computing students from LJMU provide additional support on floor two during extended placements. It is generally felt that co-operation between LRC staff, computing staff and LJMU students is good. Concerns mainly relate to lack of consistency in user support resulting from varying levels of IT expertise among LRC staff and varying levels of customer care among computing and LJMU staff.

There has been a noticeable change in general reference enquiries. Whether this is due to the positioning of the collection on the ground floor, or to users answering their own general queries electronically, is unclear. Some LRC staff report that they are increasingly unable to answer queries at the first floor desk which are becoming more and more IT-related. They worry that users are receiving inconsistent levels of help there, depending on which member of staff is on duty. They feel uncomfortable having repeatedly to send queries up to the second floor (computing staff) desk. They are very keen to receive more IT training for this reason.

At the same time, LRC staff have territorial feelings about the first floor desk, being reluctant to give ground to computing staff. Some rethinking of enquiry desk staffing may be necessary in order to achieve the best service for users, exploiting both the close relations between the two groups of staff and the opportunity offered by the building to combine traditional bibliographic with IT-related expertise.

A significant proportion of library users at remote sites are mature, part-time students, many with low IT skills and awareness. CD-ROMs on the two other sites are mounted on standalone terminals, so that access is less than on the networked main site. The personal service offered at remote sites is felt to go some way to counterbalancing that disadvantage. The expense of providing full networked access to remote sites is considerable, but LAN/MAN initiative funding has been secured which has facilitated much improved networked links to the two smaller sites.

Staff Training and Development

LRC staff (both at senior and library assistant levels) consider that opportunities for staff development are generous. They receive every opportunity to take up training, and to attend workshops and conferences, and the centre has its own staff development fund. The main development and training needs created by the growing electronic library are felt to be in IT and in management – how to make best use of resources available. The college itself offers a well developed programme of training, from which many staff have benefited, the main constraint being time, particularly to keep abreast of new electronic sources. Staff are encouraged to do an hour's training per week but this proves increasingly difficult to sustain. Normally, the LRC has to try to accommodate time for training alongside normal service delivery. In July, some essential training takes place when the LRC opens late on a limited basis to facilitate vacation access in the evenings for part-time students; however, staffing availability is also limited then. The ideal would be to have agreed closure times specifically identified for training purposes throughout the year.

The increasing teaching role, both with students and teaching staff, is recognized; the possible take-up of courses and material offered by the national JISC eLib Programme, through the EduLib Project is under consideration. Edge Hill has its own postgraduate Certificate in Teaching and Learning, accredited by SEDA, and three of the LRC liaison librarians have already undertaken it. There is considerable interest from other staff in following the course in future years, as it offers the practical advantage of being based in the institution, and also offers the opportunity to study alongside teaching staff and other academic-related staff. One member of senior staff has undertaken the Netlinks (Sheffield University) online networked learner support course in 1997/8.

Staff on remote sites are perhaps somewhat disadvantaged in terms of training and development, missing out on close daily contact with peers. Technological support is less than at the main site and a great deal of pressure was experienced when the automated library system was introduced. Staff exchanges and joint training are facilitated to help with this problem wherever practically possible.

The use and exploitation of the Internet has been highlighted by the development of Edge Hill's Web site. Senior LRC staff have had training and have developed extensive school-based links, and in some cases they are working with academic staff on the identification of Web-based information sources. The Head of Research is also working with them to develop research links. Increasingly, LRC staff are demonstrating relevant Web-based information to staff and students in the context of total information handling, whereas computer services staff continue to focus more on the technical aspects of creating Web pages. There is discussion currently taking place on the format and content of the Web site as a whole, and who should have editorial responsibility within Edge Hill for its style and updating. LRC staff would like easier access to the library services pages than is currently the case, because of the importance of the information within to all staff and students. Increasingly, publications and guides are being added to the Web site by LRC staff to increase access to relevant information.

Managing Change

The college and the LRC in many ways display excellent practice in managing change and adopting appropriate cultures. Their particular strengths are:

- taking to heart a vision for the role of IT in teaching and learning;
- adoption of a flat institutional management structure;
- retention of the teaching and learning process as its focus, incorporating technology and new teaching methods as appropriate;
- exploitation of the different skills of the ASSIST group;
- development of an institution-wide Information Technology Strategy and an emerging Information Strategy;
- building a state of the art Learning Resource Centre, incorporating IT with books and journals;
- maintenance of a high profile for the LRC within the institution;
- development of new partnerships – with other institutions, with academic departments through the liaison service, with computing, MediaTech and Learning Support;
- adoption of a multi-skilling approach in LRC;
- adoption of pragmatic and flexible attitudes in order to make best use of resources;

- non-adherence to traditional library hierarchies, through the involvement of all levels of staff;
- empowerment of LRC staff;
- recognition of the importance of training and development for staff;
- focus on user needs and new ways to respond to these;
- encouragement of use of networked information sources.

Conclusion

With the pressures on resources set to continue, the LRC needs to pursue increasingly creative ways of meeting challenges and delivering services in an effective and efficient manner. This will no doubt include increasing the emphasis on self-service, self-instruction and on services delivered via the network.

The casualization and outsourcing of some 'backroom' processes are already taking place, and these will continue and increase. Collaboration and partnership with other higher education organizations in delivering services will have a higher profile, as will charges for certain services at the point of use or by subscription.

The LRC building itself was designed to cope with changing information needs, and, following Dearing, students will apparently need to plug their laptops into the network infrastructure. They will do this in the LRC, but only if they continue to find there the high quality support and relevant service delivery methods which meet their changing learning support requirements. Supporting students in this will continue to be the primary *raison d'être* for the LRC, whether the students study on campus or elsewhere.

Increasingly LRC staff are seeking to develop online support for students, especially for part-timers and those based on remote sites. The development of structured Web links had already enabled students to access a range of relevant resources more easily, and it is hoped that the development of the Intranet will facilitate the growth of networked learner support for specific groups of students. The school liaison librarian are piloting the use of Web-based links to tutors' notes, reading lists, LRC 'help sheets' and an electronic help desk. The pilot will concentrate on teaching information-handling skills, and also on supporting students as customers of the service.

Working in partnership with academic teaching staff is critical to the process of encouraging and supporting students and their learning needs, particularly in an electronic environment. Edge Hill has many benefits in being small enough to seek out and encourage co-operation and collaboration between staff, and to embrace institution-wide approaches to teaching and learning developments. Much still depends, however, on the skills and enthusiasm of LRC staff to ensure that the opportunities which the electronic library offers are fully understood and exploited.

References

eLib Website: http://ukoln.bath.ac.uk/elib/

Joint Information Systems Committee (1995) *Guidelines for Developing an Information Strategy*. Bristol: HEFC

Resourcing and Budgeting Issues

CHAPTER ELEVEN
Overview: Resourcing and Budgeting Issues
Thomas W. Graham

Introduction

'Planning for the electronic journal is like shooting at a moving target' (Nisonger, 1997, p.59). Such a sentiment which will be readily echoed by librarians, who would also apply it to the extending range of other information sources in electronic form. Nevertheless, shoot we must, and the development of practical resourcing and budgeting strategies will be necessary as we move into an environment in which electronic communication becomes increasingly common. It has become commonplace to assert that scholarly communication is being changed radically, and there is no doubt that this will happen. At this early stage in that process, however, we have on a practical level to acknowledge that most of what our users read is still in printed form, and that our practices have to reflect that hybrid state. Traditional activities have to continue while the capabilities of digital information provision are taken on-board. Analysis of the nature of the change which is taking place has to be a continuous process, perhaps requiring a series of changes in our resourcing and budgeting practices. This is not an easy situation for libraries (and for many institutions) whose systems tend to operate in a relatively steady-state mode. These practices will also have to reflect the realities of both the changing information world and changes in our user (whether that be education or any other) environment. We therefore face a situation where there will be conflicting pressures for change and stability operating on our libraries, and we have to steer our budgeting methods on a course which will both enable us to operate effectively now and also lead our libraries through that changing world. While much has been written on the scholarly communication process itself, on the economics of the new information environment and on collection management in the context of electronic materials, a consensus is far from emerging on the key issues which will set the framework for resourcing libraries in this new environment, and not surprisingly, much less has been written on this subject.

The New Information Scene

Library budgeting has, at least in general terms, had a consistent shape in most institutions for some time. National and institutional budgetary and political frameworks may have led to changes from time to time, but library budgets have been built round a few key lines, primarily staff, materials and operating costs, with a growing amount also being devoted to equipment. The major change has been that in most countries the actual resources available for library services have declined in relative terms. This has been one of the factors which has led to reconsideration in many institutions of the way in which materials budgets have been allocated, along with increasing demands for accountability and some changes in, for example, the balance between the use of monographs and serials in some disciplines. Nevertheless, the shape of library budgets today would not be wholly unfamiliar to librarians of the 1970s.

The introduction of electronic resources of various kinds may well change that situation, in terms not only of funding for the materials themselves, but also in terms of funding for equipment, for staffing and for space. The whole infrastructure may eventually have to alter if it is to be responsive to the changing methods of communication implied by these new media. This is because they create the possibility of quite different ways of operating for teachers, students and researchers, and therefore a new model of communication and learning. Perhaps most important, as librarians (and this is also true of other players in the information business) we must recognize that 'we shall never again control information' (Morino, 1996, p.17), and our patterns of operation and budgeting will have to be shaped against that background.

Electronic information sources are appearing in a variety of forms. The book, as a substantial entity meant to be read as a whole, is perhaps the format which is most resilient against migration to the electronic environment. At the research level, however, American university presses have identified a crisis in conventional publishing as a result of sharply dropping sales and print-runs (Renfro, 1997). Various proposals have been made for changed publishing models, such as the Committee on Institutional Co-operation (CIC) proposal for collaboration between presses, libraries and computing centres and more radical ideas for different models of communication such as the use of interactive media and new relationships based on the Web, rather than the linear form of print monographs (Renfro, 1997) or Hawkins's ideas for a 'national electronic library' in the USA (Hawkins, 1994).

In the teaching and learning environment, the potential for meeting the demands of large groups of students requiring access to material over a short period by the use of electronic reserve collections is extremely enticing, given that there is no possibility of doing this really effectively by print media, and that the need for this is increased by the development of mass higher education in the UK. The related concept of on-demand publishing, focused on a client group such as students on a particular course and often related to readings from books, articles, etc., also has a place. Projects such as SCOPE and ACORN, funded under the eLib programme in the UK, have explored these models of provision in different ways, and they have considerable resonance in the United States, where the pattern of higher education supported by reading organized in this way, is long established. In both cases, the linked issues of digitization costs, the potential loss of sales for publishers, and of the copyright implications of such collections have financial, and therefore, resource implications.

The most dramatic developments have taken place in the area of electronic journals. In addition to the growth of new electronic and dual-format journals, a significant number of existing publishers have in the past few years made their print journals available in electronic versions. The striking feature of the last two years indeed is the speed with which publishers have taken up the idea of parallel publishing. In the UK, the Funding Councils' Pilot Site Licence Initiative (PSLI) has acted as a catalyst to this development. Publishers, who were previously uncertain as to how to move forward, have seized on the opportunity provided by the Internet and Web technology to launch electronic versions of their titles (Hitchcock, Carr. and Hall, 1997). The key point about such publishing is that, because it has made available well-known and respected journals in electronic form, the idea of electronic publishing is gradually being accepted by academics. These electronic versions are also increasingly available in a multiplicity of forms. They may be available individually, or through a publisher's package deal, as with Elsevier's *Science Direct* or the Institute of Physics service; or they may be aggregated with a number of publishers' products in a third-party service, such as Blackwells' *Electronic Journals Navigator* or the BIDS *Journals Online* service. These are increasingly likely to be arranged by some subject classification in response to user needs. In some cases too, these products are linked to other services in an attempt to provide a more integrated approach to accessing the information.

This variety in the products has obvious implications for budgeting, since they do not fit existing publication patterns. As with books, different models of journal publishing, based on different combinations of players and sometimes involving different methods of financing, have also been proposed, such as Stevan Harnad's 'scholarly skywriting', using a preprint archive prior to full publication (Harnad, 1995), Quinn's idea of library co-publication (Quinn and Macmillan, 1995) or Hobohm's proposal for a journal supported purely on sponsorship and advertizing (Hobohm, 1997).

Electronic document delivery was envisaged early on as a likely 'product line' from the electronic library, and has been made possible, using for example the Research Library Group's Ariel software. Some eLib projects in the United Kingdom are at the time of writing already operational (LAMDA) or about to become so (EDDIS). This kind of service has also quickly become associated with development of electronic Table of Contents (TOC) services, such as the CARL *Uncover* Service, provided in the UK by Blackwells, and SwetsNet services. Commercial suppliers and the British Library Document Supply Centre are all linking their TOC services to a document delivery service to provide alternatives to conventional inter-library loan. These are available both to libraries and directly to end users, thus obviously introducing the questions both of 'who pays' and comparative costs and quality into the resourcing issue.

A further development has been the creation of electronic databases of primary material. Some of this has been in the form of primary texts, particularly of literary texts. The Oxford Text Archive in the UK and centres at, for example, Rutgers University, the University of Virginia and the University of Columbia in the United States are examples of such databases (Gaunt, 1995). Others contain different forms of primary material, such as archaeological data or digitized copies of manuscript material, such as the material being collected under the Arts and Humanities Data Service initiative within the eLib programme. Projects in image digitization are also in progress in various countries.

The development noted above of aggregator services, integrating access to a number of journals or services originating with a range of publishers or to a number of databases through a standard interface, is both a very significant new development and an indication of the growth of all these products and services. OCLC FirstSearch and the RLG's Eureka service both provide access to a range of secondary databases. Examples have already been given above of services providing a route into a range of electronic journals. Chadwyck-Healey's LION does the same for a number of full-text literary databases. Links between the services, as happens between OCLC FirstSearch and Electronic Collections Online, provide a further example of integration, an important characteristic of the electronic environment.

The existence of the Internet and Web access to information on it has led to the development of other less formal sources of information. Some of these, such as Paul Ginsparg's pre-print physics archive, are substantial databases in their own right, but there is a whole spectrum down to papers held on departmental or individual Web sites.

A key feature of all these developments has been the move from local holding of data, in formats such as CD-ROM and even mounting on local servers, towards network provision using the Web as an access mechanism. The availability of information across the network means that the idea of holdings and access as two competing alternatives is gradually being diluted. Although document delivery from a database held elsewhere is clearly 'access', should the same be said of the process of pulling down an article from a journal for which you have rights of access via a licence but which is held on a server elsewhere?

These developments (and this is a very brief summary of the variety of forms) are fluid: new services are appearing at intervals so it is difficult to know when to take up new services, and indeed which to take. They may overlap with each other, and the same material can be provided through several sources. This is a trend which seems likely to become established. However, it can mean that the overlap between the services raises issues not only of choices and funding, but also about how a varied suite of services can be integrated into a coherent whole for users. Finally, it must not be forgotten that providing access to these services – looked at negatively – is itself a further burden on hard-pressed library finances unless it substitutes in some way for existing expenditure. Several recent writers have stressed the need to make clear to funders that, during this interim period, libraries will simply require significantly increased funding, and will be expensive (Lancaster and Sandore, 1997), which is not an easy message to give to higher education institutions. What is certain, however, is that resourcing information in these forms does not necessarily fit into budgeting patterns of the past. Given the fluidity of the development of information provision and the funding difficulties which libraries face, we have to acquire some understanding of, and view on, the costs of these new media.

Cost in the New Environment

There is little published information on the costs of electronic books and even the costs of electronic document delivery. The picture for serials is very different. The increasing prices of serials in the print environment triggered a major debate on the cost of serials production over the past ten years. The appearance of electronic journals has begun to change the nature of that debate, with the focus now being on the effect on costs of electronic production. It has produced a mass of literature, although the light cast on the problem cannot yet be said to be proportionate to its scale. The focus has been very much on the costs of electronic journals. The literature suffers at times from a failure to distinguish between different kinds of journals (see for example, Garson, 1996, and O'Donnell, 1996), so is worth reviewing briefly.

The distinction between kinds of journals is an important one, because it may critically condition both costs and prices. An obvious distinction is that between journals in subjects where writing is text-based and those in which there may be extensive illustration or where the writing may include, for example, mathematical formulae. There may also be a distinction drawn between journals intended for purely scholarly use, defined by Steven Harnad (1995) as 'esoteric journals' where the writer may be purely concerned to get his or her work as widely circulated as possible, and journals which are used by both academic researchers and, say, pharmaceutical companies. A commonly-recognized difference is that between journals produced by commercial publishers and those produced by learned societies. An obvious distinction, but one not often articulated, is that between journals in a field where there is a high-volume readership and therefore high sales and those in a field where subscription volumes are generally low. An even less frequently made difference, but one remarked on by Schad (1997), is that between journals in disciplines where there is traditionally a high reject rate, and also possibly has a lower growth rate, and those in disciplines where the purpose is to preserve the archive of the discipline. Schad exemplifies this in the print environment by contrasting the prices and volume of the *American Historical Review* and the *Physical Review: A*. Whether this, and indeed the previous distinction, reflects a science–arts divide can only be proved by a larger sample than he uses. There are no doubt other differences based on size of publishing companies, etc. and potential economies of scale. In the context of the new environment, of course, the obvious distinction is that between journals produced in print, those in parallel print and electronic forms, and those journals which are produced solely in electronic form. The last may take a variety of forms. Some may simply mimic print; others may introduce new elements, such as moving images, hypertext links, the ability to change illustrations, multiple ways to present data and the capacity for users to respond to points made in a paper. The number of these is certainly increasing rapidly, but so far, the majority of them are carried out as relatively small-scale enterprises with various forms of support, and they have yet to become fully established and gain credibility at the level of the established print journals. At this stage, the dominant form, as illustrated in the previous section, is parallel publishing, mainly, though not entirely, mimicking the print versions exactly.

Not surprisingly, it is publishers who have most strongly argued that the cost of electronic journals will not be significantly less than that of print journals. Robert Marks, of the American Chemical Society, has claimed that 82–86 per cent of the production costs are accounted for by the fixed copy cost, and the cost for production in print on paper is 14–18 per cent of the whole. By his analysis, the basic costs are the same whatever the medium, involving management of the editorial and refereeing process, editorial work and production (Marks, 1995). The same approach is taken by Janet Fisher of MIT Press, in comparing the costs of an electronic journal with those produced as print journals. The median cost of production of an article in an electronic journal was estimated in 1995 as reducing to \$3,200 over three years, while the median figure for print articles was \$4,500. These estimates include editorial support, overhead costs, production expenses and marketing and mailing costs. In her view, the heavy marketing and overhead costs of the electronic journal 'overwhelm' any savings in production costs (Fisher, 1995). There are interesting variations between Marks' and Fisher's views. While Marks' claims that costs would be little or no different, Fisher's own figures suggest that production of electronic journals might cost 70 per cent of the cost of an average print journal of the same kind, a figure supported by her statement that printing, binding and mailing account for 30 per cent of the cost (although her account of the relative balance between cost elements has some internal inconsistencies). Fisher too is more willing to accept that there may be scope for savings.

The opposite view – namely that electronic publishing on the Internet could result in massive savings – has been strongly articulated by a number of authors, particularly Steven Harnad and Andrew Odlyzko. Harnad (1995) has claimed that the cost of a purely electronic journal could save

70 per cent of the cost. His thesis is based on the premise of a free electronic preprint swapped for a refereed reprint text, with various funding models being possible, including page charges built into research funding. This is a radical approach and has not yet met with acceptance in the academic, let alone the publishing, world. As Harnad himself accepts, it requires 'a cognitive and behavioral paradigm shift that most people have difficulty contemplating'. Odlyzko, in an article which looks at the total costs to all those involved of the production of an article, suggests that the first copy cost of the production of a conventional mathematics article is around $4 000, a figure not far removed from Fisher's median figure for the average production cost of an MIT Press article, especially when the difference between average and first copy costs are taken into account. In comparison, the cost of production of an electronic journal article could be between $300–$1 000, made cheaper by the economies possible from improving technology and from different views of what is necessary to produce an acceptable product: in his view, jettisoning a few features would save considerable sums. He also directly challenges some of the publishers' claims. In his view, for example, the claim that costs cannot be reduced much because so much of the cost is first-copy cost is refuted by the widely different costs among publishers. He also claims that the disparity in costs is a 'sign of an industry which has not had to worry about efficiency' (Odlyzko, 1997). Vijay Jog, reviewing the evidence for comparative costs of social sciences and humanities journals in 1995 in a thoroughly-researched report which is based on a more conventional view of the possibilities, suggested that the cost of production and distribution of an electronic journal could be 28–48 per cent lower than a comparable paper-based counterpart, though he recognized that the estimated savings from this might be offset by reductions in subscription revenues (Jog, 1995).

This debate is important because, as electronic publication develops in a variety of ways, there will have to be a greater understanding of the economic basis of the new environment.

The variety of publication forms however means that no one economic model can be regarded as the norm. Even if we limit the discussion – as I have done – to electronic journals, it can be seen that the range of publication models makes it impossible to determine one pattern of costing. Part of the disagreement illustrated above stems from the fact that the authors are discussing different publication models. As the outline of publication forms given above indicate, however, the variety of forms goes beyond electronic journals. As it becomes clearer which possibilities for new publication models are realistic, it may become possible to look at their economics in a more objective way. It is certainly clear that more work on the economics of multiple forms of electronic publishing needs to be carried out, and it is to be regretted that more economists do not take up this challenge. At the same time, the existence of vested interest will ensure that the debate about costs will continue.

Pricing in the New Environment

The growth of new methods of information provision inevitably raises issues of pricing which, while related to the costs of production, include other factors more related to commercial policies. Inevitably too, the debates about prices which began in the print environment, have been carried over into the new environment, carrying over some of the same arguments and generating some new ones as well.

The basic element is of course the product itself. As has been demonstrated earlier, the range of products in the electronic environment is extensive and growing. This will itself determine a range of pricing models. Archives of primary material of various kinds, organized under various funding regimes, are likely to be available in ways which reflect these regimes, ranging from free access to licensed arrangements with the producers. These are quite different from electronic journals and, as we have seen, the range of these is itself quite extensive and therefore likely to be priced in a variety of ways. The aggregation of such publications under various 'badges' may produce further variety. Electronic books or collections of material from books will produce further pricing variations. How the ownership of intellectual property in the electronic information world develops will also impact on pricing.

Pricing levels

A key issue remains that of pricing levels. Those writers who claim that the greatest element of the costs is first-copy costs also claim that this justifies both existing prices, and further, since the basic production costs are the same, that this pattern has to be replicated in the electronic environment (Marks, 1995).

Not surprisingly, where there is a belief either that costs in the print environment are higher than are strictly necessary or that electronic publication can cut production costs, this is usually reflected in an expectation that prices can be lower than those to which we are accustomed. Odlyzko, as well as challenging publishers on costs, points out too the existence of large profits, quoting Elsevier's pretax profits of over 40 per cent and indicating that even professional societies earn substantial profits on their publishing operations. He notes that some publishers keep over 75 per cent of the revenues from such societies' journals just for distribution. In his view, this is a sign of an industry that operates in an environment without price competition, and that therefore there is scope for substantial price reductions in the electronic publishing environment (Odlyzko, 1997).

There is some agreement between the two camps, in that both recognize that the growth in the scholarly literature is a (in some cases stated to be 'the') cause of the crisis. The disagreement is over the solution. In Marks' case, his argument is that the cost of publication is a tiny fraction of the total cost of research, and the basic problem is that most library budgets are not keeping pace with the continued growth in the amount of published literature. Ways must be found to pay for the production and dissemination of research results. (Marks, 1995). While one might agree with this assessment of the problem factually, its flaw lies in assuming that funders will accept publishers' figures for either costs or prices *and* will be willing to pay these prices. All the evidence is that they will not do so. If this means that access is increasingly not being provided to all the literature which is wanted, they will demand that librarians and scholars look for cheaper ways of accessing the research literature. Odlyzko concentrates on the other side, that of what he sees as excessive prices. He points out that there are perverse incentives built into the information chain; scholars have no incentive to maintain it since they are not aligned with the interests of publishers, and he believes that cheaper methods of making material widely available and of obtaining the prestige of publication could lead to the system's collapse. Equally, as he admits, they also have no incentive to dismantle it, and believes that the system will not change until decision makers realize that there are other cheaper ways to make the information available (Odlyzko, 1997).

There are other perversities in the present system. For example, in what other market does a supplier respond to a drop in sales by increasing prices? This may reflect the fact that competition in the journals market does not operate in a simple way on price competition, but rather on quality and prestige, and this has effectively created monopolies.

The rapid expansion in Web-based access to electronic versions of existing print journals has involved publishers in determining charging policies on a very conventional conservative basis. For example, some publishers, such as Elsevier and the American Chemical Society, have based prices on print price *plus* an electronic surcharge *plus* in some cases projected inflation increases. The PSLI effectively operated on that basis in that the total sum paid by the institutions and the funding councils together amounted to more than 100 per cent of the printed price for the journals. Although some users are finding this acceptable, if not palatable, there is a groundswell of opinion against this approach. The International Coalition of Library Consortia (ICOLC), building on the work of a German and Dutch coalition, have argued that this approach makes libraries carry the full financial burden of the research and development involved in bringing these products to market. For the future, the Coalition claims that pricing models must result in a significant reduction in the 'per use' cost of information and that, over time, savings accruing through electronic information production should be passed from the provider to the customer (ICOLC, 1998). Others have pointed out that there is no reason why pricing of electronic information should bear any relation to models designed for a print environment, (Hitchcock, Carr and Hall, 1997).

A more imaginative approach to the pricing of electronic products might involve taking advantage of the flexibility of the product to adopt differential pricing. Hal Varian (1996) proposes this in the context of learned societies concerned about membership loss if their electronic journals are mounted on networks. While such differentials could be exercised in a negative way by providing a cheaper subscription for use within a library only, he proposes positive methods which instead enhance the value for members, such as the provision of hypertext links, more powerful search engines, earlier release, etc.

Pricing mechanisms

The growth of electronic information has also engendered new mechanisms for pricing products. Some titles continue to be available on subscription, particularly where the material is actually acquired in physical form as a CD-ROM or as data for local loading, and where therefore the parallel with the print environment is closest.

Increasingly, however, with the growth in network access where the material cannot be 'owned' in the same way, this has led to a substantial growth in the use of site licences. These can be for individual titles, but is increasingly being used for a range of titles either from a single publisher, or through an aggregator on a publisher or subject basis. This approach has the advantages of price predictability, it is not dissimilar to subscriptions and is therefore familiar, it is free at the point of use, there may be access to more journals than otherwise might be the case (as happened with the PSLI) and there are fewer problems of access or copyright. The key difference between subscriptions and licences is that the former works on the basis of copyright law, whereas the latter replaces this with a legal contract which supersedes copyright law (Davis, 1997). This is a key change because it makes it particularly important that such contracts protect users' rights as copyright law would have done. There is some evidence that publishers are aggressively trying to strengthen their control and weaken users' rights. Librarians in the USA have been at the forefront of moves to resist such changes (Case, 1998). While the licence concept has been welcomed in the short term, it has been argued that it can be a way to perpetuate the 'serials crisis' into the electronic future, and also of encouraging payment for journals which are not wanted,because the licence terms may restrict copyright and inter-library loan user rights (Rouse, 1997).

The option of paying per use is available from document delivery services through electronic TOC services and from products such as BioMedNet Information Services, with the payment including an element for the service and a fee to cover copyright. The same concept of pay-per-use (though this is sometimes changed to pay-per-view) is also sometimes available when a journal is mounted on the Internet but the individual or the institution does not have a licence to access the whole product. Concern about intellectual property rights has delayed such services moving into a fully electronic mode, but developments in electronic commerce are moving us towards a position where such an approach could be handled in a practical way. The advantage of this approach is that it is based on the concept that you pay only for what is wanted (the advantage always claimed for the 'access' model of library service). The disadvantage is that it is highly unpredictable and the accepted wisdom at present is that librarians cannot consider approaches which do not give predictable expenditure (Bide *et al.*, 1997).

Most of these pricing models are concerned with access to electronic journals. As has been shown earlier, there are other electronic products which raise different issues, and attention is beginning to be paid to these. For at least some time, for example, we shall be faced with the need to digitize material which is already available in printed form, and which may or may not be in print. A study for the joint JISC/PA Working Party looking at digitization issues has suggested that two charging models be adopted. The 'textbook purchase substitution' model would be a limited term licence linked to student numbers, and would be appropriate when the content involved would be the sort of material which students might buy in multiples. It would therefore be expensive, but some money might be recouped by paying for printing elements of the material. The 'library purchase substitute' would involve a perpetual licence for a one-time fee, and would be more appropriate when the material was of reference or research use. The basic charge unit in both cases would be the printed page. (Bide *et al.*, 1997).

The complexity of new information models together with the prices problem has acted as a catalyst to a process which already established itself in the United States – the rise of consortia. Originally intended as resource-sharing groupings, these have gradually taken on new functions, particularly that of negotiating deals for services and (increasingly) electronic content. The American pattern of regional consortia has been repeated here in groupings covering the Southern universities, the North East (of England) and Yorkshire, Scotland and Wales, though these are only now turning to common purchasing of electronic material. Other groupings with perceived common interests, such as the Consortium of University Research Libraries (CURL), are also considering such possibilities. The major activity has been at the national level, where the combined Higher Education Software Team (CHEST) has negotiated common terms for access to databases. The PSLI was negotiated by HEFCE on behalf of all the Funding Councils (HEFCE, 1997). Its successor, the National Electronic Site Initiative (NESLI) will, as its name suggests, focus on the electronic product, an indication of how times are changing (Friedgood, 1998). The advantage for libraries of consortia deals may be that lower prices can be negotiated (indeed in the long run, this has to be the prime purpose of such arrangements for libraries). For publishers, the advantages should be the administrative savings and the additional penetration into the market. The disadvantage for both is the potentially slow process of achieving agreement.

Consortia continue to fulfil the resource-sharing role and to move into other areas of importance for the resourcing and budgeting for electronic information. The LAMDA consortia, one of the UK eLib projects, aims to achieve lower costs for electronic document delivery and is fully operational now, although the full costs have not yet been identified. The Scholarly Publishing and Academic Resources Coalition (SPARC) in the United States is looking to develop a more competitive marketplace in the electronic environment (Case, 1998). What might be seen as the ultimate library consortium, the ICOLC, is concentrating on principles and preferred practices for library consortia in the future concerning pricing, licences, access, intellectual property and archiving (International Coalition of Library Consortia, 1998).

Running through the debate about pricing is the issue of copyright in the electronic environment, since producers will be seeking to ensure that the their rights are protected by authentication and authorization, that use of data can be tracked, security of data is guaranteed, and that they make a commercial return on the process. Where they contribute to the process, they will reasonably require payment for their work. At the same time, the evidence of rights owners aggressively advocating an increase in their rights as against those of the user has triggered such developments as SPARC and the ICOLC Statement (Case, 1998).

Resourcing and Budgeting

Infrastructure and staffing

The previous sections have illustrated some of the factors which will have to be included in considering the resourcing and budgeting of such material. These concentrate purely on the content. Other issues will also have to be considered. Amongst the areas of capital funding are such areas as the provision of appropriate network infrastructure and the availability of standard software which is required for the use of such electronic materials within both the library and the institution. The library must have an input to decisions on such matters at an institutional level. Similarly, but more parochially, the library – whether converged or not – will be a heavily IT-intensive building and service. The regular cycle of replacement of both PCs and servers will be a major funding commitment, even if it is spread in such a way as to be treated as regular recurrent expenditure. The recent introduction of charging for network traffic may also impact on the library. The growing amount of transatlantic traffic generated by information retrieval, even if it is ameliorated by the existence of mirror sites, means that information service business will contribute considerable to these costs. Institutions will differ in the way in which these are handled, but the library will certainly be involved unless the costs are handled through some other central budget.

It is likely too that changes in staffing patterns will be required in response to changing electronic developments, as the need for evaluation, for digitizing information managing access and, perhaps particularly, for developing new ways of teaching the use of these resources as a key element in information skills training as the library's role becomes more integrated with teaching and learning processes. The range of skills associated with these activities will be embedded at all levels of staff, and relationships between posts will change. This may require a different approach to staff budgeting, as greater flexibility is needed and as projects become a more common mode of developing services.

Budgeting and resourcing therefore has to take into account the infrastructure and charges which have traditionally not necessarily been part of the library budget, and to think in different ways about how the staff budget is built up and distributed

Electronic resources

The most significant changes may be required in the budgeting framework for the electronic resources themselves. Libraries, suppliers, publishers and users all tend to favour the familiar, to look for approaches which most nearly conform to the systems they have employed in the past. Where tried and tested systems work well, this is a reasonable approach. These may, however, perpetuate the weaknesses of the recent past. There are many constraints operating against change: these include patchy understanding of both the increasing failure of the existing system and the possibilities for new models, protectionism operating round scarce resources, caution amongst librarians, the immaturity of the marketplace and the fragility of new economic models. If the pattern of information does change markedly, as may happen albeit slowly over time, then there is no reason why we should expect resourcing and budgeting patterns to fit a model which is no longer dominant.

In the first place, the means by which funding is provided for information provision might be re-assessed. It can be argued that, if Odlyzko's argument that the costs and trade-offs in the scholarly communication system have to be made clear to scholars is accepted, the most straightforward approach is to adopt a system for the funding of such provision through devolution to academic units. The probable growth of services based on pay-per-use might be said to support such an approach.

However, there are a number of factors which, in practical terms point clearly in other directions. The example which Odlyzko (1997) quotes to illustrate his point about the way economic incentives operate perversely – in which an expensive journal took over from a cheaper one as the 'journal of choice' in a particular subject area because the latter (although it had lower overall costs) had page charges – indicates that the incentives for the individual scholar or team are often in direct opposition to those which should operate for the research enterprise or the institution as a whole. It is clear that the mechanisms do not exist to inform users of the complete picture in such a way that a devolved system can work more effectively than a more centrally-controlled one, and indeed Odlyzko does not argue for that change of approach.

The changing modes of provision, such as the use of aggregator services, purchasing/acquiring rights to resources through consortia mechanisms and the increasing use of licences of varying kinds all argue very clearly for a funding mechanism handled initially through a central body with specialized skills. In terms of managing the change to the new environment, the corporate shifts in provision which may be required cannot be easily handled within a funding system which is initially devolved. Central co-ordination is required to manage what is likely to be a complex meshing of purchase and licence arrangements mediated through a number of agents and suppliers.

At the most mundane level, there is little sign that, with the growing pressures on academic staff, they are likely to be able to devote the time to consider the complexities of the economics of each decision which may be required to optimize the availability of information. That task will remain one for librarians, and other ways will have to be found to ensure that scholars and those who determine budgets are made aware of the need for change and are given the background for them to understand the new marketplace.

For many years, institutions and their libraries will operate in a hybrid environment, and we are only at the beginning of the change. For that reason, methods of budgeting within library services have not changed significantly in recent years. In some cases, electronic sources are frequently handled in the same ways as their nearest print equivalents.

Book material has been handled within the book budget, periodicals along with print periodicals and document delivery along with inter-library loans. In other instances, separate budget lines have been set up to deal with these. This may have been done so that the library can control and monitor any shift towards the electronic library and possibly even to make the handling of VAT easier or, less convincingly it may simply be a reaction to new models of provision.

It remains open to question whether this will be a suitable approach for the future. It is indeed probably too early to propose new models of budgeting with any confidence because of the immaturity of economic models for scholarly information and the fact that we still operate in an environment in which print remains dominant and, while electronic provision of information is common, it has not yet achieved critical mass. The most appropriate approach at this stage is therefore to identify key issues for the future.

One of these is the need to consider the provision in a much broader financial framework. The rationale behind the JSTOR project, for example, was not only to provide access to backruns of major journals but also to enable libraries to discard print runs of these titles and thus to save capital expenditure on buildings and shelving (Guthrie, 1997). Leaving aside the political implications, libraries will increasingly have to consider capital and recurrent funding as part of the whole, represented in this case by space and content. The need for adequate bandwidth and provision of PCs on a suitable scale to make this improved access a reality is a further element in this equation.

A second issue is the possibility and likely need to shift towards thinking more routinely about cost-per-use. In a print environment based on purchase, the information on use is not available. In an environment where knowledge about use, at least in quantitative terms, is more available, then decisions about how provision is to be made between methods which involve up-front payments as purchases or through licences and those which operate on the pay-as-you-go principle can become more firmly based on evidence.

The emergence of aggregated packets of information in a variety of forms raises several issues. These may be based on a title by title approach, allowing an element of choice, or on a block basis where there may be much less, or indeed, no choice beyond the packet as a whole. In a volatile world, it is attractive to prefer models which provide groups of material for an all-in price (with administrative savings in staff time) rather than those which involve an element of picking and choosing (which is what happens just now with periodical selection). The Academic Press model in the PSLI provides access to all AP titles, though at present institutions are paying sums related to their individual current print holdings. The evidence of use shows that users have taken advantage of access to titles to which their institutions did not previously subscribe. Once the top-slicing which was a feature of the PSLI is removed, the basis of pricing for this model of provision will change. At the end of the day, librarians will have to choose whether they are willing to pay for material to which they do not need continuous access in order to gain the benefits of simplicity. In the context of ever-tightening budgets and the need to demonstrate value-for-money, this approach has at least to be questioned. One approach may be negotiating licence agreements which take account of the fact that the demand for the material included may range from heavy to zero.

The aggregators have introduced a further new element in that, by introducing a middleman between producers and users/libraries, there is a further link in the chain which affects the pricing. For the first time, a product such as a periodical title or a table of contents or document delivery service may be available through several sources: direct from a publishers, through several commercial aggregators, or possibly through specific consortium agreements. Decisions on which of these to adopt these may be based on price, on access mechanisms, on licence conditions, etc. Each library will have to determine which combinations of these provide it with an appropriate mix of material and delivery mechanisms.

Each library will of course not be making these decisions wholly in isolation. The growing importance of consortia will mean that, for most, there will at least be consultation, and at best the opportunity for negotiating appropriate pricing models and levels which provide optimal value for money for the consortia members.

The way in which services are increasingly linked means greater complexity for budgeting. Electronic TOC services with integrated provision for document delivery will involve a combination of original payments for access to the service plus a pay-as-you-go element as individual items are obtained by users. Apart from the issue of integration of these quite different payment mechanisms (which may not be a major problem in practical terms), two other things follow from this. Firstly, to what extent should we adopt pay-as you go, given the problems of unpredictability. Secondly, it also highlights the issue of 'who pays' which, although it is an issue which has been addressed in the past, will now take on a sharper focus. Both of these have of course been considered in many libraries in the context of inter-library loan, but they take on a new perspective in the electronic environment.

The same is true of provision for creating digitized texts in, for example electronic short loan collections, where eLib projects such as ACORN and SCOPE have illustrated the problems of setting up a system which can work with the requisite speed and still provide adequate return for rights owners. Possible solutions designed to meet this need are being proposed (Bide *et al.*, 1997). The important feature in terms of budgeting is that such provision introduces a new factor into budgeting within the library.

All of these will also impact on the overall budgeting structure. Many of these models of provision operate in ways which cut across the subject structure which is often used as the basis for internal budgeting, in that payment is made for groups of materials which cut across disciplinary boundaries.. Given that both good resource management and the pressure for accountability requires that some such subject approach is needed, means will have to be found to marry that approach with the realities of more aggregated and varied models of information provision. What can perhaps be said at this juncture, flowing from the variations in the way that information can be provided, is that a greater integration of budgets will be required, both at the macro level because of the increasing use of aggregators of various kinds, and at a more detailed level in the form of resources allocations. Similarly, there is a need to look at costs in a less simplistic way than has been done in the past, with a greater emphasis on cost-per-use and value for money than has been previously possible.

Conclusion

This chapter does not give answers. Indeed it could be argued that it simply raises more questions. I would respond that, while we are conscious of considerable changes, we are in reality at the beginning of a period of even more substantial change and we do not know how that will impact on all the stakeholders in the system. It is not surprising therefore that, in these circumstances, libraries have not yet developed new models for resourcing and budgeting. This chapter has therefore concentrated on identifying important features of the economic landscape of the changing information scene and identifying how these will have to be taken on board in developing appropriate funding models within libraries in the future. This will not happen quickly, because the transition to an electronic environment will probably only slowly take on a significantly new shape. Nevertheless, there are sufficient signs of new models of provision to make it likely that new funding and budgeting patterns will be required in the future.

References

Bide, M., Oppenheim, C. and Ramsden, A. (1997) *Charging mechanisms for digitised texts: second supporting study for the JISC/PA.* http://www.ukoln.ac.uk/services/papers/pa/charging/

Case, M.M. (1998) ARL promotes competition through SPARC: the Scholarly Publishing and Academic Resources Coalition. *ARL* **196**, 1–5

Davis, T.L. (1997) License agreements in lieu of copyright: are we signing away our rights? *Library Acquisitions: Practice and Theory,* **21**, 19–27

Fisher, J.H. (1995) The true costs of an electronic journal. *Serials Review,* **21**, 88–90

Friedgood, B. (1998) The UK National Electronic Site Licensing Initiative. *Serials,* **11**, 37–39

Gaunt, M.I. (1995) Literary text in an electronic age: collection development issues. *Collection Management,* **19**, 191–215

Guthrie, K.M. (1997) JSTOR: from project to independent organization. *D-Lib Magazine,* http://www.dlib.org/dlib/july97/07guthrie.html

Harnad, S. (1995) Electronic scholarly publication. *Serials Review,* **21**, 78–80

Hawkins, B.L. (1994) Creating the library of the future: incrementalism won't get us there! *Serials Librarian,* **24**, 17–47

Higher Education Funding Council for England (1997) *Report on phase 1 of the evaluation of the UK Pilot Site Licence Initiative.* Commonwealth Higher Education Management Service (HEFCE M3/97). Bristol: HEFCE

Hitchcock, S., Carr, L. and Hall, W. (1997) Web journals publishing: a UK perspective. *Serials,* **10**, 285–299

Hobohm, H.-C. (1997) Changing the galaxy: on the transformation of a printed journal to the Internet. *First Monday*, **2**, http://www.firstmonday.dk/issues/issue2_11/hobohm/index.html

International Coalition of Library Consortia (1997) *Statement of current perspective and preferred practices for the selection and purchase of electronic information.* http://www.library.yale.edu/consortia/statement.html

Jog, V. (1995) *Cost and revenue structure of academic journals: paper-based versus e-journals.* http://schoolnet2.carleton.ca/english/biz/economics/vijayjog.html

Lancaster, F.W. and Sandore, B. (1997) *Technology and management in library and information services.* London. Library Association Publishing

Marks, R.H. (1995) The economic challenges of publishing electronic journals. *Serials Review*, **21**, 85–88

Morino, M. (1996) Costs and benefits of investments in technology: how can technology serve the public interest? In *The economics of information in the networked environment*, eds. M.A. Butler and B.R. Kingma, pp.17–21. Washington: Association of Research Libraries

Nisonger, T.E. (1997), Electronic journal collection management issues. *Collection Building*, **16**, 58–65

Quinn, F. and McMillan, G. (1995) Library copublication of electronic journals. *Serials Review*, **21**, 80–83

Odlyzko, A. (1997) The economics of electronic journals. *First Monday*, **2**, http://www.firstmonday.dk/issues/issue2_8/odlyzko/

Renfro, P.E. (1997) The specialized scholarly monograph in crisis, or, how can I get tenure if you won't publish my book? *ARL*, **195**, 6–7

Rouse, K. (1997) The serials crisis in the age of electronic access. *Newsletter on Serials Pricing Issues*, 177

Schad, J.G. (1997) Scientific societies and their journals. *Journal of Academic Librarianship*, **23**, 406–407

Varian, H.R. (1996) Pricing electronic journals. *D-Lib Magazine*, http://www.dlib.org/dlib/june96/06varian.html

Case Study: A Stealthy Crusade: Resourcing and Budgeting for the Electronic Library at Southampton University

Bernard Naylor

Introduction

One day, maybe, Southampton University will have a fully electronic library, one in which the only use of paper will be to receive printouts of electronic information. That day seems unimaginably distant; no one, so far, has attached a firm date to that prediction of ultimate 'paperlessness'. In our time, therefore, managing the electronic library is about managing a process of change; the electronic library as *status quo* (if such it ever becomes) is a long way in the future.

The change we are currently seeing is one in which an increasing range of electronic services is becoming available. The experience of Southampton University Library (SUL) supports the common complaint of academic librarians, that the process is by no means a relatively simple one of substituting electronic services for more traditional ones. The level of demand is growing greatly, and matching the growing range of available electronic information products, but the demand does not arise as a result of being displaced from other non-electronic parts of the library service. The enthusiasm for paper shows little or no sign of diminishing.

SUL is also feeling the multiplying pressures on higher education, as student numbers grow and the overall level of resources declines in real terms. New approaches to the management of higher education resources are being developed. The competition for resources within the institution and with other institutions becomes ever more intense. Proposals for innovation are likely to be judged by severe cost-benefit criteria, imposed by high-level managers to whom speculative developments must be justified by the efficiencies they can deliver, or the competitive edge they can provide. Just as elsewhere in the British way of doing things, the timescale in which returns are expected is not generous. Investment for long-term success may be fine in theory, but funding councils, and teaching quality authorities are no more impressed than the City when apologies for the state of things today are embellished with promises of how things could be, given a bit more time.

Historic Background

The process of migration from the paper-based library to one in which electronic technology lies at the heart of so many services has been going on for some time. The first electronic service (for the control of circulation) at SUL was introduced more than thirty years ago. The age of access to paperless scholarly information was gently ushered in in the mid-70s when mediated online searches for scientists, engineers and medical researchers began to feature on the service menu. Although the storm clouds of financial constraint were already visible if you looked closely, that was a time when funding for innovation was easier to come by. In the Library of the mid-70s, there were already established staff positions for the support of automated library systems, and for carrying out electronic information searches.

It was also possible to make appropriate financial provision in other parts of the budget. Since the library's acquisitions, circulation and medical cataloguing systems ran on the administration computer alongside payroll and student registration, and since the university's financial control arrangements were already highly devolved, there was also a line in the estimates for computer use, against which the regular financial transfers from the library to the administration were charged. This line included provision for a 'sinking fund' to provide for the eventual capital cost of machine replacement. There was also a budget for 'computerized information services' intended to cover the costs of online searches for those who did not have a research budget against which they could be set.

Setting out the historic scene cannot disguise the fact that the surging increase in the availability and significance of electronic services has substantially altered things in recent years. It is impossible to pretend that all we are doing is continuing to make marginal adjustments to arrangements set in place over twenty years ago. The challenge of resourcing adequately the new forms of service – alongside the continuation of the existing ones – is striking ever more deeply into the heart of budgeting and resource distribution.

Funding the Infrastructure

While the overall picture is undoubtedly one of increasing financial need, there are some offsetting trends in the other direction. There is no doubt that, in real terms, the cost of the actual systems which run the main library processes of acquisition, cataloguing and circulation, has fallen, while the systems themselves have improved immeasurably in flexibility and power, and the ubiquitous OPAC has emerged, a new core service for a barely noticeable marginal cost. Furthermore, the former anxiety that there would be additional, untimely mid-term costs, as activities outgrew machine, has been soothed or even laid to rest altogether, now that additional machine memory, processing power and disk space are so cheap. However, as the cost of the hardware and software at the heart of systems has fallen in real terms, there has been an inexorable rise in the demand for the provision of peripherals. If the electronic library is to function satisfactorily, most library staff members must have access to a terminal in order to carry out their responsibilities properly, and the same demand is also quite rightly arising from the community of library users.

Some of this user demand is at present met on terminals provided partly for other purposes in the library or across the campus, as part of the institution's general IT provision. A whole bundle of resource allocation and budgeting questions is arising from this. Fundamentally, the electronic library is utterly dependent both on the adequate availability of terminals and the adequate provision of networking. So far there seems no evidence that the institution thinks it worth its while to tease out what this means in the sense of allocating the costs of terminal and networking provision correctly across the range of services which are dependent on them. This certainly does not amount to saying that provision is adequate to the need. However, provision of the networking spine (certainly) and local connectivity and terminals (to a lesser degree of certainty) are treated in financial terms as strategic matters, and funded 'off the top' as a result of institutional decisions, rather than at individual activity level.

When the university first installed its fibre-optic network, it was argued at the time that networking connectivity should be seen as an integral aspect of accommodation provision, along with heating, lighting and telephones. That demand has not been fully met; there are people who must work in offices where the connectivity is inadequate or non-existent, but they are neither in the dark nor shivering with cold. So, if it wants to provide electronic services which satisfy users' reasonable aspirations about access, the library is dependent on policies which are in the end actually funded from elsewhere in the institution, even though the library may vigorously advocate them. This is obviously part of the argument about the convergence of services, which is discussed in Section 2 of this volume.

For a library which, with respect to its budget, is not part of a converged service, the battle lines are drawn up on different terms. If they are worth their salt, senior library staff ought to be ahead of the institution's general managers in seeing how fundamental IT infrastructure provision is and will be for the future provision and future development of library service. Until recently, there was a different institutional pocket from which equipment money could be taken, namely the separate equipment grant made to each university by the Funding Council. This has always been seen as financial provision particularly needed by equipment-intensive science. When computers first began to be a regular charge on institutional finances, it was again the number-crunching demands of science which it was at first considered most important to satisfy.

Against this background, the library has found it difficult to secure acceptance that, in the institutional IT strategy, there has to be a dimension devoted to needs arising from library service development. It has, however, fought hard to establish its fundamental need for IT provision, most of all in respect of IT provision within the walls of the library. Given an institutional policy (entirely defensible in itself) which favours the dispersal of workstation provision in relatively small clusters of fifty machines or fewer across the campus, the library has had to press for recognition that mediation of Web-based services to users who need expert guidance, or group instruction of library users, or continuing enhancement of the expertise of library staff, absolutely require that workstation provision in the library should reach a certain minimal level. The tendency is rather for the institution to assume that, within an overall IT strategy, the needs of such as the library will inevitably be taken care of in an appropriate way – subject, of course, to the overall availability of resources. Handing any share of these resources to the library is not readily seen as an appropriate step to take, even in the age of the 'electronic library'. The struggle for adequate resourcing of the infrastructure requirements and especially of peripheral equipment is, therefore, on-going and ultimately a political matter, which is being fought out at institutional level.

Resourcing the Staff Needs of the Electronic Library

Provision for staffing in academic libraries has always been a more controversial matter than, say, the funding of an acquisitions budget for books and periodicals. The two equations 'spending on staff = bad, spending on books and periodicals = good' have been widely and readily endorsed by teaching staff and university administrators. At the University of Southampton, as had already been remarked, the general atmosphere of growth of the late 60s and early 70s made it possible to create posts for the support of automated systems and online information retrieval. By the early 80s, with the library's growing dependence on equipment absolutely clear to library staff, there was nevertheless a reluctance elsewhere in the institution to accept that proper arrangements for supporting and servicing this equipment were essential if the library's services were to be sustained. As we have pressed on through the 90s, it has become ever more clear that, with major services increasingly IT-based, a new approach is needed to meet the increasingly technical staffing demands thrown up by the support needs arising from the advance of the electronic library.

In so far as this support is to be found from within the library, staff must be reassigned from other functions, provided they have the competence and the commitment to fill the bill. Alternatively, the library can look to colleagues in the computing service, but may then have to accept that the priorities of the other service may not always match the library's perception as to what is most urgently needed. A third possibility is the creation of entirely new library staff positions, but, if, as previously indicated, there is institutional opposition to capital spending on the Library's IT needs, the opposition to new recurrent spending on staff is even more stern.

Electronic library services are also demanding a change in the way staff carry out more traditional professional tasks. Being a subject specialist in an electronic library environment is not necessarily the same as doing that job in a print-on-paper environment. At Southampton, the library has declared a preference for electronic services 'all other things being equal', as evidence of a commitment to the likely shape of things to come. At the micro-level, where the eventual shape of services is determined through a multitude of individual staff responses and efforts, questions of personal preference, judgments about priorities, and professional skills all play their part. The task of managing staff resources in the changing situation is complex and challenging and calls for deft handling. It is made more complex by the fact that, with the overall level of resource remaining static or declining, there is little or no possibility of deliberately introducing new staff members as catalysts for change.

In the end, however, the staff resourcing issues must probably be resolved within the library, and will involve creating a whole new cadre of staff who have an acute awareness of the potential, which electronic information has, to change the library's traditional shape. Some of these will be existing staff who have successfully adapted to these new demands. All of them will acknowledge the crucial importance of close alliance with colleagues in the computing service.

Purchasing Information

Notwithstanding problems of equipment and staffing, the 'option for electronic' is also presenting considerable resource allocation problems in respect of the purchase of materials. As early as the mid-70s, there was already a budget line for online information services. From then on, for more than ten years, it was policy to increase that budget line

disproportionately by comparison with other budget elements. But the total was so small in relation to the overall
budget that the impact was hardly noticed. When an expenditure item accounts for less than two per cent of the overall
allocation, major deliberate movements in budgeting for that
item are totally overshadowed, even by accidental over-
spends or underspends on such preponderant items as staff
or print-on-paper materials.

A major change in the situation occurred in the late 80s
and 90s. By that time, it is fair to argue that mediated online
searching had reached a plateau. Any attempt to increase the
scale of that service would have been blocked by limits on
staff resources as much as limits on spending with the data-
spinners. The major change which took place was in the
funding basis of the online services themselves. Online
searching had always been a pay-as-you-go service for the
most part. Each individual search attracted a charge for
connect time and a separate, additional telecommunications
charge. However, the offer of CD-ROM versions of online
databases presented the opportunity to make this service a
pay-up-front service, with an annual institutional subscription, allowing unlimited use by the institution's members,
subject only to observance of the terms of a licence. This
change was further reinforced by the inauguration in the
early 90s of BIDS-ISI services, different in that access to a
remote server was the basis for the service, but similar in
that an up-front payment bought permission for quasi-unlim-
ited use within the subscribing institution. Finally, the
introduction of JANET (in the mid-80s) as a national electronic network, connected to similar international networking
services, meant that telecommunications charges no longer
accrued on a pay-as-you-use basis.

For some time, this change has dominated the question of
resourcing information retrieval. The change to an annual
subscription basis placed a ceiling on library costs, which had
not been there under the pay-as-you-use regime. This in its
turn made it possible to allow end-users to carry out searches
as much as they wished, because no additional expenditure

was implied. With end-users doing their own searches, there was a massive increase in the number of searches without a commensurate increase in the demand on library staff time. In fact, a thirty-fold increase in service take-up was achieved with no significant increase in 'materials' budget or staff cover. Disregarding (for a moment) any discussion about the quality of end-user searching, this has to be counted a rare episode in the history of library and information provision.

The launch of subscription-based CD-ROM and BIDS services also brought the substitution question into focus. The claim that the electronic library has to find room to grow, alongside a paper-based service which refuses to shrink, is not one hundred per cent true. From the moment the new subscription basis became possible, the question of possible cancellation of subscriptions to paper-based reference tools, such as abstracting and indexing services, had to be on the agenda. In the Southampton context, this had the potential to foment tension between the library and teaching departments. Traditionally, the library had controlled and managed the online services. It was also in the library that the policy of encouraging electronic services had been formulated. By contrast, the library's influence over budget for purchasing more traditional materials was weaker, and correspondingly stronger in the teaching departments.

There was, and is, therefore, a difficult resource management question to deal with, a question which has a high political content. Any policy of substituting electronic resources for print resources requires the library to engage with the teaching departments in a more open debate about the overall policy of pursuing electronic options. Since the teaching departments already exercise more control of the larger funding resource currently spent on printed materials, opening a wider debate on substitution necessarily opens the possibility of handing a greater measure of influence to the teaching departments where the enthusiasm for the policy favouring the electronic library is not necessarily so great and is certainly not consistent and uniform.

Changes in Funding Methodologies

At Southampton, the funding climate has changed radically for the library in recent years. The library was formerly complete master of its own financial destiny, for better or for worse. It was funded by a central allocation from the University, from which it had to resource everything, from library attendants to the library van. A Library Committee was nominally the ultimate financial authority, empowered to monitor and oversee the library's efforts to achieve its financial targets. It had the power to vary spending proposals drawn up by the library's staff, but found it difficult to do so because it was insufficiently aware of the financial implications of various policy options.

Since the financial constraints of the early 80s, and the change from grants committee to funding council, the basis for the allocations made to universities at national level has become ever more transparent. In line with that, Southampton University has moved towards mirroring the allocation model of the funding council in its own distribution of resources. In the funding council resource allocation model, there is no explicit place for library funding as such. Library expenditure is seen as ancillary spend, appended in an unquantified amount to the money made available to support particular subject interests. Within the university itself, this has sharpened the development of the recharging model, by which the costs of support departments such as administration, the library or the computing service are seen as being charged against revenue earned by the teaching and research activities of the teaching departments.

Some of this recharging is notional, carried out by the use of comparatively arbitrary drivers such as staff or student numbers, or, in the case of estate maintenance costs, space occupied. How otherwise can you charge back the cost of looking after the grounds, for example? In the case of the library spend on books and periodicals, however, the expenditure is itself accounted for by the library according to faculty or departmental subject interests. This represents an open invitation to charge those costs back strictly in the proportions in which they are incurred, that is, as 'actuals'. This complex story is tending towards a simple conclusion. Disregarding for a moment the extensive evidence of the interdisciplinary use of library materials, teaching departments increasingly know precisely how much the library spends on 'their' books and periodicals. They also increasingly regard this money as 'their money'. Hence, they expect to play an increasingly decisive role in how much money is allocated and how it is spent.

Broadly speaking, in Southampton as in so many of the older universities, they may be seen as knocking on an open door. It has long been accepted that the library broadly speaking buys what the teaching departments recommend for purchase. Through the recharging model, however, the departments' role in determining the choice of information medium, whether electronic or printed, is being further strengthened. The question is to what extent the library can manage to harness and aggregate these diverse power centres where purchase recommendations are formulated, in order to pursue a homogeneous and harmonious policy of preferring the electronic option. At the time of writing, the library's ostensible position, of being the sole manager of its own financial affairs, is intact, but, under the surface, it is coming under increasing pressure.

In this situation, it is tempting to conclude that if something like coherent and consistent criteria are to be developed to drive this important process of change affecting forty or more departments, as unlike as music and reproductive medicine, then it has to be mainly an internal process. It can be revealed to people outside the library, but exposing it to judgment could be the prelude to a casual derailment of carefully thought out policy by casually assembled comments. At large, it has to be expected that the print-on-paper products will be spoken for in the teaching departments because they are familiar and because they are perceived to be at risk from rising prices and therefore in need of protection. Within the library, there is a continuing search for financial devices which will in effect allow continued pursuit of the agenda for change in ways which can be made to appear to have minimal effect on the main spending agenda.

The funding and control picture which has been described is not the best setting in which to develop proper decision support systems for budgetary control. In the increasingly transparent funding picture, each student counts the same amount. However, the costs of library provision in any subject area do not rise linearly in relation to numbers of students or staff, any more than teaching costs do. Formulaic models of resource allocation may be a convenient truce mechanism to bring an end to unfruitful strife between subject interests about library resource provision. But no one model has ever triumphed over any others which leads one to assume that none has any particular validity over the others. Likewise, there is a multiplicity of arguments which resourceful and clever academic staff can bring to bear against any particular methodology for judging the effectiveness of resource deployment, including deployment in favour of the electronic option. That being the case, the arguments must always be handled in a manner which takes the fullest possible account of the complexities of the political context.

Quality and Value for Money

The changes taking place do not arise solely from the development of the recharging model. Directly, it is the teaching departments which are called to account through Teaching Quality Assessments (TQA), and the Research Assessment Exercise. Indirectly, the library is also involved at every call, especially in the assessment of teaching quality. Indeed, the library has had to handle so many calls to participate in TQA exercises that it is rightly regarded by some as the best repository of experience as to how to handle those visitations. Still, the headline burden of the outcome of the visitation is carried by the subject discipline every time.

Practical experience tends to confirm that visiting TQA teams are very limited in their outlook on library matters. Either they are working to a very stereotyped model, and are therefore likely to discourage innovation and individuality, when they visit, and deter it in advance of their visit, through a foreshadowing effect, or they tend to have an outlook which reflects the particular standpoint of the library of their home institution, not necessarily the worse for that, but not necessarily the unarguably correct model to take round the country and argue for at every other institution. Electronic services however are fundamentally about change. Hence, if the major quality assessors from outside are conservative and stereotyped in their outlook, this is not usually an encouragement to put one's own library at the cutting edge of development. The safest place to be is somewhere in the middle; the safest course to follow is to ensure there is a solidity of provision in the basic services. Some of them, it is true, will be electronic, but the quality will be the quality of low risk.

In this relationship with teaching departments, it is very difficult to achieve a consistent and coherent approach to value for money. Every department comes with its own agenda, indeed with several agenda at times. The member of teaching staff whose job it is to serve as conduit of communication between library and department will approach the task with his or her own agenda. The job itself may be associated with a particular status in the department, not untypically that of the most recent recruit. This could prove, helpfully, to be the person who has most recently worked intensively with information resources, in a period of postgraduate research. However, it is a task which may be laid aside at the first opportunity, since this will signify a rise in the departmental pecking order. Finally, in the particular cycles of TQA and Research Assessment, different priorities may come to the surface in the teaching departments, priorities which do not accord with those preferred by the library, as it pursues the policy of preferring the electronic option.

A Stealthy Crusade

It would be nice to believe that universities were places in which rational systems of evaluation could be agreed and put into place and that people handling the outputs from such systems would invariably be driven by a cool and high-minded objectivity. Unfortunately that is usually not the case. In the event, handling the resource and budgeting issues of this enormously important change process is more like managing a crusade than minding a decision support system. The distinguishing characteristic of people who manage crusades is that they have a burning conviction that they are right. It is this burning conviction that carries them along when more rational considerations might inspire them to call a halt. Conviction is certainly a very desirable quality in those who are keen to involve themselves deeply in the realization of the electronic library. Crusades have been known to fail for economic reasons, but the point of failure more often lies somewhere below and beyond that fabled bottom right-hand corner of the balance sheet. Crusaders have also been known to be wrong. Success at the time may not always be the best criterion on which to judge that. Most important, crusaders are not always the best people to judge whether their cause is right. Meanwhile, whatever the ambiguities and the doubts, pursuit of the electronic option continues to occupy a very high place on the library's agenda.

CHAPTER THIRTEEN

Case study: Sheffield Hallam University

Graham Bulpitt

A National Professional University: an Introduction to Sheffield Hallam University

The University was designated in 1992 and may be characterized as a national professional university where teaching takes place within a strong environment of scholarship. Formerly Sheffield City Polytechnic, the institution is one of the six largest teaching institutions in the unified higher education sector. The University has strong links with the City of Sheffield and the surrounding region which are reflected in collaborative arrangements with local companies, the partner college network, as well as in the institution's own culture and style.

Undergraduate and diploma courses are provided across almost all disciplines (with the exception of medicine and some specialisms such as pharmacy and librarianship) and the University has a strong portfolio of postgraduate and post-experience courses – it is the fourth largest provider of taught postgraduate programmes in the UK. The partner college network includes a number of regional colleges as well as special hospitals and the UNISON Open College. There are collaborative links with universities in Europe, the Middle East, South-East Asia, the United States and Australia. Sheffield Hallam has also been the most highly rated new university in the 1992 and 1996 Research Assessment Exercises carried out by the Higher Education Funding Councils.

The professional orientation of the University is reflected in all its activities. Programmes of study are linked firmly to industry, commerce and the professions and the University's graduates have a very high employment rate. The University is the largest provider of Business and Technician Education Council awards and is the largest provider of sandwich education in Europe – Sheffield Hallam students normally spend one year of their undergraduate course in industry. The University's research is generally applied rather than theoretical in nature, and many projects are carried out in collaboration with industry. There is also an established programme of consultancy work and post-experience training programmes.

There are twelve Schools of Study which are responsible for some 23 000 students. The student profile reflects that of the broader university sector: half of the University's students are mature (i.e. over 21 years of age) and one-third are studying part-time; 4000 students are enrolled on postgraduate courses. There are some 2500 staff based on three campuses in, or near, the centre of Sheffield. The University's annual budget is approaching £100 million (Sheffield Hallam Univ., 1997).

A distinctive feature of Sheffield Hallam University has been its focus on institutional mission and strategic priorities. The institution has adopted a number of strategies which anticipate the changes currently affecting universities: the continued pressure on funding, increased competition across all institutional activities and the changing requirements of students and other users of university services.

A new academic framework has been adopted for programmes of study which develops core skills (in the context of subject competence), emphasizes student-based learning and provides enhanced student choice. Postgraduate work, consultancy and research have been developed and expanded. The Learning and Teaching Institute was established to work with academic staff on innovative approaches to course delivery.

House services and commercial activities have been consolidated into a new Facilities Directorate, which has delivered considerable economies in operations. A major part of these economies has come from a rationalization of the University estate: two small campuses have been closed, leased accommodation has been relinquished and the main city centre campus has had a major refurbishment and redevelopment programme to provide high quality, purpose-designed accommodation.

The University faces a number of challenges in the immediate future. The pressure on finance is likely to continue and will be exacerbated by a further expansion of student numbers in the sector and changes to the funding regime. As the higher education sector becomes increasingly segmented, it will be essential to maintain a distinctive institutional profile in a market where the competition will grow and will come increasingly from overseas institutions.

However, the major challenge will be to develop programmes of study so that they meet the needs of a more diverse student body. They must also be affordable within a reducing unit of resource, and quality must be maintained. Establishing the Learning Centre as a new department, and the opening of the new Adsetts Centre building on the city campus, were regarded as key strategic investments by the University in responding to these changes.

From Library to Learning Centre: the Development of the New Department

In common with many former polytechnics, library services at Sheffield Hallam had been integrated with audio-visual production services in the former department of Library and Learning Resources. When the University's internal quality review system was extended beyond Schools in 1993, the department was the first academic service to be the subject of an Area Review.

The recommendations of this exercise, which echoed many of the concerns expressed by the department's staff, were to prove highly influential in the department's development (Sheffield Hallam Univ. Academic Board, 1993). The report suggested that the level of resourcing should be increased and a clear funding rationale should be developed; the department should be a priority for improved accommodation; and that strategies should be developed for information and teaching and learning in which the Library and Learning Resources should be regarded as a key component.

At the same time, the recommendations of a Staffing Review carried out in 1992 were being put into effect (Sheffield Hallam Univ., 1992). There was a substantial increase in the number of staff and a new team structure was introduced. A new career scheme was put into place for librarians and the responsibilities and grading of all posts was reviewed. A major aim of the Staffing Review was to develop more open and responsive working arrangements which encouraged individuals to assume more responsibility for their work.

A further aim, in the context of continued budgetary pressure, was to review tasks to ensure that they were carried out by staff at the appropriate level. There had been a tendency, as demand for front-line services continued to grow (10 per cent increases year on year were common), for tasks to be carried out by staff who were more senior than the work required, and this was proving to be expensive. Targeting many of the new appointments at routine tasks liberated a considerable amount of staff time.

In September 1996 the Library and Learning Resources department was integrated with the University's Learning and Teaching Institute and some user computing provision to form the Learning Centre. The development of this new department followed the concept for the new building on the city campus, which was designated the Adsetts Centre (after Norman Adsetts, the prominent Sheffield businessman and Chair of the University's Board of Governors). A summary team structure is given in Figure 13.1.

The new building was seen as an opportunity to create a new learning environment which would anticipate changes in two key areas: teaching and learning and new technology. The rationale for the building – and the new department – was to bring together a range of provision and services which would stimulate student learning and provide practical support for academic staff in programme design and delivery, particularly the use of innovative approaches.

The Learning Centre operates across all three campuses and employs a total of approximately 250 people (including students and weekend staff), has an annual budget of some £4 million and generates income approaching £500 000 each year. Plans are currently in hand to extend the integrated model of provision to the University's second largest campus, at Collegiate Crescent, in the Summer of 1998.

After considerable debate, the term *library* was dropped from University nomenclature and *Learning Centre* was adopted to emphasize that the department would be different from a traditional library. In addition to providing an integrated physical environment, the Learning Centre contains a range of staff skills and expertise which can be used to deal with educational problems: library, computing, media production, curriculum development, educational research and project management. The integration of these skills has been supported by the introduction of a new career scheme for Information Assistants and Information Advisers, the use of project teams, the staff training programme and common working practices.

Resourcing for Teaching

The integration of services in the Learning Centre is a key element in the University's approach to teaching and learning.

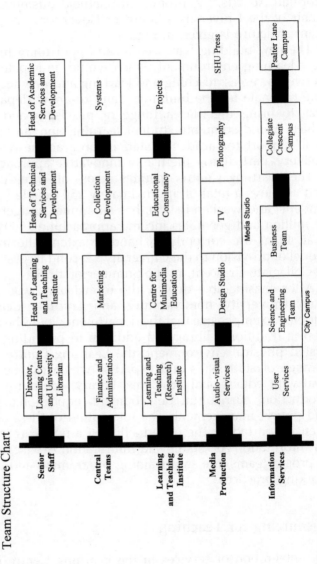

Sheffield Hallam University

Learning Centre
Team Structure Chart

Senior Staff
- Director, Learning Centre and University Librarian
- Head of Learning and Teaching Institute
- Head of Technical Services and Development
- Head of Academic Services and Development

Central Teams
- Finance and Administration
- Marketing
- Collection Development
- Systems

Learning and Teaching Institute
- Learning and Teaching (Research) Institute
- Centre for Multimedia Education
- Educational Consultancy
- Projects

Media Production
- Audio-visual Services
- Design Studio
- TV
- Photography
- SHU Press

Media Studio

Information Services
- User Services
- Science and Engineering Team
- Business Team
- Collegiate Crescent Campus
- Psalter Lane Campus

City Campus

Figure 13.1 Learning Centre team structure chart

Teaching provides over 80 per cent of the University's income, and the development of new approaches to course delivery is a priority in responding to increased pressure on funding and maintaining a high quality student experience.

The continuing trend away from classroom-based activities towards resource-based work by students reflects both educational thinking and practical resourcing problems. Independent work by students makes them active in their learning and enables them to develop the personal skills sought by employers. The Dearing Inquiry recommended that 'all institutions of higher education give high priority to developing teaching and learning strategies which focus on the promotion of students' learning' (NCIHE, 1997). In addition, the pressure on institutional funds, particularly staff salaries, encourages institutions to find alternatives to high levels of student-tutor contact.

The effect is familiar to all librarians: students spend less time in timetabled teaching sessions and increasingly depend on libraries and computer centres for their work. The annual surveys carried out at Sheffield Hallam show that 50 per cent of students visit a Learning Centre every working day during semesters – this represents 10 000 visits each day; and 92 per cent of students visit a Learning Centre at least once a week (Sheffield Hallam Univ. Learning Centre, 1997).

It is useful to place these figures in the context of the student working week. A survey of undergraduate students at Leeds Metropolitan University suggested that students spent some 30 hours each week on activities related to their course, of which only 20 per cent is spent in lectures, seminars and tutorials (Leeds Metropolitan University, 1996).

These changing patterns of teaching and learning impact at two levels on the resourcing of the Learning Centre at Sheffield Hallam University. At an institutional level, the department is seen as offering a cost-effective way to support students which could justify an increased share of teaching funds. This needs to be done on a rational basis, and the University model for the allocation of teaching funds is being examined to see if could be developed to resource student-based activities outside Schools.

At departmental level, the continuing increase in demand for Learning Centre provision and increased pressure on funds makes it necessary continually to seek new approaches to the delivery of services. The University has adopted a devolved budgeting system, where the costs of central departments are attributed back to Schools and this also places all elements of the Learning Centre budget under scrutiny.

Although the rationale for the integration of services within the department was primarily educational, the rationalization of service points for library, computing and audio-visual provision has enabled the department to control operating costs. Indeed, a number of School-based services and collections have been consolidated within the department, and accessibility to all provision has been improved through increased opening hours and staffing support. A similar approach has been taken with electronic information services, which have been used both to contain costs and deliver services more efficiently as well as improving the quality of provision.

The interaction between Learning Centre staff and students has been significantly affected by the impact of services based on communications and information technology. There is a high level of integration of front-line support by Information Advisers for the use of information and computing provision. Teaching activities by Information Specialists, which are subject to the same increases in student numbers as other teaching, have moved away from traditional activities based on taught sessions with small groups.

Introductory sessions use demonstrations of electronic information services and video presentations to explain the potential of the Learning Centre to new students; in fact, these presentations are now increasingly being used in open days to promote the University to prospective students. Information skills work is integrated as far as possible within programmes of study, with sessions often being organized in the form of drop-in database workshops. More specialized help is arranged through project tutorials with specialist staff.

Multimedia tools have also been developed to provide self-help for students. The ERiS (Electronic Resources/ Information Skills) programme provides help with using computers, finding information and identifying specialist databases, and hyperlinks from the programme to networked information services are being developed. A multimedia guide to the Adsetts Centre has been developed, which is accessible through the Campus-Wide Information Service.

A number of projects have been carried out to explore the potential of multimedia materials for teaching and learning. The multimedia development team has prepared a range of material for use by students within the Learning Centre. A variety of sources of material have been used: some material has been purchased from commercial suppliers, some has been acquired through the Funding Councils' Teaching and Learning Technology Programme and has then been customized for use by Sheffield Hallam students. A number of programmes have also been developed inhouse.

An example of a local production is the Adsetts Centre Case Study, a resource bank relating to the new City Campus Learning Centre building which includes material such as specifications, briefs and minutes, building plans, a history of the site, a record of the construction project in still and moving images and video interviews with members of the design team. This material provides a real case study for student investigations. One approach, for example, has been for teams to compare the actual performance of the building against the original specifications.

There has been a substantial growth in the number of multimedia programmes available within the Learning Centre, from four pilot programmes which were available when the department was established in September 1996 to over 40 programmes by the end of 1997. It is likely that the role of front-line staff, which has already been extended from dealing with information enquiries to supporting the use of computing services, will increasingly move towards providing learning support for students. The growth of resource-based learning will also require a greater contribution to course design and development from Learning Centre staff, for example, to identify appropriate learning materials. Distance learning programmes, which are already supported by a dedicated team within the Learning Centre, will increasingly require remote help. The increasing emphasis on the educational role of Learning Centre staff is recognized in the initial proposals for qualifications to be recognized by the proposed Institute for Learning and Teaching in Higher Education.

An integrated approach to the funding and provision of information services has been developed within the department as electronic services have grown in significance over the past few years. The funding of all information provision is now combined in a single budget head (the former 'book-fund') and approximately 30 per cent of these funds were allocated to on-demand services (such as inter-library loans and document delivery), electronic information sources and copying licences in 1997/98. The funding of support for Schools of Study and Research Institutes is also integrated, so that Information Specialists are able to buy an appropriate mix of conventional, electronic and on-demand services from a single budget allocation.

The range of electronic services available through the Learning Centre are integrated as far as possible at the PC desktop. A new library management system, due for implementation in the Summer of 1998, will enhance access to full-text documents, electronic source materials and Internet-based resources. The potential to enrich the database with externally produced records for journal articles, from a source such as the British Library's *Inside* service, is also being explored. This would provide a useful first-line tool for undergraduate students by encouraging them to track down material already in stock before requesting material held in other institutions. A similar approach has already been used with Internet information. Information staff maintain a series of home pages for each major discipline which provide hyperlinks to selected and evaluated information sources on the Internet and also make use of subject gateways such as EEVL and SOSIG.

Resourcing for Research

In common with other new universities, research activity at Sheffield Hallam has increased substantially over the past ten years, and has been stimulated by the establishment of a single university sector and the separation of Funding Council support for teaching and research. Strategically, the development of research has been linked to the need to maintain the institution's reputation as a national professional university and to underpin teaching programmes. As noted earlier, the University achieved the highest overall rating of new universities in both the 1992 and 1996 Research Assessment Exercises. The expansion of research activity is also consistent with the University's aim of diversifying its income sources – particularly to reduce its dependence on teaching funds.

The funding of Learning Centre support for research distinguishes three types of research activity. Scholarship, which is pursued by all academic staff, is included within the core allocations related to teaching in Schools. Support for contractual research is funded as a standard part of the institutional overhead. Funded research is supported from a proportion of the University's total research allocation.

The University policy on Learning Centre support for research, which was agreed in 1994, recognized that electronic and other on-demand services offered the best way forward. It was agreed that core printed material, including key journals, reference sources and monographs, should be acquired to meet the immediate needs of researchers, but it was noted that collection development would need to be highly selective, and should reflect long-term institutional priorities.

For most research needs, on-demand services, such as database searches, inter-library loans and documents in electronic form were accepted as the most appropriate solution, and the increasing amount of material available in this way has done much to overcome the limitations of the print collections. These services have been complemented by reciprocal access agreements, most notably with the University of Sheffield, which allow borrowing by academic and research staff.

Accepting the principle, reaffirmed by the Follett Committee, that 'the prime responsibility for meeting the library and information needs of researchers should continue to rest with the home institution' (HEFCE, 1993), Learning Centre staff have nevertheless supported the approach suggested in the Coopers and Lybrand Study (Coopers and Lybrand, 1997) that there should be a compensation system for the major net providers of research collections in return for providing access to all higher education researchers.

Learning Centre staff have now built up useful experience of substituting electronic information services for collections of print material. It was evident in 1994 that there would be a crisis in library support for research in science as a result of high journal inflation. The subscription costs of maintaining the existing journal collection were estimated to be over £100 000 for the 1995 calendar year – more than the total bookfund allocation for science. It was clear that a more radical solution was required than the conventional approach of trimming the number of journal subscriptions and discussions were opened with academic and research staff to agree a strategy for information provision.

The proposal made by Learning Centre staff was to reduce the journal collection to three small core collections, each costing no more than £15 000, to serve the main disciplines of physics, chemistry and biomedical sciences. It was suggested that researchers' main information requirements would be satisfied through providing desk-top access to a range of electronic information services backed up by document delivery. The proposals were accepted by the research groups who acknowledged that they would allow individuals to obtain a much greater variety of material whilst containing costs.

A number of practical arrangements were put in hand. Networking arrangements were reviewed to ensure that all staff had access to the services they required and training sessions were arranged, on a one-to-one basis if required, to develop their search skills. Some additional licences were taken out to new electronic services, and arrangements were made with a number of scientific and medical libraries for the fast supply of photocopied articles from journals. Although the British Library was used for some material, it was considered important to use a range of suppliers. A system was introduced to allow researchers to send requests for articles electronically to the Learning Centre and very fast delivery, using premium services, was offered. In fact, these were used only occasionally, since research staff were generally satisfied with the normal supply time and were reluctant to see money spent on the additional costs of fast delivery. Some material was also obtained from commercial suppliers, and it was clear from their reaction to some of the issues that were raised by Learning Centre staff at that time that they were breaking some new ground in their use of these services.

The cost of providing these on-demand services was estimated to be £20 000, which left £35 000 from the original bookfund allocation to be spent on monographs. A review was held after the first year of operation and, although many staff missed the convenience of being able to browse printed material, the new approach was generally held to be a success. It has since been extended to some other disciplines, such as engineering.

Electronic services have also been a major component of an approach to collection development being piloted with the School of Cultural Studies. This School developed a strong research profile relatively quickly, and it was necessary to agree a long-term strategy for Learning Centre support which would match researchers' ambitions and yet keep within the budget that was likely to be available.

The work with the School was designed to produce a collection development plan which would provide a framework for Learning Centre and research staff. The first step required researchers to map out, in some detail, their activities for the medium term – a five year horizon was used in the first instance. This blueprint was then used to set out the range of information provision which would be required for the research targets to be met.

Although much of the infrastructure was visualized in terms of conventional collections of books and journals, the requirement to temper ambition with realism forced staff to look carefully at alternatives. There had already been good experience with one research group of buying the *Corvey* collection of nineteenth century material on microfiche. This relatively modest purchase had provided researchers with an invaluable tool which had attracted external project funding – even though the material's format was unfriendly and tiring to use. Research staff were receptive to the prospect of new electronic services in the humanities, and the collection development plan specifies a range of information resources and services in both conventional and electronic forms. This has provided a base for planning expenditure over a number of years, which takes account of priorities as well as developments which are more difficult to predict, such as the emergence of new electronic services or opportunities to acquire collections of specialist material.

A major benefit of this work has been the improved partnership between Learning Centre staff and researchers. Good links were already in place, but the task of developing the plan has improved mutual understanding of individuals' skills and expertise. The resulting plan should also remove the potential for tensions relating to the support provided to researchers, particularly the difficulties of making provision which will keep pace with the ambitions of research staff. A further benefit is the opportunity to bid for additional funds. Everyone associated with the work has a clear picture of the resources required in this area, and is well prepared to seize funding opportunities and make joint cases.

Income Generation

Given the continuing pressure on university and library budgets, it is appropriate to conclude this case study with some consideration of income generation activities, which have been a significant element of the Learning Centre's activity (Bulpitt, 1996). In 1997/98 the department had an income target of £400 000 out of a total departmental budget of £4 million.

A range of activities is used by the department to generate income. Approximately half of the income is derived from traditional library activities such as photocopying and fines; there is, however, an established policy not to charge for mainstream services, such as reservations and inter-library loans. Such charges have been regarded as discriminating against students who need resources which are not available inhouse.

External funding for projects and consultancy activity accounts for a further £60 000 of annual income, and the remainder of the revenue comes from sales and contracts for the production of material. Sheffield Hallam University Press operates as the University's publishing house and produces a range of material for niche markets. The original rationale was for the Press to sell material produced inhouse to external markets. The former unit, PAVIC Publications, was an established supplier of materials, which had been originally developed in the School of Education, to primary and secondary schools. Sheffield Hallam University Press has now developed a number of lists for specific markets and produces material in a variety of formats, including video and audio tapes, computer software and multimedia.

Much of the material sold by Sheffield Hallam University Press is produced by specialist studios within the Learning Centre, including television, photography and graphics. The primary purpose of these units is to support mainstream teaching and research activities, and they are funded and staffed at an appropriate level to fulfil this function.

External work is carried out both to exploit spare capacity and also to generate additional income. Commercial experience is also regarded as providing an opportunity for staff to maintain a high level of skills in order to compete with other organizations, including staff based in the private sector. Experience gained from external activity, including the application of new technology to the design and production of material, can then be applied to internal projects.

References

Bulpitt, Graham (1996) Making the most of what you've got: income generation in university libraries In *Proceedings of a conference on Income generation '95: the challenge ahead (London, 14 December 1995)*. Grimsby: Effective Technology Marketing.

Coopers and Lybrand (1997) *Study of the level and costs of use of higher education libraries by external researchers*. [Carried out for the Joint Funding Councils]. Scottish Higher Education Funding Council.

Higher Education Funding Council for England, et al. (1993) *Joint Funding Councils' Libraries Review Group: Report*. (Follett Report). Bristol: HEFCE

Leeds Metropolitan University (1996) *Diary survey: how undergraduate students spend their time*. Leeds: LMU.

National Committee of Inquiry into Higher Education (1997) *Higher Education in the Learning Society*. (Dearing Report). London: HMSO

Sheffield Hallam University (1992) *Library and Learning Resources, Staffing Review*. Sheffield: Sheffield Hallam University.

Sheffield Hallam University (1997) *Annual report and accounts, 1996/97*. Sheffield: Sheffield Hallam University.

Sheffield Hallam University Academic Board (1993) *Library and Learning Resources Area Review. Final report.* Sheffield: Sheffield Hallam University.

Sheffield Hallam University Learning Centre (1997) *A report on the 1997 Learning Centre user survey.* Sheffield: Sheffield Hallam University.

Management Information

CHAPTER FOURTEEN

Overview: Management Information for the Electronic Library

Peter Brophy

Introduction

The selection and use of management information for the electronic library raises a series of issues which are very different from those posed by the management of traditional libraries. Although at first glance it may appear that all that is required is a set of data, and a series of performance indicators, which parallel traditional library requirements, research has shown that the whole concept of the 'library' needs to be redefined if management information is to be meaningful in the electronic context. Thus initial ideas that a performance indicator such as 'books issued per user per annum' might be paralleled by 'electronic documents delivered per user per annum' disintegrate once the concept of 'electronic documents' is examined. What are we to count? Perhaps where an electronic journal is structured in the same way as its printed equivalent we could count 'papers'. But what happens when the paper contains links to images, perhaps held on another server and equally accessible as separate 'documents'. Do we count the paper and all the images as one 'document', or are they separate 'documents'? What happens with a linked set of web pages? In any case, even if we could count web page accesses reliably, what is the point of the exercise? A high count might indicate that users are having difficulty, being forced to navigate around web sites and using commercial search engines to try to locate the information they need. A low count could indicate that the library has provided excellent front-end services with direct links to useful sites.

A further consideration is that electronic library services impact on traditional services, so that traditional indicators may become unreliable. For example a common indicator for the traditional library is 'number of visits to the Library per user per annum' with a high count being regarded as indicative of a good service. But if the aim is to deliver services electronically to the desktop, then having to visit the library could indicate failure.

Approaches to Electronic Library Management Information

There have to date been two major strands of research into the management information and performance measurement needs of the electronic library, one in the USA and the other in Britain. Work has also been done by the National Library of Canada, which has made a suggestion to the relevant ISO Committee (TC46/SC8) that it should develop electronic library performance indicators to sit alongside the traditional set which is to be published during 1998. Individual libraries have also been experimenting with the use of different indicators.

The major US work has been led by Charles McClure at Syracuse University. The key publication from this work, *Assessing the Academic Networked Environment: strategies and options*, appeared in 1996. It is important to note that the work addresses the whole academic networked environment, and not just the library element. The study poses the following questions as a foundation for assessing networked services:

- What is the volume and type of networking taking place on a particular academic campus?
- Who are the users that access the academic network and what types of services do they utilize?
- How much do the various types of network activities and services cost?
- How has access to and use of networked information resources and services affected teaching, research, learning, service and other aspects of traditional academic life?

The work, which is ongoing, aims to equip managers with the tools to answer these types of question by achieving the following objectives:

- to describe a range of techniques that assess the academic networked environment;
- to provide procedures for collecting and analysing the data needed to produce an assessment of the academic networked environment;
- to identify and discuss data collection issues and problems that may be encountered when conducting such assessments;
- to encourage academic institutions to engage in a regular programme of ongoing evaluation and assessment of their computing networks;
- to provide a baseline for conducting network assessments as a means for improving academic networked services.

In order to meet these objectives, the publication is divided into five parts, of which part 1 is an introductory overview. Part 2 presents guidelines and suggestions for appropriate data collection techniques, and combines both quantitative and qualitative methodologies. It may be noted that the document as a whole lays heavier stress on qualitative techniques than has been usual in the literature of performance measurement, and the document may consequently be considered to offer library managers a richer choice of evaluation techniques than has previously been available. Part 3 presents the performance measures which the original study devised, as well as six key assessment areas in which quantitative data can be collected. The measures themselves are each laid out in a standard form which includes definition, issues, data collection, data analysis discussion and additional suggestions, while the six areas suitable for qualitative assessment techniques include:

- users: the number and types of users of the network and the frequency of their use;
- costs: the total and types of financial resources necessary to operate the network;
- network traffic: amounts and types;
- use: amounts and types;
- services: the applications which are available on the network;
- support: the types of assistance which are available to network users.

Part 4 of the manual addresses the importance of user surveys in network assessment, and links back to the discussions of data collection methods earlier in the work. Part 5 summarizes the importance of ongoing assessment and suggests directions for further research.

Further work in this area by McClure *et al.* was reported verbally to an Expert Workshop for the *Management Information for the Electronic Library (MIEL)* Programme at the University of Central Lancashire (see below), held in May 1997. In addition, the Coalition for Networked Information (CNI) launched a programme of field-testing of *Assessing the*

Academic Networked Environment in March 1997, involving a range of institutions, including universities institutions and community colleges. Interestingly, Kings College London is a member of the group.*

Work by Brophy *et al.* at the Centre for Research in Library and Information Management (CERLIM) at the University of Central Lancashire initially and currently at the Manchester Metropolitan University has been reported in two formal reports to JISC and in a number of conference papers. The work has been undertaken partly under the UK Higher Education Funding Councils' (HEFCs') Joint Information Systems Committee (JISC) Electronic Libraries Programme (eLib) and is continuing with part funding from the European Commission's Libraries Programme and from other sources. This work is described in the next section.

It is also worth considering in this context the approaches taken by publishers and other commercial information suppliers when they offer electronic products. In order to arrive at appropriate charging regimes they must find ways to measure the amount of use being made of their services. At present a very wide range of mechanisms are used, including charging by connect time, by items downloaded, by session and by the number of users permitted simultaneous access. The economic models behind these charging policies are complex and not always well understood in what is a rapidly evolving marketplace. Work in this area will undoubtedly influence the future development of management information systems for the electronic library.

The MIEL Programme

The MIEL Programme has been underway at CERLIM for some time. MIEL, as presently conceived, has five major phases:

- MIEL1, a Scoping Study carried out under the eLib Programme, which included an expert seminar attended by UK university librarians with experience in the field of performance measurement. The Scoping Study recommended a basic model for work on this subject. Briefly this would involve consideration of the needs of library managers for management information in support of three functions: operational, or day-to-day, management; forward planning; and evaluation and review, and would develop indicators appropriate to these requirements;

- MIEL2, a follow-on to the Scoping Study, which was funded as a Supporting Study under the eLib Programme. Because of the JISC funding for this work, it was tied very closely to the earlier, traditional library performance indicator report from the Joint Funding Councils' Ad-hoc Working Group on Performance Indicators for Libraries, known as *The Effective Academic Library* (1995). The Report on the MIEL2 Study (Brophy and Wynne, 1997) has been published recently on the Web (see http:www.ukoln. ac.uk/models/studies/). Its key results are described in Section 5 below;
- MIEL3 consists of international standards activity designed to provide agreement on electronic library performance indicators, paralleling work on traditional indicators by such bodies as ISO and IFLA. This work is being funded by the European Commission as part of the larger EQUINOX Project which will run from 1998 to 2000;
- MIEL4 is examining the issue of management information requirements in co-operative networked electronic environments such as clumps and hybrid libraries;
- MIEL5 is researching the management information needs which arise when electronic libraries are delivered to dispersed and remote populations, with particular attention to the provision of services through multi-agency agreements – for example these might include university and further education college libraries, public libraries and community centres or schools.

The last two phases are still very much at the preparatory stage.

MIEL also relates to a number of ongoing projects in CERLIM, most notably in the area of quality management. Again, this work has received funding from both the British Library and the European Commission and a number of papers (e.g. Brophy and Coulling, 1997) and a book (Brophy and Coulling, 1996) have been published.

Models of the Electronic Library

In order to develop an approach to management information for the electronic library, Brophy and Wynne (1998 and in process) have been undertaking a theoretical model development exercise. One formulation of this model is shown below in Figure 14.1:

Resource Discovery	Resource Delivery	Resource Utilization	Infrastructure Provision
Resource identification Location identification	Request Acquire Deliver to user	Exploitation tools	Space Equipment Networks Support services
← .... **Resource Management** .... → Prioritization, Budget control, Value for Money			

Figure 14.1 A model of the electronic library

If we assume that the principal role of the academic library is to enable its users to identify, locate, gain access to and use the information they require, then the 'electronic library' may be identified and characterized by a series of five functions:

- it provides tools* which enable users to view the 'electronic information landscape', through the sources of metadata which have been provided either directly by the

---

*   By 'tools' we include (human) advisory services as well as IT-based mechanisms.

library or to which it provides access. This is a 'resource location' or **'resource discovery'** process. It may be seen as a two stage process of *resource identification* and *location identification* i.e. the user may identify a resource and then identify a location which holds it. The second locating process may be left to the library to perform (as when a user completes an inter-library loan request but does not specify a holding location);

– it provides tools which enable users to gain access to the information which they have identified as being of interest to them. This is a 'resource provision' or **'resource delivery'** process. In some cases resource delivery may be a three-stage process, whereby the user, having discovered an item, first requests it, the library then acquires it, and the library then delivers it to the user – this is the classic traditional library process expressed, for example, in a reservations or inter-library loan service. In an electronic context these processes are usually, but not always, concatenated;

– it provides tools which enable users to exploit the information content to which they have been given access. This is a **'resource utilization'** process. In an electronic context the tools will include word processing, spreadsheet and database software together with filters and specialist display software such as Adobe Acrobat;

– it provides, possibly through third parties, the physical infrastructure and support services which users need to exploit information resources. This is the **'infrastructure provision'** process. One of the functions of the electronic library will be to provide network infrastructure, PCs, printing facilities and so on. It will also provide support in the form of helpdesk and advisory services.

Finally, the electronic library has management structures and procedures which ensure that the resources available to it are used to provide the maximum possible value for money to its users. As part of the management function, decisions will be taken on which resource discovery tools to provide, on how specific resources should be delivered (for example, should they be held locally or accessed from remote servers?) and on which tools should be provided to enable users to exploit the information. In addition, managers will provide procedures to handle the economic and legal aspects of information provision. As identified in the MIEL1 Scoping Study, it is helpful to consider this management requirement under three headings:

- **operational management**, by which is meant the detailed day-to-day organization and control of services and resources, including the management of exception conditions as they arise;
- **forward planning**, which includes the medium to long term planning of services and resource requirements and requires the extrapolation of current trends, an analysis of the external environment and the ability to carry out "what if?" analyses;
- **evaluation and review**, which requires analyses of recent and current activity, with close reference to user requirements and user satisfaction, and increasingly looks to comparisons with similar service providers elsewhere (whether through formal benchmarking or more informally).

If these management tasks are placed alongside the model of the electronic library outlined above it is possible to draw up a grid of management decision types (Figure 14.2) and to start to identify both the datasets needed to provide management information and the performance indicators which may derive from them.

For example, an operational manager concerned with resource discovery might want to monitor utilisation of PCs in the Library to ensure that numbers were adequate. The forward planner might be interested in tracking the changes in use of different services over time so as to plan future provision. The evaluator/reviewer would be examining data on user satisfaction with each aspect of the service.

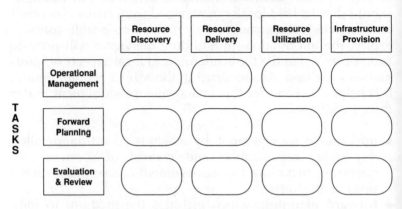

Figure 14.2 Grid of management decision types

Work at CERLIM on modelling is continuing and the basic electronic library model described above has been refined as shown in Figure 14.3 below.

This expansion of the model takes into account the need for a continuing process of access negotiation, an element of resource capture and storage (for example in mounting CD-ROMs on the network), explicitly recognizes the provision of advisory services and adds in a function concerned with resource preservation. At the time of writing this model was still being developed and as the earlier model informed the MIEL2 work described below it is not discussed in more detail here. Its main implication for the MIEL Programme's work is to indicate areas where some further development and definition of datasets and indicators is needed.

Access Negotiation	Resource Capture and Storage	Advisory Services	Resource Discovery	Resource Delivery	Resource Utilization	Infrastructure Provision	Resource Presentation

Figure 14.3 CERLIM modelling

One of the key issues identified in MIEL2 was that in the electronic environment it is necessary to find new, reliable indicators of 'service provided'. For example, use of electronic services could be measured by reference to connect time, number of sessions, number of concurrent sessions, number of hits, cost, number of active users or a variety of other factors. Care has to be taken with each of these possibilities, since it is quite likely that each could be affected by irrelevant and indeed uncontrollable variables. For example, connect time may well depend on network response times outside the control of the individual library, while if number of hits was used to measure the value of a library's own database, the result could be a drastically lower value if a cache came into use – even though the service was of great value.

After a great deal of discussion, including a debate at the Expert Workshop referred to above, the CERLIM team chose to use as its principal measure the number of sessions (or a variant on it). This has a number of advantages:

- it is time- and process-independent, in that it measures each occasion a user tries to do something (find information or whatever) rather than how (in)efficient they are at it or how they go about it, or whether the network infrastructure is efficient;
- it enables sub-measures to be defined easily (e.g. by internal department);
- it gives an (admittedly rough) idea of comparative use between services;
- it gives the possibility of building up time series, although clearly only with great care;
- it may facilitate inter-institutional comparisons, especially where the same service is provided to a number of institutions (as with JISC Dataservices such as those offered by BIDS).

However, it is recognized that relying on sessions can only be a temporary expedient. If 'push' technologies become common, it is difficult to see how the concept of a session can survive.

Management Information Datasets and Performance Indicators

Using the analysis outlined above, a number of datasets and performance indicators were identified by the CERLIM team as being of potential application to the electronic library. Selected examples are given below to indicate the type of management information which is likely to be required.

Management Information for Operational Management

A process model approach (in which inputs become outputs through the application of processes) may be particularly appropriate since at the operational level the key issue is to manage the use of resources (people, money, information, and so on) through processes to produce outputs (books lent, web pages accessed, etc.). To some extent operational management will also concern itself with outcomes – the effects of its outputs. However, in general indicators will be concerned with tracking the amount of service being provided per unit of resource (e.g. in the traditional library, books issued per member of staff employed at the service desk). They will also facilitate 'what if?' comparisons to enable alternatives to be explored. The MA/HEM tool is a good example of a software product which enables such comparisons to be made to assist alternatives to be evaluated (SCONUL, 1996).

Increasingly, operational managers are putting in place Service Level Agreements (SLAs) which define the type of service and the extent of that service, both in relation to internal and external customers. It is to be expected that each SLA will require one or more performance indicators to be devised in order for both the provider and customer to monitor compliance.

The actual indicators chosen by operational managers will be a matter for local decision, although the acceptance of common measures, as when JISC services report the number of sessions with a particular dataset, will facilitate inter-institutional comparisons if used with care. Thus, for example, the lists of institutional total accesses in datacentre annual reports may raise questions for management about usage levels (see http//:www.jisc.ac.uk for access to datacentre information and reports).

It is useful for operational managers to consider their choice of indicators in relation to the five-fold functional model of the electronic library presented earlier (although, as noted above, this may need to be extended further).

Resource Discovery

In this category we include bibliographic sources, other indexes and tools such as Web crawlers. There are two key issues here:

- the range of such resources, which defines the 'map' provided to users of the information landscape and therefore limits the landscape features to which they can gain access;
- the quality of such resources, equivalent to the accuracy and scale of the 'map', which defines whether items can be retrieved and, if they are retrieved, whether they are accurate, reliable, and so on.

For operational management it can be assumed that the range of resources has been planned to meet as much demand as the resources available permit. The issue will be to manage the use of those resources. Therefore, the basic indicator for resource discovery services will be

Sessions per service per time period

Complemented by

User satisfaction with service results

the latter enabling the manager to monitor whether the quality of each service is adequate. Time periods will vary according to the need of the manager but might typically be a month for counts of sessions or longer for user satisfaction measures. These indicators should form the basis of the performance indicators used for operational management of resource discovery.

Resource Delivery

The indicators used for resource delivery will again depend, of course, on the services offered. As in resource discovery (and recognizing the overlap between the concepts) the 'sessions per service' and 'user satisfaction' indicators will be central. Each service (i.e. each external dataset to which access is provided, each internal dataset including CD-ROMs) will thus be defined in a similar manner. Where it is possible to do so, it may be desirable to maintain a parallel indicator:

Items downloaded per service per time period

Some services, such as Web pages, are not amenable to this type of analysis (see above) and there are severe problems in defining the concept of an 'item' or 'document' in the context of electronic resources. Any attempt to measure activity of such information services must be taken with extreme care, especially if a time series is being compiled. As an alternative, for services where 'items' cannot be defined and 'sessions' is inappropriate or cannot be measured, it may be necessary to use

Number of 'hits' per service per time period

where 'service' could include objects such as web pages. It may be noted that McClure and Lopata suggest this type of measure as a means of indicating use of network applications (e.g. word processing packages) over time. This is a particularly appropriate indicator for 'front end' services, such as Web pages provided by the library and giving links to high quality Web resources, where the effects of caching etc. are likely to be less pronounced (although again they cannot be ruled out).

Resource Utilization

Under this heading managers may wish to have information on the availability of tools which users need to exploit resources (such as personal bibliographic software) and the extent of use of those tools. Therefore it may be helpful to define two indicators:

User satisfaction with resource utilisation tools

Percentage of users using each tool

The first indicator will provide information on whether the right range of tools is available: the second on the utilization (or market penetration) of each.

Infrastructure Provision

Operational managers will need information on the adequacy and use of the infrastructure provided. This will include whether sufficient workstations are available, whether the network is adequate and reliable, whether support services are available and adequate and so on. The type of measures required will be:

Queuing times for access to workstations

Downtime (as percentage of total time) per month

Availability (as percentage of attempted accesses) per month

'Downtime' can be defined as the amount of time that the service is not available to users, either through planned hardware/software maintenance or through a system/network crash. 'Availability' is slightly different, as it measures 'immediate access', which may be denied where the library subscribes on the basis of a limited number of concurrent users, even though the physical connection is available.

Another useful measure will be to assess output generated by monitoring print, still a favourite form of output with most users:

Pages of print per time period

One of the key services for the electronic library is the provision of some kind of 'help desk' service. In general it will be necessary to monitor this through the collection of data on amount of activity and on user satisfaction. The latter may be measured by a negative, 'number of complaints' received, although this will not generally be satisfactory. So, for operational service management, there might be two indicators:

Number of enquiries received per time period

User satisfaction

Forward Planning

Forward planning will encompass a considerable amount of 'intelligence' gathering concerning the environment in which the library operates (both in institutional and broader sectoral and societal terms) and likely developments which will have an impact on the library service. In respect of the electronic library the rate of change will make qualitative measures, and especially assessment of such issues as relevance, currency, etc., vital. It will be important that the manager of the electronic library maintains a 'technology watch' function to predict the impact of new technologies and new products on the services offered.

To an extent forward planning will also depend on the extrapolation of current trends, and it is in this area that hard management data may be of most use. Typical data in this category might be:

- changes in the size and composition of the market;
- extrapolation of market penetration;
- extrapolation of individual service usage.

For example, the manager may wish to develop a set of time series of the type shown below (using year 0 as the current year):

Size of market
Number of students in years -2, -1, 0, 1, 2, 3 . . .
Number of staff in years -2, -1, 0, 1, 2, 3 . . .

Market penetration
Proportion of students as active users in years -2, -1, 0, 1, 2, 3 . . .
Proportion of staff as active users in years -2, -1, 0, 1, 2, 3 . . .

Resources
Available budget for services in years -2, -1, 0, 1, 2, 3 . . .
Available budget for staff in years -2, -1, 0, 1, 2, 3 . . .

Use of services
Total number of sessions in years -2, -1, 0, 1, 2, 3 . . .
Number of sessions per service type in years -2, -1, 0, 1, 2, 3 . . .

Cross-sectoral data will be important for forward planning, both to enable comparisons with the sector as a whole to be made and to point up particular issues which may indicate that the local service will need to consider a new approach or new service. More generally benchmarking approaches, using data from the local and comparative libraries (or a carefully constructed group of comparator libraries) will be important. It is worth stressing that performance indicators must be used to *indicate* issues that the manager needs to address, not to build up spurious league tables which then form the manager's real agenda.

Evaluation and Review

The aim of the CERLIM team was to build on the approach taken in *The Effective Academic Library*, which uses a five-fold structure to gauge overall library effectiveness, as shown below:

Overall Library Effectiveness =
- P1 Integration
- P2 Quality of Service
- P3 Delivery
- P4 Efficiency
- P5 Economy

McClure (1997) has suggested that a similar set of criteria might be appropriate for the electronic networked environment, as follows:

- Extensiveness;
- Efficiency;
- Effectiveness;
- Service Quality;
- Impact;
- Usefulness;
- Adoption.

A major issue will be the definition of the boundaries of the 'electronic library'. For example, an important aspect to be considered in reviewing services will be the assessment of user satisfaction with the IT infrastructure, since without adequate infrastructure services cannot be delivered. So the manager will need to assess:

- satisfaction with end-user equipment (e.g. is a PC available and if so is it of adequate specification?);
- satisfaction with end-user software (e.g. is Adobe Acrobat available to enable .pdf files to be manipulated?);
- satisfaction with network performance (e.g. availability, response times).

This immediately brings into focus issues like convergence: is the service that the user receives a 'library' service or a 'library + IT' service? If it is the former, what happens when the infrastructure severely constrains the service being offered? Should the user be forced to differentiate between content and infrastructure? Or does a user-centred approach force service convergence?

In developing management information and performance indicator definitions for this type of decision, the CERLIM team undertook in-depth analyses of a number of issues. What, for example, do we mean by the 'effectiveness' of the electronic library? The number of electronic documents downloaded (even assuming that we have managed to resolve the definitional problem of what an electronic document is) cannot be regarded as an indicator of effectiveness. Unlike, for example, a traditional inter-library loan service, where it is reasonable to assume that the majority of items delivered will have some value to the user, this may not be the case in the electronic environment. For example, Web pages are accessed to determine their relevance (they currently act as their own metadata), are accessed accidentally, or are used as a route to other information. Furthermore, it often matters little to the library how many items are accessed since so many services are now provided under unlimited access contracts and released to users as 'free at the point of use'. The same argument applies even where licence restrictions allow access only to a specified number of concurrent users.

The CERLIM team concluded that what is important to the user is the *range* of resources available and their *depth*. These issues should therefore form the focus of effectiveness indicators. They are equivalent to indicators of the range and depth of traditional library collections.

The team therefore suggested that, for UK academic libraries which are offered subsidized subscriptions to a wide range of JISC datasets, a useful indicator might be

Proportion of JISC datasets available to users

Clearly such an indicator would need modification outside the confines of UK academia, but the principle of defining a 'basket' of relevant electronic services and examining the proportion to which a particular library's users have access remains valid. To balance this indicator, it might also be useful to count major services available to users:

Total major electronic subscriptions

which will be the total numbers of

JISC or equivalent dataservice subscriptions
Networked CD-ROMs (or equivalent)
Commercial service subscriptions (above an agreed threshold value)
etc.

As in *The Effective Academic Library*, consideration was given to measures of efficiency. For example, it might be useful to calculate performance indicators such as:

Total library expenditure/PC hours used per time period

Total major subscriptions/FTE staff numbers

Total expenditure/Total major subscriptions

A considerable number of other indicators were suggested and will be found in the MIEL2 Report (Brophy and Wynne 1997).

Conclusions

Management information and performance indicators for electronic library services are as yet in their infancy. Recent work has identified what may be key indicators and the datasets which would support them, but as yet there has been no rigorous testing of these suggestions. Further work is clearly needed to validate the chosen indicators and to extend the initial set. The MIEL Programme will provide a focus for this work, particularly in the EC funded EQUINOX project (MIEL3) which will bring a European focus to the work and will involve a wide variety of different types of library.

Because electronic libraries are an emerging concept it is to be expected that definitions of management information and performance indicators will change as experience is gained of the management challenges that these new libraries represent. To add to the complexity, the dominant concept may in fact be that of the 'hybrid' library, serving its users by offering a managed range of print, video, audio, electronic and other services supported by staff with a wide range of expertises. Managing such services will represent a major challenge, in the achievement of which the availability of suitable management information will be an essential support.

References

Brophy, P. and Coulling, K.C. (1996) *Quality management for information and library managers.* London: Gower.

Brophy, P. and Coulling, K. (1997) Quality management and benchmarking in the information sector. In *Quality management and benchmarking in the information sector.* ed. J. Brockman, pp.33–119. London: Bowker-Saur.

Brophy, P. and Wynne, P.M. (1997) *Management information systems and performance measurement for the electronic library.* Final report.

Bristol: JISC. (http://www.ukoln.ac.uk/services/eLib/papers/ supporting) (Printed version published by LITC, South Bank University, 1998)

Brophy, P. and Wynne. P.M. (1998) Libraries without walls: from vision to reality. In *Libraries without walls 2: the delivery of library services to distant users, 17–20 September 1997, Molyvos, Mytilene, Greece*. London: Library Association Publishing.

Brophy, P. and Wynne, P.M. (1998) Performance measurement and management information for the electronic library. In *Northumbria international conference on performance measurement in libraries and information services, 7–11 September 1997*. Newcastle: Information North.

McClure, C.R. (1997) Information services in the networked environment: recent evaluation efforts, methods, and future prospects. *Paper prepared for the expert workshop on management information in the electronic library, University of Central Lancashire, UK, May 16 1997*.

McClure, C.R. and Lopata C.L. (1996) *Assessing the academic networked environment: strategies and options*. Washington: Coalition for Networked Information.

SCONUL (1996) *MA/HEM. Methodology for access/holdings economic modeling: acquisitions decision support tool. User manual*. London: SCONUL.

Managing the Just-in-Time Library

CHAPTER FIFTEEN

Overview: Managing the Just-in-Time Library

John Blagden

The buy or borrow decision lies at the heart of many of the management issues surrounding the electronic library. What librarians in all sectors, across all developed countries are having to grapple with is how far do we travel down the virtual library road, in which all required information is delivered to a user's personal computer? This virtual scenario raises many questions, including:

- is this what users want and, more importantly, is this what users need?
- is it technologically feasible?
- is it affordable and, conversely, can UK universities compete effectively if they fail to capitalize on the enhancements to information access and delivery that new technology can confer on academic staff and students?

The virtual library debate has, of course, developed a great deal of discussion, with Miksa (1989) baldly stating that 'A library, if anything, is a collection. If there is no collection there is no library.' This, of course, is in contrast to the concept of the 'library without walls', but in reality the debate is really about altering the mix between local holding and access. Beardman (1996) defines, in much less dramatic terms, these two approaches in the context of journals:

- Ownership model – a higher level of subscriptions supplemented by traditional inter-library loan;
- Access model – a lower level of subscriptions supplemented by rapid document delivery services.

It should be emphasized here that the ownership model appears to be the dominant way of managing UK libraries at present. According to SCONUL (1997), the percentage of inter-library loans of all lending is running at 2.2 per cent and has been around this level for some time now. So around 98 per cent of lending is from within the stock of the individual library. It is interesting to note here that Parry (1997) maintains that in public libraries the figure is even higher, with only 0.12 per cent of total lending being accounted for by inter-library loans. These figures are in sharp contrast with the figures at Cranfield University which, on the campus which is admittedly exclusively postgraduate, the figure is 17.3 per cent (Blagden,1997b). Approaching 1 in 5 requests go outside at Cranfield, whilst the norm for the sector is 1 in 50. It should be stressed here that the purpose of these comparisons is not to suggest that any particular approach is right or wrong, but to use it as a diagnostic tool – this is how we compare with other institutions. What can we learn from this?

One apparent paradox here is that although the general level of inter-lending is low when compared with the volume of borrowing from stock, the user success rates in using local stock leave a lot to be desired. Line (1996) reports that availability studies in both the UK and USA have shown that only about 70 per cent of material requested is held in the library and that only 60 per cent is available at the time it is requested. Some university libraries in Canada (Oral presentation made at the 1997 SCONUL annual meeting) try to set service targets for different groups, e.g. 100 per cent self-sufficiency for undergraduates, with lower figures for post-graduate students and faculty. The paradox that does emerge is, of course, how are all of these unfulfilled requests being satisfied if inter-lending is at such a low level?

Later in this chapter, data will be reviewed that will present an overwhelming case for many more libraries placing a greater reliance on inter-library loans – the just-in-time, rather than the just-in-case approach. Just-in-time pre-supposes of course that the requested item is used, but clearly in some instances the requested item will be hoarded on a just-in-case basis. However, as more and more libraries cancel journal subscriptions, so the subscription price for these journals will continue to rise above the rate of inflation, leading to even higher subscription prices. Publishers will, of course, want to maintain their revenues and if most UK university libraries were to embrace fully the just-in-time approach, the residual holding libraries could face huge price rises. This in turn could lead to the holding libraries, including the Document Supply Centre (DSC), charging much higher prices for copies and/or the publishers increasing their copyright fees. Carrigan (1995) quotes 150 US dollars deliberately to discourage the just-in-time approach. He concludes that the just-in-time model will succeed providing it does not become too successful. Bernard Naylor (1994) also warns that

'If just in time carries no penalty or delay in the electronic environment, it seems obvious that the balance of cost and price between just in case and just in time provision, will have to reflect this. Each type of access will have to generate its own reasonable share of the revenue needed to keep the information source economically viable. The possibility of getting from a remote source a 'fair dealing copy' of an article without paying the publisher, will have to be curtailed.'

As Maurice Line (1996) notes, the costs of access and ownership are not stable' and he suggests that charging the full costs of document supply will become the norm, implying significant increases in document supply prices in the medium term. It should be noted here that this debate about access *vs.* local holding is largely conducted in terms of scientific, technical and medical (*STM*) journals and this will be the focus of this contribution.

However, before examining in detail the strong case for the just-in-time approach, it is worth examining some of the contextual factors in which these decisions are made. The Joint Funding Councils Review (1994, pp.1–21), which is also known as the Anderson report has recognized that 'it is neither feasible nor desirable to expect each institution's library to provide for all the research needs of its staff and students.'

The report goes on to argue however of the danger of some institutions 'free loading' on the system. What appeared to emerge from a LINC (Library and Information Co- operation Council) conference on the Anderson report (1996, pp.1–69) is that there is a need for a national policy which can discourage free loaders whilst at the same time ensuring that *bona fide* users are not denied access to the nation's library resources.

Free loading does pre-suppose that there is a case for some statutorily enforced standards for local holding which is totally at odds with the high degree of autonomy that universities enjoy. Free loading also needs to be defined – is paying for inter-library loans free loading? Free loading has to be seen in the context that most library resources are provided out of public funds and is there not a case, therefore, for more liberalized access to these collections as the Joint Funding Councils' libraries review (HEFCE, 1993) partly suggests (this is also known as the Follett report). It is interesting to note here that this cannot be seen simply as a higher education problem. One illustration of this is the large amount of use that students make of public libraries, reference to which is made in the Apt report (1995). What is clearly happening in the electronic library is a huge explosion in electronic activity. Figure one, drawn from Cranfield data, demonstrates this (Blagden, 1997b) and it should be emphasized that these figures exclude access to the Internet, the online public access catalogue and a number of other

Table 15.1 Increase in electronic access

Mode	Cost (£)	No. of searches/sessions
Dial-up (1987–88)	30,000	1,000
CD-ROM (1995–96)	37,000	15,000
BIDS (1995–96)	5,000	4,783

Note: 20-fold increase excluding access to internet, Opac and other service

electronic services. It is not unreasonable to suggest that a 40-fold increase in electronic access over a ten-year period is in the right ball park and this is at an institution where student and staff numbers have remained pretty well constant during that period. Electronic access is going to continue to increase demand and this is going to put more strain on university libraries, perhaps pushing them further down the access road.

The higher education (HE) sector has, of course, successfully used its purchasing power to negotiate preferential deals for accessing information via its BIDS (Bath Information Data Services) facilities. This is funded by a combination of top sliced money and institutional subscriptions, but the impact is of increased access at lower cost.

BIDSs primarily delivers electronic databases which, of course, will inevitably lead to increased demand for items unless that demand is artificially constrained by price or some other mechanism (i.e. request limits). One of the possible suggestions for the lack of growth of inter-library loans is that demand is being artificially constrained in this manner. Line (1996) argues against this:

'For a library to charge users for access [to inter-library loans] other than a small fee to deter frivolous use is to penalise them for poor selection. It is no more logical than charging them for use of the stock in the library. In any case, if users are charged a realistic price why should they go to the library at all?'

Burke and McGuinness (1997) however, report that in four Irish libraries surveyed, all users were expected to pay for inter-library loans. This apparently was based on the some-what dubious premise in my view, that 'materials obtained from outside the library are not considered a core element of the library service'. They also report that there is little evidence of a switch to access in Irish university libraries, but this is a somewhat self-fulfilling prophecy as clearly charges will inevitably deter a significant amount of demand. The issue here is whether charges will eliminate trivial requests as Line (1996) suggests or whether it will deter legit-imate requests. This issue of triviality is a difficult area and is certainly counter to the spirit of unfettered academic enquiry which perhaps some universities still encourage. There is, of course, a danger that if prices are not imposed demand will explode and many articles may be acquired on a just-in-case basis which may, in the medium term, destroy the economic advantages of the just-in-time approach anyway.

Although this discussion has focused on the current access model in which items are identified via a bibliographic data-base, sooner rather than later STM journals will be available in full text. The problem at the moment is that a large propor-tion of journals are not available electronically and those that are, are delivered in a multiplicity of different modes via a bibliographic database, via subscription agents and direct from the publisher. Not only are a number of journals still only available in print form, but this fragmentation of delivery modes means that take up is inevitably somewhat slow.

This move towards full text journals was recognized by the UK university funding councils when they set up the Pilot Site Licence Initiative. This Initiative is still under way and involves four publishers: Academic Press Ltd, Blackwell Publishers Ltd, Blackwell Science Ltd and the Institute of Physics Publishing Ltd who have made some of their jour-nals available to the HE sector. The preliminary evaluation of this scheme (HEFCE, 1997) has recently been published in which the question is posed as to whether this £2 million investment has resulted in more use. This in itself is not an easy question to answer as both Brophy and Wynne (1997) and Goldberg (1997 private communication) make clear. There are a number of issues identified in this report:

- the experiment was based on publishers' output rather than user information need – a subject approach might have been preferable;
- the need for a common licence;
- the problem of network congestion;
- the need for a good IT infrastructure and good user support;
- the need for a common user-friendly interface;
- the threat of the imposition of value added tax on electronic delivery;
- the problems of copyright.

The report also claims that 80 per cent of publishers' costs are in the acquisition, reviewing and sub-editing of papers so electronic publication only has a limited contribution to make to reducing costs. Kutz (1992), however, estimates that if a journal were not transformed into paper copy at all, savings of 30–35 per cent could be achieved. Publishers are, of course, proceeding very cautiously here and the Site Licence Initiative (HEFCE, 1997) report describes an arrangement in Ohio where 40 university libraries have negotiated extensive electronic access, but only by guaranteeing the levels of existing print subscriptions. This, of course, is because publishers wish to maintain revenues, but it is doubtful whether electronic access to full text will really take off unless a bolder view is taken. One opportunity for publishers is to take advantage of the cost savings by only delivering electronically and reaching a wider market by charging on a pay as you go, i.e. just-in-time basis. Revenues for this access would go to the publishers, although these might have to be shared with a partner who would be responsible perhaps for ensuring seamless access to many different publishers' output. This would, of course, divert revenues away from such document delivery agencies as the

DSC, with possible adverse consequences for the UK HE library sector. McGrath (1997) has estimated that if the DSC loses 100,000 requests a year, 7.5 pence will need to be added to the cost of a DSC request in order to recover relatively fixed overheads. The possible demise of printed copy also raises the issue of archiving – how can access to retrospective files be maintained in the long term? Clearly there are other technical issues, i.e. obsolescence of software and whose responsibility is it to guarantee such access in a wholly electronic environment?

The Site Licence report (HEFCE, 1997) also warns against the pay as you go means of charging for access as this poses budgetary control difficulties for library managers. One option here would be to charge academic departments for this access, or to give academic departments part of the library budget to support this. If charges are introduced this will usually mean that demand is curtailed and devolved budgets will need to be 'ring fenced' in order to avoid the library budget being used for non-library purposes. The issue of inter-disciplinary access is another problem related to devolved budgets. Generally what appears to happen is that any increase in inter-library loans and/or electronic access is taken from the materials budget rather than devolving budgetary control.

However, as a recent eLib study has suggested (Fishwick, Edwards, and Blagden 1997) there may be a number of marketing innovations that publishers could introduce, ranging from subscriptions to core electronic journals (much as now, although the core might be much smaller), pay as you go for marginal journals with perhaps reduced charges on a sliding scale for those that subscribe to X per cent of a publisher's output. Many variations on these two options could also be developed, i.e. low rates for out of hours access, special trial offers, etc. Electronic publishing can also provide an added value product by including such features as links to cited references, integration with databases and multimedia add ons. However, such enhancements will not come cheap and will largely nullify the savings to which reference was made earlier.

Top slicing of money to provide access to electronic journals at the national level is another possible approach. Given that the focus of the HE sector tends to be international in its outlook, particularly in research, co-operative acquisition of electronic journals at the regional or local level may not be the way forward. However, it will be interesting to monitor what impact the development of Metropolitan Area Networks have on sharing of electronic services, a good example of which is what is happening in the CALIM (Consortium of Academic Libraries in Manchester) project. CALIM as Blunden-Ellis (1994) makes clear, consists of five academic libraries all located within two square miles of each other in Greater Manchester. Together they serve a user population of over 70,000. Delivery of networked full text information to CALIM users features strongly in their initial plans.

Differing modes of delivery, copyright and VAT issues and caution on the part of the publishers may slow down electronic access to full text STM journals. DJB Associates (1996) have argued that by the year 2015 about 50 per cent of STM journals will still be available in print mode. There is, of course, always the assumption that one medium will totally replace another and clearly this may not prove to be the case, particularly in the case of less developed countries who may still wish to rely on hard copy.

Given this uncertainty about full text electronic publishing, university librarians need, therefore, to address the issue of how far they should move towards an access model, i.e. a greater reliance on inter-lending. Line (1996) suggests four criteria by which such decisions should be judged:

- speed of supply;
- reliability – i.e. probability of getting an item;
- ease of use;
- costs.

In terms of speed of supply, librarians will need to be aware of the impact of the 'instant gratification' culture and, of course, of the definition of the perfect library that provides everything that a user wants immediately, in the right place, in the right format, etc. Although the focus of this section will be based on delivering items through the mail or courier services, electronic delivery and fax will also need to be evaluated. Electronic delivery can pose the problem of format and inconvenient delivery points to the user and fax is often inappropriate for illustrations and formulae. Almost certainly these problems will be resolved, probably in the short term. Grossen and Irving (1995) report a delivery time of between 3 and 7 days as being acceptable, whilst Truesdell (1994) quotes two studies in which 77 and 75 per cent respectively of users were willing to wait between one and two weeks. The problem here is the emergence of premium high-priced services for speedier delivery, particularly for material not held in the UK which will place even greater strains on library inter-library loan budgets.

Although reliability of supply is an issue, if it is an issue for inter-library lending it will almost certainly be an equally difficult problem if the decision is made to purchase the item. Ease of use is an issue, but seamless downloading from a database to an inter-library loan module within library automation systems will become a standard feature of most, if not all library systems. This too could have a big impact on inter-library loan demand.

In terms of the comparative costs of ownership *vs.* access Beardman (1996) in Australia has demonstrated that 36 per cent of titles subscribed to in biological sciences were cheaper to borrow than to buy. Out of those journals cancelled the most heavily requested cancelled journal would have cost A$1683 per use, compared with an access cost of A$22 per use via an external document supply agent.

A similar pattern is evident in the USA. Grossen and Irving (1995) used the much quoted Association of Research Libraries figure of the average costs of an inter-library loan of $18.62 for the borrowing library and $10.93 for the lending library. However, the authors calculated that if the University of Albany had relied entirely on inter-library loans it would have cost the University $2,900,456 compared with a total subscription cost of $1,273,531. It should be noted here that these average inter-library loan costs disguise dramatic variations with many libraries either much higher or much lower than the $18.62. However, considerable savings were identified for low use items – $102,979 is quoted in the 1995 survey. The authors recognize the difficulty of determining accurate figures for journal use and assume that one use equals one inter-library loan. This, of course, may not be accurate. A user could read three articles from the same journal issue or, conversely, consult a journal without finding anything of interest. This is a methodological minefield and reference should be made to the excellent review of this area by Geoffrey Ford (1990). Grossen and Irving (1995) re-calculated the savings by assuming that use of journals subscribed to by the library was doubled and yet there would still appear to be significant savings to be made. Although perhaps a single in-house use could be regarded as an unfair comparison between ownership and borrowing, it is salutary to note (Ford, 1983) that 25 per cent and 30 per cent of the stock acquired by Southampton and Sussex universities respectively had not been used ten years after it had been acquired. The best predictor of future use is, of course, past use, so the likelihood of these items ever being used must be doubtful. This is made more difficult however because, as Ford (1990) reports, there is a very weak correlation between use as reflected in recorded borrowings and use within library. Another problem is when academic staff are questioned about which journals should be retained in hard copy within the library, there often appears to be significant contradiction in what users say they want and what they actually use. This is certainly the case at Cranfield, but may or may not apply elsewhere.

Ferguson and Kehoe (1993) in a study of scientific journals and monographs concluded that if a monograph is only used once, it was five times more expensive to own than to borrow. It is interesting to note here that this is *without* taking storage and processing costs into consideration. For STM articles it was estimated again by Ferguson and Kehoe (1993) that it was 21 times more expensive to subscribe than to acquire articles through inter-library lending for biology, 31 times more expensive for physics and 20 times more expensive for electrical engineering. These figures were calculated by comparing actual costs of inter-library loans at Columbia with the costs of retaining the less used journals in the library. These figures again assume only one use per journal issue. If this assumption of one use per item looks dubious, consideration should also be given to their analysis of inter-library loan requests where 72 per cent of periodical titles and 92 per cent of monographs were only requested once. This study was conducted over a reasonably long time scale – 20 months.

Kingma (1996) does go into greater detail of the costs associated with borrowing and owning. He quotes labour costs of borrowing articles from $0.91 to $4.06. On ownership he assumes an average of 2.25 minutes processing time plus storage rates, based on current costs per square foot of renting space within similar buildings to the library. He also attempts to determine user costs, but perhaps one should restrict such analyses to the direct costs of borrowing and the subscription costs.

At Cranfield University a blanket access policy was adopted in which *all* the journals for a small research group operating in biotechnology were cancelled. These cancellations were agreed with the head of the group on the understanding that the journals would be reinstated if the experiment proved to be unacceptable to the users. This is a somewhat more cautious approach than that adopted by Widdicombe (1993) who cancelled all journals and relied entirely on electronic access backed by fast delivery. This series of studies known as BIODOC, have been reported more fully elsewhere (Harrington, 1995; Nicholls, 1995; Evans, Bevan, and Harrington, 1996; Harrington, Evans, and Bevan, 1996), but it is worth highlighting some of the key results. It should be noted here the 'UnCover'' service was provided to all the biotechnology users at the time these cancellations were made.

Table 15.2 Buy/borrow decisions

	1995	1996
Requests for cancelled journals (% of total)	3.4%	7.0%
Cost of requests	£ 856	£ 1099
Savings made on cancelled journals	£11760	£14192

The data shown in Table 15.2 reinforce the findings reported earlier in that it again seems overwhelmingly cheaper to borrow than own. What is also interesting is that the number of periodical titles borrowed doubled from around 500 in the pre-BIODOC year to over 1000 in the two BIODOC years. This was caused by the increased awareness of what was available through the use of UnCover and a dramatic increase in demand for inter-library loans as Table 15.3 shows.

Table 15.3 Inter-library loan demand

	1994	1995	1996
Pre-BIODOC requests	1849		
1st year BIODOC requests		4849	
Increase in demand over 1994		162%	
2nd year BIODOC requests			3139
Increase in demand over Pre BIODOC year			70%
Decrease in demand over 1st BIODOC year			35%

However, the overall costs of the service increased in 1995 by 42 per cent and *decreases* in 1996 by 25 per cent as Table 15.4 shows.

It should, of course, be emphasized here that the case for cancelling the journals is still as strong as ever, but enhanced electronic access leads to a dramatic increase in inter-library loan demand and this has to be taken on board. It may be more cost effective to borrow rather than own, but access

Table 15.4 Costs

	1994 Pre-BIODOC	1995	1996
Journal subs	£10729	£ 460	£ 875
ILLs	£ 7846	£26000	£13000
Total	£18575	£26460	£13875
1995 percent increase on 1994 42%			
1996 percent decrease on 1994 25%			

policies are not necessarily going to lead to net savings unless artificial constraints are placed on demand.

There are also a number of caveats that should be taken into account when examining these 25 per cent cost savings in year two as I have indicated elsewhere (Blagden, 1997).

- In year one users were allowed to e-mail requests to the library which were then entered by library staff into the Libertas Artel system. In year two we reverted to the normal procedure where users had to do this for themselves. Now if this is the main reason why demand has fallen it could be argued that if users cannot make the effort to key in their own requests then the requests cannot be that important anyway. In my view this is a dangerous argument. It has been well documented by Allen (1977) as to how important an impact the principle of least effort has on information seeking behaviour. If we make systems difficult to use by erecting physical or mental barriers many users will be deterred from using these systems. It does not necessarily follow that most of that potential use was unimportant, and use has to be put in the context of the time pressures under which most of our users are having to work;
- The figures given in Table 15.4 do not take account of inflation and, given the strength of sterling in 1996; Cranfield has been borrowing from mainland Europe thereby getting more loans for the money invested;

- The costs do not include the higher degree of staff costs involved in both training and servicing inter-library loans, which do not apply to the more passive 'holding' situation;
- I also believe that there was a 'Hawthorne' effect (Roethlisberger and Dickson, (1937)) in year one in which the heavy intervention by library staff raised the level of information awareness amongst academic staff and students leading to a greater use of services;
- It should also be noted that as access policies become more prevalent the runs of hard copy journals retained in 'access' libraries like Cranfield will diminish. That being the case demand will increase given the emphasis on more recent titles;
- The hidden costs of the IT infrastructure which are required to ensure users have complete access to these electronic services.

In these BIODOC studies most users appeared to prefer electronic access as a means of browsing. In a more extensive study, however, Beardman (1996) reports that in 9 per cent of 709 cases a useful reference was identified by casual browsing of journals held in the library. However, the actual titles browsed generally corresponded with the high use titles which would not have been cancelled on financial grounds anyway.

If the case is accepted that borrowing rather than buying is often more cost effective, it also has to be accepted that university libraries should provide comprehensive access to electronic sources so that these items can be identified by the user. If, however, this happens, library managers should not be surprised if this leads to significant increases in inter-library loan demand. One question that will, of course, be asked is what is this increased activity delivering in terms of improvements in learning and research? Earlier studies in two special libraries (Blagden, 1980), a public library service for the housebound (Wigmore, 1989) and a medical library (Marshall, 1992), have all demonstrated that most library use appears to confer beneficial outcomes on their users. More recently in a medical teaching and research environment, Urquhart and Hepworth (1995) have demonstrated that access to information can save lives and you cannot get a more beneficial outcome than that.

The cost beneficial argument for a greater reliance on inter-library lending is a strong one, but Line (1996) argues that libraries who move too far down the access route are selfish. Bruce Kingma (1996), however, maintains that:

'It is difficult for the library director at a single library which has a trivial influence on the price of a journal subscription to estimate and incorporate the possible price of a journal subscription increase that other libraries may suffer when the library attempts to determine whether or not to subscribe to a particular journal.'

It may well be that if there were a dramatic switch to the just-in-time approach, that this would encourage publishers to take a more positive stance on moving into electronic publishing.

One other option that has not been explored in this contribution is to encourage users to visit libraries, providing of course, access to these facilities is not regarded as 'free loading'. This clearly puts a strain on the visited library and Fox (1996) notes that 53 per cent of Cambridge University's registered users are drawn from outside the university. This is an issue that is currently being addressed by Coopers and Lybrand on behalf of the implementation group of the Anderson report (1994). If the costs of servicing external users is significant, some compensation needs to be given to the major holding libraries. This does, however, need to be put in to some kind of perspective – currently university libraries are spending £389,476,000 per annum (HESA, 1997) and costs of servicing this additional use are somewhat trivial in comparison. Furthermore, the benefits to the user should not be forgotten and the expenditure figure above largely excludes the costs of buildings, IT infrastructure and general overheads.

A reliance on access should be encouraged, whatever form that access takes and, above all, it should be recognized that what is needed is a national framework under which this could flourish. This is currently being addressed by the Library and Information Commission, supported by the work of the Library and Information Co-operation Council. In the meantime, the individual library manager must put at the top of his or her priority list, the key client group that the library is attempting to serve. This is not, in my view, a selfish line to take because publishers, librarians and users have to understand that it is in everyone's interests to capitalize fully on the many benefits that the electronic library can confer on both its users and ultimately UK plc.

Acknowledgements

I would like to thank the entire librarian team at Cranfield for their contribution to this chapter. Although it is somewhat invidious to pick out individuals, I would like particularly to mention Simon Bevan, Louise Edwards, Janet Evans, Valerie Hamilton, John Harrington, Emma Nicholls and Heather Woodfield, together with Dr Frank Fishwick with whom I worked on the eLib electronic publishing study.

References

Allen, T.J. (1977) *Managing the flow of technology*. Boston: MIT

Apt Partnership (1995) *The Apt Review: a review of library and information co-operation in the UK and Republic of Ireland for the Library and Information Co-operation Council (LINC)*. Sheffield: British Library Board

Beardman, S. (1996) The cost-effectiveness of access versus ownership: a report on the Virtual Library Project at the University of Western Australia Library. *Australian Library Review*, **13**, 2, 173–181

Blagden, J. (1980) *Do we really need libraries?* London: Bingley

Blagden, J. (1997a) Enhancing access: a national priority. In *Proceedings of the Anderson Report Seminar* (Cranfield 1996), ed. Pat Wressell & Associates, pp.37–43. Bruton: LINC

Blagden, J. (1997b) Access versus holdings. *Interlending & Document Supply*, **25**(4) 179–182

Blunden-Ellis, J. (1994) The Consortium of Academic Libraries in Manchester (CALIM): strategic and development planning of new consortium. In *Proceedings of the 16th International Essen Symposium: Resource Sharing: new technologies as a must for Universal Availability of Information* (Essen, 1994), ed. A.H. Helal, and J.W. Weiss pp.99–114. Essen: Universitatsbibliothek

Brophy, P. and Wynne, P.M. (1997) *Management information systems and performance measurement for the electronic library*. Final report. Bristol: JISC.

Burke, M.A. and McGuinness, C.M. (1997) An investigation of the paradigm shift from ownership to access in academic libraries. *International Journal of Electronic Library Research*, **7**(1), 3–24

Carrigan, D.P. (1995) From just-in-case to just-in-time: limits to the alternative library service model. *Journal of Scholarly Publishing*, **26**(3), 173–182

DJB Associates (1996) *The future of electronic information intermediaries*. [s.l.]: DJB Associates

Evans, J., Bevan, S. J. and Harrington, J. (1996) BIODOC: access versus holdings in a university library. *Interlending & Document Supply*, **24**(4), 5–11

Ferguson, A.W. and Kehoe, K. (1993) Access *vs.* ownership: what is most cost effective in the sciences? *Journal of Library Administration*, **19**(2), 89–99

Fishwick, F., Edwards, L. and Blagden, J. (1997) *Economic implications of different models of publishing scholarly electronic journals for professional societies and other small or specialist publishers*. Draft report to the Joint Information Systems Committee

Electronic Libraries programme. Cranfield: Cranfield University Information and Library Services

Ford, G. (1990) *Review of methods employed in determining the use of library stock.* British National Bibliography Research Fund Report 43. Cambridge: Cambridge University Press

Ford, G. (1983) The framework of research – in house research. In: *The academic library in times of retrenchment,* ed. C. Harris and L. Gilder pp.27–50. London: Rossendale

Fox, P. (1996) Access versus holdings: a new perspective from an ancient university. In Access Versus Holdings: A Virtual Impossibility? UC&R Conference 1996. *Relay* (44), 3–8

Grossen, E.A. and Irving, S. (1995) Ownership versus access and low use periodical articles. *Library Resources and Technical Services,* **39**(1), 43–52

Harrington, J. (1995) Access versus holding: a report on the BIODOC current awareness and document supply experiment at Cranfield University. *Managing Information,* **11**(2), 38–39

Harrington, J., Evans, J. and Bevan, S.J. (1996) BIODOC: a preliminary user analysis. *Serials,* **9**(2), 170–177

Higher Education Funding Council for England, et al. (1993) *Joint Funding Councils' Libraries Review Group: Report.* (Follett Report). Bristol: HEFCE

Higher Education Funding Council for England) (1997) *Report on Phase I of the evaluation of the UK Pilot Site Licence Initiative.* HEFCE Ref M 3/97. Bristol: Commonwealth Higher Education Management Service

HESA (Higher Education Statistics Agency) (1997) *RESOURCES of higher education institutions 1995/96,* Cheltenham: HESA

Joint Funding Councils' Libraries Review (1994) *Report of the Group on a national/regional strategy for library provision for researchers.* The Anderson Report. Higher Education Funding Council for England Circular 17/94. Bristol: HEFCE

Kingma, B.R. (1996) *The economics of access versus ownership: the costs and benefits of access to scholarly articles via interlibrary loan and journal subscriptions.* Binghamton, NY: The Haworth Press Inc.

Kutz, M. (1992) Distributing the costs of scholarly journals: should readers contribute? *Serials Review*, **18**(1 and 2), 73–74, 96

Library Service Provision for Researchers (1997). Proceedings of the Anderson Report seminar organized by the Library and Information Co-operation Council (LINC) and the Standing Conference of National and University Libraries (SCONUL) at Cranfield University, 10–11 December 1996, Ed. Pat Wressell & Associates. Bruton: LINC

Line, M.B. (1996) Access versus ownership: how real an alternative is it? *IFLA Journal*, **22**(1), 35–41

Marshall, J.G. (1992) The impact of the hospital library on clinical decision making: the Rochester study. *Bulletin of the Medical Library Association*, **80**(2), 169–178

McGrath, M. (1997) Resource sharing at the crossroads. *Sconul Newsletter*, **10**(Spring), 24–27

Miksa, F. (1989) The future of reference II – a paradigm of academic library organisation. *College and Research Libraries News*, **50**, 780–790

Naylor, B. (1994) Just in case vs just in time: a librarian ruminates about journals, technology and money. *Logos*, **5**(2), 101–104

Nicholls, E.J. (1995) BIODOC: an interim evaluation of a rapid document delivery and electronic current awareness service. MA Thesis, University of Sheffield

Parry, D. (1997) *Why requests fail – interlibrary lending and document supply request failures in the UK and Ireland.* Newcastle-upon-Tyne: Information North for CONARLS

Roethlisberger, F.J. and Dickson, W.J. (1937) *Management and the worker.* Boston: Harvard University Press

SCONUL (1997) *Annual Library Statistics 1995–96*. London: SCONUL

Truesdell, C.B. (1994) Is access a viable alternative to ownership? A review of access performance. *Journal of Academic Librarianship*, **20**(4), 200–206

Urquhart, C.J. and Hepworth, J.B. (1995) *The value to clinical decision making of information supplied by NHS library and information services*. British Library Report No. 6205. Boston Spa: British Library

Widdecombe, R.P. (1993) Eliminating all journal subscriptions has freed our customers to seek the information they really want and need. *Science and Technology Libraries*, **14**(1), 3–13

Wigmore, H. (1989) *The captive reader: a study of the housebound reader service in Harrow*. Cranfield: Cranfield Press

CHAPTER SIXTEEN

Case Study: London Business School

Helen Edwards

London Business School Library (LBSL) is a specialist research library with a strong academic focus. It is also a business data resource, providing access to the primary data needed for business intelligence: news, economic, financial, market and trade information. The nature of its subject area and the requirements of its users make many 'just-in-time' issues particularly applicable to LBSL. This chapter looks at the access versus ownership debate from the perspectives of the different types of literature of interest to the Library users and the impact of just-in-time on collection development. It also covers service delivery and library management issues associated with the just-in-time model.

The School and its Library

London Business School is a graduate business school and a full college of the University of London. It is a single subject institution, engaged in teaching and research in the business and management studies area, employing over a hundred full-time faculty. There are approximately a twelve hundred full- and part-time students at any one time studying on the PhD, MBA and MSc management and finance programmes. The Masters programmes are restricted to students who have a specified minimum of work experience, three years in the case of the full-time MBA leading to an average age on entry of 28. In addition, there is a portfolio of non-degree post-experience ('executive education') open programmes. The workplace experience of the students, together with the cost of the School's programmes, means that expectations of library services are high. Specifically there is there is the expectation that commercially available business information services, which many users have experienced previously at work, will be available to them and that service delivery standards, for example response times, will meet commercial norms.

LBSL is part of the Information Systems Division, comprising library, computing, telephone and audio-visual services. Its primary purpose is to serve the faculty and students, but it is also open to members of the School's Alumni Association and there are a number or corporate subscribers. The collections consist of about 25,000 monographs, 1000 current journal subscriptions, a number of working paper series, government publications, an extensive hardcopy annual reports collection, corporate directories and market research publications. Electronic resources managed from the library but also available over the campus network include bibliographic (including full-text) sources and numeric data. Real-time data available in the library includes newswires and financial market data.

Impact of 'Just-in-Time' on Collection Development

As is the case for every library, LBSL is subject to spatial and financial constraints. The former, especially in central London where space is at a premium, imposes serious limitations to the amount of hardcopy material which can be stored. Nor can budgets keep up with the range of material of potential interest to library users now being produced. The library thus has to define its remit in terms of the level of information provision and associated services it is able to offer, with the goal of making the best possible use of the funds it has available. The beginnings of just-in-time management lie in the acceptance of the library's responsibility for meeting information needs for a wider range of requirements than those covered by the library's own stock. It extends the traditional collection development policy to incorporate material not owned by the library but which can be made available on an 'as needed' basis to its users. It is then, within the parameters of its budget, that the library has to decide what to own, what to rent and what to borrow. Also important, the library needs to make clear what it disowns, that is those information needs it is not able to support; and whether any mechanisms will be put in place to assist users in acquiring, at their own expense, this material. Once these parameters are clear, the Library can then operate a document supply policy which does not distinguish, from the perspective of the user, how the material is obtained. It is the library's job to decide which supply option is appropriate in each instance; minimizing any knock-on penalties to the user. Thus LBSL does not charge users for any inter-library loan requests or online searching which falls within the library remit; the Library having decided that these ad hoc supply methods are the most suitable for the specific requirement.

Thus just-in-time management has been around ever since libraries decided to keep back some of their budget to acquire material at the time it was needed rather than in advance. The traditional inter-library loans service was the first just-in-time service to form part of the School portfolio. The availability of inter-library loans relies on other libraries being committed to buying material so that it is available to others to rent. This model of co-operation is of potential benefit to both the supplying and user libraries. The suppliers benefit by making their expensive collections available (at a price) to a larger number of users and the user libraries by having a means of making accessible to their readers material as needed.

The British Library operates a national service from its extensive collection of books and journals, and the network it has of second line libraries. Figures for the last six years show that the British Library Document Supply Service has been able to supply seventy five per cent of the interlibrary loan requests submitted to them by LBSL, accounting for seven per cent of the books and serials budget. The Library has recently started using the LAMDA (London and Manchester Document Access) service to provide journal articles at a discount to the British Library price. LAMDA is a consortium of university libraries, originally funded by eLib, which are co-operating to leverage investment in journal collections by supplying scanned images of journal articles amongst themselves and to other requesting libraries. LAMDA members use the Ariel software, together with optical scanner technology in the supplier libraries, to pass images to each other over the Internet, usually within 48 hours. Analysis of London Business School requests to LAMDA over the last six months show eighty per cent of these requests were turned around within this timescale. Other document supply options available to the Library using post or fax delivery are the Bath Information Data Service (BIDS) and the UnCover document delivery services.

These services are all based largely on hardcopy collections, paper still being the only format in which most of the older material is available. Pricing models also come from the paper days, where copying is a cumbersome and somewhat self-limiting physical process, and from times where administrative mechanisms were, of necessity, kept simple. Many services still operate on fixed pricing, with the main variables being the speed (urgent action) or means of delivery (post or fax). However the UnCover charge consists of a fixed service element based on the type of delivery and a variable copyright fee. An informal analysis conducted by LBSL on a range of peripheral titles indicated a variation in copyright fee from under $4.00 to over $50.00 per article. As will be discussed later in this chapter with reference to business data supply where variable charging is commonplace, the introduction to just-in-time services of sophisticated pricing models, based on individual content valuations, requires a more complex management environment than has been needed previously.

The increasing availability of full text journals in electronic formats opens new possibilities for document delivery of journal articles. Services such as ProQuest Direct over the web disaggregate the article itself into components and formats, including abstract, text, text and graphics, pdf, all separately priced. Commercial intermediaries such as online hosts are including more and more full text journals (both academic and trade) in their services, enabling the identification of material and its acquisition to be a one rather than two stage process. Subscription agents too are expanding their focus from the provision of electronic contents pages to supplying electronic full text of journals, and their services to include both the subscription and the ad hoc supply models.

So why, with the availability of efficient inter-library lending and document delivery services, does LBSL continue to maintain an extensive journals collection? Firstly the Library is itself a specialist research library and a source for the British Library in some areas, notably finance. Secondly, as a higher education institution with a very active research faculty, the size of the journals collection is still an important factor in the School's ability to provide an environment to attract researchers world-wide. For several years the Library has been carrying out a detailed annual review of journals subscriptions with teaching and research faculty. What is obvious from this process is that researchers are not willing to accept any of the alternatives to an inhouse paper collection available at present. Few journals are ever identified as candidates for cancellation. The very fact that the collection is still in paper makes it difficult to assess actual usage and present figures justifying the financial case for just-in-time. Finally the strength of an institution's journals collection is still an element of assessment in exercises like HEFCE (Higher Education Funding Council for England) Quality Assessment, by which the quality of the research environment is measured.

However, while the research profile of the School has dictated caution with regard to any significant move to just-in-time for its core business and management journals collection, in other areas flexible acquisitions options have been of much more interest. Indeed part of the reason for investigating pay-as-you-go models in these areas was precisely the need to find money from elsewhere in order to maintain the journals collection in times of rising periodicals prices and static budgets. The first 'casualties' to just-in-time were general reference sources and material from disciplines impacting on but not central to the School's primary teaching and research needs. These include social science and humanities coverage in areas such as education, psychology, and law, and reference products with a multi-disciplinary focus such as indices to theses. Of course any specialist library needs to maintain a small general reference collection on its own site for the immediate convenience of its users. However LBSL now relies on online access when needed, together with reciprocal agreements with other libraries, to support the wider ranging humanities and social sciences reference needs rather than subscribing itself to many of these more general publications.

Current awareness tools also play a part in ensuring that individual researchers are able to keep up to date with specialist areas from other disciplines applicable to their work, and are able to follow journals of interest whether or not the Library has a subscription. Electronic contents pages services allow individual profiles, determined by journal title or subject, to be set up, extending the exposure to new materials beyond the bounds of the library's physical collection. Not surprisingly one of the immediate (and ongoing) effects of moving from an inhouse paper-based alerting service, based on the contents pages of the library's own subscriptions, to an electronic alerting service, based on a much more extensive title list, has been a sharp rise in inter-library loan requests.

The net consequence of just-in-time, from the academic perspective, is that the library has become more specialized. Collection building, in terms of buying material for retention, has been able to focus on key areas, enabling the Library to maintain and develop its core collections. This has been paid for, in part, by the availability of just-in-time services to support necessary access to other materials, in cases where usage costs are lower than subscription costs.

Business Information

In addition to its academic collection, London Business School needs to make available to its users a comprehensive collection of business data. Business data consists of the company annual reports and financial statements; financial market data; market research; press coverage; trade literature; government publications; grey literature emanating from a wide range of trade, professional and official or regulatory bodies; statistical and economic data of all kinds. This material is used by students for assignments and project work, as raw material by researchers and for commercial purposes (subject to contractual agreements) by alumni and corporate subscribers.

Most of this information is still available in paper form, prices ranging from free, in the case of company annual reports acquired individually, to hundreds, or even thousands of pounds for specialized market or broker research. Print sources include the many directories, reference works, data books etc. together with the press, trade and ephemeral material. Business data is also at the forefront of the electronic revolution. The commercial value of this data has meant that suppliers have found it worthwhile to make substantial investments in making the data available electronically and in a variety of delivery formats. The interactive and data manipulation capabilities of electronic data give these formats significant added value over conventional publishing, in particular for numeric datasets. Electronic distribution mechanisms such as satellite, ISDN, leased lines, X25 and TCP/IP also enable the delivery of real-time or near real-time services, especially in the areas of news and financial market data.

Many of the collection development criteria relevant to academic collections also apply to business data collections. There is the need to define the core material to be made available without restriction, to identify the range of additional material to be acquired as needed, and to recognize the material beyond the library's scope. Often currency of information is important and the version to be supplied by the library needs to be established. However in many areas of business information, especially for data in electronic formats, the concept of collection building gives way to the requirement to ensure access is and remains available, both to current and historic data.

It is necessary, also, to recognize that the primary customer for business data services is not higher education but the commercial sector. With the business customer in mind, many services are based on a different paradigm for using and charging for information than that of the conventional academic world. Business users are often able to make a commercial judgement about the value of different types of information to them, and expect variable pricing to reflect accepted commercial valuations. Electronic formats also facilitate pricing on a per unit of information basis. However these valuations are often completely prohibitive in the education context. Nor may the mechanisms be in place in many higher education institutions to manage per unit billing, or the authorization of expenditure issues that necessarily accompany this kind of pricing. Thus there is the need to negotiate with those suppliers with some interest in the education market to find an affordable way of providing educational access to commercial information.

At London Business School a number of different types of deals have been offered by business information providers covering the whole range of the just-in-case/just-in-time spectrum:

- fixed price, unlimited use. This is the traditional 'just-in-case' model, often provided by 'educational edition' CD-ROMS using less frequently updated information. Indeed acceptance of non-current data, ranging from superseded editions of market research reports to financial market prices delayed fifteen minutes, often offers an affordable way to make valuable data available for educational use;
- upfront purchase of hours, often at a discounted price. This model allows the library to estimate how many hours it needs of the service and contract for their supply at a fixed rate. This is a just-in-time model managed by time rather than material. Its advantage is that it extends library access to a larger range of material than it would be able to own, but limits the time within which it can be used;
- the 'carnet' system, in which the library contracts to buy, at a fixed price, a certain volume of material. An example of this is a market research service which allows users to select market research reports, as needed, up to an agreed number;
- core service provided at a fixed price with add-ons extra;
- variably priced online services up to a predefined limit, based on user category. This provides the mechanism for decisions about resource use to be devolved to enduser groups, yet the overall management to be kept within the library;
- commercial online services at academic or commercial 'as used' prices;
- 'showcase' deals providing access to new products, free or at a low price, in return for user exposure and feedback. A problem with this type of deal is that, after expectations amongst users have been raised, the supplier may return to commercial pricing;
- alerting services priced by number of search profiles. This is an example of the 'ahead-of-time' or server push model.

Further complications are caused by overlap and duplication of the information resources themselves. Thus a single resource may be available in its own right in a variety of formats and a number of versions, themselves variably priced, and as a part of a number of packages provided by different commercial intermediaries. This leads to multiple permutations of just-in-case/just-in time scenarios. Selection of electronic resources requires far more than an analysis of the information content. There is a need to identify, for each prospective service, content issues (current and historic); version issues (currency of information and frequency of update); user interface issues (ease of use for endusers); technical issues (networking, delivery mechanisms, maintenance etc.); and pricing issues (fixed and marginal costs for content, networking fees, communications charges). To enable a holistic focus on this complex group of products, London Business School now employs three Electronic Resources Specialists to manage and support the Library's electronic resources.

Service Delivery

This chapter has so far focused on the collection development issues raised by the just-in-case/just-in-time debate. However there are also significant service delivery and management issues from both the user and library administration perspectives.

User perspective

Users need not only to discover resources of interest but also to access them. Different resources within the library perform different functions and pose their own problems of integration:

• catalogues and indexing and abstracting services used to identify material often stop short of providing access to the documents themselves;

- primary full-text sources may not be well integrated with the tools for locating material;
- commercial intermediaries go some way to integrating information from different primary sources but may introduce new problems themselves in terms of their charging structures;
- print resources need to be referenced electronically for inclusion in the virtual library framework; these references can be independent of physical location.

Implementation of just-in-time delivery, so as to minimize the discontinuities between resource discovery and resource access, is central to the development of a useful service environment. The objective of this service environment is to present users with all available delivery options for an item. These include:

- immediate delivery in electronic format (pdf, rich text, ASCII etc.);
- reference to print location (library shelf mark);
- notification of information available in electronic format for a further charge (payment/approval mechanism required);
- notification information not immediately available, but which can be requested (inter-library loan, reserve, order, internal document delivery);
- combination of delivery options with time/cost variables (reserve from library/premium document delivery service/available at alternative site).

Decisions about how to make material available need to take into consideration the available service mechanisms, the impact on the user in terms of both delivery times and request processing (number of forms to fill in, repeat visits necessary etc.). The ability to integrate resource discovery with efficient mechanisms for, if not immediate delivery of, resource access is critical to any move to an access rather than holdings strategy.

This model of an integrated service environment was central to LBSL's requirement specification for its new library system, procured in 1996. Features supporting this, now available in commercial library management systems, include Z39.50 functionality, enabling cross searching of other catalogues, and Web-based user services, supplying request functionality. These services are now being implemented at London Business School. At the national level, the concept of the hybrid library, integrating a wide range of traditional and electronic resources, has been identified by JISC (Joint Information Systems Committee) as one strand of phase 3 of the eLib programme. LBSL, in conjuction with partner sites the London Business School at Economics and the University of Hertfordshire are developing one model of the hybrid library in the JISC funded project, Headline.

Management perspective

From the management perspective the ability of the service environment to streamline request processing is also important, if the administration costs of a service at item usage level are to be contained. This is especially important as numbers of requests increase faster than they can be processed to the required service levels. Work flows supporting user selection of a resource from a catalogue or index and the automatic transmission of the request to the library administration system save rekeying and reduce error levels. One serious constraint holding back the development of automated document request systems is the need to collect user signatures for copyright purposes. This necessitates the user submitting a signed paper copyright declaration in addition to any electronic request. Thus, even if an automated document delivery system is in effect, a parallel paper system still has to be maintained, with all the overheads of managing the two systems. There are also additional copyright issues regarding materials in electronic formats.

Secondly the automation of the collection of usage statistics and the availability of tools to analyse this data provide, as a by-product of an electronic service environment, valuable management information. Automated tracking and analysis techniques, applied to a largely electronic environment, make into an exact science what was once a matter of guesswork. There is the possibility of constructing useful models of the point at which it is worth moving from an ad hoc to a subscription model or increasing the number of simultaneous users able to access a resource. Thus the decision to move to just-in-time in some areas but not in others can have an economic basis, based on measurable usage patterns.

However this methodology has to be used with caution. Access and request rates for information are not in themselves measures of its actual usefulness. Nor should users of more esoteric resources be penalized as long as their needs fall within the library's scope. At London Business School monitoring techniques are used not to define the library remit itself but to determine the most cost-effective way of fulfilling user needs. The pattern of usage is a key factor dictating *how* material is made available, ranging from unrestricted access over the network to a search conducted by an intermediary of a full-priced commercial host, not *whether* a user is entitled to the information.

Conclusion

LBSL is an academic library operating also in the business environment. In the academic world there has long been the tradition of information 'free at the point of use', of minimizing the disadvantage to those users who need access to expensive or unusual resources. Any charges levied at users, for example in some libraries for inter-library loan requests, tend to be based on administrative rather than information content costs. This model has always been difficult to apply in the context of business information. One challenge faced by LBSL has been to operate a coherent service in the face of different supplier philosophies about the value of information. Paradoxically the Library's long experience of negotiating with business data suppliers, the need to countenance a range of deals covering the whole spectrum of just-in-case/just-in-time, is now coming in useful in the academic context, as commercial models, enabled by technology, become more prevalent.

In the subject areas covered by LBSL, more and more material is becoming available in electronic formats, and, especially, Web formats. Once access to material becomes independent of location, the just-in-time/just-in-case debate becomes increasingly irrelevant. With its origins in inventory management just-in-time is most applicable to paper based collections where the choice to own is absolute. An item either exists in stock just-in-case or is acquired when it is needed just-in-time. In the virtual world this kind of ownership is being replaced by a variety of access agreements of the types described in this chapter. Instead of the dichotomy of just-in-case/just-in-time, the library requires an access model. The purpose of the access model is to optimize the use of resources based on, firstly, the library's remit, that is the information needs it is contracted to satisfy, and secondly user demand at resource level. It is to this model that LBSL is working across both its academic and business data collections.

CHAPTER SEVENTEEN

Case study: University of Newcastle upon Tyne

Keith Webster

Introduction

'Before World War 2 interlending was regarded as an optional extra
... any research library considered it an admission of failure to have
to obtain any item from elsewhere.'

(Line, 1989, p.1)

Traditionally, libraries were considered a success on the basis of size – biggest was best. However, over time, a realization dawned that this was not an accurate reflection of good library performance, and that changes in funding, publishing and scholarly practice meant that sharing of resources in some form was essential. Every library now accepts that it cannot be self-sufficient. In 1996/97 the British Library alone supplied almost three million items to British libraries, an increase of one million items since 1986/87 (British Library, 1997). Inter-library lending is no longer an optional extra, but a mainstream activity of the modern library. The term inter-library lending reflects the origins of the service where one library loaned an original item to another. The introduction of photocopiers in the 1970s led, more commonly, to the supply of a retention copy, and this form of 'lending', properly called document delivery, dominates today.

At present, inter-library lending and document delivery in most libraries retains its traditional features, and technological developments are only beginning to make their mark. This chapter considers the development of document delivery in British academic libraries, and places it in the context of the emergence of the electronic library.

Opportunities and Constraints

The pace of change in higher education and the worlds of publishing and scholarly communication, and their impact on academic libraries has been described elsewhere (Webster, 1997a). A range of factors, both opportunities and constraints, have had a direct impact on collection building and access to information.

The number of publications issued each year has grown dramatically, reflecting the upward spiral of the world's knowledge base. For example, in the United Kingdom, 102 000 books were published in 1996, compared to 68 000 in 1991. Meanwhile, journal and book prices have continued to increase at well above inflation rates. The average periodical subscription increased from £150 in 1991 to £264 in 1996 (Library and Information Statistics Unit, 1997a), and in the UK, book prices increased by 70 per cent during the past 10 years (Library and Information Statistics Unit, 1997b). Periodical prices have given particular cause for concern, with average annual percentage price increases as high as 22 per cent in 1994 (Blackwells, 1995) and forecast as 11 per cent in 1998 (Blackwells, 1997).

Against this pattern of increased publishing activity and soaring subscription prices has been a picture of falling library budgets. Cancellations to periodical titles, limiting onsite physical access, have become the norm for many libraries, and book purchasing has fallen significantly. An

Association of Research Libraries (ARL) study (Case, 1997) of journal cancellations showed that 59 per cent of research libraries surveyed (in the United States) planned to cancel some titles during the year.

Student numbers have increased too, from just over 1 million in 1990 to 1.7 million in 1995, with, significantly, a growth in the number of postgraduate students of 80 per cent in the last five years, reflecting the general expansion of the UK higher education sector (Department for Education and Employment, 1997).

This growth in student numbers has led to a major shift in teaching style: students are being asked, more than ever before, to conduct small-scale studies and project work depending greatly upon literature searching and extensive reading. Meanwhile, free access to electronic bibliographic indexes and abstracts across electronic networks has become widespread. Library users can quickly tap into the scholarly publications of the world and generate long lists of 'essential reading' necessary for the completion of their assignment or research project. The growth in academics' research activity has had a great impact on literature supply and inter-library loan requests in major research universities show peaks in the period leading up to the publication deadline for Research Assessment Exercises. There is also a frequent phenomenon of the inter-library loan office being swamped with requests for items when access to a new database has been provided (Rutstein, DeMiller and Fuseler, 1993, p.48).

It is the advent of new technology that offers libraries the opportunity to respond to the constraints described above. The proliferation of electronic information sources, and the increase in electronic publishing and electronic document delivery, coupled with improved networking within and beyond universities will enable libraries to transform the process of information supply. One traditional response to journal cancellations but increased demand for literature was to place greater reliance upon inter-library lending services. Technological advances provide the opportunity to introduce a major change with planned moves towards greater access to information just-in-time, rather than local holding of materials just-in-case.

Access and Holdings

The move away from extensive local holdings is not a recent phenomenon. The common use of inter-library lending services started in the 1950s and by 1975 a move towards access was gathering force. DeGennaro (1975, p.950) claimed that 'the traditional emphasis on developing large local research collections must be shifted toward developing excellent local working collections and truly effective means of gaining access to needed research materials wherever they may be'. The Atkinson Report (University Grants Committee, 1976) introduced the concept of the self-renewing library and reduced the expectation of constant growth of library collections. In the UK, this view was confirmed in the Follett Report (HEFCE, 1993, p.51): 'It is neither feasible nor even desirable to expect each institution itself to provide for all the research needs of its users.'

The access and holdings debate is complicated, and certainly does not depend upon access being electronic (Cornish, 1996, p. 83), but it is worth remembering that access and ownership are points on a continuum, not opposites. The library's image as a warehouse or supermarket of information has now lost validity. In the just-in-time library, materials are only acquired which users need immediately, freeing up funds to buy access to peripheral material for a wider range of users. Libraries are evolving rapidly to a model where it is not what a library owns that is important, but what it can provide access to. The Association of Research Libraries in the United States has been reported (Rutstein, DeMiller and Fuseler, 1993, p.52) as considering an amendment to its membership criteria where new members will be admitted not merely on the basis of the size of local collections but also on their ability to provide access to online resources or other networks.

This directly affects the ways in which collections are developed and managed and the challenge for collection managers is to balance between access and purchase, whilst serving the needs of their primary users. To complicate matters further, it is not uncommon to see an overlap between different formats of the same information, for example printed and electronic versions of indexes. Different forms may serve different types of users (for example, novices or experts) or people in different locations (in the library, or in the laboratory). One extreme view is that collection developers should expand access through database subscriptions, inter-library lending and shared collecting arrangements, reserving purchase for items that cannot be obtained except through ownership. (Intner, 1989, p.8)

User expectations have increased in recent years. As a result of increased computer literacy, people are happy to use terminals to locate and retrieve information, and it is through this technology that many would wish to access information. Rosenthal (1992, pp.10–11) outlined a model of common user expectation:

1. Users believe that their library's online catalogue contains everything held in the library, whether this is true or not, and whether or not other resources such as card catalogues are available.
2. Users want to be able to use one terminal for all information retrieval: catalogue records, abstracts and indexes and, ideally, full-texts of journal articles and reports.
3. Users want to find whether or not information relevant to their needs exists, regardless of where it is physically stored.
4. Users want to be able to select data from files, organize information from multiple sources, download or print the results and transmit it to others.
5. Users want to be able to do all of this in locations and at times convenient to them, through a reliable service, and at little or no direct cost to them.

However, despite these wishes, at present we have rapid bibliographic access, but not rapid document delivery. The aim of the just-in-time library in the electronic environment will be to complete the model of electronic access and document delivery in the manner most appropriate to the user's needs and the library's resources.

The University of Newcastle upon Tyne

The University of Newcastle upon Tyne is typical of many British civic universities, although it did not come into separate existence until 1963. Before then the University had had a long existence which can be traced back to the formation of a medical school in 1834 which became part of the University of Durham in 1852. By the turn of the century, a wide range of subjects in medicine, arts and science were being taught in Newcastle, and continued growth ultimately led to the establishment of the separate University of Newcastle upon Tyne. Today, the University is one of the country's leading research institutions, with strengths in fields such as medicine, dentistry, engineering, pure and applied sciences and the arts.

The university library service is provided from the Robinson Library, a large, modern building opened in 1982 and extended in 1996, and from divisional libraries for medicine and dentistry and for law. The Library holds a stock of around 1.2 million volumes, and has some 20 000 registered borrowers. It is one of the British Library Document Supply Centre's largest customers, and its inter-library loan sections process in excess of 35 000 requests each year, an increase of 20 000 on 1987 levels. Users pay a small contribution, currently £1, towards each request satisfied. Copyright regulations permit restricted copying by libraries on behalf of readers, and no copyright fee is payable for the supply of the majority of items through the inter-library loan service.

More than half of these requests are made by postgraduate students, with the remainder split evenly between undergraduate students and academic staff. Almost 90 per cent of requests are satisfied by the British Library, 5 per cent by the British Medical Association Library, and the remainder by libraries approached to satisfy one-off requests.

Despite the fact that the term inter-library loan suggests that something is sent from a supplying library on loan, 75 per cent of requests are satisfied by the supply of retention copies, typically photocopies of journal articles.

It is clear that the access and holdings debate is entering a new era and the pressures described above are forcing libraries to challenge long-established practices. Technology is offering a range of opportunities which could only be dreamt of in the past and the time is, perhaps, ripe for change. However, central to any change in service delivery must be the views of the user. In the access world it is essential to know who the library's users are, how they use information, what are their information needs and how these needs are likely to change. Libraries need to ask how best to meet these needs, and to examine the relationship between collection building in its traditional sense and inter-library lending. There needs to be a look at current inter-library loan use and practice to allow the system to survive until the future arrives, and to allow the incorporation of new services which best meet users' needs.

A local survey

The electronic library incorporates the need for librarians to increase outreach and programming in order to better determine users' needs and become responsible for the creation and operation of systems which facilitate access (Brin and Cochrane, 1994). To inform any change in inter-library lending practices, such as a move towards electronic document delivery, a survey of users at the University of Newcastle was conducted between November 1996 and May 1997, following an earlier pilot study carried out in May and June 1996, and Webster (1997b) reported initial findings at a FIDDO (Focused Investigation of Document Delivery

Options) seminar. The aim of the survey was two-fold: firstly, to monitor the impact of electronic bibliographic databases on the nature and volume of inter-library loan requests, and, secondly, to assess the speed of delivery (in relation to the user's needs) and the relevance of the item supplied.

The survey consisted of a two-part questionnaire. The first part was issued to a fixed-interval sample of users submitting interlibrary loan requests. The second part was sent to respondents willing to participate further shortly after their request had been satisfied. 280 initial responses were received (51 per cent) from which 230 people agreed to participate in stage two. 100 completed questionnaires were received during stage two, representing 5 per cent of the inter-library loan service's regular user population.

In Part one respondents were asked to identify the source of the reference which they were requesting. The results are presented in Table 17.1, where paper sources (footnotes from books and journal articles and reading list items) represent 43 per cent of sources, while electronic media (CD-ROM and electronic databases) form 57 per cent of sources. These findings support the perceived impact of electronic databases on literature searching.

The purpose for which the item was required reflected the predominance of postgraduate users of the service, as shown

Table 17.1   Source of reference

	%
Electronic sources	
Online database	36
CD-ROM	21
Paper sources	
Book/journal article	31
Reading list	7
Printed index	5
Total	100

in Table 17.2. Student activity such as thesis preparation and assignments accounts for almost three quarters of requests, whilst academic purposes represents 17 per cent of requests.

Part two of the survey was designed to examine the shift in user opinions of the item at the time of request to their assessment of its usefulness when the item had been supplied. There was some concern that users were ordering many items without considering how useful they really would be, partly due to the lack of abstracts in many databases. When submitting the request one third regarded the item as crucial, one half as very important and the remainder as fairly important.

After the item had been supplied, only 15 per cent of respondents regarded the item as crucial to their needs, whilst more than half regarded it as very important and one third fairly important. An 'expectation measure' was calculated to demonstrate the shift in user opinion before and after seeing the item (see Table 17.3). A positive score would indicate a greater degree of satisfaction, a negative score a lower satisfaction, and a score of zero would show that the item met the user's expectations.

It is of some concern that one third reported a negative score. Although detailed analysis has not been undertaken, it seems that many of these were reported when details about

Table 17.2 Purpose of request

	%
Thesis	58
Assignment	13
Background reading	12
Research	9
Publication	5
Teaching	3
Total	100

Table 17.3 Expectation measure

Expectation measure	%
–2	4
–1	31
0	56
1	6
2	3

the contents of the item, such as an abstract or review, had not been available to the user at the time of ordering. A survey of the users of electronic tables of contents services (Brunskill, 1997) supported this observation.

Every respondent confirmed that the item requested had arrived on time. All of these items had been processed using the normal British Library Document Supply Centre (BLDSC) service, with the item being delivered by post to the requester, or by van to the library for collection. Interestingly, 71 per cent of respondents said that they would refer to the item for some future piece of work.

A cross analysis was made between the source of reference and the extent to which user expectations had been met. The results in Table 17.4 show that online sources provided the highest volume of satisfactory items.

Table 17.4 Satisfaction vs source of reference

	Online	CD-ROM	Paper	Total
Completely	14	2	18	34
Satisfactorily	23	9	24	56
Slightly	5	2	2	9
Not at all		1		1
Total	42	14	44	

A move towards the future

British academic libraries are intensive users of inter-library loan services but their inter-lending procedures continue to be predominantly paper-based. A survey carried out as part of the Electronic Libraries Programme FIDDO project found that all academic libraries had access to the BLDSC, with 85 per cent using its services on a daily basis. Occasional use is made of other services, such as the British Medical Association, local and regional libraries, other academic libraries and commercial document delivery services. Inter-library loan practices remain broadly traditional: requests from readers are most commonly made on paper forms (to obtain a signed copyright declaration), and notification of request status and receipt by library to reader also remains paper-based in most libraries. Requests to potential suppliers are normally submitted electronically, especially to the BLDSC and commercial services. The most popular method of receiving documents from suppliers is through the standard postal service, or by van delivery from BLDSC. Some commercial services use fax or e-mail, and electronic delivery using the ARIEL software is becoming increasingly common – 40 per cent of libraries are considering the introduction of some form of electronic document delivery (FIDDO, 1997). These findings mirror the current picture at the University of Newcastle. Like many libraries, much thought is being given to future practices, and the remainder of this paper will consider how these practices might emerge.

Although BLDSC has extensive collections, the purchase of some overseas materials has been reduced due to financial constraints, and increased competition from other document delivery services may force it to increase its standard fee for supplying an item. The British Library's Document Supply Service has strong supporters (Prabha and Marsh, 1997), but equally strong critics. (Mowat, 1997, p.59), for example, argued:

'I have an awakening appreciation of how much of a dead hand the Document Supply Centre has been on access in this country. It may

have restricted the development of access arrangements . . . we have
a national model which restricts access for users.'

Others have expressed concern about the impact of serial
price increases and funding cuts on BLDSC's collections and
services:

'There has been a feeling in the UK library community that we
should have an alternative source for document delivery, in case
we are not able to rely on Boston Spa as heavily as we have done
in the past to provide a high-quality cost-effective service.'

(Friend, 1994, p.17).

Changes at BLDSC are not the sole impetus for change.
All universities are under a constant challenge from the
Funding Councils to find further efficiency gains each year,
and schemes such as the Charter Mark award, which was
received by Newcastle University Library in 1995, place
emphasis on obtaining value for money, demonstrating innovative service development and offering choice to service
users. Part-time students, especially at postgraduate and
research level, now form a major sector of academic library
users, and their mode of study is forcing libraries to review
services which may have been established to cater for a
predominantly full-time student body and adapt them to
meet the needs of non-traditional user groups.

Document Delivery – a Changing Picture

Harer (1992) described an 'Information Cycle Network', a
three-part process which comprises the identification of a
document, the location of the document and finally its
delivery. Ideally, all of these functions could be carried
out from the end-user's workstation and demonstrator
projects to develop services such as these have been funded
by a number of bodies, notably through the European
Commission's Telematics for Libraries Programme and the
(UK) Joint Information Systems Committee's (JISC) Electronic
Libraries Programme. Publishers have experimented with

electronic services, as have enterprising academics seeking to break the traditional scholarly communication model.

A typical document delivery system consists of a number of functions:

- searching for bibliographic details, often performed by the end-user;
- requesting by linking the bibliographic reference to the user's particulars;
- locating the source of the required document;
- ordering the document;
- copying the document, either by retrieving it from store or scanning it;
- delivering the document to the requester;
- managing the whole process including copyright management, fee payment, reporting to the user (Lor, 1996, p.275).

Some services have been developed which provide electronically each of these functions, but many current developments offer only part of the complete document delivery process. It is not possible to provide an exhaustive list of electronic document delivery services here, but a detailed review has been provided as part of the FIDDO project (Price, Morris and Davies, 1996) and the FIDDO Website provides links to further details of many experimental and commercially available services.

The most common type of electronic document delivery system in British academic libraries is current awareness service–individual article supply (CAS–IAS), based around electronic tables of contents services, in which the searching, requesting, locating and ordering of desired documents is carried out electronically. End-users can access the service through an Internet interface, and either browse the contents pages of selected journals or search for articles by using a keyword search. Notable services include UnCover, operated by the Colorado Alliance of Research Libraries (CARL) and the Blackwell subscription agency. Other CAS–IAS services of note are OCLC's ContentsFirst and ArticleFirst (Mitchell,

1993), Pica's RAPDOC service (Costers and Koopman, 1993), SwetsDoc from Swets and Inside Information from BLDSC. It is notable that whilst several of these services are operated by libraries, a number have been established by periodical subscription agents.

A different form of electronic delivery is provided by services which handle electronically the copying and delivery of documents. The most significant development in British academic libraries has been the LAMDA project, funded by the Electronic Libraries Programme (Friend, 1996). The LAMDA service is now fully operational, and allows libraries to search an electronic union catalogue of serials holdings in a number of libraries in London and Manchester, request an article by e-mail and receive the document electronically to a local laser printer. The LAMDA scheme uses the ARIEL software which has been developed by the (American) Research Libraries Group (RLG) (Bennett and Palmer, 1993; Landes, 1997). The ARIEL system enables the scanning and transmission of documents from the sender through the Internet to the recipient's computer. The system is more versatile than fax – documents do not need to be photocopied before transmission, and documents can be sent and received simultaneously. Both sender and recipient must have access to the Internet, and have ARIEL installed on their computer, but these limitations are offset by a very high standard of document reproduction. ARIEL has been used by a number of services, such as the RLG SHARES service. More recently, the BLDSC has offered to transmit requests to customers using ARIEL at the same price as their standard photocopy and post service (BLDSC, 1997, personal communication). Other services which have delivered documents electronically include EDIL (Braid, 1994) and Marcel (Smith and Delaney, 1996).

A further stage of current developments is the type of service which merges a separate CAS–IAS type service with a copying and delivery system. This has been demonstrated by the SurfNet Project (SurfNet, 1995).

A more complete electronic document delivery service is that which integrates electronically all stages in the process, from initial searching to delivery, whilst offering management support systems. One of the earliest of these systems was ADONIS, a full-text, CD-ROM based database of biomedical journals (Braid, 1989). More experimental services include EDDIS (Larbey, 1997) and Ariadne (Roes and Dijkstra, 1994). The TULIP project (Elsevier Science, 1996) is an example of a publisher-driven scheme to provide an integrated electronic service.

Running alongside these developments which seek to deliver electronically predominantly paper-based materials has been a huge change in scholarly communication, itself having been prompted by technological advances. Even in advanced forms, printed journals can take several months to appear after acceptance of articles for publication. Electronic publishing can reduce greatly this delay, and facilitate easy scholarly collaboration. Many authors are turning to electronic media, such as electronic journals and e-mail discussion groups to overcome the print world's inability to keep up with the information explosion. Some academics have set up electronic journals, such as the Web Journal of Current Legal Issues, based at the University of Newcastle, and there have been some enterprising developments such as an Internet depository of journal articles which are awaiting peer review and print publication (Winclawska, 1997). It is possible that in the future some specialized disciplines will only communicate electronically. If these materials are produced and distributed electronically, sharing of materials will be easier than at present, but the kind of texts available in this way at present represent only a small percentage of acquisitions or requests.

This is electronic publishing in its most pure form: the information is being published electronically in the first instance, and may never be produced in any other form. A variant form is the simultaneous publication of both print and electronic forms of the same information. This is most commonly seen in electronic journals made available by commercial publishers, and, in the UK, has been the subject of a number of site licence agreements through which libraries can make available electronic journals (HEFCE, 1997). There are also schemes which seek to convert to electronic form materials which were originally published in print form. The most notable of these schemes is JSTOR, an American consortium service which is digitizing back runs of a number of journal titles (Guthrie and Lougee, 1997). JSTOR is currently being made available, by JISC, to universities in the UK.

The phenomenon of electronic publishing brings with it a whole new range of issues for library managers, beyond the scope of this paper. Although the end-user is likely to gain direct access to materials, libraries will have a role to play in cataloguing and making available access to electronic publications, and there is the as yet unresolved issue of who will be responsible for the long-term maintenance of electronic back files.

A number of studies have reported implementations of some form of electronic document delivery, often on a trial basis and frequently in response to heavy serials cuts. Kilpatrick and Preece (1996) reported the experience of cancelling subscriptions to 1241 periodical titles in an American university library and providing alternative access through services such as UnCover and BLDSC. In the United States, commercial document delivery services often provide cheaper access than traditional inter-library loans (there is no American equivalent of the BLDSC, and inter-lending services are based on regional and national co-operative resource sharing schemes), and offer additional benefits of a one-stop-shop rather than the need to check a range of libraries for holdings. Kilpatrick and Preece found that access could replace the holdings of the journals cancelled, but that there was a need to mix the use of commercial vendors and inter-library loan services. These findings were supported Pedersen and Gregory (1994) and by Hughes (1997) who reported a 93 per cent fill rate, and acceptable delivery time in supplying articles from journals where subscriptions had been cancelled. In the Hughes study, the initial scheme, which provided unlimited access, proved so successful that restrictions had to be imposed to save costs. Fax delivery was also curtailed when it was found that articles could be received through postal delivery within an acceptable three to five days. The ARL price cuts survey (Case, 1997) showed that 56 per cent of libraries are using collection funds to support commercial document delivery services, at an average of $30 000 per institution. Subsidized document delivery appears to be a strategy that more and more libraries are using to trim their collections and support their community's needs.

These studies have looked at document delivery in its present form: a combination of traditional inter-library loan and some electronic delivery. Further work has concentrated on the use solely of electronic document delivery on a trial basis. Williams (1997a; 1997b) described the trials of a number of electronic document delivery services including UnCover, the BLDSC Urgent Action Service and TUDELFT (the Delft University of Technology Document Delivery Service) at the University of Bath. Also in the UK, the Cranfield University BIODOC project has examined the feasibility of introducing electronic document delivery systems in academic libraries (Evans, Bevan and Harrington, 1996). Sellers and Beam (1995) reported on a trial of UnCover at Colorado State University, and Orr and Dennis (1996) reviewed the use of a number of CAS–IAS services at Central Queensland University. Fill rates tend to be high – frequently over 75 per cent – and the services tend to be user-friendly. Delivery speeds vary, but receipt within 48 hours of request is common. However, some problems have been found: network delays meant that ordering items took a long time, the cost was high in British terms, at an average price per article of $18, and the quality of the document received by fax was often poor. Other services, however, are more attractive: LAMDA, for example, offers document delivery at a rate per article lower than that of the BLDSC, and with a quality of transmission superior to fax.

The price of many electronic document delivery services at present makes their widespread adoption in British academic libraries unlikely. However, they do have a role to play in delivering urgently required items, and as an alternative to existing suppliers if they are unable to satisfy the request. There is a tendency to believe that expensive services should not be used, but care must be taken to ensure that access to information is not unreasonably denied solely because the desired item is available only from an expensive source of supply.

Managing the Just-in-Time Library

Clearly, there are a number of developments which will provide the means for libraries to offer rapid and reliable document delivery in the future, but there remains the question as to whether or not access is an adequate substitute for ownership.

There are three criteria which should be borne in mind by library managers when considering the performance of the just-in-time library: cost, turnaround time and fill rate. (Truesdell, 1994, pp.201). There have been a number of attempts to measure the costs of document delivery, both in traditional inter-library lending systems and, more recently, in electronic document delivery services. Useful benchmarking data for American libraries was gathered by the ARL and the RLG (Roche, 1993), showing an average cost of $18.62 to borrow an item or purchase a photocopy of an article through traditional inter-library lending services in the United States. This figure corresponds closely to the costs of electronic document delivery services (Mancini, 1996, p.127). More recently, in the UK, the Electronic Libraries Programme sponsored the development of MA/HEM (Methodology for Access/Holdings Economic Modelling), an acquisitions decision support tool (SCONUL, 1996). MA/HEM allowed managers to compare the costs of acquiring the same information from different commercial sources. Kingma (1996) developed an economic model of access and ownership and provided a set of decision rules for access to information.

'Access delayed can be access denied' (Rutstein, DeMiller and Fuseler, 1993, p.51). This widely quoted statement implies that acceptable document delivery services will be able to provide materials as quickly as it would take a reader to go to the shelves to consult a locally held item. However, it is important to recognize that just because the technology exists, it is not imperative to deliver everything as a matter of urgency. The study of inter-library loan users at the University of Newcastle showed widespread acceptance of a delivery time of a few days. Of course, there will always be some items which are needed urgently, but many can be delivered using a less speedy service.

Conclusion

Libraries are at a point of change, merging the technologies of the nineteenth and twenty-first centuries. This combination of print and electronic resources, and the services required to provide access to both, will be offered in the foreseeable future from a hybrid library, and experimental projects to develop paradigms of hybrid libraries have been sponsored by the Electronic Libraries Programme. 'Library leaders want the library of the future to be a hybrid institution that contains both digital and book collections' (Benton Foundation, 1996).

In the hybrid library the need for librarians will continue, but librarians will have to market their services to entice readers. Publishers will want to cut out intermediaries, thus increasing their profits, and libraries will become competitors rather than intermediaries. Users will not perceive a need for librarians, but will search for, request and receive documents sitting at their desks.

If technological developments in document delivery take 'place in a haphazard manner, the co-operative spirit which underlies our present national inter-library lending system could be threatened and the economy and efficiency of the system lost.' (Coopers & Lybrand Deloitte, 1988).

There are some concerns about the implementation of electronic document delivery services. If their costs are higher than those currently paid by libraries, will there be any real incentive for libraries to use them? If the true potential of technological developments, through which users can bypass the library, are to be realized, will users pay the full cost when they can obtain the same document much more cheaply through the library? Copyright issues, which have largely been ignored in this chapter, must be resolved. 'Resource sharing . . . could disappear in libraries governed by the non-commercial publishing model.' (Drabenstott, 1993, p.130).

The long-term commitment of publishers to electronic document delivery is unclear. They have been happy to experiment, but 'electronic document delivery does not bring in the revenues which publishers need to support the subscription revenues . . . electronic document delivery is a parasite on the mother journal draining out its life blood with every cancelled subscription it facilitates.' (DJB Associates, 1996, p.176).

Until all documents that are required by our clients exist in electronic format on universally available, user friendly delivery systems, libraries can expect to act as intermediaries in some way between our clients and paper documents and between our clients and electronic forms of documents that they are unable to access themselves. 'As our clients increasingly have access to networks themselves . . . the library may act as an intermediary only for the out going request – the document supplier may deliver the document directly to the client' (Blinco, 1995).

This chapter looked at possible trends in the development of the just-in-time library. Many foresee that the future will really be one of just-in-time information, with the library playing a role only in ensuring subscriptions to electronic document delivery services which are used remotely by users. This day, if it ever comes, will be long in the future. At the present, the challenge for the manager of the electronic library is to ensure that the right information is delivered to the right user, just-in-time!

References

Bennett, V.M. and Palmer, E.M. (1993) Ariel on the Internet: enhanced document delivery. *Microcomputers for Information Management*, **10**, 181–193.

Benton Foundation (1996) *Buildings, books and bytes: libraries and communications in the digital age.* Washington: Benton Foundation.

Bevan, S.J. and Harrington, J. (1995) Exploring the potential of new partnerships for document delivery at Cranfield University Library: report of a trial with Delft University of Technology. *Program*, **29**, 177–181.

Blackwells (1995) *Periodical price index for British libraries 1994.* Oxford: Blackwell's Information Services

Blackwells (1997) *1998 business forecast.* http://www.blackwell.co.uk/business_forecast.html

Blinco, K. (1995) *Some recent initiatives in electronic document delivery.* http://www.gu.edu.au/alib/iii/docdel/online.htm

Braid, A. (1994) Electronic document delivery: vision and reality. *Libri*, **44**, 224–236

Braid, J.A. (1989) The ADONIS experience. *Serials*, **2**, 49–54

Brin, B. and Cochran, E. (1994) Access and ownership in the academic library environment: one library's progress report. *Journal of Academic Librarianship*, **20**, 207–212

British Library (1997) *Bibliographic services and document supply: facts and figures.* Boston Spa: British Library

Brunskill, K. (1997) Measuring researchers' preferences for CASIAS. *New Review of Information Networking*, **3**, 93–102

Case, M.M. (1997) Projections of Libraries' 1997 Purchasing Strategies. *ARL Newsletter*, **191**. http://www.arl.org/scomm/prices.html

Coopers & Lybrand Deloitte (1989) *Modelling the economics of inter-library lending*. Boston Spa: British Library

Cornish, G.P. (1996) Resourcing academic libraries – is IT the answer? Electronic document delivery services. *New Review of Academic Librarianship*, **2**, 83–90

Costers, L. and Koopman, S. (1993) The Dutch RAPDOC project: from interlibrary loan to electronic document delivery. *Interlending and Document Supply*, **21**, 4–6

DeGennaro, R. (1975) Austerity, technology and resource sharing: research libraries face the future. *Library Journal*, **100**, 917–923

Department for Education and Employment (1997) *Education statistics for the United Kingdom 1996*. London: The Stationery Office

DJB Associates (1996) *The future of electronic information intermediaries*. London: JISC

Drabenstott, K.M. (1993) *Analytical review of the library of the future*. Washington: Council on Library Resources.

Elsevier Science (1996) *TULIP final report*. New York: Elsevier Science

Evans, J., Bevan, S.J. and Harrington, J. (1996) BIODOC: access versus holdings in a university library. *Interlending and Document Supply*, **24**, 5–11

FIDDO (1997) *ILL Survey – Summary of findings*. http://dils2.lboro.ac.uk/fiddo/illsumm.html

Friend, F.J. (1994) Electronic document delivery thorough library co-operation: a trial using SuperJANET and future possibilities. *Interlending and Document Supply*, **22**, 17–21

Friend, F.J. (1996) LAMDA: questions and some answers. *Interlending and Document Supply*, **24**, 27–29

Guthrie, K.M. and Lougee, W.P. (1997) The JSTOR solution: accessing and preserving the past. *Library Journal*, **122**, 42–44

Harer, J.B. (1992) Information delivery in the evolving electronic library: traditional resources and technological access. *Collection Management*, **17**, 77–91

Higher Education Funding Council for England, et al. (1993) *Joint Funding Council's Libraries Review Group: Report.* (Follett Report). Bristol: HEFCE

Higher Education Funding Council for England (1997) *Report on phase 1 of the evaluation of the UK Pilot Site Licence Initiative.* Bristol: HEFCE

Hughes, J. (1997) Can document delivery compensate for reduced serials holdings? A life sciences library perspective. *College and research libraries*, **58**, 421–431

Intner, S. (1989) Differences between access vs. ownership. *Technicalities*, **9**, 5–8

Kilpatrick, T.L. and Preece, B.G. (1996) Serials cuts and interlibrary loan: filling the gaps. *Interlending and Document Supply*, **24**, 12–20

Kingma, B.R. (1996) *The economics of access versus ownership: the costs and benefits of access to scholarly articles via interlibrary loan and journal subscriptions.* New York: Haworth Press.

Landes, S. (1997) ARIEL document delivery: a cost-effective alternative to fax. *Interlending and Document Supply*, **25**, 113–117

Larbey, D. (1996) Project EDDIS: an approach to integrating document discovery, location, request and supply. *Interlending and Document Supply*, **25**, 96–102

Library and Information Statistics Unit (1997a) *Library and information statistics tables for the United Kingdom 1997.* Loughborough: LISU

Library and Information Statistics Unit (1997b) *Average prices of British academic books January – June 1997.* Loughborough: LISU

Line, M.B. (1989) Interlending and document supply in a changing world. In *Interlending and document supply: Proceedings of the First International Conference* (London, 1988), eds. G.P. Cornish and A. Gallico, pp.1–4. Boston Spa, IFLA Office for International Lending

Lor, P.J. (1996) Document supply. In *Library and information work worldwide 1995*, eds. M. Line, G. Mackenzie and J. Feather, pp.259–298. London: Bowker Saur

Lynch, C. (1993) *Accessibility and integrity of networked information collections*. Washington: Office of Technology Assessment

Mancini, A.D. (1996) Evaluating commercial document suppliers: improving access to current journal literature. *College and Research Libraries*, **57**, 123–131

Mitchell, J. (1993) OCLC interlending and document supply services. *Interlending and Document Supply*, **21**, 7–12

Mowat, I. (1997) Contribution to a plenary session discussion. *Library service provision for researchers: proceedings of the Anderson Report seminar*. Bruton: LINC

Orr, D. and Dennis, C. (1996) Unmediated document delivery and academic staff at Central Queensland University. *Interlending and Document Supply*, **24**, 25–31

Pedersen, W. and Gregory, D. (1994) Interlibrary loan and commercial document supply: finding the right fit. *Journal of Academic Librarianship*, **20**, 263–272

Prabha, C. and Marsh, E.C. (1997) Commercial document suppliers: how many of the ILL/DD periodical article requests can they fulfill? *Library Trends*, **45**, 551–568

Price, S.P., Morris, A. and Davies, J.E. (1996) An overview of electronic document request and delivery research. *Electronic Library*, **14**, 435–445

Roche, M.M. (1993) *ARL/RLG interlibrary loan cost study*. Washington: ARL and RLG

Roes, H. and Dijkstra, J. (1994) Ariadne: the next generation of electronic document delivery systems. *Electronic Library*, **12**, 13–20

Rosenthal, J.A. (1992) Crumbling walls: the impact of the electronic age on libraries and their clienteles. *Journal of Library Administration*, **14**, 9–17

Rutstein, J.S., DeMiller, A.L. and Fuseler, E.A. (1993) Ownership versus access: shifting perspectives for libraries. In *Advances in Librarianship* Vol. 17, ed. I.P. Godden, pp.33–60. San Diego: Academic Press

SCONUL (1996) *MA/HEM User manual*. London: SCONUL

Sellers, M. and Beam, J. (1995) Subsidizing unmediated document delivery: current models and a case study. *Journal of Academic Librarianship*, **21**, 459–466

Smith, J. and Delaney, T. (1996) Marcel: a MIME prototype study in electronic document delivery. *Interlending and Document Supply*, **24**, 24–27

SURFNet (1995) SURFNet SURFDoc final report. http://www.surfnet.nl/surfdoc/surfdoc-eng.html

Truesdell, C.B. (1994) Is access a viable alternative to ownership? A review of access performance. *Journal of Academic Librarianship*, **20**, 200–206

University Grants Committee (1976) *Capital provision for university libraries: report of a working party*. London: HMSO

Webster, K. (1997a) Research collections. In *Resource management in academic libraries*, ed. D. Baker, pp.137–157. London: Library Association

Webster, K. (1997b) End-user requirements of document delivery services. In *Proceedings of Issues in Document Delivery: a FIDDO Workshop* http://dils2.lboro.ac.uk/fiddo/webster.html

Williams, F. (1997a) Electronic document delivery: a trial in an academic library. *Ariadne* (web version), **10** http://www.ariadne.ac.uk/issue10/edd

Williams, F. (1997b) Electronic document delivery: a review and comparison of different services. *Ariadne* (web version), **11** http://www.ariadne.ac.uk/issue11/edd

Winclawska, B.M. (1997) Fourth revolution in scholarly communication? In *Porozumiewanie sie i wspolpraca uczonych*, eds. J. Gockowski and M. Sikora, pp.303–315. Kraków: Secesja

Managing Reference and Information Services

CHAPTER EIGHTEEN

Overview: Managing Reference and Information Services

Terry Hanson

Introduction

Reference and Information Services can, and should, be considered at two general levels. The first level is that of direct service provision on a reactive basis. We are there to respond to requests for information whether they are at the desk(s), by telephone, etc. The second level is the proactive one. This level of service is characterized by expectations of demand and by subject librarians working with departmental colleagues in order to anticipate and encourage them.

Into the former category we can place our enquiry desk services, inter-library loans, current awareness services, and mediated searches; whilst in the latter category we can consider user education at all levels, contributions to course and curriculum design, academic staff development workshops, liaison with departmental colleagues on reading list and assignment matters, attendance at course committees, etc. Another way to describe this split is by employing the well worn phrase just-in-time vs. just-in-case.

Before taking this distinction any further it is worth clarifying the terminology. The use of the term reactive to describe enquiry services is based on the expectation that people will come to the Library and, while there, wish to ask questions about finding information or using Library services. We react to this expectation by placing reference librarians at appropriate points throughout the building. The service is reactive then in the sense that people have to come to the Library and then come along to a reference desk to ask a question. We react with the answer. This does not mean that we cannot be proactive in such situations. We may, for example, go looking for questions by walking along the banks of PC workstations and asking how people are getting on. Or we may notice, in any part of the Library, that somebody looks confused and offer assistance. These are examples of a proactive approach within the context of a reactive service.

Having made this distinction it is clear that the two types of service require different management approaches. In carrying out their proactive functions subject librarians need to be flexible and creative and to operate with a considerable degree of independence. Reactive services on the other hand, and in particular reference desk services, are more akin to the provision of basic services such as would be found in any well run high street service such as a bank or department store. In these we expect that there will be people there to deal with our questions or transactions.

However, it is also important to stress that these two levels of service combine together and constitute the whole that can be described as 'those services which are designed to actively exploit and promote the library and its collections'. The move towards subject librarianship in the UK in the 1960s and 1970s had this aim as one of its principal justifications (Crossley 1974; Woodhead and Martin, 1982) and it will be this broad approach that will be examined in this chapter. It will address the organization and management of reference services and will seek to identify the key questions and discussion points that will need to be addressed in academic libraries as they seek to plot a pathway into the uncertain and very different future.

The Expanding Agenda

For some years now the professional literature has been warning of the need for libraries, and librarians, to change and of the danger of becoming marginalized if we do not (Campbell, 1992; Campbell, 1993; Ewing and Hauptman, 1995; Kong, 1995; LaGuardia, 1995; Lewis, 1995; Riggs, 1997; Rockman, 1991). In the UK there have also been more focused comments from, for example, the Fielden report (John Fielden Consultancy, 1993). The broad thrust of these comments is that many of the present (typical) management and service arrangement in academic libraries need to adapt to changes in teaching and learning methods, to the increasingly complex needs of 'networked learners', to the emerging situation of multiple information providers on campus and to the many challenges presented by the Internet.

As is often the case in change situations, standing still equals losing ground. The library's standing in the University is based on the traditional role as information curators and exploiters. But as technology strips away the uniqueness of this role, adaptation is necessary. The library can no longer claim the role of sole information provider and sole place of access to that information. Strategies for the future need to accommodate this new situation and they should be positive and assertive.

So what are the challenges? Some are in the reactive domain, pointing to ever increasing need for reference desk service, while others are more proactive in nature and represent a challenge for subject librarians in particular. Some have an impact in both areas and some are clearly challenges for the library's senior management. I will mention some of, what I consider to be, the main challenges.

Integrated access and support

Technology is taking us rapidly to the point where the multi-functional networked computer (the 'scholar's workstation') will become the norm. At such a machine the student will be able to communicate using e-mail, write papers using word-processors, use other software tools for data manipulation, retrieve references from bibliographic databases, read and download the full text from journals and books, use computer-based learning materials, browse the Internet, etc. As universities develop their online learning environments so they will need to consider access arrangements that are predicated on this integrated online activity. The obvious challenge here is to plan for the incorporation of large numbers of suitable workstations in the Library. This is a major challenge not least because it questions assumptions about the role of the library and of librarians.

Hitherto libraries have dealt in only part of the picture because the various tasks described above were, if they were possible at all, distributed between the library and computer facilities elsewhere on campus. Now, the trend is towards integration of access via multi-functional workstations collected together in 'learning centres', or re-defined libraries. It is a trend that emphasizes user convenience and one of the principal challenges for librarians is to engage fully with this process and to apply their strong tradition and philosophy of service and support.

The support implications for this model are, in fact, very significant and need careful and extensive debate. The challenge is to incorporate support for the whole range of activities in the online learning environment, building on the concept of library as workplace as well as information access point. It is to consider support for general purpose software applications, teaching and learning materials, navigating the Internet, etc. At a more general level this redefinition process needs also to consider the potential for decentralizing information access: A series of learning centres perhaps, strategically located around campus, rather than one central facility.

This consolidation of access is one of the driving forces behind convergence of academic support services in British universities. And though there is as yet no standard model of how to proceed, more than 50 institutions have converged to date (Law, 1998). At this level it is a challenge for the whole University, and for the library in particular it is an opportunity for vision and leadership.

Internet support

At a simple level the challenge of the Internet is fairly straightforward. Librarians can deal with it at this level as long as it is seen as an access tool to traditional scholarly information, such as bibliographic databases or electronic journals. At this level the challenge is to provide more machines, to develop the 'collection' of resources, to design the service to make it logical and simple to use, to devote sufficient technical and clerical support and to develop staff expertise for both personal development and user support.

But there is much more than just scholarly information of course, and though in some ways it may be desirable to deploy this service in such a way that it is limited to such sources, to do so would be to deny access to many other valuable forms and sources of information and forms of communication. However, to take this broader view suggests a broadening of the library role generally, and this is the challenge. If unlimited access to the Internet is provided through a library Web service, which bits of it are to be seen as the library's domain, and therefore requiring support, and which bits are to considered somebody else's problem?

This immediately takes us back to the discussion in the previous section about support for the integrated learner. An integrated support model for the Internet would mean an extension of our role, and skill range, to offer advice on:

- General Internet terminology and organization;
- General use of the browser and how to configure it;

- Appropriate file formats and associated helper applications and plug-ins;
- How to Telnet;
- How to FTP files and knowledge of the main FTP sites;
- How to discover discussion lists and sign up to them;
- Knowledge of the best search engines and how to use them.

It is also part of the challenge to offer e-mail and news-group access and to prevent illicit uses such as game playing and downloading pornography. And then there are the grey areas, if those listed above are not grey enough, of using Internet Chat or multi-user domains (MUDs) for informal scholarly discussion. Should the library take on the whole range of access and support or will there be limits, and if so how and where?

Changes in teaching and learning

As university teaching and learning strategies develop, in line with national and international trends, the library is called upon to respond. The main developments will be:

- Increasing proportion of non-standard students;
- Increasing proportion of part-time courses;
- Increasing use of open and distance learning;
- Increasing use of resource based (student centred, independent) learning;
- Increasing use of (electronic and printed) study packs as substitutes for conventional reading list approaches.

Libraries will need to respond at both the reactive and proactive levels.

- Desk reference services will need to be open longer, as will other reader services, to help cope with an ever increasing demand for reactive services;
- Better arrangements will be needed for supporting part time students generally;

- Better arrangements will be needed to support remote, and sometimes very distant, users;
- There will be a greater need for proactive discussions with departmental colleagues, and on the various departmental and general university committees, on the subject of the information needs of students in the changing situation;
- Librarians will be called upon increasingly to go beyond the information aspects of the student assignment to provide more comprehensive support and guidance;
- Librarians will need to develop and co-ordinate network access arrangements to online course materials and related information.

Service levels and quality

The challenge in this area is to adopt the customer care approach of banks and shops. Libraries too are service organizations and need to debate some key issues in the areas of service levels and their quality. They include:

- Whether service level agreements should be devised that guarantee a minimum stated level of service;
- Whether this means reducing the number of desks according to the staffing available;
- Whether to employ quality audit, Total Quality Management and Continuous Quality Improvement methods to analyse work routines in particular areas;
- How to employ user surveys to assist in service planning.

Personalised services

Librarians have traditionally provided current awareness, or selective dissemination of Information (SDI) services to academic staff and researchers in their universities. And it has long been possible to personalize and automate this process via the online information hosts such as Dialog and STN, but at a cost which prohibits widespread usage. The challenge now is to identify available technologies and services that will enable librarians to make these services available beyond those who can afford them, and in the process to make a more direct, and personalized, contribution to the research work of the institution.

Information skills teaching

All subject librarians are involved to some extent in teaching students the rudiments of information retrieval and management. Some go significantly beyond the basics and some go beyond just information skills and into related areas such as study skills and Internet usage. As university teaching and learning strategies focus on the learning process so there is a greater emphasis on the acquisition of key transferable skills by students as part of the higher education experience. This work is going to assume even greater importance in the future, perhaps to the extent of an assessed learning resource module in every course.

This has been the holy grail of subject librarians for many years but success in establishing these skills as a standard component of the new curriculum raises problems of workload. The amount of extra teaching could be enormous, beyond the subject librarian resources available.

Academic staff development

Transferable skills are needed by academic staff as well as students. In fact, for many their need is somewhat greater as they perceive rapid change all around them and their young students coping without apparent difficulty. The staff have an identifiable set of skills that they need to acquire, whether they are young or not so young and whether they are new to the institution or not. Librarians have a significant role in this area with many of the core skills relating to information access and management. Whether this is done on an informal staff development basis, or as part of a formal programme to equip all new academic staff to teach in higher education (very popular since the Dearing Report (NCIHE, 1997,

Recommendations 13 and 48)) it is an important opportunity to bring information skills and awareness to academic colleagues with, hopefully, beneficial effects in terms of their advice to students.

Information strategy development

This is perhaps the biggest challenge, and the one that encompasses all the others and more besides. The encouragement from JISC (1995), Follett (HEFCE, 1993, p.28) and, more recently, Dearing (NCIHE, 1997, Recommendation 41) to develop all-encompassing information strategies has provided a tremendous opportunity for universities to assess the importance of information, whether academic or administrative, to their mission. In particular this presents the opportunity to redefine the role of the library as part of a larger re-engineering of the learning support infrastructure. The main question is who supplies the leadership.

Service Response

Having examined the main challenges and opportunities facing libraries in the months and years to come, it is time to consider possible responses.

Proactivity and the subject approach

The expanding agenda discussed above is predicated on a belief in, or commitment to, the proactive approach to reference librarianship as embodied in the subject specialist model that has developed since the 1960s. As a model it is not without its critics; there are no doubt plenty of subject librarians who could do with an injection of proactivity, but if we believe in the power of librarianship to play a constructive and genuinely valuable role in the higher education process then this model, or some variation upon it, has to be part of the service response.

For the sake of this discussion I will assume that subject librarians are part of the picture and thus that the management of the reference and information service involves the co-ordination of both the proactive and reactive elements. The first general question to discuss is the extent to which the reactive and proactive services are integrated. The classic subject librarian model suggests high level integration, seeing the continuum of reference activity, from enquiry services to liaison, as exploitation of the library and its collections. In this arrangement subject librarians would bring their knowledge and expertise to bear on all reference activities plus collection development and, often, cataloguing and classification policy in appropriate subject areas, in a vertically integrated manner. And, crucially, this method of operation is seen as giving a direct line into Library policy making and service activity generally for university staff and students. This will be ensured by formal and informal links to the academic departments and their students. With this brief subject librarians are normally appointed at a senior level in the Library and are expected to exercise a great deal of initiative and leadership and to be ambassadors for the library on campus. This general model is very common in the UK university libraries.

At the other end of the spectrum is the horizontally integrated approach which sees each activity in the Library as separate, and performed by different departments or sections. In this model there would be a reference department to run reactive reference services and the responsibility for collection development and liaison would be located elsewhere. This model is the norm in United States universities, and not entirely unknown in the UK.

Staffing issues

This chapter began with the split between reactive and proactive services and with the observation that these different services require different management approaches. However, we have also stressed the need for the continuum of reference activity to be managed as a whole, using the subject model as our guide. We need now to look at how this model can be implemented, on staffing terms, taking into account the stresses of the expanding agenda. In this context I want to suggest a general approach to staffing reference and information services. This concerns the analysis of work and the allocation of tasks and responsibilities to different levels of staff.

The work of the subject librarian is of course very varied and often requires absence from the Library. It is also increasingly demanding, in terms of the amount of information and the array of skills that one is expected to acquire. Subject librarians are, for these reasons, the most highly paid category of staff in any library. In thinking about staffing issues in relation to reference services it is useful to start with questions relating to the role of this group of staff, and indeed most of the discussion will be easy and non-contentious. Liaison, collection development, user education and reference work are all in the subject librarian's domain. The question for debate is whether he or she has time for all of this, not to mention the expanding agenda items discussed above, and if not, then how can other staff be utilized to allow the subject librarians to concentrate on their 'core' activities? This takes us on to the question of 'drift down' and the process of work analysis that it suggests.

Drift down (borrowed from Michael Gorman, 1991)) is a simple process that posits that in any stratified organization the contribution of staff at all levels can be maximized by freeing each level of the tasks that can be done just as well (or even better) by staff at a lower level. In the university library we would begin at the subject librarian level with the questions:

- What are the core skills of the subject librarian?
- What tasks can be carried out by the subject librarian and by nobody else?
- What is the key contribution that subject librarians make to the work of the University?

The answers to these questions will provide a generic subject librarian job description. Next we would look to see if the subject librarian has any time left after doing all these things and then ask if there were any tasks still being done by the subject librarian that could be done just as well by other staff. If yes then this work would 'drift down' to the next level. The process would continue, looking at each level of staff until the point is reached where work could be passed down to the level of a machine. With such a process it is easy, and genuinely useful, to identify burdensome tasks at every level that could be usefully passed to the next level but in the university library the process quickly leads to some contentious questions. In particular: who does reference work and who does teaching?

Within the guidelines established so far it is clear that reference work cannot be left to subject librarians alone because of their varied workload. Moreover, a large proportion of reference work in most university libraries is at a low level such that the non-subject librarian could handle it very well. Put another way: Is it a good investment to place the library's most expensive resource on a reference desk where perhaps 10–20 per cent of the questions would benefit from their level of knowledge and expertise?

Drift down would suggest a redesign of enquiry services around the concept of front line filters (non-subject librarians, paraprofessionals) and an efficient referral process for questions requiring a particular subject librarian's expertise. Perhaps subject librarians should be excluded from the front-line rota and work on a referral (appointment) basis only (Arthur, 1998; Massey-Burzio, 1992; Shoebridge, 1998).

The same approach can be applied to teaching. Is it a good use of subject librarians' time to conduct endlessly repeated induction/orientation tours? Could other library staff take on some of this work too? With staff working in subject teams, there can still be a subject approach: *A* subject librarian rather than *The* Subject Librarian. The notion of the assistant subject librarian is a popular approach to this problem.

We then get to the question of which levels of staff can and should be included in reference teams. This debate has been running in the profession for some years. A clear indication of it can be seen in the recent Fielden report where it is noted that staff at all levels will need to be more flexible and where all categories of staff will be 'upskilled' to help meet the new challenges (John Fielden Consultancy, 1993, p.20 and p.31; Oberg, 1992). Thus it is now quite common in Britain and the United States for reference teams to include specially trained library assistants, or para-professionals.

This analysis, coupled with our desire to manage the reference process as a whole, leads to a team management arrangement, stratified by drift down to include the different levels of staff discussed above. The teams would be led by a subject librarian and would take on responsibility for all aspects of reference work (reactive and proactive) as it relates to the subject. Fielden also promotes the idea of team working as a necessary alternative to hierarchical structures if the challenges are to be met and the necessary changes made (John Fielden Consultancy, 1993, p.32).

Learning Centre or Library?

Thus far we have dealt with conventional university library services and situations but as indicated above one of the new challenges is to redefine the library as information access point in a broader sense. In practice this service concept can be seen in a number of new 'learning centres' that have emerged in recent years (Bulpitt and Oyston, 1997; Robertson, 1997; Kendal *et al.*, 1997; Parmenter, 1996; Sykes, 1996; Dye, 1996). In these, and many other 'new libraries', the library's historic role as information access point and scholar/student workplace has been extended and redefined to incorporate access to new forms of information and to the range of software tools necessary to manipulate that information.

These developments affect the provision of reference and information services by raising questions about how the necessary support for software applications etc. is incorporated into the traditional reference service arrangements. The choice is between integrating the software and technical support into basic front-line reference work or maintaining separate desks for reference and software/technical support. A further consideration is whether to see the software support role as an extension of the work of existing technical staff from the computing centre (in a typical 'convergence') or to make a distinction between the work of a technician (installing and fixing computers) and a software support specialist (performing an educational role). Traditionally, technicians have taken on both roles if only because they were based, visibly, in public access computing facilities, and because there were no other staff with software support as a clear responsibility. There is an opportunity with the design of new services to reconsider the software support role as a very important component of student support in the new increasingly electronic, and resource-based, learning environment.

Clearly, on the basis of the drift down discussion, subject librarians would not be expected to take on this work. The choice of whether to integrate with other front-line staff will still be difficult as this represents a major change. Experience to date indicates that these developments require careful management. Some universities, such as Bath, have adopted the separate desks approach, while others, including Birmingham, Liverpool John Moores and Hertfordshire, have implemented forms of integration (Shoebridge, 1998; Sykes, 1998; Arthur, 1998). Those opting for the separate approach will avoid much of the difficult 'change management' or 'culture change' taken on by those that have chosen to integrate.

Core competencies

The core competencies of each level of staff involved in the reference process will be determined by the staffing and service model adopted. In a designed subject model, using the principles of drift down, core competencies would match the intended function. In most areas this would be straightforward. The main area so far unresolved is the impact of the Internet on the work of the reference staff.

Earlier we considered this question and identified the aspects of Internet use that might be supported. With the service model emerging so far it is clear that many 'technical' aspects of Internet use (such as how to ftp a file) would be allocated to the staff responsible for software applications support. This still leaves, however, the broad question of the Internet as information resource and no matter how critical librarians may be about the chaotic nature of the Internet it cannot be ignored. Nothing is more certain to guarantee the marginalization of the profession than such a blinkered attitude.

Librarians have the opportunity to bring to the Internet their understanding of how information is organized and generated, even when these processes are haphazard as well as formal. The main Internet search engines should be as familiar to librarians as the Silver Platter SPIRS interface. Similarly, the process of discovering online discussion lists and newsgroups should be routine. In fact, subject librarians in most university libraries would normally take on the responsibility of maintaining a section of the library Web site to collect together useful links by subject for the benefit of their academic colleagues and students.

Number of reference desks

In libraries that are organized by subject, in terms of stock and staff, it is common to locate a reference desk on each subject floor of the building. This provides an admirable level of service convenience and customization but it is obviously very difficult to maintain with any level of service guarantee.

The advantages of the distributed subject model are listed below:

- The most obvious benefit of the subject model is the coincidence of subject questioner meeting with subject specialist librarian. The quality of service in such a situation is commendably high and remains high even when it is not the perfect coincidence, i.e. when the questioner is greeted by a different subject or reference librarian from the same team. It is likely of course that all librarians working on a particular team will gain a good knowledge of the sources available;

- A sense of belonging, or identification with a particular part of the library, is promoted. To the economics students, for example, the social sciences floor is where they will bump into their subject colleagues, friends, lecturers, and librarians. This fosters a community spirit within what might otherwise appear a monolithic and unfriendly Library. We manage to personalize our services through this approach, an attractive compromise between the larger impersonal central library and every academic's ideal: the departmental library down the corridor (though clearly for some they would still hold out for the latter no matter how we organize our services);
- Another significant benefit is that the subject library per floor approach promotes knowledge of the book and journal collections as well as of the reference sources, including the electronic ones. This brings benefits to the students when a librarian is able to suggest particular books and journals, and even particular issues of journals, as part of the answer to their question, and is able, because of their proximity, to walk over to them and point them out. In so doing this furthers the librarian's collections knowledge.

These advantages may be compelling but they must be set against the one major disadvantage of affordability. The distributed subject model is clearly labour-intensive and beyond the means of most libraries. Compromises include distributed desks but not to the extent of one per floor, and desks that have guaranteed staffing for a limited number of hours per day, with informal arrangements in between those times. Whichever arrangement is adopted the staffing policy should be made clear to the users.

With the one desk option the logistics are straightforward and the advantages clear. All reference services would be concentrated in one place with a referral arrangement to subject librarians when appropriate. This arrangement is very common in British and, especially, American university libraries. A whole floor, or large area, would be given over to reference services with a desk, collections of printed reference materials in all subject areas and large numbers of PCs for access to electronic services.

The compelling advantage of the one-desk model is its efficiency in the deployment and organization of resources. Its major weaknesses are that it does not have the advantages inherent in the distributed model as indicate above. More specifically it requires all staff at the desk to operate as generalists rather than specialists. Gaining and maintaining familiarity with resources across all subject areas, to an adequate level to offer quality service, is increasingly demanding, and perhaps unrealistic.

The desk service configuration becomes a trade-off between large and efficient and small and personalized.

Electronic reference

In the increasingly electronic library reference staff are called upon to provide services electronically in order to serve users whether on or off campus. Several techniques have emerged and are often referred to collectively as networked learner support (Powell and Levy, 1995). A well organized Web site, with links to local and Internet resources is, of course, a major part of such support and, as already mentioned, subject librarians will play a major role in selecting resources for this service. Beyond these links other initiatives have become popular; in each case they transpose standard reference functions, such as enquiries and user education, to the network environment. They include:

- *Online or e-mail enquiries* Also called 'Ask a librarian' services, these have become standard practice on university library Web pages in the last year or so. From a management point of view the main considerations are clarity of service definition and clarity of responsibility. The users will need to know what type of enquiries they can submit and how soon they can expect a response. Among the reference staff it will need to be established who is responsible for checking the mail box(es), filtering the questions and referring on as appropriate;

- *Virtual Reference Desk (VRD)* The VRD is an attempt to provide a reactive reference service in a proactive fashion. The central feature would be a Frequently Asked Questions (FAQ) list which would be based on typical questions collected by reference staff. This might be one alphabetical list or it may be structured by subject. The answers might take the form of a couple of sentences or they may refer the reader to a short library guide. For example a question might be 'Where can I find statistics on employment?' And the answer might take the form of a link to a printable one-page list of sources;
- *Online information skills tutorials* These may take the form of general purpose introductions to information retrieval techniques, without referring to any particular software. Or they may be database/product specific. Either way they offer an excellent method of offering information seeking skills on demand, when the need arises;
- *Service requests* These include the direct input of service requests such as Inter-library loans, book purchases or booking a place on a library workshop. Many libraries have developed this type of service with special online forms to streamline the process.

A good collection of electronic reference, or networked learner support, initiatives can be seen at the Netlinks Web site at Sheffield University (University of Sheffield 1998). The list of information skills tutorials is particularly interesting.

Current awareness services

As noted previously current awareness services and automated SDI services have long been a standard component of
library reference services but the latter have been limited,
typically, to those willing to pay. It is now possible, however,
to create and manage an automated SDI service on the basis
of locally mounted databases using software supplied by the
principal database publishers (such as Silver Platter and
Ovid). Hitherto, locally customized electronic current awareness services were only possible using very labour-intensive
techniques.

In addition, there are many free services now available on
the Internet that will allow the individual user to register to
receive contents pages from their favourite journal titles as
and when they are updated. For a fuller discussion of these
services and techniques please see Chapter 33.

Conclusion

Managing reference services in university libraries has never
been more challenging than it is at present. The expansion
of higher education on its own represents a major challenge.
But for this to be accompanied by a shift in focus from
teaching to learning and the massive changes in the processes
of information production and organization magnifies the
challenge enormously. Few professions face this magnitude
of change.

The purpose of this chapter has been to examine some
of the major challenges and to discuss possible service
responses from the perspective of the 'typical' British university library. Clearly there can be no standard response;
each library will need to react individually, taking into
account local circumstances, but the questions and challenges
discussed here, and perhaps others too, apply to all.

References

Arthur, J. (1998) Managing Reference and Information Services: Case study: University of Hertfordshire Learning and Information Services. In: *Managing the electronic library*, T. Hanson, and J. Day, pp.369–389. London: Bowker-Saur.

Bulpitt, G. and Oyston, E. (1997) The development of the Adsetts Centre, Sheffield Hallam University. *DeLiberations.* http://www.lgu.ac.uk/deliberations/lrc/

Campbell, J. (1992) Shaking the conceptual foundations of reference: a perspective. *Reference Services Review*, **20**, 29–36.

Campbell, J. (1993) In search of new foundations for reference. In: *Rethinking reference in academic libraries* Ed. A.G. Lipow, pp.3–14. Library Solutions Press.

Crossley, C.A. (1974) The subject specialist librarian in an academic library: his role and place. *Aslib Proceedings*, **26**(6), 236–249.

Ewing, K. and Hauptman, R. (1995) Is traditional reference service obsolete? *Journal of Academic Librarianship*, **21**(1), 3–6

Gorman, M. (1991) The academic library in the year 2001: dream or nightmare or something in between? *Journal of Academic Librarianship*, **17**(1), 4–9

Higher Education Funding Council for England, et al. (1993) *Joint Funding Councils' Libraries Review Group: Report*. (Follett Report). Bristol: HEFCE

John Fielden Consultancy (1993) *Supporting expansion: a study of human resources management in academic libraries*. Bristol: HEFCE

Joint Information Systems Committee (1995) *Guidelines for Developing an Information Strategy*. Bristol: JISC

Kendal, S. *et al.* (1997) Learning development environments: the academic versus the student perspective in 1994. *DeLiberations.* http://www.lgu.ac.uk/deliberations/lrc/

Kong, L. (1995) Reference service evolved. *Journal of Academic Librarianship*, **21**(1), 13–14

LaGuardia, C. (1995) Desk set revisited: reference librarians, reality and research systems design. *Journal of Academic Librarianship*, **21**(1), 7–9

Law, D. (1988) Convergence of academic support services. In: *Managing the electronic library*, eds. T. Hanson and J. Day, pp.49–62. London: Bowker-Saur

Lewis, D.W. (1995) Traditional reference is dead, now let's move on to important questions, *Journal of Academic Librarianship*, **21**(1), 10–12

Massey-Burzio, V. (1992) Reference encounters of a different kind: a symposium. *Journal of Academic Librarianship*, **18**(5), 276–280

National Committee of Inquiry into Higher Education (1997) *Higher Education in the Learning Society*. (Dearing Report). London: HMSO

Oberg, L.R. (1992) The emergence of the paraprofessional in academic libraries. *College and Research Libraries*, **53**, 100–101

Parmenter, J. (1996) The development of the Rivermead Learning Centre, Anglia Polytechnic University. *DeLiberations*. http://www.lgu.ac.uk/deliberations/lrc/

Powell, S. And Levy, P. (1995) Developing a new professional practice: A model for networked learner support in higher education. *Journal of Documentation*, **51**(3), 271–280

Riggs, D.E. (1997) What's in store for academic libraries? Leadership and management issues. *Journal of Academic Librarianship*, **23**(1), 3–8

Robertson, S. (1997) The Learning Resources Unit at Chichester Institute of Higher Education. *DeLiberations*. http://www.lgu.ac.uk/deliberations/lrc/

Rockman, I.F. *et al.* (1991) Reference librarians of the future. *Reference Services Review*, **19**(1), 71–80

Shoebridge, M. (1998) Managing reference and information services: Case study: Managing converged reference services at the University of Birmingham. In: *Managing the electronic library*, eds. T. Hanson and J. Day, pp.357–368. London: Bowker-Saur

Sykes, P. (1996) Liverpool John Moores' Aldham Robarts Learning Resource Centre. *DeLiberations.* http://www.lgu.ac.uk/deliberations/lrc/

Sykes, P. (1998) Managing reference and information services: Case study: Converged Working at Liverpool John Moores University. In: *Managing the electronic library*, eds. T. Hanson and J. Day, pp.63–78. London: Bowker-Saur

University of Sheffield (1998) Netlinks Resource Base http://netways.shef.ac.uk/rbase

Woodhead, P.A. and Martin, J.V. (1982) Subject specialisation in British university libraries: a survey. *Journal of Librarianship*, **14**(2), 93–108

CHAPTER NINETEEN

Case Study: Managing Converged Reference Services at the University of Birmingham

Michele Shoebridge

Introduction

The publication of the Follett Report in 1993 prompted the University of Birmingham to re-assess its approach to academic information support services. The growing functional overlap between libraries and other information services, pressure to optimize financial and human resources and the need for a more integrated approach to learning support all prompted the University to review the way library and information services were delivered on campus. After much discussion and consultation it was decided to converge the principal academic services (excluding administrative computing) from October 1995.

The converged structure

Four units were converged. The University Library (consisting of the Main Library and ten site libraries), the Academic Computing Service, Television and Film Services and the Centre for Computer Based Learning. This created one large unit of over 270 fte staff. It was decided to call the new unit Information Services.

The Birmingham convergence saw the newly-created Information Services divided into five divisions. Collection Management (CMD), Learning and Research Support (LRSD), Information and Computing Systems (ICSD), Planning and Administration (PANDA) and Public Services (PSD) (see Figure 19.1).

It was a fairly radical exercise which had a considerable impact on existing staff. Some staff remained in their old posts, others moved between the divisions having applied for, or been designated to, newly created posts. Any posts not filled internally were advertized externally.

CMD and PSD existed pre-convergence but were given additional areas of responsibility. Within CMD, special collections (rare books and manuscripts) were added to the acquisitions, cataloguing and bindery functions.

PSD, which had operated along fairly traditional 'reader services' lines, underwent some re-organization, with two new teams being created alongside the long established Lending Services team. The new teams were Enquiry Services and Publications and Marketing. In addition, the line management responsibility for all the site libraries was transferred to the PSD in order to achieve a more consistent approach to activities and procedures across the service as a whole.

The new divisions, PANDA, LRSD and ICSD were set up in response to particular demands being made on the University. ICSD covers most of the old Academic Computing Service activity, responding to the University's need to remain in the forefront of information technology developments, particularly in network and server technology. LRSD advises on the full range of services available through Information Services, ensuring that electronic and printed sources are integrated into all aspects of teaching and learning. The Division is made up of both subject and functional teams and this enables it to deliver a wide range

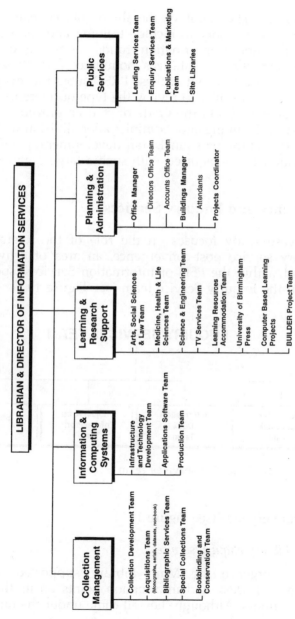

UNIVERSITY OF BIRMINGHAM

Information Services

LIBRARIAN & DIRECTOR OF INFORMATION SERVICES

Collection Management
- Collection Development Team
- Acquisitions Team (Monographs, serials, datasets, non-book)
- Bibliographic Services Team
- Special Collections Team
- Bookbinding and Conservation Team

Information & Computing Systems
- Infrastructure and Technology Development Team
- Applications Software Team
- Production Team

Learning & Research Support
- Arts, Social Sciences & Law Team
- Medicine, Health & Life Sciences Team
- Science & Engineering Team
- TV Services Team
- Learning Resources Accommodation Team
- University of Birmingham Press
- Computer Based Learning Projects
- BUILDER Project Team

Planning & Administration
- Office Manager
- Directors Office Team
- Accounts Office Team
- Buildings Manager
- Attendants
- Projects Coordinator

Public Services
- Lending Services Team
- Enquiry Services Team
- Publications & Marketing Team
- Site Libraries

Figure 19.1   University of Birmingham Information Services

of services. The remit of the three subject teams extends beyond the advisory to include training and some management of subject information funds alongside designated 'departmental representatives' nominated from the academic staff. The development of these LRSD subject teams gave the PSD the opportunity to review the type of reference services being delivered and the grade of staff employed.

A larger Planning and Administration division was created to handle all the personnel, staff development, planning and financial activity required with such a large organization.

Reference and Enquiry Services

This case study focuses on the role of the reference and enquiry service post-convergence, an area of activity now located within the PSD of Information Services, specifically within the Enquiry Service team (see Figure 19.2).

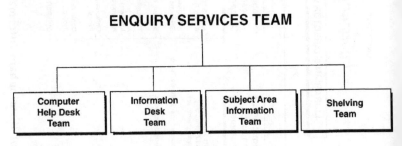

ENQUIRY SERVICES TEAM

| Computer Help Desk Team | Information Desk Team | Subject Area Information Team | Shelving Team |

Figure 19.2 Enquiry services team

Pre-convergence (see Figure 19.3)

Main Library enquiry services

Pre-convergence the Main Library supported a central information desk and information points on its three main subject floors. Although they all came under the umbrella of

PRE-CONVERGENCE

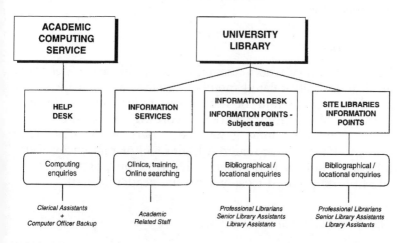

Figure 19.3   Pre-convergence

Reader Services each service point had a certain amount of latitude. All the information points were staffed by a mixture of professional and para-professionals (senior library assistants and library assistants) who were responsible for answering reference and directional enquiries, supervising the re-shelving of books etc., and undertaking other housekeeping-type duties.

The staff also offered some day-to-day low level support for the Library's extensive range of electronic sources i.e. networked and stand-alone databases. They were not responsible for the hardware and software associated with them. This was the responsibility of 3 software assistants who formed part of the Library's dedicated Systems Unit.

In addition, a small team of academically-related staff undertook online searches, ran training sessions and clinics. The latter were mainly aimed at academic and research staff, and postgraduates. They were also responsible for writing a large number of subject-related publications and developing an electronic guide to the University Library and its collections.

Site libraries

Each site library was managed by a site librarian, generally an academically-related member of staff, assisted by senior library assistants and/or library assistants. The relationship with the Main Library varied according to the site library history and how long it had been part of the University Library. Each site provided a high level of reference service (although not all had separate information points) and the site librarian liaised closely with the academic staff.

The Academic Computing Service

The Academic Computing Service ran a Computing Help Desk and Helpline (see Figure 19.3) from their Information Office in the computing building. The Information Office acted as a reference library for computing manuals and journals for teaching and research staff, co-ordinated computing publications, administered and sold site licensed software and assisted in the Microsoft Select scheme. A senior computer officer was given responsibility for the combined Help Desk /Information Office service assisted by three clerical support staff.

The Help Desk's remit was to support all information technology on campus and disseminate information about computing services. ARS (Action Request System) software was implemented to enable the logging, tracking and escalating of queries and to provide a way of identifying frequently asked questions. The software runs on a UNIX server with Windows clients.

It took considerable time and effort to set up the Help Desk and convince staff that it had a legitimate role. This process has not been completed. The ARS software required a considerable amount of configuring and maintenance to make it work effectively and deliver the kind of management information required to run an efficient service. The recruitment and retention of staff with relevant skills was a challenge. Extensive training was required to support the University's distributed computing environment and lack of standardization in hardware and software. The network infrastructure, proliferation of electronic mail servers and e-mail registration procedures, complicated remote dial-in arrangements, large departmental servers all increased the burden on the Help Desk.

Post-convergence

General and subject enquiries

Convergence presented the opportunity to take a much more integrated approach to reference and enquiry services. The emergence of the subject teams within the LRSD division created another layer of subject expertise available to users, and gave the opportunity to review the staffing structure of the Enquiry Services team. This, coupled with feedback from Main Library staff and supported by statistics collected on long and short enquiries, led to the conclusion that the kind of enquiries received at the main Information Desk and in the subject areas were fairly low-level and did not necessarily require the presence of a permanent professional member of staff. This trend was supported by a literature review undertaken on trends in reference services in North America. However, it was clear that any new strategy would only be successful if liaison between PSD and LRSD worked well.

As a result of this review, professional staff were withdrawn from the subject areas and information assistants left to run the service point with back-up from professional PSD staff based at the Information Desk and adjacent area and LRSD staff. When more detailed queries occur in these areas they are referred to a member of PSD professional staff or, if it is a specific subject enquiry, they are referred to clinics run by the LRSD liaison librarians who can also be contacted by telephone if a more immediate subject response is required. Since each site library is covered by one of the LRSD teams (e.g. the site librarian for the Education Library works closely with the liaison librarian for the Education Faculty), the same referral procedure works in the sites.

Assessment of users' needs and the change in the grade of staff at information points led to further changes. Two new service points were established, one to support official publications, statistics, the European Documentation Centre and German Documentation Centre, and another aimed at providing more detailed support to academic staff and research postgraduates requiring detailed advice on bibliographies and national and international catalogues. Both of these new service points are supported by professional staff, the latter by cataloguing and acquisitions staff from the CMD. Both have required considerable publicity and are still not being fully exploited.

Considerable effort has gone into making information, particularly reference and enquiry-type information, available on the World Wide Web via the Information Services Web Site. A 'frequently asked question' section aims to answer the most common questions received via the information points and the Help Desk. It is intended to make these electronic resources more interactive and to use them to supplement information points in certain areas.

Finally, responsibility for re-shelving (which is an extremely busy area of activity at Birmingham), has become the responsibility of a separate, dedicated, shelving team led by a senior information assistant. This has allowed the information assistants to do more interesting work in the subject areas.

The deployment of different grades of staff at information points will continue to be monitored to ensure that the user receives the most appropriate level of service.

Computing enquiries

One of the practical aims of convergence was to remove the barrier between the library and the computing service for the users. It became another 'plank' in the new approach to Enquiry Services to merge the main Information Desk and the Computing Help Desk to deliver a 'one-stop shop' approach and present a highly visible example of convergence. Consequently the Help Desk was moved from the computing building (located on the edge of campus) into the Main Library, a more central location.

It took a considerable time to get any interaction between staff that had been recruited to work at the 'computing enquiries' end of the Information Desk with those that worked at the 'library enquiries' end. This situation has improved and staff can now provide basic cover for either type of enquiry. Inevitably it will be some time before the two services become truly merged but this trend should continue as more computer-literate graduates with transferable skills appear on the job market.

Planning for the Help Desk move was carried out by a small project group consisting of key staff and a user of the service. The actual move took place in January 1996 with users responding well to the improved access. However, some important operational issues i.e. the re-configuring of the ARS software, updating lists of experts supporting the Help Desk, and defining a proper remit for the Desk were not progressed partly because financial constraints prevented the appointment of a Help Desk Manager. This post has now been created and has had a tremendous impact on the development of the service, not least in gaining support for the Desk from other members of staff.

The transfer of the site licensed software operation away from the Help Desk took a lot of pressure off the service and at the same time enabled the procedures for distributing the software to be streamlined and work more efficiently. Over 30 software titles are now distributed via the Sales Counter in the Main Library and this has brought positive feedback from users who also find it more convenient to collect from a central point.

Staff development and training

One inevitable outcome of convergence was the need for more staff training at all levels, both to enable staff to undertake their duties and for staff development.

At the library assistant (or information assistant as they are called post-convergence) level the Library had always run an induction training course for new staff and ad hoc training sessions on a variety of topics. A more structured approach was taken within PSD to ensure that staff could carry out their duties confidently and one professional member of PSD staff was given the task of creating additional training courses for information assistants. In order to target training more efficiently staff in Enquiry Services were no longer expected to work evening and Saturday duties on the Issue Desk, thus relieving them of the need to know the intimate details of the Talis circulation system and complicated Lending Services procedures. Instead they undertake their duties on the main Information Desk, a more familiar environment.

For the subject areas and Information Desk the training aimed to give a better understanding of the Internet, World Wide Web, databases on CD-ROM, along with printed resources. This is inevitably an on-going process. With assistance from the University's Staff Development Unit, staff 'away-days' were organized for the Enquiry Services and Lending Services teams for the first time in 1997. They provided the opportunity to cover issues like customer care in more depth and assisted in general team building.

The training programme for staff working on the Help Desk has been more detailed and involved both on-the-job and bought-in training. Again this must be on-going if the staff are to remain abreast of new services etc.

Another initiative aimed at involving staff at the information assistant level in decision-making involved the setting up of Quality Enhancement Teams which looked at areas of the service where there were problems and came up with recommendations for improvement. The first two teams looked at the shelving process and monograph ordering. The exercise has been very successful and will be extended into other areas of IS activity.

User feedback

The Library has canvassed feedback on library services via an annual user survey for a number of years. This has now been extended to reflect all Information Services' activities. The purchase of the Libra software has assisted in the main survey and allowed smaller, more focused surveys to be undertaken on different parts of the service. The inclusion of focus groups in the whole process has delivered a better view of what users want and allow Information Service the opportunity to explain its policies. The intention is also to get users involved in major changes and this has already started with the Help Desk move project.

A formal 'comments' procedure also provides users with feedback. There are Comments boxes in all Information Services libraries and all comments received in this way are logged onto a database. Replies are communicated in writing or via a public notice board.

Other channels involving LRSD staff exist to obtain direct feedback from academic and research staff. These include representations on a wide range of Faculty and School library and computing Committees; discussion via e-mail lists, e.g. Science/Engineering computer contracts list and participation in the University Academic Audit process.

Service levels

Traditionally the library has published service level targets for all the Public Services activities and for budget centres. Again this will be extended to all areas of Information Services activity over the next two years with the creation of a student charter and service level agreements with individual Schools. The targets relating to reference and enquiry services will be revised after consultation with the appropriate staff.

Conclusion

Convergence has had a profound effect on the reference and enquiry services at the University of Birmingham. The new structures still continue to evolve in response to the changing demands for the University and from users. Staff will constantly need to be ready to respond to these changes and this requires the adoption of a 'flexible' culture and a dynamic staff development and training policy.

References

Oberg, L. R. (1993) Rethinking reference: smashing icons at Berkeley. *College and Research Library News*, **54**(5), 265–6

Ford, B. J. (1992) From discussion to action: changing reference service patterns. *Journal of Academic Librarianship*, **18**(5), 284–855

Rettig, J. (1993) Academic reference service astride a fault line. *Wilson Library Bulletin*, **67**(9), 53–6

Yu, X. (1996) Advancing reference information systems on the Web. *Internet Reference Services Quarterly*, **1**(3), 67–74

CHAPTER TWENTY

Case Study: University of Hertfordshire Learning and Information Services

Jane Arthur

Introduction

At the University of Hertfordshire (UH), computing, library and media services were converged into a department called Learning and Information Services in January 1997. The department delivers converged services through campus Learning Resources Centres (LRCs). This case study is concerned with the delivery of reference and information services at UH.

IT has had a major impact on the delivery of reference and information services. These services are increasingly available in electronic form. Simultaneously users require IT applications to manipulate, analyse and present information derived from both hardcopy and electronic sources. We therefore provide a wider range of services than is traditionally part of library reference and information services and concomitantly their organization is different. At UH, the terminology 'campus information services' is used to cover the range of services provided to users within and remote from the LRCs. This case study looks at the process of designing services for the new Hatfield LRC, the layout of resources, user support and initial evaluation.

The impetus behind a review of computing, library and media service design and delivery was twofold: a new 11 000 sqm building at the Hatfield campus as part of the Follett building programme (HEFCE, 1993; SCONUL 1995) and the university's decision to merge computing, library and media services into a single operationally-converged department. This new department delivers services through LRCs at Hatfield, Hertford, St Albans and Watford. The new Hatfield LRC, on which this study will focus, opened in September 1997 and is the largest, supporting approximately 9000 full time equivalent (FTE) students in 5 faculties: Art and Design, Combined Studies, Health and Human Sciences, Natural Sciences, Engineering and Information Sciences.

Key Issues Influencing Service Design

There were a number of key issues driving service design for the new Hatfield LRC. Firstly, the university determined upon a converged computing, library and media service. The vision behind this was of an integrated service providing seamless access to information and the resources to manipulate, analyse and present this information. In addition, there were advantages in terms of staffing and of building and security costs, because fewer separate service points would be open for long hours (4 LRCs instead of 9 libraries and computer centres).

The second key issue was a corollary of convergence: the size of a building providing combined library, computing and media services to 9000 students in 5 faculties was larger than many traditional library buildings. This had implications for the layout of facilities, navigation around the building and user support. There are no design standards for LRC provision, but there has been a lot of debate on designing LRCs, including discussion of whether traditional library building standards may be applicable. See, for example, University Grants Committee (1976) for traditional library standards, and the Institute of Advanced Architectural Studies (1995) and the Higher Education Design Quality Forum (1996) for LRC design. With few norms to follow, the design process continually challenged assumptions, which was both refreshing and time consuming.

The third key issue was the drive for integration of learning resources within the academic process. The Subject Librarian was a key role in the library's original structure. This had to be developed to meet the requirements of teaching quality and research assessment exercises. Integration of computing, library and media elements of learning resources was therefore addressed in the layout of services and arrangements for user support.

Consultation

Integration within the academic process meant consultation with users. How did academic staff and students see learning and teaching needs developing within the next 5–10 years? What should be deemed to be part of a learning resources centre? For example, should the careers service, originally in the same building as Library and Media Services and with a small reference collection of careers-related materials, be located in the LRC? What about resources for disabilities' support and learning support? What about facilities and support for staff developing multimedia teaching materials? Or language laboratories? These are just some examples. The design process was helped by the pro-vice-chancellor giving a clear message that the building was for independent study. It was not to be a building for teaching, although facilities for skills training would be provided, to ensure that students would make the best use of the resources available. Is teaching versus skills training a meaningful distinction or merely semantics? Making this distinction served a purpose in providing a pragmatic basis for decision making in terms of service design. Thus facilities for disabilities' support, learning support and developing multimedia materials were to be provided on an open access basis, but not offices for staff providing learning support or careers services.

With this clarification that the building was to support independent study needs, consultation had a clear framework. How did students and staff envisage using a learning resources centre: Would they use books/journals and computers together, or would the noisier environment of an area with computers and printers be distracting for those preferring to work in silence? What did staff anticipate would be the balance of group work/individual study in the future, and therefore what balance of group study rooms and individual study places was required? How far would the use of video and image become commonplace in production of coursework and what implications would this have for equipment and its layout?

Consultations were held with various groups of staff, including a sub-group of the Learning and Teaching Committee, the university committee with responsibility for these aspects of policy. Presentations were given at Faculty Boards. The research community was specifically targeted, via the university research newsletter. The Users Committees of the Library and Media Services and of the Computer Centre received regular presentations. Open meetings were held on every campus with presentations from the architects.

Few clear guidelines came from these consultations, as users held contradictory opinions and tended to find it difficult to envisage how a building with library, media and computing facilities together in one physical location might be used differently from physically separate services. However, two clear messages did come across. The first message was that users wanted a single named point of contact for a constituency of users (one or more departments), similar to the traditional role of the Subject Librarian. This role was accommodated in the new staffing structure with the establishment of Information Consultants. The second message was that users wanted a large informal area, where food and drink would be allowed and users might choose to relax or study, individually or in groups. Consequently the coffee bar was extended to 125 seats. In general, however, user views were uncertain and contradictory, so what was very apparent was the need for multifunctional and flexible space, which could be adapted to meet the needs of different courses, constituencies of users and times of day or night. Flexibility became one of our key building criteria.

The consultation process had another important benefit. Academic staff said loudly that there was no point in having a new building and additional equipment without staffing to provide effective user support. It was therefore determined that the staffing budget would be the combination of the budgets of the two original departments. Service quality improvements would be sought, but not simple efficiency gains from a reduction in staff numbers.

Trends in use of services

Consultations with users, together with our experiences of current trends in use of services, were developed into our criteria for service design. We were observing a number of trends, common to many UK university libraries and computing centres. These included an increasing use of IT and a greater complexity of information sources. There was increasing demand, related in part to higher student numbers, but also related to the increase in 'student centred learning', i.e. less academic staff contact time and more self-managed time for individual and project work. So there was an increased need for both single and group study spaces. This increase in demand, much of it from students following atypical study and attendance patterns, raised many questions about the length of opening hours, service continuity and levels of service. Also, the additional IT provision planned for the building and the increased use of facilities experienced in many new buildings (Revill, 1995), led us to expect further increases in the use of services at Hatfield. Changes in teaching patterns mean many more students on placements for larger parts of their courses. Remote access/delivery of materials and support and dial-up access to electronic services were therefore crucial. There is some evidence of the development and use of locally produced learning materials, primarily for use by distance learning students. Whilst the demand for this is not yet great, we anticipated a growing need to support such developments.

Criteria for service design

These trends in use, in conjunction with limitations on staffing, the anticipated increase in demand and the expanded IT base through capital provision, led to the definition of a number of service criteria for the new LRC. Firstly more user support was needed. Much of this was at a routine level and at this level it was to be multi-skilled, covering enquiries ranging from how to operate equipment (photocopiers, laminators, camcorders, reader-printers), to locating items from a reference on the automated library catalogue and on the shelves, to using various standard computer packages, e-mail and CD-ROMs. This is the one-stop-shop.

In addition to front line support, more information and computing support was needed at a specialist level, in support of research, new teaching initiatives and student projects. This was not seen as multiskilled-, although in practice many computing, library and media professionals were beginning to develop overlapping skills.

Secondly, and complementing increased user support, there was a need for greater emphasis on self-service for all routine aspects of service. This was a significant cultural change that needed careful communication, and on which the layout of services had significant impact. The drive for self-service routines must be seen as enabling more specialist support and not as a reduction in services provided. This is a difficult message to communicate to both academic staff and to Learning Information Services staff.

We therefore saw the LRC as following a 'department store' model, a model which is fundamentally self-service, but which incorporates specialist departments where expert advice is available. The LRC would be a one-stop-shop for all requirements, with self-service routines, enquiries handled by multiskilled staff at the basic level, and more complex problems referred to professionals/consultants with complementary specialist skills who would deal with queries on an appointment or surgery basis.

Longer opening hours were needed to meet the changing patterns of study. This had implications for security of equipment and people (staff and users) within the building. Given restrictions on staffing resources, it also required more services to be self-service, if a full range of services were to be provided when staff were not available.

A strengthened working partnership with the academic staff was needed. A reactive role in relation to new course and research developments would be too slow, a proactive or experimental role was wasteful if it did not tie in closely with academic developments, since staffing resources are at such a premium. The process needed to be better integrated.

These criteria for service design – more user support, self-service routines, longer opening hours and integration with the academic process – led to key building requirements of:

- flexibility;
- ease of use;
- high quality environment;
- security of people and resources.

These had impact throughout the building design process, for example from underfloor flood wiring for flexibility to access control to the building for security. I shall address here some of the ways that two of the key building requirements – flexibility and ease of use – were translated into layout of services and user support. Further examples are given in Arthur (1997).

Flexibility

From consultations with users, it was apparent that flexibility was a key criterion. We should continue to expect changing attendance patterns, methods of teaching and courses taught at the university. The ability to change the designated use of space was therefore crucial.

Space allocated to shelving and study places was liable to future change, so task lighting was provided to shelving on the first floor to accommodate the different lighting levels needed for book stacks and study places with computers. All floors were designed to take bookstacks and bookstacks are free-standing. Thus shelving is designed to be easily moved.

Study environments needed to accommodate both multiple uses from day one and different future study requirements. The building therefore has 15 group study rooms to take up to 10 people, 3 IT suites for teaching the information and computing skills needed to use LRC resources, 40 single study rooms and open access study areas. The study furniture used throughout is modular. A core study space is 1000 mm wide by 800 mm deep. To this, side and middle partitions can be added to create study carrels and task lighting can be fitted to the middle partition; study spaces can be slotted together to create large open plan working areas; semi-circular shaped table segments can be fitted together to create round study tables, or core study spaces slotted into them to create large oval group study tables.

To meet the different study requirements, the intention has been to zone the building. For example, a quiet study area was designated adjacent to back issues of periodicals. This is entirely single study carrels with no computers or printers. Similarly, group study tables are located on the busy ground floor.

Ease of Use of Facilities

Ease of use of facilities was a key criterion, so that as many facilities as possible would be self-service and enable limited staff resources to be most effectively deployed. Ease of use was addressed through layout, signing and guiding, user support and self-service access to facilities.

The physical location of resources within a large 11 000 sqm building on four floors was a key issue to ensure ease of use. The architects came up with a system of banners hanging in the atrium indicating subject areas, to help people orientate themselves and navigate through the building. We used the model of the department store guide, or list of resources on each floor with a floor plan and located this by the stairs on each floor.

The Dewey sequence was used to arrange stock and there were no plans to change this. Subject areas based on Dewey were established, following the Dewey sequence and moving up through the building:

first floor
Computer Science
Psychology
Social Sciences
Languages
Sciences
Medical Sciences

second floor
Engineering
Management
Arts
Periodicals A – Z

The names for these areas generated a huge amount of discussion. Dewey is not intuitive, therefore people looking for materials on a specific topic will not necessarily easily identify in which subject grouping they will find the resources they need. Therefore banners indicating main subject areas also list some of the topics located in the area. The intention was that the user should use the catalogue for specific searching and the subject areas to facilitate browsing and to identify with an area as being their prime use area, to help make a large building more scaleable, user friendly and less intimidating. In the recent past, there have been a number of departments setting up local LRCs and reasons given have included the impersonal nature of the library building and the difficulty in finding resources.

Within each subject area, materials are located within a single main sequence (books, videos, pamphlets, oversize, CD-ROMs). In addition, each subject area has a separate Subject Reference section of dictionaries, directories and handbooks. There may be some duplication of materials between the subject reference areas (primarily dictionaries) to address the size of the building. Eventually, most of these sort of resources should be replaced with electronic services. Current periodical issues are also located in subject areas to facilitate browsing and to promote their use.

Back issues of periodicals are located in a single alphabetical sequence on the top floor, with a standard cut off date, initially 1980, for stock located in the closed access rolling stack on the lower ground floor. The question of heavy use journals having all the back issues on open access, versus ease of use of a standard cut off date, was given considerable debate. It was felt that a single sequence for back issues was preferable to a subject arrangement, since the use of back issues tended to be from a given reference (from a reading list, an abstracting service or from other journals and books) and not for browsing. Stack requests over October – February 1998 were running at the low level of about 100 requests a month, with the majority related to Natural Sciences.

On the ground floor, there is a collection of high demand short loan and reference materials, called the reserve collection. This is controlled by a book security system, so that materials are kept in this area, which is provided with study spaces, photocopiers and computer workstations. This prevents materials being taken throughout the building and effectively 'lost' until located when tidying. It also provides a core collection on the ground floor, should long opening hours and security of people and resources prove incompatible: thus if only the ground floor were accessible for certain hours, there would be a core collection available. Initially, all floors are open from 08.30–02.00, with different service levels at different times of the day.

A small collection of general reference materials is provided on the ground floor, including multi-disciplinary encyclopaedias, telephone directories, newspapers. This is considerably reduced from the previous library collection, most of which has been dispersed to subject reference in subject areas. In time, this should become all electronic based.

Computer workstations are located adjacent to subject areas according to what hardware is most used by the relevant faculties: for example, Suns adjacent to Computer Science; Macs adjacent to Arts. Standard software and electronic databases are available from all workstations, except where it is restricted to stand-alone machines for technical or licensing reasons.

Electronic services are provided uniformly, so that from a single log-in users are presented with a standard range of services: word processing, spreadsheet and presentation packages; e-mail; an Internet browser; programming languages; interactive learning packages; bibliographic databases; and the library management system. Software and databases managed locally (at UH) are loaded on file servers and networked, wherever technically feasible and licences permit. Printing is decentralized, with approximately one laser printer to every 20 workstations. Users have individual print accounts, managed using GPAS software.

These subject areas are designed to be flexible, to adapt to space needs as more study spaces with computer workstations are required or to cater for growth of hard copy collections in certain areas. Journal expansion is catered for by the rolling stack: the cut-off date for materials on open access can be changed, as necessary.

The core of the building is open plan and each subject area is adjacent to some individual study and group study rooms. Subject areas also have notice boards and leaflet display racks for the information consultants to use to define and distinguish their subject areas and to promote services. It is hoped in this way to make the building more scaleable and to create an environment more conducive to study.

User support is an important issue for a building this size and on four floors. How much needs to be provided and where should it be located? Too often library layouts have been designed for a number of help points which staffing resources have been unable to support. It seems to be an axiom that the more support that is provided, the more is expected. For example, students and staff at the smaller campus of Watford have traditionally received – and therefore have come to expect – a far higher level of user support than at the larger Hatfield campus.

We are aiming for access to as many services as possible to be self-service. This includes the use of vending machines for the sale of consumables and the provision of self-help guides to many services. Ideally, such guides would be incorporated on Web pages, but we find that many users prefer written guides or to ask for help. The layout is designed so that there are hardcopy guides available between the entrance to the building and the Help Desk.

The help desk is located on the ground floor, to handle first-line enquiries, in person or by telephone from other floors. On the first and second floor, there are information points. They have a telephone linking directly into the Help Desk and self help guides available.

The Help Desk is staffed by Information Officers. These posts do not require library or computing professional qualifications. These staff provide the multiskilled first level help and refer on specialist enquiries via appointments or surgery times to Information Consultants (qualified librarians), Computing Consultants or Media Consultants. See Appendix 1 for the list of practical skills required by Information Officers. Initial indications are that it is difficult to recruit people with the full range of skills for information officer posts, so there is a major ongoing training commitment.

The Help Desk has networked computers set up with the same range of services and interface as seen by the users. It was intended that the help desk should not be easily by-passed in favour of the consultants, as they are in staff offices with access control. We are trying to develop a culture whereby the consultants are seen as specialists whose time is valuable and available by appointment. This has enabled specialists to better manage their time, as many enquiries can be answered by Information Officers. This becomes increasingly important for the Information Consultants as their departmental constituencies become larger and as they take on new roles. Given the enhanced role for Information Officers, this has necessitated largely freeing them from routine jobs, e.g. shelving, tidying, processing of new books, filling photocopiers with paper, issue/return of items and delivery of classroom equipment. These jobs are now largely performed by Resources Assistants, some of whom are students working up to 8 hours a week on casual contracts.

In addition to the Help Desk for enquiries in person or by telephone from elsewhere in the building, there is a telephone helpline for users elsewhere in the university, on placement or calling from home. This is available to users from all campuses to answer front-line enquiries.

Evaluation

The LRC opened for the first week of the 1997–98 Autumn term. Six months from opening, data available on usage patterns and user evaluation is limited and should be treated with caution. However, some interesting patterns are emerging.

Occupancy figures compared to the library and computer centre, for the same time(s) in 1996 have more than doubled. Gate figures, for those entering the LRC, are more than double those for the library for the same times in 1996 (people entering the computer centre were not monitored).

Patterns of enquiry numbers and type are known to vary throughout the academic year. However, there is a consistent pattern emerging of a strong IT bias with few traditional 'library' queries at both the helpdesk and the university wide telephone helpline. The following data is based on March 1998 only.

For March enquiries, about 7 per cent are 'library' and 39 per cent IT based. This has implications for recruitment and training. Enquiries also show high levels of general queries which indicate that more work needs to be done to intercept

Table 20.1 Percentages of types of enquiry to the Help Desk and telephone helpline

Enquiries (%)	Help Desk	Helpline
General	18	23
Roombk	3	3
Sales	36	7
Printers	26	12
Copiers	2	2
Libertas	3	7
Oth.lib.	2	4
CDRoms	1	2
Q/Ref	0	1
Network	1	3
Password	3	12
Dialup	0	3
Email	2	6
Web	1	2
Disks	1	4
Systems	0	3
Word	1	3
Excel	0	2
Othapps	0	2
Total	100	100

these queries before they get to the Help Desk, e.g. through displays of self-help guides; notices and information on the web.

Whilst a full user survey has not yet been attempted, a survey of undergraduates on two courses, Psychology and Cognitive Science, was carried out (Vallee-Tourangeau, 1998, unpublished) soon after the building opened. This asked students to rate on a scale from 1 (very poorly or dissatisfied) to 8 (very adequately or satisfied) a number of services and features offered.

The top rated features by both groups are Layout, Lending services and Journals. The lowest rated features are books (Psychology students) and software (Cognitive Science students). These results indicate a relationship to changes made (or not made) to LRC services, compared to previous library and computer centre facilities. For example, the arrangement of the journals is different from the library, in that current issues have a front-on display, adjacent to the relevant subject area. By contrast, the bookstock and range of software are unchanged from previous facilities. The

Table 20.2 LRC services

Survey	Label
1. How well does the LRC suit your needs for books?	Books
2. How well does the LRC suit your needs for periodicals (journals?)	Journals
3. Rate your satisfaction with the inter-library loan services	ILL
4. Rate your satisfaction with the short-loan collection (reserve collection)	SLC
5. Rate your satisfaction with the Helpdesk services	Helpdesk
6. Rate your satisfaction with the Lending services	Lending
7. Rate your satisfaction with the software provided in the LRC	Software
8. Rate your satisfaction with the organisation and layout of the LRC	Layout

Table 20.3   Mean satisfaction rate for Psychology and Cognitive Science Courses

	Psychology	Cognitive Science
Layout	5.9	6.2
Lending	5.8	5.8
Journals	5.5	5.8
Software	5.4	3.6
SLC	5.2	4.6
Help	5.2	4.0
ILL	5.2	4.6
Books	4.9	4.7

ratings by the individual courses are consistent with the balance of book/software use, in that the students are more critical of the resources of which they make greatest use. Experiences in new buildings elsewhere support the observation that satisfaction with a new building tends to be associated with increased criticism of library stock and Help Desk services.

Help Desk services are developing. In designing the service, it was envisaged that in order to solve many queries, Information Officers would need to go to the user's workstation. Thus all study places are numbered for ease of identification. Information Officers would carry either radios or mobile phones to maintain links with the helpdesk and also to enable them to contact technicians or consultants if they could not solve a problem. In practice, because of the length of queues at the Help Desk, this has not happened at Hatfield, although going to assist users at their workstations is common practice at the smaller campuses. Plans for roving or peripatetic support at Hatfield are under consideration. The jury is still out on the best way to manage helpdesks (Clegg 1998).

Conclusion

The question one always asks about a case study is: how far is the experience it contains transferable? As building and service design for converged services has few norms there are many different models appearing in the sector for both building design and converged management structures. However, the trends in use of services are broadly similar across the sector and thus the key service design require-ments of flexibility, ease of use, high quality environment and security of people and resources are common to most academic libraries. Ways of implementing these design requirements are variable across the sector. As Brindley said (1995):

> 'the vision of the electronic library and its grand planning, difficult though it is, is relatively easy when set against the difficulties of gradual implementation in the context of uncertainty'.

At UH, convergence of different learning resources became a design imperative. Some universities have determined on a continued physical separation of IT and traditional library facilities – often an economic decision, because of the costs of raised floors for wiring and also sufficient floor loadings for bookstacks. In perhaps 10–20 years time, I anticipate this separation will be a cost effective solution, as a large propor-tion of teaching materials will be in digital form accessible from a workstation. Students can then use the hardcopy sources on an occasional basis, in the way that rolling stacks tend to operate today. Until then, I anticipate we will see an increasing number of users working with hardcopy and elec-tronic facilities in conjunction. We therefore need to design and manage services to meet this trend. Whether the imple-mentations described in this case study are effective will be tested with the ongoing heavy use of the Hatfield Learning Resources Centre.

References

Arthur, J. (1997) Designing a university library for the 21st century. In *Libraries of the Future: Seminar CASLIN PEW IV* (Dlouhe Strane, 1997), pp. 29–58. Brno & Olomouc: MOLIN.

Brindley, L.J. (1995) Introduction, In: *Building libraries for the Information Age: based on the proceedings of a symposium on the Future of Higher Educational Libraries* (York, 1994). York: University of York, Institute of Advanced Architectural Studies. pp.1–4.

Clegg, S. (1998) Converged enquiry/help desks: rhetoric or reality? *RELAY*, **45**, 7–10.

Higher Education Design Quality Forum (1996) *The development of learning resource centres for the future: proceedings of a conference.* (Royal Institute of British Architects, London, 1995). London: SCONUL.

Higher Education Funding Council for England, et al. (1993) *Joint Funding Councils' Libraries Review Group: Report.* (Follett Report). Bristol: HEFCE

Institute of Advanced Architectural Studies (1995) *Building libraries for the Information Age: based on the proceedings of a symposium on the Future of Higher Educational Libraries* (York, 1994). York: University of York, Institute of Advanced Architectural Studies.

Revill, D. (1995) The effects of a new 'library' building. *SCONUL newsletter*, **5/6**, 40–44.

SCONUL (1995) Funding for library buildings. *SCONUL newsletter*, **5/6**, 37–39.

University Grants Committee (1976) *Capital provision for university libraries: report of a working party under the chairmanship of Professor Richard Atkinson.* London: HMSO.

Appendix 1

Skills required by Information Officers in UH Learning and Information Services

1. Basic competence in PC, Macintosh and Unix operating systems: including switching on/off, login/logout, formatting disks, window management, use of mouse and menus, file management (directories, deleting, moving), printing, backup.

2. Basic familiarity with a designated range of software packages available to users; understanding of their appropriate usage and the hardware platform(s) on which they are available.

3. Ability to use the main functions of a specified range of software applications including:
   a wordprocessor   (currently Word 6 for Windows)
   a spreadsheet   (currently Excel 5 for Windows)
   a presentation package (currently Powerpoint)

4. Ability to use email, including reading, composing and sending messages and files, groups and lists, saving and printing

5. Ability to access and use a range of networked electronic sources including:
   – use of a Web browser to access the Internet, search for specific addresses and subjects and use bookmarks.
   – telnet, ftp commands
   – access to BIDS, Uncover, Medline and other information database services

6. Ability to access networked and stand-alone CD Rom

databases and multimedia CD Rom including: switch on/off, loading disks, login/logout, access commands, printing, downloading to disk.

7. Ability to use the automated library system Libertas to:
   - to look for materials on a specific subject or for a specific item
   - to check stock holdings, copy availability and shelf location
   - to place a reservation for an item
   - to issue, return and renew items
   - to understand and deal with individual user records, intercept messages, fines queries
   - to input and deal with inter-library loan requests
   - to enter orders for materials, receive items and check progress of orders
   - to create/acquire basic catalogue record and add local data

8. Basic familiarity with copyright and licencing requirements and with UH codes of practice

9. Ability to operate and carry out basic maintenance procedures for the following equipment and processes:
   photocopiers (black and white and colour)
   printers
   scanners
   fax machines
   binding machines
   laminators
   microfilm/microfiche reader/printers
   audio replay/tape to tape copying
   video replay/video copying
   camcorders
   overhead projectors
   slide projectors
   mobile radios

satellite reception/recording
off-air recording

10. Basic technical awareness including checking connections, visual safety checks, dealing with common faults and problems

11. Ability to carry out systematic information retrieval to locate specific items and subject materials in the library collections

12. Understanding of bibliographic references for books, journals and other materials and ability to use designated sources to locate full bibliographic and purchase details of a book

13. Ability to use a specified range of quick reference sources (both printed and electronic) to answer routine enquires

14. Ability to use a specified range of indexes and abstracting sources (both printed and electronic) to locate information on a specific subject.

15. Ability to recognise when to refer enquiries on for more specialist assistance

Managing User Education and Training

CHAPTER TWENTY ONE

Overview: Managing User Education and Training

Margaret Watson

Introduction

Lifelong learning is not a new concept, but in a world where information has become a primary commodity and technological innovation has completely changed the way in which we access information, we must be sure that everyone has the necessary information skills to equip them for that learning. At every level of education information skills are being addressed and librarians have a key role to play; librarians can facilitate the process by which students become fully independent information users but they cannot do this in isolation. We must work with educators and computer specialists to provide a learning environment in which students are given help, advice and support to find the information they need. Increasingly that information is available electronically. The vision of the user – student, researcher or teacher, sitting at their work station searching databases, writing papers, taking part in an electronic discussion etc. is exciting but can also be terrifying initially to the user. Support for learning must be the guiding principle for librarians; providing training on how to access and use all the resources that are available is a primary requirement in order to produce lifelong learners.

Information Literacy

Information literacy is a term commonly used now to express the required end product and, as with most labels, there is disagreement over its use, but, as Snavely and Cooper (1997, p.10) remark there 'seems to be agreement, however, that librarians have embarked upon a trend in instruction which recognizes the need to ensure that students (and graduates) are capable of independently (and in groups) recognizing and refining their information needs, finding the information they need, and evaluating and using the information they need throughout their lifetimes'. The process by which this outcome is achieved has also been given many labels! Bibliographic instruction is most common in the USA, user education and information skills training are more common in the UK. In a recent book Kirby (1998) refers to the term empowerment; a term which stresses the importance of information skills in the range of transferable skills. The term user education has been criticized as it sounds rather patronizing and suggests that we make libraries so difficult to use that we need to educate people to use them; however the term has the advantage of putting user first and relating that to education. In this chapter user education is taken to encompass any activity which enables the client to become an efficient and effective user of information and will refer to activities mainly in the higher education sector.

The Higher Education Environment

The principal changes in HE in the UK – changes in teaching and learning, impact of information technology, increased student numbers, changes in student profile and reduced resources – have obviously all affected the library and information services in universities. The Electronic Libraries (eLib) Programme, set up following the Follet Report (HEFCE, 1993), addresses this whole area. A recent review by Day *et al.* (1996) outlines the impact of these changes. The Dearing Report (NCIHE, 1997) has added to the debate about standards and quality of provision. Although ' it is inconceivable that the inquiry will fail to consider the increasing role and significance of library and information services in HE' (Day *et al.*, 1996), the report appears to pay little direct attention to libraries; however it does envisage a learning environment increasingly based on technology.

All of these changes have impacted on user education. For example, increased student numbers has seen a move away from the traditional library tours as part of induction; changes in student profile have made it much more important to focus on the user to provide more relevant programmes for mature students, overseas students, disabled students, part-time and distance students. Information technology has enabled the development of computer assisted learning and online guides to using references sources. However it is the changes in teaching and learning plus the development of the electronic library which perhaps have made a more dramatic and exciting impact on user education.

Teaching and Learning

There has been a movement away from traditional lecture-based methods towards open, flexible and student centred learning (Day *et al.*, 1996 pp.167–174). Rather than being solely dependent on knowledge transfer from their teachers, students are encouraged to make use of wider resources. 'Much detailed discipline content is now secondary to an ability to find, analyse, understand and apply information' (Pollard, 1996, pp.58). However we still need to know more about how people learn. Cowan (1994, pp.16) makes a plea that all of us involved in education should meet the challenge to 'be involved effectively with all aspects of the teaching and learning relationship, and to see teaching ... as the purposeful creation of situations from which motivated learners should not be able to escape without significantly learning or developing as a result from our efforts' and he goes on to say that this definition of teaching and learning 'covers instruction – aye, *and* facilitation and student support in all forms and places, *including libraries and information centres'*.

At present very few students embark on their university courses with the necessary knowledge and skills to enable them to take advantage of an information-rich learning environment. Many universities offer study skills courses to all first year undergraduates and very often information skills play an important element in that course. It is interesting to note the changes of title from Library to Resource Centre, Learning Resource Centre, Learning Support, Information Services Department etc., which underlie the changing role of the library within teaching and learning.

Additionally we also have the increased use of information technology in delivering teaching and learning. Peters (1996, p108) comments that 'the provision of IT services to individuals using desktop PCs is effecting a momentous shift in the way students learn and find information, which in turn is forcing not only libraries but educational organizations in general to reconsider their pedagogic methods'.

Many students at present need to be taught basic IT skills before they can begin to take advantage of the new resources. Study skills courses should also include these basic IT skills. Students need to be computer literate and information literate. As well as having access to information online via CD-ROM and the Internet, students can access lectures via video or a department's Web page, lecture notes are available on the local network, even assessment can be done on-line. The enthusiasm displayed by students for using the Internet can to be used to good effect in user education (just as it did earlier with the introduction of CD-ROM services). Developments in methods for teaching distant learners have been incorporated into teaching materials for on-campus students. Students are expected to undertake activities, including information seeking, and to reflect on their own performance; formative assessment is very important in the learning process. By using self-paced learning materials, in concert with lectures, seminars, workshops etc., students can have much more control over their own learning. New teaching methods can be as difficult for staff as for students!

The Electronic Library

What do we mean by the term electronic library? Discussion and debate will occur in other chapters of this book, and in other fora. 'Electronic library' seems to blur with 'virtual library'. In his introduction to the 1st ELVIRA Conference, Collier (1995, p2) says 'if the electronic library is so universal in scope, multimedia in presentation and unrestricted in time and space, is it all things to all people, or is it even capable of being defined?' Librarians involved with user education need to plan both for the needs of their users at present and for the future; most libraries are moving along the continuum from traditional to electronic library and will be for some time. Biddiscombe (1996, p.3) reflects that 'between the utopian promise of a fully liberated and self sufficient end-user, and the prospects for the library of the future, there lies the present reality'. Technological developments seem to offer the virtual library in the near future, but for many of us the reality is a hybrid library, both a real space where printed and electronic resources will be available as well as a cyberspace where access to resources worldwide are available. La Guardia *et al.* (1996, p.10) define the 'New Library' quite succinctly:

- In part it will be a physical place called a library;
- 'In part it will be a network accessible space called a library;
- Therefore readers will access it by walking in the front door, moving to and through via networks, call it on the

telephone, FAX to and from it, send e-mail to it, and video-conference with it;
- The New Library will contain information in the traditional physical forms of books, magazines, microformats, visual formats, etc.;
- The New Library will provide access to network information resources by providing users with logical and sensible means to navigate the networks;
- Librarians will work in both the physical and the electronic library. They will locate materials, some of which will be physical, and some of which will be electronic. They will acquire these materials, organize them, and give readers physical and electronic access to them;
- Finally, librarians will teach each other and users about how to use the New Library.'

The Educational Role of the Library

There are three aspects to the educational role which are inter-related: user education, reference and support services, and liaison with academic staff over course content. Academic librarians have been involved in supporting learning for a long time, providing courses and workshops for undergraduates, postgraduates, researchers, academic staff and increasingly other support staff. Because of the changes mentioned above it is even more important now that librarians work with academic and other support staff to develop courses which facilitate lifelong learning, and to give support to academic and other staff in the university to update their own skills and knowledge. Academic librarians need to work in close liaison with academic staff on the design of study skills modules for undergraduate students. (Approaches to developing these courses will be discussed later.) Academic liaison will vary from person to person, and from institution to institution but it is important that all students are given the opportunity to learn the core skills they will need both at university and beyond: 'the emphasis

on open and flexible approaches to learning and the acquisition of core skills by learners recognized that they needed
both the skills for learning and the skills to enable them
to operate effectively in the world of work' (Kingston, 1994,
p.74).

New researchers and academic staff may also need to
enhance their information skills; librarians are involved
with induction programmes for new staff but with the advent
of the compulsory teaching qualifications for academic
staff perhaps information skills might be included in that
qualification. In addition, workshops on new or changed
information services should be offered to all users of the
library. It is equally important that all library staff also have
an opportunity to update and enhance their information
skills.

It is also vital that as Heery and Morgan (1996, p.132) say
'helping to connect people with the required information
regardless of format will remain a basic tenet of academic
librarianship. The time that students and academic staff
interact regularly and effectively with library and information sources without the need for guidance and advice is a
long way off'. So as well as providing courses and workshops etc. in formal user education programmes, librarians
will also need to continue to offer more individualized
support at the point of need, whether in person or electronically. Surgeries or appointments with appropriate subject
staff, electronic reference desks as well the more traditional
enquiry points or help desks (most users do not want to
differentiate between asking for help in using the software
or how to find relevant information) are becoming more
popular.

The third and possibly most exciting aspect of the educational role could be the integration of librarians within the
departments or schools in discussion of course design and
delivery.

This would involve team work involving the academic
subject expert, the subject librarian and colleagues from
computer services and/or learning support services. As

Creth (1993, p.125) says the 'combined efforts of technologists and librarians could have a significant impact on the development of new approaches to instruction on university campuses'. Many academic staff are already developing new and exciting courses using information technology, encouraged in UK higher education by government sponsored programmes like the Computers in Teaching Initiative, Information Technology and Training Initiative and Teaching and Learning Technology Programme, but there is still long way to go. Librarians can play an important part in developing appropriate resources for the new styles of learning if they are involved from the design stage, and not just called in for remedial help for learners.

User Education in the Electronic Library

'The virtual library raises questions which go to the heart of educational provision. Will staff and students feel liberated (or terrified) by this freedom? Will they be able to cope with using technology for the main element of their studies ... ?' (Peters, 1996, p.120). Helping people to cope is where user education starts. Users need to become familiar with resources available in the library and how to access information from beyond the library. Their need for user education will depend largely on their prior experience and training and on the subject area, on the way it is taught and how the literature of the subject is presented. Any programme of user education should start with a needs analysis; in order to do this successfully target groups should be established and their user needs defined. The planning for user education in the electronic library is no different from that of the traditional planning cycle: user needs analysis, establishment of aims and objectives, consideration of resources and facilities, content and method, delivery of programme, monitoring and evaluation of programme and modification of the programme.

Who needs user education?

Undergraduate students are the obvious category; new to the university and most of them new to the self-directed learning on which they are about to embark. We should ensure that all students 'irrespective of module choice, programme of study or degree route have a broadly similar experience of teaching and learning during their time at university'. (Pennington and O'Neil, 1994, p.11) Part of this experience is to acquire information skills which will enhance their personal and professional development; 'this includes the need to understand technology, networks and methods of access to information as well as acquiring enhanced personal skills and a knowledge of teaching and pedagogic methodology' (Day *et al.*, 1996, p.158).

The most successful user education at this level is fully integrated into the course, as a study skills course or effective learning programme, and is part of the teaching and learning strategy of the institution. User education in the USA is part of the culture of the university, but there is evidence still in the UK that user education is often seen as an add on or peripheral to the subject discipline. People learn best when they need to learn, when they practise what they have learnt and can reflect on it, and when they get feedback on what they have learnt. Heery and Morgan (1996, p.50) list the four ingredients of success as RITA: relevance, integration, timing and assessability. Even among undergraduates there will be a variety of experience and attitude towards learning and information technology, so it is useful to keep in mind the three levels: novice, knowledgeable but intermittent information user, and frequent user as suggested by Day (1994, p.141). However with an undergraduate study skills programme it is best to start with the novice level but allow for flexibility of programme to enable students to learn at their own speed; any expert users can be used to support and encourage other students. Such a programme could be designed by subject specialists in the library, learning support staff and computer support staff in collaboration with academic staff. The course might then be delivered by the appropriate academic staff with help where appropriate. Even at this level there is a likelihood that user support will be networked and that users will be increasingly remote.

Once initial user education is provided there will only be the need to offer help and advice as mentioned earlier, personally or electronically, and to offer workshops on new resources and services. Often such help is required when students are faced with final year projects or dissertations. However it is always imperative that students continue to practise and develop their new information skills throughout their course, so it becomes instinctive and part of their portfolio of transferable skills.

Postgraduate students and researchers will hopefully already have good information skills but once again it is dangerous to place everyone into a homogeneous group. Perhaps with smaller numbers of postgraduate students and researchers it is easier to draw up user profiles and to develop support material more specific to their needs. Modules on research methods can include enhanced information skills elements and workshops or demonstrations can be given to specific groups as appropriate.

Academic staff will need to know what resources and services are available through the electronic library, and may require help and guidance in using them. New staff, including administrative and support staff, are usually given an induction programme and it is important that the library is able to make a contribution to this programme. However nothing is better than one to one discussion. Academic liaison can start here with subject librarians, or other appropriate members of library staff, getting to know the information needs of the academic staff, the courses which they will be teaching and their research specialisms. Academic staff need to understand the support that the library can give to their students. Many librarians take this opportunity to compile a user profile so that current awareness services etc. can be developed.

The final category of people who need user education or staff training are, of course, other members of library staff.

New library staff should be included in the institutional induction programme which helps them to see how the library contributes to the teaching, learning and research of the university. Other staff training should be on-going. Any member of staff likely to be on a help desk or enquiry point will need quite specific training on networked information and resources, as well as more traditional library routines. Once again a needs analysis is important to decide on the level of training required. 'A training strategy should identify what level of knowledge and skill is needed by each staff member' (Day, 1994, p.143) Nothing is more frustrating for the user to be passed from one member of a staff to another in order for an information need to be satisfied. There may be qualified or experienced trainers or teachers in the library and they can be used to help train others, as Byron (1995, p.243) suggests 'instruction librarians (responsible for managing and educating other library instructors) creating a comfort zone in cyberspace is a growing and vital element of the job'.

Who should teach user education?

All staff need to be able to give help and support to users of the library but not everyone is required to be a teacher or trainer. Very few librarians are formally trained as teachers, but more and more are being required to help design and deliver information skills modules. La Guardia *et al.* (1996, p.59) comment 'when multiple online systems hit the library arena, the multitudes began, quite rightly, to clamor for training, training, training. Training in e-mail, word processing, spreadsheets, alternate character sets, Windows, graphics packages, statistics packages, database searching, database creation, OCLC, RLIN, UNIX, HTML, SGML and any number of other initials. Yet amidst all this tumult, we have as yet to hear a strong unified voice calling out for training in what seems to us a most basic library need. Teaching'. They go on to devote a whole chapter to 'Finding, Creating, Becoming Library Teachers'. There has been a similar reaction in the UK and a need for librarians to understand the process of teaching and learning, and to acquire associated skills, has been voiced.

Data the from the Impact on People of Electronic Libraries (IMPEL2) (See Section 3) reveals a need for trainers in libraries to undergo some formal teacher training. Some comments from interview transcripts include: 'staff involved in training users suggested they could benefit from learning more about how people learn and they would welcome any advice from experts in the teaching profession', 'a more systematic approach to appraising skills as educators would assist us', 'I think it does put a lot of strain on the staff who do information skills training', 'I think, well I did my best, I am not a teacher'.

This form of training can be part of an institutional teacher training programme, but many universities do not offer places to librarians; it can be offered through masters courses in education, or other certificate and diploma courses offered by colleges or the Open University. Some information and library studies departments offer modules on user education or learning resource centre management. More specialist course for librarians and other learning support staff are also available. The following chapter on the eLib project EduLib will discuss this further; however it is clear from the take-up of the EduLib programme that many librarians are keen to improve their knowledge and skills in this area.

Whilst emphasizing the importance of this kind of training for librarians and learning support staff, it is also important to repeat the need for collaboration and partnership with academic staff so that the learning environment supports students, researchers and academic staff.

Another group of possible trainers are of course students themselves. Peer tutoring and training can be seen as an additional level of learning support. Students who are already expert in the use of IT are often employed on help desks in computing labs.; this could be extended to online support for information skills.

How should user education be taught?

Perhaps the answer is – *in any way* which provides clients with the skills and knowledge to define their information need, refine their need into a search strategy, recognize the most appropriate resources to use, find relevant information, analyse and evaluate it and add to the knowledge and understanding of their subject. Information skills as part of an integrated study skills course for undergraduates has already been mentioned; but, even within that, variety of method and approach is recommended. The combination of demonstration, hands-on, discussion and formative assessment supported by both printed and online documentation is most appropriate. There is no point in teaching information skills for the electronic library if you do not use information technology both in content and delivery. Heery and Morgan (1996) give some very useful guidelines in Chapter 3 of their book; they comment that 'there is a high degree of overlap between criteria under which learning takes place, the content of the programme or unit, the methods used, the support provided and the skills and attitudes of the librarian. The library that has worked out the recipe and provides a balance across each of these variables has indeed developed a highly marketable product'. La Guardia *et al.* (1996) also give some useful advice about teaching in the electronic classroom and types of remote instruction.

There are useful computer assisted learning packages produced by Glasgow University Library, under the national Teaching and Learning Technology programme, which can be purchased quite cheaply and networked in any institution. The CTI Centre for Library and Information Studies (CTILIS) regularly reviews, in both its journal *Infocus* and the *Resources Guide*, information skills packages; many of these packages can be borrowed or tested at CTILIS in the Department of Information and Library Studies at the University of Loughborough . NetSkills, another important eLib project, has just revised TONIC, the online tutorial for using the Internet, and other learning packages are currently available free of charge to higher education institutions.

NetSkills also organizes workshops and other events. Further information can be found on the web at http://www. netskills.ac.uk.

Cox (1997) in a review article discusses how the Web can be used for library user education. It echoes the feeling that, as students are excited about surfing the Net, we should be using this tool to teach the important information skills that lifelong learners will need.

Whatever approach is taken aims and objectives must be articulated; the learning outcomes for each session or element of the programme must be clear. Usually information is given first, often with a demonstration, and then students are asked to practise the skills and to apply them to a piece of course work or assessment, but Atton (1994, p.310) suggests that 'given that education at all levels is now striving to develop the independent learner through student-centred styles of learning, it can be argued that critical thinking should precede any knowledge of information sources and retrieval techniques'. He designed a course where students began with identifying the problem and discussing how they could resolve it. Once again close collaboration with academic staff was required, but the end result was very positive.

Some Examples of Methods and Approaches.

An example of the integrated approach was described by Hunter at the 2nd International Symposium on Networked Learner Support at Sheffield University in June 1997 (available at http://netways.shef.ac.uk/rbase/papers/hunter.htm.). 'The University of Lincolnshire and Humberside has developed a University Skills and Capability Curriculum that is core for all students at all three levels of study. At level one there is an Effective Learning Programme (ELP). The main aim of ELP is to develop independent life long learners.' The programme ran for the first time in 1996 and is currently being modified. A computer-based networked learner support system provides profiling tools, self-diagnostic tests, automated assessment, feedback to the student, feedback to the tutor, information on ELP and electronic materials delivery. Students do not learn the skills in isolation but use them immediately within the context of the subject programme. ELP is the responsibility of academic departments but Learning Advisors are to be appointed to subject areas to assist in delivering an integrated approach to the development of students' learning and study skills.

The great advantage of networked learner support (NLS) is that the tools are always available on the network and that all students are offered the same support. Students can do remedial work if they need to; students who move from one institution to another, or who join a course in the second year, are also able to follow the programme. Links can be made from the programme to other Web sites, other networked information and other computer assisted learning tools. Guides to the (physical) library can also be made available on the network for as we have mentioned earlier, many students will continue to use the library and printed texts for some time to come. Many libraries who do not offer full networked learner support do have training suites, which are linked to the network, where students come for study skills/information skills programmes. The NetLinks project (Levy *et al.*, 1996) at Sheffield University provides a forum for interesting discussion on NLS and can still be accessed through the web at http://www.shef.ac.uk/~np/ although the project finishes in 1998.

Other examples of integrated information skills programmes in the UK include the University of Wales Institute, Cardiff described by Welsh *et al.* (1996) where implementation of the programme depended on ' fulfilment of a number of specialist roles. Professional librarians were responsible for writing the content; professional photographers provided conventional and digital pictures; the Learning Materials Development Officer provided expertise in the application of advanced computing techniques; the Head of Learning and Teaching used his expertise in learning styles and methods to draw the project together and thus create a coherent, structured, fully interactive programme'. Also Wade (1996, pp. 96–109) describes training the end user at Sheffield Hallam University which has recently opened the Adsetts Centre, 'a flexible learner support centre'.

Biddiscombe (1997, LRE23) describes how 'subject based teams of computer and library services staff have been created to provide support for teaching and learning across the faculties and schools of the institution'; he gives details of three Web-based projects: ArtsWeb, which has created 'a focused interface for subject-based information services' and brought together 'the skills of the whole team in support of the user' and 'encouraged the interaction of Information Services and academic staff in support of the teaching and learning process (ArtsWeb can be accessed via http://www.bham.ac.uk/arts/); Information Services Guide which can be found at http://www.bham.ac.uk/isg/; and finally, the work of the Effective Learning Group which hoped to produce an in-house guide to study skills but at present uses appropriate commercially produced packages and other established information skills programmes and is available at http://www.bham.ac.uk/eig.

A very useful discussion list for anyone interested in information skills teaching can be found on the Mailbase discussion list: lis-infoskills.

Assessment and Evaluation

It is a commonly held view that students only do something if there is a mark attached to it! Although not subscribing totally to this view, it does appear that we all learn best when we get feedback on how we are doing; both formative and summative assessment can be used to apply the information skills we learn but generally, for initial study skills courses, formative assessment would be preferred. Time should be given to discussing work that has been done and feedback should be given either in person or electronically. Sometimes it is useful to discuss progress within a small group to encourage people to learn from each other and to establish peer support groups. If assessment is used in the programme, that assessment must be course related so that the student experiences a seamless join between the information skills programme and the subject course; feedback must always be given as quickly as possible. Assessment criteria must be clearly given and feedback structured around those criteria. Assessment is used to mark the progress of an individual towards the learning outcomes and is not a substitute for evaluation, although it can form a part of evaluation.

Many of the examples referred to in this chapter are pilot projects or are in the process of being evaluated. No user education programme should be offered and not evaluated; how else do we know if the user needs have been satisfied and that learning has taken place? Evaluation has always been the 'Cinderella' of the implementation of user education but Hopkins (1995, p.8) reports on a CTILIS survey which showed that an increase of 40 per cent of university libraries are now evaluating their programmes. Interestingly the same survey revealed that 95 per cent offered IT oriented user education for existing users but only 31 library reported using IT to teach information skills.

A variety of methods can be used to evaluate programmes including observation, questionnaires, discussion or focus groups, keeping a log of enquiries either manually or electronically, feedback from academic staff and assessment as mentioned earlier. This variety should give a richer picture of the end product and enable the librarian to modify the programme for the next time. As information technology advances we need continually to revise and update our programmes, as well as try to use the new technology in the delivery of the programmes.

Conclusion

The Dearing Report is entitled *Higher Education in the Learning Society* and this report will influence the development of higher education into the 21st century. In Section 20 of the executive summary it states that 'new technology is changing the way information is stored and transmitted. This has implications both for the skills which higher education needs to develop in students, and for the way in which it is delivered'. (NCIHE, 1997). User education for the electronic library is therefore very much on the agenda.

It is clear that the only way forward is for librarians to become more closely involved with the teaching and learning process, and to work in collaboration with academic staff and other learning support staff to enable students to acquire information skills which will enable them to become self-sufficient information users. If librarians do not seek to integrate user education into the teaching programmes and work with other staff to develop networked learner support, then the library will be failing in its education mission and may gradually become only a storehouse of printed material. It is an exciting challenge for academic librarians to develop their role in the learning culture of the university, providing information in all formats, navigational tools, user education and helping to design courseware and learning support materials. In some ways this is not very different from what we have been trying to achieve for many years; however now with the electronic library we have an advantage of being at the fore-front of developments.

References

Atton, C. (1994) Using critical thinking as a basis for library user education. *Journal of Academic Librarianship*, **20**(5/6), 310–313

Biddiscombe, R. (1996) (ed.) *The End-User Revolution: CD-ROM, Internet and the changing role of the information professional*. London: LAPL

Biddiscombe, R. (1997) Support for the Web in arts teaching. *Library Association Record*, **99**(5) pp.23–24

Byron, S. (1995) Preparing to teach in cyberspace: user education in real and virtual libraries. *Reference Librarian*, 51/52, 241–247

Collier, M. (1995) Defining the electronic library. In *Electronic Library and Visual Information Research: ELVIRA 1: Proceedings of the First ELVIRA Conference* eds. M. Collier and K. Arnold, pp. 1–5. London: Aslib

Cox, A. (1997) Using the World Wide Web for library user education: a review article. *Journal of Librarianship and Information Science*, **29**(1), 39–43

Cowan, J. (1994) The student and the learning process. In *Colleges, Libraries and Access to Learning*, eds. M. Adams and R. McElroy, pp. 1–20. London: LAPL

Creth, S.D. (1993) Creating a virtual information organization: collaborative relationships between libraries and computer centers. In *Libraries as User Centered Organizations: Imperatives for Organizational Change*, ed. M.A. Butler, pp. 111–132. New York: Haworth Press

Creth, S.D. (1995) A changing profession: central roles for academic librarians. *Advances in Librarianship*, **19**, 85–98

Day, J.M. (1994) Training end-users for CD-ROM. In *CD-ROM in Libraries: Management Issues*, eds. J.M. Day and T. Hanson, pp. 137–157. London: Bowker Saur

Day, J.M. *et al.* (1996) Higher education, teaching, learning and the electronic library: a review of the literature for the IMPEL2 project: monitoring organizational change. *New Review of Academic Librarianship*, **2**, 131–204

Heery, M. and Morgan, S. (1996) *Practical Strategies for the Modern Academic Library*. London: Aslib

Higher Education Funding Council for England, et al. (1993) *Joint Funding Councils' Libraries Review Group: Report*. (Follett Report). Bristol: HEFCE

Hopkins, T. (1995) *User Education in Academic Libraries: Results of 1995 CTILIS Survey*. Loughborough: CTI

Kingston, P. (1994) The role of the librarian in student learning and assessment. In *Colleges, Libraries and Access to learning*, eds. M. Adams and R. McElroy, pp. 68–73. London: LAPL

Kirby, J., Liddiard, L. and Moore, K. (1998) *Empowering the Information User*. London: LAPL

La Guardia, C. *et al.* (1996) *Teaching the New Library: a How-To-Do-It Manual for Planning and Designing Instructional Programs*. New York: Neal Schuman Publishers

Levy, P., Worsfold, E. and Fowell, S. (1996) Electronic libraries programme: networked learner support. *Library Association Record*, **98**(1), 34–35

National Committee of Inquiry into Higher Education (1997) *Higher Education in the Learning Society*. (Dearing Report). London: HMSO

Peters, J. (1996) The IT literate user. In *Providing Customer-oriented Services in Academic Libraries*, eds. C. Pinder and M. Melling, pp. 105–122. London: LAPL

Pennington, G. and O'Neal, M. (1994) Enhancing the quality of teaching and learning in higher education. *Quality Assurance in Education* **2**(3), 13–18

Pollard, N. (1996) The learning framework. In *Staff Development in Academic Libraries: Present Practice and Future Challenges*, ed. M. Oldroyd, pp. 54–67. London: LAPL

Snavely, L and Cooper, N. (1997) The information literacy debate. *Journal of Academic Librarianship*, **23**(1), 9–14

Wade, A. (1996) Training the end-user. Case Study 1: academic libraries. In Biddiscombe, pp. 96–109

Welsh, J. *et al.* (1996) User education: accessibility and the integrated approach. *Infocus*, **1**(2), 7–13

CHAPTER TWENTY TWO

Case Study: The EduLib Project and Implications for the Management of Change

David McNamara and Jane Core

Introduction

The EduLib Project, located at the Universities of Hull and Abertay Dundee, has been funded within the Training and Awareness Strand of the Electronic Libraries Programme. It is not possible within the compass of this chapter to provide full information about the project, the 'philosophy' which informs its operation, its organization and *modus operandi*, its progress and what has been achieved. More detailed information about the project is available in Core and McNamara (1996) and McNamara and Core (1997). For those who prefer electronic sources, all the important documents produced thus far are available at our World Wide Web site (http://www.hull.ac.uk/edulib/). The purpose of this chapter is to provide higher education librarians with managerial responsibilities and other people interested in the provision of Library Information Services with:

- Some background information about the EduLib Project;

- An account of some of the pertinent issues we have encountered with reference to the management of training for new expertise;
- An exploration of the relevance of some of the issues we raise within the context of library management.

The essence of what we wish to consider is the extent to which it is possible for higher education librarians to acquire new expertise associated with their role as educators and disseminate that expertise among their librarian colleagues.

Background Information

In 1993 the document was published which set the agenda for the eLib programme, namely the Joint Funding Councils' Libraries Review Group: Report (HEFCE, 1993). A key recommendation of the report was that the exploitation of information technology was essential to create an effective library service in the future. If library end-users, both academic staff and students, are to make the most effective and productive use of networked and electronic information services they need education and training in the selection, evaluation and use of information in these forms alongside generic information skills. Librarians must, therefore, become key agents in the provision of training in the employment of networked information. This entails an extension of the higher education librarian's traditional role. While library staff have already evolved a training role, the substantial technological and cultural changes being wrought within the system indicate that librarians must now become the key educators and trainers who will develop the training and support required to enable users to make effective use of networked information. Moreover, in the longer term, if librarians are to be equipped to work in effective partnership with their academic colleagues it is not sufficient for them simply to receive some training in educational methods and learning strategies. There needs to be a sea-change which recognizes that the profession, namely university and college librarians, should take over the responsibility for developing librarians' educational capabilities. This must, of course, entail more than the efforts of individual librarians. There should also be an institutionally managed approach which ensures that the development of librarians as educators and managers of learning is integrated within institutional policy.

In brief, what is distinctive about EduLib is that it arises from the conviction that in order to fulfil their mandate to enhance end users' capacity to make effective use of networked information, higher education librarians themselves need to do more than acquire additional knowledge about networked systems. They must also develop the capability to become effective educators of end users. This requires, in particular, that they develop the educational knowledge and understanding that will help them to facilitate their clients' learning of networked information.

The purpose of EduLib is to contribute to this process and is best summarized under its original aims which were:

a) to specify and provide to librarians working in higher education institutions the skills and capabilities which will enable them to execute their training and awareness-raising roles, and to communicate effectively with client groups in ways in which will ensure that these end-users, staff and students alike, can adopt and incorporate new information resources and the skills to utilize them within their own teaching, learning and research;

b) to foster, within the higher education library community, a professional culture which recognizes that, with the advent of the digital library, professional roles will change and that librarians will need to acquire training in teaching methods and staff development skills, and that in the longer term librarians will need to develop the capacity to take a measure of responsibility for their professional development in order to fulfil these new roles;

c) to produce a training programme and associated learning materials which will be disseminated and continue to be in the public domain after the completion of the project.

Informing Principles

No programme of educational training can be introduced into an intellectual vacuum or be value neutral in its implementation and execution. Rather than let these matters come about by default or be implied, EduLib has, from the outset, been based upon a set of explicit principles. These are:

- that librarians associated with the project will come from and work within higher education institutions where there will be variations in: institutional missions, especially as regards the balance between teaching and research; levels of library provision and the use of information technology to support library services; the organization and management of academic services generally; and the provision of staff development and training support for both library and academic staff. Librarians must be trained to work effectively in their particular institutional circumstances;
- that the programme we offer must be an exemplar of the 'good practices' which we aim to engender among librarians, and should also employ wherever appropriate the same technologies which the Electronic Library programme is endeavouring to promote;
- that the project is designed in such a way as to ensure that the requirement for dissemination throughout the higher education system is integrated into the project from the outset and is not merely added on as a separate activity at the end.

These principles arise from a number of educational considerations. First, the evidence of over quarter of a century of educational research (from, for example, the ground-breaking studies of Gross *et al.* (1971) to Fullan (1993) suggests that seeking to engineer educational innovation and change through some crude top-down delivery model will be ineffective, even if, as in some cases, the parties involved claim to be committed to the new practices. The circumstances under which librarians teach and carry out their educational responsibilities are to some degree peculiar to the special institutional circumstances in which they work. For example, librarians acting in a tutorial capacity are likely to teach students in 'batches' rather than develop a longer term relationship with them and not to assess students' learning; hence librarians may have a particular problem in terms of gaining feedback on their teaching and being able to offer feedback and support to their users directly. Change cannot be imposed from without. It is essential that EduLib works in collaboration with librarians so as to identify their training requirements and to offer training, advice and support which recognizes their remit for teaching and the sorts of issues they face and the circumstances in which they work.

Second, it is important that the library community has an investment in and 'ownership' of the programme materials and in due course takes responsibility for the wider dissemination of educational expertise among practising librarians. To this end EduLib must help develop a professional 'culture' within which key librarians become prepared to take over the responsibility for their own professional training in teaching skills.

We have, therefore, actively involved librarians in the development, testing and implementation of our teaching materials.

The Development and Dissemination of New Expertise

In order to focus upon the management issues we wish to address we consider the pivotal stage in the project when the twelve members of our Development Team had completed a substantial part of their own formal programme of educational training and were preparing to organize themselves to disseminate their new-found expertise among librarian colleagues on a regional basis. This is because the wider dissemination of the EduLib programme depended crucially upon the capability of the members of the Development Team (a) to take responsibility for the educational training of those librarians who have teaching responsibilities, and (b) where feasible to influence educational development programmes and frameworks offered and planned at an institutional level. During this phase we established regional workshop programmes which were available for librarian colleagues in their localities. We have provided teaching materials and resources which form the basis for these workshops. There is a number of factors which had a direct bearing upon the successful dissemination of EduLib at this stage. For the purposes of the present analysis it is convenient to make a distinction between three key factors, while recognizing that they are interrelated. These are what may be termed the higher education library community, the capability of members of the Development Team and the institutional context. They will be considered *seriatim*.

Preparedness for the innovation

The introduction of a new area of expertise among higher education librarians depends crucially upon its reception among its potential recipients. It was essential, therefore, for EduLib to work in association with library professionals, and to generate awareness about our programme, generally raise the profile of the project, and communicate what we thought was EduLib's worth and relevance for librarians. All the evidence that we have acquired both formally and informally from the Training Needs Analysis (McNamara and Core, undated), national Awareness Days, local consortium-centred awareness meetings and national conferences demonstrates that librarians were and are keen to take advantage of the support and training which EduLib has to offer.

It is, of course, a moot point as to whether the welcome EduLib has received was generated by our activities or whether librarians themselves were already coming to the view that they needed training in educational methods independently of EduLib's efforts. It is worthwhile to note in this respect that the needs of librarians ranged from those associated with acquiring new skills for new roles to having, in the case of longer standing professionals, the opportunity to validate and consolidate twenty or more years of practice in an educational role. There can be no doubt that librarians have been working in this field for too long to leave the future development and recognition of their skills to chance.

Capability to disseminate expertise

The Development Team members were carefully recruited at the outset because of their demonstrable interest in the training and awareness dimension of their work. They underwent a substantial programme of training so as to develop their own educational expertise and have the capability to communicate their educational expertise to colleagues.

The programme they completed was more extensive and testing than the one they were delivering to the library community. Nevertheless, as we prepared for the dissemination phase, it was necessary to discuss with our team how well prepared they felt they were to teach other librarians about teaching. In order to assess as parsomoniously as possible their capability to deliver EduLib within their own regions they were asked a number of key questions at a meeting of the Development Team. The questions and the responses are given below.

1. In the light of your experience with the Workshops and the programme thus far do you think that at the end of Phase Two you will be able to take responsibility for delivering and an accredited course and qualification (a) yourself and (b) with others?

Replies	Yourself	
	No	1
	Probably not	4
	Probably	5
	Yes	3

	With Others	
	No	0
	Probably not	0
	Probably	7
	Yes	5
	(No response	1)

2. In the light of your experience with the Workshops and the programme thus far do you think that at the end of Phase Two you will be able to offer individual workshops on some key topics?

Replies	No	0
	Probably not	0
	Probably	2
	Yes	11

The responses clearly indicated that the vast majority of Development Team members judged that they would be able to offer a programme of educational workshops for librarians in their region. The delivery of a full accredited programme would be a considerable challenge for team members and it was reassuring to know that they all (leaving aside the non-respondent) at least felt able to offer a programme in association with others; Although it must be noted that only three members offered an unqualified 'yes' as far as delivering the programme on their own are concerned. When it is borne in mind, however, that many of the established experts who organized the training provided for the team themselves made it clear that they wanted to work with a partner, it was both realistic and sensible for team members to reply that they wished to work with other colleagues. In sum, the information indicated, as far as the Development Team members' capability was concerned, that they felt able to deliver educational training for librarians.

The institutional context

If EduLib was to be successfully established within the wider community it was not sufficient that there was interest among potential participants and that we had the capability to deliver training. In addition, there needed to be the capacity and preparedness for potential participants' library services or sections to support the project and sponsor library staff who asked to attend our courses.

Feedback from members of our team and other information indicated that in most institutions library managers were willing to support staff who wished to develop their educational skills and that arrangements could be made to release them to attend our courses. In general, however, there were not the local resources which would enable us to mount comprehensive programmes of training leading to a recognized higher education teaching qualification. We came to the firm view that a comparatively short and intensive programme was what would be most acceptable. There were a number of reasons which lead managers to this view. The particular mix of circumstances which rendered the introduction of a full programme of accredited training problematic differed from institution to institution, depending upon matters such as their academic traditions, committee structures, administrative modus operandi and available resources. Nevertheless, a number of recurring problems were identified, namely:

Economic retrenchment

A factor which could not have been foreseen when the project was initiated was that the higher education system as a whole would be facing significant financial cutbacks consequent upon the reduction in Government funding.

This resulted in some institutions placing a moratorium upon any new developments and often, in addition, requiring all sections, including the library, to reduce expenditure. This meant that it was difficult to introduce an innovatory programme unless it could be demonstrated that it was financially viable and contributed directly to the economy of the institution.

Time scale

There are occasions when institutions can move rapidly (indeed opportunistically) in order to approve innovations, but generally proceeding through the due process of course approval may take a long time, up to two years in some cases. Among other things, new courses have to be approved by faculties and departments (and in the case of a library based course there could be problems over ownership' and whether the appropriate body, such as Continuing Education or the School of Education, would be prepared to take it on), quality standards committees, validation committees and senates. Such committees need to satisfy themselves, among other things, that course numbers could be ensured for a number of years and that the staffing and resources were in place to support the new venture. In addition, of course, accreditation needs to be sought although this may proceed in tandem with internal processes.

Institutional characteristics

In a number of institutions we wished to work with there were distinctive problems which made it all but impossible to found a full programme of training leading to a qualification. For instance in one they simply did not permit vocational courses; in one there was no tradition or precedent for providing teaching courses; in one a single member of staff could not be allowed to take responsibility for a course; in one all courses had to be faculty based and the library was not regarded as a faculty; and in another the section of the university in which the programme would have to located was facing drastic restructuring.

Time for individual librarians

In one significant respect the EduLib model did not provide a good guide for further dissemination. This is because throughout, and especially, during their crucial period of training, the members of the Development Team were seconded from their posts for two days per week so that they could attend the workshop programme and undertake the substantial work required for assessment purposes – if they were, in due course to achieve the accredited qualification. It was extremely unlikely that such opportunities could be routinely available to librarians who wish to pursue an extensive course. Time and again it has been reported to us that however keen individual librarians may be to acquire a formally recognized higher education teaching qualification, this simply could not be possible unless they could gain sufficient release from their normal duties and be provided with the necessary resources to support their attendance and study over a long period of time.

A further complication

The ever changing context in which EduLib has sought to introduce its programmes has now been positively influenced by another crucial factor unseen when the project was devised. The publication of the 'Dearing Report' (NCIHE, 1997) would seem at first sight to provide a particularly favourable climate for the reception of our training programmes. The report recognizes and makes appropriate recommendations on, among other things, the key role of information technology in the learning environment, the importance of good teaching and the need for higher education staff to acquire formal teaching qualifications.

If librarians are to play their full part in the provision of a quality learning environment for students in a mass higher education system relying, in part, on networked information, then librarians must become trained and qualified educationists as much as their academic colleagues. We now regard it as part of EduLib's purpose to promote this view and we hope that library managers will also appreciate the now increasing need for their staff to participate in educational training courses.

In summarizing these comments it should be noted that if any educational innovation is to be established effectively local circumstances must be well disposed towards it and have the resources to be able to accommodate change. In our case, local factors have often been beyond the control of library managers and affected by unforeseen events. As far as EduLib is concerned, over a comparatively short time scale we have been adversely affected by factors associated with economic cutbacks in higher education, but we hope that the 'Dearing Report' (NCIHE, 1997) will have a beneficial influence upon institutions' dispositions to avail themselves of our courses.

Library Management for Change

One must always be wary when generalizing from one particular case and exploring the extent to which the EduLib experience may generate issues of broader interest and relevance to others. Moreover, space does not permit a sustained discussion of our project within the context of the library management literature (for a more extensive electronic source see the discussion with Jane Core in *Ariadne* (Bailey, 1997) and for extensive discussion among librarians about the development of educational skills within a library management context see the discussion titled 'The value of user education some jaundiced views' archived on *Mailbase* (1995). We feel, however, that the following issues are worth raising.

Preparing the ground

Any educational innovation, if it is to have any impact, must be favourably received by those individual librarians who may benefit from it or see some professional advantage in associating with it. In our case we deliberately built in an Awareness Raising Phase at the beginning of the project. All our evaluations indicated that the events associated with this phase were well received and in the event about a quarter of the librarians who attended our programmes noted that they had attended one of our awareness sessions. The negative reaction was that people felt that we should have been ready to offer our courses as soon as we had raised awareness. (An important reason why we had decided in advance not to do so was that we had assumed that library managers would prefer considerable advance notice if they were to be asked to release a member of staff on a regular basis over a long time.)

Capability of the innovators

If any change is to be wrought throughout the wider system the capability of those charged with bringing it about is crucial. Central to our project is the belief that librarians can disseminate new-found expertise among colleagues. To what extent is this possible? In recent years there has, within the wider educational system, been the need to disseminate rapidly and economically new expertise among teachers in order rapidly to effect change. In particular it has become necessary for the national teaching force to be trained to teach the National Curriculum. The main way to achieve this has been nominating, say, a staff representative to attend a central training programme and then 'cascade' what they have learned among colleagues back in their school. The extent to which such efforts are successful is problematic and it is certainly questionable whether the rhetoric of educational cascading may be introduced into the higher education context. On the basis of our experience we have to ask to what degree it is possible for librarians to disseminate new-found expertise among colleagues.

It is demonstrably the case, as far as EduLib is concerned, that our members can, when working in a team with colleagues, very effectively organize and present educational workshops on teaching and learning which are well received by the library community. Moreover, in a number of areas, they do have distinctive expertise comparable with that of any educationist. They would probably be the first to acknowledge, however, that they are not expert education-ists with years of training and experience behind them. Because of this the training materials (McNamara and Core, 1998) we are producing provide an essential support for their educational work and the members of the team use these to a greater or lesser extent, depending upon their own knowl-edge and experience of the theme being introduced. We are confident that when our teaching materials are used by librarian educators who have themselves attended work-shops covering the same theme as the materials that there is no problem with their use, or of our team's capability to diversify educational expertise onwards to colleagues.

We are unsure, however, to what extent this process of collegial dissemination may or should extend or 'ripple' out-wards from EduLib. For instance, we know that many of the participants who attend our regional programmes will, themselves, wish to convey their knew knowledge among colleagues in their institutions. To what degree will they feel confident to do so on their own, or will they wish to have the support of colleagues? It remains to be seen whether those colleagues who may engage in support activity will come from the same institution as the programme leaders or whether there is something so distinctive about librarians that they cannot be mutually supported by their teaching colleagues. Of more concern, it must be remembered that our materials are to be freely available within the higher education community in both paper and electronic formats. We will be concerned if librarians and others tried to use our materials for training purposes (or even as self-study teaching materials) if they either had not attended one of our courses or had not gained the requisite background knowledge by other means. (An irony beginning to emerge is that some members of our team are being regarded as educators in their own right and our materials may have a place in educational development training beyond the confines of library services.) Our materials cannot be regarded as standalone 'scripts' to be delivered. They provide support for those librarians who already have some familiarity with them and who are carrying out educational development which seeks to add to librarians' professional repertoire of skills.

We suggest that the theme that we are raising may have more general applicability. At this stage we can do no more than raise a number of issues. To what extent and in what ways is it possible for new knowledge and skill drawn from another discipline (in this case education) to be disseminated within the library community? To what extent is it necessary to rely upon outside expertise and to what degree can librarians, with appropriate training, undertake the training themselves? To what extent do we need to provide supporting training materials? Furthermore, what other methods of support, for example inter-professional and inter-institutional personal networking might be usefully employed?

Managing for or in response to change

It has to be recognized that for much of the time we have had to react to change, rather than manage the EduLib programme so as to help in the process of bringing about change in the library community. We have had to respond and adapt to emerging events and circumstances which could not have been foreseen when our project commenced and over which we have no control. If we had doggedly persisted in following the original project proposal we can be reasonably confident that we would not have established our workshop programmes as effectively as our evaluation evidence suggests that we have. Possibly the most important lesson for management arising from our project it that managers must be flexible and adaptable if they wish to bring about change in the ever changing world of higher education (see, for example Fullan, 1993), and accept that a state of change is a permanent condition.

Finally, we welcome and support the 'Dearing' recommendation (NCIHE, 1997, recommendation 42) which highlights the responsibility of senior managers to promote and support the change process. Librarians' responses to EduLib have demonstrated that they are able and willing to take a measure of responsibility for their own development. The extent to which they are successful in doing so may be associated with the preparedness of library and institutional managers to set and respond to the emerging new agenda for staff and educational development. We suggest that this agenda should integrate recognition and reward for excellence in teaching, learning and support with opportunities to acquire, practise and formalize the educational knowledge and skills that will enable universities and colleges to continue to enhance the quality of educational provision they make available for its students. In what should be a co-ordinated institutional endeavour librarians have a key educational role.

References

Bailey, C. (1997) Interface: Jane Core. *Ariadne* 8, p.3

Core, J. and McNamara, D. (1996) EduLib: a model of staff development for higher education librarians as teaching and learning partners in the electronic library, *The Tenth Annual Computers in Libraries International 96, Proceedings.* (Novotel, Hammersmith, London)

Fullan, M. (1993) *Change Forces: Probing the Depth of Educational Reform.* London: Falmer.

Gross, N., Giacquinta, A., and Bernstein, M. (1971) *Implementing Organisational Innovations, A Sociological Analysis of Planned Educational Change.* New York: Harper & Row.

Higher Education Funding Council for England, et al. (1993) *Joint Funding Councils' Libraries Review Group: Report*. (Follet Report). Bristol: HEFCE

McNamara, D. and Core, J. (1997) The EduLib Project: Staff Development for Higher Education Librarians' Teaching Expertise: Progress and Issues. in *Proceedings of the Conference New Tricks ? Staff Development for the Electronic Library*. ed. B. Knowles Bournemouth University. Occasional Papers

McNamara, D. and Core, J. (undated) *Higher Education Librarians as Educators: A Training Needs Analysis*, EduLib, Universities of Hull and Abertay Dundee.

McNamara, D. and Core J. (1998) (eds.) *Teaching for Learning in Libraries and Information Services: a series of educational development workshops*, EduLib, The Universities of Hull and Abertay Dundee (In press)

Mailbase (1996) Discussions on lis-infoskills [online]. Available: http://www.mailbase.ac.uk/lis-infoskills/1996–10/index.htmlj.

National Committee of Inquiry into Higher Education (1997) *Higher education in the learning society*. (Dearing Report). London: HMSO

CHAPTER TWENTY THREE

Case Study: University of Newcastle

John Morrow and Jill Taylor-Roe

In discussing how user education and training is managed in Newcastle University Library we will divide the subject into two distinct but closely related parts. Firstly we will consider the staff training and development needs of Library staff in being able to carry through programmes of user education successfully and how those needs are met. Secondly we will look at the methods and programmes of user education which are currently carried through by Library staff or are in preparation.

Staff Training and Development

As the scope of the electronic library increases, so too do the training needs of the Library staff to enable the delivery of the training which both academic staff and students require to make the most effective use of current resources. The strengthening role of networked information sources in the daily working life of academic staff and students alike make this inevitable.

Over recent years Newcastle University has put considerable time and effort into staff development and training, regarding it as one of the most important ways in which the Library can ensure that it has a flexible, informed and committed staff who are continually developed and who can adapt successfully to rapid change and future developments in the provision of a quality service. The Library's defined role of supporting the University's objectives by providing services to meet the University community's current and future book and other information needs as effectively and economically as possible within the resources available, requires such a commitment to staff training and development if it is to be achieved. The commitment to staff development is also fundamental in helping Library staff work more effectively towards meeting the Library's annual aims and objectives.

A number of principles underlie the Library's approach to staff training and development. These include each member of staff having his/her training needs identified and agreed annually; acknowledging that staff development and training is the joint responsibility of the individual concerned, the sectional line manager and the Library's Staff Development Group (comprising staff from across the Library), and that all should lay emphasis on its importance; encouraging the development of staff by financing relevant courses and events; and maintaining a record of the Library training needs, with individual staff keeping a record of their own progress. Professional and Personal development includes attendance at externally provided courses, workshops and conferences; visits to other libraries; staff exchanges; work related professional qualifications; management training; and participation in the activities of professional bodies. The Library's Staff Development Policy is made generally available with a statement of commitment, distributed to all staff to communicate the above philosophy.

Within Newcastle University Library it is the Liaison Team who are largely responsible for the provision of programmes of user education. So how and what do the Library staff need to learn? Firstly they need to become familiar with the variety of electronic resources available, acquiring the necessary skills in the process, e.g. how to use the sources available through BIDS, and secondly they need to acquire the teaching skills which will allow them to provide effective user education. Traditionally concentration has been on the former but the value and importance of learning how to teach is increasingly being recognized, e.g. by the eLib (Electronic Libraries) EduLib programme.

Specific skills and database awareness is achieved in a number of ways. Newcastle University Library staff attend launches of new products, taking the opportunity to discuss the product with developers and also to discuss appropriate applications with staff from other libraries. Attending events like these is important in helping the Library make initial assessments of how a particular product will fit in with the other databases already provided and what it will offer the University community. If a new database is considered potentially valuable a trial and evaluation is scheduled in the Library in consultation with Library users. There are also the product fairs, e.g. the Library Resources Exhibition, attendance at which can provide useful general information on trends and progress in specific areas of development. Library staff are also encouraged to attend local and national workshops and training days, e.g. on FirstSearch. Specific workshops are also held within the Library to refresh skills and introduce new sources of information, e.g. on the Social Sciences Information Gateway. These are attended by a variety of staff and not only by the Liaison team in order to increase information skills and database awareness which are essential for enquiry work across the Library, and which allow Library staff to know when they should refer to the Liaison team and when they can answer for themselves. An accompanying feature of using new sources is the cascading of learning within the Library through the production of the necessary documentation, e.g. help-sheets and leaflets available on paper or via the Library's Web home page, to help students and academic staff make the best use of a new database.

The opportunity to develop the necessary skills required to use networked information sources effectively has been greatly enhanced by the Netskills programme, part of the eLib programme and based at Newcastle University. Netskills offers a variety of opportunities which address general Internet skills and increasingly cover more specific subject areas, e.g. medicine, and which Newcastle Library staff use regularly. There is also the eLib NetLinkS project which provides the opportunity for Library staff to work through a distance-learning online professional development course. Library staff participation in such activities is positively encouraged and supported. Having academic departments feel confidence in the member of Library staff with whom they work directly is of obvious value to the fulfilment of the Library's role within the University.

Acquiring the specific skills to use electronic resources is, however, a relatively simple process compared to having the necessary teaching skills to show others how to use them well. We have been teaching our academic staff and students how to make the best use of library materials for years without necessarily considering the nature of teaching or teaching methods, but with the growth of the electronic library has come an awareness that we need to understand those too. The teaching role of library staff is becoming increasingly important and is one which Newcastle Library staff have taken up. There have been a variety of approaches to user education in the past, and there is much continuing discussion, but now we are starting to see the formalizing of best practices and the sharing of them. All Library staff have access to the Internet and are able to participate in discussions on the best use of teaching resources. In Newcastle University Library the e-mail lists are divided between members of the Liaison team so that pooled experiences are more easily acted on.

Newcastle University Library regards EduLib as an important development and as such our colleague Graeme Arnott, who as the Science Liaison Librarian is a member of the Liaison team, has been seconded to the project for 3 years, ending in December 1998 (See Chapter 22). As one of the 12

EduLib development officers Graeme has been taking the postgraduate Diploma in Teaching and Learning in Higher Education. Much of the final year of the course will be spent delivering workshops to other library staff on a regional basis. The workshops will cover a variety of directly relevant topics, including understanding how students learn, how to plan a training/learning event and how to evaluate the effectiveness of the teaching and the feedback received. Having the expertise available to offer development course such as those for our own staff is something on which Newcastle University Library will need to build. As always there are staff resource implications in terms of the time taken to attend but the need is there and is being addressed.

One of the EduLib workshops will be on evaluation and feedback. This has always been an area of staff training and development in which Libraries have been relatively unsuccessful. We have been comfortable with 'happy sheets' which provide immediate feedback and good line managers have always checked to see if training has been successful in terms of getting the job done effectively. However, being able to evaluate our staff training and development in terms of its effect on our services to Library users and its contribution to the fulfilment of the University's objectives is another and more complex matter. Training our staff to be able to provide effective user education for both students and academic staff gives us an avenue to explore in establishing such methods of evaluation and taking action on the results. User education is an increasingly important part of our services and knowing how well or poorly the Library performs is essential if we are to improve. Evaluation and feedback are also part of the training cycle which helps us assess how appropriate the training itself is regarded by our users and how effectively we are spending our valuable resources.

Having considered how Newcastle University Library addresses staff training and development needs in the provision of user education for the electronic library, we now need to consider the methods we employ and the programmes we carry out.

Delivering User Education in a Modern Academic Library

'Change is constant'. Thus observed Disraeli in 1867, but he could just as easily have been talking about the Higher Education (HE) sector in the 1990's. (Disraeli, 1867). As an academic service, the work of the University Library is inevitably shaped by the circumstances which affect its parent institution, and this is particularly true of 'front-line' activities such as user education. Over the last five years, we have radically reviewed the way we organize and deliver user education in the Robinson Library, largely in response to changes affecting the University as a whole. In so doing we have endeavoured to balance operational needs with customers' requirements to provide a timely, relevant and cost-effective service.

There are many factors which have shaped, and continue to shape, our user education programme. Not the least of these is the sheer range and diversity of electronic services which are now available; each with their own strengths, weaknesses, and idiosyncratic modes of access. Library staff spend a considerable amount of time comparing and evaluating these services, as well as promoting or explaining them to users. Each new release of software can bring enhancements which render existing help-sheets out of date, or worse still, have the odd quirk which turns a hitherto trouble-free database into a source of constant queries.

The shift to modules and semesters has increased students' study options and given them more opportunities to comment on the quality of their educational experience. Whilst these changes are most welcome, we have found that it has become much more difficult for the Library to secure meaningful blocks of students' time for user education. Increased choice has made timetabling such a complex operation, that we have to work much harder to win space for user education because there are so many other options competing for attention. That battle won, we then face the far more difficult challenge of convincing the students that it is worth their while turning up for what are often regarded as peripheral activities.

In our attempts to secure library slots in the crammed curriculum we have been greatly assisted by the Total Quality Assessment exercises to which all academic departments are now subject as part of a rolling programme. The Library is assessed under the heading of Learning Resources and one of the areas in which assessors have been prompted to ask questions is the level and range of skills training which the Library provides for students and staff. (SCONUL, 1997). At the start of each academic year, we make contact with the departments who are going to be assessed, to offer our help and support. The subsequent briefing meetings have enabled us to gain a greater understanding of the objectives of their teaching programmes, and provide an ideal opportunity to discuss the information skills training which would best support them. In addition to the Library sessions for students that arise from these meetings, we find we are often asked to run advanced or updating sessions for academic staff.

Although the Library is very mindful of the dangers of 'questionnaire fatigue', we have nevertheless revised and extended the use of our printed and electronic evaluation forms to encourage more feedback from staff and students. We have learnt that whilst users generally find the traditional demonstration sessions and handouts to be a useful introduction, what they really want is an opportunity to try out library resources and services for themselves, with library staff on hand to deal with any questions or problems which might arise. Furthermore, they want training that is timely, customized, and wherever possible, embedded in the curriculum so that its relevance is immediately apparent. We have also learnt that many mature students, who may have been out of HE for a long time, feel they need more 'one to one' support, but sometimes feel too embarrassed to keep asking for help when they are part of a larger and potentially more experienced group. There is also a growing number of part-time students who require access to training sessions in the evenings and weekends, because they are unable to attend our regular weekday slots. We recognize that it is impossible to provide the level of personalized, seven-days a week, service which our users would like, but have nevertheless borne their comments in mind when reviewing our user education and training programmes.

For example, we now have several teaching suites, equipped with networked PCs, which liaison staff can use for practical teaching sessions. We work closely with academic staff to try and ensure that sessions are delivered at the most appropriate time – for example, training in the use of relevant bibliographic resources is offered just before students are due to embark on a major extended essay or research project. We have also revised a popular series of lunch-time 'Show and Tell' programmes that we have been running for several years. The basic format is a half hour demonstration of electronic databases or services, followed by a question and answer session. The programme is aimed at postgraduate students and academic staff, although undergraduates are always made very welcome if they choose to attend. In response to user feedback, we now offer a much shorter programme of 'Show and Tells', backed up by a series of complementary afternoon workshops, which we endeavour to run the day after the demonstration session. The workshops are run on a 'drop in' basis, so users stay for as short or as long a time as they can spare. The workshops are very popular, and very demanding, as we invariably find that they require two members of staff to run them, and if more than 20 people turn up, even two people can be over-stretched.

As far as mature students are concerned, we encourage them to make contact with their Faculty Liaison Librarians, who will provide as much one-to-one help as they can, often using one of our smaller teaching rooms, which can seem less intimidating. We are very much aware of the increasing number of part-time students, and try to meet their needs in several ways. We provide take-away help sheets and workbooks for many of the key bibliographic services, which we use in our training sessions, and these are widely available around the library. There are also electronic versions which are accessible from the library Web pages. Where there are sufficiently large numbers, we will try to run additional or alternative sessions on weekday evenings between 6pm and 8pm, or on Saturday mornings. However, with so many other demands on staff time, our ability to offer these out of office hours sessions is very much dependent on the good will and flexibility of library staff.

One of the most innovative and challenging training initiatives during the last two years has arisen from the library's involvement in the Postgraduate Research Training Programme run by the Faculty of Law, Environmental and Social Sciences (FLESS). One of the key factors which influenced the development of this programme was the concern expressed by the Economic and Social Research Council (ESRC) and other funding bodies, about the time it was taking for graduate students to complete their doctorates. It was generally agreed that new students required some additional training to help them make the transition from graduates to researchers. Social Scientists have always been amongst our heaviest library users, and liaison with the Faculty is excellent, so we were delighted when the Faculty Liaison Librarian was invited to join the small team of academic staff charged with developing a research training programme. The programme they devised was designed to run over two semesters, and covered a wide range of topics including research methodology and thesis preparation. The Library elements were awarded a total of twelve hours on the timetable, and as all of the sessions were run by two members of staff, we in fact committed to provide 24 hours of teaching. Some of this teaching was done in the evenings to accommodate the high number of part-time students.

Although we were delighted to be involved in such a programme, the staff concerned had to devote a considerable amount of effort to preparing the library modules, which included a marked assessment exercise. Students were asked to prepare a bibliography of at least twenty items derived from at least ten different bibliographic sources. Whilst this was not a particularly challenging assignment, given the range of resources available to Social Scientists, it was time consuming to assess, because of the large numbers of student involved, and the range of different subjects they chose to research. When the research training programme was evaluated by participating students at the end of the year, it was gratifying to note that the library elements scored very highly – a fitting tribute to the care and commitment which Chris Hagar, the Faculty Liaison Librarian, and her team of trusty helpers, put into preparing and delivering them. The FLESS training programme is about to enter its third year of operation, and a similar programme has also been running for two years in the Faculty of Arts. It will not be long before other Faculties require us to run equivalent programmes for their students.

Part of the challenge in setting up and running successful user education programmes within a Faculty teaching programme can be convincing academic colleagues that library staff have the necessary teaching skills. In our case this was not a problem because the Faculty already knew and valued the work of their Liaison Librarian. However, if there had been any doubts, it would have been helpful to be able to point out that two members of the Library Liaison team have successfully completed the Certificate in Teaching and Learning in Higher Education Course (specific to the University of Newcastle), which is compulsory for all new members of academic staff at Newcastle University. The Library had two objectives in seeking to be involved with this programme; one was to reinforce academic perceptions of our teaching role, and the other was to ensure that new staff were made aware of the existence of Library Liaison staff at the earliest opportunity. Thus far, our involvement with the programme has fulfilled both objectives, and we hope to build on this by encouraging more of our Liaison Librarians to participate in future.

The Robinson Library offers a wide variety of user education programmes, which are as flexible in terms of delivery and as subject specific in content as we can make them, because that is what our users want. Although the work is very rewarding, it is extremely demanding, as time has to be allocated to prepare, assess and evaluate sessions as well as deliver them. Wherever possible, we try to utilize existing materials. For example, we find the computer programmes created by Glasgow University Library under the Teaching and Learning Technology Programme extremely useful for introducing new students to the concept of literature searching. However, we know that our users want training material to be relevant to them, so we do prepare a lot of material ourselves. We save some time and effort by using templates for helpsheets and workbooks, so the format is the same; only the searching examples and other details are varied. We are also mounting an increasing amount of material on the Library Web pages, where it can be more readily updated.

So what does the future hold? The long-awaited Dearing Report (NCIHE, 1997) into the future of HE has highlighted the importance of lifelong learning and the need to equip graduates with a range of skills which will enhance their future employability. Information management and retrieval skills are clearly part of this skills package, and it is helpful to have this endorsement. Perhaps the greatest challenge we face is to find ways of delivering a wider programme of timely, relevant, user-centred training, in a more cost-effective manner. In this we may be helped by the advent of more common interfaces, for example, the ATHENS authentication system for accessing BIDS databases on the World Wide Web. The commercial services currently being marketed by major subscription agents as gateways to electronic journal collections should also help to minimize the number of different access techniques we have to explain to users. Technology may also provide us with additional means of communicating with distance and part-time users, for example, by facilitating live video-links with in-house training sessions, and enabling trainers to dial in in real time to remote users' screens to help them get out of difficulties. The demands on liaison staffing may be partially eased by bringing in colleagues from elsewhere in the Library to assist with user education. The Library Assistants who work for the Liaison Team already help out with training sessions, when other work commitments permit, and find the work most enjoyable.

Whatever we do in the next few years, we are committed to taking an innovative approach to user education, and above all, to being responsive to user needs. The future may be challenging, but with solid teamwork, adequate resources, and a dash of imagination, we will be more than equal to the task!

References

Disraeli, B. (1867) Speech at Edinburgh, 29 October, reported in *The Times*, 30 October 1867

National Committee of Inquiry into Higher Education (1997) *Higher Education in the Learning Society*. (Dearing Report). London: HMSO

SCONUL (1997) Working Group on Quality Assurance. Aide Memoire Working Party. *Preparing for the Learning Resources aspect of TQA: a guide for teaching staff*. London: SCONUL.

Managing Technical Services

CHAPTER TWENTY FOUR

Overview: Managing Technical Service in the Electronic Library: modernization before transformation

Will Wakeling

Introduction

These are heady times in the Hybrid Library, with many technical services (TS) staff feeling they are managing versions of transitional chaos in the present volatile information environment. In their analysis of the future of TS, Allen and Williams (1995, p.174) propose the shift from paper to the digital as just one of six major agents for change (the others are the search for savings, the pressure on library space, user demand for access, pressures on the organization and advances in software). This chapter looks at some of the impacts of the transition to the electronic library, that 'shift from paper to the digital', on TS, what type of adaptations have been introduced or are being planned for. An interesting distinction is that made by Clifford Lynch (1993, pp.7–8) between 'modernization' and 'transformation' – the former capturing how the Internet can help us do better and more effectively what libraries have always done, the latter representing how it will, in the long run, effect a fundamental change. In this sense most library managers in the TS environment would probably admit hitherto to carrying out mainly 'modernization'.

McCombs (1994) noted the relative slowness with which technical services librarians at that time were seeking to exploit the opportunities offered by the Internet. She advocated more exploration, collaboration and lobbying (e.g. for Z39.50 and cataloguing standards, for funding for hardware). At that time the power and ubiquity of the World Wide Web and the browser could only dimly be imagined. But it is possible to see some of the factors that applied then applying still in the present debate about the role of TS in the electronic library – slow development of open-systems or web-based products by integrated library system (ILS) suppliers, shortage of funds to implement them and upgrade workstations, incremental progress only on the development of standards of importance to technical operations, relentless pressure on staffing levels meaning shortage of time to commission exploratory projects. On the other hand, more recent consortial, national and international developments on a broad horizon (the Dublin Core, eLib, CHEST, the Pilot Site Licensing Initiative (PSLI)) have now triggered local activity in the TS area at many sites, and offered scope for much rethinking.

There are many points of contact between conventional technical services and the key features of the electronic library. This chapter works through the ways in which the services are being adapted to the changing environment, and points to some of those areas where more radical amendment must surely follow.

Technical Services Organization, Staffing and Structure and Staffing

Library managers will be well aware both of the enormous variety of TS organizational structures that pervade their institutions, and of the individual elements and activities that have subsisted at their heart – ordering, claiming, receipting, cataloguing and classification, serials control, database maintenance, processing (labelling, etc.), binding and preservation. No matter how libraries are organized, 'the fact remains that there are certain tasks that we group under the rubric of *technical services* that will go on in libraries for the foreseeable future.' (Gorman, 1990, p.2). It is important to recognize this in considering how handling increasing volumes and proportions of digital material should affect the way we manage the totality of information resources, printed and non-print. Few libraries currently devote more than 10 per cent of their purchasing budget to electronic resources, so reconstructing work flows, processing patterns and staffing structures to optimize the treatment of these at the expense of conventional printed material would be misguided, as long as the latter continue to represent the majority of users' preferred medium of information transmission. A huge expansion in genuinely high-quality and potentially low- or no-cost teaching and research resources made available over the Web will require treatment significantly different from that needed for administering printed acquisitions. But until that critical mass develops technical services have to be able to cope with the vigour of the Hybrid Library, printed and electronic.

That said, we should certainly consider whether there are advantages inherent in some variations of TS organization that will better support the development of the electronic library. One key and recurring aspect of the management of electronic resources from the TS point of view is the greater extent to which communication and joint decision-making is necessary, indeed vital, between the multiplying number of interested parties within the library. Those several academic libraries which have team-based structures focusing on selection, acquisition, bibliographic control and reference service activity by faculty or broad subject may be better placed to avoid the difficulties that can arise from the extra decision-making requirements involved in securing a Web-based or a networked CD-ROM resource. Interactive working relationships between staff variously (and often simultaneously)

selecting electronic resources, managing licensing, negotiating for access through the local consortium, and cataloguing or compiling Web pages need to be underpinned by
new organizational support modes. These can typically
include the redrawing of team boundaries or reworking of
patterns of interplay between existing function-based departments, the introduction of matrix-based non-hierarchical
management or empowered teams (see e.g. Bloss and Lanier,
1997), or the superimposition of cross-divisional panels to
review, inform and approve decisions.

As we shall see, the advent of the Hybrid Library with its
increasing digital information component implies new modes
of TS activity, but is not the only engine of change. Shifts
in the institutional mission and funding model, the drive
for greater efficiency and value for money, the siren call
of outsourcing, and radical IT developments all require TS
managers to embrace change. There is a significant body of
literature illustrating how these conditions can be turned to
advantage in the re-engineering process (e.g. Atkinson, 1992;
OCLC, 1994; Boissonnas, 1997). One immediate manifestation
over the last few years has been the invention of a new category of 'digital' or 'electronic resources' librarian, often
located in or straddling technical services, and responsible
for co-ordinating the selection and implementation of electronic resources. This is the clearest possible recognition that
traditional processes have to be transformed to accommodate
the new media. In personnel terms the process of adaptation
can have other profound effects – consider two related
aspects: the impact of IT, and changing roles of different staff
grades.

ILS suppliers are moving uniformly (though at differing
paces) towards the provision of Web-based OPACs (able to
provide direct access to a range of electronic products) and
the true integration of their component modules based on
multi-tasking. Local area networks integrate the activities of
different functional departments, as well as opening TS staff
to increased user contact (e.g. via an advertized presence
for TS departments on the Library Web site or via personal

e-mail). In acquisitions and cataloguing, the trend towards lowering the unit costs of their characteristic technical operations by using less highly trained and less expensive staff (effectively deprofessionalizing those operations) has been under-way for years (Allen and Williams, 1995, p.168). But now, with the increased sophistication of the ILS and local systems, with staff access to bibliographic resources and the Web via Windows-based workstations, and with complex new electronic products to be assimilated, trained for and coped with (as tools or options for TS staff themselves, like BookFind or Amazon.com), the trend seems to be in the process of reversing. Support and para-professional staff in TS will increasingly be required (and will expect) to exercise a new range of multiple skills and expertises, reflecting the diverse nature of the resources the library itself promotes. Herein lies a considerable challenge for TS professionals charged with leadership and management (Goulding, 1996). Few libraries have budgets that allow them to contemplate increasing their overall staffing load to cope with the growing complexity of operations. So it becomes a key responsibility to train and deploy staff who can work with varied formats and be sufficiently competent, interacting as they must in new ways with colleagues in other teams and divisions. The electronic library has a natural tendency to draw technical and public/reference services into convergence, because of that greater complexity in the selection and implementation process and because library users are responding in new ways to the new range of data being made available to them. In order to acclimatize to this environment, librarians at all levels must, as McCombs (1992) points out, develop a certain tolerance for ambiguity, and that requires training and understanding.

The Link with Collection Development

Hitherto, academic libraries in the UK have variously adopted a range of management approaches to collection development, based on selection (and deselection) by subject librarians or subject teams, sharing responsibility with (or passing it to) academic colleagues, and the deployment of formal (or informal) collection development policies (see Law, 1991, for one of the rare discussions of these issues in the UK context). Traditionally, TS librarians knew where they stood in all of this, and got on with the purchasing, cataloguing, processing and preserving.

The electronic library, as the other chapters in this book demonstrate, subverts these (relatively) well-ordered relationships in its shift of emphasis from collection management to content management. It centres on its function as a gateway to local and external resources; its focus is less on the familiar access vs. holdings distinction and more on institution-wide access to a core of locally held physical resources or networked data (which may or may not be on-site, and may be free or 'owned' or 'leased'), with less important material accessible through the gateway via document delivery or pay-for-view (see, for example, Harloe and Budd, 1994, p.86, or Gorman and Miller, 1997). In this user-centred approach the old lines of demarcation defining where responsibility lies for selecting a source, acquiring and maintaining access to it and registering its location can start to blur. So a crucial safeguard against inefficiency for libraries moving strongly into the electronic environment lies in ensuring that knowledge and skills developed by acquisitions, serials and cataloguing staff are properly applied at the selection stage.

Selection criteria for new electronic products need to be well informed, well defined and well advertized, and the selection process broadly participative. It is not only vital that the criteria allow issues of, say, systems-related technical implementation to be taken into account, such as the level of networkability of a CD-ROM, or any requirement for a Web-based product of local downloading of printing software. TS issues such as reliability of supply and support, comparative costings data, negotiated discounts, licensing and the implications for bibliographic control and navigation (e.g. the need for analytical or item-level indexing of a compilation product) also need to be reviewed as a matter of course. That acquisitions and bibliographic services librarians should be actively engaged with academic colleagues in these evaluative processes (no back-room role here) only serves to highlight how trends towards openness and accountability go hand in hand with the accessible, networked approach that delivers information as widely as possible to users cross-campus.

The need for detailed collection development policies that foster a consistent and coherent approach to all library resources including the digital is also compelling, the more so given the array of new formats for information delivery (Johnson, 1997, p.86). TS librarians would expect to be regularly engaged in co-operative or consortial activity looking at the group purchase of electronic products or aspects of the development of bibliographic databases. As a result they are well-placed to contribute to the broadening of collection development policies to subsume information resources beyond the local and the printed.

Acquisitions in the Digital Environment

It is worth looking in a little detail at some of the key features of acquiring electronic resources, to clarify how the TS manager may need to reform existing practice into moving into the ambit of the hybrid and electronic library. Staff may already in their day-to-day work be relying on sophisticated electronic systems to facilitate acquisitions, check-in and processing. Most of the major ILS suppliers already offer a version of Electronic Data Interchange for online book and serial ordering; automated invoicing (e.g. for handling annual subscription renewals) will often already be in place.

But interestingly, this functionality is still almost entirely directed towards acquiring printed material. When it comes to electronic products, these systems, and the processes they mediate, are as yet ill-constructed to handle and control (e.g. for audit or internal tracking purposes) the range of formats and platforms, particularly those remotely hosted. They are not designed to respond to the circumstance, already familiar to acquisitions and cataloguing staff, where even finding out at which point the library has actually 'acquired' access to a product may be shrouded in mystery. They offer no means of processing Web-based or locally networked bibliographic sources, full-text databases, e-journals, interactive learning packages, electronic add-ons to print titles (such as CD-ROM supplements or cumulations), digital textbooks, locally digitized text (in or out of copyright). These are currently a test of staff ingenuity at working round system limitations. Acquiring these products and implementing them in a hybrid library also requires a series of additional considerations before they can be offered to users as part of an integrated and coherent 'collection'.

Content

Evaluation in advance and on implementation needs to examine, for instance, the match in content between a printed title and its electronic counterpart; the situation with full-text journals in both formats is particularly complex and subject to disparity (Luther, 1997). There are also genuine issues to be addressed in ensuring that electronic products as received or made accessible via the Web deliver what they advertize. Packaged or bundled products, combining a number of datasets or titles, may gain some elements and lose others over time and unannounced; where the electronic product has been leased on subscription to replace a printed equivalent the short- and long-term impact of such alterations may be significant.

Costs

No part of the process of constructing the electronic library is so fraught with complications at present as the comparison of cost-benefits from competing electronic products, or indeed the justification for spending on any one electronic product. There is no clear rationale yet apparent for costing the added value inherent in electronic information, or for establishing what are the appropriate proportions of an acquisitions budget to devote to this added value. Publishers are promoting their electronic initiatives according to no single pattern (or even a limited number of them) but relying on what the market will bear. For librarians, the extra costs must stack up in terms of quality of content and interface, ease of access and networking.

In some areas, the calculation of these benefits is relatively straightforward and the equation of outlay against utility can be balanced: for instance, in the provision of CD-ROM versions of reference tools. In the case of some Web-based abstracting and indexing databases intermediated by companies such as Ovid and SilverPlatter, it is clear that there is a significant financial premium that libraries are prepared to meet in order to provide cross-platform desk-top access to high quality core data, especially when it is linked to full text. In other areas, such as the provision of bundled suites of e-journal titles by specific publishers at an additional premium in excess of 10 per cent of the basic printed subscription price, resistance has been more widespread amongst libraries and their consortia. In this confused market-place, libraries have to rely on the expertise and judgement of reference staff in analysing the value of new products, and acquisitions staff in analysing the costs and means of access to them.

Dealing with intermediaries

Librarians working in this area and charged with making decisions about modes of electronic access to the primary literature have a jungle of mediating options to consider. In picking their way through the range of new products being launched, revised or re-badged by the established serials agents, specialist (e.g. CD-ROM) suppliers and new-age content intermediaries, they have also to be aware of the increasing range of choices for individual article supply

(Davies, Boyle and Osborne, 1998). The process of sifting and evaluating the appropriate options to offer the widest access to their own users, with the greatest assurance of budgetary efficiency, integrity of content and security of delivery, represents as great a challenge now as there has ever been for professional staff with acquisitions responsibilities.

Registration and access

Librarians need to develop a clear and measured understanding of the implications for local access of the various security and control options offered by a electronic resource, including password, IP address and domain name. The same applies to the extent to which access may be limited for some users by the software platform on which a product runs or the reconfiguration it may imply for their network-connected computers. Here is an area where Systems and TS staff have to be in regular and detailed collaboration – as with the related process of negotiating licensing, dealt with below, there are new skills in interpreting technology and documentation which need to be added to the acquisitions librarian's armoury.

Usage data

It remains for librarians to assert themselves in routinely requiring of the publishers and suppliers of remotely-accessed products (such as e-journals) adequate levels of usage data. These should be at least equal to what they would themselves expect to be able to capture for products running in their local library or institutional network environment. There are sensitivities (and data protection and privacy legislation) to be taken into account in establishing how finely detailed that usage data should be. However, if there is any lesson to be learned from the PSLI it is that access without usage data effectively nullifies subsequent review and informed decision-making.

Year 2000 compliance

This issue, while certainly a factor to be taken into account in current purchasing for the next few years, is much more of an issue (and likely to be one for TS to resolve) in respect of one-off electronic products acquired in previous years, or products running on older software.

Before moving on to consider the related issues of licensing, co-operative activity, resource discovery and archiving in sections below, we need briefly to review a category of electronic material which poses special and characteristic challenges to libraries and to TS managers: electronic journals.

Electronic Journals: Adapting to Cope

E-journals are now arriving with a vengeance. The latest (seventh) edition the ARL Directory of Electronic Journals (Mogge, 1997) lists over 3400 serial titles, twice as many as for 1996, of which 1465 are categorized as e-journals and 1002 as peer-reviewed; even these numbers may fail to do justice to the number of new (often parallel print-and-electronic) arrivals during the year. For libraries in the UK, there has been the added impact of the PSLI since 1996, boosting the size of the immediately available serials corpus. [The result has for some libraries been not far short of a wash-out, redeemed by the cost savings – many libraries have struggled to make the most for their users of the new resources, have promoted them modestly and have only relatively late in the initiative implemented the procedures necessary, for example, to provide Web-based and bibliographic links to the Initiative's electronic titles.]

As Duranceau (1997, p.1) points out on behalf of serials librarians (but speaking as well for all those dealing with the TS aspects of the electronic library), 'The digital revolution demands, but also offers, a defining moment for serials librarians. We have a new opportunity to demonstrate our value, for electronic serials ask us to do more and be more: electronic serials are more complex to buy, more complex to bring into the library, more complex to provide access to, more complex to regulate, and more complex to renew'. She offers a detailed analysis of the changes implied for all aspects of serials management, with revised workflows and staffing requirements, methods of addressing URL and Web link management, the construction of a licences database, new approaches to dealing with periodicals agents and publishers, provision for negotiating archiving terms and indications of new processes for the cataloguing of these and other electronic resources. This thorough-going, radical revision of existing practice, repeated and reflected in a multitude of libraries, is a demonstration of the way in which Lynch's modernizing spirit is extending itself into transformation, with the management of a new environment causing staff to redefine, or have redefined, their own function.

Woodward *et al.* (1997) make a number of interesting points in the course of disposing of fifteen myths about e-journals. Myth seven is that e-journals will bypass librarians and make them redundant: the rebuttal shows how serials librarians, however they may in future be designated, will continue to have a key role to play in facilitating and enhancing access, in influencing and unifying the variety of publishers' user interfaces, and in controlling local financial management.

Managing Licensing

Licensing, like copyright observance, is important, not just from the Library's point of view but as an aspect of the administration of the whole institution. Proper negotiation of licence terms, the promotion of those terms to library users and the diligent maintenance of reference files will loom increasingly large as a central responsibility of the Library. This is in circumstances where litigation or the imposition of penalties by licensers can be seen as the counterbalance to the extended freedom to exploit data available to the user in the emerging electronic environment.

Because it has a bearing on the conduct of the whole institution, and because it can raise complex legal issues, many libraries have already opened a channel of communication between the staff in technical services usually responsible for the detailed management of licensing and the institution's legal advisers, and that channel can expect to become ever more active. The example of the USA, with its more fevered litigious ambience, serves to provide librarians in the UK and elsewhere with instruction in the exegesis of licence details, and with guidelines (ARL, 1997) to inform library decisions on licensing. These complement the efforts of the JISC/ Publishers Association Working Group that produced its much proclaimed but so far little exploited 'model licence' (JISC/PA, 1997).

Managing licensing in TS is not new. What is new is the explosion of detail and complexity which makes reference to these guidelines important, and the proper assignment of responsibility for working over and signing off licences is crucial. Libraries would do well to develop a checklist of those aspects of all licences that need to conform to their own preferred terms and definitions: agreement on what is a 'site', a 'user', the payment terms, ownership and rights, restrictions and disclaimers. Negotiations over these issues can take time and require the commitment of senior staff resources, particularly in respect of 'local' or one-off agreements. Even the range of variations in nationally negotiated licences such as those for CHEST, JSTOR, and the PSLI needs detailed attention for local implementation.

The Rise and Rise of the Consortium

Collaborative, co-operative and consortial undertakings form such a large part of TS activity now that it is important to give a few simple examples to explore how the move towards the electronic library may affect them.

TS staff are already engaging in collaborative, inter-institutional projects and transactions across the full range of service operations. In the area of preservation there are examples like the eLib-funded Internet Library of Early Journals (ILEJ, 1998) with its four-partner consortium scanning and digitizing 18th and 19th century journals. In the realm of cataloguing and resource discovery, it has been the interaction and co-operation of cataloguers, and their collaborative contributions in building content and agreeing structures for new standards, that has allowed important bibliographic utilities to thrive. This is true for a whole range of utilities, from those at the heart of commercial integrated library systems like the bibliographic database offered and maintained by the UK systems supplier BLCMP, to the databases of not-for-profit membership corporations like the Research Libraries Group.

For acquisitions and serials management staff there is close involvement in consortial purchasing activity. A development already well established in the USA, and with a growing currency in the UK academic library environment (e.g. CALIM in Manchester) is the selective purchase of individual or packaged electronic products, databases or datasets from a local or regional consortial base. This process asks special questions of those tasked with representing both the interests of an individual institution and, in negotiation with the publisher or supplier, the consortium.

It is crucial in these circumstances to have developed a clear view of the key advantages and disadvantages of co-operation, and for the consortium to have agreed *and to operate* according to well-defined and comprehensive terms of reference. Klinger (1997) gives a valuable checklist of the pros and cons of consortial database use, and points to be taken into account in the process of selection, licensing, funding, loading, access control, client support, etc. What is revealed is how much more complex and densely layered than for handling the joint acquisition of print or microform material are the internal terms under which a consortium has to operate in order to function successfully in purchasing for the digital environment.

Acquisitions and serials management staff are equally well aware of the need for close attention to detail from their experience of consortium-based book and serial tendering and procurement exercises. Many academic libraries are now participating regularly in such exercises as members of the various University Purchasing Consortia, and at least one (the Midlands) has included supply of digital products in a recent specification. There is a particular benefit from the mutual exchange of information that informs the work of these groups and feeds back, via the agreed standards incorporated into the tender specification, into the working arrangements of the member libraries. Similarly TS staff have a key role in the local implementation of the whole range of CHEST and BIDS-negotiated deals for electronic products; the same will be true when the higher eduaction community starts to engage with JISC's Distributed, National Electronic Resource (DNER) (see JISC, 1997).

Cataloguing the Electronic Library and the Internet

'The primary function of the library is not so much to provide access to information, as it is rather to reduce the amount of time needed by local clientele to gain such access.' (Atkinson, 1991, p.38). When libraries comprised printed material alone, ownership was the surest way of reducing that time, and the catalogue was the key tool promoting access. In the world of the hybrid or electronic library, how do things change?

The way they have changed so far is largely by increments. Libraries have extended the reach of their OPACs (especially as they have moved to a Web base) by having cataloguers add selected Internet resources using (when they have access to it) the MARC 856 field. Web sites have been created to contain lists of hyperlinked e-journals (e.g. the pioneering work in the UK of Glasgow and Loughborough, or see Ellwood and Thompson, 1997) or a wider range of local electronic or digitized resources, or Web-based subject catalogues linking to selected Internet resources. Such sites also often include pointers to some of the national gateways such as NISS NetFirst, SOSIG or OMNI, taking advantage of the efficient collaborative cataloguing effort that has compiled them (Woodward, 1996, offers a comprehensive if early review, esp. pp.195–205).

It is clear that libraries would be able to devote very substantial staff resources to Internet and other electronic resource discovery work, including listing, cataloguing and pointing to local and remote sources, and still have barely scratched the surface of the Internet information load. What elements should go into the management strategy governing these activities, and what role is there for TS?

There are strong arguments, first of all, for seeing the Library Web OPAC as the primary user tool for locating electronic and Internet resources, as it is for a significant proportion of the Library's physically held material; the Library OPAC can also potentially or actually function as a Gateway to other resources and metadata repositories (Xu, 1997). Against this, especially in the absence of a Web-based OPAC, there may already be an elaborate and effective locally-constructed Web site listing, arguing in the short- or medium-term in favour of a plural approach (Hanson, 1998). There needs to be a consolidated strategy on the use that will be made of links to nationally compiled gateways, as opposed to locally created links direct to the target object, taking into account the URL maintenance work that is implied for all locally established links. Local policy on the use of metadata has to be agreed, with active involvement and training in the application of Dublin Core, SGML, EAD and any other appropriate schemes incorporated into working practices and schedules (for a helpful introduction to metadata issues, see Miller, 1996). Likewise, local expertise needs to be fostered on the application of unique identifiers like the PURL (persistent URL) and DOI (Digital Object Identifier) (see Green and Bide, 1997).

At the same time, managers have to strike a balance between the effort to be devoted to supporting resource discovery for Internet resources, and the continuing call on staff to catalogue printed and other material. In many libraries it has been subject and systems librarians and reference staff who have taken the initiative in developing Web site resource listings, not least because of the unyielding pressure on cataloguing staff to process printed material. Cataloguers are well placed by experience and training to adapt to the changing environment of the Dublin Core and to exploit it. However, it may take a further shift in the transfer of cataloguing responsibilities to para-professionals and support staff (or outsourcing), and even more intense exploitation of the major shared bibliographic utilities for record retrieval, before professional cataloguers can in general make the transition to high-volume electronic text or Internet cataloguing.

Preservation (and the Digital Archive)

The genuine impact of the electronic library on those TS staff who have traditionally been engaged in preservation activities – the book binders and binding preparation staff – will be relatively slow in coming. It will appear as the (gradual) falling off of journal binding as e-journals begin to predominate and a reduction in rebinding work as a greater number of heavily used textbooks are superseded by their digital or digitized equivalent. Meanwhile, there will be scope for scanning and digitization activity to preserve (and promote) fragile and embrittled special collections material, but if existing practice in the UK is followed, such activity will not necessarily be located in the bindery; the key relevant expertise may already be available in the library's Systems or Reprographics staff complement, or in a separate facility dedicated to scanning and digitization for all purposes; or the work may be contracted out (to the Higher Education Digitisation Service, for example.)

In the meantime, a growing concern amongst other TS staff is and will be the best means of determining the long-term preservation of digital material for which at present only the flimsiest archival future is secured. It should be a core element of the library's preservation strategy that conscious decisions are taken at the point of acquisition about the retention and archiving of electronic material not bought on lease.

Some licences for e-journals (for example with OCLC's Electronic Collection Online) do provide for access in perpetuity, and the relevance of such considerations has to be included in initial purchasing decision. Where permanent retention and physical archiving is the preferred option, then another set of issues will arise: how to ensure long-term provision of the hardware and software needed to mount or copy the original. It is some small comfort to know that nobody has good solutions yet to all these problems: librarians throughout the UK await the outcome of the Consortium of University Research Libraries' CEDARS project on this subject with interest (CURL, 1998).

Conclusion

Much is still obscure about the problems and challenges that the move to a digital base will bring into academic libraries. But changes in technology, radical developments in the commercial and not-for-profit publishing and dissemination of electronic material, and the continuing need to administer substantial print collections mean that technical services operations, like the libraries they sustain, will be modernizing significantly in the next years, with staff having to retain and adapt old skills while preparing to learn and exploit new ones.

References

Allen, N.H. and Williams, J.F. (1995) The future of technical services: an administrative perspective. *Advances in Librarianship*, **19**, 159–189

Association of Research Libraries (1997) *Principles for licensing electronic resources.* http://arl.cni.org/scomm/licensing/principles.html

Atkinson, R. (1991) The conditions of collection development. In *Collection management: a new treatise*, eds. C.B. Osburn and R. Atkinson, pp.30–38. Greenwich, CT: JAI Press

Atkinson, R. (1992) The acquisitions librarian as change agent in the transition to the electronic library. *Library Resources and Technical Services*, **36**, 7–20

Bloss, A. and Lanier, D. (1997) The Library Department Head in the context of matrix management and reengineering. *College and Research Libraries*, **58**, 499–508

Boissonnas, C.M. (1997) Managing technical services in a changing environment: the Cornell experience. *Library Resources and Technical Services*, **41**(2), 147–154. [This issue has several useful contributions on change management in tech. services departments.]

CURL Exemplars for Digital ARchiveS (1998). http://www.curl.ac.uk/cedarsinfo.shtml

Davies, M., Boyle, F. and Osborne, S. (1998) CAS–IAS services: where are we now? *The Electronic Library*, **16**, 37–48

Diedrichs, C.P. (1996) Acquisitions management in changing times. *Library Resources and Technical Services*, **40**, 237–250

Duranceau, E. (1997) *Beyond print: revisioning serials acquisitions for the digital age.* http://web.mit.edu/waynej/www/duranceau.htm

Ellwood, C. and Thompson, S. (1997) *York Information Connections: an attempt to catalogue the Internet.* http://www.ariadne.ac.uk/issue11/york/

Gorman, G.E. and Miller, R.H. (1997) (eds.) *Collection Management for the 21st Century: a handbook for librarians.* Westport, CT: Greenwood

Gorman, M. (1990) (ed.) *Technical services today and tomorrow.* Englewood, CO: Libraries Unlimited

Goulding, A. (1996) *Managing change for library support staff.* Aldershot: Avebury Press

Green, B. and Bide, M. (1997) *Unique Identifiers: a brief introduction.* http://www.bic.org.uk/bic/uniquid.html

Hanson, T. (1998) The access catalogue: gateway to resources. *Ariadne*, 15, 6–7.

Harloe, B. and Budd, J.M. (1994) Collection development and scholarly communication in the era of electronic access. *Journal of Academic Librarianship*, **20**, 83–87

Internet Library of Early Journals (1998) http://www.bodley.ox.ac.uk/ilej/

Johnson, P. (1997) Collection development policies and electronic information resources. In Gorman and Miller (1997), pp.83–104

Joint Information Systems Committee (1997) *An integrated information environment for Higher Education: developing the Distributed, National Electronic Resource (DNER).* http://www.jisc.ac.uk/cei/dner_colpol.html

Joint Information Systems Committee and Publishers Association (1997) *Proposed 'Model licence' between UK universities and publishers.* http://www.uksg.org/pa.htm

Klinger, T. (1997) *Sharing the Load: the pros and cons of consortial database use.* http://www.library.kent.edu/~tk/consort02.html

Law, D. (1991) The organization of collection management in academic libraries. In *Collection management in academic libraries*, eds. C. Jenkins and M. Morley, pp.1–20. Aldershot: Gower

Luther, J. (1997) Full text journal subscriptions: an evolutionary process. *Against the Grain*, **9**(3), 18,20,22,24

Lynch, C.A. (1993) The transformation of scholarly communication and the role of the library in the age of the networked information. *Serials Librarian*, **23**, 7–8

McCombs, G.M. (1992) Technical services in the 1990s: A process of convergent evolution. *Library Resources and Technical Services,* **36,** 135–147

McCombs, G.M. (1994) The Internet and technical services: a point break approach. *Library Resources and Technical Services,* **38,** 169–177

Miller, P. (1996) *Metadata for the masses.* http://www.ariadne.ac.uk/issue5/metadata-masses/

Mogge, D.W. (1997) (ed.) *ARL Directory of electronic journals, newsletters and academic discussion lists,* 7th edn. Washington: Association of Research Libraries

NISS NetFirst Service. http://www.netfirst.ac.uk/

OCLC (1994) The future is now: the changing face of technical services. Proceedings of the OCLC Symposium, ALA Midwinter Conference [February 4], 1994. Dublin, OH: OCLC

Woodward, H. *et al.* (1997) Electronic journals: myths and realities. *Library Management,* **18,** 155–162

Woodward, J. (1996) Cataloging and classifying information resources on the Internet. *Annual Review of Information Science and Technology,* **31,** 189–220

Xu, A. (1997) *Metadata conversion and the library OPAC.* http://web.mit.edu/waynej/www/xu.htm

CHAPTER TWENTY FIVE

Case Study: UMIST Library and Information Service

Keith Renwick

Introduction

Academic libraries, particularly the 'old' universities, tend to use organizational structures that are based on bureaucratic models which are relatively inflexible to the demands of present-day information management requirements. This inflexibility has predominantly been due to historical factors, but has been exacerbated by the financial constraints imposed upon universities over the past twenty years, combined with vastly increased student numbers and high levels of inflation for academic journals. Limited resources for all types of academic activity and the costs of implementing new technology have not allowed for flexibility and the continuous review required of the organizational and management structures of academic libraries. In addition, the past decade has witnessed a rapid escalation in the development of electronic formats of information, thereby necessitating a steep learning curve for many traditional academic librarians who have been relatively unfamiliar (and perhaps uncomfortable) with computer-based information formats.

There is no doubt that many of the processes which have evolved into the traditional technical services activities of acquisitions, cataloguing and serials administration within libraries are less relevant when applied to electronic resources than is the case with printed materials. For library staff too, the division of functionality between user and technical services has become less distinct when applied to networked and online information resources.

This case study outlines the organizational structure and administration relating to the management of electronic information resources within the Technical Services Division of UMIST Library and Information Service. It attempts to focus upon the problems involved in retaining traditional organizational structures in the acquisition and processing of newer forms of information dissemination at a time of diminishing resources.

Organizational Structure

When the author joined UMIST Library as an Assistant Librarian in 1973, the Senior Management Group was composed of six senior members of staff, comprising the Librarian, Deputy Librarian and four Sub-Librarians with responsibility for Reader Services, Acquisitions (including the Periodicals Section), Cataloguing and Library Systems.

The departure of a number of senior members of staff during the financial cuts that occurred within higher education in the late 1970's and early 1980's resulted in the non-replacement of the posts of Deputy Librarian and two Sub-Librarians. The functional responsibilities of these posts were absorbed by the remaining two Sub-Librarians who became Heads of two new divisions, Reader Services and Technical Services. The members of staff responsible for the library automated housekeeping systems had formerly been responsible directly to the Librarian, but this responsibility was absorbed into the Technical Services Division in early 1993. At the same time, the Head of Technical Services position acquired responsibility for Administration, which encompassed responsibility for the building fabric and refurbishment, furniture and equipment and other matters relating to the day-by-day administrative functioning of the library. This is the organizational structure retained to the present day (Figure 25.1). Almost all posts indicated in this organizational structure chart are involved in staffing duties on the Issue Desk (non-professional staff) or the Information Desk (professional staff). This reduces the time available for work in the sections of the Technical Services Division by periods of between 25–30 per cent, although this fluctuates between vacation and term times.

The merging of responsibilities for acquisitions and cataloguing into a Technical Services Division was an entirely logical development that reflected the organizational structure that existed in many academic libraries at the time. During periods of diminishing (or inflation-reducing) university budgets, it was frequently the posts of senior academic-related grades of library staff that remained unfilled whilst other staff continued to absorb the additional workload caused by increasing student numbers, rapidly changing technology and escalating loans and reservations.

In 1965 UMIST (formerly a College of Advanced Technology) became a University in its own right, although it retained the status of the Faculty of Technology of the University of Manchester, until gaining full independence from the University of Manchester in 1994. The only formal relationship presently existing between UMIST and the University of Manchester is that UMIST degrees continue to be conferred by the University of Manchester.

Up until the early 1980's, all expansion of UMIST Library had taken place within the Main Building by taking in additional space on an ad-hoc basis. It was clear by 1981 that UMIST was in desperate need of either a new library or considerable expansion and refurbishment. At the time, however, a new purpose-built library building was precluded on the grounds of insufficient funding, falling student

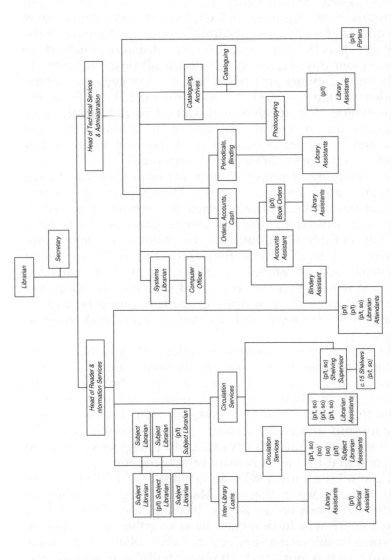

Figure 25.1 UMIST Library and Information Service organizational chart

numbers and lack of a suitable location. The expansion and refurbishment of the Library therefore took place within its existing and additional space between the period 1984 to 1987, providing the opportunity not only to enhance the environment of the Library, but also to produce a development plan that formulated library policy and planning for the ensuing decade, although technological innovation has to a large degree dictated the development of IT-based library services. The introduction of an integrated automated housekeeping system in 1984 resulted in the re-evaluation of many processes and systems that had evolved from manual systems of ordering, cataloguing and processing library acquisitions. The Adlib system (little known in the UK, but popular in the Netherlands and Australia) had been selected predominantly due to the fact that it could be mounted on a Prime mainframe computer, of which UMIST had spare capacity. In addition to its comparatively low cost, Adlib had the advantage of being relatively straightforward to configure to the particular requirements of the Library. Partly for this reason and partly due to insufficient support from the supplier, a considerable amount of development of the system specific to the needs of UMIST Library was carried out internally by our systems librarians.

In 1993 UMIST transferred its automated housekeeping system to the BLCMP Talis UNIX-based system, operating through Sun hardware using Client-Server architecture. Although at the time in its early stages of development, Talis offered the long-term potential for a fully-integrated housekeeping with a leading systems supplier in the academic sector. Also important was the fact that the same system had been adopted by the John Rylands University Library of Manchester one year previously. In addition, it was likely to be the system migrated to in the future by the other local academic libraries of the Manchester Metropolitan University and University of Salford, a key factor in the development of the Manchester academic library consortium. Among the initial problems relating to electronic resources management was the fact that few electronic materials were held in UMIST

Library in 1993, almost none of which had ISBNs (used as BLCMP control numbers). The conversion of catalogue records from Adlib (non-MARC) to Talis (MARC) format was predominantly by ISBN control number, therefore matching of records for electronic materials had to be done by author-title mnemonic, resulting in a very low percentage of correct matches for these records.

Development of Electronic Information Resources

Electronic information resources in UMIST Library can be categorized into the standing order type of material, which may be in one of a number of formats or accessible via a network and the 'one-off' items which often accompany printed monographs, now increasingly supplied in CD-ROM format.

During the 1980's, library-based research activity academic libraries became dependent upon the use of online databases as the principal source of secondary information, to a large degree replacing the traditional manual sources of printed abstracts and indexes. By the late 1980's, there were more than 2000 online databases available for searching, normally using experienced librarians acting as intermediaries between the search requester and the database host. Although library users were required to cover the cost of a online searches (at the time, this was the only charge made by the library for any of its services) users often preferred it to the alternative of carrying out time-consuming manual searches of printed abstracts. In many cases the searches were funded from research grants or by academic departments, therefore from 1983/84 the number of online searches carried out annually in UMIST Library rose from 130 to a peak of 466 by 1990/91.

By the mid-eighties, a new information format had appeared on the academic library scene which brought about a major revolution in the way in which librarians and library users disseminated and manipulated information, particularly of a bibliographical nature. The CD-ROM (Compact

Disc – Read Only Memory) was developed from the Compact (audio) Disc by Phillips Industries, the first commercial products appearing in 1985. However, like many of these products, its take-up was relatively slow, mainly due libraries being unwilling to gamble on a new technology format demanding expensive investment in equipment where few software products existed. It was not until 1989 that UMIST Library acquired its first CD-ROM products, these being mainly CD-ROM alternatives to traditional printed abstracts and indexing sources, such as Compendex (CD-ROM version of Engineering Index) and Metadex (Metals Abstracts). It was these products, and especially ABI-Inform (a management/business database), which stimulated an enthusiastic response amongst library users. Whereas previously, searching of printed abstracting and indexing sources had been confined to a small number of users (mainly postgraduate research students), CD-ROM databases offered a format that was considerably faster to use and more user-friendly than printed versions. More importantly, CD-ROM database searches could be undertaken by the user, producing instant results at no cost to themselves, therefore their popularity quickly increased with both undergraduate and postgraduate research students.

Within a short period of time, academic members of staff in departments such as the UMIST School of Management began to set project work and essays which necessitated CD-ROM searches. Occasionally it became obvious that inexperienced students were undertaking searches of CD-ROM databases that were totally unsuitable for the subject enquiry they were undertaking. However, by 1994/95, the number of mediated online searches carried out by UMIST Library had declined to 91, but the number of recorded CD-ROM searches on the network had reached a staggering 63 000.

The escalation in the volume of material on CD-ROM within ten years has been remarkable and has contributed to the dramatic increase in user-operated computer-based information resources in libraries. In 1989 it was estimated there were almost 400 commercially-available CD-ROM databases

(Hartley, 1990), but by 1997 the CD-ROM Directory listed over 24 000 titles.

The popularity and usability of CD-ROM databases was to some measure offset by a lack of standardization in the search engines used by the database providers, although the BRS search engine (used by Books in Print Plus, Ulrichs Plus and BLDSC Conferences databases, amongst others) increasingly became the most commonly used. In addition to the bibliographic databases, the CD-ROM collection increased rapidly in its coverage to include a number of full-text newspaper and popular journal back-files including the Times, Financial Times and the Economist.

Another important development in the provision of access to electronic information resources has been the growth of national networked database services, the most successful of which in the UK has been the BIDS (Bath Information and Data Service) which provides a networked alternative to many online and larger CD-ROM databases. BIDS was originally initiated as the agency to provide networked access to the ISI Citation Indexes, but now also includes online bibliographic resources such as Compendex, and the Royal Society of Chemistry databases. In addition to solving the problem of providing adequate resources in-house for the networking of the CD-ROM versions of these databases, BIDS has also developed search interfaces which are more user-friendly than the CD-ROM equivalents.

The vehicle for negotiating purchasing arrangements for BIDS and other software, data, information and training materials on behalf of the higher education sector is CHEST (the Combined Higher Education Software Team) which, like BIDS, has its headquarters at the University of Bath. CHEST has been successful in negotiating deals for a wide variety of materials that have enabled academic libraries and computing services to stretch limited budgets and make resources available that otherwise may not be economically viable.

A further significant event for the UK higher education community was the HEFCE Pilot Site Licence Initiative (PSLI), now in its third year of existence and likely to be extended in Mark II form under the auspices of the Joint Information Systems Committee (JISC). The PSLI was an agreement initiated by the HEFCE with four publishers (Blackwell, Blackwell Science, Academic Press and Institute of Physics) whereby the higher education budget was top–sliced to fund enhanced access to the journal collections of these publishers at a lower cost to individual institutions. An additional benefit of the initiative was access to the electronic full-text journal databases of the four publishers at no or little additional cost, however specific terms relating to access, coverage and financial terms varies between the individual publishers. It is estimated that the average saving for a higher education institution is in the region of £11,000, although for UMIST it is calculated to be approximately £7,130. There is some uncertainty as to whether the present arrangement of top-slicing the higher education budget will continue for the Mark II version of PSLI, particularly if it is now to be administered through the JISC.

Alternative sources of access to electronic databases, at present in the early stages of development, are the services offered by 'aggregators', such as serial subscription agents and specialist database providers. All four major subscription agents now offer services providing access to electronic databases mounted on their own systems or interfacing with publishers' servers, although this is likely to result in further duplication of databases accessing identical resources via different interfaces.

The Manchester Academic Libraries Consortium

The four higher education institutions in Manchester (including Salford) form one of the largest educational conurbations outside of the United States of America, with a student population in excess of 60 000. The majority of these students study in the square mile around Oxford Road, comprising the institutions of the University of Manchester (including Manchester Business School) and the Manchester

Metropolitan University. Only a few hundred metres from these two institutions is the campus of UMIST, with the University of Salford located approximately three miles to the west.

In 1992 the libraries of these institutions established the Consortium of Academic Libraries in Manchester (CALIM) with the aims of:

1. Encouraging resource sharing in a spirit of enlightened self interest;
2. developing an infrastructure including computer networking, common catalogues and systems of document delivery;
3. regulating access on the basis of formal agreement whereby defined members of one institution can use the library of another;
4. agreeing policies of collection development preventing unnecessary duplication;
5. encouraging and seeking funding for research projects of common interest;
6. identifying and implementing information policies which assist the students and staff of Manchester institutions.

One significant success in the area of consortium access to electronic information resources has been the negotiation of a CALIM–wide deal to provide access to the Information Access (IAC) database consisting of approximately 1000 periodical titles in full text, mostly social science and management titles. Another CALIM consortium deal provides access to the Technical Indexes database of World Wide Standards which consists of 147 CD-ROM discs locally mounted in a jukebox at the University of Salford and accessible throughout CALIM via the G–MING (Greater Manchester Interformation Network Group) network .

Although the benefits of consortium purchasing arrangements through CALIM, particularly for networked electronic materials, are extensive, they have created a number of difficulties for library staff with responsibility for acquisitions and accounts. The most important of these has been to ensure that any financial commitment is correctly recorded, particularly on occasions when agreements are negotiated verbally by a member of CALIM who may have no direct accountability to UMIST. Another problem has been to ensure that the invoices for recharging joint arrangements between the member libraries are correctly administered to ensure that the financial regulations of each institution are adhered to and documentation conforms to library requirements.

CALIM Council has recently approved a broad strategy for the next three years, the key objective of which is to create the concept of the 'virtual research library'. One of the goals relates to the joint purchase of both physical and electronic materials that will be 'a fundamental activity of the consortium'. This goal has already been partially achieved by deals on electronic materials previously negotiated and by a consortial tender for periodicals which came into effect from 1997/98. However, it is the opinion of the author that the goal of joint purchasing is unlikely to be successfully achieved without either the amalgamation of administrative processes involved in joint purchasing or by devolving responsibility for administering joint purchasing to one of the member libraries. In addition, the problems involved in recharging and administering the significant sums involved, particularly where it involves the payment of Value-Added Tax, are likely to be considerably reduced through a centralized operation.

By the end of the decade there will need to be fundamental rationalization of both printed and electronic resources to reduce unnecessary duplication within the CALIM libraries. This will not be easily achieved until the CALIM librarians can demonstrate to academic staff of the five institutions that document delivery or remote access can provide a more efficient and economical service than is achievable by duplicating resources within each library. To this end, it is of the utmost importance for CALIM Libraries to gather and evaluate usage data for both printed and electronic materials in order to analyse which format of information is used and/or preferred by users.

Selection and Acquisition of Electronic Formats

Functionality relating to the majority of procedures and controls within the Acquisitions Section of UMIST Library is well defined and involves a small number of staff in a limited number of processes. Orders for monographs and standing orders originate within a small team of subject librarians who co-ordinate the information requirements for the relatively limited range of subjects studied in UMIST, predominantly in Science and Engineering, but also including a substantial Management School. Subject librarians select the titles to be ordered and pass requisition slips to the Acquisitions Section, where records are downloaded for requested items from the (BLCMP) Talis database of approximately 14 million records. For the small percentage of titles not contained on the database, records have to be manually input by the acquisitions staff. At present, orders are allocated to approximately six or seven suppliers, some of whom are selected for their ability to supply a service based upon subject, publisher or geographical location. Library staff involved in the acquisition process used their expertise and experience of library purchasing and knowledge of library suppliers to obtain the required resources and materials in the shortest possible time and at the lowest possible price. Until the recent demise of the Net Book Agreement, the ability of libraries to negotiate with suppliers on price was limited, although some advantage could be gained by including servicing requirements within the scope of the purchasing arrangements.

There is little doubt that the development of electronic information formats, particularly online and CD-ROM databases, involved subject librarians in considerably more direct contact with the resource supplier than had previously been the case with printed materials. In the early days of CD-ROM development, the merging of the functions of database selection and acquisition evolved within UMIST Library due to the allocation of responsibility for the installation and networking of the databases. The highest level of expertise (largely self-taught) in the setting up and configuration of computer systems for operating CD-ROM databases resided with one of the subject librarians (not a member of the library systems staff). Working with her opposite number at the John Rylands University Library of Manchester, they developed a level of expertise that enabled the two institutions to develop one of the most advanced CD-ROM networks in the UK academic library community. Many of the procedures relating to the acquisition of CD-ROM databases evolved through informal procedures established through the need to liaise directly with the publisher or supplier, thereby by-passing the normal ordering procedures. In a number of cases, this resulted in situations where invoices would be delivered to the Accounts Section (part of the Acquisition Section) relating to materials for which no order or requisition details existed. As these invoices were often of substantial value, it became difficult to maintain accurate records of financial commitments, as well as occasionally contravening the requirement to adhere to UMIST financial regulations. A recent audit of library financial procedures highlighted the requirement to raise an official order for all material purchases and support it with a properly authorized requisition.

In the early days of CD-ROM systems, it was understandable that there would be some degree of interaction between subject librarians and the product suppliers, due to the need for information on subject coverage or supplier support relating to installation and networking. Often this support from suppliers was minimal and the situation for both librarians and users was exacerbated by the variety of search engines in the databases and the differing configurations required on the library CD-ROM network. Once products and search engines became more standardized, the need for this interaction between librarian and supplier diminished.

By the early 1990's, a number of companies specializing in the supply of CD-ROM products had been established, in addition to a few traditional library suppliers and subscription agents who were beginning to build up expertise in this area. Initial use of general library suppliers for the supply of CD-ROM databases resulted in a few problems, although these were often due to the lack of established procedures on the part of the library as well as teething problems on the part of the suppliers. By 1994, serious consideration was being given by UMIST Library to the possibility of a tender for the supply of CD-ROM databases as part of the Library's policy of ensuring maximum financial benefit in the acquisition of library resources. The establishment of a CALIM Tendering Group, initially to initiate tendering for journals and presently to prepare a tender for monographs and serials, is likely to result in a future tender for CD-ROM and other electronic resources on behalf of the Consortium.

Although Technical Services and Acquisitions librarians have traditionally had responsibility for negotiating the purchase of information resources from library suppliers, the responsibility for the negotiation and purchase of electronic materials within UMIST and the other CALIM libraries now resides predominantly with the User or Information Services librarians. This has come about principally due to the diminution of functionality between selection and acquisition activities and the evolution of a CALIM Committee as the principal body for not only selecting electronic resources for purchase, but also negotiating financial purchasing arrangements with suppliers.

In terms of the basic processes attached to the ordering and handling of electronic materials, most appear to cause no problems to staff in the Acquisitions Section. Occasionally a computer disk or CD-ROM received as part of a book/disk package may be found to be corrupted, thereby necessitating its return to the supplier. If received as a set (usually with a set ISBN) this usually necessitates the book being returned to the supplier with the disk, which can cause problems if the item has been in stock for some time and the book is on loan to another reader.

Licensing Issues

For most academic libraries, one of the major changes relating to the development of electronic information has been the fact that these resources, whether supplied in the form of CD-ROM, online or locally networked databases, are now commonly supplied on a licensed lease rather than purchase basis. Their use is strictly controlled through these licences, which may impose limitations upon the way in which academic libraries provide services to the user populations, such as the requirement to impose user names and passwords in order to exclude use of databases by non-registered members of the library user population. UMIST Library has for many years, implemented a policy of admitting any person requiring use of the Library for reference purposes, the only condition of entry being proof of identity. Unfortunately for librarians, not only are the conditions of use attached to the licences quite restrictive, they also vary in respect of the terms attached to each licence, thereby necessitating considerable study of small print in each licence.

The development of an extensive and sophisticated network of electronic resources that is accessible not only throughout the UMIST campus, but also from student halls of residence, has resulted in additional costs for networking which have added to the increasing costs for the library of electronic resource provision. These additional charges are often of the order of 50 per cent, usually being based upon the number of concurrent users or networked workstations.

Periodicals Administration

In addition to the blurring of responsibilities and functionality for staff involved in activities within the Acquisitions Section, there has been a similar effect with regard to the staff in the Periodicals Section. This has resulted in a situation where the Head of Section has responsibility for administering the printed periodicals collection, but has not been assigned equivalent responsibility for titles in electronic format. To some degree, this has evolved due to the interest and acquired expertise of the Head of User and Reader Services and his responsibility for developing user services in this area.

There has been considerable discussion recently among the library community, particularly on e-mail lists, concerning the subject of whether or not to include records on the library catalogue for journals or other materials in electronic format not held or directly subscribed to, but which can be accessed by users of the library. The policy adopted by UMIST Library has been to add records to the database for all journals which can be accessed directly from the Web OPAC catalogue. To this end, considerable effort has been expended recently in ensuring that all electronic journals accessible by UMIST Library, whether as paid subscriptions or freely available (e.g. as part of the PSLI) have entries on the catalogue and links from the Web version of the OPAC.

Although cataloguing of all other materials, irrespective of format, is undertaken by the Cataloguing Section, the cataloguing of periodicals and serials is a responsibility of the Periodicals Librarian, although the bulk of the entries for electronic journals accessible over the Internet were input as a centrally–funded student project over the 1997 summer vacation. Although many librarians, particularly cataloguers, regard the integrity of the catalogue record as sacrosanct, the catalogue record is essentially a finding tool to enable the user to locate the information they seek. It may in the future be difficult to reconcile the conflicting demands of the integrity of the catalogue record with the need to ensure electronic resources can be located through a simple catalogue search by novice library users.

Cataloguing and Servicing

The cataloguing and processing of electronic information resources has been an increasing burden on the small number of staff available in the Cataloguing Section. Although the number of items added to stock on an annual basis is not particularly high, the time required to catalogue and process electronic information resources is disproportionately greater than for other materials.

During the financial year 1991/92, UMIST Library begun to acquire computer disks in 5.25 inch format, usually accompanying research monographs or textbooks in computing-related subjects. This form of supplementary and/or support data for printed books became increasingly popular with library users, although 5.25 inch disks were notoriously susceptible to damage or corruption. After considering the copyright position and obtaining the views of a sample of disk suppliers, it was determined that library staff could make a single copy for the purposes of backup in the event of damage to the master copy.

By 1994, most of the PCs available to users in the Library and all new machines purchased by users had adopted the 3.5 inch disk format, which were both more robust and had greater capacity than 5.25 inch disks, thus resulting in an increasing demand by users for material in this format. Problems relating to the handling and use of computer disks were mainly related to their corruption through misuse or, occasionally through becoming accidently wiped by the de-sensitizer attached to the security system, a recurring problem with all forms of magnetic tape materials. In addition, the 3M Tattletape security system did not have any security devices available to protect the disks against theft, although losses did not appear to be particularly high. Demand for replacement disks, mainly due to damage or corrupted data, averaged about two disks per week, a minor task in addition to the normal processing and copying of newly-acquired material.

Computer disks gradually became less popular as the format for support material for mongraphs as CD-ROM became progressively cheaper to produce. During the year 1996/97, UMIST Library acquired 185 CD-ROM programs, mainly as support material for textbooks or multimedia databases, compared with only 170 programs on 3.5 inch computer disk. The advantages of CD-ROM format over computer disk are principally related to processing and security issues, although the format is popular with library users and has stimulated considerable demand. In addition, the secure format of information contained on CD-ROM has resulted in a considerable saving in staff time due to the removal of the necessity (and feasibility) to make a backup copy. Unlike the computer disk, CD-ROMs can be easily protected from theft by the use of an inexpensive security trigger. There is only one known example of a CD-ROM being rendered inoperative through misuse and this was probably caused by an act of vandalism. Whereas initially CD-ROMs were principally published as support material for computer-related subjects, they are now increasingly supplied with textbooks on a wide range of subjects related to the subjects taught or researched in UMIST.

Conclusion

The problems faced by library staff operating in the traditional roles encompassed within the Technical Services Division of UMIST Library seem typical of the situation affecting many other academic libraries in the UK. The author's involvement over many years with the National Acquisitions Group and United Kingdom Serials Group combined with discussions with colleagues in other institutions, confirm the view that electronic information resources are treated differently to print and other non-book materials, particularly for information resources accessed directly by users over a network or via the Internet.

The difficulties of long–term strategic planning for academic library services are obvious in the light of the evolutionary nature of the electronic revolution. This situation is exacerbated by the trend towards monopolization of electronic information, a recent example of which was the proposed merger of Reed Elsevier and Wolter Kluwer. Librarians are already starting to take a stand against this trend, assisted by the consortialization of information purchasing arrangements. It is the view of the author that control of information dissemination needs to be returned to the environment from which it originates, that is the higher education sector. In addition, the problem of the long-term archival and storage of digital information can probably only be resolved by using the extensive computing resources that exist within the university environment, perhaps on a regional, subject-based approach utilizing existing regional computing centres.

The management of electronic information resources should no longer be a problem for librarians and library systems. Automation system manufacturers should be designing systems with the flexibility to incorporate all the elements relating to the ordering, cataloguing, accounting systems (including VAT), processing and user access functionality which will enable libraries to provide the desired information, irrespective of format, access method and distribution medium. Library catalogues of the future will not only be able to access the holdings of their library (or CALIM libraries in UMIST's case) but will be the principal interface between the user and a multiplicity of electronic information resources.

The traditional academic library organizational structure based upon sectional/divisional responsibilities relating to technical library activities and processes, particularly those oriented around functions (acquisitions and cataloguing) or format (printed periodicals and serials) appear less relevant to the electronic age. It will be difficult to introduce radical change into a bureaucratic system at a time of financial uncertainty whilst maintaining essential services, but it is important that librarians carefully consider the ideal organizational structure to manage all formats of information in an efficient, economic and effective manner. It is also crucial that the skills and expertise of library staff, gained over many years of traditional library activity based upon the print medium, continue to occupy a position of value and importance in the electronic library of the future.

References

Hartley, R.J. *et al.* (1990) *Online searching: Principles and Practice*, p.3. London: Bower-Saur

UMIST Library and Information Service Web site: http://www.umist.ac.uk/UMIST_Library/

CHAPTER TWENTY SIX

Case Study: Glasgow University Library

Colin Galloway

Introduction

Since the opening of a new library building in 1968 Glasgow University Library has had a strong Reader Services ethos which, arguably, put the Library in the forefront of such developments in the UK. From the mid-1980's the emphasis has changed from a relatively passive Reader Services environment (responding to expressed need) to a highly pro-active Reader Services role with, at its core, the liaison programme of a team of 16 Subject Librarians. Furthermore, the posts of Head of Reader Services and Head of Technical Services no longer exist, part of the policy of breaking down the barriers, real and imagined, that existed between the two areas. An IT Services department, non-existent a decade ago, now has 7.5 staff, three of them professional.

By way of contrast, as recently as 13 years ago the Technical Services areas of Glasgow University Library (by which I limit myself to the four areas covering Acquisitions, Serials, Cataloguing and Classification) had the FTE equiva-lent of 11 professional members of staff (numbers varied over the years as did duties). Today there are 4.5 professional FTEs. Even that number should be qualified in any comparison with other institutions as 1.5 are based in the classification unit where our own in-house classification system is used. The existence of this has limited our ability to make use of external classification from imported bibliographic records and left the remaining input at professional level higher than it might otherwise have been, although we do make full use of imported Library of Congress Subject Headings (LCSH). The other 3 professional staff head the areas of Acquisitions, Serials and Cataloguing (the latter designated in this Library as Bibliographic Services).

There has been no reduction in the numbers of non-professional staff to parallel that of professional staff. In fact the number of promoted non-professionals has increased as they have taken on duties that were formerly undertaken by professionals (although, as we shall see, in a rather different set-up). Some of these changes might well have happened anyway in the move towards increasing liaison with academic staff, but this would in itself have been difficult to implement in an era of static staff budgets without the redeployment of professional staff from areas of Technical Services made possible by the use of new technologies as the Library moved into the electronic age.

Cataloguing

One of the first areas where this trend was seen was in cataloguing and the sharing of machine readable cataloguing (MARC) data. In Glasgow University Library at present bibliographic records are searched for online from three major co-operative databases. Our first choice is the Consortium of University Research Libraries database (CURL), failing which the Research Libraries Information Network (RLIN) database of the Research Libraries Group or the OCLC database would be used. These databases are searched by Acquisitions staff at the pre-order stage and records are downloaded into our database via CURL, where the RLIN and OCLC US MARC records are automatically converted to UK MARC, giving us a full bibliographic record in our OPAC (including LCSH) while the material is still on order. This avoids keying of bibliographic data for records at the ordering stage only for it to be jettisoned when the material is received and properly catalogued. Disadvantages lie in the number of downloaded records that may require deletion if items are reported as out of print or otherwise unavailable. This is a relatively minor inconvenience, but financially might be an important factor for some libraries. Some items have no bibliographic record available at the time of ordering (or in the case of certain categories it has not proved worthwhile searching at the pre-order stage e.g. Cyrillic). These have skeleton records provided by Acquisitions staff. On receipt of the material these items have a full bibliographic record overlaid by staff from Bibliographic Services. About 17 per cent of our records are still created in-house; this figure includes theses, official publications and international agency publications but excludes additions to our Special Collections. Almost all this work is now done by higher grade non-professional staff.

So there have been three major effects of technological change in this area: (1) Many fewer records are created in-house (2) Acquisitions staff perform some of the functions that would hitherto have been considered the prerogative of cataloguing staff, and (3) The grade of staff who perform these functions is generally of a lower level than formerly.

As a member of CURL and RLIN, the records we create in-house are added to these databases for use by other libraries. As our records created at the pre-order stage are sub-MARC in standard, we do not want these added to the above databases. Fortunately our current automated system, innopac, enables us to code those records that are full standard and can be transferred to other databases and those of sub-standard that will not. If this were not possible on our system, the whole question of pre-order records would have to be reconsidered.

Management Information

Management information is far more readily available from automated library systems today than it was formerly, even if what we require often seems to be a stage ahead of what is possible to retrieve! The increased sophistication of the Innopac system installed at Glasgow University Library in summer 1995 has given us the opportunity to extract a much wider range of information than was possible hitherto.

The acquisitions and cataloguing processes now allow the inclusion of many more management information codes against each order or catalogue record to yield the information that a modern library requires in order to make appropriate decisions. We can, for instance, track ordering patterns in different subject areas, unit cost of purchases, and establish countries of origin of material by subject to help us in our predictions of likely inflation rates in the year ahead. This is increasingly important as Glasgow University Library moves over to a system of devolved funding. At present funding for core areas such as undergraduate provision, document delivery service, and reference and information resources of a general nature or in non-print format are top-sliced from the University budget and allocated to the Library. Funds, formerly topsliced, for research material including the bulk of our serials and standing orders as well as over 50 per cent of monograph purchases in areas such as the humanities are no longer top-sliced, but are allocated directly to Planning Units (Faculties). The Library then negotiates with the various Planning Units the funds required to provide the level of Library research provision deemed necessary for the coming financial year. This has implications for Technical Services not least in the need to provide details of how the Faculty's money is being spent, and perhaps to justify our sources of supply, discounts obtained etc. This formerly laborious process is somewhat ameliorated by our ability to combine management information codes on Innopac to obtain tailor-made lists that can be e-mailed to recipients or downloaded into a word processing package manipulated and forwarded as attached documents. Likewise statistical information can be downloaded to a spreadsheet package for manipulation and onward transmission.

At present we do not regularly report the state of individual funds unless specifically asked. With devolved budgeting this will almost certainly change. However we do now provide two services that partially address this: expenditure, commitment and free balances against all funds and groups of funds (the latter in any combination as defined by the Library) have been established on the system with subject librarians passworded to view the information which is updated at about 4 pm each day by Technical Services staff. The second area where we are providing an enhanced service is in the provision of regular accessions lists on demand, tailored to the needs of the department or individual who requires them. For example they could be lists of material bought from a particular fund, or classified in a certain area, or in a particular format, or a combination of all or some of these. The lists can be in full MARC format, or limited to any catalogue and order fields that the list compiler selects. The lists can be e-mailed direct from Innopac or, more normally, downloaded for word processing and sent as attached e-mail documents.

The use of a wide range of management information codes has not added significantly to work at the ordering or cataloguing stage as we have taken full advantage of the facility on Innopac to enter sets of default codes for material at the time it is placed on order or catalogued. For example material ordered from our standard French supplier has details of country of origin, type of material ordered, fund to be debited, vendor code, whether the order is to be printed or sent electronically, suggester's status, number of copies and site locations, all automatically added according to parameters set up by professional technical services staff. Any of these codes can be overwritten if necessary for individual orders. In addition prompts can be made for non-professional staff to insert data, e.g. a note on catalogue card number to our Italian supplier. In addition codes have been set up that can be inserted and which will automatically produce a longer message without need to key it each time. For example coding %e in the Library note field of the order record generates the message 'Pass this book to Bibliographic Services for overlay with full Marc record'.

Thus these codes give us much useful management information but avoid non-professional staff having to key information repetitively and only require keying when certain elements need to be overwritten or added.

New Formats of Material: The Hybrid Library

Ever increasing amounts of material are available electronically from remote hosts or on CD-ROM. This has opened up new areas where problems can arise: For example, leaseholding of information rather than direct purchase, checking and ensuring adherence to licence agreements for database access, networking costs, estimates of the required number of simultaneous users of a database and relative cost vs. benefit of different formats. There are also consortium issues that are increasingly raised by the above, for example special deals that may be offered to CURL or the Research Libraries Group, giving libraries access to databases at an advantageous price, but offering a different mix of databases from those the Library has and/or would ideally require. Additionally, many of these services are not obtained through traditional Library Suppliers but direct from publisher. However in the area of CD-ROMs at least, there is a clear trend for these to be obtained through Library Suppliers rather than direct from publishers. In some cases this can expedite matters but use of an intermediary can sometimes muddy the waters if licence agreements are required.

The provision of, and access to, electronic journals is an area of rapid development. Although at a relatively early stage, future preponderance of e-journals in subject areas such as medicine, science and engineering in tandem with cancelling of print equivalents or the complete abandonment by publishers of the option of the latter format will mean savings at the clerical end of Library operations (receipting, claiming, binding, shelving) with increased responsibilities, at least in the early years, at the professional end (negotiating deals, pursuing consortium arrangements, advising readers on access and downloading, mounting Web pages and dealing with passwording issues). Publicizing of e-journals has been a prominent activity at Glasgow where 'electronic journal parties' have been organized attended by academics who come along to the Library and have hands-on experience of latest developments while enjoying a glass of wine.

Cataloguing of such material is not a major issue. If we can access the full text of an e-journal, information to that effect is available in the catalogue on the same record as the print copy if we have both formats. Likewise journals from CD-ROM databases such as *BPO (Business Periodicals On Disk)* appear in the catalogue as they are available full text. The text of datasets, e-journals, and networked CD-ROMs are available through our Merlin Work Stations which provide integrated access to our catalogue and other information resources.

For the present and, I believe, the next few years at least the primary medium of delivery of monograph material will be in print form. Even in this area the electronic revolution has transformed processes and the speed with which we expect to acquire material. Starting with bibliographic checking, we are accustomed now to a networked CD-ROM of English language books in print, updated monthly (in Glasgow's case currently Bookdata's *Bookfind*). This is a great advance over printed sources although currency and accuracy about availability are still not all they could be, presumably because publishers do not update or actually misinform Bookdata with overoptimistic publication dates etc. This problem will arise with any such database in any format. Nevertheless, we can see at a glance the choices available between hardback and paperback format and British and American editions, formerly a labour-intensive and thus debatably not cost-effective business, and take our purchasing decisions accordingly. This is a role that has been devolved at Glasgow from professional to senior non-professional staff working within parameters set for them. Internet access is now available to databases such as *Verzeichnis Lieferbarer Bucher* and full use is made of this facility.

Increasingly use is being made of other information available over the Internet, whether checking stockholdings at some major suppliers, checking external databases available through the web pages of others as well as material available from sources such as the Internet Bookshop. To verify existence of publications and their correct bibliographic details, sources such as OCLC Worldcat prove invaluable. The wide range of publishers' catalogues available over the Internet prove useful too, although their currency is not always much better than that of regularly produced print equivalents. Many of these catalogues are available through Book Industry Communication's home page although we have them bookmarked for ready access. Our only current limitation in this area is in the relatively few terminals in Technical Services that have Internet access at present, but this is a problem that is currently being addressed with a large upgrade of staff terminals soon to start.

Glasgow University Library, in common with many others, has an active programme of acquiring out of print material. In this area one of the main problems has been obtaining material that has recently gone out of print, often undergraduate textbooks in heavy demand for taught courses. Easy online access to the stockholdings of major bookshops makes the task of identifying copies that may be held there quicker and easier than before and in most cases we can order the book immediately over the Internet.

This brings us into the area of digitized resources and electronic reserves. We have recently purchased the Innopac electronic reserves module which we hope to have operational by the beginning of the 1998/99 academic session. Electronic reserves far from reducing the work of Technical Services staff will only alter it. In fact the role of the professional here will be increased in the early stages as negotiations with copyright holders are conducted and the mechanics of the operations are worked out. (It must be hoped that the Higher Education Copying Accord drawn up jointly by the Committee of Vice-Chancellors and Principals (CVCP) and the Copyright Licensing Agency (CLA) will soon be extended to digital formats.) Technical Services staff will also have to ensure that not only the data itself, but also details of what is available, in what medium it exists, and where to find it is available to library users. This is being done by using the Course Reserve List facility on Innopac, a feature of the system that enables readers to check by course name or lecturer name in order to retrieve a list of set texts with details of where and in what format that material is available. Electronic material available on the Course Reserve List will be accessible by hot-linking and signing on by entering ID and PIN code. There will be an option to print to a system printer or to view the material on screen.

To benefit from work elsewhere and avoid duplication, we are alert to developments in eLib sponsored and other projects on digitization and on-demand publishing. In a Scottish context, but of much wider interest, the Scottish Collaborative On-Demand Publishing Project (SCOPE), on which we have a representative, has been closely monitored to see how developments there will affect any in-house developments in this area. Similar attention is being given to successor projects to SCOPE.

We have also given preliminary thought to electronically-produced theses and the issues this raises for storage and access, not to mention how one identifies the official 'archival' version. This is currently being investigated on a wider stage by the University Theses On-line Group (UTOG) of which Glasgow University Library is a member.

Electronic Ordering

The Innopac system supports electronic ordering, a first stage for libraries towards full electronic data interchange (EDI).

Two methods are available, one by ftp and the other by e-mailing orders directly off the system to suppliers. The latter is our preferred option. Suppliers are set up on the system either to accept printed orders or electronic orders. The latter have their e-mail address and, if required, the appropriate Standard Address Number (SAN) keyed into the appropriate field of the vendor record. A supplier that receives both printed and electronic orders has to be established on the system as two separate suppliers. For example a supplier that handles some of our map orders as well as monograph orders receives the former in printed form and the latter by EDI. The processing of book recommendations on the system is identical as far as the non-professional staff are concerned. It is the system that sorts these orders by supplier code into EDI and printed orders.

A problem we do have with electronic ordering is that the Innopac system still currently supports only the American BISAC format rather than the UK TRADACOMS or the emerging international EDIFACT standards. This is good news for North American suppliers but less so for British and European ones. With only some minor difficulties, however, our main British suppliers have developed interfaces with our BISAC orders, in the case of our larger suppliers converting our records to TRADACOMS format on receipt. Our main European suppliers started accepting our orders in BISAC format in spring 1997. This is perhaps not the place to sing the praises of EDI, but turnaround time for orders sent in this way has been reduced by 8–14 days depending on source of material.

Unfortunately the BISAC format still used by Innopac has severe limitations, some but not all shared by other EDI formats. Firstly only the first ISBN transmits, so it is essential that this is the ISBN that fits the format required or that it covers an entire multi-volume work or only one volume of it as appropriate. Fields are limited in length, so sub-titles are often dropped, and imprints truncated after the place of publication omitting the far more important information of publisher and date of publication. The edition statement is not transmitted either. However the benefits still far outweigh the disadvantages: the electronic orders once keyed by non-professional staff are automatically assigned to a file by the system where they are checked by senior non-professionals against the original order request. A key stroke can then transmit scores of orders to a variety of suppliers by e-mail. Even the e-mail address of the recipient does not have to be keyed as it is an integral part of the supplier record as set up on the system. We follow up transmission of our requests with an e-mail to our suppliers stating the number of orders sent and asking for e-mailed confirmation of receipt. About 85 per cent of our monograph requests are now sent electronically. Twice in the course of 18 months a file has been lost in transfer. As we temporarily store the suggestion slips for electronic orders, it is a straightforward process to reset them on the system for transmission again. It does not, thankfully, require rekeying.

Although standards are now in place in Europe for interchange of invoice data and order reports, system developments will be necessary before we can take advantage of progress in this area. However the Innopac system does already support the receipt of serial invoices from major subscription agents and our 'one-line' invoices for early payment are loaded onto Innopac by file transfer. We are also developing electronic serial claiming with two major agents.

There was a time in the not too distant past when recommendations for purchase had to be submitted on a standard Library recommendation form. A few years ago we agreed that, as long as information given was adequate and intelligible and that proper authorization for purchases was clearly given, that recommendations could be sent by submitting publishers' fliers, marked up catalogues, e-mailed messages, or by use of the book recommendation facility on Innopac. We have now taken this a stage further by setting up a book request template on our Library Web pages to facilitate ordering. Hot-links have been attached so that suggesters in each field know to which academic library representative or subject librarian they should forward their request, with the latter forwarding the request to Acquisitions. A default for automatic transmission from the suggester to Acquisitions has been established for those who are unclear to whom they should be forwarding their request. Acquisition staff then forward as appropriate for authorization before ordering. There is the problem that e-mailed Library forms do not contain the required signature of the authorizer. We have adopted the policy that if a suggestion is e-mailed from the authorizer's own e-mail address that this is sufficient. It is probably less open to abuse than the traditional signing of printed forms has been.

The book recommendation template is currently being linked to Web pages with details on purchasing policies and procedures and links to publishers' catalogues available on the Web as well as to the available databases of major booksellers. We hope that this will not only help suggesters identify material they wish to order, but also to check details before submission if they are unsure of them thereby reducing the perennial problem of trying to trace what someone has asked for when they have provided inadequate information.

Summary

As far as job satisfaction is concerned, the changes that have been and are being introduced as a result of technological change have in general enhanced the self-esteem of the staff working in the area. Apart from the basic keyboarding skills which perhaps in themselves are no longer seen as any greater than literacy and numeracy, competence in the use of CD-ROM, database searching of remote hosts, file transfer, Internet searching and the like have added a new dimension to the work for many and given them useful transferable skills when applying for posts elsewhere.

The emerging electronic library has taken much of the labour intensiveness out of traditional technical service operations, but new expectations have arisen from our readers. The quicker and more cost–effective we are, the greater the demands for even greater speed and value for money. Justification for our actions, much derived from management information functions, is increasingly required. Today everything is being driven by the basic fact that student numbers and materials price inflation outstrip library budgets. Newer, cheaper, easier, less labour-intensive methods of delivery of information are required as a way round these two problems. We realize we are in a transitional phase – the hybrid library is not yet properly established – but this does present us with continuing challenges to which we must endeavour to rise.

Managing Library Systems and Technical Support

CHAPTER TWENTY SEVEN

Overview: Managing Library Systems and Technical Support

Robin Yeates

Introduction

Library systems are not merely technology. A system is 'a set of connected things or parts that form a whole or work together' (Willoughby, 1996). Although the complexity of electronic library issues is daunting, genuine improvements in systems will improve manageability at the same time as enhancing user services. Management involves some technology, but also and more importantly, people, contacts, procedures, thoughts, ideas and planning.

A systems librarian helps the library derive benefits from information technology (IT). Benefits must be for library staff and users, as well as other stakeholders, such as publishers and suppliers. Work involves strategy, operations, dissemination, concertation, training. IT can be used for training, resource provision and to provoke cultural change.

What are libraries?

Libraries are *multi-purpose, managed communities of extensive organized resources* [Table 27.1]. This is true of traditional and electronic libraries. We now have actual valuable experience in the latter area.

Libraries are information led, not technology led, and concerned with information management rather than processing (Heseltine, 1994). The Information Society is about 'possession, transmission, exploitation' (Dugdale, 1997).

Libraries are no longer merely passive repositories, but are about organization of information for re-use. This raises issues of so-called granularity: we still handle books and journal issues but now deal with individual articles, chapters and smaller units of information. Efforts need to scale to match this shift (Yeates, 1996; Whalley, MacNeil and Landy, 1997).

Electronic records management and librarianship converge. Published and unpublished material overlap. Internal information tends to be made available externally on a restricted basis and then more widely. News and alerting are important. IT needs to capture and manage content, context and structure. Systems need to cope with a wide

Table 27.1   What are libraries?

	Multi-purpose	Managed community	Organized resources	Extensive resources
Libraries	✓	✓	✓	✓
Bookshops	✗	✗	?	✗
Internet	✓	✗	✗	✓
Cybercafes	✗	✗	✗	✗
Web sites & special conditions	✗	✓	✓	✗
Museums	?	✓	✓	?
Educational courses	✗	✓	✓	✗
Publishers	?	✓	✓	✗

variety of media, long-term storage, obsolescence and volatility, manipulation, compound documents and virtual documents (Shepherd, 1996).

User Focused Library Automation Management

Three things are vital for user focused electronic library management: perception, personalization and performance.

Perception

The Internet has raised expectations of global information services. Digital libraries may take more of the limelight than traditional libraries (Springthorpe, 1996). Many users see e-mail and the Web combined as a potential source for all information and students may be too easily satisfied.

We must successfully manage user perception of library services. This covers access, availability, reliability, security, convenience, cost and quality. Quality is often proportional to effort and cost, and cannot be handled separately from other factors affecting user perception. Experimentation is often useful, such as when deciding on the quality of scanning of paper documents or level of optical character recognition (OCR) checking required for adding printed journals to the electronic library (Emly and Jupp, 1997).

There is a general growth in expectations of self-service facilities. The Decomate research project involving electronic full-text journals provision at the London School of Economics in 1997 found that only one per cent of researchers wanted to make use of terminals in the library rather than in their own rooms (McDonald and Stafford, 1997).

Personalisation

Past deficiencies were often the result of inflexible systems. Future systems will be closely tailored to group and individual needs, preferences, budgets as we move towards 'just for you' systems and full desktop integration of digital library services as network components.

IT has affected science through the process of research and communication of it. Electronic libraries will affect science itself more directly in future (Meadows, 1996). IT has also affected the humanities: academics have been waiting for invention to catch up with need. The greatest impact of IT so far in this sector will be access to resources through the electronic library (Deegan, 1995).

Personalized services are non-discriminatory, open to all (Cross, 1996). In practice, many new difficulties and barriers to equality arise. How can we make terminals available to all? All should have equally fast network access and high quality printing facilities. Charging for printouts or information disadvantages poorer users. How can we ensure remote users have suitable equipment or are computer literate and appropriately trained (Dugdale, 1997; Myhill and Jennings, 1996)?

Projects are addressing special needs, such as those of the visually impaired. Many such needs can be catered for by simple awareness of issues and solutions, and Web services are a powerful potential means of improving the design and delivery of services for those with special needs, although they also present new difficulties all the time (Livesey and Fisher, 1997).

Performance

Managers must be proactive in building and developing systems. Lead times, for example to install network bandwidth for networked multimedia or video-conferencing, require us to predict future user needs and to project current technology trends.

Security and reliability should be managed in conjunction with user support and help systems, but they rarely are. Taking a user focused view of downtime, single points of failure, backups and redundancy involves full integration of help functionality with operational systems management.

Users need to be warned of impending work which may affect them, alerted to current problems, trained to understand backups and recoveries and participate in the formulation of institutional strategies. Users can play a valuable feedback role, reporting bugs, errors, downtime, failure events and difficulties. If communication channels are properly set up and moderated, they can assist users to help other users without involving extensive staff time.

What Needs Managing?

Old things

Electronic libraries still need to manage physical stock objects, limited metadata to assist retrieval of physical stock, limited personal information to control circulation and passive raw data. The object is to enhance systems, relate them better to user needs and extend the use of them to new users through wider networking: i.e. more of the same as we have seen for a decade or more.

New objects

New functions will manage digital stock objects, extensive metadata and links for various purposes, users as individuals and groups, staff, physical space and equipment.

New environments

Library systems to date could be viewed as autistic: there has been an excessive attention to detail at the expense of broader understanding and the environmental context; systems do not support sharing and collaboration through creation and communication of views of the world. Libraries now need to create the learning environment (Bob Banks, 1997, unpublished paper); the information searching environment (Pollitt, 1996); the document management environment;

perhaps the information management environment or the knowledge management environment. Knowledge management goes beyond information management, is based on an organizational approach, exploiting hidden knowledge assets to facilitate organizational learning (A. Foster, 1997, unpublished paper).

The primary purpose of a system will govern its initial design, the amount of funding and effort devoted to it and its promotion and support; it will also govern its perception by users.

This fact will become increasingly important as networking becomes more widespread and users tend to have the technical means to access to all Web resources: in practice they will only make use of a few primary services, such as a learning or public library environment, through which they will expect to gain access to others.

As it will become possible to offer several environments at a single physical site, managers will consider the integration of these. 'Information landscapes' seek to extend this kind of integration across the services of multiple institutions.

Architectures

New technologies support integration or separation of systems which might be delivered to the same users. Conventional library automation systems may be retained and supplemented by new separate servers for new functions. Open, standards-based service architectures need to be developed which can support ongoing enhancements most efficiently and most effectively.

Integration

Local/remote resource integration is already a major issue and a major challenge. CD-ROM hybrid publishing developments demonstrate how cheap, easy to use local resources can be usefully combined with up to date online resources (Reisman, 1995). The desktop operating system will offer a full hypertext environment; hybrid services will allow local holdings to be linked to remote databases. Managers need to control mirroring and caching, search engines and agents which can operate across local and remote databases and can handle temporary disconnection from the network. Major factors are the performance and costs involved, which may vary for different user groups, information types and applications.

Decision support

Systems need to support more varied information purchasing options and economic models and help managers create and operate new services.

User support

User support systems must be greatly improved in the electronic library. Support for remote users is a particular growth area, and work on distance learner support may lead the way for other areas (Myhill and Jennings, 1996).

Feedback

Systems to measure or indicate performance will show usage levels and user satisfaction. Facilitating information transfer and communication can often improve management and control.

Social relationships and shared interests are especially important in the electronic library, since its geographical reach is so wide, but managers must balance privacy with improved communication.

Management Aims

Management should be fun. IT can provide the means for managers to produce worthwhile outcomes. Managers will foster:

- teamwork: to achieve growth, development, popularity, service;
- community building: to match innovations with user needs;
- comprehension: seeking common features of disparate systems and common needs to derive critical success factors which can drive new objectives;
- a feeling of control: to satisfy all stakeholders;
- breadth and depth of service usage: to justify investment.

Involvement

Service definition

Service boundaries are blurring but need definition to provide the focus for service excellence–libraries cannot/do not manage all end-user information activity.

Resources

Experience shows that resources follow success. Never take without giving, and always try to kill two birds with one stone: these are good ways to involve people and attract resources.

Teams

Effective management requires multidisciplinary skills best provided by teams brought together for particular tasks–skills include in-depth IT skills, applications experience, knowledge of users, project management, creative design, monitoring and evaluation. Optimal teamworking involves excellent networking and will benefit from long-term collaboration within and outside the library's parent organization.

There is a useful trend for libraries to be involved more with more parts of the computer industry: libraries are closer to users, more application-oriented and have a support and service culture. On the other hand, generic network computing products are of increasing importance to libraries: for example, Netscape/Internet Explorer browsers, standards-based directory services, metadata registries, access control systems, information service ratings systems, filtering software and information delivery technologies such as push publishing standards and agents based on these. Libraries are also affected by well funded efforts to increase usage of cable and telecommunications networks to benefit the global information society. They may even benefit from recycled cyber-profits, as in the case of the Gates Library Foundation.

Teleworking

Some element of teleworking may be appropriate for aspects of library automation management. It may even assist in building effective teams through the use of expertise when it is most needed. It may encourage individuals to gain breadth of experience. Library systems staff should lead the development of improved support for teleworkers generally in the library, perhaps using teleworkers to maintain Web sites, provide graphic design skills, write manuals or produce training courses.

Driving Forces

Strategy

Some librarians extol the benefits of an IT strategy (Gallimore, 1997), others see grand plans as posing unacceptably high overall risk. Improvements in networking will help maintain control, but pragmatic interim solutions are often needed.

Plans, priorities

In either case, the usefulness of frameworks, guidelines and documentation is acknowledged. The long-term nature of many of the problems of setting up electronic libraries requires systems staff to develop and use frameworks for planning. An example is the ongoing work on better management information and performance indicators and measures (Brophy and Wynne, 1997).

Library automation systems managers will advise, represent, monitor, assess, liaise, develop, carry out tasks based on their IT skills and experience. As providers of support for others, they will facilitate much work of other managers. The UK Library and Information Commission's '2020 Vision' talks of Connectivity, Content and Competencies, all very much the concerns of library automation managers (Cotton, 1997).

Legislation

IT often raises the need for new legislation, particularly as we move from print to a digital information society. IT managers often have to implement changes as a result, and need to be actively involved in legal developments affecting information handling. Copyright is one such area.

Funding

In future, more investment needs to be made in research and development by library and information managers, and new capital expenditure will be required more frequently than in the past. Extra funds will also need to be found for skilled specialist staff. Much of these funds will come from passing management and control to end-users, and in some cases charging them for services.

Competition

Managers will be more aware of competitors in the global information sector. Services which add value near the user interface, such as fuzzy logic enhanced query systems, will tend to attract users and be perceived as good value.

Self-service systems have their dehumanizing aspects, but they have become popular with many library users and staff alike and are altering user expectations, for example of opening times and systems availability (McDonald and Stafford, 1997).

Standards and consistency

Web sites and e-mail lists are raising the profile of standards. Local choices have to be made. Often standards activities will result in demands for new systems or enhancements to existing systems, and they can also be used as part of benchmarking activities and performance monitoring.

Standards are a fundamental part of the electronic library and arrangements for their management should be given appropriate priority.

The Z39.50 standard is fundamental enabling technology for sharing information and databases of all kinds, and has been applied already to many important library catalogues. It will underpin the development of clumps (MacColl, 1997; Russell, 1997).

Metadata is another important area. Various types of structured data about network objects will allow links to be developed to build complex structures with low central maintenance overheads. Libraries need to apply cataloguing and classification skills and be involved in developing and using identifiers for digital objects and standards for description and subject control of information.

Rights clearance and copyright management standards for Electronic Document Interchange (EDI) have been developed by publishers working with librarians, and codes of practice are recommended, covering, for example, formats for cleared documents (JISC/PA Clearance Mechanisms Working Party, 1997).

Technology

A wide range of new technologies will influence managers: distributed client-server systems, intranets and full-text/ image handling generally. We are already approaching having the required critical mass of electronic full text in some libraries, thanks to large publishers. Java-based software can offer cross-platform support, allowing users to access systems from all types of terminal. Suppliers will need assistance from libraries to enhance their products to meet real needs (Cibbarelli, 1997).

Librarians have to make best use of existing technology. Most libraries are still catching up with basic features which users have found useful at leading sites, and may need to focus on such limited enhancements for financial or practical reasons:

- New functionality might consist of full text retrieval for a Web server or community information system; Web access for online public access catalogues (OPACs), but also for network administration, user registration and information updates;
- Z39.50 servers to support inclusion of the library's catalogue in larger virtual library systems, perhaps as part of a regional clump;
- hyperlinking from traditional bibliographic records, so that users may access Web resources directly from titles, or from corporate, conference or personal author names.

Much work may also be involved in deploying systems to support appropriate browser plugins such as the Adobe Acrobat viewer without compromising security. Finally, attention in many research libraries will need to be paid to digitization of backfiles to allow access to legacy printed materials: such efforts may be best accomplished on a co-operative basis, as in the American JSTOR project or at least using specialist expertise from the appropriate sector, such as is available in the UK Higher Education Digitisation Service (Guthrie, 1997).

EDI services can be used as the basis for more advanced electronic commerce services, and library systems are being enhanced to support them (Talis 7 released, 1997).

Research projects are increasingly producing software products which can be usefully applied by libraries, given the appropriate skills and system platforms. Web sites show what is available and how to obtain materials (Tools for the library community, 1997).

New Digital Functions

Some new functions have manual equivalents from which experience we can learn. Others are new territory altogether. Research programmes are becoming an accessible way of discovering new ideas.

Access control, user authentication and permissions

Library system suppliers are only just beginning to offer electronic library management software, moving up from operating system to network operating system to generic applications to specialist applications and tools. Systems will allow all networked services and resources to be made available in the right place at the right time under strict management control, and tailored to the needs of user groups or individuals. These moves may be encouraged by new style learning resources centres with large quantities of personal computers (PCs) provided as network environment access tools (Yeates, 1997; Akeroyd, 1997).

Tools to protect intellectual property and assist in its exploitation are becoming available. Use of these high security systems must be restricted to cases of need, when the intrinsic value of information is high enough to warrant such investment, such as in commercial image archives (Lyon, Maslin and Baker, 1997; Pitcher, 1997; Tuck, Oppenheim and Yeates, 1996).

User authentication lets users navigate freely around and use resources to which they are entitled, without requiring repeated entry of passwords or use of very general group entitlements; for example the Athens authentication service.

Local systems should interwork with developing national and international ones. Smart cards may play a role in the future, but are as yet unproven in the multi-function campus card role (Myhill, 1997).

One aspect of control which is already important yet difficult to administer is the use of styles, templates and other re-usable software objects. These have the potential to enforce high standards of graphic design and a common look and feel for services managed by distributed individuals. Managers may begin by specifying graphics which are permitted on Web pages, but may move to full stylesheets combined with centralized document repositories in future for assisting with republication of material according to user profiles, as supported by, for example, the Basis Intranet product.

Agents

Software agents automate simple, regular tasks, but are growing in sophistication. They are system components which may support collaborative browsing, machine-assisted cataloguing and authoring, exception reporting, replication and mirroring of information, updating of software, push publishing and more. They reflect our knowledge of users and can implement policies, standards and permissions, leaving librarians more time for assessment and training tasks (Gordon, 1997).

Alerting and current awareness

Digital libraries will need to operate a wide range of alerting and current awareness services. Users expect alerts via e-mail or Web services rather than via traditional library automation systems, even if content may include new additions to stock or service information held in such systems (Stoker and Secker, 1997).

Scope for new collaborative alerting services will depend on libraries implementing improved vocabularies and thesauri, metadata generation and authoring tools and network services which will deliver material to end users in forms most convenient to them.

Projects such as Decomate have shown that users need alerting services to be integrated with electronic journals, but they are not the exclusive preserve of libraries.

Alerting systems are also likely to prove useful in the management of distributed information services. Traditionally services such as the GABRIEL or M25 Consortium pages showing opening hours and subject coverage of academic libraries in London have depended for accuracy on review by distributed staff, who have had to maintain information in multiple places for differing purposes (to produce local brochures, notices, etc.). Agent-based alerting systems offer the potential to reduce the effort needed to maintain accuracy of distributed information, which will encourage usage and justify investment in setting up such systems (Jefcoate, 1996; Sykes, 1996).

Communications

Geography is less important in electronic libraries; there are fewer one to one messages, and more one to small group/ large group messages, requiring address book management.

Mirroring and caching services need to be managed. These can improve performance, awareness of content, collaboration, reliability (through redundancy) and reduce network traffic and related costs. However, they require time and effort to administer and face technical and legal problems. It is no longer desirable, however, for libraries to leave such matters to network computing staff (Kirriemuir and Knight, 1997).

Network management equipment is constantly improving, to support secure remote access to networked services from dumb terminals or older PCs and to improve management of legacy equipment such as CD-ROM players.

Copyright management

The complexity of copyright management in the electronic library places it at the centre of current research and development. Managers need to assess its importance for specific applications, such as Web publishing or use of electronic journals. The cost of setting up various compliance arrangements, licence management, rights allocation systems, print, view, cut and paste management environments affects overall investment policy and the speed of development of the digital library as a whole. Librarians have always managed copyright to some extent, such as by placing notices near photocopiers, or obtaining signatures for inter lending of journal articles. Managers are now moving into realms formerly the preserve only of publishers and the media. They will need both systems and skills appropriate for managing intellectual property.

Not all materials can be treated the same way, and not all uses of libraries require similar copyright arrangements. The rule will be to keep things as simple as possible, but this can be hard to achieve. For example, a decision to print a copyright statement on each page printed via library terminals may require many systems to inter-operate which currently do not. At the other end of the scale, fully encrypted documents may require specialized user environments which require active user support services as well as central management (Tuck, Oppenheim and Yeates, 1996). Electronic information is self-renewing, plentiful, but valued only in a specific context, but how many library systems can determine or make use of such a context, and do so without invading individual privacy (Arnold and Arnold, 1997)?

Customization

Personal or group profiles filter information, but managers have to instil confidence that source coverage is comprehensive.

We must acknowledge that there is an element of advertizing in all publishing: if users become too successful at filtering out material, the authors or publishers affected will constantly seek alternative means of reaching users.

All networking involves some degree of openness. Systems must support helping people make contact with others for collaboration and yet help users retain appropriate levels of privacy. Differing levels of privacy for differing circumstances are required. Control over privacy may rest with the individual, the library systems administration, network administrator or library staff–but only if the systems in place allow all these.

Developments in language handling have enabled libraries to offer multiple user interfaces for different languages, although most OPACs and services offer only one and none offers a very wide range. Once services can support multiple languages, appropriate metadata, machine translation and automated summarization software will allow services to be offered to a much wider community.

Customization is linked to access control functions and should be a fundamental consideration of local network architectures.

Decision support

Suppliers such as BLCMP and Ameritech have responded to user demand with integrated products based on standard databases and query languages. Newer, non-numeric systems supplement or provide detail about our understanding of users (see issue 103 of **VINE**, 1996).

Document delivery

Document delivery services provide on-demand access to remote full-text and electronic ordering and delivery of printed materials. Emphasis is on ease of ordering, high fulfilment rates, good print quality, reliability, quick delivery and low cost (Morris, Hirst and Davies, 1997; Malinconico and Warth, 1996).

Electronic communities

Software to support management of electronic communities is being built using experience from Web servers, conferencing systems, document management systems and information retrieval systems. Models such as the Ei Village for engineers and its localized British Engineering Centre are developing for other communities. The nature of their future impact on campus library services is still uncertain, but library automation managers will need to understand how such communities fit in with local provision, what affect they might have on user expectations, client software, printing, training and support.

Electronic reserves

The idea of special support for heavy use materials seems to apply in the electronic library as much as in the physical library world. Library suppliers have begun to offer commercial modules to support this function, although issues surrounding it are many and varied, ranging from copyright and printing arrangements to content formats and maintenance (Innovative Interfaces unveils Electronic Reserves, 1997)

Fee management and billing

Libraries are becoming more commercially minded. User accounting is important even if no fees are actually charged to end users. Managers design systems to support increased usage at little or no extra cost. They try to make free or very low cost information at the point of delivery be perceived as of high value. Fee income must be flexibly related to user satisfaction.

Facilities for cost apportionment are important in the development of electronic reserves and other information services. Some library management systems support invoicing for resources used (Grant for course materials study, 1997 Swiftbase announces SwiftLIB and SwiftTEXT, 1997).

Information gateways

Support requirements for geographically distributed cataloguing of network resources and the need to offer users clear starting points on the network have given rise to subject-oriented information gateways, sometimes called Access to Network Resources (ANR) services. These will increase in number and scope and in depth of coverage. More library staff will become involved in their maintenance and development, and local systems will need to support this activity. Requirements include not just contributions and records, but support, training and quality assurance, which must be very closely linked to other feedback systems, through use of e-mail, workshops, documentation of search strategies and other methods (see ROADS Web site).

There is also a need for automated services to support client activities: for example, use of Z39.50 information retrieval services requires a knowledge of target hosts and databases which can be provided by collecting structured information about resources and using it to configure information retrieval client systems. These could be multi-user gateways or desktop clients for individuals. Increased automation will require libraries to describe themselves in a more structured manner.

Integration

Academic library managers are progressively developing the Scholar's Workstation concept introduced in the 1980s. This focuses on the needs of a user in a particular context (Davies, 1997).

One-stop shopping depends on improvements in producing and publishing electronic information. There is a need to avoid single points of failure. Online bookselling has taken off as a result of networking efficiencies. The SuperJournal project found that users use a wide range of journals, but are more fickle with electronic journals than they are with integrating Web sites (Pullinger and Baldwin, 1997).

Licence management

Serials agents offer intermediary services for libraries subscribing to electronic journals. Managers decide how to integrate such services with their own direct licences and with local full-text holdings. Some library systems support local/remote holdings integration. Managers study model licences, case studies, regional bodies and consortia arrangements to build new forms of acquisition and procurement, which local systems must support.

Publishing and authoring

Libraries are becoming publishers and document managers. Managers must enable authors to present information effectively even if the context is unknown at the time of authoring. Information can then be re-used more effectively.

Document standards should be managed. For example, theses could be submitted as SGML or HTML documents for easier handling. Images and multimedia objects should be created in a restricted number of formats to reduce the need for specialist viewing or manipulation software (Ubogu and Wilson, 1997).

On-demand publishing from resource banks or locally held collections of electronic journals appears to offer the potential to satisfy student demand for course materials more efficiently, but raises issues of culture change, copyright and moral rights and charging, as well as technology, collaboration and economic modelling (Decomate; Halliday, 1997).

There is a growing need to automate the creation of certain types of metadata to reduce costs, extend services and support up-to-date services, although humans will always be needed to enhance it. Such tools create document summaries on demand, cluster retrieved documents for browsing, format material for agents to handle or simply reduce repetitive keyboarding and reduce errors. In some cases, the work could not be done any other way, such as when generating metadata to be used for content-based image retrieval

Personal bibliographic software tools such as EndNote and ProCite also have a role, and can be promoted by staff as standards, or used to import and manipulate bibliographic data, produce and format references and bibliographies for various research and publication purposes (Eakins, 1997).

The library may need to provide support for peer review, as part of publishing management activity. Requirements have been explored by eLib projects such as ESPERE (see ESPERE Web site), indicating links with access control, standards and communications work.

Testing and prototyping

Managing change requires involving library staff and users in the design and prototyping of systems and information products.

Facilities need to be made available, with appropriate access control and security. The effects of testing on operational services must be considered. Videoconferencing and multimedia services in particular tend to involve much increased usage of network bandwidth and may need to be separated from live systems.

User support

New networked systems are needed for enquiry handling, fault recording, collaborative help provision and network-wide context-sensitive status information.

Asking a person may be better than searching a database, but support for this needs to be arranged via the network. Videoconferencing or telephone hotlines may be needed on top of e-mail, database or conferencing systems (Gleadhill, 1997).

Some raw data can be derived from usage logs, but these are notoriously hard to interpret correctly, and will need to be supplemented by increasingly sophisticated techniques. For example, publishers are beginning to use external auditing of their Web sites.

Web OPACs

The most basic of electronic library services is the Web OPAC. How local OPACs relate to national ones such as the British Library's OPAC97 or the co-operative COPAC service depends on local implementations. Issues relate to underlying systems capabilities, staff skills and time, available tools, environment and integration generally. Features of other dedicated Windows-based graphical user interfaces, such as the highly graphical Ameritech Kids Catalog or ALS Meritus library floorplans will tend to be implemented as Web OPACs, as underlying standards evolve, reducing or eliminating the need for special function software on client PCs.

References

Akeroyd, J. (1997) Ready to take on new roles. *Library Technology*, **2**, 15

Arnold, S.E. and Arnold, E.S. (1997) Vectors of change: electronic information from 1977 to 2007. *Online*, **21**(4), 19–33

Athens authentication service. Described at http://www.athens.ac.uk/

BIBDEL–Libraries without walls: the delivery of library services to distant users. Research reports available at http://www.duc.ie/library/bibdel/

Brophy, P. and Wynne, P.M. (1997) *Management information systems and performance measurement for the electronic library: eLib supporting study (MIEL2) Final Report.* University of Central Lancashire, Centre for Research in Library and Information Management. Available at http://www.ukoln.ac.uk/models/studies/

Cibbarelli, P.R. (1997) Library automation vendors: today's perspective. *The Electronic Library*, **15**, 167–168

Cotton, R. (1997) The Library and Information Commission. *Library and Information Briefings*, **70**, 1–19

Cross, A. (1996) Towards the cyber-library? *VINE*, **102**, 5–8

Davies, J.E. (1997) Learn by wire: managing network access to learning materials. *The Electronic Library*, **15**, 205–214

Decision support systems. *VINE*, **103**, whole issue

Decomate–Delivery of Copyright Material to End-users. Information available at http://www2.echo.lu/libraries/en/projects/decomate.html

Deegan, M. (1995) IT and the humanities. *Information UK Outlooks*, **14**, 1–19

Dugdale, C. (1997) Equality in an electronic environment. In *Electronic library and visual information research – ELVIRA4* (Milton Keynes, 1997), ed. C. Davies and A. Ramsden, pp.23–30. London: Aslib

Eakins, J. (1997) The shape of things to come: automatic retrieval of similar shapes. *British Library Research and Innovation Centre Research Bulletin*, **16**, 6–7

eLib–Electronic Libraries Programme. Information about projects is available at http://www.ukoln.ac.uk/services/elib/projects/

Emly, M. and Jupp, Bill (1997) The Internet Library of Early Journals. In *Electronic library and visual information research–ELVIRA4* (Milton Keynes, 1997), ed. C. Davies and A. Ramsden, pp.167–175. London: Aslib

ESPERE–Electronic Submission and Peer Review. Information available at http://www.ukoln.ac.uk/services/elib/projects/espere/

ECUP Copyright Focal Point is available at http://www.kaapeli.fi/~eblida/ecup/index.html

Ei Village is available at http://www.ei.org/

Gallimore, A. (1997) *Developing an IT strategy for your library*. London: Library Association Publishing

Gates Library Foundation. Information is available at http://www.glf.org/

Gleadhill, D. (1997) Does the Nerd have the answer? *Library Technology*, **2**, 35–36

Gordon, E. (1997) Verity agent technology: automatic filtering, matching and dissemination of information. *VINE*, **104**, 40–44

Grant for course materials study (1997) *Library Technology*, **2**, 47

Guthrie, K.M. (1997) JSTOR: from project to independent organization. *D-Lib Magazine*, (July/August), available at: http://hosted.ukoln.ac.uk/mirrored/lis-journals/dlib/dlib/dlib/july97/07guthrie.html

Halliday, L. (1997) Scottish Collaborative On-demand Publishing Enterprise: mid-term progress. In *Electronic library and visual information research–ELVIRA4* (Milton Keynes, 1997), ed. C. Davies and A. Ramsden, pp.49–55. London: Aslib

HEDS–the Higher Education Digitisation Service (and Centre) began operation at University of Hertfordshire in 1997 with eLib funding. Press release available at http://heds.herts.ac.uk/

Heseltine, R. (1994) Library automation. *Information UK Outlooks*, **9**, 3–15

Innovative interfaces unveils electronic reserves (1997) *Library Technology*, **2**, 3

Jefcoate, G. (1996) Getting the message from Gabriel. *Library Technology*, **1**, 33–34

JISC/PA Clearance Mechanisms Working Party (1997) *Copyright clearance and digitisation in UK higher education: supporting study*. JISC. Available at http://www.ukoln.ac.uk/services/elib/papers/pa/

(1997) JSTOR and OCLC to co-operate over scholarly journals. *Library Technology*, **2**, 24

Kirriemuir, J. and Knight, J. (1997) Mirroring and caching network-based resources. In *Electronic library and visual information research–ELVIRA4* (Milton Keynes, 1997), ed. C. Davies and A. Ramsden, pp.133–143. London: Aslib

Livesey, S. and Fisher, S. (1997) Included, equal and independent? *Library Technology*, **2**, 83–84

Lyon, E., Maslin, J. and Baker, R. (1997) Audio and video on-demand for the performing arts: Project PATRON. In *Electronic library and visual information research – ELVIRA4* (Milton Keynes, 1997), ed. C. Davies and A. Ramsden, pp.177–185. London: Aslib

MacColl, J. (1997) CEI looks for bold response. *Ariadne*, **8**, cover, also available at http://www.ariadne.ac.uk/issue8/cover/

Malinconico, S.M. and Warth, J.C. (1996) Electronic libraries: how soon? *Program*, **30**, 133–148

McDonald, A. and Stafford, J. (1997) (eds) *Self-service in academic libraries: future or fallacy*. Proceedings of a conference organised by Information Services, University of Sunderland, in conjunction with SCONUL (Sunderland, 1996). Sunderland: University of Sunderland Press

Meadows, J. (1996) IT and the sciences. *Information UK Outlooks*, **18**, 1–19

Morris, A., Hirst, S. and Davies, E. (1997) Electronic document delivery–friend or foe? In *Electronic library and visual information research–ELVIRA4* (Milton Keynes, 1997), ed. C. Davies and A. Ramsden, pp.65–73. London: Aslib

Myhill, M and Jennings, S. (1996) The electronic library and distance resourcing: the Exeter experience. *Program*, **30**, 111–120

Myhill, M. (1997) Smart move at Exeter University. *Library Technology*, **2**, 42

Pitcher, G. (1997) The Cactus system. In *Electronic library and visual information research–ELVIRA4* (Milton Keynes, 1997), ed. C. Davies and A. Ramsden, pp.187–197. London: Aslib

Pollitt, A.S. (1996) Taking a different view. *Library Technology*, **1**, 20

Pullinger, D. and Baldwin, C. (1997) SuperJournal: what readers really want from electronic journals. In *Electronic library and visual information research–ELVIRA4* (Milton Keynes, 1997), ed. C. Davies and A. Ramsden, pp.145–153. London: Aslib

Reisman, R.R. (1995) CD-ROM/online hybrids: the missing link? *CD-ROM Professional*, **8**, April 1995. Available at http://www.teleshuttle.com/cdpart.htm

ROADS–Resource Organisation and Discovery in Subject-based services. Information available at http://www.ukoln.ac.uk/roads/

Russell, R. (1997) Searching in clumps. *Library Technology*, **2**, 64

Self-service systems. (1997) *VINE*, **105**, whole issue

Shepherd, E. (1996) The management of electronic records. *Library and Information Briefings*, **69**, 1–14

Springthorpe, M. (1996) Public information systems: serving the wider community. *VINE*, **102**, 9–14

Stoker, D. and Secker, J. (1997) The design and content of an electronic current awareness service for information professionals: the NewsAgent project. In *Electronic library and visual information research – ELVIRA4* (Milton Keynes, 1997), ed. C. Davies and A. Ramsden, pp.57–64. London: Aslib

Swiftbase announces SwiftLIB and SwiftTEXT. (1997) *Library Technology*, **2**, 47

Sykes, J. (1996) M25 information flows in two directions. *Library Technology*, **1**, 75,78

Talis 7 released (1997) *Library Technology*, **2**, 47

Tools for the library community (1997) *Library Technology*, **2**, 53–54

Tuck, W., Oppenheim, C. and Yeates, R. (1996) *Electronic copyright management systems*. London: Library Information Technology Centre, South Bank University

Ubogu, F.N. and Wilson, D. (1997) Digital library initiative in a South African university. In *Electronic library and visual information research–ELVIRA4* (Milton Keynes, 1997), ed. C. Davies and A. Ramsden, pp.39–48. London: Aslib

Whalley, W.B., MacNeil, J. and Landy, S. (1997) Running a 'pure' electronic journal on the World Wide Web. In *Electronic library and visual information research–ELVIRA4* (Milton Keynes, 1997), ed. C. Davies and A. Ramsden, pp.155–165. London: Aslib

Willoughby, S. (1996) Electronic public information. *VINE*, **102**, 3–4

Yeates, R. (1996) Library automation: the way forward? *Program*, **30**, 239–253

Yeates, R. (1997) Managing access to the digital library: the CaseLibrary project. In *Electronic library and visual information research–ELVIRA4* (Milton Keynes, 1997), ed. C. Davies and A. Ramsden, pp.207–218. London: Aslib

CHAPTER TWENTY EIGHT

Case Study: University College Cork

John Cox

Introduction

This study examines the approaches taken by the Library IT Services division at University College Cork to providing systems support for an expanding range of electronic information facilities and services. It begins with a snapshot of the main activities of the division, followed by a description of staffing arrangements. The greater part of this study focuses on a number of strategies, with examples of their practice, which guide activities.

The Library IT Services Division

The Library IT Services division is based in the Boole Library at University College Cork. Its remit is to ensure the availability, reliable functioning and development of library systems and to facilitate their use. All of its activities are focused on meeting and anticipating customer needs. Primary customers are the 1700 staff and 11 000 undergraduate and postgraduate students of the college. Student numbers have doubled in the past ten years and research activities have also been thriving, challenging the library to support greatly increased and varied demand. Expansion of access to electronic information services has been a key focus and has helped to shift the balance of Library IT Services' customer base from a largely internal one in the library to one embracing campus-wide and external audiences.

Support for the activities of library staff continues to be a major focus, however. There are over 90 staff, mostly housed in the Boole Library building in the centre of the campus. The only other concentration of staff at present is at Cork University Hospital, two miles away. Provision of systems support is certainly made easier by the current consolidation of library staff in two locations.

Activities

The activities of the IT Services division can be broadly categorized under the headings of systems support, development and training. The Innopac integrated library system was implemented in 1996 as a replacement for Dobis/Libis and provides OPAC, cataloguing, acquisitions and circulation facilities. Serials control and inter-library loans procedures are currently operated through the ISIS and Lancaster systems respectively, although the feasibility of integrating them with Innopac is actively under examination. Indeed, purchase of the Innopac serials control module is imminent. Configuration and maintenance of Innopac are ongoing activities for the division.

The division provides hardware and software support for the library's public access database facilities, including management of the Electronic Reference Library (ERL) server through which campus-wide access to a range of SilverPlatter databases is delivered. More than 20 other databases are available on a single-user basis at workstations within the library. Many of these public access workstations offer Internet access. The library has its own Web site, Booleweb, and IT Services staff manage the Web server and load new or updated information regularly. To these core areas of activity is added the considerable effort of ongoing maintenance and configuration of more than 130 networked PCs and terminals used by library staff and customers for access to the facilities already outlined and, in the case of library staff, to word processing, spreadsheet and other office software applications. Library staff and users depend heavily on the availability of access to networked applications and IT Services staff work with Computer Centre staff to ensure that access to the campus-wide network and to the Internet is reliable. The library also has its own sub-network through which shared access to documents and other electronic resources can be provided for library staff use.

Beyond core activities the division maintains a watching brief on possible areas for developing existing systems or adopting new ones. Innopac offers great scope for development and the division is regularly involved in projects like expanding the facilities accessible through the Web OPAC, optimizing the configuration of individual modules and investigating the feasibility of new services such as electronic ordering, self-issue and electronic reserves. Database networking is clearly a live area and IT Services staff frequently pursue and advertize trials of new databases either within the Innopac and ERL services or through Internet delivery from the publisher. Interestingly, networked delivery through the CD-ROM medium is rarely a factor in our calculations nowadays! The whirlwind rate at which Web technology is developing provides opportunities all the time for enhancing services. For example, we have been happy to move from manual HTML editing to the richer possibilities offered by the Microsoft FrontPage editor and to take the lead in planning and initiating a library intranet.

The training and educational role is one we take seriously and one we view as part of the operational overhead for every system implemented. The value of any system is vested in its effective use. Training for library staff is an ongoing activity to meet specific needs but is also formalized into practical sessions on areas of common need such as word processing, e-mail and Internet searching. More recently the IT Services division has identified a need from research and teaching staff outside the library for training in areas such as access to electronic resources, bibliographic software and use of Internet search engines. These areas are not necessarily subject-specific and our coverage of them has been complementary to, rather than competitive with, training offered by other library staff. Attendance levels at the sessions run so far indicates a need for this type of coverage. All of our training activities have been supported by the provision of learning materials in printed form and on our local Web pages.

Staffing

The staffing complement of the IT Services division is three posts: the Head of the division and two assistants. The Head's post is at sub-librarian level and includes membership of the cross-divisional Library Planning Team, an important factor in communicating policies and winning support for future plans. Other responsibilities include project planning, budget management and development of relationships with departments and suppliers, themes which are discussed later in this study. The assistants provide day-to-day administration and support for the hardware and software in use in the library. They also assist and train users and are well placed to identify new requirements both in terms of equipment and training. Their expanding knowledge of networking and of equipment and applications is the lifeblood of systems support and it is interesting to note that, although they are not trained librarians, these people are highly influential in the development and sustainability of electronic library initiatives. They are accustomed to rapid change and versatility is an essential quality in their jobs. The most effective staff in the electronic library are likely to be those who are most versatile and flexible.

In a small unit such as this there needs to be flexibility both in terms of rapid response and of ability to deal with diverse systems needs. Therefore, although there is a recognition of an inevitably increasing need for specialism given the number of diverse systems involved, expertise is shared as far as possible rather than concentrated. This is facilitated by a programme of weekly training sessions at which one member of the team shares with the others the details of using a particular program or supporting a specific category of equipment. Thus, although only one person administers the ERL server in depth, the other staff know how to load database updates, ensuring that customers do not have to wait unnecessarily for the latest information available. Our weekly sessions alternate between specific practical sessions, as described above, and participative discussions of more general themes such as training methods, analysis of our customer base or trends in database networking. The aim is to maintain staff development in the division by ensuring flexibility, open-mindedness and an awareness of technology trends. All of these attributes are absolutely essential in supporting and developing the electronic library and in operating in an environment where rapid change is the norm.

Strategies

Having sketched in some background in terms of our range of activities, customers and staffing, it is opportune to look in more detail at some general strategies which guide our specific activities and plans.

Standardization and integration

The IT Services division administers the library's computing budget and co-ordinates the purchase and support of all computers and applications. The need to keep up with the rapid pace of technological development, coupled with our limited staffing and budgetary resources, forces us to try to make savings on technical support by standardizing where possible on selected software or hardware. This approach is not new and is not always popular. The integration of serials control procedures into the networked Innopac library system perhaps holds more appeal for systems administrators than for staff familiar with a specialist standalone serials system. Critically, this integration is justifiable in that it benefits the customer by making information about serials issue receipts accessible through the OPAC. The adoption of ERL as our primary database networking solution can appear limiting to advocates of databases not immediately available through this system. SilverPlatter, however, provides the best coverage of the main databases we need and offers a single user interface. The gains that standardization and integration can bring in terms of efficiency actually allow us to offer more in-depth support for those products we have selected and enable us to make time for examining in detail the implications of new technological possibilities.

Ironically, by limiting the range of products supported for existing applications we can provide a wider view on new opportunities. This would not be possible if all our time were devoted to supporting more options than are necessary to do the same job. Equally, we have learned from our experience with Dobis/Libis that ploughing hours of technical support into a system that is well outside the mainstream of current library systems architecture is counter-productive in terms of its restriction of electronic library development. The adoption of Innopac has shown us and the customers of the library what is possible if reliable, expandable applications are in place. As a result we have opted for the mainstream in many cases in our choice of hardware, operating systems and software. Innopac, ERL, Windows 95, MS Office, Eudora and Netscape therefore represent standard applications on Dell PCs in the library. Our aim is also to deliver access to electronic resources through a standard interface. Most of our users are conversant with the Web and we have worked to ensure that core services like the library catalogue, ERL databases and Booleweb present a familiar Web interface to the users.

There are, of course, limits to what is possible or desirable in terms of standardization. We can only integrate if Innopac offers the necessary functionality and brings benefits to library users. Equally, we look beyond SilverPlatter for networked access to popular databases. With software development and delivery greatly expedited by the Web it would be folly not to explore new applications and indeed this possibility is open to all staff with a hard disk and Web access. The establishment of hardware and software standards is nevertheless an important part of our work and ensures that a sustainable platform is in place from which we can explore and expand to new possibilities.

Developing partnerships

The electronic library can only develop in technological terms through partnerships within and outside libraries. The traditional organizational structure within libraries has been highly compartmentalized with one section dealing with automation, and others with acquisitions, cataloguing, information services and so on. Automation has been seen as a separate entity controlled by a few people who took all the decisions about library technology. This structure is still visible at University College Cork but the highly fluid environment of the electronic library is moving us away from its rigidity.

The whole library now has a stake in technology and there is a growing recognition that technology is an underpinning and liberating influence for library activities rather than an appendage imposed by systems people. Today's open library systems offer opportunities for flexible configuration and interoperability. Even within a degree of standardization it is possible for library staff to have the facilities they want as opposed to the systems they are given. In our case the latter situation largely obtained with Dobis/Libis but the former has become possible through Innopac.

Service development throughout the library increasingly means electronic service development and the challenge for

IT Services is not only to deliver what library staff want but to communicate to them both proactively and reactively the range of possibilities that exists. A good example here is the development of the library's Web site, a project to which all staff can make a contribution. Our aim must be to forge partnerships with other library staff so that they see us as allies rather than afterthoughts in developing their services. Freer communication between sections, facilitated by easier access to staff through e-mail, is the key and it will be no bad thing if the end result is a less clearly-defined and rigid divisional structure. The IT Services division clearly has a role to play not just in systems integration but also in library staff integration!

Partnerships outside the library are also crucial. Interestingly, our relationship with the college computer centre has been able to undergo a healthy evolution from dependence to partnership in recent times. Computer centre staff previously managed the Dobis system on behalf of the library, creating a climate of dependence which gradually became difficult to sustain for both parties. The implementation of Innopac has passed systems control to the library and this has enabled the development of a relationship based on collaboration in shared areas of interest like networking, security, server administration and Web service development. There is regular dialogue but there are no plans to develop a converged service.

Partnership with users is something we are actively trying to develop. Until recently, the IT Services division had tended to operate mostly within the library and to have little contact with staff in other departments. The delivery of a greatly increased range of electronic information services has given people outside the library a major stake in the products of our activities. The traditional 'backroom' nature of our activities meant that we received very little feedback from users of these systems. We considered this a serious deficit and have taken a number of steps to take us into closer contact with users. These steps have been the publication of a newsletter in printed and electronic format (http://booleweb.ucc.ie/onlib.html), the provision of training courses for research staff and a change of name from Library Automation division to Library IT Services division. There is a long way to go but already our links with users have increased and their feedback is helping us to improve our systems and services. Increasingly, we receive requests from academic departments for advice on projects like setting up a database of publications or making course materials available through the Web. We take a positive view of this development and try to help when we have the knowledge and resources to do so.

The continued development of partnerships with systems suppliers is central to our activities if we are to get the systems we want. In the case of Innopac we pay a substantial sum annually for help-desk support and it makes sense to participate in systems development through regular dialogue with Innovative Interfaces about our needs. Participation in user groups and listservs has enabled us to lobby for new facilities in Innopac and ERL and it is essential to make time for this kind of activity rather than passively hoping that what we want will materialize. This can also mean working with more than one company, aiming to bring them together to deliver a facility like Z39.50 access from one service to another. Such negotiations can be time-consuming but rewarding in building better services and should be considered part of the job. Another area of collaboration with suppliers is in the arrangement of trial access to database services or beta-testing of software. We try to allow time for this type of activity and to provide meaningful feedback to suppliers.

Lobbying for system improvements is often done in partnership with other users. Involvement in collaborative ventures with other libraries is facilitated by networks and is an increasingly important activity. One such national project is IRIS, a service which provides Z39.50 access to the catalogues of Irish university libraries.

Project planning and management

The need to optimize our resources and to pursue new technological solutions systematically has led us to develop a regular project planning process and to communicate our plans to library staff well in advance of implementation. Possible implementation projects come forth all the time and it is essential to examine the most likely and affordable ones in detail before committing resources to them. Every six months our divisional management team reviews candidate projects and nominates those to be pursued. These are then timetabled and planned in financial and human resource terms. A Gantt chart (see Figure 28.1) is produced showing the main projects in which the division will be engaged, the stages involved and the anticipated timeframe for each. Once agreed, this chart is circulated to all managerial staff in the library.

The project planning process provides a helpful framework for IT Services staff. It helps to focus our efforts on what can be realistically achieved and enables us to monitor progress by reference to the chart. It also serves an important communication function by setting forth our plan of action to other staff. They become aware of what should happen and when in relation to projects which in many cases have been nominated by them. The adoption of a structured planning approach enables us to take charge of our activities and makes it less likely that staff will be successful in rushing through projects which will lead us down blind alleys or whose timetables are unreasonable!

Our aim is to anticipate and respond to real needs and to take a considered rather than impulsive approach to developing the library's electronic systems and services. This can cause frustration in some instances but it does mean that serious projects have a good chance of being carried through thoroughly rather than being implemented in a half-baked fashion that serves nobody's interests. It is important to note also that we recognize the need to build flexibility into our operations. Our project plans rarely run exactly to time and

	Task Name	Duration	22/12	12/01	02/02	23/02	16/03
16	**Serials system migration (JC,JP)**	**57d**					
17	analyse data migration, archiving requirements	15d					
18	data extraction, specification, testing	42d					
19	ongoing transitional support	57d					
20	**Electronic ordering (JC,JP)**	**42d**					
21	familiarise with procedures	20d					
22	configure and test suppliers	32d					
23	**Developing Computer Room (JC)**	**62d**					
24	investigation of air conditioning	20d					
25	planning of partitioned area	42d					
26							
27	**Database, e-journal networking (JC)**	**62d**					
28	BIDS Compendex password admin	20d					
29	ongoing support for trials	62d					

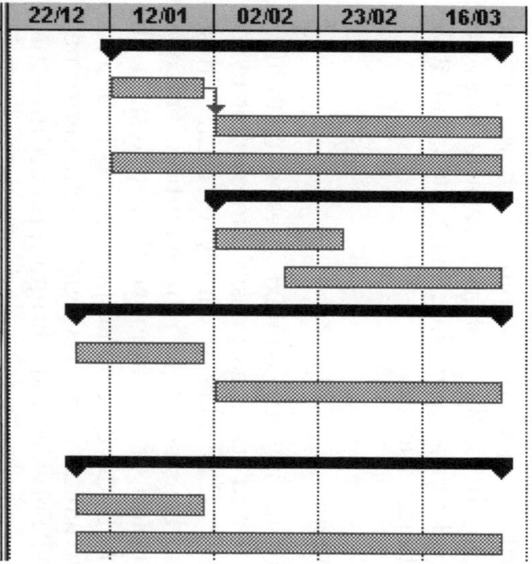

Figure 28.1   Extract from an IT Services Division project plan

act primarily as a guide within which we aim to operate. Flexibility is obviously vital in such a fast-developing area and we need to accommodate major new initiatives quickly if circumstances dictate.

Empowerment

Empowerment in our context means enabling as many library staff and users as possible to exploit technology for their benefit. This takes a variety of forms. In some cases it might be considered to be devolution. For example, the implementation of the Innopac library system afforded an opportunity to devolve some procedures to other sections of the library which had previously been performed on their behalf by IT Services staff. Printing procedures for the generation of circulation notices and of purchase orders are far simpler under Innopac than Dobis/Libis and it made sense to enable other staff to carry out printing at their own convenience rather than to have to wait for IT Services staff to do it for them. Although this idea was initially unpopular, on the grounds that groups were now being asked to carry out an extra procedure without additional staffing, the fact that it is easy to do and that it enables printing to be done on demand rather than when designated staff are available seems to have sold it successfully. One result has been a necessary freeing up of time for IT Services staff. Another has been the stimulation of interest in alternative approaches such as electronic purchase orders and e-mail circulation notices. This is a favourable outcome since it represents a positive embracing of new technology rather than a feeling that it is being imposed.

Effective training is vital to empowerment and IT Services staff are committed to its delivery both to library staff and to users. Training is a time-consuming effort, particularly in terms of preparation, for a small unit like ours and we are always examining ways of making it more effective and less time-intensive. The Web is a major ally in this since it makes it possible to deliver interactive training materials to our whole constituency and to encourage a self-service approach to learning. This also enables us to offer better targetted and more in-depth training. Instead of trying to run training sessions for all library staff, for example, we now ask the Heads of other divisions in the library to nominate staff to attend a fixed number of sessions at beginner and advanced level for topics such as Microsoft Office, e-mail and the Internet. Limited numbers make it possible to run highly practical sessions and to have a follow-up session at which experiences of actual use resulting from set coursework can be shared. For IT Services this has the effect of maximizing our limited training resources and ensuring that what is taught is put to definite use. It puts the emphasis on active learning and ready access to training materials in electronic form helps to facilitate a situation where library staff can actively take responsibility for their own learning.

As mentioned earlier, we have also developed training sessions and learning materials (http://booleweb.ucc.ie/guides/guides.html) for staff and researchers outside the library. Although our training resources are limited, it is healthy to develop our links with these groups. While one might argue that training in the use of bibliographic software and the intricacies of Internet search engines could or should be offered by other groups, the fact is that this training was not being provided to people who could benefit from it. A gap was waiting to be filled and we moved to fill it. One of the exciting things about the evolving electronic library is that such opportunities exist and that they enable units like ours to move beyond traditional and limiting roles. A lot of territory remains to be staked out and systems staff can benefit from this if they take an outward view.

Communication

IT Services staff recognize a need to do more than implement library technology. We have an important role to play in selling its benefits and in communicating new developments. The transition from Dobis/Libis to Innopac provided us with first-hand experience of this. The old system had been in use for 13 years and, despite its limitations, was familiar to library staff. Although IT Services staff embraced the imminent move to Innopac enthusiastically, this feeling was not universal in the library and there was a considerable amount of apprehension about the forthcoming change, especially among library assistants who had participated less in the system selection process. We felt it necessary to run some awareness sessions at which we could communicate the anticipated practical benefits of Innopac for library staff and its implementation timescale, as well as offering a forum for issues of concern to be raised. Reference to experience at other Innopac sites, including demonstrations of how their OPACs had been developed, proved reassuring.

These sessions showed us the value of being aware of other people's concerns and working at selling technology positively within the library. They have stood us in good stead as we continue to look at new possibilities like self-issue, integration of serials control under Innopac and intranet development. We see a clear need to demystify technology and to concentrate on its benefits rather than promoting it as an end in itself.

Ongoing communication of developments to staff inside and outside the library is a vital activity. IT Services staff often get news of new technology or electronic resources sooner than other library staff and need to take the time to communicate it when relevant. We use the library Web pages and our newsletter, *The Online Library*, as channels for information like database trials, new software features or significant Internet resources of general interest. Within the library we commonly use e-mail to circulate project plans, database usage statistics or new database updates. The development of a library intranet, which our division is leading, should facilitate communication further. Regular communication has not always been a strong point of systems staff but it is a habit we need to develop in the dynamic environment of the electronic library. Given that other players in this area may also be slow to take up the communication role, this is another of those areas where the door is open for us to play the leading part.

Bridging to the future

Futurology is also expected of library systems staff. library technology continues to evolve very rapidly. Managing current systems and keeping up with today's developments may seem difficult enough but our decisions must always take account of the future as well as fulfilling immediate needs. A regular reading diet of periodicals like *Personal Computer World*, *Byte* and *Online*, along with various Internet resources is a must, of course, in order to get a picture of what can be done today and where technology is leading us. Ultimately, however, we have to make our own decisions within local contexts, limited budgets and time constraints.

In 1996 we were in the fortunate position of being able to make major investments in technology, precipitated by the decision to fund implementation of a new integrated library system. We were conscious, however, that this was a rare opportunity and that funding on this scale would not be available for a long time so we had to make the most of our chance. In consultation with users, the library opted to purchase applications like Innopac, ERL and Microsoft Office, all of which represented leading brand products which had strong development paths, were based on standard protocols and, critically for ourselves and our users, were well integrated with World Wide Web technology. Our judgement was to play relatively safe. We have not been disappointed in terms of system stability, improved service to customers and ongoing product development. These systems have given us a solid platform and they have not precluded development of other services like Internet access to a wider range of databases from different publishers.

In many ways we were fortunate to be able to make our decisions at a favourable point in the technology cycle of these products. Each product was mature and tested at other sites and was well advanced in terms of integration with the

World Wide Web. We hope to benefit from a similar maturity in terms of other products like self-issue systems and electronic ordering and invoicing. Limitations on our staffing and budgetary resources will tend to curtail our ability to jump on bandwagons too early and this may not be a bad thing.

Inevitably there are other areas in which we shall wish that we could have invested a little later. One of these is likely to be client hardware for library staff and users. In 1996 we purchased 60 Pentium PCs and 30 terminals. These have proved highly serviceable and will doubtless continue to do so for some time. Nevertheless, we would like to have been able to consider investment in the new breed of network computers which promise lower acquisition and maintenance costs and which appear highly suitable for supporting standard applications like searching or, with the increasing proliferation of Java applets, word processing. Unfortunately, this technology was not sufficiently developed in mid-1996. If it develops rapidly we may soon wonder at the need for our over-specified client hardware. Equally, Digital Versatile Disk (DVD) may prove to be a highly viable storage medium through which to deliver networked access to databases, obviating the need to copy data from CD-ROM to hard disk as we currently do with ERL.

In each of these cases, however, we had to make a purchasing decision within a given time frame, assessing the best technology available and ensuring that our customers benefited sooner rather than later. There is no single right time to make technology purchasing decisions and there is an acceptance that total future proofing is not possible. The best we can do is to make carefully considered and informed judgements based as far as possible on definite or anticipated user needs and technology trends. The nature of this business is that we should be prepared to take the plunge and expect advances in technology to deliver more power for less cost a year or two later. If nothing else, this keeps our feet firmly on the ground!

Conclusion

These are interesting times for the IT Services division at University College Cork and it is no curse to live in them. The pace of technology change provides a huge challenge in terms of meeting current needs and anticipating future possibilities. We need to plan and manage our resources highly efficiently to meet this challenge. Our work is now much more varied and we are taking the opportunity to reinvent our role from one based primarily on support of systems for use within the library to one with a far higher profile throughout the campus. The range of applications and customers we support and work with has expanded and will continue to do so as networking pervades even further. Already we have seen gaps in the electronic landscape, notably in training and in communication, that we can fill. As our library becomes more electronic so our position in its strategic development becomes more influential. It will be vital, however, for us to use this influence constructively and to help encourage a favourable view of the electronic library among staff and users who are adjusting to it and need to be see the benefits of technology rather than be blinded by it.

Finally, it is questionable whether the model of concentrating systems support and development in a single discrete unit of the library will endure. Increasingly, all sections of our library have a stake in technology as an underpinning influence in carrying out their work. Distinctions between parts of what might be considered information services and the services operated by the IT Services division, in the areas of training and communication with users for example, are becoming blurred both within and outside the library. It may be that IT support staff will need to work within, rather than separately from, service teams which will want to take responsibility for shaping their own technological future within an overall strategy. The one certainty is that there will be change and that the future will be even more interesting.

CHAPTER TWENTY NINE

Case Study: University of Sheffield

Kath O'Donovan

Introduction

Three themes run through this case study of system management and technical support in a university library:

- the rapid and all-pervading nature of change in information systems and IT;
- the need for systems team members to communicate widely within and outside the library;
- the importance of training and documentation in supporting the work of the team.

These themes overlap and intertwine throughout this chapter, emphasizing the place of the systems team at the heart of the modern academic library.

The Context

The university

The University of Sheffield, with some 18 000 students, is amongst the group of pre-1992 universities known as 'major civics with medical school', or 'red brick'. Other members of this group include Manchester, Birmingham, Leeds and Newcastle. The university is explicitly research led and has been successful both in the 1996 Research Assessment Exercise and in teaching quality assessments. In common with other higher education institutions, there is a major shift in the student population to mature students, part-time and distance learning.

The library

The university library has 4 major branches and 7 minor sites, mainly on the city centre campus, but with a branch of the Health Sciences Library located in a hospital across the city. A new branch of the Health Sciences Library may open on a site 15 miles from the main campus in 1998. The main library, a 1959 Grade II* listed building, accounts for around 50 per cent of library activity. The library is a member of the Consortium of University Research Libraries (CURL) and the US based Research Libraries Group (RLG).

The library has some 165 staff, 125 FTE, with 25 staff on academic-related grades.

The systems team

The systems team, which carries out the majority of system management and technical support, in addition to system development, consists of the following:

Sub-Librarian: Information Systems and Technical Services
Systems Manager
Assistant Systems Manager (p/t)

Head of Bibliographic Services
Assistant Librarian: Information Systems
IT Support Officer

The library system

In 1996 the library migrated from BLS to BLCMP's Talis library management system. The circulation system handles loans in all but 3 branches. The catalogue is complete for all stock purchased since 1974, and the retrospective conversion of the catalogue should be complete within three years. Serials checkin operated for the main library in the previous system and this was extended to include all appropriate branches in within 6 months of the migration. Inter-library loans were introduced into the major branches 8 months after the migration. The OPAC, known locally as STAR, is World Wide Web based.

The library was not able to introduce inter-library loan or self-service options in the previous system because of restrictions on the power of the equipment available, but these were a priority when the new system was implemented. The ability to include reading list information on the OPAC is seen as a major service to users and implementation of this is a priority.

The electronic library

Since the early 1990's the library's policy has been to deliver as much library service as possible to the user's desktop. This includes both information services such as CD-ROM and BIDS, and information about library services provided through LibWeb, the library's Web-based information service. Rapid developments in electronic journals have recently come to the fore and increased the value to the user of networked information services.

Relationships within the university

The changes sweeping through both computing and university administration have, if anything, affected these departments rather more in recent years than the library. The MAC initiative in administrative computing, and the move from mainframes to networked personal computers in academic computing services, have transformed old ways of working. These developments have placed several aspects of computing, information, software and computing power, directly in the hands of end users. In Sheffield, the strategic importance to the university of the computer network has been recognized by the creation of a new administrative department, Corporate Information and Computing Services (CICS), which incorporates the former Management and Administrative Computing Service and Academic Computing Services. This department also manages the university's Web presence and the introduction of a single card system across campus. The central system hardware for the library system is located in the CICS machine room.

The library's long-standing relationships with almost all the constituent parts of this new department have continued to develop within this new environment, taking on increasing significance.

The university network

The university has a well developed ethernet network, run by CICS, which extends to all areas of the campus. Around 90 per cent of the personal computers on campus are PCs. The primary interface for users is the Windows 3.11 desktop, which is available to all users, both staff and students. The desktop, which is identical over a number of Novell file servers, includes the full range of office software from Microsoft, World Wide Web (currently via Netscape) and library CD-ROM services. More specialist software, such as teaching materials are additionally available on some servers. Users therefore have a comprehensive information environment. They can search BIDS or a CD-ROM, read electroni journals and synthesize their findings into an essay during a single login. The drawback with this unitary system has been the lack of flexibility imposed by the need to run all the services side by side, but for some time the benefits to users outweighed this. However, Windows 3.11 is now a dead end, and CiCS are wrestling with the very substantial difficulties presented by a move to Windows 9x or NT. For its part, the Library Systems Team is considering the cost, training and support issues in what will inevitably be a more distributed environment.

The Planning Framework

In 1997 the university library defined a new planning framework. This began with the production of a strategic planning document for the period 1997–2000. This document will be revised annually, becoming a three year rolling plan. The strategic plan will be supported by operational objectives set within working groups, teams and branches throughout the library. These operational objectives will be reviewed by the library management group to produce a set of objectives for the library as a whole. The systems team is developing its own operational objectives and the remainder of this case study is based upon the discussions taking place during this process. I am grateful to my colleagues on the systems team for their contributions to this process, and for their willingness to allow me to use our discussions for this paper. Any errors which emerge here are, of course, my own.

The process has been particularly fruitful for the systems team. It comes at the very end of the Talis installation period during which day-to-day problem solving absorbed all our energies. This first stage is now complete and systems staff have regained the level of expertise they enjoyed with the previous system. The requirement now is to develop our management procedures and set up systems which will give the library the management information it requires using Talis's almost unlimited capacity in this field. A range of functionality remains to be implemented, and we need to consider how this can be done effectively.

Systems team strategic plan

The team has only been formed in its current configuration for 12 months, linking together the traditional systems work of supporting the library's computerized activities, with the rapidly developing areas of information systems support and Web activity. Whilst it is clear that we cannot expect stability or a period of consolidation in this area of library work, it seemed important to draw together the areas of our activity. The first task was therefore to define the functions of the team. The following statement is our working definition:

The Systems Team:

- supports the library and its staff in delivery of high quality services to library users, both on and off campus;
- manages, directs and develops IT in the library:
  - Talis software and related hardware;
  - Libweb;
  - PC hardware and software and other related equipment;
  - campus network related matters;
  - procedures for IT related tasks;
  - documentation for library systems;
  - training co-ordination and development for relevant areas of IT use;
- advises the library on future developments in IT and their implications;
- communicates widely within the library, across the campus and with external agencies:
  - all sections of CICS;
  - other parts of the university administration, particularly those relating to student services;
  - BLCMP;
  - hardware suppliers;
  - information service suppliers.

We identified the following as the major areas of activity which are discussed in more detail below:

Communication
Talis
WWW
Hardware and technical support
Training support and documentation
Campus network and open access PCs
MIS

Communication

The inclusion of this as a separate and major area of activity emerged during the objectives setting meeting, as each team member outlined areas important to them individually. The idea contrasts sharply with the conventional view of systems personnel wedded to their computers and scarcely able to talk to anyone at all!

COMMUNICATION WITHIN THE LIBRARY
Within the library the systems team act as a focal point for system development. Reader services staff are responsible for public aspects of services, but dialogue with systems team is essential for them to understand what Talis can do, and how this can be set up within the constraints of the library itself. This is particularly significant in a complex system with a number of large branches, where the need to vary practice according to local conditions must be set against the need for consistency across the library as a whole. The systems team is already represented on all of the major library committees and working groups and this is considered essential given the centrality of IT to library developments.

COMMUNICATION WITHIN THE UNIVERSITY
The library's relationship to CICS is clearly central to the success of the library's activities as more and more of our

service is delivered directly to the desktop. The library needs both to ensure that its own priorities are made known, and also to remain aware of strategic thinking within the department to ensure that the library is positioned to take advantage of developments. The university has recently consolidated cross-representation of all service departments on the relevant university committees, and this ensures that appropriate information is available quickly. Nonetheless, personal relationships remain of critical importance.

Links can be characterized as follows:

Management level	Strategy, space planning, joint developments,
MIS Development	Transfer of data (student names and addresses etc.) between systems
User Services	Development of training for library staff and users
Student Information Systems	Analysis of student categories for single card system
Open access areas	Space planning
Network Support	Installation of network points in Libraries
Desktop Support	Networking of CD-ROMS and library presence on the desktop, kiosk mode operation of library based OPAC PCs
Technical Services (UNIX)	Support of the library's central system machines
Special projects	Information services developments (CD-ROM caching etc.)

COMMUNICATION OUTSIDE THE LIBRARY
Systems staff links to other agencies outside the library have always been important, but perhaps overlooked. Links with

the systems supplier are clearly vital to ensure that library needs are recognized, and that system developments are promptly incorporated into library activities. Where the system supplier is a co-operative, as is the case with BLCMP, other staff within the library maintain links, and it is important to ensure that relevant information is circulated to all interested parties.

Systems staff play an important role in discussing equipment requirements with suppliers. This extends from central system equipment, terminals/PCs, barcode scanners, and the whole range of other IT equipment, such as flatbed scanners and digital cameras, important to the library's functioning.

Talis

This area represents the traditional core of technical support: setting system parameters, users and enablements, sending out notices, routine maintenance. As many of the tasks associated with this operation are more straightforward in the new environment, the team is looking for ways to spread expertise more widely through the library staff to make the system more robust. In-house documentation for Talis is not yet complete, and the development of networked solutions for presentation of this and other library documentation will be a major part of the work of the team over the next year or so.

WWW

The World Wide Web is perceived by the library as of major strategic importance, not least because WWW and associated software will be the preferred delivery method for the majority of services currently available through the Windows desktop.

The Systems Team is responsible for development of LibWeb, the library's Web presence and the major entry point to the library's information services. There are close links here with the library's Electronic Library Group, where much of the strategic thinking about information services is carried out. The systems team and the Electronic Library Group have a joint task in spreading the skills and knowledge in this area to more members of library staff. Without a determined effort in this direction, this activity risks becoming ghettoized, when it should be part of the thinking of all members of library staff.

Hardware and technical support

The move to Talis, and the decision to standardize on the Web OPAC for presentation of catalogue information within the library, required a move from terminals to PCs as the standard interface to the library system. As part of the procurement exercise, the period 1996/7 saw a flood of PCs coming into the library, putting a machine on the desk of almost every member of library staff. The technical support load has shifted from the need to make sure terminals remained in touch with the mother ship, to the wider range of work associated with PC management. Not least of these issues is security. All our machines are clamped, and key management is a major headache. At the end of the line comes that recurring management issue: where do you put the Strepsil tin which contains the key to the key cupboard? There has been no increase in technical support staff, and so our whole mode of working must concentrate on enabling staff to recognize and resolve their own problems before contacting systems team members. Links with CICS have again been helpful in enabling us to 'buy in' hours from postgraduate students working part-time in that department to help with unpacking and checking of large equipment deliveries. We plan to continue this flexible arrangement.

Maintenance of stand alone CD-ROM workstations continues to absorb effort. Although our policy is to select networkable services wherever possible, networking can in some cases be too expensive for anticipated levels of use, or unfeasible for technical reasons. A growing number of titles appear which do not fit into existing models of service in this area. Booking a machine for 30 minutes or an hour works reasonably well for bibliographical titles. Where titles cover a large corpus, such as *Patrologia Latina*, longer periods of study are required. Multimedia is increasingly common in titles we are requested to mount on the workstations, with implications for workstation specification and operation.

We have always offered print facilities with our CD-ROM workstations, but keep this policy under review, as central printing policies change.

With the proliferation of CD-ROM in all subjects, library users have begun to bring titles into the library expecting to find a machine they can use. Our internal discussions on such provision has centred on difficulties of support for users where titles require installation, maintenance of the hard drive and protection against both deliberate and accidental damage, not to mention assisting users with the software itself. Despite our concerns we have put out a multimedia PC for standalone open access use on an experimental basis. This service is not currently available elsewhere in the university.

Systems staff also support specialist equipment and software purchased for staff and users. Consideration should be given when purchasing such equipment to the amount of skilled support which will be needed to establish and run a service based upon it, and if possible (a vain hope) adequate staff time provided to develop and maintain such a service.

Training support and documentation

Systems team staff are sometimes overwhelmed by the pace of change in IT, but at least we have chosen to be in this fast moving area and are in a position to influence the direction of that change and learn about it first hand. Other library staff can feel that systems staff are making changes just to keep them on their toes!

Clearly in this environment training and staff development are crucial to the day to day running of the library, and to ensuring that its staff are equipped to adapt to continuing change. The move to a new library system is a difficult one for library staff, and this section describes the programme developed by the library's Staff Development Group and systems team in the migration period.

We realized at an early stage, even before going out to tender, that our new system would be likely to run on PCs, and to operate in a graphical environment. As the majority of library staff, particularly in reader services and technical services, were used to terminal access to the library system, and were not familiar with the campus network, we embarked on a training programme to build up staff expertise in this area. This programme, known as WinTrain, was carried out over a 6 month period from November 1995 to April 1996. It was divided into 5 sections: the campus network, basic Windows, handling your files, using an application (e-mail) and advanced Windows. This course was delivered to around 120 people, and some parts of it, notably file handling, are still presented from time to time as demand emerges.

The WinTrain programme terminated just as MigTrain–the collective name for training for the new system–entered the station, and all library staff completed a series of sessions on Talis.

These two training programmes were staff intensive, but were essential to the smooth running of the library. In order to deliver MigTrain, we identified a number of trainers throughout the library system. These staff, many of whom had not delivered training before, worked from prepared scripts, and were very successful.

Following these major exercises, systems team has identified an ongoing commitment to training. Firstly, documentation must be completed. It is easy for documentation to fall behind in a dynamic situation, but we are working on procedures which will ensure that documentation is kept up to date and made easily available to those who need it. Our current plan is to switch from Word to HTML format in line with our strategic approach to WWW. Secondly, there is the need to keep staff up to date with system developments.

Simply noting changes in a staff newsletter is not sufficient, as staff find it difficult to relate such announcements to their own work. We plan to revive the group of Talis trainers, organizing regular updating sessions for them, and asking them to disseminate good practice in their own branches and departments.

Campus network and open access PCs

The campus network and open access PC clusters are run centrally by CICS. Systems team members liaise closely with their opposite numbers on CICS technical staff to arrange access to shared space for library documentation, shared IDs for counter PCs, CD-ROM networking, access to WWW server and many other areas. As a result of this centralized arrangement, library staff have not found it necessary to build up technical network skills. This has worked well for the library as IT skills are in short supply, but can leave us vulnerable when resources in other departments are limited.

Open access PC clusters originally developed outside libraries on campus. Over the last two years the library has been keen to establish open access PC areas within libraries and now each branch has at least a few machines, with some offering a substantial number. Plans are in hand to extend provision in the main library in particular. These developments make sense from an educational point of view, as students have access to print and electronic materials in one location. Also, in an institution where convergence has never really been on the agenda, it is still useful for the two services to co-operate in this explicit way.

Management information systems (MIS)

The three themes noted in the introduction to this chapter, change, communication and training, come together in the area of MIS. The whole of the higher education sector is subject to scrutiny in the form of teaching quality assessments and research assessment exercises. Costs have never been monitored so closely by academic departments under pressure to maximize their income. In this competitive environment the need for timely provision of management information about library activities is greater than ever before. Because of the developments in IT, the systems team are in a position to respond to this need. The importance of MIS development has been recognized by the appointment of a Project Officer for one year to get the programme off the ground. This involves a review of national initiatives such as Minstrel.

Newer library systems based on industry standard relational database systems, such as Talis, can provide data in abundance, but skill and judgement are needed to transform this data into an effective tool to support library management. Here is an opportunity for the systems Team to use their skills to provide just such a service. Systems staff have an intimate knowledge of how the library works through their close links with circulation and other system-related activities; they are familiar with the software which can take data from the library system and other areas such as turnstile figures, and present it in an accessible way; and they have contacts within library staff to gather details of the information required.

Awareness training may well be required to make library staff aware of what can be achieved, and continuing dialogue will be needed to ensure that reports continue to meet the needs of library management. Within a few weeks of such an awareness session in Sheffield, we eliminated the need for local listings of periodicals, essential under the previous system because of its lack of flexibility, in one branch library, with consequent savings of time and effort. There is little doubt that there are similar savings to be made across the library system.

We are also able to use easily understood interfaces, such as Access or WWW queries to enable staff to run regular queries themselves, allowing more time, perhaps, for the discussion of one-off or more difficult requirements. Incorporation of regular statistical surveys, such as the SCONUL statistics is also within reach.

Conclusion

System management and technical support have always been vital to the library. I hope that I have shown that these activities are moving from being the preserve of boffin-like figures carrying out dark rituals in secret machine rooms, to an open process involving dialogue not only with colleagues in the library but with colleagues in support departments across campus and beyond. The new information systems environment requires team work and commitment from staff at all levels within the library and it is the role of the systems team to encourage this process. It is, after all, what we do.

Managing Specific Electronic Services

CHAPTER THIRTY

Managing Electronic Reserve Collections

Paula Kingston

Introduction

The development of electronic reserve collections is a relatively recent activity for academic libraries in the UK. There
are several projects and services under way but definitive
findings on the costs and benefits of these services are not
yet available. However, the experiences of a number of developmental services have provided some clear evidence on the
type of management issues they raise. This chapter provides
an overview of these issues and outlines some of the decisions and options managers face. It refers to the experiences
of a number of projects and to issues which are currently
being addressed through wider initiatives.

Background

Traditional short loan or reserve collections have largely been
developed by academic libraries as a way of coping with periods of intense student demand for access to recommended

course readings. Their main purpose is to increase access to recommended readings when the number of copies held by the library, available for the normal loan period, do not alone suffice to meet the users' needs. Additional pressures have been placed on these services by the sharp rise in student numbers in recent years, and by moves to modularization of courses in many institutions.

Between 1988/9 and 1992/3 there was a 57 per cent increase in student numbers in the United Kingdom, from 517 000 to 811 000 (Brown, 1996) while modularization has led not only to an increase in choice and flexibility, but has also concentrated demand for access to key materials into a shorter timespan. Both the numbers of part-time students and the number of courses offered via distance learning have increased substantially. In each case traditional reserve collections are often unable to meet demand without specific further provision, such as acquiring copies for loan to part-time students only. The pressures created by this situation have also been exacerbated by reductions in university funding per student.

The potential for electronic delivery to enable the library to meet students' needs for access to essential texts has been recognized and explored by a number of libraries. This type of service is perceived as one which could potentially meet intensive demand by providing for multi-user access, twenty-four hours a day, seven days a week, from points across the campus where networked computer facilities are available. The potential for access from beyond the campus for part-time and distance students has also been recognized.

Overview of Developments

The project which pioneered electronic access to course materials was Electronic Library and Information Online Retrieval (ELINOR) based at de Montfort University. It began in 1992 and by 1995 contained over 120 textbooks and other materials including examination papers and journals (ELINOR, a).

More recently, the Electronic Libraries (eLib) Programme has supported a number of projects exploring the development of electronic 'short loan' collections, including Access to Course Readings via Networks (ACORN), Edbank, Research Information and Delivery (ResIDe), Performing Arts Teaching Resources Online (PATRON), and Quick Information for Part-time Students (QUIPS). QUIPS and Edbank in particular are developing services to part-time and distance students, while PATRON is exploring the electronic delivery of multimedia materials across a campus network.

Some of eLib's on-demand publishing projects, such as the Scottish Collaborative On-demand Publishing Enterprise (SCOPE), On-Demand Publishing in the Humanities, Electronic On Demand (eOn), Eurotext and Phoenix have explored the electronic delivery of material, in some cases across different sites and institutions. Some have also explored the electronic production of course packs, delivered in printed form to the end user (SCOPE and Phoenix). Outside the eLib Programme a number of UK universities are exploring the development of electronic collections. For example, Leeds University has developed an Online Counter Collection, and the universities of Derby, Wolverhampton and Birkbeck College, London, are all in the process of developing or piloting electronic services to deliver course materials.

Issues Raised in Developing Electronic Collections of Materials

The development of electronic collections requires careful planning as at each stage of the process decisions and options are available which need to be assessed in the light of local circumstances, costs, available skills and technology and copyright clearance issues. In summary, service development needs to take account of the following:

- identifying users' needs;
- identifying appropriate material;

- developing copyright clearance procedures;
- publishers' charges;
- creating electronic materials;
- managing the delivery of electronic copyright materials;
- promoting the service and training users;
- monitoring and evaluation.

Identifying users' needs

Before embarking on developing a system it can be useful to consult potential users about their needs, as this not only raises awareness about the planned service in advance, but also provides information which can help shape the design and specification of the system. Interviews and focus groups have been used successfully (ResIDe, 1997a; ResIDe, 1997b; PATRON, 1997) to facilitate this type of input into the development process, with participation from both academic staff and students. System design can be usefully influenced, for example, by finding out how users prefer to search for course readings, and ascertaining their views and preferences for reading on-screen, printing out materials, or downloading portions of documents electronically. This approach also enables the library to explain the issues raised by copyright clearance and digitization at an early stage, and to indicate the timescales required for making materials available electronically. The interest of potential users can be stimulated by this approach, and their commitment to providing feedback in later stages of development may therefore be easier to secure.

Identifying appropriate material

Most services have opted to identify high demand readings, such as book chapters and journal articles on course reading lists, for inclusion in electronic services. The timely identification of this material can pose problems, and close liaison with academic staff is needed to identify material well in advance of the start of the course. However, academics' patterns of working and timescales for updating reading lists may not easily lend themselves to the timescales required for developing an electronic collection. For example, ACORN found that 54 per cent of academics updated their reading lists immediately before the start of the course (ACORN, 1997a).

Where academic staff do co-operate actively, their involvement has been found to be one of the crucial determinants of successful services as not only do they help ensure that the content of the service is appropriate, but they also encourage their students to attend training sessions and to make use of the service.

In order to avoid the particular problems raised by copyright clearance, some services have opted to include or to focus on non-copyright materials. Examination papers, lecturers' notes and materials, and tutorial questions and solutions are examples of these types of materials. Some materials may not be suitable for electronic delivery, or may require a specialized approach. For example, the eOn project chose to focus on open learning materials for electronic delivery, but subsequently found that the interactive approach inherent in these materials was not facilitated by the format they had chosen for the electronic versions.

Developing copyright clearance procedures

Having identified appropriate material, permission to make an electronic copy needs to be acquired from the copyright owner, who is normally, but not always, the publisher. Until very recently there has been no central clearing house for electronic copyright clearance, so copyright owners have had to be identified and contacted individually. This process can be lengthy, and normally entails the use of an appropriate contract, or possibly a Heads of Agreement where the service is a pilot or experimental one. Both ELINOR and SCOPE have developed model licence agreements (ELINOR, b; SCOPE, 1997) the former of which which may be modified for use by other institutions. In contrast, a Heads of

Agreement approach provides a statement of intent by both parties to work together and allows co-operation to start, without entering into a legally binding contract where neither party is certain of the detailed clauses which should apply. Project ACORN has used a Heads of Agreement (ACORN, 1997b). To date, a relatively small number of publishers have developed their own contracts.

More recently a joint working party of the Joint Information Systems Committee (JISC) and the Publishers Association (PA) has developed, and is inviting comments on, a model licence agreement (JISC/PA, 1997a) containing a wide range of clauses to cover different circumstances. The intention is that publishers and libraries will select from this agreement those clauses which they wish to apply in their particular situation.

These efforts to facilitate the copyright clearance process underline the difficulties experienced by libraries to date, and the delays inherent in what can become difficult and complex negotiations. Publishers may need to check carefully the rights they hold, to consult with the original authors and check who owns the rights in any illustrations included in the original printed material. Before they agree a contract and a price with the requesting library, they need to take into account how electronic licensing might affect their commercial and strategic interests. This can lead to delays in providing clearance which then affects the timely availability of material in the electronic service. For example, Leeds University requested permissions for 158 items and was still waiting for a response on 68 items several months after applying (Wellesley-Smith, 1997, unpublished data). Project ACORN calculated that on average it took 66.5 days to obtain copyright clearance for a journal article (ACORN, 1997c). The time required to monitor progress with requests and to chase non-responding publishers should not be underestimated.

A recent report from another JISC/PA working party (1997b) makes a number of very useful recommendations on how the process of clearance can be facilitated. On the library side, a clear indication to publishers of the type of service to be offered, the numbers of students involved, the format in which the materials are to be made available and the arrangements for security, can help speed the process. A key recommendation in the report is the authorization of a central agency to handle electronic copyright clearance on behalf of publishers, as currently happens in the print environment. The Copyright Licensing Agency has recently been endorsed by representatives of the Authors' Licensing and Collecting Society and the Publishers Licensing Society as the central body to license the digitization of existing print material, and plans are underway for the development of specific licences for specific sectors in consultation with UK rightsholders. These should be available from mid-1998 (CLA, 1998) and will simplify clearance procedures for librarians.

With regard to fair dealing, a JISC and PA working party (1997c) has been established to consider this issue and has developed guidelines on fair dealing in electronic materials.

Publishers' charges

Another area of uncertainty for libraries is the nature and type of charges publishers may make for their materials. There is no standard approach to charging and different projects have different experiences of pricing structures and charging levels. This indicates that there is as yet no consensus on the value of electronic copies, and insufficient experience and evidence on which to base price calculations. Charges can vary both between publishers and between agreements which a single publisher may have with different institutions. The types of charges made to different projects have included charges to digitize the material, an up-front charge in the form of a licence fee, charges per printed page, or a combination of one or more of these. Experience has shown that fees are negotiable, although publishers are generally concerned to set 'commercially viable' rates. Although libraries can undertake to negotiate, there is clearly a significant cost involved in the staff time and skills required to do this on a publisher by publisher basis.

A paper by Sykes (1996) sets out factors to take into account when agreeing a price with publishers. These include the degree of security provided for the electronic texts, affordability by the library and/or the end-user if charges are passed on, possible loss of revenue to publishers from sales of printed texts, volume of use, whether an electronic copy is provided or has to be made, and the duration of the agreement. For journal articles, subscription to the paper copy and whether the author of the article works in the requesting institution has influenced the charges applied. It may be easier to obtain permissions for journal articles than book chapters as the former do not affect publishers' income from journal subscriptions, which are selected by and large on the basis of research rather than teaching needs. Leeds University found that publishers charged lower rates or sometimes made no charge for older items while requesting large fees for newer material and material sill in print (Wellesley-Smith, 1997, unpublished data). It is clear that careful selection of materials for inclusion in an electronic service can reduce costs significantly. A further JISC/PA study on charging mechanisms for digitized texts has recently been completed (1997d) and these guidelines will serve to reduce the complexity of negotiation in this area.

Permission may, of course, be refused outright, and this can leave serious gaps in provision as well as raising more general concerns about access to materials identified as essential for teaching and learning. One project, when faced with a refusal, identified a different textbook covering the same subject area for which permission could be obtained. However, the academic concerned still recommended the original to students, and the electronic copy remained unused. Other projects have asked academic staff to recommend an alternative when faced with a refusal, while one project found that provision on some of its target modules could be seriously impaired by a refusal from one publisher. Project Phoenix (1997) found that it was easier to secure permissions for producing course packs, where the numbers produced were predetermined, than for texts which would be delivered electronically to end-users.

Refusals may result from publishers' uncertainty about how to respond to requests for electronic permissions, particularly if they have not yet developed a policy covering this area. Hopefully, as more publishers develop policies the numbers of refusals should decline, along with the numbers of non-responding publishers. Progress made by the JISC/PA working parties and the development of a central body to license digitization of print material will also contribute to more positive responses from publishers.

Creating electronic materials

In general, publishers are rarely able to supply electronic copies of materials originally published in printed form, so the requesting library generally has to arrange for an electronic copy to be produced. This situation will change over time as more electronic material becomes available from publishers, but given the date-spread of materials in reserve collections, digitization is likely to be required for many years to come.

The need to digitize material raises the issue of which document format to choose and whether the copy should be produced as an image or text file. Image files are more straightforward, and therefore cheaper to produce, being simply an image of the original page, although problems have been encountered if the quality of the original copy is poor. The disadvantages are that the files created in this way are large and hence slower to display and to print. There may also be some problems with on-screen legibility. Image files are used by a number of projects and the Leeds Online Counter Collection has been able to mount hand-written material from lecturers very easily using this format.

An alternative to image files is digitization to text, which requires optical character recognition, a process which does not currently produce a high degree of accuracy, making very careful proof reading and correction essential. These files are therefore much more costly to produce than image files. The accuracy of text files is influenced by the quality of the printed copy used in the scanning process, whether complex tables and mathematical formulae are included and the size and types of fonts used in the original. However, the advantages of text files are that they are searchable and take less time to display on screen and print out. In addition, and where allowed by the agreement with the publisher, they can provide the option of 'cut and paste' and electronic downloading, thus enhancing their usability.

Estimates of the time and costs of digitization vary, but in all cases are a significant cost element to electronic reserves. Project ACORN has estimated 30 minutes per page, amounting to a cost of between £3.75 and £5.00 per page for text files, compared with £1.00 per page for image files (ACORN, 1997, unpublished data). On-Demand Publishing in the Humanities has estimated between 30 minutes and one hour for the whole process of digitization to text (Porter, S. 1996a). It is clear that digitization costs can greatly increase the overall costs of electronic reserve material where digitization to text, rather than image files, is the chosen option.

Adobe Acrobat's Portable Document Format (PDF) has become an increasingly popular choice as it keeps the appearance of the original printed copy, an important factor for both publishers and authors. It has rapidly become a de facto standard for delivering full-text documents in a Web environment and Acrobat Reader software is often already available on universities' networks. Files in this format can be either image or fully-converted text files. Some services have chosen HTML format, where the need to reproduce the exact appearance of the printed original has not been required by publishers.

Managing the delivery of electronic copyright materials

Some form of electronic copyright management system is fast becoming an essential item, not only to manage the process of rights clearance, but also to provide for user authentication, document security, monitoring of usage and, where appropriate, the charging of end-users. Several projects have developed in-house systems incorporating some or all of these features, but a cheap and proven off-the-shelf product is not yet available.

Document security is an important feature within these systems and they include features such as access limitation to specific machines, encryption of documents, username and password access only, limitations on electronic downloading and 'cut and paste' facilities, on-screen copyright statements and the watermarking of print outs with usernames and copyright statements.

The Electronic Reserves Copyright Management Systems (ERCOMS) project has undertaken to develop a generic system capable of transfer to other institutions, which can be tailored to interface with local systems, and which will include a PC-based rights clearance system. ACORN has developed CLEAR, a Microsoft Access database, which handles rights clearance and interfaces with the ACORN system to produce reports on usage and calculate payments to publishers, while SCOPE has developed a system called Cactus which enables electronic documents to be securely delivered to end-users at different participating sites. Other commercially available electronic copyright management systems, as well as those being developed as part of European projects are reviewed by Tuck, 1996. The main challenges for a generic system appear to be in the areas of printing, charging for printing and user authentication, where different institutions are likely to have very different arrangements and approaches.

Proprietary systems have been used in some projects to make materials available to users, but the benefits of using World Wide Web tools and integrating access to electronic course readings with access to other Web-based materials have made this approach increasingly popular. ACORN and Phoenix, for example, provide direct access to electronic texts held in Adobe Acrobat format, through their Talis Web OPACs. Some projects have mounted their full-text documents on existing university machines, while others have opted for a dedicated server which can improve access times and allow for the development of more sophisticated features. PATRON has opted for IBM's Digital Library product to meet the particular requirements for delivering multimedia materials across networks.

The availability of networked PCs to enable users to access electronic reserves materials has not yet been reported as posing significant problems, but as pilot services aimed at particular subsets of students are expanded, access may begin to present problems, especially if on-screen reading of documents proves significant. Similarly, as service use increases, the number and quality of networked printers required may well increase, particularly where users prefer to read from a printed page rather than from the screen.

Promoting the service and training users

As with all new services, promotion and training are important to encourage awareness and use. Working with academic staff to identify material can be followed up with regular reports on progress with copyright clearance for their courses. Involving them in arranging training for their students, and providing them with feedback on service usage, can ensure their continuing interest. Promotion of the service to students via academic staff is a very effective method to use and it can be supplemented with posters in departments, items in university newsletters and e-mails to groups of students where this facility is available.

The needs of users for training in the use of electronic readings has been addressed in a number of projects and the IT skills of students have emerged as an important factor in service usage. On-Demand Publishing in the Humanities found that some humanities students needed a very basic introduction to the Windows environment, before the service itself could be presented (Porter, 1996b). Eurotext's student focus groups' findings indicate that students themselves report lack of awareness of electronic resources and lack of knowledge about how to use them as reasons for non-use (Eurotext, 1997). Consultation with academic staff, and investigating the type and levels of IT training different students have received as part of their courses is a useful prerequisite to designing training.

While it is possible to design and deliver targeted training courses as part of specific projects, looking to the future, when electronic readings have become part of standard library services, the library needs to consider how this type of training can be integrated into ongoing provision, and the support materials required.

Monitoring and evaluation

Developing an evaluation strategy is clearly important for any new service in order to be able to assess costs and benefits. Under the eLib Programme, several projects have worked with the Tavistock Institute to develop comprehensive evaluation strategies for their services using focus groups, questionnaires, interviews and observation (Tavistock Institute, 1996). Preliminary findings are beginning to become available although it is not yet possible to draw firm conclusions.

The production of course packs by conventional means has encountered high costs, both for copyright clearance and production. University College London found that the production of printed study packs by conventional means was not cost-effective, and while acknowledging that there was a demand from students for packs, determined to wait on evidence of reduced production costs through using electronic means (Friend, 1997). However, with regard to electronically-produced course packs, projects have again encountered the unpredictability of price due to variable copyright charges by publishers and pack sales have proved unpredictable as they depend on both the price and the extent to which the lecturer promotes the pack to students. Packs are seen as particularly convenient for part-time and evening degree students, but SCOPE found that a majority of students indicated that they read 50 per cent or less of the articles in a pack (SCOPE, 1996). Course pack projects are now also exploring the development of electronic resource banks offering students the option of selecting material themselves rather than buying a pre-packaged product.

Some preliminary information is available on the usage of electronic reserves, and on users' perceptions of their value, although several projects have reported low inital usage. ELINOR has compared the use of complete electronic books with printed books, and preliminary findings indicate that while users find it easier to find a known item through the Electronic Library System rather than the conventional OPAC, they find specific information more quickly in the printed book than in the electronic version (Zimin, Ramsden and Zhao, 1995). From usage data based on its first eight weeks of service operation, ACORN found that students did not appear to be reading whole articles on-screen, and while viewing activity was intitally high, printing activity increased, especially during the examination period (ACORN, 1997d). Some of the key issues affecting usage appear to be lack of awareness of services, technical problems affecting access, lack of IT skills, time constraints, and in some cases a dislike of computers. However, those who do use electronic services successfully are keen to see them futher developed with a wider range of materials. The need to achieve a critical mass of material in order to make the electronic service compelling has been highlighted within several projects.

The issue of whether users are willing to pay charges over and above institutions' standard rates for printing is still uncertain. There are some indications that if charges are comparable with photocopying charges, this could be perceived as acceptable, but this can only be confirmed by implementing charges and monitoring usage. Many librarians feel that access to core course resources should be free rather than determined by ability to pay, while some feel that it is appropriate for users to pay for value-added services as long as the traditional 'free' service is still available to those who are not able or willing to pay.

Developments in the USA

Experiences of electronic reserve collections in the USA provide some useful points of contrast with UK developments because of the diversity of approaches adopted and the more established nature of some services (Soete, 1996). Some libraries use commercially available proprietary electronic reserve systems, whilst more recently there have been significant developments of in-house Web-based services, more akin to practice in the United Kingdom, which can provide greater flexibility along with wider accessibility to students.

Some significant differences from UK approaches include the involvement of academic staff in scanning and mounting materials from their department and in taking responsibility for copyright clearance. In some cases a wide variety of material is included in electronic reserve collections, such as lecturers' notes, Powerpoint presentations and digitized images. For example, the ERes system at Santa Clara University enables faculty to create their own Web pages and enter a wide range of material formats into the system.

At Northwestern University Library, a Web-based system enables the library to link to academic staff Web pages, while students are linked from the electronic reserve collection to newsgroup discussions to enable online discussion with their classmates. At Colorado State University, Xerox's Document-on-Demand system enables copyright clearance to be requested electronically from the USA's Copyright Clearance Center. UMI is developing a product which will enable direct electronic access to full-text items in their databases, thus circumventing the need for scanning.

A number of different approaches are taken to copyright by academic libraries in the USA, including not mounting copyrighted materials at all, securing permission for copyrighted materials, or applying the same policy for electronic as for paper materials, in particular following the American Library Association's model policy of 1982 which states that the first time an item is placed in a reserve collection is a fair use, while permission must be sought for subsequent use (ALA, 1982). The Copyright Clearance Center, referred to above, has now begun to offer clearance for electronic copies from those publishers who are authorizing them to act on their behalf.

Conclusion

While electronic reserves are more widespread in the USA, and more likely to be a mainstream library service rather than a special project, little evaluative information is available. The approaches outlined above indicate that the integration of electronic course readings with other materials is more advanced, and the potential impact on approaches to teaching and learning is therefore greater. Experiences to date in the UK suggests that electronic reserves are a value-added service providing enhanced access to course texts, and in some cases enhanced usability, rather than cost savings.

Developments in the areas of digitization and copyright clearance over the coming years may well significantly affect development and management costs, while the effects of scaling up will need to be closely monitored in terms of institutional IT infrastructures and student access to networked computers. Further information on costs, service usage, users' reactions and impact on traditional reserve collections is needed before an overall assessment can be made, but despite the drawbacks outlined, pilot services seem to represent an enhanced level of service where increased accessibility is appreciated by users. The Electronic Libraries programme is shortly to fund a project to set up a national digital resource bank to further facilitate and support the development of electronic reserve collections.

What is emerging is that electronic services will not only affect the usage of traditional library services, but will also have a wider impact on approaches to teaching and learning. This will be particularly significant where links can be readily made to other types of electronic information, leading to the creation of electronic 'study packs'. The potential for access to these by distance learners from home could solve some of the access problems referred to earlier. Such developments signal the increasing involvement of librarians in course planning, working alongside their academic colleagues to ensure that appropriate electronic resources are available, and that students are provided with the skills to use them.

References

ACORN (1997a) *Academic staff survey report.* http://acorn.lboro.ac.uk/reports/acadfi.htm

ACORN (1997b) *Heads of Agreement.* http://acorn.lboro.ac.uk/hoa.htm

ACORN (1997c) *Summary of ACORN Permissions Information Report. Phase one, semester two, 1996/97.* http://acorn.lboro.ac.uk/perm/summar.htm

ACORN (1997d) *Phase one usage report* (unpublished data)

American Library Association (1982) *Model policy concerning college and university photocopying for classroom, research and library reserve use.* Chicago: A.L.A.

Brown, D. J. (1996) *Electronic publishing and libraries,* pp. 18–19. London: Bowker-Saur

Copyright-Licensing Agency (CLA). Rightsholders support CLA moves to license digitization. News release. 23rd January 1998. Http://www.cla.co.uk/www/press16.htm

ELINOR (a) http://ford.mk.dmu.ac.uk/Projects/ELINOR/

ELINOR (b) *Model licence agreement* http://ford.mk.dmu.ac.uk/Projects/ELINOR/copyrt.html

Eurotext (1997) *Eurotext evaluation : students.* http://eurotext.ulst.ac.uk/background/eval/stud/index.htm

Friend, F. (1997) *Re : course packs* . Electronic mail message on course packs, from F. Friend, University College London, ucylfjf@ucl.ac.uk

JISC/PA (1997a) *Proposed 'model licence' between UK universities and publishers.* http://www.ukoln.ac.uk/services/elib/papers/pa/licence/intro.html

JISC/PA (1997b) *Copyright clearance and digitization in UK higher education : supporting study for the JISC/PA Clearance Mechanisms Working Party.* http://www.ukoln.ac.uk/services/elib/papers/pa/clearance/

JISC/PA (1997c) *Report of the Joint information Systems Committee and Publishers Association Working Party on fair dealing in an electronic environment.*   http://www.ukoln.ac.uk/services/elib/papers/pa/fair/intro.html

JISC/PA (1997d) Charging mechanism for digitized texts. Second supporting study for the JISC/PA, by Mark Bide, Charles Oppenheim and Anne Ramsden. Http://www/ukoln.ac.uk/services/elib/papers/pa/charging

McRory, L. M. *On-Demand Publishing in the Humanities Project. Eliciting feedback.* http://www.livjm.ac.uk/on_demand/eval-web.htm

PATRON (1997) *Application development.* http://www.lib.surrey.ac.uk/eLib/Patron/Patron.htm

Phoenix (1997) *Project Phoenix Milestone 3 Report* p.15 http://www.hud.ac.uk/schools/phoenix/web_docs/ms3r.pdf

Porter, S. (1996a) *Progress update : optical character recognition* On-Demand Publishing in the Humanities Project http://www.livjm.ac.uk/on_demand/progress.htm

Porter, S. (1996b) *Progress update : student responses.* On-Demand Publishing in the Humanities Project. http://www.livjm.ac.uk/on_demand/progress.htm

ResIDe (1997a) *ResIDe user survey.* http://www.uwe.ac.uk/library/itdev/reside/usersrvy.htm

ResIDe (1997b) *ResIDe student focus group report.* http://www.uwe.ac.uk/library/itdev/reside/studntfg.htm

SCOPE (1996) *Annual Report : Project Year 1, 1 Apr 1995 - 14 May 1996, updated to 31 July 1996.* http://www.stir.ac.uk/infoserv/scope/docs/annrep/year1/

SCOPE (1997) *Model contract for licensing on-demand publishing in academic libraries.* http://www.stir.ac.uk/infoserv/scope/docs/contract/v4.htm

Soete, G. J. (1996) *Issues and innovations in electronic reserves.* Transforming Libraries Series. Washington: Association of Research Libraries

Sykes. P. (1996) *Agreeing a price for electronic documents.* On-Demand Publishing in the Humanities Project. http://www.livjm.ac.uk/on_demand/pricing.htm

Tavistock Institute (1996) *Guidelines for eLib project evaluation.* http://www.ukoln.ac.uk/services/elib/papers/tavistock/evaluation-guide/

Tuck, W. (1996) *Electronic copyright management systems : final report of a scoping study for eLib.* http://www.sbu.ac.uk/litc/copyright/ecms.html

Wellesley-Smith, H. (1997) unpublished data

Zimin, W., Ramsden, A. and Zhao, D. (1995) The user perspective of the ELINOR electronic library. *Aslib Proceedings,* **47**, 13–22

CHAPTER THIRTY ONE
Managing the Evolving Map Library

Patrick McGlamery

Introduction

At the 1994 Meeting of the Groupe des Cartothécaires des
LIBER in Zurich a discussion of the role of the map librarian
in the 'information' age isolated two divergent approaches.
One consideration described, and advocated, an approach
which depended on the cartographic object–the map–as the
essential and primary carrier of spatial information (Perkins,
1995). The other consideration argued that the map was a
carrier and storage object of spatial information, as are
gazetteers, travel guides, air photos and, in fact, telephone
books. The argument that the emerging 'print media' of
digital spatial data was having a profound effect on the
librarian's role in spatial data was the focus of the meeting
(McGlamery, 1995). In fact, the two considerations reflected
the traditional passive and active approaches our profession
takes in response to change. In this case the passive role was
described by a professional geographer serving as the curator
of a university geography department map collection. The
active role was argued by a university map librarian whose

professional interests are information science, especially spatial information. The considerations bear a thorough discussion, as they are at the heart of the ability, or inability, of libraries to respond to changing information needs.

The conservative, or passive, approach focuses on the medium of the information, and takes to heart the categorization of information in libraries by format. In fact, in the paper world, a strong consideration of *how* materials are stored makes good economic sense. The library edifice as a storage facility is the clearest and first concept of the library. Only after the collection is built, and the user begins to access the materials, does the information component of the material collection begin to take form. Is the information stored in the collection timely? Is it comprehensive? Is it readable ... accessible? As much as libraries use the organization of materials by format, it is the information which most interests the user. In a map library it might be the location of a site – an archaeological or historical site, an engineering project or Aunt Tillie's birthday party. Timely, comprehensive, readable maps enable the seeker to convert the information carried by the map into knowledge. Only a small component of our user community is interested in the map for the map's sake. The overwhelming majority of users are interested in the dense information features of cartography. Most users augment the information from the map with information from other sources, often because the paper map is capable of limited storage and display. Until recently (with the advent of desktop mapping computer programs) authors called upon the services of trained cartographers to create the knowledge they needed to communicate in books and papers. Users more generally made throw-away sketch maps of the route to Aunt Tillie's house, or more carefully rendered maps depending on their education and training–their cartographic skills. Perkins' argument that map-making should be left to the cartographer is wise counsel indeed. But it is not the making of maps that is the critical issue before us.

The critical issue for librarians today is to make accessible information that will never be printed. Data is simply not available as hard-copy. Nor will it ever be because the nature of working with spatial information has been fundamentally changed by GIS (Geographical Information Systems). GIS enable the user to work with dynamic, timely and comprehensive information. Digital spatial data, an information phenomenom of the computer technology, enables the storage and access of multivariate data, expanding the constraints of the paper map. In fact, the map becomes primarily a report or communication device for the database. Data gathering and compilation has always been the greatest challenge of the cartographer. With a wealth of digital spatial data available to the regular user, the burden of good cartographic presentation is passed on to the regular user. These bottlenecks to spatial information impede librarians in providing service to their users. There are a number of reasons for spatial information bottlenecks:

- radical technological advances in data collection (such as satellite imagery), have created simply too much data to print;
- in the past, printing was the only distribution method. A press-run of one or five hundred was the same. Today specialized maps for limited groups of decision makers have resulted in 'one-off' plots, reducing the number of published maps which find their way into map libraries;
- GIS offer an entirely new and evocative way to analyse data for decision making, which might, or might not, be output as a map;
- issues of copyright and intellectual property model the paper environment.

Paper maps have been a part of library collections for centuries. In the last decade, digital mapping, geospatial data or geodata have begun to be a part of information services in libraries. Geodata can cover a range of types of information, including digital maps, tabular data such as census tabulations, point data as varied as temperature, street addresses or species locations, and other sorts of numerical data which have spatiality. This chapter will describe levels of service, explain the types of geodata, their general availability, issues relating to access of data and spatial metadata.

Much of the mapping we see on paper has been in a digital format for at least a decade. Maps are, by their nature, numeric and therefore inherently digital. That is, they are geo-referenced to the earth's surface by some sort of co-ordinate system such as latitude and longitude. In addition, in order to represent these numbers on flat paper (or a flat screen), the co-ordinate system is rendered through a projection, such as Mercator's or Lambert Conformal. There are a number of co-ordinate systems depending on the needs of the map makers and their clients. Lat/Long, based on the number twelve (as are our calendar and time systems) is not particularly friendly for either computers or people. Decimal co-ordinate systems, such as 1000 meter grids, have emerged over time to resolve calculations and to provide for finer levels of gradation. A point, line or polygon on a map is represented in a digital file by a number or series of numbers representing the X/Y value of that point or points. A single set of numbers can represent the central point of a city, while two sets of numbers represent a street and a more than three sets of numbers represent a city block or the boundaries of the city.

These data sets often have little or no textual information, therefore are not compatible with text-based search engines such as Websearchers or harvesters. Additionally, each software program uses its own proprietary format, not necessarily ASCII, for storing the data. These software programs are called Geographic Information Systems. A GIS is a 'computer system capable of holding and using data describing places on the earth's surface. ... An organized collection of computer hardware, software, geographic data and personnel designed to efficiently capture, store, update, manipulate, analyze and display all forms of geographically referenced information.' (ESRI, 1990). Because a GIS is a spatial database management system, the user is able to query, assess, reconfigure and generate new datasets. GISs enable the user to use geospatial data in exciting new ways, but not without extensive mediation.

Levels of Service

As with any other library operations, it is of primary importance to determine the needs of the client group before determining either the collection or level of service for geospatial information. These levels are more or less cumulative. A hierarchical range of geospatial services might be:

1. general reference tools such as routing programs, general electronic atlases or maps on CD-ROM. These services can be provided on a stand alone machine, a local area network or via the Internet;
2. More specific reference tools based on thematic or regional needs of the client group such as natural resources data, social science or business data;
3. Specialized input and output devices such as scanners and large format printers and plotters;
4. Lab situation for editing and manipulation of data especially proprietary data.

Level 1

General reference tools generally fall into three categories; viewing a map, accessing some other type of spatial information such as routing and simple mapping of thematic data. There are a number of map viewing packages available, for example various Bartholomew's products (http://www.geo.ed.ac.uk/~barts_twr/maincont.html) and DeLormes' Global Explorer (http://www.delorme.com/). These use CD-ROM as a medium for distributing maps of countries of the world down to a city level. They work best on stand-alone machines. These packages and most other mapping packages are best provided with a colour inkjet printer. Interacting with a map interface provides the quickest method of accessing geospatial information, but often the user will make use of a gazetteer to get to the data.

Routing software is a good example of a gazetteer interface and of accessing another type of spatial data than a map. Microsoft's AutoRoute on CD-ROM, or AutoRoute Express and MapQuest on the Internet (http://autoroute.msn.com/) are good examples of these sorts of application programs. MapQuest will calculate a 'best route' from one street address in the United States to another. These sorts of routing packages often allow the user to determine fastest, shortest routes with several variables such as no high-speed highways (a good choice for cycling). The user is presented with an itinerary and/or a map of the trip.

Mapping thematic data, such as demographic data has become extremely simple with computer mapping. The challenge has been to enable the user to create maps which communicate information rather than cartographic objects which look like maps, but which mis-inform. Good examples of thematic mapping in a controlled program are the US Bureau of the Census' mapping programs LandView II (http://www.census.gov/ftp/pub/geo/www/tiger/lv2info .html) and Demographic Data Viewer (http://plue.sedac. ciesin.org/plue/ddviewer/). LandView is a CD-ROM package which works on a stand- alone machine with a printer. The staff of the Bureau of the Census have taken much of the cartographic decision-making out of the process. It is a simple, easy-to-use program that does not allow the user to do much more than map variables and present those maps as clear cartography. In the United States LandView is sent free to over 400 libraries.

Level 2

The next level of service is enhanced collection development. Narrowing in on the state and city, or topical level, the greater the detailed information, the lesser the likelihood that the data have been published in any real manner. This is not necessarily a bad thing, but it is difficult. The library will have to contract for data. This often means determining who the data producer is and working through the problems of providing reference services to the data. It might simply mean directing the library user to a state or local agency. It might mean working out a budget in support of this service. At the University of Connecticut it has meant working with the data producers of the Connecticut Department of Environment Protection to put their data on a Web site and manage it. This co-operative relationship has meant quicker access to data in a number of formats. In fact, the relationship has its antecedents in the strong partnership of libraries as distributors of public government information, a partnership that goes back 60 years in the United States. These partnerships exist in all countries and renegotiating the social contract between libraries and government can be a beneficial thing. In any event, in Sharing Geographic Information (Onsrud, 1995) the clear consensus of the specialists was that the impediments to sharing spatial information are more social than technical. Making the data available in-house, on the Internet or both is more a reflection of the user community than the collection development decision. In any event, it is most important to have the data on a network. The files more often than not exceed the capacity of standard floppy drives. A good example is UKBorders via EDINA (http://edina.ed.ac.uk), a co-operative boundary file archive managed by the University of Edinburgh. This archive of boundary files down to the administrative level is available to consortia members in a number of formats for research use. The datafiles are owned by the Crown copyright and made available to the academic user only. In Canada a similar process is emerging to make geospatial data whose copyright is held by the government available in university research libraries. The important piece to consider in each of these cases–Connecticut's, the United Kingdom's and Canada's is the contract, negotiated by the library for the user community.

Level 3

Input and output devices define the next level of service. Large format scanners and printers and plotters are expensive even in today's climate of declining prices. Conventional paper maps are large and maps generated on a computer are also large. The computer will not release us from large pieces of paper.

Scanners are much like copy machines, except that they copy to a file rather than to another piece of paper. A good desktop scanner will copy aerial photos at high enough resolution for archaeological use, and at a reasonable price. Depending on the granularity of the information (aerial photographs have very high granularity, whereas navigational charts are rather low) the object can be scanned at 100 to 600 dpi (dots per inch). After the object is scanned, it can be geo-referenced, that is, an appropriate co-ordinate system and projection can be added to the file and it becomes a dataset of 256 grey scales. The geo-referencing points are taken from maps or an information technology called GPS or Geo-Positioning System and entered into the image using image analysis software such as ERDAS Imagine, ER Mapper or Idrisi. Scanners are the interface between the library's paper collection and its digital use. The files, depending on the dpi, will be rather large (over 10 Mb) and will need a powerful machine to capture and process the data. Users of this type of data usually invest in a IOmega zip drive with a capacity of 100 Mb per disk. The library's machine should have either an internal or external drive. The service provided is great, access to a collection of analogue spatial data, its copy and conversion, resulting in a file which the user can plug into.

Another input device is the digitizer, or digitizing tablet or table. This device is a surface upon which the map is fixed and, using a puck, the information is traced. It is an electronic light table. The work is as slow and tedious as it was to work with tracing paper. This device negates erasures and white-out however. Often, especially for limited projects, this sort of intensive input is the only way to go. Tablets can be circulated to the user for their use at home, their office or lab. GIS software packages generally support a digitizing module.

Plotters are large printers. There is a range of paper sizes which these plotters support, from sizes A to E (36 × 48 inches). The least expensive plotter is a pen plotter. This can often be obtained for free from engineering companies that are trading up to an inkjet plotter. The pen plotter is a slow proposition, drawing each line of the map with an appropriately coloured pen. The inkjet plotter uses the same technology as an inkjet printer, but with larger paper and more ink. It lays down colour as the paper feeds through. A pen plot can take up to three hours to draw, depending on the complexity of the map, whereas the inkjet plot will take a fraction of that. The service to the user is a shared machine, often the only one available. Cost for copy can be passed on to the user.

Level 4

The highest level of service provides a lab with appropriate and up-to-date software packages, input and output devices, user workspace and storage and staff for consultation. A lab is much like a reading room for digital geodata, with one very important caveat: it is a lot more costly. Supporting hardware and software and doing consulting can take at least two highly trained people in addition to the librarian. The University of Minnesota's John Borchert Library is an example of this sort of service.

Types of Geodata

The varieties of geo-spatial data are significant enough to describe in some detail. The need for the librarian to have a passing understanding of data formats and data models increases depending upon the level of service, of course, but a fundamental grasp of vector, raster and attribute data is imperative. These three forms of data are joined together in a GIS. Co-ordinate systems and projection are foundations of geo-spatial data; they provide the geographical context. Vector data, or nodes connected by arcs, and raster data, or columns and rows of data values each require co-ordinates and projection to link to the earth's surface. Vector data are most relevant for line features. These primitives join together to form street or hydrographic features for example. Topology is information which indicates to the line primitive what its neighbour is, thereby creating networks, perhaps hierarchical or perhaps a tree structure, depending on the data model. ArcINFO is an example of a GIS which uses topology, MapInfo is an example of a GIS which does not. Both use vector data, each have their client group. It is generally accepted the topological GISs are more powerful tools for analysis than those which lack topology.

Polygons are line features which come together to form a closed unit. They are vectors with a body and often form boundaries or spatial units such as soil types, voting districts or plant colonies. Choropleth mapping, maps that shade districts by quantiles, link attribute data to the identification code of the polygon. These simple forms of computer mapping are often used to display demographic information. Once the boundary file exists any sort of data can be joined to it. The town boundary files from MAGIC, the University of Connecticut Library's Map and Geographic Information Center, can be used to map attribute data from a variety of state agencies such as incidences of Lyme disease or rabies from the Department of Public Health, well drilling permits or deer counts from the Department of Environmental Protection, burglaries from the State Police and per pupil cost of education from the Department of Education. Additionally private data such as real estate transactions, sales and so on can be mapped and these data can be co-related with demographic data to give new perspectives of the State's consumer profile. Attribute data need a variable to link them to the polygon or line feature.

General Availability

Geodata have emerged as a substantial contemporary market. Competition is fierce among publishers to produce quality products for various user groups. Educational, home use and academic products abound, with more coming to the marketplace each year. Most geodata begin at the governmental information level. Data at the national level in Britain are maintained by the Ordnance Survey (http://www.ordsvy.gov.uk). Educational use of British Ordnance Survey geodata is clear:

5. What the licence permits–digital map data:
    5.6 The use of Ordnance Survey mapping in machine readable form is included in the licence subject to the following conditions: digital mapping is used solely for teaching, lecturing and university research projects only; and prior written permission must be obtained from Ordnance Survey in order to digitize detail from any of our maps. If permission is given, further royalties may be payable.
6. What the licence does not permit:
    6.1 The licence does not cover: copies made for any purpose other than teaching, for example, mapping in a school brochure or prospectus; copies reproduced by outside printers; any work intended for sale or distribution to the public or any outside organization; the transfer of Ordnance Survey material onto computer media for other purposes; and digitizing and scanning of Ordnance Survey mapping or copying of Ordnance Survey data by outside firms or computer bureau.
    6.2 On each occasion that you wish to make copies that come under any of the above categories, prior permission must be obtained from Copyright Licensing. (from http://www.ordsvy.govt.uk/services/index.html).

The Ordnance Survey Interactive Atlas of Great Britain is an interactive general reference atlas of Great Britain. It is intended for family and educational use and offers a wide range of mapping detail including full coverage of Great Britain at 1:625 000 scale (1 cm to 6.25 km or 1 inch to 10 miles) and 1:250 000 scale (1 cm to 2.5 km or 1 inch to 4 miles). It is described at http://www.microcolour.com/osatlas.htm.

The primary mission of the Combined Higher Education Software Team (CHEST, http://www.chest.ac.uk/) is to obtain quality software and datasets for the UK higher education and research community at low prices and attractive terms. Although the community CHEST serves is primarily that of UK higher education and research institutions, it will normally make its agreements available to all of education where this can be achieved. CHEST has been responsible for negotiating many agreements for datasets, including the ISI Citation Indexes, Embase, Compendex, OCLC and FirstSearch.

CHEST has negotiated agreements for geodata from Harper Collins (Bartholomew's Digital Map Data), Ordnance Survey (digital data from sample areas); the National Remote Sensing Center (satellite data from Landsat and SPOT) and most recently from GeoInformation International (Cities Revealed, digitized aerial photography); and for GIS software from ESRI (ARC/INFO and ArcView), Erdas (IMAGINE) and GE Capital IT Solutions (eXceed, X windows emulation).

EDINA (http://edina.ed.ac.uk/) at Edinburgh University Data Library provides national online services for the UK higher education and research community. Services range from bibliographic data to research metadata and geographic information systems, and include UKBORDERS, a database of digitized boundaries, as mentioned above. Academic staff and students at UK higher education and research institutions may make use of the most comprehensive set of UK boundary data as yet assembled. These are particularly well-suited to computer-aided mapping of the small area statistics from the 1991 Population Census but will have many other uses also. As well as allowing users to map 1991 Census data systematically at any scale from small area to the whole country, the digitized boundary data (DBD)can be used to design new zones from the small area building blocks and to integrate census data fully in geographical information systems.

Other commercial publications

The *Times Electronic World Map*. It is described at http://www.geo.ed.ac.uk/~barts_twr/maincont.html This product, produced by the Electronic Publishing Department of Bartholomew/Times, is a dedicated database asset system for interactive maps and statistics. The database features over 5000 places and geographical locations, 50 statistical categories, 6 map scales, over 1000 map views, over 400 000 different map combinations, and country descriptions covering politics, current affairs and economic information. The Bartholomew London 1:5000, Great Britain 1:250 000, Europe 1:1 000 000, World 1:20 000 000, *GB Maps on CD-ROM* and *EuroMaps on CD-ROM* products are currently available through the CHEST scheme at a fraction of the normal prices. Bartholomew have specifically extended the coverage of the scheme to include all European universities and other similar educational establishments. Contact your institution's CHEST co-ordinator for further details, e-mail CHEST, or visit the CHEST web site.

AutoRoute Express is available as a stand-alone product and is now available via the Internet at http://autoroute.msn. com/ It is a route planner and gazetteer.

The Digital Chart of the World, ed. 1 is a set of geodata in the global public domain. It is at a scale of 1:1 000 000 and at the University of Pennsylvania server (http://www. maproom.psu.edu/dcw/) is downloadable by country in ArcINFO export format.

Chadwyck-Healey distributes the *World Climate Disc*, a CD-ROM product. The disc was published in 1992. It uses data assembled by The Hadley Center for Climatic Prediction and Research of the Meteorological Office, UK and the Climatic Research Unit at the University of East Anglia. The disc contains mainly meteorological data sets, some of which are relevant to oceanography.

British Isles from the Air, a CD-ROM published by Anglia Multimedia Ltd. holds over 200 aerial photographs of man-made and natural features in the British Isles. Some of the photographs are historical, the earliest dating back to 1922. Occasionally both oblique and vertical views of the same feature appear.

Earthscapes in Time–The See-Through Satellite Atlas, a CD-ROM product (http://www.hyperdrive.com/time/index.html) provides 26 case studies of geographical change over time. Each case study contains a map, two or more satellite images (from different times) and background information on the images, area, the satellites used and sources of imagery. These are presented so that the user can compare the images and maps to investigate the changes over time. Examples include the effect and regeneration after Mount St. Helen's eruption, deforestation in the Brazilian rainforest and pollution around Mexico City.

Encarta 96 World Atlas, (http://microsoft.com/catalog/products/EncAtlas/), another CD-ROM product is published by Microsoft. It is a good undergraduate general atlas.

Issues Relating to Access of Data

Size, copyright and format of the data are major issues. Geodata can be large. Vector and raster coverages of high resolution spaces can easily exceed 50 Mb. Storage has become less of a problem as storage costs plummet. In 1997 a 9 Gigabyte drive sold for $1,700. Transporting these large files will continue to be a problem. Zip drives and writeable CD-ROM will alleviate the problem, but for most of the user community, networks will provide the best solutions. MAGIC, at the University of Connecticut, is an example of an Internet library of digital geodata. It stores over 15 000 files of spatial data of the State of Connecticut for free use. The data are generally produced by state and federal agencies and in the US public domain. Occupying over 10 Gb of storage, it is readily used and re-used by its client group. The user is transferring the cost of storage to the library, while absorbing the cost of telecommunications. Size will continue to be a major issue for geodata, as map size is a hallmark of paper map collections.

Copyright and intellectual property rights are as important in the digital library as they are in the conventional library. Availability of spatial information on the Internet is a function of availability of public use data. MapQuest (http://www. mapquest.com/) can make street and address level information available because in the United States federally produced spatial data is more often than not in the public domain. The 1990 decennial census made available fairly good street and address information for the country at a scale of 1:100 000 through its TIGER project. The general availability of geospatial data in the United States has made for a very innovative environment. New uses of geospatial data emerge every day, forecasting the entrepreneurial use of geodata, albeit free.

Data formats, that is, proprietary formats, are varied and provide challenges for the user. The Open GIS Consortium, Inc. (OGC, http://www.opengis.org/) is a unique membership organization dedicated to open system approaches to geoprocessing. By means of its consensus building and technology development activities, OGC has had a significant impact on the global geodata and geoprocessing standards community, and has successfully promoted a vision of Open GIS technologies that integrate geoprocessing with the distributed architectures of the emerging global information infrastructure. Hopefully, as geographic software developers co-operate with the philosophy of OGC, the impediments to sharing information will minimalize.

Spatial Metadata

Metadata is data about data. This simple sentence does little to convey the complexity of metadata in general and spatial metadata in particular. The past four years have seen a drive to create and standardize various forms of metadata. Most recently there have been a number of co-operative efforts, including The 'Dublin Core,' shorthand for the Dublin Metadata Core Element Set, is a core list of metadata elements agreed at the OCLC/NCSA Metadata Workshop in March 1995. The workshop report forms the documentation for the Dublin Core element set (http://www.oclc.org: 5046/conferences/metadata/dublin_core_report.html>). Projects and publications of the UK Office for Library and Information Networking (UKOLN, http://www.ukoln. ac.uk/metadata/) are also helpful. The most comprehensive spatial metadata format, and a starting point for international co-operation of spatial metadata standards is the *Content Standard for Digital Geospatial Metadata*, known as the FGDC Metadata Standard. *A Solicitation of Comments for the Revision of the Content Standard for Digital Geospatial Metadata* is available at http://www.mews.org/nsdi/. The form of the metadata is inclusive and comprehensive, including as it does fields from the USMARC Maps format.

Spatial metadata is a catalogue record for large numeric electronic files. The files, typically non-textual, require metadata for two important purposes; as searchable records on an on-line catalogue, or Clearinghouse, and as narrative text describing the dataset for the user. A good example of the Clearinghouse concept is the National Spatial Data Infrastructure (NSDI, http://www.fgdc.gov/clearinghouse/ index.html). The Clearinghouse activity, sponsored by the Federal Geographic Data Committee (FGDC), is a decentralized system of servers located on the Internet which contain field-level descriptions of available digital spatial data. Clearinghouse uses readily available Web technology for the client side and uses the ANSI standard Z39.50 for the query, search and presentation of search results to the Web client.

A fundamental goal of a Clearinghouse is to provide access to digital spatial data through metadata. The NSDI Clearinghouse functions as a detailed catalogue service with support for links to spatial data and browse graphics. Clearinghouse sites are encouraged to provide hypertext linkages within their metadata entries that enable users to download directly the digital data set in one or more formats. Where digital data are too large to be made available through the Internet or the data products are made available for sale, linkage to an order form can be provided in lieu of a data set. Through this model, Clearinghouse metadata provides low-cost advertising for providers of spatial data, both non-commercial and commercial, to potential customers via the Internet.

The Clearinghouse enables individual agencies, consortia, or geographically- defined communities to band together and promote their available digital spatial data. Servers may be installed at local, regional or central offices, dictated by the organizational and logistical efficiencies of each organization. All Clearinghouse servers are considered 'peers' within the Clearinghouse activity–there is no hierarchy among the servers–permitting direct query by any user on the Internet with minimum transactional processing. The Clearinghouse concept resembles a loose federation of libraries. Some libraries in the United States are involved in the NSDI, while others are beginning to learn of the service.

Summary

Geographic information system, and geodata are transforming the way society deals with geographic information. There will continue to be maps, of course. Cartography is more important as the number of potential cartographers move into the information arena. The role of libraries should transform to reflect changes in the information society. A management strategy is to scale the levels of service depending on the clients served and the resources available. Levels of service range from general reference to highly specific laboratories. There are a variety of types of geodata, sharing the common constraints of co-ordinate systems and projections. Vector, raster and attribute data must be understood and managed as data. Each have its strengths and weaknesses, each have their special needs from a library management point of view. Geodata are not necessarily accessible. New relationships need to be fostered between data producers and publishers and libraries. Finally, spatial metadata is cataloguing, and libraries need to understand and become involved in the metadata discussions, perhaps even managing metadata collections or clearing houses.

References

Environmental Systems Research Institute (ESRI) (1990) *Understanding GIS: The ARC/INFO Method*. ESRI: Redlands, CA

McGlamery, P. (1995) Maps and spatial information: changes in the map library, European Research Libraries Cooperation: *The LIBER Quarterly*, **5**, 229–234

Onsrud, H. J. and Rushton, G. (1995) (eds.) *Sharing geographic information*. New Brunswick, N.J.: Center for Urban Policy Research

Perkins, C. R. (1995) Leave it in the labs? Options for the future of map and spatial data collections, European Research Libraries Cooperation. *The LIBER Quarterly*, **5**, 312–329

CHAPTER THIRTY TWO

Managing the Web – The University of Exeter Experience

Martin Myhill and Ian Tilsed

Introduction

The University of Exeter Library offers, according to recent
user satisfaction surveys and Teaching Quality Audits, an
excellent subject-support service. Like most British university
libraries, Exeter has suffered the pressures caused by large-
scale expansion of student numbers, declining book funds
(in real terms) and the relentless demands resulting from
the introduction of new technology. Through the LIBERTAS
system, the library has provided a fully-networked online
catalogue since 1990 complete with remote access capability.
In 1992, the library launched one of the first UK-based
campus-wide networked, bibliographic CD-ROM services
using the Multiplatter system. In 1993, after discussions with
the then computer unit, one of the senior library staff became
joint *gopher master* for the University with a remit to explore
the possibilities afforded by this latest technology. It was not
long before links were made with other gopher servers. And
then, in 1994 attention was turned to the Web, as described
elsewhere (Myhill, 1995).

Libraries and Changing Technology

The University of Exeter Library relies on a team of subject librarians to provide subject support. Seven of these are based in separate site libraries and six are located in the main library. Most were career-trained in the use of catalogue cards, filing rules and typewriters rather than Java, Active X and HTML. Like many library colleagues elsewhere, they have experienced many stages of development including microfiche catalogues, retrospective cataloguing, increasing adoption of computer technology and on to the more recent introduction of online datasets and Windows-based programs including Web browsers. In each case, library staff (not just subject librarians) have had to learn to exploit these information systems to the full.

There have been a number of catalysts which have promoted this change, many of which apply to other libraries.

- Subject librarians are justifiably proud of the service they provide to users. They have a deserved reputation to maintain and this includes using all available technologies as appropriate to the need of the moment;
- The technology itself is useful in assisting their work. Compare manually checking the printed version of the ISI Social Science Index with a quick flit through the online BIDS-based version;
- Libraries tend to implement simple-concept yet 'killer applications' (such as online catalogues) with widespread appeal and can rarely afford to experiment with the latest 'state-of-the-art' thinking. Most of the technology introduced into libraries has worked (some with significant teething troubles) and created the inevitable demand for more and better systems;
- Expectations of the 'virtual' library are encouraging use of 'front-ended' systems offering one-stop access. While use of the Web is especially important here, sophisticated search engines such as those using Z39.50 standards are

also catalysts because they make the search for information a more effective process;
- Users themselves are coming to libraries with an increased
  expectation of information technology provision (whether
  they know how to use it or not). While this leaves librarians in a difficult position regarding reinvestment in technology and training when faced with declining budgets,
  fees from users pay many of the library's running costs
  and their corporate views should not be ignored;
- Aware of the constant change taking place, librarians have
  put in place all sorts of training schemes to support their
  staff. As well as training courses organized by professional
  associations, most libraries now have training officers and
  training plans. Provision includes continuing development
  for established staff and detailed induction programmes
  for new staff. Most librarians offer their staff some form
  of personal development plan and set aside resources to
  support it.

If this helps to explain why subject librarians have been
able to adopt new technologies so readily it also raises the
important question of management. Frequently the changes
referred to above have been the result of a 'knee-jerk' reaction–perhaps fear of losing the competitive edge or demands
for up-to-date bibliographic systems from vociferous departments. In the case of the World Wide Web there are similar
reasons, such as special interest by a small group of staff,
why development might be haphazard and unplanned. It
has widespread acceptance in many walks of life. While
much of the information it contains might be classified as
useless, misleading, of dubious importance or illegal, there
is much to commend some of its resources to the information professional. Unlike the gopher system with (in
hindsight) its seemingly more limited capabilities, continued
advances in Web browsers (such as the latest 'desktop'
features of Microsoft's Internet Explorer version 4) linking
word-processing to Web publishing and electronic mail
merge the three most important functions of this phase of

the information revolution. The Web browser already provides the front-end to many varied information systems. Search engines such as Alta Vista or Lycos offer complex retrieval systems to this global library of information. Librarians cannot afford to ignore the vital nature of these developments in the same way that they could not ignore a spilt card catalogue tray.

Managing this change in a regulated manner is a difficult business. Since 1994, the University of Exeter Library has developed a substantial set of Web pages to exploit the possibilities afforded by this particular information concept. These pages are heavily used by both staff and students within the university and others world-wide. They consist of local guides, general links to catalogues, Web indexes and the like, specific links to sites of popular interest such as virtual museums and galleries, and highly developed subject trees reflecting the current faculty structure of the university. Creation of the subject pages is the responsibility of the respective subject librarian, while the general pages fall to the library's own Web Editor (who combines this post with that as Library Computing Development Officer). Management can be divided into macromanagement (those areas relating to layers of Web management, people, provision of technology and finance) and micromanagement (covering page structure and layout, HTML usage and style, and system management and liaison). Both types, in the Exeter experience, involve considerable discussion and committee work.

Macromanagement

Given the factors influencing the adoption of new technology by subject librarians and the growing, global appeal of the Web, the University Librarian established a Web Management Group in 1995. The remit of the group was to develop an appropriate Web strategy for the library including appropriate pages and subject trees. The membership of this group included those with an already clear vision of the uses of the Web, including the Education Subject Librarian (*gopher-master* and member of the university Electronic Information Working Group), the Library Computing Development Officer, the Science Subject Librarian and the Systems' Librarian. This ensured links with subject librarians and the emerging 'official' University development of the Web as well as the library's IT Steering Group as a forum for discussing equipment purchases.

Top level web management

This is a key management issue because it relates to respon-sibility. Previous gopher experience at Exeter uncovered a number of vital issues which had to be resolved before progressing Web development. Most of these concerned the University in general rather than the library but discussions were carried out by the Electronic Information Working Group, at which the library was represented.

The decisions followed a relatively logical path.

1. There would be official university pages and unofficial pages. Library pages would be regarded as official pages.
2. The University Registrar would be ultimately responsible for the legality of official university pages.
3. Although individual page styles would be allowed, each official page would contain a statement of ownership and would offer a path back to the University Web home page and its disclaimer.
4. The author of each page would be responsible for its main-tenance including checking links.
5. Originally the Head of the External Relations Division expected to oversee each page but this idea was soon abandoned in view of the sheer volume of pages published.
6. All electronic documents were to reflect existing paper versions (e.g. University calendar) – including errors.

Personpower

It was decided at an early stage to involve all subject librarians in the Web development process. The reasons for this relate entirely to the nature of the Web–it would have been unprofessional to ignore the needs of any one of our subject areas–and the special knowledge of each subject librarian. In practice, some areas developed faster than others. This was often the result of different technical abilities rather than time pressures.

The key personnel issues in this global approach were:

Editorship

The library was fortunate to have appointed Ian Tilsed as Computing Development Officer in 1995 in order to promote and support the growing use of microcomputers by library staff and users within the library. He had followed the early Web and gopher developments and was well versed in the use of Hypertext Mark-up Language, HTML. Having established a Web Management Group that included him (the other members all had some degree of subject involvement), it was a relatively simple task to add the role of Web Editor to the duties of this willing Computing Development Officer. Responsibility for the library's general Web pages (guides, announcements etc.) was also vested in him.

Training

Gopher development had been a comparatively simple matter. The University gopher master, Martin Myhill, had sole access rights and any information submitted had to be added by him. While this partly explains the short life history of the gopher system at the University of Exeter, it also confirmed that a much wider group of individuals would be necessary to support a parallel Web-based development. For the reasons described above, it should be clear that there was considerable (although not universal) enthusiasm amongst the subject librarians to be involved in Web development.

However, very few subject librarians had any HTML knowledge at this stage. It should be noted that although use of word-processing software was commonplace amongst this group at this time there was no access to any HTML converter software. Having established the library Web Management Group and an editor, it was also necessary to offer training and on-going advice to all subject librarians. Training was provided in formal teaching sessions by the library's Web Editor and informally by a series of mentoring sessions where each member of the Web Management Group took responsibility to assist individual subject librarians in their production of Web pages.

Maintenance

The Web may be regarded as an animate object. The pace of development, both in technical advance and in the number of pages added or developed, likens it less to the work of a spider and more to the growth of a highly vigorous creeper. It is not enough to develop one set of pages, however sophisticated, and then leave them alone. Style changes introduced by the Web Management Group, usually at the bidding of the Electronic Information Working Group or university Web Master (http://www.ex.ac.uk/EAD/Extrel/wwwregs4.htm) have encouraged subject librarians to keep their pages up-to-date. At the same time, no doubt prompted by having to access their pages, subject librarians have added further links and improvements. As more users discover the benefits of the various Web engines, however, the impetus for ever-evolving subject trees is slowing. A further maintenance factor which has to be considered is frequently checking the functioning of existing links. Technical factors have precluded the use of software such as MomSpider to assist this task although recent software announcements (see later) will make this an easier process before long. Instead, library staff have either made the most of times of slack demand (such as evening duties) or passed the task to other staff such as graduate trainee library assistants in return for Web training.

Technology

Web management and personnel-related issues are closely linked to technological issues. For use of the Web to be effective, it is necessary for there to be sufficient computers to allow access (both to authors and users), for these to be of an adequate standard and for server or local response times to be acceptable. In this context the pace of global Web development is out-stripped only by continued advances in computer processing power and this raises its own challenges to anyone seeking to manage Web development.

At the University of Exeter Library there were a number of specific challenges. The library has a very good relationship with the university agency responsible for information technology – IT Services (formerly the Computer Unit). All the library's Web pages are stored on the UNIX-based central University Web server managed by IT Services. Unlike the earlier gopher system, as day-to-day responsibility for each page rests on its author, each author had to be registered as a user of the central Web server, allocated file space and taught some basic UNIX commands to assist file management and access control. This involved registering over twenty library staff and a considerable amount of liaison between library staff and IT Services's Web Master.

In 1994, the library was only just beginning to invest in Widows-based PCs for some of its staff. The LIBERTAS system was linked in majority to non-windows-based 'dumb' terminals which also allowed access to the Web server. In the early days of our Web creation, therefore, nearly 50 per cent of the pages were written as ASCII files on such computers. As these could not support anything other than a text-only browser, the author then had to find a 'spare' Windows-based computer running a Web browser to check layout.

In view of this cumbersome process, the library accelerated its introduction of windows-based PCs for its subject librarian team and for users. Not until recently, however, did all subject librarians have access to their own PC and many of these are comparatively modest models (8 Mb RAM 486 PC compatible). As more staff gained this access, it became necessary to standardize the browser. Originally the University had preferred Mosaic but during 1995 Netscape gained increasing popularity and this remains the library's choice. To prevent considerable extra loading on the Computing Development Officer, all library staff PCs will soon be linked to a library server which manages much of the network software centrally.

Finance

At the University of Exeter no additional resources were initially allocated either in terms of staffing or specific equipment to support Web development. While technical specifications for computer purchases have been influenced by Web browser requirements, some subject librarians had to wait for many months before being given their 'own' PCs. While it may be interesting to reflect on what has been achieved at Exeter without directly targeting additional resources, it would be useful to speculate on what might have been achieved with extra staffing and better equipment. By way of example at the time of writing, the University of Exeter Library Web pages make no direct use of Java, frames, video or sound files. The library owns a number of 'treasures' including a substantial, rare sound archive. In this case there are few copyright implications and, finance permitting, this archive would now be available (in part) on the Web. Similarly, our pages would be more interactive and animated which would lead in most cases to more efficient use and be of greater benefit in the desired development of open learning resources.

The University of Exeter uses a model of devolved funding involving an internal financial market. Web development continues to involve members of different university departments. Costs have been absorbed by each department in a spirit of co-operation rather than devolution. Without this (or alternatively targeted resources), development of the Web at Exeter would have been impossible in the current era of financial restraint.

Micromanagement

The strategic decision to publish information on the Web poses considerable micromanagement issues, covering such areas as style, maintenance, training, resourcing and relentless technical developments. In the fast-changing Web environment a mere two years is a 'lifetime' and this poses considerable challenges in any commitment to a Web presence.

Content and purpose

As with any Web site, it is important to establish its purpose. Essentially, it can be said that there are two general 'audiences' for a university library – those within the wider university (staff, students and external borrowers) and those beyond the institution (such as potential visitors and those searching for specific resources). It is often the case that the two are amalgamated in the minds of Web authors, leading to the projection of a sometimes confused and unclear Web strategy. During the early development of the library Web site, the library Web Management Group decided that the nucleus of the online information should be developed from existing hard-copy documentation, thus addressing the information needs of the library's primary 'audience'. This took the form of library user guides and information leaflets, giving such diverse and yet essential information as borrowing rights, opening hours and details of collections. This necessitated both the conversion of word-processed documents and the re-working of the text to suit the nature of the Web. The former posed some problems because of the crude nature of early conversion tools. However, with advanced conversion tools (such as the Internet Assistant for Microsoft Word) now being much more available via familiar desktop software, the problems of simple document conversion are very much a current topic of debate. The Web demands a particular style of writing that reflects the non-linear nature of hypertext documentation. The simple conversion and publishing of a Web document, converted from a word-processed file with little or no editing, does not do justice to either the original text or the possibilities of the computer medium. It was, and continues to be, essential therefore that the conversion of existing texts was carried out in conjunction with the original author in light of the demands of the Web medium.

Beyond the conversion of existing documentation, it was decided to develop new documents specifically written and designed for the Web. A considerable and ongoing commitment to the development of a 'subject tree' (http://www.ex.ac.uk/~ijtilsed/lib/subjecttree.html), listing Internet resources by subjects as taught within the University, has become one of the main examples of a new resource within the Web site. As documented elsewhere (Tilsed, 1996) this enterprise has involved considerable discussion of issues regarding resource classification, evaluation of quality and the resourcing of continual maintenance. The intention of the Web Management Group to encourage and instigate the development of online teaching resources in conjunction with academic departments is another example of the opportunities the Web offers libraries beyond the simple provision of existing user information.

The existence of both hard-copy and electronic information within the library service has posed a challenge to all staff responsible for writing guides and documents. Decisions continually need to be taken regarding the primacy of a particular medium – should the hard-copy document take the lead, or should the material be written for the Web and reworked as necessary for hard copy? Whilst not significantly involving any duplication of effort, thanks to the power of modern office software, it has necessitated a continued commitment to training and the development of differing but appropriate writing styles and techniques.

Style

It is now commonplace for most institutions to have corporate identities, with logos and unusual typefaces gracing everything from stationery to vehicles. The Web, perhaps fortunately, has not escaped this particular practice. The University's Web Master, in conjunction with a sub-group of the Electronic Information Working Group (including the library's own Web Editor), developed a standard structure and style for the 'home pages' of the various departments within the university. Aimed primarily at the academic departments, the University guidelines defined the order and content of the official departmental pages, offering a consistency of style and information provision. The guidelines also provided advice on the use of the University logo and made available versions of the same in computer-readable format. The style guidelines have been amended to reflect developments in HTML and the corporate image of the institution but essentially they have remained constant.

The library, together with many other service-oriented departments, found that the suggested structure and content of the University pages were not always appropriate to the services offered. To this end, the library's Web Editor developed a set of style guidelines specific to the library Web presence, adopting the broader principles of the University guidelines alongside more specific recommendations suited to the content of a library Web site. Where necessary, additions have been made to the guidelines in light of further Web development (such as the 'Exeter Subject Tree' of Internet resources, which demanded its own particular layout and style). The library 'home page' has been designed to reflect the University Web guidelines (at the time of writing a graded light blue background with a darker blue left hand column containing contact details, together with the University logo), whilst offering links to information particular to the role of the modern library service. Instead of offering access to prospectus information, the page offers links to service details; instead of access to course module information there are links to electronic information resources. The design of the 'home page' is frequently reviewed, to ensure that it both reflects the changes in the broader University style and the developments within the library's own Web pages.

The crafting and documentation of a style for a set of pages is only half the battle. To assist in the implementation of the guidelines, templates were made available to those authoring Web pages. In addition, the ability to view document source code within Web browsers and the ingenious use of 'cut and paste' with Windows significantly eased the application of particular HTML 'coding'. The importance of this cannot be overstated. The successful application of a 'corporate iden-tity' or, in our case, a library style is determined in the main by the resources offered to those implementing the guide-lines. The provision of support, through training, documen-tation and resources assists those with the job of authoring the documents that constitute the Web site and ensures the development of a uniform style.

Style is, in part, determined by the version of the HTML used to create the documents. The fast development of the HTML code poses a particular set of problems for those managing a Web site. The problems could, perhaps, be best distilled in the phrase 'design versus accessibility'. As is often the case with fast changing technologies, it can be tempting to be at the 'leading edge', implementing the latest developments in HTML to produce a visually impressive and multi-faceted site. However, the potential audience is very much determined by the adoption and use of the latest in Web browsers in order actually to *see* the creation. It is most often the case that the 'technological elite' will often have access to such software, whilst the majority of poten-tial readers will be using older, less featured software. Indeed, a minority on the Internet still use text-only browsers such as Lynx. It is the tension, therefore, between access and design that frequently occupies the mind of many a Web site editor.

During early development the decision was made within the Web Management Group to use HTML version 2.0, with use of proprietary 'extensions' and proposed HTML 'tags', such as that for tables, where appropriate. This has meant that, in places, the Web pages seem at first glance to be fairly plain. However, this policy has ensured that the majority of

Web users (including those still using text-based browsers) can read the information provided on the Web pages. This is in accord with the information role of the library. Of course, this does not mean that the nature of the pages is forever fixed in stone. As more capable browsers are adopted by the majority of Web users (including our own staff), the developments in HTML (such as those in versions 3.2 and 4) will be implemented as appropriate to enhance further the nature and delivery of the library Web site.

Hardware and Software Requirements

As anyone who takes a remote interest in the Internet knows, there is a never ending stream of new software developments, all proclaiming to be the 'best', 'fully featured' or 'most powerful' of their type. This is particularly true of the Web browser market. Every eight to twelve months there is the announcement of a new version of Netscape Navigator or Microsoft Internet Explorer, as two of the market leaders do battle for supremacy. These developments, whilst valuable in themselves, pose considerable challenges to both managers of IT facilities and Web authors. As already mentioned, Netscape Navigator was adopted by the library as the browser of choice. With the introduction of Microsoft Windows 95 the Internet Explorer browser has also begun to appear on staff desktops. This is no bad thing in itself, although it presents the inevitable support and training considerations.

The considerable developments in recent HTML and the increased use of proprietary 'tags' has meant that the use of more than one Web browser has become increasingly necessary. It is all too common to come across a Web site that proclaims to be best viewed using this or that browser, usually because of the implementation of Active X, Java or some other browser-specific feature. 'Plug-ins' and 'helper applications' also abound. Some of these, such as the Adobe Acrobat Reader for the viewing of PDF files, have become a standard component of a browser configuration. This is certainly true of the University of Exeter Library, in keeping with other UK higher education libraries, as online electronic journals increasingly demand the use of third party software to view the resources. However, keeping up with new developments and new versions is a time-consuming and challenging issue. Use of a centrally managed file-server running networked software can certainly ease the burden of frequent software updates, but decisions need to be made about what 'plug-ins' and 'helper applications' to install in the first place. Frequent software updates may keep up with technical developments but at what cost? Each new version of a Web browser and each new file format demands a training commitment, otherwise the software is not used effectively or perhaps even used at all.

All this takes its toll on hardware. A commitment to a Web presence and the distributed authoring approach undertaken in the library requires significant investment in hardware. As a result, the library has significantly increased the number of windows-based PCs during the last two to three years that are available to staff (and indeed to readers, via the creation of a 24 machine PC cluster). The technical specifications have increased dramatically with each order of equipment over this time, with more facilities and greater speed at often lower prices, leading to a variety of PC specifications within the library service. With increasing hardware demands from Web browsers and other software, not least in the amount of disk space physically required for installation, decisions regarding software need to be taken carefully. The implementation of the latest software, which only the newer PCs could handle, would lead to a fragmented service and increased support and training overheads. It is with this in mind that the Computing Development Officer, in consultation with the library IT Steering Group, implements software that is perhaps a step back from the leading edge and yet accessible by all.

Training

The decision to create a Web site where many are involved in the authoring of pages carries with it a substantial training commitment. The library is perhaps fortunate in that the Computing Development Officer (in his role as the library's Web Editor) is responsible for teaching the University-wide IT services courses on Web authoring. This responsibility requires the library Web Editor therefore to keep abreast of developments in HTML authoring and of the latest in authoring tools. This knowledge is subsequently applied to the library's own Web site and the support of colleagues responsible for Web pages. In addition, the library uses the courses (which are open to all University staff and students) as an opportunity for its own staff to enhance their own authoring skills.

The actual task of HTML scripting can be greatly assisted by the use of Web authoring software packages. These tools (such as HTML Assistant) can greatly speed up the actual tagging of text and often apply HTML rules as documents are authored. The installation of these utilities is essential to the support of those who author pages, and continual updating of the tools to match the fast development of HTML and browsers is a necessary commitment if the tools are to be of continuous assistance. However, despite these tools and conversion packages, all those involved in Web authoring are trained in the raw, manual creation of Web documents in the first instance, to ensure a proper grounding in the principles of HTML.

Maintenance

The creation of Web pages, as already indicated, involves a continuous responsibility to maintain both the content of the documents and the 'accuracy' of the hypertext links, especially those to sites beyond the host server. The former involves considerable liaison between the Web Editor and those responsible for the various departments within the library. All central information on the Web is the responsibility of the Web Editor, even though he may not be the original author. This decision was made to ensure the consistency of both style and information content. The latter responsibility is perhaps the one issue that has yet to be resolved to the satisfaction of both the library and IT services. The University of Exeter Library is not alone in experiencing this problem, especially in regard to the subject tree. The issue of 'link checkers' is very much a perennial discussion topic on some of the relevant electronic forums. Until recently staff have made use of quieter periods to check links within the various subject resource lists. Recently, however, use of Web site tools, such as Net Mechanic (http://www.netmechanic.com) and Dr HTML (http://www2.imagiware.com/RxHTML/), have gone some way to addressing the issue of link maintenance, but there is no doubt that this is an ongoing and labour intensive commitment. This is a good example of how the management of a Web site must look beyond the initial creation to the continual resourcing of development and maintenance, on both the macro and micro levels.

The Future

In the existing financial climate it is unlikely that there will be major revisions of the University of Exeter Library Web pages in the near future. However, continued technological advances particularly relating to advanced authoring tools such as 'Hot Dog' (http://www.sausage.com) and the developing drive towards using Web technology to promote more open methods of teaching and learning, will be catalysts for further developments. Above all, Web development of our library pages will continue to be a partnership, working alongside academic colleagues to engineer a resource suited to the continued demands of teaching, learning and research. Without such a context, the library's Web pages would be a mere plaything.

References

Myhill, M. R. *et al.* (1995) Keeping the threads together: use of the World-Wide-Web at the University of Exeter Library. *Vine*, **99**, 15–18

Tilsed, I. (1996) Subject trees – the Exeter Experience. *Ariadne – the Web Version*, (5), http://www.ariadne.ac.uk/issue5/subject-tree/

CHAPTER THIRTY THREE

Managing Current Awareness Services

Terry Hanson

Introduction

Current awareness services, in one form or another, are a feature of information service provision in most academic libraries, and have been for many years. The purpose of this chapter is to discuss those services that are primarily electronic, in terms of the sources that are used, the method of delivery to the end user and in terms of the methods used by the recipient to manage the information. In particular our concern is with the role of the library in mediating this process and its management implications.

The concern is primarily with:

- Bibliographic information supply to academic researchers in higher education institutions, but clearly the techniques and services discussed are applicable in many other service environments;
- The notion of service, whereby the researcher is provided with information on a regular basis, rather than the end-user regularly logging into a favourite database and

running a search manually. The service element may be the result of human or machine mediation, or it may be a combination of the two;

- Awareness of the existence of documents, not so much with the document delivery though this is of course related. Many current awareness products exist for both purposes with built-in document delivery facilities using post, fax, e-mail or direct on-screen display using, for example, the Acrobat format. Examples include the various CAS IAS (Current Awareness Service with Individual Article Supply) services such as the British Library's Inside-Web service or CARL UnCover (Davies *et al.*, 1998), and also the conventional bibliographic databases, such as those from SilverPlatter, are also beginning to incorporate IAS services using their 'Silver Linker' Internet linking technologies.

The Purpose of Mediation

The purpose of a mediated search is to use the expertise of the librarian to provide a high quality information service. In the old days of online searching, before end user CD-ROM services came along, all searching was mediated, if only because the techniques were esoteric, and it paid to be quick–both factors that led search customers to be all too willing to leave it to the experts. In the end-user age the situation is very different, at least in respect of the greater friendliness of the search interface and the absence of the ticking clock. The need for mediation too is affected by the greater exposure most academics now get to search interfaces, on a variety of products. Most users would, by now, have acquired a basic familiarity with search procedures. But few would describe themselves as expert searchers, and even if they did claim such distinction they would normally be so busy that they would happily have their subject librarian take on the task of searching for new material in their subject areas, through a mediated current awareness service (Brunskill 1998).

A mediated current awareness service in an academic library would normally begin with the subject librarian working with the researcher to construct a subject profile. This may range from a couple of keywords to a couple of hundred keywords. It may also involve author names and specific journals. The subject librarian will recommend the most appropriate database(s) for the search and will then turn the keyword list into a formal search strategy for this database.

The advantages to the library of this approach are that it involves subject librarians more closely in supporting research and, through the need to discuss subject profiles, in liaison work generally. The principal disadvantages are that it can be either very expensive or labour intensive according to the methods and sources used and as a result such services are not common in university libraries (Hanson, 1990; Cox and Hanson, 1992; Hanson, 1994; Hewett, 1997). However, this situation is beginning to change at least in respect of locally run services with the recent releases of enhanced database administration tools from SilverPlatter and OVID (see below).

Online Databases via Commercial Hosts

If the selected database is not available as a locally mounted, or otherwise free-at-the-point-of-use, service then the librarian would have to opt for a commercial arrangement with one of the main online hosts such as STN or the Dialog Corporation. These companies would allow the local creation of the profile which would then be stored by the host and run automatically, against either one or many databases, at a frequency determined by the creator. Any records retrieved would then be mailed, by post or e-mail, to the local researcher.

At the time of writing an SDI from STN run against, for example, the Inspec database costs £1.13 per week, or £4.52 per month. This price would include up to 20 prints. An SDI run against ABI-Inform from the same service costs £3.76 per week or £9.40 per month. The same two databases run monthly by Dialog cost $6 (with unlimited prints) and $16 (with 20 prints) respectively. Clearly a major mediated current awareness strategy at a typical university, serving perhaps hundreds of researchers, managed on this basis would be very expensive.

Another important player in the commercial SDI market is ISI (the Institute for Scientific Information), producers of the various Citation Indexes and the Current Contents series. These databases are available from a variety of online hosts, and so the SDI arrangements discussed above would be available for these databases. However, in recent years, the company has introduced its own SDI facility. Initially called the Research Alert Direct service it is now known as the Discovery Agent. This tool allows the user to create, revise and manage personal search profiles from the local site. ISI also offers contents page services within the Discovery Agent and an add-on service called Personal Alert which mediates the process of profile creation using company staff. Users can opt to receive results by e-mail or, as Discovery Agent is Web based, they may log on from anywhere and see the results from the six most recent weeks of each profile.

The Discovery Agent is extremely impressive, everything the current awareness service manager could dream of in terms of functionality, accessibility, ease of use and attractiveness. But, unfortunately, dream is the operative word as the profiles cost $350 each, coming down to $290 each for 6 or more. This may not be a realistic option for a managed current awareness service in universities.

The facility to manage profiles (revise as well as create and delete) in a client server situation is a relatively new facility for bibliographic database hosts. The conventional arrangement would not permit profile revision; instead it would require a new profile to be created to replace the old one. Both Dialog and ISI (and the UnCover Reveal service, see below) offer this very useful facility. It effectively localizes the management, if not the finances.

Finally in this section it is worth mentioning the Inside Web service from the British Library. This is a general current awareness service covering the most frequently requested 20 000 journals at the British Library Document Supply Centre. At present the facilities for automated current awareness are fairly crude but are due to improve in the near future. The user can create search profiles and set frequencies at which they should be run. Then, at the next login, the user would be prompted to run any overdue profiles. Later (within 1998) it is intended that the profiles would be run automatically.

Locally Mounted Databases

Running the service against locally mounted databases has the great advantage of not incurring any further costs once the service has been purchased or subscribed to. It is also true that this kind of service will ensure greater use, and thus value for money, from the investment already made in the databases. However, there is a downside and it concerns labour. This process can be very labour intensive because of the relatively (compared to the online hosts) unsophisticated search management software used with most CD-ROM databases (Krishnananda 1995). Though this situation is in the process of change, with the recent release of software enhancements from Silver Platter and Ovid, the great majority of CD-ROM databases will not benefit from the improvements. We shall look first at the management process for a non-automated service and then move on to the new automated techniques.

Manual techniques

Once the profile has been created for use with a local CD-ROM database it would be stored as a file in the search software (e.g. a .HIS file in SPIRS). This pre-supposes that the software used to search the database concerned is capable of storing profiles. Most now have this capability but by no means all. Notable problems include the UMI software (used for ABI-Inform and Inspec etc.). Having created and stored the search strategy it would then be passed to the staff who will run the strategies on a regular basis. The subject librarian will have determined the frequency with which the strategy will be run. This will vary according the database used and its update frequency. In the case of some services, such as Current Contents or the British Library's Inside-Web, this may as frequent as weekly.

The profiles would be run manually, one by one, according to the procedures used for the database concerned. Any records found would be downloaded for transmission to the researcher. At this point two further considerations arise:

- *The suitability of CD-ROM databases for running profiles.* This is not a problem for the majority of CD-ROM bibliographic databases but there are still some (such as UMI again) within which it is not possible, using any search or limit facilities, to identify the records added in the most recent update, against which the profile needs to be run. Although it is still possible to identify the new records it becomes an even more labour intensive process and for many this will exclude these products from the service.
- *File formats* and the manner in which the researcher will be managing the references received. A fully electronic service would facilitate the management of bibliographic references using specialist, end-user software such as ProCite, Reference Manager, EndNote, and Papyrus. If the university has adopted one or more of these packages, perhaps on the basis of the library's initiative, it would be appropriate to consider the provision of records in a compatible format. Depending on the circumstances this may or may not be straightforward. All the packages mentioned have the ability to import records from a variety of sources. They also have tools for customizing the import process to recognize additional formats. In the case of ISI databases such as Current Contents on Diskette

and the Citation Indexes on CD-ROM, the process is made even easier as download formats are offered for the leading bibliographic software packages.

Having downloaded the records, in whatever format, they would be transmitted to the user either by diskette or electronic mail. New users would also receive instructions for importing into whichever package was being used. And, as the final part of the process, the library might design an output format from the bibliographic software that would act as a document request form for interlibrary loans or photocopies of journal articles from library stock. Using this form the researcher would be able to select references to follow up and print them for dispatch to the library.

As Internet-accessible databases incorporate document delivery facilities by direct links to article suppliers the local current awareness service could include the field containing the URL in the format of records delivered to the user. Then, the recipient could connect to the supplier either direct from the e-mailed reference or from the record once imported into the personal database. Internet linking is now a feature of the leading bibliographic software packages.

One other important consideration at the start of the process for each customer is whether they require a retrospective search to be run in order to establish a core database to which the regular updates would then be added. Once the profile is established and up and running it would then be the responsibility of the subject librarian to keep in touch with the researcher and to make sure that the profile is producing suitable results. If not then amendments may be necessary.

Automated techniques

The SDI services offered by commercial hosts are fully automated. It would be unthinkable for these companies to offer such services on the basis of labour intensive approaches such as those described above. Not until very recently, however, have automated SDI management facilities been readily available within the software for managing local installations of CD-ROM databases. The two leading database publishers, Silver Platter and Ovid, have for the last couple of years been developing these facilities and the products have recently appeared.

The SilverPlatter SDI facility made its appearance as part of the ERL suite of software and requires the presence of a local ERL server. The SDI tools are made available as part of the WebSpirs client (version 4 onwards). In fact the tools comprise both an SDI service, for customized profiles for individual researchers, and also an Alert facility which allows the librarian (administrator) to create search strategies on general topics that may be of interest to many users, undergraduate students as well as researchers, and to which they may subscribe. The SDI facility is available as an end-user service while the Alert is an administrator's tool only.

The first step in the SDI procedure is to create a search using the normal routines in WebSpirs. Any search, once run, can be designated an SDI simply by clicking in the appropriate box next to the search statement. The search may be on a single line or it may be a complex search strategy comprising several lines. If it is the latter it would be necessary to bring the appropriate sets together in the final line, using 'or' links. The SDI would then be created on this final set.

Having selected the search statement to use for the SDI, an information screen appears requesting, among other things, the profile name, frequency with which it should be run, the format of the records, and the e-mail address to which the results should be sent (see Figure 33.1). And that is all there is to it. What was a very labour intensive process has, from the point at which the profile is created, become a fully automated process, just as it is at Dialog and STN. The profile will be run at the pre-determined frequency and the user will receive results by e-mail in a fraction of the time taken hitherto. A service that would probably have been considered by most libraries to be too expensive in terms of staff time now becomes an easy, and very attractive, option.

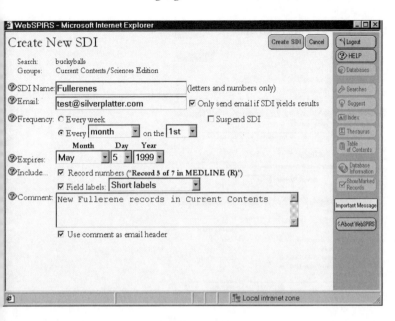

Figure 33.1 Creating an SDI in WebSpirs

The Ovid AutoSDI service is conceptually very similar to SilverPlatter's. It too allows the user or administrator to create profiles (as Saved Searches) for later running against newly updated databases with results sent automatically be e-mail (see Figure 33.2). Alerting services with user subscription however are not, at the time of writing, part of the service.

Given the extent to which major databases are becoming available via national academic hosts such as BIDS, EDINA and MIDAS it would be of great benefit to the university community if there were to be an automated SDI facility available from these services.

Clearly not all databases are available from Silver Platter and Ovid, so it may still be necessary to run the current awareness service using the more laborious techniques. Or it may be decided that the service will only be available on products that can run in automated mode. In which case the

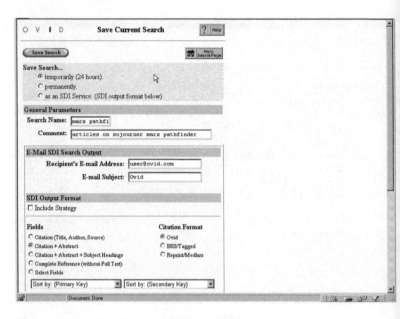

Figure 33.2   Creating an SDI in Ovid

strategy might be to subscribe to an all-subjects service, such as Current Contents so that all sections of the university may benefit.

Automated Contents Page Services

Thus far we have discussed mediated services that are based on the construction of detailed subject profiles designed to retrieve articles by a mixture of keyword, author or journal source. This is clearly the premium level service. There are however other possibilities which are easy to manage and still very useful, and popular. They are based on the delivery of the contents page of one or a range of journals each time they are updated. Journal contents can easily be included as a feature of the mediated services discussed above but there are now many sources of contents page updates. Some are based on general current awareness databases while others are direct from individual journal publishers.

Perhaps the best known of the general services, over many years, has been Uncover Reveal (http://uncweb.carl.org/). The user can select the journal(s) required and indicate the e-mail address for automated delivery as and when they are published. Recent enhancements to Reveal include the ability to store not just journal titles but also a keyword search strategy for automatic updates and a books element, in conjunction with the American Book Centre, known as Books-in-Reveal. The keyword search strategy, however, is limited to 75 characters. The costs vary according to the category of user. An individual would pay $25 per year to maintain a profile. Site licences are also available.

Other contents page services include the recently introduced AutoJournals from BIDS and services from Swets, EBSCO and Faxon. Publishers themselves are also offering contents page services. Examples include Elsevier's Contents Direct service (http://www.elsevier.com), IDEAL Alert from Academic Press (www.europe.idealibrary.com) and a similar service from Oxford University Press (http://www.oup.co.uk).

These services are clearly designed to be end-user based. There is however still a mediation role for the library to bring them to the attention of the local academics as part of the local strategy and as part of a portfolio of services.

Books Services

Book databases, such as Books in Print or BookData, can be included in either the commercial or locally managed SDI services listed above. Two recent arrivals on the online book current awareness scene are UnCover Reveal: Books-in-Reveal (see above) and a service from Dawsons (http://www.dawson.co.uk), the library subscription agent and bookseller, inviting users to submit detailed subject profiles via their Web site and receive information about newly published books.

This service, known as Dawsons Advance, will run the profiles free of charge and send the results via e-mail.

Another very important component of the local service is a customized update listing recent local acquisitions. Librarians have typically provided a general accessions list, containing all recent acquisitions. Traditionally this has been supplied in printed form but more recently it has become popular to make it available as an electronic service, perhaps as a feature of the online catalogue.

The ideal situation for selective dissemination of recent local acquisitions information would be for the type of automated facility discussed above to be built into library management systems. Unfortunately this is not yet a standard feature in such systems. It is not unknown however and products such as Sirsi Unicorn do offer this facility. The user can interact directly to select appropriate class numbers, author names or keywords for a personal profile and submit this for regular e-mail updates. Alternatively it may be a mediated feature only whereby it becomes necessary to produce and distribute, physically or electronically, an application form.

A practical alternative, in the absence of automated features, is to arrange with the systems librarian for a file to be produced on, say, a monthly basis of all newly added records. If this is produced as a tagged ASCII file it may be imported into a separate database, using, for example, ProCite. And, using this package's ability to store and re-use search expressions and search profiles, a service could be offered. The results would be downloaded and dispatched by e-mail. This, like its labour-intensive counterpart above, is not the most streamlined operation but it does work, and it provides a popular service.

Push Services

We cannot leave the subject of current awareness without making a nod in the direction of the new Internet 'Push' facilities, and 'intelligent agents', for keeping people up to date. Push is a new name for the concepts of selective dissemination of information or alerts as discussed above. It refers to information being 'pushed' out to those requiring it rather than the potential user needing to log in to a service, find the information and 'pull' it back to his or her own PC (Bing, 1997a; Bing, 1997b; Brenner, 1997). In this sense the concept is also referred to as a broadcast facility, similar to TV or radio. Unlike TV and radio however many push services allow the user to specify information needs precisely. A good example of this is Profound Livewire, covering business information, from Maid plc (http://www.maid-plc.com). Like the sophisticated administration tools discussed above for bibliographic information so Livewire has facilities for precise profile definition, end-user control or administrative mediation. An example of a general news service on the same model is the PointCast Network (http://www.pointcast.com) or the 'My Yahoo' service from the popular Yahoo search engine (http://www.yahoo.com)

Netscape and Microsoft have now incorporated push services into their Internet browsers. Netscape offers Netcaster while Microsoft has incorporated channels into Internet Explorer. Both services offer companies a method of pushing information to their customers via broadcast channels. Initially companies such as Elsevier, Dun and Bradstreet and Dow Jones have signed up for this new method of information dissemination. Perhaps the most interesting early example from our perspective is the Science Channel from Elsevier. This new service provides the tables of contents of all Elsevier journals. The user can select those of interest and receive updates automatically, by e-mail. The personal profile can also include information about upcoming scientific conferences and even news and views on current scientific topics. Use of the Science Channel is free (http://www.elsevier.nl/locate/Science).

Conclusion

Until recently the university library manager has had a limited range of choices for offering current awareness service to their local researchers. Where the service model has been ambitious, in offering personalized service with complex profiles, the management implications have been prohibitive in either financial or staffing terms.

In this context the University of Portsmouth Library has, since 1989, offered its Electronic Current Awareness Service (ECAS) to local researchers (Hanson, 1990; Cox and Hanson, 1992; Hanson, 1994). The service currently provides around 300 researchers with a customized update using a wide variety of major database sources covering all subject areas. All ten subject librarians are involved in setting up profiles and the work of running the profiles is undertaken by a team of library assistants equivalent to approximately 1.5 FTE.

ECAS has been very popular among researchers but the service has been, from a library perspective, very difficult to sustain in terms of staff commitment. It has operated, of necessity, on an unavoidably labour-intensive basis, in the manner discussed above. It is hoped now that with the new Silver Platter SDI facilities the service can benefit from greater automation, freeing up library assistants for other, equally important, work. Then perhaps the holy grail of current awareness services, a combination of high quality, personalized updates, minimal administrative effort and low cost, will be realizable. And mediated current awareness services will become a standard feature of the electronic library of the future.

References

Bing, M. (1997a) Implementing Webcasting as a communication tool. *Database*, **20**(6), 42–44

Bing, M. (1997b) Push: a technology with staying power. *Database*, **20**(4), 27–30

Brenner, E. (1997) A 'Push' by any other name (continued). *Information Today*, **14**(8), 10, 62

Brunskill, K. (1997) Measuring researchers, preferences for CASIAS. *New Review of Information Networking*, **3**, 93–102

Cox, J. and Hanson, T. (1992) Setting up an electronic current awareness service. *Online*, **16**(4), 36–43

Davies, M. *et al.* (1998) CAS–IAS services: where are we now? *Electronic Library*, **16**(1), 37–48

Hanson, T. (1990) The Electronic Current Awareness Service and the use of ProCite at Portsmouth Polytechnic. *Online Information 90: International Online Information Meeting* (London, 11–13 December 1990), pp. 277–287 Learned Information

Hanson, T. (1994) Role of academic libraries in supporting research. *New Review of Information and Library Science*, **1**, 197–206

Hewett, S. (1997) The future for mediated online search services in an academic institution: a case study. *Online and CD-ROM Review*, **21**(5), 282–284

Krishnananda, M. *et al.* (1995) Automated SDI service using CD-ROM databases. *Online and CD-ROM Review*, **19**(3), 137–141

Stanley, T. (1997) Pushing your luck? *Ariadne: the Web Version*, (8) http://www.ariadne.ac.uk/issue8/search-engines

SECTION 12

General Case Studies

CHAPTER THIRTY FOUR

General Case Study: The University of Wales Swansea

Andrew Green

There is a Welsh proverb 'hanner y daith, cychwyn' – 'starting out is half the journey'. To those most closely involved, the beginning of the journey towards the electronic library carries a special significance, a taste of the excitement felt by the Edwardian polar explorers:

> '... the period of preparation, of loin-girding, of feats of arms: the explorers work in their hut by the hiss of gas-lamps through the long darkness of the Antarctic winter, readying equipment and sallying out on preparatory journeys' (Spufford, 1996).

University of Wales Swansea is a largely unexceptional seat of higher learning. The only league table it could claim to top is proximity to the sea. But in its very ordinariness it could be regarded as a paradigm of a research-cum-teaching institution feeling its way, in its chosen means of transmitting knowledge, from a print monopoly to the hybrid – part-print, part-digital – academic communication of the future.

Strategic Planning

In parts the path has been laid out with map and compass, in parts it has wandered with the contours. Strategic planning, though it has its critics, has proved an important navigational instrument. In 1993, for the first time, the library devised a comprehensive strategic plan, intended to plot the course of its development over the coming five years. Its chief feature was an insistence – dangerous obsession would be the preferred description of one humanities professor – that researchers and students could and should benefit from the electronic tools already in evidence. With the exception of the LIBERTAS library management system, which was beginning to offer information services beyond the traditional online catalogue (OPAC), the Library at the time could boast very little in the way of visible electronic services. The plan was welcomed by the University (it appeared at the same time as the Follett Report), and coincided with an expansionary phase in its finances, which allowed relatively swift progress to be made.

The original strategic plan has been revised annually on a rolling basis, and, if anything, the electronic theme has intensified in the five years since its publication. Librarians tend to overestimate the impact of their carefully crafted strategic documents, but certainly anyone reading our plan could hardly have failed to notice that a major change of direction was under way.

Content, Connection, Consciousness, Competence

From the beginning it was recognised that the promotion of the 'electronic library' depended on the interrelationship of four 'C' factors: content, connection, consciousness and competence.

The supply of electronic content was accelerating, especially in the form of CD-ROMs, although possibly the most important single stimulus, as in other institutions, was the advent of the Institute for Scientific Information (ISI) citation databases on the Bath Information and Data Services (BIDS) service. Most of these early services were broadly biblio-graphic in nature. They were therefore familiar to library staff, who felt comfortable exploring and later promoting them to academic colleagues, despite the variety, and often awkwardness, of their interfaces.

Connection (or connectivity) soon became an issue. Though stand-alone CD-ROMs often offered a more sophisticated and pleasing experience than BIDS, it became obvious that BIDS was far more popular, and not only because of its wide subject appeal and simple interface: the fact was that researchers could, even with an underpowered computer, connect directly to the service from their own rooms. Librarians found they needed to make common cause with their computer service colleagues in encouraging the perva-sive networking of the campus and the extended ownership of personal computers (PCs) or their equivalents. When CD-ROMs began to be networked (Swansea was relatively late in doing so, and benefited from the pioneering work of other institutions) the dependence on network connections for successful use became more obvious still. The same could be said of the library's automation system, LIBERTAS, where many of the new service developments, such as self-reservation, Internet access to the catalogues of other libraries, and later e-mailed distribution of new accessions lists, assumed easy remote network access by staff and students.

Connection on its own, however, was not enough. Consciousness, the third factor, was also needed so that users could take full advantage of the new electronic services. Swansea, though its campus is compact and its computer network was comparatively well-developed, had what can fairly be described as a conservative electronic culture, and much effort was put into persuading academic staff in partic-ular of the benefits to them of investing time in exploring and adopting networked information. This was done through the subject librarians, through leaflets and newsletters, and by formal means such as the establishment of an 'electronic library' sub-committee of the Library Committee.

Finally, competence in using the new tools and services could not be taken for granted, despite the fact that many of them enjoyed intuitive and friendly interfaces and that increasing numbers of students had already encountered computers and their basic applications before entering the University.

Staffing the Electronic Library

Behind all these factors, though, the management of the transition to a proto-electronic library relies crucially on the qualities of the staff – in the library and outside it – responsible for implementation.

Here Swansea was particularly lucky. After almost a decade when virtually no fresh appointments had been made to the professional library staff, the period 1993–95 saw the retirement of many long-serving staff, and the opportunity, in the wake of the expansion of student numbers, to restructure the staff and make some additional appointments. A succession of younger professionals joined the Library. Whereas in the past they might have undergone a ritual apprenticeship in the cataloguing department, they now found themselves in demanding, multifunctional roles, typically within the newly formed subject teams – with some cataloguing duties, but also involved in information skills teaching, information work, and writing guides to the new electronic sources. Information technology (IT) skills – not merely keyboard and word-processing, but Internet and CD-ROM skills – were essential requirements of successful candidates. A decision was taken early on that most of the generic skills needed to advance the electronic library would be needed by *all* staff ('non-professional' as well as professionally qualified): it would not be sensible to concentrate skills in the hands of a few 'IT librarians' who would find it impossible to act as IT lifeguards for all their struggling colleagues.

At the time the library had – and still has – only one full-time professional 'IT librarian'. He had started as a traditional 'systems' librarian, but the increasing stability and ease of use of the library management system allowed him to diversify into CD-ROM networking, the library's intranet and Web pages, and other, project-related work.

As well as insisting that candidates for professional jobs possess relevant IT skills, the Library is also concerned that it recruits staff able to promote, teach and communicate well with users. Interpersonal and communications skills figure prominently in selection decisions – all assets crucial to successful development of the electronic library. All candidates shortlisted for professional posts are invited to give brief presentations, such as mock information skills sessions, to Library staff.

Training and development are even more important than wise recruitment in preparing staff for new roles in a new environment. A new Deputy Librarian appointed in 1995 – in contradiction to the fashion for 'flat management structures' – was given the high-profile task of developing new staff training and development policies and programmes, and very quickly these became established as an accepted part of Library life. Inevitably IT-related skills featured strongly in training needs assessments and the programmes that resulted, for all types of staff. The relevance of these skills became apparent to all once PCs began to multiply within library branches, and when IT invaded and then took over the Library's internal communications.

The PC Invasions

The electrification of internal Library communication was gradual but decisive. At first only the senior management team possessed networked desktop computers. As funds allowed, more and more staff (not only 'professional' staff) joined them, and once a critical mass had been achieved by 1995 a high proportion of documents and messages passing between staff avoided the use of paper (or would have, were it not for an irresistible urge to print out anything of 'significance'!). An insistence on standard software and other tools also played its part.

In Swansea, as no doubt elsewhere, the Library seized the opportunities presented by electronic mail and standard word-processors and the like well ahead of most other University departments. In retrospect it was over-reticent in not offering itself as a model to other departments, and indeed to the University as a whole, where even now a chaotic medley of systems and packages flourish simultaneously.

This easy and cheap communications revolution allowed staff to be kept informed of developments in the rest of the academic library world – the early days of the Mailbase service were dominated by the 'lis' community – but they also opened up library information and developments to the staff, at a time when a centralized management style had given way to more dispersed modes of decision-making. The Library continues to experiment in this direction, most recently with World Wide Web-based 'intranet' tools that allow easy posting and editing of online internal documents.

All this was invisible to the Library's users. What could not be ignored, even by the most casual user, though, was the spread of personal computers within the Library's branches. The first suite of 24 PCs appeared in the Main Library in December 1993. These were the first computers on campus that were truly open-access and could be used by any student, from any department, without formality (even registration or logging on). The introductory Windows screen was divided into two main categories of application, 'production' tools like a word-processor, and 'retrieval' tools like the library catalogue and BIDS. This all-inclusive approach was deliberate and was continued in other suites. The Library held to the idealistic principle – often belied, as the Vice-Chancellor was fond of pointing out, by the dominance of simple word-processing and the use of e-mail not to download bibliographical references but for social calls to friends in foreign parts – that one of the highly desirable features of the electronic environment was the ability to interrelate tools of difference types and uses, and to manipulate information at will, while working at a single workstation.

Though acclaimed by users the PCs soon proved problematic to the Library. It had been intended that IT Services staff would support them within the building. These, however, did not materialize and it was necessary to improvise by training a number of library assistants to respond to the frequent routine queries and requests that arose from use of the new machines. Before long the main information desk was fielding both traditional 'library' enquiries and also questions (between 15 per cent and 20 per cent of all verbal requests) about lost files, quirky printers and aberrant software. All staff rota'd for the desk were expected to have attained a standard level of IT competence, with the aid of a checklist familiarly known as 'The Knowledge'. This example of 'internal convergence' proved a portent of things to come.

Each of the library's smaller branches has gone through a similar process of PC 'adoption and fostering'.

Another early field of electronic activity for the library was the Campus-Wide Information System (CWIS) – a software package that in retrospect appears remarkably primitive, which was intended to be used to mount on the campus network information about the university for the university. It was fortunate that no staff time was available to gather and organize data to be added to this system, since it was rapidly swept away by the advent of the World Wide Web.

The World Wide Web

The Web epitomized a phenomenon that now haunts all who attempt to manage electronic information: a technology so swift and pervasive in its triumph that it could not be antic-ipated or planned for. However, once a University site had been established, the Library was one of the first departments to exploit it. A member of staff was seconded part-time to develop a basic set of pages about the Library and its services, with access to the catalogue and a feedback mechanism, which could stand comparison with the Web pages of much larger university libraries. At the same time the Library was represented on a University body, the Web Development Group, charged by Senate with the task of designing and organizing the institution's Web site: this participation continues today, with the Director of Library and Informa-tion Services a member of the group and a staff member of Library and Information Services (LIS) as the operational manager. An interesting tension exists between the Univer-sity's view of the Web site as primarily a promotion and marketing tool, and LIS, which is more concerned with devel-oping it as a gateway for Swansea staff and students to usable electronic information, internal and external.

As the importance of the Web grew as a source of acade-mically valuable knowledge in almost every discipline, the conundrum of whether the library should seek to organize access to this knowledge on behalf of its users, and if so how, became more pressing. One option was to do nothing, and rely on the work of others, or users' own ingenuity. Another route, followed by a few academic libraries, was to organize their own 'subject trees' in subject areas taught by their parent institutions. This kind of large-scale arboriculture was clearly beyond Swansea's means, and we chose a more pragmatic approach – constructing a basic classified and annotated list of key Web sites of potential value to all staff and students, and for each subject area a short list of key sites, many of them gateways themselves. This policy has stood the test of time, as subject gateways, many of them products of the Electronic Libraries Programme, have sprung up to supply services more comprehensive and sophisticated than any one library, however single-minded, could devise independently.

Electronic Materials

A key managerial issue was whether the Library should 'force the pace' in the direction of a more electronic future in areas where it lacked independence of action.

In Swansea most decisions on selecting research and learning material lie in the hands of academic departments. However, in order to boost the acquisition of CD-ROMs and other electronic resources, at the Library's suggestion a top-sliced 'Electronic Fund' was set up as a pump-priming sum against which departments could bid for electronic purchases. This tactic succeeded in its aim of drawing departments' attention to their existence and advantages, and after two years the Fund was abolished, having achieved its purpose of establishing electronic sources as a natural and equal partner with printed material.

By this stage electronic purchases and subscriptions had broken out of the ghetto of bibliographic and other secondary sources. The next frontier – the Library was under no illusion that monographs would easily fall under the digital onslaught – was periodicals. The first opportunity to make a real impression on users was the introduction of the Periodicals Pilot Site Licence Initiative, launched by the Higher Education Funding Councils in 1995. For the first time significant numbers of academic periodical titles began to appear in parallel electronic form, available to any network-linked member of the university. Substantial staff effort was dedicated to embedding and promoting this new service, including references in catalogue records to the availability of electronic versions, with as yet uncertain results. Serious problems include the lack of a unified and consistent interface, the complexity of the pathway to the actual article sought, the lack of a Web-based online catalogue giving a direct link from title to text, the uneven subject coverage, and the difficulty of giving enough prominence to electronic journals in a Web environment.

This remains the most difficult hurdle to overcome: how to advance beyond electronic meta-information – the catalogue record, the abstract, the index entry – to the text or other primary object of study in digital form.

Among the assets of the Library is an archive collection called the South Wales Coalfield Collection. It is a remarkable assemblage, in many media, including banners, posters, photographs and audio and video recordings, documenting the economic and social history of the South Wales Coalfield, from the point of view of the miners, their organizations and their communities. With financial help from the British Library and the Higher Education Funding Council for Wales an online catalogue of part of this collection has been constructed which finally gives adequate access worldwide (a Web version is available) to summaries of the rich contents of the collection. The Library, however, has always seen this catalogue as only a preliminary to mounting on the Web simulacra of the most significant objects in the archive, whether in the form of text, or still or moving image, or sound recording. This remains the ambition, although it requires additional resources for us to realize in any significant way. Even so, the progress made so far represents a considerable achievement in an area not traditionally associated with digitisation and electronic access.

Spreading the Word

Our concern with the archives has been to extend knowledge and use of them outside the university via electronic means, but in most cases our task is to spread the word about external electronic sources of information to our own staff and students. This is a campaign on many fronts: talks to heads of departments on 'The Library of the Future', the establishment of an IT sub-committee of the Library Committee, articles and notes in the termly 'converged' newsletter *Inform*, dissemination of the Follett Report and its evangelical message on the digital library, a joint library/IT student orientation programme, and the use of the library's subject teams to promote the take-up of information sources in academic departments.

The subject teams were also instrumental in developing an ambitious programme of courses and training sessions entitled 'Information Access'. These were aimed initially at postgraduate students and offered through the university's newly formed Graduate School, but were later extended to staff and advertized through the Staff Development Unit. They concentrate heavily on electronic sources, either generic, like BIDS or the online catalogues of other libraries, or subject-specific (such as CD-ROMs in specific disciplines); they offer introductions to tools such as personal bibliographic software or electronic mail, and how to use and write for the World Wide Web. Perhaps more than any other single initiative 'Information Access' succeeded in fostering a culture among researchers receptive to new ways of seeking and using academic information.

'Information Access' courses are offered equally to all postgraduates and staff: although some other courses form part of academic courses the Library has not yet found a satisfactory standard means of integrating information skills teaching as core elements of departments' undergraduate modules.

Gradually the term 'electronic library' began to gain currency. (In fact the phrase is misleading, suggesting as it does that the world of print is obsolete, and the more recent term 'hybrid library' seems preferable.) The Library, though not a lead organization in any of the projects in the Electronic Libraries Programme, has participated in several of them, and, as the Programme has matured, has done its best to keep itself informed of developments, by hosting seminars and by nominating 'monitors' among its staff to keep abreast of projects in specific programme areas.

The Impact of Convergence

The Library's thinking and practice on matters electronic were therefore already quite well developed when the University decided in summer 1995 to split the existing IT

Services department and unite half of it, responsible for academic computing, computer networking and media services, with the Library, under the management of a single Director of Library and Information Services. The new body, following a successful rearguard action by a professor who could not tolerate the loss of the word 'library', was named 'Library and Information Services' (LIS) and came into being on 1st January 1996.

The usual mix of principle, fashion and expediency informed these decisions. The principle – roughly, that the worlds of libraries and computer services were beginning to overlap and that the process should be helped on its way – was not followed up in any rigorous way by the University, and for the most part it was left to LIS to work out its own destiny. No attempt was made to force a rapid marriage between the library and the computing parts of LIS, and the first year was spent on thinking about convergence (a large heap of convergence thoughts was amassed) and on two large infrastructural tasks.

The first was an attempt to put together, for the first time, a comprehensive strategic plan covering all aspects of information and communication technologies throughout the university (not simply within LIS itself). Specifically library concerns were deliberately excluded on the grounds that a well-established plan for the Library already existed, and to this extent a converged approach to strategy was postponed. Nevertheless, the new plan, christened *Rough Magic* to convey the awkwardness as well as the wonder of the new technologies, tried to lay the foundations on which could be built elements of the electronic library of the future: better network access for students, a new structure for IT support and training, the embedding of IT in teaching practice. Making it was a long and time-consuming process. Whereas the library strategic plan had been developed and written over a short period by a small number of insiders, *Rough Magic* was distilled from the investigations of seven Task Forces, consisting of staff from central services, academic departments and central administration as well as students

– over 50 people in all, over a period of almost nine months. The result was a plan that could fairly be said to represent the views of a broad group of users and providers. Its weakness, however, was its failure to gain the real commitment of the University authorities. This, combined with general financial restrictions, has made implementation of an ambitious plan an extremely difficult process.

At the time work on the plan was started thought was given to the idea then being advocated by the Joint Information Systems Committee (JISC) of information strategies. There was general agreement, however, that the concept was too all-embracing to be manageable. The boundary line between an information strategy and a general institutional strategy was ill-defined, when 'information', in its broadest sense, was the common currency and *raison d'être* of the whole university. It was also unclear how a strategy could be devised and put into operation in any practically useful way without enormous time and staff effort.

The second preoccupation of the first year of convergence was physical planning. Both the university authorities and LIS management agreed that an essential key to successful convergence and a better and more integrated service to users was bringing together staff, facilities and services in the same location. This was not only for the obvious reasons – economies of scale, administrative efficiencies and combined public services – but also because it was felt that longer-term benefits depended on breaking down the social and psychological distances between library and computer services staff, which, even with the best possible existing relations, will inevitably persist when almost the length of the campus divides them. The precedent of some other universities where physical convergence did not occur was not encouraging.

Attached to the Main Library is a four-storey block of office accommodation. By good fortune the two academic departments occupying it moved out in 1996 to new accommodation nearby, and plans were formed to reuse the floors to house mainly behind-the-scenes LIS staff, while reorganizing space within the existing Main Library building to create a new joint machine room, joint information points and new accommodation for student PCs.

Plans were also prepared to reflect these physical changes in the organizational structure of LIS. These acknowledge the separateness of some (mainly technical) library and IT functions, but combine central administrative functions and, most important, all direct public services, with an expected improvement in the quality of user support. The pace of change for staff will increase. This is not necessarily problematic: IT support staff, after all, have already undergone, and survived, the massive change from centralized to distributed computing, and library staff have also adapted quickly to new roles.

Funds available to realize these changes were restricted to the necessary building adaptations – there was no money available for any significant increase in the number of student PCs – and therefore most of the impact of convergence on users will inevitably be in the longer term.

The Future

Library and Information Services will continue to be a place, as well as a service, and not only because the printed collections will continue to be needed and to grow: the building will provide a single secure, safe environment, open for long hours, for students to seek and use existing knowledge (printed and digital) and to generate their own knowledge. It will also be, as now, a convivial, social centre – and therefore a noisy as well as a studious place.

At the same time LIS will press ahead with the parallel model of the distributed, electronic library: adding more primary research and teaching material to the network, extending remote access to library systems (e.g. remote document delivery), working towards more consistent and intuitive user interfaces. New tools, including a new-generation library system, will be acquired. Convergence will add new concerns, for example the extent to which the hybrid library can be managed by hybrid staff, equally at home in the traditional librarianly skills and in the technical skills of information and communication technology. Another will be the attempt to strike a new balance between staff devoted to face-to-face services, and those planning and delivering remote, distributed services, working collaboratively with academic colleagues.

Perhaps the most profound change to come for librarians will be that, whereas in the past they could afford to take for granted the pedagogic process, and concentrate on the separate function of learner/researcher support, in future they will not be able to escape involvement in the difficult issues of academic development and planning.

Acknowledgements

With grateful thanks for their comments on drafts of this chapter to my colleagues: Sara Marsh, Lis Parcell, Martin Price, Paul Reynolds and Chris West.

Reference

Spufford, F. (1996) *I may be some time: ice and the English imagination.* London: Faber

CHAPTER THIRTY FIVE

General Case Study: The University of York

Elizabeth Heaps

The University of York is characterized by its excellence in teaching, being second only to Cambridge in Teaching Quality Assessment, and in research, where its position is well established in the top ten universities. The University at York dates from 1962, and has developed in size in a controlled manner, to the current number of around 7000 students, and with the intention of continuing to grow in a manageable way. The library contains around 700 000 volumes and over the years has taken a pride in delivering a high quality and cost effective service. There have never been opportunities to develop the depth and richness of the historical collections of older and wealthier institutions, therefore it is necessary for us to maintain a judicious balance between the materials we hold in printed form, and those electronic resources we 'hold' or to which we provide access. Electronic information is a key part of our strategy to provide support to the education and research mission of the University. We have made considerable progress towards being able to call ourselves an electronic library while still maintaining a commitment to printed resources appropriate to a library with which users can identify. The issues and choices facing us will be very familiar to other libraries, especially in the higher education sector, in the UK and beyond.

It is our objective to provide access to the major information resource in each of the main subject areas taught or researched in the University, whether printed or electronic, though as time goes by increasingly the expectation is that it will be electronic. This objective has financial, staffing, management and training implications which will continue to challenge us. Our strategy is based, as it should be, on the objectives of the University as they appear in the Corporate Plan, and as they will be further articulated in the teaching and research strategies of the University currently being produced.

Managing Information Services on the Campus

Following several lean years in the 1980s and early 1990s in terms of resourcing, it became apparent that inflation, particularly for periodicals subscriptions, had once more outstripped funding by a critical amount and a cut of 25 per cent in subscriptions was proposed. As a result a Library Review was set up to investigate the funding and budgeting processes both to and within the library.

The review was wide-ranging and the report issued in 1994 was positively received. Implementation began immediately. The library's budget was for the first time linked to a percentage of the University's turnover (adjusted) and set at 3.66 per cent. However, this represented a considerable increase which could not be achieved immediately, so a schedule was agreed which will allow the target to be reached in 1998–99. Unusually in the University this is a one-line budget, including staff salaries. A resource allocation model was devised so that the funding structure for individual subjects would be formula based and more transparent. A new and more coherent staff structure was accepted allowing for better management and communication within the library.

Another outcome of the review was the recognition of the closer relationship between information services and information systems, and it was decided to change the University's committee structure to reflect that. A new Information Committee was created, combining the former Information Systems Committee with the Library Advisory Committee. The library and the computing service both report to the Information Committee which is chaired by the Deputy Vice Chancellor. The Library Committee is the users' committee with representatives from all the departments, centres and students' unions; the Computing Committee is a different style of body and has an advisory function to the Director.

Following the Library Review, it was decided that a similar exercise was needed into the funding and structure of the computing service. The outcome was different in significant respects. The response to the acknowledgment of the under funding of the library was for the University to accept responsibility for providing adequate funds from the centre. It was similarly agreed that the computing service was under-funded, but full funding from the centre, which is to say top-slicing, was not supported. A basic level of funding linked to a percentage of turnover was provided for a core service, including the network infrastructure, PC classroom support, and training in software applications. Beyond this the computing service was instructed to charge departments for software, services and connections. However, there is a perceived danger of fragmentation of the overall network and information infrastructure, so implementation has been slowed down pending the production of an Information Strategy.

The Librarian, Tom Graham, resigned to take up the post of Librarian at the University of Newcastle in April 1997, and it was decided to link the process of seeking his successor with the outcome of the Information Strategy, which would logically have an impact on the management and committee structure surrounding the providers of the information services. An Acting Librarian was appointed and the

Information Committee was charged with creating the Information Strategy. The University's Corporate Plan had identified five core processes within the University: teaching/learning, research, external interface, statutory obligations, and finance and funding matters. The approach adopted by the Information Committee was to tailor the Information Strategy to the core processes. Teaching and research committees were asked to develop their own written strategies and the Information Committee will draw on these to create both an Information Strategy and a management structure, which includes the consideration of convergence between the library and the computing service and any other appropriate services. The timetable for the production of the strategies is Summer 1998.

Whatever the outcome of this discussion, the library and the computing service will continue to work closely together. At York the tradition has always been for close and fruitful co-operation between the two academic service departments. Communication is direct between staff at all levels, and many shared projects have been successfully undertaken, including student registration and the Mondex smart card, often in an informal way.

The Library's Management Structure

The library is divided into three divisions: User Services and Administration, Bibliographic Services, and Subject Services and Information Systems. There are advantages in having systems and subjects in the same division, in that the structure facilitates the flow of information, with the additional advantage that the head of the section has an intimate knowledge of both these areas and can more easily keep them working in the same direction in support of services to users. The systems team consists of the Information Systems Librarian and the Systems Librarian responsible for the Dynix library management system, with a part share in a library assistant.

Subject librarians are the first point of contact with departments. This works extremely well, with close relationships being formed between library and academic staff. Departmental library committees, of which subject librarians are members, are expected to take a key role in the management of the subject allocations, especially monitoring the balance between recurrent expenditure on subscriptions and capital expenditure on books, and to preside on a regular basis over periodicals reviews and cuts as required. In this way it is hoped to avoid the old-style crises leading to the threat of large-scale cuts across the board.

Subject librarians and the departmental library committees have between them produced departmental Information Resources and Access Policies (IRAPs), which are designed to help departments to address the balance between the provision of material for research and for teaching across the various research groups and courses in the department. Special attention has been given to the information requirements of the departments, and the ways of supplying access in the most appropriate way. The IRAPs have raised awareness of strategic planning, and of the need to balance holdings and access.

Resourcing and Budgeting

Once the library budget has been calculated as a fixed percentage of turnover, an information budget is set and is approved by the Information Committee. The ring-fencing of the library's budget will end in 1999/2000 when it will be added to the percentage paid to the computing service and disbursed between the services by the Information Committee. Within the information budget, funds are identified for the purchase of extra copies of student texts, for inter-library loans, expensive purchases, strategic developments in electronic form, which could be new databases or new services, and for special purchase especially in the humanities.

The main materials fund consists of the book and periodicals funds. At the initial stage, the fund is divided in this way to enable calculations of recurrent periodicals subscriptions, taking account of deals, such as the Periodicals Site License Initiative (PSLI) and consortium purchasing deals, such as that of the North East and Yorkshire Academic Libraries. The decision was taken at the start of the PSLI deal not to cancel the journals replicated in electronic form, until the future became clearer, in order to avoid the expensive possibility of runs being split, and until archival issues were more satisfactorily addressed. The remaining money is available for purchase of books and other monograph material.

We operate a resource allocation model where all subject areas are represented. The materials fund is first top-sliced to create a general purpose fund from which are purchased reference works, bibliographies and abstracts, government publications, and electronic resources, with network licences, including the subscriptions to nationally networked services such as BIDS. The formula is then applied to the remaining funds thus: 25 per cent based on numbers of taught course students, 25 per cent based on numbers of research students and research staff and the remaining 50 per cent calculated on volume of publication in a subject area and the average cost of books and periodicals in that subject.

New databases are proposed by subject librarians after discussion with departments and a case made on academic grounds. The Electronic Services Group ensures a technical evaluation is carried out, and then prioritizes the databases for approval by the Resource Management Group. The first year's subscription is normally paid for from the strategic development fund, though there is provision for some new subscriptions to be funded from the subject allocations.

Just-in-Time

Electronic document supply has been temptingly close for some time, but it is only relatively recently that it is becoming a practical reality on any scale. At the same time, the 'monopoly' of the British Library Document Supply Centre (BLDSC) is being seriously challenged for the first time in around thirty years. In York we rely quite heavily on inter-library loans owing to the relative youth and small size of the University Library. One full-time and two part-time library assistants process over 20 000 requests per year using the Lancaster management system, ILLOS. The service is as streamlined as we can make it: requests are made on paper forms so that the copyright declaration signature can be obtained at the time of application. Ideally an electronic signature would be acceptable, but sadly this still seems to be some way off.

The majority of our document supply is from the BLDSC so a minimum of staff time is taken to locate sources. Were we to change to using one or more of an increasing range of suppliers, such as the British Library's Inside service, UnCover from CARL, or the eLib funded LAMDA, we would use more staff time in searching catalogues and identifying sources of supply. Also we borrow a significant number of books and theses, whereas alternative suppliers deal for the most part in articles. To lend or supply material in any significant amount, we would need to create a staff infrastructure to support the increased activity. We are not yet persuaded that the savings in costs would be sufficient to fund the extra staff and management input, but we are maintaining a watching brief.

Reference and Information Services

Subject librarians have the key role in evaluating sources of information, for content and technical specification. They are responsible for promoting awareness of the resources within departments and for training staff and students to make the best use of them. They also take responsibility for identifying Internet resources to add to the subject pages on LibWeb, the Library's World Wide Web service. The enquiries service is provided by subject librarians as a general rule, with support from three library assistants. Subject enquiries are frequently referred to the subject librarians, who are in any case directly accessible to members of their departments. They are finding that their services and time are in increasing and conflicting demand for information skills teaching, information work with individuals, and maintaining their own awareness of resources in their subjects. Prioritizing work within the whole range of their activities is becoming increasingly difficult for them and certainly their educative role is becoming more significant. To help them we will be seeking to increase the small number of library assistants available for subject support.

Information Skills Training and Awareness

Traditionally the subject librarians at York have worked closely with academic departments in user education. This takes place at different levels: for undergraduates and other taught course students, for research students, and for staff, in various ways according to need. At the beginning of each academic year, introductory tours are timetabled for all students, and the attendance rate is gratifyingly high. Later, by arrangement with departments, subject librarians organize workshops or demonstrations of library skills, bibliographical resources and research techniques. This has now become formalized into a programme of information skills designed and delivered jointly by the computing service and the library, called Information Literacy in All Departments (ILIAD).

The ILIAD course is designed to cover information discovery, handling and management techniques, including use of library and information resources, word processing, databases and presentation software. The original idea had been to deliver ILIAD as a pilot which could later be scaled up and offered to all students. However, funding was not available at such a level, so different costing and sponsorship models have been explored. A working group in the

University has been looking at transferable skills acquired within and outside the curriculum and has put together a package of courses and activities which count towards a portfolio of skills. ILIAD exists inside that structure, but is considered by the library and the computing service to be so integral to the learning experience that it continues to be delivered independently as well. It is taught in units, so participants can select those units they wish to follow, or it can be integrated into the course structure. The delivery is a combination of tutorial and hands-on sessions with workbooks allowing students to learn at their own speed.

The library's information skills programme is not confined to ILIAD. Subject librarians devise and deliver sessions on more subject specific resources and information handling techniques, which are tailored to the needs of departments.

Library Web Services

When the World Wide Web emerged, the library and the computing service immediately realized its power and potential. The University has always had a highly developed network infrastructure, so the Web seemed a natural development as a vehicle for information. Broadly speaking the technical expertise was provided by the computing service and the organization of the site and linked resources by the library, a natural division of labour in our environment, although there is much overlap in practice.

The importance of the Web as both an external information resource and an internal communications device was soon recognized more widely by the University, and a Web Steering Group, chaired by the Deputy Vice Chancellor, was formed to provide strategic direction and the impetus for academic and administrative departments to develop their own home pages, containing information directed at external as well as internal users.

LibWeb is the University of York Library's Web information service (http://www.york.ac.uk/services/library/). From the start it was designed as a comprehensive site which would bring together information on library services, staff and collections, and provide electronic versions of the library guides. Its precursor, the campus-wide information server had been developed to include bibliographies and other resources downloaded (with permission) from remote sites and this formed a useful collection which we wished to retain. The question arose as to how best to organize the resources to make them accessible to our users.

Our solution was the York Subject Tree, a collection of links to resources of interest to staff and students at this University. As well as pointing to specific resources, the Subject Tree contains links to other more comprehensive sites and collections so that it provides a starting point for those who wish to search more widely. The site has been further developed into York Information Connections, which combines the resources from the Subject Tree with a section on exploring the Internet with pointers to search engines (http://www.york.ac.uk/services/library/subjects/subjects.htm).

Cataloguing the Internet is obviously beyond the realm of any individual library, but just as a library has a collection of its holdings, we have made a selection of the Internet resources which we believe are of particular interest to our users. The choice is made in partnership between the subject librarians and interested parties in the departments, similar to a collection policy for hard copy. However, where printed sources are classified by subject, we have taken the pragmatic solution to link resources to departments of the University, for reasons of staff time and ease of use. The development of and rationale for LibWeb are described in an article by Christine Ellwood and Sarah Thompson (1997).

Electronic Journals

Following the eLib programmes and PSLI, the increased availability of electronic journals presented challenges for organization and access. We considered whether to include them in our catalogue database, but decided not to do so, as at the time the Dynix Web OPAC was not sufficiently well developed for us to wish to purchase it. We would obviously wish to provide direct links to them via the Web and could not afford to duplicate our efforts. The access route is therefore via LibWeb. Initially an alphabetical list of titles was provided with links to the sites wherever they might be located. More recently LibWeb's gateway to electronic journals has been updated, and now offers subject lists of e-journal titles, again based on departments of the University, to make browsing easier (Figure 35.1). The subject lists also provide links to the e-journal home pages. In addition to these lists, there are also pages devoted to online newspapers, to major publishers of e-journals and to other directories of e-journals.

Networked Information and YorkDataNet

Our aim has been to provide access to information resources via the network wherever possible. Following from BIDS, we

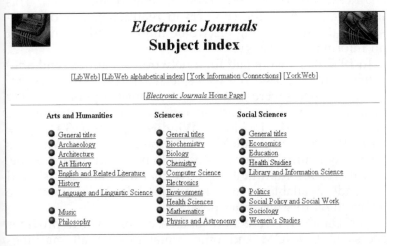

Figure 35.1 University of York Library electronic journals subject index Web page

have made use of national deals where there was a choice, for instance transferring Biosis to EDINA at the first opportunity to offer wider access than we were able to manage at that time with CD-ROM. Registration and authentication are close to our hearts, and we welcome the appearance of Athens3 on the scene, although it has required some local programming to make it more appropriate for our use. The administrative burden of authentication cannot be ignored, and Athens3 places this with the site administrator, so a system which removes some of the burden and generates user names and passwords is required.

From the outset the intention was to network the CD-ROMs as soon as the technology was within our reach. A library information network (LIN) was installed in 1991 using Novell and Optinet. At the time it was thought to be the configuration most suitable for the purpose, tried and tested, and potentially compatible with future campus network provision. In the event this did not prove to be the case as PC-NFS was the choice two years later for the campus networking solution, and it was not possible to network the CD-ROM service campus-wide on that configuration. This illustrated at once the conflicts in requirements and provision in the fast-moving electronic market, and the need for an information strategy.

In 1997 plans were laid for a networked solution, and after a tendering process, ITS was selected to provide a system. The key aspects were that the system must support a variety of different platforms and operating systems in use on the campus network, including Windows 95 and 3.11, Unix workstations, and AppleMacs. The penetration of Windows 95 was not sufficient for a solution to be based on that alone, and it was an important objective that the databases should be made available as widely as possible. Using winframe technology, this was now possible.

YorkDataNet is the new database host which provides access to CD-ROM and other databases on all machines across the campus network. The system is based on two NT servers, using the proprietary CD-ROM networking package

Ultra*Net. The CD-ROMs are cached onto one of the servers, and users with Windows 95 connections have direct access to the server. The databases are mirrored on the other server. Users with other connections, such as AppleMacs and Windows 3.11 machines, access the databases using 'thin-client' technology and the system is started from a Web page.

The Web page, Databases at York (Figure 35.2) lists all the database host services we subscribe to or provide, including BIDS, MIDAS, and YorkDataNet, together with the e-journals. Direct connection to some of the services is possible via this page, and we hope eventually to provide access to all the services through this route.

For technical or funding reasons it is still not possible to move all the databases on to the network. Not all the CD-ROMs to which we subscribe were designed for networked use and a small number have proved unduly recalcitrant and will continue to be provided stand-alone for the immediate

University of York Library

Databases at York

[LibWeb] [LibWeb alphabetical index] [York Information Connections] [YorkWeb] [Collections]

𝒩𝑒𝓌! YorkDataNet now available 𝒩𝑒𝓌!

● List of Databases - database host services, databases available at York, and links to individual database guides.
● Access to Databases - how to connect to database host services and how to download software if required.
● Database FAQ - answers to frequently asked questions about databases available at York.
● York Information Connections - finding information on the web, including freely available subject resources.
● Electronic journals - full-text electronic journals and tables of content services.
  Please email us if you have any queries about any of our database pages.

Page maintained by Sue Cumberpatch (ext. 3891, email scl7@york.ac.uk)
Last updated 14 April 1998

Site maintained by the Library Web Coordinator (libweb@york.ac.uk)

Figure 35.2   Databases at York Web page

future. Others are outside our budget. Nevertheless, with YorkDataNet, the service to users has been much improved and our aim to provide access over the network to the majority of electronic resources is being achieved.

Electronic Reserve–Remote Access Library Project Hosted at York (RALPHY)

Most libraries have a collection of photocopies which is heavily used and quite labour intensive to maintain, and York is no exception. The obvious solution is to provide an electronic collection on the Web, with the advantages of accessibility at all hours, multiple access without the need for duplication, and access from across the campus network. Technology can support this, but copyright problems are still being addressed. While eLib projects, such as ACORN at Loughborough, are investigating and, we hope, resolving the technological and copyright management issues, at York we felt that a small scale electronic reserve project was timely.

The idea was first explored with the Psychology Department, which makes great use of the photocopy collection. Since all the reading lists and other departmental resources were already provided over the Web, it was felt that the students would find it perfectly normal that articles should be provided in the same way. So it proved, and a small number of articles were copyright cleared and scanned. A balance had to be reached between practicalities of scanning, readability on the screens of a variety of equipment, adequate print quality for those who wished to print, and speed of loading the file. This small-scale experiment, piloted in Spring 1997, was successful and proved popular, which encouraged us to seek funding from the University's Teaching Innovation fund for a scanner of our own and a small amount of extra staff time to manage the copyright applications. This having been granted, the project under its new name RALPHY was begun.

We are working with several departments on the implementation of RALPHY and it is being received with great enthusiasm, especially by the student representatives on the departmental library committees where it has been discussed. Many of us see it as the way forward, though in the library we are fully aware of the potential scale and difficulties, and are keeping our options open to adopt any solutions provided by the eLib projects. We have had helpful discussions with project ACORN and are using a copyright management system created for the project.

eLib Programme

The eLib programme has provided welcome resources and support to a wide variety of initiatives, all aimed at bringing the electronic library to reality with all possible speed. The University of York has participated in a number of these, notably the e-journal *Internet Archaeology* (http://intarch.york.ac.uk), and two non-formula funded projects: an archives project based at the Borthwick Institute of Historical Research, and the retrospective cataloguing of the York Minster Library.

In the latest round, the Yorkshire and Humberside Universities Association (YHUA) libraries bid successfully for one of the 'clumping' projects which is under the programme of resource discovery. The project has been named RIDING. The intention is to create a virtual catalogue so that users in any of the sites will be able to search a range of catalogues simultaneously. This involves the use of the Z39.50 protocol and will entail mapping the respective catalogues, collection profiling to enable users to select the catalogues most likely to be useful to them for searching, and library profiling so that prospective users can readily obtain information about access arrangements. The project is possible owing to the Yorkshire and Humberside Metropolitan Area Network which is being installed in 1998 to most sites. Membership of the RIDING group consists of the YHUA university libraries, with the welcome addition of Leeds Library and Information Services, which is the Leeds public library system, and the BLDSC. RIDING will draw on and co-operate with the UNIverse project, under the Telematics for Libraries programme, where the BLDSC is one of the lead sites.

At York we feel we are moving ahead successfully on several fronts in what could easily become a bewildering range of projects. We are proud of what we have been able to achieve already and are encouraged by the way new ideas and initiatives are embraced with quite a degree of enthusiasm by library staff, academic colleagues and students. Clearly the information world will continue to develop at an ever increasing pace, and we are glad that we are able to respond to the challenges creatively and positively with the benefit of improving the service to our community.

References

Ellwood, C. and Thompson, S. (1997) York Information Connections: an attempt to catalogue the Internet. *Ariadne: the Web version*, 11. *http://www.ariadne.ac.uk/issue11/york*

CHAPTER THIRTY SIX

General Case Study: The University of East Anglia

Jean Steward

A 'new' university, established in the 1960s, the University of East Anglia currently has over ten thousand students. Teaching is based in Schools of Study, with many interdisciplinary courses across a broad range of subjects (excluding engineering and medicine) and the university's research rating puts it in the top twenty in the United Kingdom. With the introduction of a School of Health, including nursing studies, the single campus university now also has smaller nursing sites in Norwich and at Kings Lynn, forty miles away. The Norwich Research Park is centred next to the campus and there are close links with the research institutes based there. The library therefore faces the challenge of supporting a very broad subject base, growing student numbers, high quality research activity in most disciplines and three sites in a geographically isolated region of the country where the collaboration possible in the larger population centres is not feasible. Electronic solutions are vital to help meet the challenges and to provide access to the range of services our users demand. This case study describes library and university initiatives, which are gradually transforming a traditional library service into a 'hybrid' if not a totally electronic library. The library will remain the physical space where the process of information access is managed; it will also remain a physical space where many users, particularly undergraduates, come to borrow materials and to study. However, the benefits of present and likely future technological developments will mean that the emphasis will increasingly be on services driven by user needs and based on access, and mainly electronic access, to information and support. The key issue currently facing library staff is the management of this change. A short history of early developments is necessary to set the context for the current initiatives at UEA.

Early Developments

As with all UK libraries, technology was first introduced to assist the library with the provision of traditional services – circulation, cataloguing (allowing nationally created data to be imported), an OPAC, acquisitions, inter-lending. All involved a learning curve for the library staff, but none fundamentally altered the basic services provided by the library. The introduction of the OPAC was the first end-user service offered and it was this development that first demonstrated the potential of online searching of bibliographic information. Despite its power as a search tool, this was seen as complementary to browsing materials at the shelves not as a substitute for this.

Dialog and similar databases were used by library staff to undertake literature searches for users, but it was the advent of the ISI databases, and of BIDS, which gave UEA library the first taste of the electronic library. BIDS was a service, developed outside UEA, but which was available to the whole university community. Library staff had to develop a means of registering what was then 6000 users – no easy task – as well as providing training and support for a service which would be used across the whole campus. Subject-based training was devised in collaboration with computing centre staff and delivered to faculty and post-graduates, who were not familiar with online databases, with boolean logic or often with using keyboards and basic computer techniques. Despite the difficulties the service proved extremely popular and the numbers of registered users and searches exceeded expectations in the first year. Within two years the paper-based versions of the Science Citation Index had been removed from the shelves and the transition to an electronic library had started.

As a new university in a geographically isolated region, UEA Library has always been keen to ensure that its resources are exploited to the full and has believed that IT can play a central part in achieving this. The nationally funded TLTP (Teaching and Learning Technology Programme) initiative was seen as an opportunity to develop this potential. The School of English and American Studies developed courseware to support the teaching of poetry and the library worked in partnership with them to ensure that the courseware included access to the information sources needed to support the process, but which also provided stand-alone versions available to the whole university community. Software was developed which took the results of BIDS searches and compared it with local holdings, adding classmarks where there was a match. Instead of being given traditional reading lists, students were encouraged to search the OPAC and BIDS to find relevant materials, to download the results to create a personal bibliographic database and to share the results with colleagues using e-mail discussion lists. The results were mixed. The stand-alone software was used fairly widely across the university and ProCite software was also purchased and sold on to a number of faculty and researchers. Integration with the courseware was technically feasible, but the change was too great for the students who had no basic grounding in IT skills. The learning curve to introduce courseware, electronic mail, online database searching and related techniques at the same time was too steep and the school and library initiatives were split. The lack of a basic programme of IT training for all students and staff was a continuing problem for library staff until recently. Humanities students in particular only needed IT skills to access library services, and library staff initially had neither the time, the resources nor the skills to teach the basic skills in using IT to such large numbers. In 1994 the central university VAX computers, on which the software was loaded, were phased out and at the same time the library moved to a new system supplier. The replacement systems could not support the existing software and, with reluctance, a service that was growing in popularity had to be abandoned. It has taken three years to get to the point where it can be re-offered, clearly demonstrating the fact that the transition to electronic library services is never a straight line, but a series of steps forward, with some reverses.

From these early stages the pace of change has quickened substantially in the past three years and in that time the university has introduced an information strategy, intended to exploit the potential of electronic information sources and systems. Simultaneously the library has moved to a policy of 'access and holdings' that is leading to the development of a 'hybrid' library, as dependent upon electronic resources and services as on more traditional ones.

An Information Strategy

In 1996 the Librarian was asked to prepare an information strategy for the university. The document is about the information creation, management and provision at UEA. The objectives are to improve service and support for teaching and research and to enhance efficiency. The emphasis of the strategy is practical: that data should be prepared, keyed only once and should be disseminated according to need and must be timely; that there should be good access to national and international sources of information and that the university should exploit to the full the information it produces. The potential of IT to deliver information across the campus is one of the key themes and the university has committed to a number of projects which will turn the principles in the strategy into a working reality. The library is involved in a number of campus-wide demonstrator projects, including the development of a new financial system (which includes the electronic transfer of invoice details from the library's Dynix system to the central university system), campus cards (which will combine an identity card with building and car park access and a library card initially and will then add cashless vending), a UEA intranet (with access to all committee papers, student records and other internal university information) and an audit of all information sent to new undergraduates. This is supported by a strong programme of IT training for all staff and researchers and the development of transferable skills training programmes for undergraduates in an increasing number of sectors. The information strategy is taking library staff into many new areas of activity not traditionally associated with librarians and coping with the increased and rapidly developing workloads is a challenge.

Convergence of academic support services

One of the main outcomes of the information strategy has been the convergence of four separate academic support units – the library, computing centre, audio-visual centre and administrative computing–into an Information Services Directorate from April 1997, with the Librarian serving as the first Director of Information Strategy and Services. There was already good interworking between the different units in areas of common interest, particularly between computing centre and library staff. A reliable and well supported campus network with good links via JANET to the rest of the world has become essential for the delivery of many library services. Distinctions are blurring as more services in each unit are computer-based, and interworking is essential to provide the new types of academic support required within the university. Shared services being introduced this academic year include a much enlarged networked CD-ROM facility (which will be accessible from all networked PCs and Macs across campus and will support a minimum of 100 CD-ROMs), video-conferencing facilities and new computerized video editing facilities. All will operate to published service standards.

Managing Change: Human Resource Issues

The introduction of electronic resources and services has impacted on library staff at all levels and job content for almost all library staff has changed and developed significantly, particularly over the last three years. The library has a proud tradition of subject specialization and many of the professional staff joined to library to develop subject collections to support new Schools of Study at UEA. Although stock selection and collection management is still a very important area for subject librarians, they are now equally involved in the management of electronic resources. Web pages have been developed for all subject areas, including links to relevant sites across the globe; CD-ROMs and online database services are growing rapidly; access to electronic journals, courtesy of the eLib programme, has been introduced. Subject librarians have had to gain a clear understanding of how to manage and exploit such resources and to develop user education and training programmes to help users, sometimes preoccupied with their academic interests and unwilling to cope with change, to make the transition to using these resources in support of their teaching and research. In order to create the time for these new areas of work, subject librarians no longer classify and assign subject headings to all stock in their subject areas – a responsibility which was not relinquished lightly. They are not the only staff affected by the change. The impact on technical services and reader services staff is described in subsequent sections. Computer-based services are now impacting on all staff, including the library janitors, who from September 1997 were all expected to use electronic mail daily, to provide basic maintenance for nearly 100 workstations and associated laser print facilities, to sell computer disks and explain how to format them and to use the Dynix system for book returns – all a far cry from distributing the post, checking books as users leave the building and undertaking security patrols.

Coping with change on this scale has not been easy and there have been periods of low morale during the process. Good communications are crucial and are not always easy to achieve. A staff briefing is held every week and is open to all staff, although it is currently held when service points are open so not everyone is able to be present. The briefings attempt to explain university strategies and plans as well as new library initiatives and are very important to ensure that all staff are aware of developments and feel a part of them. Electronic mail is also used extensively and has greatly improved the exchange of information between staff in different sections of the library.

Involvement is equally important and team working is being introduced to replace the more traditional hierarchical structures in the library. All staff now work in teams, grouping staff with different skills and at different levels, and this interaction is hopefully adding to the sense of ownership of new developments.

The third strand is training, which is critical to develop the new skills required. There is an in-house training programme, which in the last year has included sessions on the World Wide Web and on Dynix for all staff. University-wide sessions providing IT training are attended regularly by staff at all levels and the training budget is increasing every year, as staff attend external conferences and training sessions on such topics as new databases, user education, electronic document delivery and the creation of Web pages.

Resourcing and Budgetary Issues

If electronic access was cheaper to provide than books and journals the pace of change at UEA would be faster! There is a growing literature on the relative costs of traditional and electronic services. With the spiralling costs of journals in particular, continued dependence on printed journals can no longer be the only option. Electronic journals subscriptions are not necessarily cheaper, and are certainly much more expensive if the costs of upgrading workstations, so they are powerful enough to support the range of software needed to access the variety of databases and full text resources, are taken into account. With shrinking budgets librarians need to be ever more inventive in finding the strategies that will stretch budgets further. UEA library is now committed to a policy of access and holdings and of achieving the most cost effective balance between the two. Access includes discussions with other local libraries about collaborative purchasing, although no formal agreements have yet been reached. Inter-lending is no longer solely with the British Library but also relies on local co-operative schemes, particularly HELIN – the Health Libraries Information Network. Recharge systems are being developed and researchers are encouraged to include the cost of inter-lending in research grant applications. The alumni fund of the university is being used to provide the hardware to support a range of specialist databases. Library subject allocations now include the ability to vire funds between stock purchase and additional inter-lending. Discussions are underway with a major publisher to develop a database of texts to support undergraduate teaching in history and the sciences. UEA does not have the answers, but is constantly looking for ways of stretching scarce resources further. Consortium purchasing contracts obviously apply to book and journal purchases – the library also formed a Regional Federation of five local HE and FE colleges when going to tender for a replacement library system. Two colleges rely on hardware based at UEA and dedicated lines provide fast links between the libraries in the Federation.

It is important in this context to consider capital budgets as well as recurrent. The library building at UEA has reached capacity and capital budgets are not sufficient to allow a new building or extension. Funding has been approved over a three year period however to facilitate improved use of the existing space. It is hoped that this will include the relegation of all older journals to remote storage, with access provided via a scan and send service, although the modelling suggests that a traditional photocopy/van delivery service may be cheaper. A final decision will be reached in the next six months. As study space and the number of workstations cannot be increased, longer opening hours are an alternative. To be affordable this is necessitating a rationalization of service points in the library, the introduction of self-service issues (with the first two units being introduced in summer 1997) and the move of all workstations to ground level. Twenty four hour opening of the workstation floor only will be possible as soon as the campus cards which will control access are introduced, hopefully in September 1998. Opening hours to the whole building will be increased this year as well – the virtual library is not yet a reality!

Access and Holdings

Building on earlier collaborative research projects with the British Library, the library is the lead partner in an eLib project EDDIS – Electronic Document Delivery; the Integrated Solution, which aims to produce an integrated, end-user driven identification, holdings discovery, ordering and electronic supply service for both non-returnable items (mainly journal articles) and returnable items (books). The consortium includes Stirling and Lancaster universities and much of the software is being developed by staff at BIDS and Fretwell Downing. This will be a crucial element of the transition to a more access-based library service. EDDIS uses the emerging standard protocols, including the ILL protocol and Z39.50 on a Unix platform, with future releases possibly available on NT. One of the main difficulties we face is that with new standards still being developed, system suppliers have not been entirely consistent in their approach, leading to inconsistent results when undertaking a search across multiple databases. Only the lowest common denominator can be used, so it is still difficult to provide the range of sophisticated searches users will require. Prototype software was available in Spring 1998 and the full software should be in operation by December 1998. Library staff are bracing themselves for the change, which (despite the difficulties noted above) we believe will transform inter-lending services by offering users choice of supplier, will provide electronic rather than paper-based requests and will facilitate the shift to access rather than holdings for many of the non-core journals provided at UEA.

Reference and Information Services/User Education and Training

The enquiry desk used to be staffed by all professional librarians on a rota basis. Many of the enquiries were practical and locational–where are the toilets, how many books can I borrow. Users needed help in finding information on topics, much of which was provided by using the catalogues or the basic reference and bibliographic works located close to the desk. With the growth of Internet, electronic databases and CD-ROMS the service has changed quite substantially. Library Web pages now contain all the basic information about the building and services and users are encouraged to use these to find the answers to such questions. Induction tours of the building are no longer given and induction sessions are provided to very large groups of students, using these Web pages, projected onto screens by a liquid crystal display panel. A team of professional and support staff has been formed to provide the reference and information service at the desk. The team provide help sheets on all the CD-ROMS available and run user education sessions for groups at lunchtimes as well as staffing the desk. As much time is spent registering users for online services, issuing stand-alone CD-ROMS, assisting with printing difficulties etc. as is spent amongst the reference books.

Technical Services

Technical services have undergone a similar transformation. As part of the access strategy the university is keen to develop links with local research collections. The library hosts the databases of a number of independent local organizations, including the Britten Pears Library, the History of Advertising Trust archives, the ANGLES union catalogue of local periodical holdings and the Norfolk Bibliography (a printed bibliography in previous editions, but now an online database of resources on Norfolk). Library staff have worked with these organizations and Dynix to agree specifications for these projects – layouts, menus, introductory and help screens, indexes – and some spend part of their time on contract creating the individual records for items in the collections.

As subject librarians have developed new roles, classification and the creation of subject headings is undertaken by technical services workflow teams, mainly comprising support staff. Staff on the basic training and entry grades now undertake much of this work. The advent of authority controlled systems, supported by training and with specialist subject librarians available to assist with difficult material, has allowed this transition. Although staff were deeply uncertain about this change when it was first introduced on a pilot basis two years ago, they have adapted to this work very rapidly and the decision to continue at the end of the pilot was unanimous.

The Zuckerman Archive and the Pritchard Papers are deposited with the library and the East Anglian Film Archive is also based at the university. This is one of the most significant regional collections in the country, with an international reputation. Two cataloguing projects are currently underway to create electronic databases appropriate to these collections, funded by NFF (the national Non-Formula Funding Initiative). This includes the creation of Web guides to the collections and of full catalogue records based on MARC but compatible with all archival description standards, including specialist software to create hierarchical links between series, sub-series, files, folders and individual items within the collections. The technical services staff in the library have worked closely with the archivists in the design of the formats necessary to provide appropriate electronic data-bases for this type of material.

On the acquisitions side the links with the university's financial system have been described above. Discussions are just beginning about the electronic transmission of orders, information from suppliers and invoice details from our main periodicals supplier.

Systems and Automation

All the above electronic services, including the communica-tions links to the libraries in the Regional Federation, have been introduced with a systems team of two. In 1997 this has been increased to three, for one year only. In the early days of the TLTP project the recruitment of systems staff was difficult – and computer centre support was necessary to specify the work, to formulate questions for the interview process and to understand the replies! Recruiting staff who are completely competent technically in so many different areas, who understand information flows and the ethos of library services, who have vision and enthusiasm, who can communicate clearly to non-technical users and who can increase the level of technical understanding of all library staff has been crucial.

Conclusion

The current pace of change means that before the EDDIS project is even at pilot stage the next phase of development has been agreed. This pace is problematic, and it is becoming increasingly difficult to protect any periods from change, to consolidate recent developments and to fine tune services.

The AGORA project, in which UEA is again the lead partner has been approved under the eLib Programme. To quote from the bid:

> we adopt the term 'information landscape' to refer to the view of resources which the library will present . . . The landscape includes a view of the library as place (local catalogue, communication with staff, description of services available) with a view of the digital spaces which the library organises on behalf of users. It will be defined in terms of logical user services (e.g. reference services, current awareness, document requesting etc.) and is independent of the underlying physical implementation of those services (e.g. CDS, web indexes, catalogues etc.). A layer of software, or middleware, which hides underlying difference and which allows the transparent addition of services and resources will provide the basis for this landscape.

The project manager has been appointed and work is underway with the prototype software expected. The project will explore the impact of a managed technical support environment on selection procedures, will develop appropriate acquisitions policies and will organize and make resources available for access by constructing the 'information landscape', creating metadata and 'plugging in' services. As a result UEA Library could look and feel significantly different in three years time.

UEA Library is not unusual, and most of the developments here are mirrored in other higher education libraries. The transition is not easy – some users are still wedded to traditional services and resent the changes. Many of the new services still have teething troubles and there is never sufficient time to refine them as we would wish. Library staff have often found the process of change traumatic. However in a three year period we have survived the introduction of many electronic services, we are developing confidence with the new technologies as our skills base increases and we know we can face the prospect of becoming truly 'hybrid' in the next three years without terror. User needs for new and better services, coupled with the need to exploit a shrinking resource base to the full, make further changes inevitable.

CHAPTER THIRTY SEVEN

General Case Study: The LRC at South Bank University

John Akeroyd

The Context

Like many new universities, South Bank University expanded very quickly from a student body of about 5000, throughout most of its life as a Polytechnic, to a peak of 19 000 in 1994/95. During that time it occupied a growing estate at the Southwark site just south of the river Thames based upon the original Borough Polytechnic building of the 1890s. Important building milestones have been the inauguration of the London Road site, completed in 1974, and the Perry library, a new 4 storey building which, though not purpose built, was adapted from its original design of light industrial units. The result of a speculative design and build exercise by Swedish architects Åke Larson, it was acquired by the university in the early 1990s to provide new and enhanced facilities to replace the limited space available in what is now the Business School.

The Perry Library is important in this case study because it represented a significant step towards the eventual construction of the digital resource centre which has become the South Bank University, Learning Resources Centre (LRC). Expansion in the late 80s was particularly rapid and caused enormous pressure on library facilities and reading space in particular. Numerous extensions had exhausted those opportunities and, increasingly, wear and tear had let to a poor quality environment. The solution was the purchase of an adjacent new building and its conversion to library use. All of this was completed quickly, in a matter of months from conception, to move, to opening in September 1992. One of the prominent features of the new library was the inauguration of the Media Centre, a multipurpose IT and Media area of about 500 sq. m providing access to a range of technology-based services such as word processing, access to the university mainframes, access to network CD-ROMs as well the provision of the more traditional video and audio cassettes.

The Media Centre proved astonishingly successful, in almost constant demand and stretching the library staff, both in technical and in tutorial skills. Applications included access to the Internet, access to advanced office software such as word-processing, spreadsheets and database management. Over a period the level of equipment provided was increased and upgraded. Further expansion in student numbers and burgeoning demand soon led to the realization that a much larger resource was required.

Building on this success, an outline proposal for a new resource centre was written but with acknowledged little likelihood of it being put into place. This changed rapidly in 1995 with the publication of the Follett Report (HEFCE, 1993).

Design Phase

Though the report of the Follett Committee on the state of university libraries in the mid 1990s has not been beyond some criticism (Akeroyd 1994; Line 1994), it was important in two ways for SBU. Firstly it was instrumental in placing the issues surrounding the digital library and its future development on university agenda. In discussion with the Vice-Chancellor a summary of Follett was placed before the Academic Board. This in turn percolated to faculties and schools. Though the discussion was limited (SBU has no great tradition of significant debate on such issues), it was effective in raising the profile of Learning Resources and placing concern about resource limitations before the university. One direct result was the doubling of the library book fund for the subsequent academic year. Secondly Follett prompted the creation of a building fund which was notified to the Executive of the university as a bidding process. The university took a quick decision to put forward a bid, based on the pre-existing idea of a multi-purpose IT centre or digital library which would utilize an existing vacant plot alongside the Students Union building and which had been bought by the university some years before. This approach was chosen, rather than attempting to expand the library, for the simple reason that there was no obvious or sensible way in which it could be so. An added benefit was to be the release of space for traditional (i.e. book-based) services in the main library. A justification for the new building was compiled and submitted to HEFCE, based to some extent on the argument of the relatively poor library space per FTE as at that time (SBU had one of the lowest figures of the new universities and historically has had a low space allocation in comparison with other new universities; to some extent it might be argued that this is a consequence of the high level of part-time students with relatively low space requirements outside core hours). Subsequent to various amendments the proposal was accepted and the new building begun in earnest in 1995.

The Design Brief

The chief arguments for building a new centre were the lack of existing space for using IT throughout the university and the need generally to improve the environment of the campus, but these together hardly constituted an architect's brief. Hence as soon as the architects were selected – these being William Gower Ltd., who had previously worked on a new hall of residence – a programme of investigation and soundings was inaugurated to firm up the outline idea. An advisory project planning group was established by the Vice-Chancellor and visits were organized to view other similar developments. Through this process the design brief gradually evolved and the architects reworked the group ideas and concerns into plans and sketches for subsequent review. This interactive process, in retrospect, was highly successful and all the potential stakeholders felt they had some view or input to the process and hence some influence in the result.

A summary of the brief at that time was compiled and put forward to the Executive for their imprimatur. Below is an extract from that and illustrates the closest the university got to a clear design brief.

Current Position

> We have now agreed that the building will contain: -
> Some several hundred open access IT facilities which will replace:
>> a) The open access Media Centre from Perry Library – this will involve the removal of approximately 70 computer terminals from Perry Library currently providing services such as word processing, CD-ROM access, Internet access and catalogue usage. This should open up approximately 500 sq. m for expanded traditional library services ie will accommodate GOS library.
>> b) The open access IT services currently within CSD, Borough Rd.
>
>> ii) At a maximum, 5 bookable teaching areas. These will replace the existing microcomputer labs in London Rd

and in Borough Rd (STHS). There is a shortfall – there are currently about 14 labs as opposed to those proposed – which will need to be bridged by:
a) Retaining some labs in London Rd
b) Turning the existing open access labs in Borough Rd into bookable rooms and
c) Bringing more of the labs into the timetable.

iii) Certain language facilities which will complement the Language Centre in London Rd (which will remain in-situ).

The whole building will be networked and attached to University and international networks and will be as flexible as possible in terms of seating, workspaces and office support. Reprographics will not be part of this building though another venue will be sought as it needs to move from London Rd.

Function and Scope

There are some fundamental assumptions which we have made but which perhaps need stating:

i) The building is essentially concerned with learning support. Even though it will host teaching sessions, these could be better regarded as directed study or directed learning.

ii) We would want to ensure maximum access and opening hours. It would not be sensible for the building to be open any less than the Perry Library given the equivalence of service.

iii) The building should provide a coherent service rather than merely housing a number of discrete services. This is important in that it is the only way support staffing and access can be maximised.

iv) The restructuring effort will be significant, will need to be in place before the summer of 1996 and someone will need to take day to day responsibility well in advance of this. A new organisational structure will be required which will need to draw upon a number of different existing support groups.

This also implies a slight redrawing of the remit of library/Learning Resources; the existing structure is not capable of sustaining this development. The IT training centre and Modern Languages should also influence developments, but do not necessarily need to be part of them.

We should not only regard the building as an advanced delivery 'platform' for a mixture of services but also as an opportunity to influence teaching, learning and information services through the development of IT based strategies.

i)   <u>Supporting Information Services</u>

Increasingly library services are being provided electronically and this is likely to expand over the next few years. At the moment we mostly provide indexes and we will need to continue this within the Perry Library as they link with the hard copy. However, many new services are being acquired which could be based and delivered almost anywhere, providing there are appropriate support staff. Within the new building we will concentrate on the delivery of such services moving towards an electronic library.

In parallel with these bought-in services, we will also need to develop more of our local resources so that not only research and scholarly material can be accessed across screens, but more basic material such as course notes, course packages and hand-outs can be provided.

ii) Supporting learning

In the first instance the Centre will serve to support the burgeoning demand for access to basic IT software such as word-processing, spreadsheets and database management. This is currently the key student requirement, though the educational value could be debated. In the medium term we should perhaps look to develop more resource based approaches to deal with core educational requirements such as IT skills, study skills, numeracy etc.

All of these should be delivered across multiple screens present so that a student could access a screen and 'click on' to, say, training in spreadsheets, training in languages, or training in word processing etc. or onto an information service, a catalogue or the Internet.

To meet the requirements above will require coherent, strategic policies to provide the necessary push to make full use of the resource.

The Specification

In many senses the building was constrained by the size and shape of the plot and by the adjacent buildings, but not least by the level of the available budget. We were concerned also that the building should feel light and open in contrast to many of the other SBU buildings some of which date from the turn of the century and can appear very oppressive. On completion of the outline design, builders were commissioned by the architects with a target of completion of some mere 12 months hence.

Additional considerations had to be given to a number of features and requirements:

- the need for high security including video cameras and other security devices;
- the need to manage glare and sunlight on screen and similar Health and Safety issues;
- a capacity for growth;
- attention to the needs of the disabled, in particular wheel-chair bound;
- a networking infrastructure and should be capable of upgrading to higher speeds if and when required;
- access issues: given the density of people and machines and the potential need to prevent theft;
- staffing support, which is the subject for another section.

The building itself is illustrated in schematic form in Figure 37.1. It occupies approximately 4,000 sq. m on four similar levels. The ground floor leads from a large open plan entrance, which includes information kiosks and monitors, into 4 training rooms and staff offices. Level 2 provides access to information services such as BIDS, e-journals and Web access. Level 3 houses a Language Centre on one side and multimedia teaching and learning capabilities on the other and Level 4 provides access to 'harder' IT such as database packages, spreadsheets and programming capabilities.

When the project began we were clear about a number of features of the new building: it would be multipurpose, it would support a mixture of technology, it would be managed as a coherent whole and not as a number of discrete units. However what was not really clear was its *raison d'être*, which showed in the variety of names given to it by all concerned and which included the Learning Centre, the IT Centre, the Information Centre, the Digital library and so on. In the end the LRC emerged as an obvious title.

In some ways the university regarded the building as one part of a regeneration plan associated with this region of South London and, clearly, creating a high quality building, where previously had been a car park, added to the general ambience of the area. By contrast, IT staff regarded it as a very high specification computer lab, whilst library staff

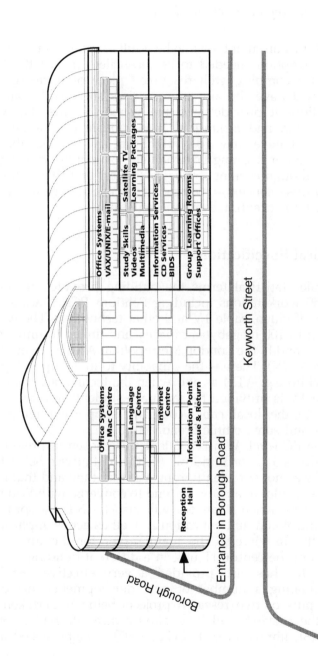

Figure 37.1 The SBU LRC

viewed it as an infant, or maybe adult, digital library. All of these perceptions needed to be reconciled. In fact the LRC remains a complex, well resourced piece of infrastructure which will never be any more or less successful than the applications it provides and the support of the staff who work within and around it. It is capable of changing to support whatever new role might emerge, whether that be as a computer learning environment, or merely as a digital library (though current strategies suggest that that will be a more diffuse concept, covering the whole university rather than being concentrated on one building).

Technical Specification

In simple statistical terms the building provides access to over 450 workstations including Pentium PCs, Macs and a mixture of video, cable TV and other technology. The whole is cabled to 100 megabytes capacity and linked to university networks and to the London Metropolitan Area Network (the London MAN). There is the capability to move up to higher band width e.g. ATM as and when the technology matures. Satellite TV is provided for language students and there are outlets to the local cable company supporting terrestrial stations and some ethnic broadcasting.

At the PC level, Win NT Client was chosen in preference to Windows 3 . . . or Windows 95, the best advice being that Win 95 was not sufficiently robust at that time and that later versions would, in any event, tend to converge with Win NT. The servers, when finalized, will also be NT and provide local control and authentication as well as act as application and software servers. The main server for the university remains in the central IT unit in a different building.

The LRC has also provided a very effective test bed for evaluating a number of new developments including the outputs of two research projects being undertaken by LITC, the research and innovation centre attached to SBU. The CASE library Project (LITC, 1997) is being tested as a potential overarching control system for centres such as the LRC or Internet centres or digital libraries. It will provide a complete management and control system at the terminal end so that we can better account for what users are doing. CASE library enables an administrator to limit access to certain resources at certain times and for certain periods of time; thus a student can be allocated 20 hours of word-processing in a week or unlimited usage at weekends or be excluded from particular networks, CDs or whatever as well as providing technical control (and management information). CASE is also capable of managing licence agreements and password access and will be extended to cope with publishers' data such as journal files in PDF format.

Another facet of the CASE library project has resulted in a Z39.50 client and this too is being tested in the LRC as a tool to provide access to a wide range of OPACs. The CASE Z39.50 client has the potential to access simultaneously a number of catalogues and cohere the result into a single list.

Ultimately each level will support appropriate clients to that particular level, so that level 1 will provide Web access to relevant information services such as electronic journals, including Web based services and the OPAC, Ultranet clients to the CD stack as well as access to e-mail. Netscape has been chosen as the appropriate Web client and Pegasus for e-mail. Vista Exceed links to the centralized Unix machines. The multimedia level is also PC-based with sound cards and CD-ROM drives, but is also Web-enabled, whilst the top level supports a complex mix of services including legacy word-processing and databases software, and, again, network access and specialist programmes such as C++ programming.

In parallel with the installation phase a number of other services have been commissioned and will gradually come online during this academic year. These include an expanded CD-ROM network based on the Ultranet software (which also uses NT as the platform) and which will be accessible through a Windows client irrespective of the base software of the CD. A SilverPlatter ERL system is also under development and this will consolidate all health related data services including CDs but also, through a Web interface, provide access to gateways such as OMNI. The health server is being largely funded by regional health contracts and should provide a coherent data service for a number of distributed health colleges. Finally the SBU Web is going through a substantial build programme commencing with university data such as regulations and codes, but leading to unit (module) documentation held in PDF format.

Staffing Issues

There was evidence that the development of the Resource Centre would have significant repercussions on existing library staffing structures and on the overarching departmental structures. The skills and qualities needed by the support staff were also of concern and, given a separate building a dedicated team would be required. The latter would need to complement the existing library team but also feel some ownership and responsibility for the new project.

Thus a primary task was to develop, from a blank sheet of paper, a structure which would provide at least a starting point for a full staff chart, with some indication of the skills and role of staff involved. This was achieved by the simple process of projecting timetables, opening hours and service points and enumerating the full staffing requirements. A relatively flat structure was proposed involving a manager, two deputies, some senior assistants and a line of support staff. Staffing skills were necessarily very general but emphasized interpersonal and communication skills, strong IT literacy and also a good organizational sense. This outline structure was agreed with the Executive and at the appropriate time, posts advertized. The selectors also looked for added value from candidates such as a particular IT skill or a strong tutorial background and these were often the deciding factors in appointments rather than a strict professional qualification. In parallel it was acknowledged that the development was also likely to impact on other sections and departments including other distributed computer laboratories which were to be assimilated into the LRC, and also Modern Languages where the open access language laboratory was also to be moved. As to the latter it was a matter of staff being re-employed into the new LRC team or in some cases elsewhere within the structure.

The computer services issue was more complex. The development team who had visited a number of universities included Liverpool John Moores, and Tilburg in The Netherlands and from these derived a notion of what a new structure might look like. Papers were produced and an analysis of the various possibilities undertaken. In substance this analysis tried to dissect the necessary functions from a user perspective rather than a functional perspective and then map the existing responsibilities onto that. The view that was taken was that current perspectives were largely historic and it was important to look at the needs of the target group and potential future needs and how best these could be met. It was argued that the background to the need for staff changes was not, in fact, the building per se but a mixture of trends which are likely to accelerate in the coming years. They included:

i)   Increasing technological convergence whereby many services and facilities now have a significant IT component including media, libraries, communications, laboratories (even in the traditional sense) and computer services;

ii) A shift of emphasis from technology (hardware + software) to information content, in that much of the infrastructure requirement is defined (if not in place) and the accent will increasingly be on provision (of information, of learning) and the definition of relevant standards;

iii) An increasing dependence on IT for the good running of the 'business';

iv) Continued devolution of IT hardware and the need to support such distribution.

Thus there were a number of functions which needed to be addressed, each of which is interdependent but for good operation needs more delineation. These included:

a) delivery of student IT and associated support;
b) administrative IT and information systems;
c) the installation and maintenance of the network;
d) the acquisition, development and support of 'soft' e.g. textual information which might include licensed databases, the Internet, discussion lists etc. as opposed to the 'hard' information of the MIS;
e) procurement;
f) training/staff development in all aspects.

We found that universities have, at the simplest level, maintained existing divisional structures but with an increasing overlap in function, perhaps mediated by executive staff or committee or drawn together through the IS strategy. With multifunctional buildings this becomes problematic, leading to diseconomy and is unhelpful from the student perspective (students see people, not librarians, technicians or whatever).

At the other extreme universities have simply merged services with the aim of providing a single coherent function. Such mergers have tended to be predicated on the underlying theme of information; its acquisition, development and dissemination. In practical terms few universities seem to have achieved a high degree of integration; indeed SBU could lay claim to existing levels of convergence as a result of earlier investment in the Media Centre.

In between are a number of models of which many examples could be found. At the minimum it was recommended that SBU must integrate the service and delivery functions, which would bring together distributed computer (technician) staff, library support staff connected with IT, media technicians and computer central support, i.e. reception staff. Job descriptions would need to be broad and flexible with a core of common duties. Staff would need service skills, even above technical know-how and might be drawn from technicians, faculty technicians, library staff and media technicians across the university.

It as also argued that delivery should include 'soft' information (textual and learning support available through the networks), its licensing, promotion and exploitation. There is a central function, which may or may not be physically part of the resource centre, to provide support to distributed information services users through e-mail, telephone etc.

Teaching and Learning

A further dimension to the new centre was to be the delivery and support of resource based, i.e. IT-based teaching and learning as a way of achieving greater economy in the delivery of common courses, and presenting learning opportunities for final year and project work. There is a sense in which the building was to be complementary to, or drive, a major thrust in teaching and learning throughout the university and be able to provide back-up and out-of-hours access to distributed delivery. Two further staffing requirements were identified which needed to be addressed as a consequence of this strategy.

The first was support within the building for directed study and directed learning. This was unlikely to be adequately provided by a core of basic support staff and various alternatives were explored. These included drop-in sessions whereby specialist academic staff are available at certain times to act on an advisory capacity. A second alternative would use para-professionals such as graduate or doctoral students particularly in support of high level computing requirements. This is potentially economic and can provide good quality support whilst opening up opportunities for research students to earn. These are not necessarily mutually exclusive.

The second requirement towards the provision of resource-based learning was to enable either the tailoring, i.e. cutting and pasting, or the origination of materials to support

South Bank programmes. Again, technology is increasingly becoming less of an issue, as the standards emerge and inter-operability becomes common. It becomes relatively easy to support and provide open learning, but to provide material which is directly relevant and potentially accessible by SBU requires a level of staff input. If any university is to progress a systematic policy of resource provision, to cope with core units e.g. study skills, research methodology, introductory maths and so on, there is a need to focus the limited resource development expertise to ensure effective delivery and co-ordination. The creation of a central team to provide that focus, drawing in existing staff either permanently or set against specific projects would be beneficial.

Figure 37.2 illustrates these functions and potential interrela-tionships. It was argued that is possible to group or disag-gragate them in whatever way is required, as long as the respective boundaries are clear. What emerged was a continu-ation of the central Computer Services Division, charged with managing networks and supporting the key and critical servers (along with administrative computing), whilst a new depart-ment, to be known as LIS (Learning and Information Services) would encompass the user end or user related services.

The Wider LRC

It was also felt that the LRC had a potential role to catalyse educational change. Many staff remain reluctant IT converts and lack the expertise to handle rapidly developing technolo-gies and understand what they might achieve. Thus the build-ing is as much a developmental centre as it is a simple student resource. At the earlier stages of the LRC project a number of consultation and discussion sessions were planned to ensure substantial involvement of all staff on all grades within the university and familiarize them with the project strategy, thus ensuring the effective exploitation post inauguration.

There is also a wider community role which is an important component of the university's mission. While the building

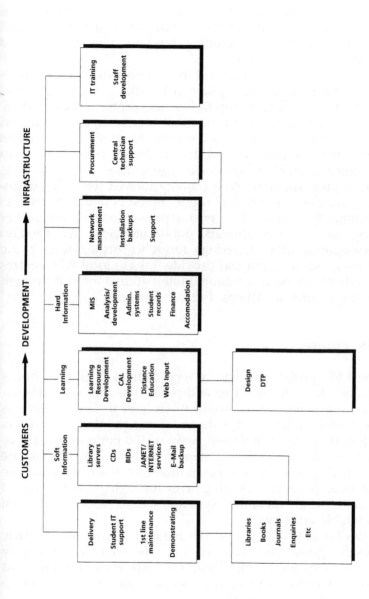

CUSTOMERS → **DEVELOPMENT** → **INFRASTRUCTURE**

Delivery
Student IT support
1st line maintenance
Demonstrating

Soft Information
Library servers
CDs
BIDs
JANET/INTERNET services
E-Mail backup

Learning
Learning Resource Development
CAL Development
Distance Education
Web Input

Hard Information
MIS
Analysis/development
Admin. systems
Student records
Finance
Accomodation

Network management
Installation backups
Support

Procurement
Central technician support

IT training
Staff development

Libraries
Books
Journals
Enquiries
Etc

Design
DTP

Figure 37.2   Function analysis

was under construction, a series of bilateral meetings was begun with Southwark local authority and with relevant business enterprises including Business Link London and with associated colleges.

These meetings culminated in a number of local initiatives including establishing a planned Internet centre in the local shopping complex, a drop-in business centre with a £100 000 grant from the DTI Information Society Initiative (aimed at providing services and facilities to small and medium enterprises (SMEs), links with new library developments in Southwark, built using single regeneration (SRB) funding, and a programme of Web training funded through 'continuing vocational education' funds, aimed both at the business community and at the general public (one of the earlier recipients being Southwark public libraries). We are also investigating other European funds to further develop the South London region and provide links to local Web centres and there has been substantial international interest through similar centres in Athens, Paris and even Beijing.

The Future

The LRC project has had a very defined beginning but is unlikely to have any clear end point. The first year of operation has been highly successful, at least if that successes is measured in terms of volume of usage. Various surveys across the year have shown peaks of 100 per cent occupancy and even higher, if the number of bodies in the building are matched against the number of machines available. There are potential problems looming with managing the volume of demand and rationing systems would seem to be an inevitable outcome.

We have also reviewed the nature of usage in the early months, given some concern that this would prove largely to be word-processing. That fear has proved unfounded though word-processing does account for a high percentage of applications in use at any given time.

Figure 37.3 illustrates the result of the survey of applications with word-processing and use of Internet the not unexpected front runners. Anecdotal evidence suggests that this pattern of usage also varies across the year as students move between assignments, literature and information searching and dissertations. No doubt in time statistical evidence will become clearer.

So in simple usage terms, the building and the investment have proved their worth to such an extent that we are now considering future expansion, perhaps through collaborative ventures. The problems encountered have been largely as a result of success, though some are worrying. Student expectations, for example, particularly as to the ability of the staff to support such a range of applications, are far in excess of what we are able to achieve. A planned referral system – to tutors for example – has never really evolved and the alternatives, such as online help or frequently asked questions, are planned for the near future. There is a need to improve the links between teaching staff and the Centre and there appears to be an increasing mis-match between what we are providing through

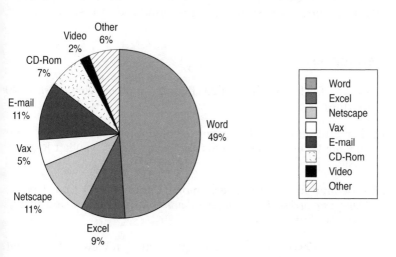

Figure 37.3　Use of LRC after two months

the LRC and what staff are recommending, all of which have shades of the experience with library text books.

Next steps will include the installation of better control and monitoring systems, including print cost recovery and the development of multimedia servers for training and IT skills support. We also need to improve the measurement of performance with a growing statistical base including figures such as occupancy levels, gate figures and prints.. The latter will be important in determining the licence agreements and monitoring the usage of expensive software. We are now developing links to other similar centres outside the university but within the local region so as to begin the process of carrying services out to the user rather expecting them to come into the Centre. This will not mean that the LRC will at some point become redundant, but merely that its role will shift over time. It will always occupy the IT high ground so as to provide access to the kind of resources and facilities which will be problematic over the networks. We expect students to have access to facilities through their own machines whether at home or whether through local centres. To an extent they may always have to come into the university to achieve access to the most innovative resources.

References

Akeroyd, J. (1994) The Follett Report: another view. *Relay*, **40** (Spring), 5–6

Higher Education Funding Council for England, et al. (1993) *Joint Funding Councils' Libraries Review Group: Report*. (Follett Report). Bristol: HEFCE

Library and Information Technology Centre (1997) *Case Library: Managing access to the digital library*. http://www.slou.ac.uk/ ~litc/caselib)

Line, M.B. (1994) The importance of Follett. A review of the Follett Report. *Serials*, **17** (1), 69–72

CHAPTER THIRTY EIGHT

General Case Study: Delivery of Electronic Services for Law at Aston University

Jackie Brocklebank

Context

Law at Aston

Law at Aston has to be considered differently from other law teaching in higher education institutions. We do not have a law school. Law is taught as part of the Management and Administrative Studies (MAS) BSc offered by Aston Business School (ABS). All students who do this degree are required to study Legal Method and Contract Law in their first year. Beyond this students can opt to study core law modules in subsequent years to satisfy Law Society exemption criteria and so proceed to a postgraduate course in Law Practice Management or go on to study for the Bar Examination. In recent years Aston Business School has developed a discrete degree in Law and Legal Practice Management in order to attract students who are looking primarily for a law degree. However, law teaching is very much a part of undergraduate teaching in the Business School with all students on the MAS doing some law in their first year. Students are expected to relate their work to a business context. There is no separate law library and all resources are grouped on the same floor as the other social science and business information. Some law teaching is also carried out in the Languages and European Studies Department e.g. French and German legal systems and European Community law for managers.

It has long been the desire of the law teaching staff to encourage the students to relate their law studies to real life situations. Consequently, the concept of the 'Law Office' was developed with students expected to use a range of resources such as those found in legal practice e.g. practitioner type books and primary sources such as the Encyclopaedia of Forms and Precedents, rather than text books.

Selection and Acquisition of Legal Information Sources

Identifying sources

Primary legal information sources

With these factors in mind we decided to carry out some bench marking to judge how well or how badly our services satisfied our law students. This initiative began in the late eighties. It soon became apparent that our law collection was in need of a major review. This took place in the context of a much larger review of information provision for the Business School. In 1989 the Corporate Library Group was set up in the library to look at business information sources focusing on support for these services. We also needed to review the physical arrangement of services and accessibility.

By 1990, reprofiling of the law collection was on the agenda of the group and work on improving the collection was approved in February 1991. It was agreed that, in principle, it should concentrate on IT based services with the focus being on business law. Funding was already available in the form of UGC monies that had been made available for improvements in books and periodicals provision in universities and we earmarked some of this for law. As there was insufficient expertise at Aston to carry out an extensive review of law services an outside consultant was approached. We employed Christine Miskin of Legal Information Resources to work on this project. Her brief was to provide recommendations on deacquisitions/acquisitions, classification, physical arrangement and documentation. Consultations would be made with staff in ABS and Languages and European Studies and within Library and Information Services (LIS), with the Information Specialist with responsibility for business information giving business law the main focus. A comprehensive report was produced with detailed appendices covering acquisitions, weeding, binding and electronic services. Several key issues emerged. We needed better access to primary source material and our journal coverage was poor. We had cancelled one major law report series in the early eighties which meant we only had the so-called 'Official' Law Reports and The Weekly Law Reports to cover the mainstream law reports plus some subject reports. One of the major strands of the report's recommendations was to take out a subscription to Lexis – a unique online and full text legal database. Lexis would cover all the major law reports series, thereby enhancing our collection considerably both by providing material we had never had in print and by providing an electronic substitute for cancelled law reports series. We would also be able to use Lexis to access unreported cases. Lexis would also offer good coverage of legislation and full text articles in some journals, thus providing some archival and current awareness information.

The provision of an electronic service which could satisfy our needs seemed irresistible as it fitted in well with two of our strategic aims–access rather than holdings policy and a move away from print to electronic, preferably networked, information.

Secondary information sources

The report highlighted several areas where secondary sources were lacking. Some recommendations were made to purchase hard copy journals, but the main area of concern was a lack of an index to periodical articles which would enable research to go beyond the holdings at Aston. At this time Legal Journals Index (LJI) was the only available UK index to the literature and was available in hard copy or electronically via Legal Information Resources.

Electronic Information Services

Lexis

At the time of introducing Lexis we were able to agree a standard academic subscription for Lexis. This meant that we purchased a set number of hours at a fixed cost plus an initial sign up fee. This fee was heavily discounted for academic institutions. Discussions with colleagues in other academic institutions indicated that usage would be well within our set limits and costs. Additional costs for downloading and printing offline were not applicable, as we disabled this facility. Lecturers were not unduly bothered by this as they agreed that students should use Lexis primarily as a reference tool for looking up information. The print screen facility was available and free. Two major decisions were taken once Lexis was bought. One was to give students maximum opportunity to access the system, the other was to locate the service on the same floor and in the same area as the other business information systems. I felt happy with this approach, but slightly concerned that people would see Lexis and imagine that it was as user friendly as other services offered at the same point. Logging on would be the same as other services using communication software called Procomm Plus, i.e. an autologon script was written. It was important that the look and feel was the same as other services up to this point. However, because of the perceived difficulty with the interface we decided to offer Lexis only to trained users. This was implemented by introducing a booking system via the service counter. Users were asked to pick up detailed documentation from the counter before using the system. They would also be asked if they had received training. If no training had been undertaken they were referred to me for a session. No actual policing of the system took place, but it was hoped that this would deter casual users and non-Aston people.

Provision of electronic legal journals coverage

Legal Journals Index (LJI) had been identified as the major source of journal material for the UK. However I was unhappy with the medium in which it was offered–hard copy or tape with fortnightly update. At Aston a campus wide network had been in place with facilities to network CD-ROM's since 1991 using an Optinet server under Novell. I wanted to find a product which would be easy to maintain and update and easily networked. The decision to purchase Lexis meant that we had limited coverage of some journals including *Law Society's Gazette, New Law Journal,* the *Lawyer* and *Estates Gazette* with an average back file of 10 years. The law lecturers at this time were keen to subscribe to the hard copy of LJI as it was seen as a serious shortcoming in our resources to have no journals index. Although I could under-stand their concerns I was in agreement with the Head of Information Services that we should either wait for LJI to be produced on CD-ROM or investigate alternatives. At this time I trialled a CD-ROM called LegalTrac which several colleagues of mine rated highly. This product is from Information Access and contains brief descriptions with some more detailed abstracts covering a wide range of journals and law reports. This is an international product with a very good spread of practice journals. Although it might seem biased towards American sources it did actually tie in with the 'Law Office' idea in that it reported current practice by law practitioners as well as the latest academic literature. The initial response from law lecturers was good and we were able to subscribe from April 1994. Over 900 journals/law reports are covered. LegalTrac has the added advantage of having local holdings software which enables users to see if the library holds journals found during a search.

EC legislation focus

Another aspect of the consultant's report focused on European Law provision. Fortunately, the European legislation on Lexis covered some aspects of this via the EURCOM library together with the French law library, which would satisfy those students on the International Business and Modern Languages degrees. Further sources dealing with European law were suggested. At the time there was a vacancy for a law lecturer with a special interest in European law and I felt that I had continuously to appraise sources as and when they appeared to see what they could offer so that I could advise on selection if and when the vacancy was filled. There was no significant pressure from the Languages and European Studies department to provide resources additional to Lexis. At the time various options were considered to supplement this provision. We could have bought one of the Justis products, possibly the Official Journal on CD-ROM, but we felt this was too restrictive and would not be used enough. Whilst I continued to trial and evaluate European law CD-ROM products I decided to take advantage of introducing an additional service by another means. At the time we were changing provision of one of our most popular business services, Textline, the international business news database. We had decided to subscribe to the service from a different host, Data-Star (now Knight-Ridder), through their Focus services. This would also give us access to a huge range of other services including EC Legislation Focus. This service consists of several databases. These are

- Celex–full text and/or references for all European Community legislation;
- Spicers–abstracts of information on a range of subjects including EC policies, initiatives and legislation;

- Spearhead–summaries of current and prospective EC measures on 1992 related information;
- Investext–company and industry reports;
- Globalbase–international coverage of companies, products and industries primarily in Europe;
- DRT EC and Eastern Europe–business and industry in the EC with the emphasis on development and expansion in Eastern Europe;
- Tenders Electronic Daily–details of invitations to tender for public supply and public works.

This seemed a good way of introducing students to a further range of sources which were both law and business related.

Budgeting Issues

In our budget a CD-ROM service is considered a recurrent cost as it is generally based on an annual fee similar to a periodical subscription. This has the advantage of being able to plan the annual budget. Not so with Lexis. Originally Lexis pricing was similar to a CD-ROM subscription with a set number of hours purchased at a fixed cost. After a period of relative stability, librarians in academic institutions were faced with a new problem. Lexis is an American product, managed in the UK at the time of our purchase by Butterworth's in London, with all the customer support and training provided by them. Because of various internal changes within the parent company, Mead Data, it suddenly became possible to buy the service direct from Mead. Mead were offering a deal direct to customers such as law schools, which amounted to unlimited access and downloading for $110 a month for one user name. The deal seemed too good to be true and generated a lot of discussion on the lis-law and cti-law mailbase lists. For those whose use of Lexis was substantial it offered a good deal. As a result many law schools re-negotiated their contracts through Mead, including Aston.

At the same time (December 1994) Mead was acquired by Reed Elsevier plc and from this time became known as Lexis-Nexis. Many universities took advantage of the news databases on offer from the Nexis part of the service, especially as they were offered at such a competitive price. At Aston I did not want users confused with yet more business news options and asked Mead to disable access to the Nexis database.

Mead were able to supply us with detailed information on their invoices about who was using the service, online times and so on. This was useful in terms of evaluating the service. However, after another relatively short period of about a year, servicing of law school subscriptions came back under the remit of Butterworth's, with charging arrangements changing once more. At present, costs are based on types of libraries (i.e. files of information) used. Butterworths decided to offer different subscriptions with different price tags to suit the user. Package A gives access to UK , Commonwealth and European material, whereas Package B provides access to these and US sources. Package C includes the Nexis services. There are also charges levied for connect time and type of access. The telecommunications charge varies according to what method is used e.g. – Internet, Compunet or other carriers. Downloading is no longer free and librarians are generally finding Lexis an expensive resource once more. Indeed, it seems particularly unfair for UK institutions since Lexis in the US is heavily subsidised and US students are encouraged full rein when using the service. The changeover for libraries transfering from Mead back to Butterworths was again the subject of lengthy discussion both on the mailbase lists and in the Law Librarian journal (Byrne, 1995, pp. 460–461).

Similar budgetary problems are currently affecting our business information services which we receive from Data-Star. It appears that Data-Star Focus will no longer be provided at such advantageous rates for business schools and we are currently reviewing provision of alternative business information. This in turn affects access to EC Legislation

Focus. As the vacancy for the law lecturer with a special interest in European law has just been filled, I expect to have to review provision in this area. It may be that we have to make do with the EURCOM library on Lexis until the lecturer has had time to evaluate her needs.

Managing Technical Services and Support

Lexis was the first of the legal electronic information services to be introduced. The system operates as a user ID controlled system. Initially Butterworths issued individual users IDs for the information specialists and law lecturers. However we did not want users to have to log in manually using individual IDs. The idea was to have access via one PC in the library running Procomm Plus communication software in which one ID would be written into the autologon file. This would ensure that the library front-end of Lexis would have the same look and feel as our other services, which all run under Procomm. We were fortunate in that, at the same time as Lexis was introduced, LIS took the decision to employ a full time Systems Specialist to support the Systems Librarian. One important role of this Systems Specialist was to support information specialists introducing new CD-ROM's and online services. This meant that the Systems Specialist wrote the Procomm autologon script for Lexis and dealt with any technical problems of access. Any problems with Lexis, which are usually due to PSS or local area network problems, are also dealt with by the Systems Specialist.

Having decided to purchase LegalTrac we gave access to all legal information services from the same machine. This would also keep the cost of Lexis under further control by reducing access times. In some ways the CD-Rom Network was a victim of its own success with many new services being introduced on a regular basis. The system had grown and eventually included an Optinet optical server and a Netware 3.11 file server with three SCSI Express towers with seven drives each and three Discport towers (one of which had a six-disc disc changer). Information specialists were becoming very aware, when planning services, that we had to cope with this shaky system which was now becoming dangerously unreliable. We were also unable at this point to network Windows products which severely restricted our choice of new CD services, which were tending to be offered as Windows based products. In 1996 we were unsuccessful in our bid for central university funds to update our network and since then we have had to use departmental funds to replace our CD-ROM server. Although this was costly we felt that the reliability of the service was so poor we had to upgrade. It also means that we are able to network Windows products.

Once access to EC Legislation Focus was possible we introduced another menu option on the Lexis machine with a Procomm script logging directly into the service.

Training

Staff training

When we decided to subscribe to Lexis we were offered training at Butterworth's training facilities in London. Four places were available – three were taken by library staff and one by the Head of Law from ABS. It was at this point that the difficulty with the interface was fully appreciated. Library staff in particular were concerned at offering to support a service where both the interface and the content of the system were so complex. Law sources, and Lexis in particular, have been the subject of regular updates in training since this time, using the dedicated training hour for library staff and the workshop facility within LIS, rather than training by the supplier.

Student training

Training of students before they used the service was considered to be essential. This in turn led to considerable time spent liaising with the department on how to do this. The best option seemed to be to offer a taster of Lexis to first year students on an optional basis. This would hook those who were either keen to exploit something extra, or those who definitely wanted to go on to the legal stream in year 2. There could be up to 300 students doing law in the first year and this would shrink to approximately 40 by year 2. Current year 2 students were offered timetabled training, which would be integrated with the departmental teaching. With this is mind, Lexis was advertized in the department and sessions were organized in the library for second years in term 2 and later for interested first years. Separate sessions were organized for final year students returning from their placement year.

All sessions were run in the library in our Information Skills Workshop. The room contained 12 networked PCs which could be monitored from a master terminal via a switching device called UTAC. The training took the form of a short talk and then a demonstration of simple searching using examples applicable to their studies. Not all students who should have attended training did so, but on the whole the first batch of training seemed successful. At this point, students were not able to do hands on for two reasons – it was not technically feasible at that time and also because it was felt that it could be too costly. Not being able to network PCs in the workshop for Lexis was a big drawback as I feel that hands on is the best way for students to learn how to use a system. Eventually the networking arrangements were improved. Part of the problem was that our PC workshop was becoming dated. Installed originally in 1988 the range of PCs had become unable to support the wide range of services we now offered. The problem with Lexis was that there were insufficient network points to support hands on. By 1995 we had secured central university funding for a re-equipping of the workshop and the work was carried out in Easter vacation 1995. At the same time we changed our ageing UTAC console for a TLS Didacnet unit. This allows us greater and more sophisticated control of the student machines, e.g. we can disable student keyboards, darken screens, view student screens and interrupt searches. There is also a teacher call facility which means that the teacher can see if someone is having trouble since they can light up a button on the master console.

Installation of the new equipment also coincided with the Lexis contract switching to Mead which meant that there was unlimited access for training on all Lexis files, not just the training files.

As far as the Business School was concerned there was no overall uniform approach from lecturers to Lexis training. Students studying different subjects within law are at the mercy of their lecturers to co-operate with me to organize training. This was particularly difficult as a good proportion of the law lecturers are visiting or part-time. I relied heavily on the lecturers' goodwill to promote the training and make it seem an important part of their learning. Some lecturers gave up their lecture time for training in the library, others left me to find a time with the administration staff when students were free. One lecturer invited me to give a lecture to students in the department and we followed this up by group work in the workshop researching particular questions which I had been able to research and discuss with the lecturer beforehand. This was particularly rewarding as the lecturer noticed the impact Lexis had on the students' work by the end of the year. However the question of unequal access did concern me and continues to be a worry. Much of the problem stems from the fact that lecturers do not always consult with each other on the learning needs of students.

Promotion and Publicity

At Aston University we have a well-established procedure for introducing a new electronic service whether it is online or CD-ROM based. As part of this information special- ists responsible for introducing a service will decide if the documentation supplied by the company is useful and can be included in a box near the terminal used for it in LIS. It may be that it is too technical or deals with issues which are too sophisticated for the user we anticipate. Most information specialists like to provide some kind of cut down version of these instructions written in jargon-free language. At Aston we have a Public Relations Quality Circle, part of whose remit is to look at material such as this, which is used to promote and publicize a service. The documentation is prepared to a standard format and is presented in A4 folders. This is then placed next to the terminal with any other information such a thesaurus of terms or list of journals covered by the system. Having a system like this helps us to have a starting point for user enquiries about searching. Some of the staff on the information point next to the business information systems are not subject specialists and need to refer users to written instructions.

LIS also produces a series of leaflets, again prepared to a standard format, covering most of the electronic services available. The leaflets are meant as a guide to what the service is and what it covers, including range of years covered, where it is available, e.g. in LIS or networked, and what the user can expect to get from it. The leaflets do not generally deal with the mechanics of searching although some indication may be given, e.g. whether you can do simple and more advanced searches. We use the leaflets for a variety of reasons. They may be handed out at the information point to supply basic information if the user does not understand the services available. For example, there is a leaflet devoted to electronic legal information which has details of the three services described in this case study. There are also leaflets on law in general, and law reports and legislation in particular, which also cross-refer users to the electronic services. The leaflets are also used by information specialists in information skills sessions to hand out as a reminder of what services are available to users. They are a useful aid at the information point both for the librarian (in case they have forgotten what is covered by a service) and also as a prompt to ask enquirers if they have attended training.

Legal information skills are taught by lecturers to new students under the title Legal Method and are quite brief without much focus on using sources in the LIS. We are working on integrating Lexis and other electronic services within this lecture programme so that awareness is raised amongst students at an early stage of the whole range of resources available to them.

Service Issues

The library is open from 9.00 am to 10.00 pm Monday to Wednesday, Thursday 10.00 am to 10.00 pm and Friday 9.00 am to 5.00 pm. The building is also open Saturday 10.00 to 5.00 and some Sundays. During this time the students have access to Lexis and EC Legislation Focus. They have 24 hour access to LegalTrac, potentially, because it is networked. My experience is that this is unusual for academic institutions. Lexis is often only available in a closed access room, often by means of an appointment with a librarian who may also do the search for them. Our students have therefore been lucky to have such freedom.

At the time of writing, contract arrangements for Lexis are set to change again, with some institutions now unable to bear the cost of such an expensive service. There could well be a big move away from Lexis provision in universities to CD-ROM based services such as Current Legal Information. Certainly the world of electronic legal information is changing all the time, with a huge selection of products all of which are not quite comparable. This means that we are constantly trying to weigh up the pros and cons of the various features to make a case for changing or supplementing a service.

Information professionals are used to doing this kind of evaluation on a regular basis, but it does mean that we need to be ever more aware of the needs of our customers

– whether they are students or lecturers. This will ensure that we provide them with a quality service which is both cost effective and timely.

Reference

Byrne, D. (1995) (ed.) Information Technology Matters. *The Law Librarian*, **26,** 460–461

Index